THE YEARBOOK OF EDUCATION LAW 2024

Charles J. Russo, J.D., Ed.D. and Jeffrey C. Sun, J.D., Ph.D., editors

EDUCATION LAW ASSOCIATION

Published by Education Law Association
Philadelphia, Pennsylvania, USA

The Education Law Association improves education by promoting interest in and understanding of education law.

Join the social learning community at EducationLaw.org.

The opinions expressed in this publication are those of the authors and do not represent the official views of the Education Law Association.

Layout Editor: Kelley A. Taksier

ISBN-13: 978-1-56534-196-8
ISBN-10: 1-56534-196-1

Education Law Association

Editors

Charles J. Russo, M.Div., J.D., Ed.D., is the Joseph Panzer Chair in Education in the School of Education and Health Sciences, Director of its Ph.D. Program, and Research Professor of Law in the School of Law at the University of Dayton. Dr. Russo served as 1998-99 President of the Education Law Association and was the 2002 recipient of its McGhehey (Achievement) Award, the 2021 Distinguished Scholar Award from the American Educational Research Association's Special Interest Group on Religion & Education, and the 2021 Lifetime Achievement Award from the South African Education Law Association. Dr. Russo authored or co-authored more than 300 articles in peer-reviewed journals; authored, co-authored, edited, or co-edited 75 books, totaling nearly 1,200 publications. Dr. Russo also has spoken extensively on issues in education law in thirty-four of the United States and thirty-one other nations. In addition, he edits two journals and serves on over a dozen editorial boards.

Having spoken in thirty-four states and thirty-one nations outside the United States on all six inhabited continents, Russo taught summer courses in England, Spain, and Thailand. Internationally, he serves or has served as a Visiting Professor at the University of Notre Dame of Australia Faculty of Law in Sydney, Queensland University of Technology in Brisbane, and the University of Newcastle, Australia; the University of Sarajevo, Bosnia and Herzegovina; South East European University, Macedonia; the Potchefstroom and Mafeking Campuses of Northwest University, Potchefstroom, South Africa; the University of Malaya in Kuala Lumpur, Malaysia; the University of Sao Paulo, Brazil; Yeditepe University, Istanbul Turkey; Inner Mongolia University for the Nationalities, Tongliao, Inner Mongolia; and Peking University in Beijing, China. He is currently a Visiting Professor at Capital Normal University in Beijing.

Before joining the Faculty at the University of Dayton as Professor and Chair of the Department of Educational Administration in July 1996, Dr. Russo taught at the University of Kentucky in Lexington, Kentucky, from August 1992 to July 1996 and at Fordham University in his native New York City from September 1989 to July 1992. He taught high school for eight and one half-years, both prior to and after graduation from law school.

He received a Bachelor of Arts degree in Classical Civilization (1972), Juris Doctor Degree (1983), and Doctor of Education degrees in Educational Administration and Supervision (1989) from St. John's University in New York City. He received a Master of Divinity degree from the Seminary of the Immaculate Conception in Huntington, New York (1978). He received a Ph.D. Honoris Causa from Potchefstroom University, now the Potchefstroom Campus of Northwest University, in Potchefstroom, South Africa, in May 2004, for his contributions to the field of Education Law.

Jeffrey C. Sun, J.D., Ph.D., is Professor of Higher Education and Law, Distinguished University Scholar, Associate Dean for Innovation and Strategic Partnerships, and Director of the SKILLS Collaborative (a research and policy center examining workforce development and legal issues to career/ professional postsecondary education) at the University of Louisville. He is also Counsel at Manley Burke.

His research and practice areas focus on higher education law and professional/career education policies and practice. Dr. Sun has served as Project Director and Principal Investigator for over $25 million in grants and contracts.

He has published approximately 100 scholarly works and is co-author of ten books, including *Law, Policy, and Higher Education* (Carolina Academic Press, 2012); Law & Education Inequality: Removing Barriers to Educational Opportunities (Information Age Publishing, 2015); *Student Clashes on Campus: A Leadership Guide to Free Speech* (Routledge); and Academic Leadership and Governance of Higher Education: A Guide for Trustees, Leaders, and Aspiring Leaders of Two- and Four-Year Institutions (Stylus Publishing, 2nd Edition, 2022).

Dr. Sun received a BBA and an MBA from Loyola Marymount University, a law degree (J.D.) from the Moritz College of Law at The Ohio State University, and an M.Phil. and a Ph.D. from Columbia University.

Authors

Joy Blanchard, Ph.D., Associate Professor of Higher Education, Louisiana State University, Baton Rouge, La.

Brian Boggs, Ph.D., J.D., Assistant Professor of Policy and Educational Leadership, University of Michigan – Dearborn, Dearborn, Mich.

Susan Bon, J.D., Ph.D., Provost and Executive Vice President for Academic Affairs, Pittsburg State University, Pittsburg, Kan.

Clarissa Bruton, J.D., Research Manager of Law and Policy, University of Louisville, Louisville, Ky.

Christine Collins-Otto, Ed.D., Senior Educational Services and Bridges Director, Multnomah Educational Service District, Portland, Ore.

Amy L. Dagley, Ph.D., Associate Professor of Educational Leadership, University of Alabama at Birmingham, Birmingham, Ala.

David L. Dagley, Ph.D., J.D., Professor Emeritus of Educational Leadership, University of Alabama, Tuscaloosa, Ala.

Gillian Foss, Ph.D., Adjunct Instructor of Higher Education Administration, Louisiana State University, Baton Rouge, La.

Beth Godett, Ed.D., J.D., Adjunct Professor of Education Law and Policy; Boston College, Chestnut Hill, Mass.; Rider University, Lawrenceville, N.J.; Farleigh Dickinson University, Madison, N.J.

Jeffrey S. Greenley, J.D., M.B.A., Superintendent, Belpre City Schools, Belpre, Ohio.

Diane M. Holben, Ed.D., Associate Professor of Professional & Secondary Education, East Stroudsburg University, East Stroudsburg, Pa.

Marigold Hudock, Ph.D., Assistant Professor of Higher Education, Stephen F. Austin State University, Nacogdoches, Tex.

Elizabeth T. Lugg, J.D., Ph.D., Associate Professor of Educational Law, Illinois State University, Normal, Ill.

Radomir Mitic, Ph.D., Assistant Professor of Higher Education, William and Mary University, Williamsburg, Va.

Allan G. Osborne, Jr., Ed.D., Retired Principal, Snug Harbor Community School, Quincy, Mass.; Editor, West's Education Law Reporter.

Barbara Qualls, Ph.D., Associate Professor of Educational Leadership, Stephen F. Austin State University, Nacogdoches, Tex.

Jeffrey C. Sun, J.D., Ph.D., Distinguished University Professor of Higher Education and Law, University of Louisville, Louisville, Ky.

Elizabeth Zagata, Ph.D., Special Education Systems Improvement Specialist at WestEd; Adjunct Faculty of Special Education Law & Policy, University of Connecticut, Mansfield, Conn.,; Sacred Heart University, Fairfield, Conn.

PREFACE

Charles J. Russo

Fifty-two years ago, in 1972, the Education Law Association—then known as the National Organization for Legal Problems in Education (NOLPE)—first published the Yearbook of Education Law (The Yearbook). It was destined to become one of our mainstays and bestsellers, serving as a comprehensive annual review of litigation in education law. However, The Yearbook's origins actually trace back to 1933, when it was published by Interstate Printers and Publishers.

The Yearbook provides attorneys, faculty members in higher education, and officials in K-12 and higher education settings with a comprehensive, advocacy-free analysis of education litigation during each given year. As in previous volumes, this edition includes chapters on a wide array of issues in education law, both domestically and, on occasion, internationally.

In addition to citations from West's Federal and Regional State Reporters, The Yearbook also includes references to West's Education Law Reporter, a valuable resource for all those interested in education law.

Having had the honor and pleasure of editing The Yearbook since 1994—and contributing as an author for three years prior—I would like to take this opportunity, in my final edition as editor, to thank my predecessors: Leroy J. Peterson (1972), Robert E. Phay (1973), Floyd G. Delon (1974), Philip K. Piele (1975–1984), and Stephen B. Thomas (1986–1994). For the past three years, I have co-edited The Yearbook with Jeffrey C. Sun, who will now take on the role of editor independently. Previously, I co-edited The Yearbook with Betsy Shaver from 2016 to 2018.

Over the years, more than 100 authors have contributed to The Yearbook, constituting a virtual "Who's Who" of the Education Law Association. Rather than risk omitting anyone, I will not list every contributor, but I do wish to recognize one longstanding author who, along with his co-author, is also stepping away from The Yearbook with this volume. Allan G. Osborne, Jr.—a Past ELA

President and McGhehey Award winner—has authored the chapter on students with disabilities since 1991. For the past 14 years, he has co-authored this chapter with another Past ELA President, Susan C. Bon. Allan and Susan, thank you for your exceptional contributions to The Yearbook and to ELA. Your work has been invaluable.

An undertaking of this size and scope requires support from many people over the years. I would like to express my gratitude to ELA's past executive directors, staff editors, officers, and boards of directors for their steadfast support. Additionally, I am grateful to my deans and colleagues at the University of Dayton for their encouragement. Most importantly, I owe my deepest thanks and love to my wonderful wife, Debbie, for her diligent citation-checking of cases throughout the years.

Finally, I want to thank ELA and our readers for the opportunity to serve through The Yearbook. I am confident that, under the capable leadership of our new lead editor, Jeffrey C. Sun, The Yearbook will continue to thrive in the years to come.

TABLE OF CONTENTS

This page is left intentionally blank.

CHAPTER 1

SCHOOL GOVERNANCE

Barbara Qualls and Diane M. Holben

Continued on the next page...

Introduction

This chapter summarizes litigation on K-12 governance issues in 2023. Compared to 2022, the total number of cases increased. The chapter is organized into two main sections: systemic governance issues and local governance issues. The systemic governance section includes 47 cases involving questions of constitutionality, elections, board meetings, board operations and authority, taxation, finance, and charter schools.

The local governance section includes 41 cases whose legal bases predominantly included state and local statutes related to breach of contract, copyright or trademark infringement, denial of insurance coverage, property rights, public records and the Freedom of Information Act (FOIA), school boundaries, school operations, transportation of students, and miscellaneous issues. Four cases were litigated in federal court, with the rest occurring in state courts. Jurisdiction frequencies mirrored the 2022 cases, with New York, Texas, and California again accounting for four of these cases each; Pennsylvania and Louisiana accounted for three cases each, with the remaining 23 cases distributed among 18 additional states. Further, the cases were largely clustered among the subtopics of property rights, breach of contract, public records/FOIA, and school operations.

Five cases related to COVID-19 issues are also included.

Systemic Governance Issues

Constitutional Issues

Religion

In *Fellowship of Christian Athletes v. San Jose Unified School District Board of Education*, the Ninth Circuit reversed the district court's decision that upheld a school district's decision revoking the local FCA chapter's status as an official student club. The school's position was that the required Statement of Faith violated the district's nondiscrimination policy. The circuit court determined that the school had engaged in selective enforcement of its policy and directed the district court to issue an order reinstating the

FCA as an official student club.[1] In another case, after investigations into fees and rental irregularities, the Eleventh Circuit upheld a district court decision barring a Jewish after-school program in Florida, finding that the program's operator did not establish violations of free exercise of religion, "class of one" equal protection violation, or due process violation.[2]

First Amendment

A Virginia parent group's challenge to a student equity ambassador program was unsuccessful in its claim that the program, which collected anonymous student reports of racism, injustice, and inequity, violated the First Amendment's guarantee of freedom of speech and the Equal Protection Clause. The respondent school board's move for dismissal was granted by the district court, finding that the program did not have discriminatory intent and did have legitimate pedagogical goals. The parents' claim that the anonymous reporting system caused students to refrain from participation was insufficient to show standing for a free speech claim. The Fourth Circuit upheld the district court's dismissal, finding in favor of the school system.[3] The Eighth Circuit reversed a district court's dismissal of claims from three Minnesota residents who disputed the conditions of an employment agreement that provided paid leave for union members to work for the local collective bargaining representative organization on a limited basis. The court agreed that the residents did not have standing to sue the school system as state taxpayers or as county residents, but they did have standing as taxpayers of the district.[4]

In Massachusetts, a private school operator sued the town, the school governing body, and three superintendents, claiming violation of academic freedom as protected by the First Amendment and procedural and substantive due process violations because the operator's application was rejected twice. The district court agreed that the operator had standing as a representative of

---

[1] Fellowship of Christian Athletes v. San Jose Unified Sch. Dist. Bd. of Educ., 46 F.4th 1075, 407 Educ. L. Rep. 416 (9th Cir. 2023).
[2] Chabad Chayil, Inc. v. Sch. Bd. of Miami-Dade Cnty., Fla., 48 F.4th 1222, 408 Educ. L. Rep. 69 (11th Cir. 2022).
[3] Menders v. Loudoun Cnty. Sch. Bd., 65 F.4th 157, 414 Educ. L. Rep. 499 (4th Cir. 2022).
[4] Huizenga v. Indep. Sch. Dist. Cnty. No. 11, 44 F.4th 806, 406 Educ. L. Rep. 182 (8th Cir. 2022).

potential pupils and their parents, but the factual record did not establish a violation of academic freedom rights. Further, there were no actionable due process violations.[5]

Elections Issues

Five election cases were resolved in federal courts. A white voter in Texas alleged that the at-large electoral system in his school district violated the Voting Rights Act by diluting the impact of votes by minorities. The district court granted the school system's motion for summary judgment and granted the school's motion for sanctions, which the white voter and his attorneys appealed. The Fifth Circuit vacated the district court's decision, finding that the voter's argument was not sanctionable, nor did his attorneys' behavior warrant sanction.[6] The remaining federal election cases were all decided in district courts. In Georgia, after a plan for establishing an at-large election scheme for all six board seats was ruled in violation of the Voting Rights Act, parties were directed to submit remedial plans. A continued dispute concerning the timeline for the remediation resulted in a decision that the school system's proposed plan for four single-member seats and one at-large was an appropriate remedy, and that the voter group's proposed plan would not remedy the existing violation.[7]

Two additional federal election cases concerned malapportioned voting districts, with the claim that minority votes were too diluted. In Kentucky, the challenging plaintiffs claimed a violation of the Equal Protection Clause in that the principle of one person, one vote was not evident. The district court found for the voters, specifically stating in the opinion that the *Pullman* abstention (federal restraint if the issue concerns uncertain state law) was not warranted and that the voting districts, as drawn, were unconstitutional under the Fourteenth Amendment Equal Protection Clause.[8] A similar case in Louisiana had a different outcome. The original district court decided that the voters' motion

---

[5] Fusion Learning, Inc. v. Andover Sch. Comm., 609 F. Supp. 3d 5, 412 Educ. L. Rep. 80 (D. Mass. 2022).

[6] Vaughan v. Lewisville Ind. Sch. Dist., 62 F.4th 199, 412 Educ. L. Rep. 931 (5th Cir. 2023).

[7] Whitest v. Crisp Cnty. Sch. Dist., 601 F. Supp. 3d 1338, 410 Educ. L. Rep. 1025 (M.D. Ga. 2022).

[8] Coleman v. Winbigler, 615 F. Supp. 3d 563, 413 Educ. L. Rep. 244 (E.D. Ky. 2022).

for a temporary restraining order and preliminary injunction was too close to the scheduled election without causing significant cost and confusion.[9] The same case was heard in state court. A month after the federal district court's action, the Louisiana Court of Appeal held that the plaintiffs' petition stated a valid cause of action for declaratory and injunctive relief.[10] The final federal case was in Wyoming, where the elected position of superintendent was vacant. Voters and a nominee for the position to finish the term brought action against the political structure, including the governor and the Republican party. The court determined that the plaintiff voters and nominee were unlikely to prevail on an equal protection challenge to the statute or the political party's bylaws and failed to demonstrate any irreparable harm.[11]

Four other election cases were decided in state courts. In Iowa, a citizens' special interest group filed for declaratory judgment to have their referendum petition on the financing of a proposed athletic stadium. The interest group appealed an initial negative judgment, but their referendum petition was declined again. The decision hinged on the calculation of the number of signatures needed. The total number of voters at the last election, rather than the total number of votes cast in an at-large school board election race, determined the number of petition signatures needed to trigger a referendum.[12] A dispute about ballot language for a state constitutional amendment proposing "open enrollment"—giving parents a protected constitutional right to select any K-12 public school in the state, including public charter schools—was decided in favor of the petitioner. The caption of the ballot title did not state that school district discretion in admissions would be eliminated, nor was there sufficient information about fiscal impact on school districts.[13] After no clear winner was named in a primary election for a school board seat, one candidate in the ensuing runoff challenged the other's residency during the qualifying period. The lower court found for the challenger, but on appeal, it was determined that the first opponent did meet residency

---

[9] Singleton v. E. Baton Rouge Parish Sch. Bd., 621 F. Supp. 3d 618, 415 Educ. L. Rep. 33 (M.D. La. 2022).

[10] Singleton v. E. Baton Rouge Parish Sch. Bd., 353 So. 3d 164, 411 Educ. L. Rep. 1246 (La. Ct. App. 2022).

[11] Speight v. Gordon, 582 F. Supp. 3d 897, 406 Educ. L. Rep. 892 (D. Wyo. 2022).

[12] Save Our Stadiums v. Des Moines Indep. Cnty. Sch. Dist., 982 N.W.2d 139, 409 Educ. L. Rep. 929 (Iowa 2022).

[13] Scott-Schwalbach v. Rosenblum, 523 P.3d 113, 411 Educ. L. Rep. 795 (Or. 2022).

requirements, so the first decision was reversed and remanded.[14] In Maryland, a county school system had a student member on the board of education. A group of parents attempted to keep the student member from exercising any voting power and challenged the legality of the student member's position. The initial judgment was for the board and the student position. On appeal by the parent group, the appellate court held that the statute providing for a student member, elected by students, did not violate the state constitution.[15]

Board Meetings Issues

Three cases challenging school board operating procedures for meetings were heard in federal district court in Florida, Maine, and Missouri. Moms for Liberty in Florida sought a preliminary injunction of the school board's operating practices, claiming that the public participation policy was unconstitutionally restrictive and vague. Further, they claimed that their participation in the meetings had been impeded in a discriminatory manner because the chair did not agree with their message. The board's response to the court was accepted, finding that the policy was reasonable, as the purpose of the participation was to provide a limited public forum. The policy was content and viewpoint-neutral, not overbroad, or vague. The Moms for Liberty's motion for a preliminary injunction was denied.[16] In Maine, a resident complained about a book available to middle school students. In the participatory portion of the meeting, he referred to the book's contents in graphic terminology and, as a result, was temporarily banned from attending board meetings. He filed a motion for a temporary restraining order. The District Court granted his motion, finding that his language was not obscene and that the ban was a violation of his First Amendment rights to free speech and to petition the government.[17] In Missouri, a political action committee brought action against the school district,

---

[14] Meisman v. Hernandez, 353 So. 3d 669, 411 Educ. L. Rep. 1269 (Fla. Dist. Ct. App. 2022).
[15] Spiegel v. Bd. of Educ. of Howard Cnty., 281 A.3d 663, 408 Educ. L. Rep. 388 (Md. 2022).
[16] Moms for Liberty Brevard Cnty., Fla. v. Brevard Pub. Schs., 582 F. Supp. 3d 1214, 407 Educ. L. Rep. 128 (M.D. Fla. 2022).
[17] McBreairty v. Sch. Bd. of RSU 22, 616 F. Supp. 3d 79, 413 Educ. L. Rep. 674 (D. Me. 2022).

superintendent, and board members for engaging in viewpoint discrimination in violation of their First Amendment free speech rights. The manifestation of the alleged violation was that the chairman of the board did not allow the PAC to mention its name or website during the participation portion of the meeting. The court granted the motion, finding that the PAC had a "fair chance of prevailing" on the merits of their claim and that the public interest and balance of harms favored granting the injunction.[18]

Board Operations and Authority Issues

Five cases dealing with issues related to board operational procedures and the scope of board authority were decided in state courts.

The Supreme Court of Louisiana resolved a long-standing dispute between the state and an oil company concerning environmental remediation of district property the oil company had leased for mineral and surface rights and had performed exploration and production for decades. Both parties appealed, and a $5 million jury verdict was affirmed in part and reversed in part by the Court of Appeal. The Supreme Court of Louisiana granted certiorari. Its holdings affirmed the Court of Appeal but acknowledged that a new trial was warranted because of confusion of extraneous instructions because of an erroneous decision on a prior appeal.[19]

An unsuccessful attempt by an Oklahoma school district to prevent the state from placing the district on probation and requiring an interim superintendent was appealed to the state's Supreme Court. The district and superintendent contended that they were entitled to a preliminary injunction to halt action on the probationary proceedings until they both had individual administrative hearings. The higher court affirmed the lower court's denial of the argument, holding that neither the district nor the superintendent had a likelihood of success on the merits of their due process claims. Their challenges to the authority of the state department of education for the probationary action for the district and suspension of the superintendent's license were also

---

[18] Brooks v. Francis Howell Sch. Dist., 599 F. Supp. 3d 795, 410 Educ. L. Rep. 662 (E.D. Mo. 2022).
[19] State v. La. Land & Exploration Co., 347 So.3d 684, 408 Educ. L. Rep. 1151 (La. 2021).

denied.[20] A similar case in Texas involved the Houston school system's performance failures and subsequent appointment of a conservator. The school system was initially successful in securing a temporary injunction against the appointment for the duration of the appellate process. However, by the time the case was reviewed by the state's highest court, amendments to the Texas Education Code made the appointment of a conservator and board of managers no longer warranted.[21]

Two other operations and authority cases were decided by lower state courts in Florida and North Carolina. An appellate court in Florida affirmed that the statute of trespassing within a school safety zone was not overbroad or unconstitutionally vague, in a case where an individual had been removed and cited for criminal trespass for standing on the sidewalk directly connected to a high school campus property, playing loud music, and shouting religious messages through a bullhorn toward students as they left the school.[22] A North Carolina thief was designated a habitual felon, in part because he pleaded guilty to possession of stolen goods from a building occupied by the county schools. The appellate court held that his larceny indictment sufficiently established that the school system was a legal entity capable of owning property.[23]

Taxation

Eleven taxation cases, with five in the states' highest courts and six in lower state courts, were decided in 2022. In Kentucky, a coalition of school boards, parents, and a nonprofit organization challenged a state program that allowed an income tax credit for donations to certain account-granting organizations (AGOs), which allocated those contributions to education opportunity accounts (EOAs) for use in various education-related expenses. The EOA funds could be used for tuition in nonpublic schools. On appeal, the Supreme Court of Kentucky affirmed the lower court's decision that the EOA Act violated the state constitutional provision prohibiting taxation for education other than for common schools

---

[20] Western Hts. Indep. Sch. Dist. No. I-41 of Okla. Cnty. v. State *ex rel.* Okla. State Dep't of Educ., 518 P.3d 531, 408 Educ. L. Rep. 1053 (Okla. 2022).
[21] Texas Educ. Agency v. Houston Indep. Sch. Dist., 660 S.W.3d 108, 412 Educ. L. Rep. 367 (Tex. 2023).
[22] Meinecke v. State, 351 So. 3d 1196, 411 Educ. L. Rep.434 (Fla. Dist. Ct. App. 2022).
[23] State v. Edwards, 879 S.E.2d 391, 409 Educ. L. Rep. 533 (N.C. Ct. App. 2022).

without voter approval of a constitutional amendment.[24] In Minnesota, a licensed early childhood center was denied its application for a property tax exemption as a seminary of learning. The Tax Court upheld the denial. On appeal, the Supreme Court of Minnesota reversed the Tax Court's decision, holding that the center was an educational institution eligible for the tax exemption by providing a thorough and comprehensive general education, as required for the designation as a seminary of learning.[25]

The Supreme Court of Pennsylvania considered a taxpayer appeal challenging a school district's method of selecting property assessments for appraisal appeal. The taxpayers contended that using a monetary threshold for recently sold properties violated the constitutional principle of tax uniformity by creating targeted subclasses of properties. Lower courts found for the school district and county board of assessment; the state's Supreme Court affirmed those decisions, finding that the selection methodology did not violate the uniformity clause.[26] A property tax incentive program, referred to as Chapter 313 because of its location in the Texas Tax Code, allowed significant property tax breaks to businesses that made eligible investments within a school district's boundaries. The specific language of the law enacted in 2001 required the comptroller to evaluate applications within 90 days of timely filing but also stipulated that no new applications could be approved after December 31, 2022. Despite planning for the anticipated influx of applications late that year, the comptroller reported that the volume of applications exceeded his capacity to process by the end-of-the-year deadline. As a result, some applications, even though timely filed, could not be evaluated and granted. The impacted taxpayers petitioned for a writ of mandamus compelling the comptroller to evaluate their applications before the program expired. The Texas Supreme Court's opinion denying the petition explained that the incentive program and its deadlines were legislative creations and not best administered by the courts.[27] After a board-approved property tax

---

[24] Commonwealth *ex rel.* Cameron v. Johnson, 658 S.W.3d 25, 411 Educ. L. Rep. 1218 (Ky. 2022).
[25] Under the Rainbow Early Educ. Ctr. v. Cnty. of Goodhue, 978 N.W.2d 893, 407 Educ. L. Rep. 272 (Minn. 2022).
[26] GM Berkshire Hills LLC v. Berks Cnty. Bd. of Assessment, 290 A.3d 238, 413 Educ. L. Rep. 362 (Pa. 2023).
[27] In re Stetson Renewables Holdings, LLC, 658 S.W.3d 292, 411 Educ. L. Rep. 1237 (Tex. 2022).

increase, eight opponents of the increase filed a referendum petition application with the county clerk's office. With an explanatory letter from the district attorney, the clerk denied the application. Reconsideration by the district attorney yielded the same result, which triggered the appeal to the Supreme Court of Utah. This court held that the argument presented by the applicants did not successfully demonstrate that the tax increase approved by the school district was subject to referendum.[28]

In lower state courts, two cases concerned challenges to the use of tax funds. Three other cases involved protests about taxes levied on specific properties. The last case examined the eligibility of a property for exemption. The first challenge to the use of funds was in California, where a district received significant reimbursement funding after the 2014 completion of a voter-approved project. The superintendent recommended that the reimbursement funding primarily be used for new capital projects, with only a small portion of it designated to retire the bonds raised for the 2014 project. Taxpayers challenged the use of reimbursement funds for purposes other than retiring existing debt but were denied. On appeal, the original decision was reversed. Among the holdings was a determination that the language governing the use of state reimbursement funds was the intent to reward savings achieved during construction, which had not happened with the project originally funded with special tax bonds.[29] In New York, homeowners lodged their protest about the use of tax funds after the election where the tax was approved. The election results contained a proposition for the construction of a public library. The homeowners contended that the proposition violated the Equal Protection Clause and their due process rights. The original request for declaratory judgment was denied; on appeal by the homeowners, the state court affirmed that decision, with clarifying language that the city was not a proper party to the proceeding.[30]

Three protests of specific tax levies were in Illinois, New York, and Ohio. The Illinois case concerned objections from condominium and townhouse associations that sought relief from property taxes

---

[28] Lord v. Salt Lake Cnty. Clerk, 519 P.3d 178, 408 Educ. L. Rep. 1081 (Utah 2022).

[29] Bates v. Poway Unified Sch. Dist., 299 Cal.Rptr.3d 828, 408 Educ. L. Rep. 949 (Cal. Ct. App. 2022).

[30] Eisenhauer v. Watertown City Sch. Dist., 173 N.Y.S.3d 774, 407 Educ. L. Rep. 890 (N.Y. App. Div. 2022).

because the school district was alleged to have an excess of various funds. Attempts at similar protests in prior years had been stymied by a lack of standing on the part of the associations to act on behalf of individual owners. Their appeal to the negative decision in this case, though, yielded a reverse-and-remand order. The appellate court determined that a homeowner's association had standing under the Property Tax Code and Condominium Property Act, and even if not allowed by the Code and the Act, the association had associational standing.[31] The New York case was a straightforward effort by a petitioner to get a review of three prior years' assessments. However, he did not comply with the notice requirements and both his original petition and appeal were dismissed.[32] The Ohio dispute concerned an increase in the value of a series of properties sold at arms-length transactions as part of a tax assessment proceeding brought by a board of education. The taxpayer appealed the decision of the Board of Tax Appeals, but the original decision was affirmed. The Court of Appeals found that the BTA acted within its scope of authority in admitting late evidence, the BTA's independent valuation was supported by sufficient evidence, and that it was not obligated to assign extra significance to a valuation provided by the taxpayer's appraiser.[33] The final taxation case decided by a state court was an appeal by a New York college preparatory school that claimed its nonprofit school status made it eligible for property tax exemption because the townhouses that comprised the property are primarily used as a school. The city assessor and board of assessment denied the exemption application. The school's appeal was successful, with the appellate court finding that the nonprofit school demonstrated that the primary use was for operation as a school, a requirement for the exemption.[34]

Finance

Two finance cases were decided by state supreme courts in Alaska and North Carolina, and two others by other state appellate

---

[31] Sunnyside Elgin Apartments, LLC v. Miller, 196 N.E.3d 418, 408 Educ. L. Rep. 995 (Ill. App. Ct. 2021).

[32] DP Fuller Family LP v. City of Canandaigua, 172 N.Y.S.3d 550, 406 Educ. L. Rep. 352 (N.Y. App. Div. 2022).

[33] Columbus City Schs. Bd. of Educ. v. Franklin Cnty. Bd. of Revision, 201 N.E.3d 367, 411 Educ. L. Rep. 771 (Ohio Ct. App. 2022).

[34] Rye Country Day Sch. v. Whitty, 182 N.Y.S.3d 206, 412 Educ. L. Rep. 266 (N.Y. App. Div. 2023).

courts in Indiana and New York. The Alaska State Legislative Council brought action against the governor because he did not execute an appropriation for public education. The Council and an intervening education advocacy group prevailed in a lower court, including an award of attorney fees. The governor appealed, and the Supreme Court of Alaska reversed the lower court's decision, finding that the state constitution's budget clauses implicitly required the budget to be determined annually without forward-funded appropriations or an exception for public education.[35] The North Carolina case centered on the constitutional right of children to have the opportunity to receive a "sound basic education" and whether funds can be transferred for that purpose by the court system. The conditions underlying *Hoke County Board of Education v. The State of North Carolina* had been litigated for years, but a consent order from 2018 produced a comprehensive remedial plan (CRP) to be fully implemented by 2028. At the end of year one, the school system had not met its CRP goals. The trial court ordered the transfer of funds to fully implement the CRP, but the 2022 Budget Act made that calculation and transfer order moot. The Supreme Court of North Carolina remanded the case to the trial court with instructions to recalculate the underfunding for years two and three considering the 2022 Budget Act, reinstate the transfer directive in the November 2021 order, and retain jurisdiction over the case to monitor compliance with the CRP.[36]

An Indiana statute that required school systems to sell or lease unused properties to charter schools or state educational institutions for $1 was challenged by two school corporations, contending that the statute violated takings clauses of the Fifth Amendment. Summary judgment was granted on the defendant state's motion. The school corporations appealed, but the appellate court affirmed the lower court's decision, holding that school corporations, as branches of the state, could not assert takings claims.[37] A New York case was triggered by adopting the Department of Education budget through the city council without the approval of the board of education and before the chancellor

---

[35] State v. Alaska Legis. Council, 515 P.3d 117, 406 Educ. L. Rep. 988 (Alaska 2022).
[36] Hoke Cnty. Bd. of Educ. v. State, 879 S.E.2d 193, 409 Educ. L. Rep. 417 (N.C. 2022).
[37] Lake Ridge Sch. Corp. v. Holcomb, 198 N.E.3d 715, 409 Educ. L. Rep. 924 (Ind. Ct. App. 2022).

had submitted estimated expenses. Petitioners challenging the city budget were granted their petition and the budget was ordered vacated regarding DOE funding, with spending levels to return to the prior year's figures pending a new budget vote. The city appealed, but the lower court decision was affirmed with modifications, namely that ordering the spending levels to revert to the prior year was unwarranted.[38]

Charter Schools

Administration

Four cases addressed issues concerning the administration of charter schools. A First Amendment retaliation case in Florida was heard in a federal district court, determining whether a husband and wife exercised expression as private citizens or as employees of the charter school. Also at issue was whether the wife suffered retaliation because of her husband's speech. The husband served on the charter school's governing board and his wife was an elementary school teacher. Over three years, both made critical comments about the school's governance and the job performance of employees. They complained that the charter school's administration forced the husband to resign from the board, while the wife was transferred to another campus and eventually her employment was terminated. The charter school's motion for summary judgment was granted, with the reasoning that the husband/board member sent emails and spoke at board meetings in his role as a board member, and the wife criticized the principal and coworker in her role as an employee. Neither of the complainants spoke as private citizens nor on topics of public concern. The wife's associational rights with her husband also were not violated.[39] In Colorado, a charter school application was denied by the county school district and that denial was affirmed by the state board of education. After an appellate court reversed the decision, the school district and state board petitioned the state's supreme court. The Supreme Court of Colorado reversed the lower court decision and affirmed the state board's final authority

---

[38] Tucker v. City of N.Y., 178 N.Y.S.3d 518, 410 Educ. L. Rep. 495 (N.Y. App. Div. 2022).

[39] Teblum v. City of Cape Coral Charter Sch. Auth., 622 F. Supp. 3d 1235, 415 Educ. L. Rep. 166 (M.D. Fla. 2022).

concerning the denial of charter applications as not subject to judicial review.[40]

Two other state court cases concerned charter school administration. In Missouri, an initial filing in federal district court dismissed federal statutory and constitutional claims concerning state vaccination and exemption regulations. That decision was affirmed on appeal and remanded to state court, where the state claims again were dismissed. On appeal, the county circuit court held that the complaining parents and students did not have standing to sue the city and county health departments, and that the regulations about appropriate documentation forms requiring an assertion of religious exemption did not violate the unbridled discretion doctrine. The holdings further affirmed that the state vaccination requirement applied to charter schools.[41] A Pennsylvania school district amended its renewal agreement with a charter school to require that the conditions of employee healthcare and teacher certification be the same as the district's. The charter school's motion for summary judgment was granted; the court found that the school district could not unilaterally amend material terms of the renewal agreement.[42]

Funding and Resources for Charter Schools

The Eighth Circuit added to a 50-year history of litigation concerning school desegregation in Missouri. The school district's motion for summary judgment was for a conclusion that the charter schools should have received their per-pupil share of special sales tax revenue, but that charter schools were required to spend such revenue on remediation programs related to the ongoing desegregation effort in the same manner as the public schools. The Eighth Circuit decision clarified that charter school students were entitled to the same per-pupil funding formula as students in the school district. Charter schools had no legacy of segregation and were not parties to a prior settlement agreement,

---

[40] Colorado State Bd. of Educ. v. Brannberg, 525 P.3d 290, 412 Educ. L. Rep. 1016 (Colo. 2023).

[41] Baker v. Crossroads Acad.-Central St., 648 S.W.3d 790, 407 Educ. L. Rep. 318 (Mo. Ct. App. W.D. 2022).

[42] Souderton Charter Sch. Collaborative v. Souderton Area Sch. Dist., 291 A.3d 447, 414 Educ. L. Rep. 612 (Pa. Commw. 2023).

so were not required to spend special sales tax revenue on desegregation programs, as were the public schools.[43]

A nonprofit corporation holding a charter granted by the Arizona State Board for Charter Schools operated two schools in the state. After a county authority made a secured loan to the local charter school on bond proceeds through a Minnesota bank, the school failed to make the agreed debt service payments for three years. The trustee for the loan began an action for a receiver on the authority of a probate court in Minnesota, after which the charter school operator appealed the appointment of the receiver. An appellate court affirmed the earlier decision, finding that the receivership was timely even with the application of a one-year statute of limitations. The Arizona court's consideration and deference to the Minnesota court's ruling that the forbearance agreement did not bar the appointment of a receiver was appropriate.[44]

Other Charter School Issues

A trademark dispute in New York involved a plaintiff who had a former relationship with the charter school using the name "Finn Academy" without her permission. Her claim of common law trademark infringement and unfair competition was dismissed. She then moved for reconsideration to amend her complaint. The federal district court, denying her motion for reconsideration but granting part of her request to amend, found she failed to state a claim under the Lanham Act for unfair competition and false designation of origin, but her claim of trademark infringement was covered by the continuing tort doctrine.[45] In Florida, a school district received several complaints about a charter school with which it had a contract. The district's legal counsel investigated the complaints and produced a public report, which prompted the charter school to seek to depose two former school district employees regarding their conversations with the attorney. The school district and former employees claimed attorney-client privilege in declining the deposition but were not persuasive in

---

[43] Liddell v. Special Sch. Dist., 65 F.4th 969, 414 Educ. L. Rep. 516 (8th Cir. 2023).
[44] UMB Bank, NA v. Parkview Sch., Inc., 523 P.3d 1261, 411 Educ. L. Rep. 1185 (Ariz. Ct. App. 2023).
[45] Thurber v. Finn Acad.: An Elmira Charter Sch., 583 F. Supp. 3d 437, 407 Educ. L. Rep. 136 (W.D.N.Y. 2022).

that argument. Their petition for a writ of certiorari was denied. The District Court of Appeal held that the conversations between the former employees and the investigating attorney were not protected by attorney-client privilege and that the discussions were not "public meetings" as defined by the Sunshine Law.[46]

Localized Governance Issues

Breach of Contract

In 2023, the types of contracts breached varied more than the previous year. The first three of the nine breach of contract cases were related to school construction. In the first, a Texas school district claimed that an athletic turf manufacturer and the general contractor breached their warranty and committed fraud when an artificial turf sports field they installed degraded within five years while under an eight-year warranty. Although the manufacturer offered to repair the field, the district installed a new field and brought claims for damages equal to the replacement cost. Upon remand after a jury verdict and state supreme court appeal,[47] the state appellate court reversed the jury's award of damages to the school district on the grounds that the clear language of the warranty relative to repair and replacement was the exclusive remedy for breach of warranty, and that the school district failed to provide evidence of damages beyond those covered by the warranty.

The second construction case involved a New York contractor performing renovation services according to a project labor agreement (PLA) with the city's school construction authority. After several unexpected delays, resulting in tradespersons working less than eight-hour days, the contractor brought claims requesting additional compensation and damages based on the PLA's requirement to pay tradespersons for an eight-hour day even if they were unable to work for the full eight hours. On appeal of the trial court's granting the defendant's motion to dismiss,[48] the

---

[46] Collier Cnty. Pub. Schs. v. Mason Classical Acad., Inc., 342 So. 3d 753, 406 Educ. L. Rep. 547 (Fla. Dist. Ct. App. 2022).

[47] Pleasant Grove Indep. Sch. Dist. v. FieldTurf USA Inc., 648 S.W.3d 608, 406 Educ. L. Rep. 1036 (Tex. App.-Texarkana 2022).

[48] Landmark Grp., Inc. v. N.Y. City Sch. Const. Authority, 186 N.Y.S.3d 16, 414 Educ. L. Rep. 692 (N.Y. App. Div. 2023).

appellate court dismissed the claims, noting that the contractor was notified in the bid solicitation letter of the requirement to follow the PLA and, upon entering into the contract, agreed to follow the provision to pay individuals for an eight-hour shift regardless of the actual number of hours worked.

The final contract case related to construction concerned a California general contractor and subcontractors hired to build a school in downtown Los Angeles. When various delays, including the discovery of cracks in the concrete foundation, caused issues with meeting the agreed-upon timelines, the general contractor sued the school district for breach of contract. Claiming that the district's faulty plans were the cause of the delays, the contractor sought compensation for the cost overruns resulting from the delays. In a two-phase process, the trial court determined that the issues with the concrete foundation were the result of the school district's inadequate plans and specifications. A separate judge and jury ruled that the school district had a good faith basis to withhold the retention fee for claims based on other delays. The superior court denied the school district's and general contractor's post-trial motions for judgment notwithstanding the verdict (JNOV) and a new trial, awarding the general contractor and one subcontractor attorney fees. The district and general contractor appealed. In a mixed ruling[49], the court of appeals reversed and remanded for retrial both the original claims and the corresponding damages awarded in the second trial. The court further reversed the JNOV ruling, ordering the court to reinstate the jury verdict and reverse the post-trial awarding of attorney fees.

Two cases supplemented the breach of contract claims with unjust enrichment claims. In the first, a New York school district failed to pay a contracted school bus company for the months during which all schools were closed due to the COVID-19 pandemic. The bus company brought claims of breach of contract and unjust enrichment, asserting that it was ready to provide services during the three months in which the schools were closed and therefore should be compensated as per the contract. The school district filed a motion to dismiss, which the trial court denied. Ruling on the school district's appeal,[50] the court opined

[49] Suffolk Constr. Co., Inc. v. L.A. Unified Sch. Dist., 307 Cal. Rptr. 3d 603, 415 Educ. L. Rep. 273 (Cal. Ct. App. 2d Dist. 2023).

[50] Pierce Coach Line, Inc. v. Port Wash. Union Free Sch. Dist., 185 N.Y.S.3d 187, 414 Educ. L. Rep. 416 (N.Y. App. Div. 2023).

that the bus company failed to state the article of the contract that the school district violated and that the district did not receive a benefit at the plaintiff's expense. Based on these two findings, the court reversed the dismissal of claims.

In the second case, an Arkansas school district brought claims against a termite-prevention service for breach of contract and unjust enrichment. In 2017, the school district previously filed a complaint against the same company because the schools became infested with termites after treatment. The court dismissed this first complaint based on the expiration of the statute of limitations. In response, the school district filed a new complaint against the same defendants and containing many of the same claims. Upon defendants' motion to dismiss, the court dismissed the new claims as well, and the school district appealed. Reviewing the motion to dismiss, the court of appeals affirmed the trial court ruling dismissing the school district's second claim based on res judicata.[51]

Another Texas case involved a school district that disagreed with the state school board association's risk management fund, claiming that the fund underpaid a reimbursement for property damage arising from a hailstorm. Although both parties acknowledged that the school district failed to adhere to the contractual requirement that necessary repairs must be made within one year of the alleged damage, the school district filed suit for breach of contract against the fund. The trial court sided with the school district, finding that the fund waived governmental immunity. Ruling on the fund's appeal of the trial court decision, the appellate court determined that the school district's waiver and estoppel assertions were defenses against the fund's claims, not claims outside the parameters of the contract.[52] Based on this reasoning, the appellate court affirmed the trial court's ruling in favor of the school district.

In a dispute over an intergovernmental agreement in Georgia, the county board of education and a separate city board of education signed an agreement authorizing, but not requiring, each board to educate "cross-over" students from one district who chose to attend school in the other district. In return, the

---

[51] Brinkley Sch. Dist. v. Terminix Int'l Co., L.P., 663 S.W.3d 807, 415 Educ. L. Rep. 382 (Ark. Ct. App. 2023).
[52] Tex. Ass'n of Sch. Bds. Risk Mgmt. Fund v. Colo. Indep. Sch. Dist., 660 S.W.3d 767, 412 Educ. L. Rep.876 (Tex. App. 2023).

agreement required the two boards to share tax revenue on a *pro rata* basis for the educational expenses incurred. After an economic downturn in 2007, the two school districts continued to educate the cross-over students but failed to exchange tax revenue as per the agreement; this status continued until 2020, when the county district requested compliance with the agreement and the partner district refused. The county school district filed claims seeking to enforce the agreement, but the trial court ruled that the agreement was unenforceable based on the state constitution's Intergovernmental Contract Clause, which only addressed provision of services, not revenue-sharing. Reversing the trial court's ruling,[53] the state appellate court opined that the revenue-sharing aspect of the agreement was in support of providing a service, namely, the education of the cross-over students. Because the primary purpose of the agreement was the provision of services, the agreement was enforceable under the state constitution.

A company that manufactured school lockers sued an Alabama school district for breach of contract. In response, the school district filed a writ of mandamus directing the court to dismiss the lawsuit on the grounds of state immunity. Based upon the state immunity laws, the court found for the school district, granting the writ of mandamus and thereby dismissing the breach of contract suit,[54] denying the locker manufacturer's request to revisit precedent, and holding that county boards of education are agencies of the state and therefore are immune under the state constitution.

In an Indiana case, a school district contracted with an auction service to sell various pieces of school district property, one of which was a scale model of a Picasso sculpture that had been donated to the school. Approximately three weeks after the winning bidder paid for the model, the auction service notified the bidder that the sale was invalid because the school district did not provide proper notice to the mayor and the emergency manager of the school district for sale of school property. When the auction service rebid the model, a different bidder won and paid substantially more for the replica. The first bidder brought claims of breach of contract, fraud, and civil conversion. Appealing a

---

[53] Jackson Cnty. Bd. of Educ. v. City of Commerce Bd. Of Educ., 884 S.E.2d 147, 413 Educ. L. Rep. 470 (Ga. Ct. App. 2023).

[54] Ex parte Jefferson Cnty. Bd. of Educ., 348 So. 3d 397, 409 Educ. L. Rep. 570 (Ala. 2021).

partial summary judgment at the trial court level, the appellate court observed that the notification requirement prior to selling the property of a distressed political subdivision was not a mandatory provision.[55] Because the contract provided the auction company with the authority to determine the successful bidder, the original bidding process was valid, and therefore the first bidder was the legitimate owner of the model.

Copyright or Trademark Infringement

The only copyright/trademark infringement case was almost identical to the one summarized in 2022. To promote reading achievement among their students, a Texas school district implemented a reading incentive program with a theme related to becoming a millionaire. Upon learning of the program, a company producing educational resources for reading instruction filed a complaint against the school district and a system of charter schools for trademark infringement under the Lanham Act, alleging that the district reading program used symbols and branding confusingly similar to their trademarked products. Citing the court's prior dismissal of similar claims against other Texas school districts, The United States Court of Appeals, Fifth Circuit, affirmed the lower court's awarding of summary judgment to the district and charter school,[56] holding that the Lanham Act's prohibitions against trademark infringement relied on the likelihood of consumer confusion between the trademarks in question and that the chances of such confusion were minimal. Additionally, the circuit court reversed the lower court's sovereign immunity decisions, ruling that the school district merited sovereign immunity, but the charter school system did not.

Insurance

A Louisiana school district rented a school campus to a charter school. The charter management organization (CMO) employed by the charter school contracted with a construction company to be the general contractor for a construction project. The general

---

[55] Paul Terrault & Gary Cmty. Sch. Corp. v. Scheere, 200 N.E.3d 490, 411 Educ. L. Rep. 333 (Ind. Ct. App. 2022).
[56] Springboards to Education, Inc. v. McAllen Indep. Sch. Dist., 62 F.4th 174, 412 Educ. L. Rep. 431 (5th Cir. 2023).

contractor then contracted with a subcontractor to perform the asbestos abatement needed to begin construction. The umbrella insurance coverage for the project specifically stated that any bodily injury or property damage resulting from the asbestos removal was an exception. After an inspection by the state environmental quality board found multiple violations, the school district and CMO filed suit to recover damages related to the contamination of property and classroom materials, as well as reputational damage. The insurance company filed a motion for summary judgment to dismiss all parties' claims for reimbursement, and the trial court granted the motion in part, only allowing the dismissal of claims covered by the asbestos exceptions in the policy. Upon review of this ruling, the appellate court granted the insurance company's request for a writ but denied any relief based on the writ.[57]

The remaining two insurance cases both considered school district liability when students alleged sexual molestation or physical/verbal abuse by school employees. In the first case, an Illinois school district was named in several lawsuits filed by minors who alleged sexual abuse by an employee of the district who also worked for a community organization renting a school facility to run an after-school program. A condition of the rental agreement was that the community organization agree to name the district as an additional insured in its general liability policy, as well as that the insurer was required to defend, indemnify, and hold harmless the district against any claims arising from the organization's use of the school. The lawsuits alleged willful and wanton hiring, retention, and supervision against the school district. The general liability insurer for the community organization filed a declaratory judgment request, asking the court to determine that it had no duty to defend the school district because of the litigation. Both parties filed motions for summary judgment; the circuit court granted the district's motion. On appeal,[58] the court ruled that the underlying complaint in the minors' lawsuits contained allegations that could fall under the category of general liability for certain negligent acts related to physical abuse and sexual molestation. Further, the clear language of the policy only imposed notice

---

[57] Choice Found. v. Law Indus., LLC, 351 So.3d 746, 410 Educ. L. Rep. 831 (La. Ct. App. 2022).

[58] West Bend Mut. Ins. Co. v. Community Unit Sch. Dist. 300, 193 N.E.3d 266, 407 Educ. L. Rep. 248 (Ill. App. Ct. 2021).

requirements on the named insured, the community organization, not the additional insured, the school district.

Similarly, the second case focused on a Michigan school district disputing the extent to which an insurance company had a duty to defend and indemnify the school district in connection with a lawsuit alleging that school district employees physically and verbally abused students with disabilities. The parent plaintiffs filed a motion for partial summary judgment, requesting that the insurer must cover costs for the defense and for claims on which the parents were successful. The school district and insurance company subsequently filed cross-motions for summary judgment, asking the court to rule that the parent plaintiffs could not seek reimbursement for the 2010-11 school year due to ambiguity in their complaint. Rejecting this reasoning, the district court denied the school district and insurer's request to modify the trial court order, retaining the ability for the parents to litigate abuse claims for the 2010-11 school year.

Property Rights

The first five property cases concern property purchases for school construction. In the first case, a Louisiana private school purchased a property with the intent to build a school. Because the charter school could not secure financing for construction, six supporters of the school formed an investment LLC to assist in obtaining financing by purchasing the property from the school and leasing it back to them through a ten-year, fixed-term lease agreement. The bank agreed to loan $1.5 million to the investment group, which then paid off the existing mortgage and used the remaining funds to build the school. Before the expiration of the lease, the school and investment group amended the lease, removing the option for the school to purchase the property, and the investment group then donated the property to a local charitable organization. The charter school sued, claiming that the sale of the property to the investment group was a financing arrangement, not an actual sale. Both parties filed cross-motions for partial summary judgment, with the trial court denying the school's motion and finding that a valid sale/leaseback transaction took place. On appeal, the court reversed the granting of summary judgment to the defendant investment group,[59] stating that there were general issues of material fact as to whether the sale/leaseback arrangement was merely a financing arrangement.

In the second case, a zoning dispute, the petitioner contracted to purchase 35 acres of undeveloped property to build a K-12 charter school in North Carolina. When the charter school presented evidence in support of its proposed major subdivision plan, the planning board and board of commissioners unanimously denied the application, reasoning that the petitioner failed to satisfy town policies related to promoting desirable growth patterns and safe vehicular and pedestrian traffic through residential areas. The petitioner appealed to the superior court, which in turn affirmed the board's denial of the plan based upon a lack of bicycle and pedestrian connectivity as required by the town community plan. In another appeal of the denial,[60] the appellate court opined that, despite the charter school no longer seeking to construct a building at the location in question, the appeal was not moot, and the trial court erred in using a whole record test to determine the sufficiency of the petitioner's evidence. However, the appellate court ultimately affirmed the trial court ruling, stating that the petitioner failed to establish an entitlement to the requested permits.

In the third property purchase case, an Ohio farmer sold property to a local school district, stipulating in the sale contract that the farmer could continue to farm the land until such time that the district commenced construction on the property. Approximately ten years later, the school district notified the farmer that it intended to occupy the property and construct a facility to support school agricultural programs, therefore providing notice of termination of his rights to use the property. The farmer filed claims for breach of contract, arguing that the bill of sale required the construction of a school and not an ancillary building. Finding that the sale contract did not require the construction of a school, the trial court granted the school district's summary judgment request. Despite the farmer's unsuccessful appeal of this ruling, the school district filed claims to terminate the farmer's use of the property based on the sale

---

[59] Cypress Hts. Acad. v. CHA Investors, LLC, 343 So.3d 736, 407 Educ. L. Rep. 375 (La. Ct. App. 2022).

[60] Schooldev East, LLC v. Town of Wake Forest, 876 S.E.2d 607, 406 Educ. L. Rep. 22 (N.C. Ct. App. 2022).

contract terms and additionally requested that the court award the planted crops and find the farmer guilty of trespass. The trial court again ruled for the school district and assessed damages to the defendant. On appeal,[61] the court determined that the trial court's application of res judicata was correct and that the finding of trespassing was warranted based on the contract language.

The fourth property purchase case addressed concerned New York homeowners who filed suit against a not-for-profit corporation that purchased adjacent land to build a private school campus. The homeowners claimed that the restrictive covenant provision in the property deed, barring the construction of an "institution" on the property, prohibited building a school. The trial court sided with the not-for-profit corporation, dismissing the plaintiffs' motion for declaratory relief. The homeowners appealed, asking the court to strike certain portions of the defendants' brief as raising issues for the first time on appeal. The appellate court disagreed,[62] finding that the trial court erred in dismissing the plaintiffs' declaratory motion because the interpretation of the term "institution" did not bar the defendant from building a school on the land, thus ordering the trial court to enter a decision for the defense.

The final property purchase case, also involving a restrictive covenant, found a county board of education in Alabama disputing the use of property sold to a nearby university. The property in question was the former campus of a high school closed by the board. The university purchased the campus for the stated use of housing various educational programs and administrative staff and also promised not to open or operate a charter school, which was reflected in a restrictive covenant placed into the sales contract between the parties but not the property deed. When a charter school organization later filed an application to operate a charter school, it identified the property as its first-choice location under the charter school statute provision giving charter schools the first right of refusal to closed school buildings. The university agreed to allow the charter school's use of the property, after which the board of education filed suit claiming reformation of deed as well as fraud and breach of contract. The trial court ruled for the

[61] Teays Valley Local Sch. Dist. Bd. of Educ. v. Struckman, 206 N.E.3d 796, 414 Educ. L. Rep. 695 (Ohio Ct. App. 2023).

[62] Gedney Ass'n, Inc. v. Common Council of City of White Plains, 176 N.Y.S.3d 702, 409 Educ. L. Rep. 316 (N.Y. App. Div. 2022).

university, stating that the property restriction sought by the plaintiffs violated public policy, specifically the aforementioned school choice statute, and that the charter school organization was an indispensable defendant not named in the proceedings. The board appealed, claiming that the application of the school choice statute to a sales contract pre-dating the statute was a retroactive application of the law. The appellate court disagreed,[63] affirming the trial court decision because the restrictive covenant was rendered unenforceable upon legislative action to adopt the school choice statute with its provision for the first right of refusal for any unused school buildings as a matter of public policy.

Two cases addressed private school requests to install outdoor athletic field lighting. In the first case, a California private school applied for the city planning commission seeking approval to add four permanent 90-foot-tall light standards to its existing athletic stadium located in a residential neighborhood. Upon review of the application, the planning commission determined that the project was exempt from California's environmental quality statute and approved conditional use that limited the number of nights a year for use and the time of day by which the lights must be dimmed or turned off. The board of supervisors affirmed this plan, imposing more restrictive conditions on the usage of the lights, the reporting for compliance purposes, and the planting of trees to screen the homes from the lights. The neighborhood association filed a petition for a writ of mandate, claiming that the project was subject to the environmental quality statute and that the conditional use was inconsistent with the city planning code. The trial court denied the petition and the neighborhood association appealed. Ruling for the neighborhood association,[64] the appellate court opined that the project did not qualify for any of the statutory exemptions, reversing the trial court ruling and requiring a project review in light of the environmental quality standards.

The second case involved a Wisconsin private school that the city re-zoned as a "Campus-Institutional District." The city provided the private school with an opportunity to submit a master plan including projected facilities and land use plans to enable the future growth of the institution. When the school decided to

---

[63] Sumter Cnty. Bd. of Educ. v. Univ. of W. Ala., 349 So.3d 1264, 409 Educ. L. Rep. 1022 (Ala. 2021).

[64] St. Ignatius Neighborhood Ass'n v. City & Cnty. of S.F., 301 Cal. Rptr. 3d 641, 409 Educ. L. Rep. 893 (Cal. Ct. App. 1st Dist. 2022).

upgrade its athletic fields by adding seating, lighting, concessions, and restrooms, the city ultimately determined that the submitted master plan did not identify athletic contests as part of the planned land use, warning the school to cease all athletic contests on the field, a ruling upheld by the zoning board on appeal. The school then applied to install outdoor lighting for its athletic field under the city's outdoor lighting ordinance. The city again refused to release the permits, stating that the fields would be rendered usable for athletic contests. The zoning board affirmed the city decision, noting that the school could choose to repeal its master plan and re-file under the same zoning classification as other high schools, which would allow the school to install lights. However, after the school repealed its master plan, city officials changed the outdoor lighting approval to a conditional use permit and grandfathered in the existing schools with outdoor lights. When the private school was again denied a permit under the new ordinance, it filed suit. The District Court for Western Wisconsin[65] denied a motion to strike portions of the school's complaint as overly lengthy or unintelligible. Further, the court denied the defendants' motion to dismiss in part, dismissing the individual defendants but not the institutional defendants.

The next two cases address environmental concerns located near a school building. In a Texas case, the state's Commission on Environmental Quality approved a standard air quality permit for a concrete batch plant site proposed by a construction materials company. An environmental advocacy group filed for judicial review of the decision, claiming that the location of the plant was not compliant with the Texas Health and Safety Code requirements limiting air contaminants within 3,000 feet of a Montessori school. Upon review, the trial court affirmed approval of the application for the concrete plant. The environmental advocacy group appealed based on the school protectedness standard in the Health and Safety Code. Siding with the defendants,[66] the appellate court determined that although the Health and Safety Code applied to the company seeking the permit, the Environmental Quality Commission did consider potential

---

[65] Edgewood High Sch. of Sacred Heart, Inc. v. City of Madison, 601 F. Supp. 3d 413, 410 Educ. L. Rep. 1005 (W.D. Wis. 2022).
[66] Boerne to Bergheim Coal. for Clean Env't v. Tex. Comm'n on Env't Quality, 657 S.W.3d 382, 411 Educ. L. Rep. 818 (Tex. App. 2022).

effects concerning the nearby school and did not act unreasonably or arbitrarily in granting the permit.

In an ongoing appeal from a case reported last year, a Louisiana school district brought an oilfield remediation action against a company due to damage caused by oil exploration and mineral leases on land owned by the school district. A jury at the trial court level awarded $5 million for breach of contract and strict liability. Both parties appealed, and the Court of Appeal affirmed in part and reversed in part the jury's verdict. Granting a writ of certiorari, the state Supreme Court affirmed and remanded the Court of Appeal's decision, stating that strict liability applied because the school district did not know about the damage more than one year before filing its claims, and that the jury verdict awarding damages for oilfield remediation and strict liability, but not breach of contract, was not inconsistent. However, the Supreme Court did remand the case for a new trial on the basis that the portion of the damages awarded for remediation was not consistent with the statutory requirements that the damages awarded were limited to the costs for remediation, and any damages above the cost of the remediation should be the subject of a new trial.

The Colorado school code provides for cooperating school districts to establish a Board of Cooperative Services (BOCES) to manage shared services. When the BOCES established a shared school to address the needs of students with reading challenges, it physically located the school in a nonmember district. That district objected and filed suit against both the BOCES and the third-party contractor hired to operate the school. The parties filed cross-motions for summary judgment for their respective declaratory judgment claims, and the trial court granted the BOCES's motion, denying that of the school district. On appeal,[67] the court ruled that the plain language of the BOCES statute did not support an interpretation that the BOCES could establish a program in a location outside of the member districts without written permission from the nonmember school district in which the program would be located, reversing the trial court decision and awarding summary judgment to the nonmember district as a matter of law.

In a unique property-based school funding mechanism, Mississippi sets aside a sixteenth section of each township as a

---

[67] Educ. ReEnvisioned BOCES v. Colo. Springs Sch. Dist. 11, 524 P.3d 324, 412 Educ. L. Rep. 329 (Colo. App. 2022).

grant to the state to provide for the public education of the children in the municipality. The board of education manages the trust properties located within that district and distributes any revenues arising from the properties. If more than one school district educates the children of a township, the state code stipulates that the funds be divided as a *pro rata* share of the enrollment in each district as documented in a year-end filing. Two school districts sharing a sixteenth-section trust property disputed whether the *pro rata* distribution of royalties from oil and gas production on the property was equitable dating back to 1978. Because the plaintiff school district recreated the required student lists from historical documents for a 20-year time period in which they did not file them, the defendant school district moved for summary judgment, arguing that the statute of limitations for submitting the lists had expired. The plaintiff school district countered with a cross-motion for partial summary judgment, claiming that the one-year statute of limitations conflicted with the state constitution. The chancery court sided with the plaintiff school district and ordered the defendant district to pay a proportionate share of the trust funds for each year in which the recreated lists were submitted. Ruling that state law does not impose a duty to hold funds in escrow until the school district provides the student lists, the appellate court reversed the decision,[68] finding that the legally prescribed statute of limitations had expired.

The final case sought to clarify the status of a North Carolina school district as a legal entity owning property. In a criminal case, the court adjudicated as a habitual felon a defendant found guilty of possession of stolen goods, based in part on a prior conviction for illegally entering a building owned by the county schools and stealing various technology devices and appliances. Upon his conviction, the defendant filed a motion questioning the sufficiency of the indictment based on the use of the term "Graham County Schools" as the owner of the property in the indictment, because the legal entity owning school property was correctly identified as the "Graham County Board of Education." The trial court denied this motion, stating that the term "Graham County Schools" implied ownership by the board of education. On appeal, the court

---

[68] Wayne Cnty. Sch. Dist. v. Quitman Sch. Dist., 346 So.3d 853, 408 Educ. L. Rep. 598 (Miss. 2022).

affirmed the trial court decision as a matter of law,[69] ruling that the original indictment was sufficient as written.

Public Records and the Freedom of Information Act

In Washington state, a parent who believed that her daughter was subjected to harassment, bullying, and intimidation filed for a protective order in court after deciding that the school's actions were inadequate. To support the request for the order, the parent made three Public Records Act requests to the school district. Because the school district was not completely responsive to her requests, the parent filed a complaint seeking damages for the noncompliance. The trial court determined that the school district incorrectly withheld 85 emails for over 600 days, imposing damages on a per diem basis at $10 per day. The parent appealed the ruling. Although the appellate court found that the school district search responsive to the first request was adequate, the subsequent two searches were not reasonably calculated to find all responsive records, and that the significant delays in producing the responsive records amounted to a constructive denial.[70] The court remanded the case, instructing the trial court to base the damages calculation on the number of records denied, not just the length of the delay, and also to calculate appropriate attorney fees.

When a parent grabbed the wrist of a student-athlete during a post-game altercation at a Pennsylvania high school sports event, a news media organization filed a request for the bus camera video of the incident. The district denied the request, citing FERPA rules pertaining to educational records. The media representative appealed this decision to the Office of Open Records (OOR), which overturned the district's decision based upon a lack of evidence that the recording constituted an educational record. The Commonwealth Court supported the OOR's position on appeal. Considering an intervening decision, the Pennsylvania Supreme Court granted discretionary review to determine whether the ruling that a school bus video could not be disclosed to parents without violating FERPA was erroneous.[71] Based upon the

---

[69] State v. Edwards, 879 S.E.2d 391, 409 Educ. L. Rep. 533 (N.C. Ct. App. 2022).

[70] Cantu v. Yakima Sch. Dist. No. 7, 514 P.3d 661, 406 Educ. L. Rep. 497 (Wash. Ct. App. 2022).

[71] Cent. Dauphin Sch. Dist. v. Hawkins, 286 A.3d 726, 411 Educ. L. Rep. 664 (Pa. 2022).

similarities between the intervening case and this case, the Supreme Court affirmed the Commonwealth Court ruling that the district can comply with both FERPA and the Open Records Act by redacting the video before releasing it.

Under the public records law, a resident in Wisconsin filed a records request for the email addresses of all persons invited to a webinar on the topic of privilege and race. The school district denied the request, citing privacy and a need to maintain its relationship with the parents in the district. The trial court granted a writ of mandamus to the petitioner, and the school district appealed the decision. Despite the district's claim that releasing the emails would chill communication with parents, the appellate court affirmed the trial court's ruling,[72] finding that the district was not persuasive as to the potential chilling effect of releasing the emails and that concerns about what ideological information the petitioner might send to the parents was irrelevant, as the purpose of the open records law was not to allow the district to maintain an ideological monopoly.

A South Carolina school board amended its policy requiring that ESL students must attend separate magnet schools outside their attendance zones in favor of the students attending school with their attendance zone peers. Because this change occurred after the deadline to request transfers, the parent of an ESL student submitted a request for the board to reopen the transfer request process so their student could remain at the magnet school for the next year. The next board meeting incorporated an executive session, after which the board acknowledged receiving the complaint and said that they would respond in writing the next day. The parent subsequently received a written denial of her request, whereupon she asked the trial court to award a declaratory judgment that the board's discussion of the matter in executive session violated the Freedom of Information Act (FOIA). The trial court concurred with the parent, and the district appealed the decision. On review,[73] the appellate court affirmed the circuit court's determination that the board violated FOIA, but they vacated the portion of the injunction requiring the board to renew

---

[72] Gierl v. Mequon-Thiensville Sch. Dist., 985 N.W.2d 116, 412 Educ. L. Rep. 341 (Wis. Ct. App. 2022).

[73] Miramonti v. Richland Cnty. Sch. Dist. One, 885 S.E.2d 406, 414 Educ. L. Rep. 1072 (S.C. Ct. App. 2023).

deliberation on the issue as tantamount to a judicial decree requiring the board to take specific legislative action.

In New York, a teachers' association sought several records from the school district in which they worked. Although the association received some documents quickly, the district informed them that others would take more time to provide. When the district finally responded with the remaining documents, it notified the association that the request was approved in part and denied in part, providing some emails that were heavily redacted. The association filed an appeal of their ruling, seeking the unredacted records and attorney fees. The trial court concurred, ordering the school district to provide both the records and fees. The school district appealed the ruling,[74] but the appellate court affirmed the lower court's decision, opining that the school district withheld documents that were not exempt from Freedom of Information Law (FOIL) requirements.

Finally, a Virginia school board held its all-day board training and strategic planning at the local College and Career Academy, a public school operated by the school district. As required by law, the board posted a public notice of the meeting. At the time of the meeting, the board, claiming COVID-related concerns, denied a community member the opportunity to attend the meeting either in person or virtually. The community member filed a complaint seeking a writ of mandamus and/or injunctive relief, alleging that the board violated FOIA because their public notice did not list any restrictions on attendance by the public. The trial court agreed, awarding both the writ of mandamus and attorney fees. The district defendants appealed, but the appellate court affirmed the trial court ruling,[75] stating that the board willfully decided to deny public access despite the room size supporting public attendance. Further, the state statute did not imply that virtual attendance only sufficed for public access to meetings.

School Boundaries

In the only case addressing school boundaries, a school district requested judicial review of a regional board of trustees' decision

---

[74] Suffern Educ. Ass'n v. Bd. of Educ. of Suffern Cent. Sch. Dist. (b), 183 N.Y.S.3d 548, 412 Educ. L. Rep. 993 (N.Y. App. Div. 2023).
[75] Suffolk City Sch. Bd. v. Wahlstrom, 886 S.E.2d 244, 415 Educ. L. Rep. 351 (Va. 2023).

to grant an Illinois property owners' petition to detach their property from one school district and annex themselves to another contiguous district. The property owners reasoned that they wished for their son to be in a larger school with larger class sizes and that the majority of his friends attended the district to which they sought to attach their property. The circuit court of review affirmed the board of trustees' decision, in part basing their decision on a review of the school district state report card demographics. The school district appealed, and the appellate court reversed and remanded the circuit court decision,[76] citing the statutory requirement prohibiting the use of school report cards as a factor in changing districts unless there is no more than a three percent difference in the three demographic categories. Given the statutory violation, the court declined to rule on the other issues brought forward in the appeal.

School Operations

When a Missouri school district adopted a four-day student week with the stated purpose of cutting costs in education and attracting and retaining qualified teachers, a taxpayer resident filed suit. The resident claimed that the four-day schedule would be detrimental to students and would reduce property values. In his filing, he asked the court to issue a declaratory judgment that the four-day school week was unconstitutional and that the board must reimburse parents for expenses incurred caring for their children on the fifth day of the week. The board, filing a motion to dismiss, claimed that the taxpayer had no standing to bring claims against the district and that state sovereign immunity protected the board from litigation. The trial court agreed and dismissed the case. After the taxpayer appealed,[77] the appellate court affirmed the trial court's ruling, noting that the taxpayer lacked standing because he was not directly and adversely affected by the ruling, and the adoption of the four-day week did not amount to child abuse that, as a minister, he had a mandatory duty to report. The court further opined that the taxpayer had no due process rights

---

[76] Bd. of Educ. of Roxana Cmty. Unit Sch. Dist. No. 1, Madison Cnty. v. Regional Bd. of Sch. Trustees of Madison Cnty., 191 N.E.3d 559, 406 Educ. L. Rep. 362 (Ill. App. Ct. 2021)

[77] Lehmann v. Bd. of Educ. of Fayette R3 Sch. Dist., 649 S.W.3d 303, 407 Educ. L. Rep. 356 (Mo. Ct. App. W.D. 2022).

violated because he experienced no prejudice based upon the board's actions.

School closures are often contentious initiatives. When a Pennsylvania school board voted to close one of two high schools in a district with declining enrollment, a local advocacy group filed a complaint objecting to the decision, arguing that the hearing on the matter should have incorporated community input and that the board never considered the possibility of closing the other high school in the district. The parent group further postulated that the board's plan to explore the construction of a new athletic field was the true reason for recommending the closure of this particular high school. The advocacy group filed a complaint alleging a violation of the group's procedural due process rights under the Pennsylvania Constitution and a breach of the board's fiduciary duty to the community, but the trial court sustained the board's objections, resulting in the advocacy group appealing the ruling.[78] Affirming the trial court's decision, the appellate court stated that the applicable state statute conferred no procedural due process rights and that no fiduciary relationship existed between the parties.

Transportation

In Pennsylvania, public school districts are required to bus resident students to any private or charter school located within 10 miles of its district boundaries. A financially challenged Pennsylvania school district decided to purchase public transportation bus passes for charter school students rather than continue to provide their transportation. In response, the charter school system contracted with a private bus service for their elementary students but had the older students use the bus passes. A grandparent of two charter school children and the charter school itself jointly filed suit, claiming that the bus passes did not constitute free transportation as required both in the School Code and the Charter School Law. The trial court ruled that the law did not require public school and charter school students to receive the same type of transportation. On appeal, the Commonwealth Court reversed the trial court's ruling, stating that the statute required the district to receive approval from the state before changing

[78] Save Our Saltsburg Schs. v. River Valley Sch. Dist., 285 A.3d 692, 410 Educ. L. Rep. 450 (Commw. Ct. 2022).

transportation methods. The district again appealed,[79] and the Supreme Court agreed with the trial court's interpretation of the public school transportation statutes as not requiring that changes be approved by the Department of Education; it reversed and remanded the case back to the Commonwealth Court for consideration of issues raised by the charter school that the court did not address.

The other transportation case concerned a Washington state man convicted of possession and delivery of a controlled substance within 1,000 feet of a school bus route stop. He was subsequently sentenced to 240 months of confinement based on the sentencing guidelines. The defendant appealed, and the Court of Appeals remanded the case for resentencing, noting that the school bus route/stop zone sentencing enhancements were not required to run consecutively. On remand, the trial court reduced the sentence to 168 months. The defendant again appealed this new sentence. The Court of Appeals, reviewing the resentencing process,[80] determined that the statute permitting the doubling of the sentence when committed within 1,000 feet of a school zone was not unconstitutionally vague and that enforcement of the sentence did not punish unknowingly innocent conduct or violate the defendant's due process rights. However, the court did remand the case for resentencing due to improper calculation of the defendant's offender score and ordered the trial court to strike community custody supervision fees imposed on the defendant.

Miscellaneous

The first uncategorized case involves the creditor of a limited liability company (LLC) that operated post-secondary art schools in Ohio. At the creditor's request, the U.S. District Court for the Northern District of Ohio appointed a receiver and stayed all pending actions by creditors. After resolving a dispute over the proceeds of a liability insurance policy, the receiver sought court approval of the settlement agreement and an order preventing third-party litigants from pursuing claims against the parties to the settlement. Students of one of the LLC's schools appealed the court's approval of the settlement and order barring further

---

[79] Bell v. Wilkinsburg Sch. Dist., 283 A.3d 245, 408 Educ. L. Rep. 934 (Pa. 2022).
[80] State v. Richter, 521 P.3d 303, 410 Educ. L. Rep. 505 (Wash. Ct. App. 2022).

litigation. The Sixth Circuit Court of Appeals[81] reversed and remanded the court-approved settlement and order barring the students' litigation, opining that such an order was outside the scope of the receiver's authority and contradicted historical practice.

The remaining miscellaneous cases concern the role and actions of attorneys within the context of school litigation. A student plaintiff in Kentucky filed suit against the school district. As the pretrial processes unfolded, it became apparent that the plaintiff's attorney was non-responsive to requests for joint reports, scheduling matters, and discovery requests. After several months of failure to meet deadlines and submit required materials, the school district filed a motion to dismiss for failure to prosecute and failure to comply with the civil rules of order. The plaintiff's attorney argued that his negligence in adherence to timelines was excusable because he thought that the parties were working toward a settlement. He also claimed that he filed the discovery responses, but that the district filed their motion before receiving his responses. The U.S. District Court for Eastern Kentucky denied the district's motion,[82] citing the court's lack of opportunity to warn the plaintiffs about the possibility of dismissal for non-response. However, the court did impose a monetary sanction on the plaintiff's attorney and formally warned him about the need to adhere to timelines and submit required materials going forward.

Second, under the California Voting Rights Act (CVRA), a local attorney sent a demand letter to a school district on behalf of local residents, stating that compliance with the CVRA required the school district to shift the voting procedure for the board of trustees from an at-large method to a district-based method to gain equitable community representation. In response, the school district's trustees adopted a resolution converting the process to a district-based method and drew its district boundaries accordingly. Upon adoption of the voting districts, the attorney who initiated the demand letter contacted the school district's attorney, requesting payment for attorney fees and other costs totaling $30,000. The school district declined payment, and the attorney filed a petition for a writ of mandate to enforce the payment for the

---

[81] Digital Media Solutions, LLC v. S. Univ. of Ohio, LLC, 59 F.4th 772, 411 Educ. L. Rep.953 (6th Cir. 2023).

[82] A.V. *ex rel.* T.V. v. Bd. of Educ. of Fayette Cnty., Ky., 342 F.R.D. 331, 409 Educ. L. Rep. 880 (E.D. Ky. 2022).

cost of work product. The trial court denied the petition, stating that the attorney lacked a prospective plaintiff on whose behalf he completed the work. On appeal, the appellate court reversed and remanded the trial court decision,[83] citing the intent of the CVRA as contrary to a requirement for disenfranchised prospective plaintiffs to pay for the legal work before filing for reimbursement. The appellate court declined to rule on whether attorney fees are recoverable as a cost of the work product, leaving that decision to the trial court.

COVID-19

Eight cases involved issues stemming from COVID-19 disputes about required vaccination, special funding, COVID-related speech issues, and mask mandates. In the first case, four school districts in Michigan sued the state's Secretary of the Department of Health and Human Services and the Head Start program, seeking a preliminary injunction for a declaration that the state's required COVID-19 vaccination rule for employees was unlawful. The federal district court denied the motion, establishing that the Secretary's authority extended to the issuance of the rule, including Head Start; the rule was not arbitrary or capricious; and that the Secretary had good cause to waive the notice-and-comment period. The decision recognized that denial of the motion favored the balance between the school districts' interest and the public interest.[84] In a qui tam action against the New York City Department of Education (DOE), other departments of education, school districts, and superintendents across several states asserted that the DOE violated the False Claims Act by submitting reimbursement requests for remote services to students during the COVID-19 quarantine. The claim was that students with disabilities were provided remote services, against the requirements of Medicaid and the Individuals with Disabilities Education Act (IDEA). Such services were presented by the plaintiffs as depriving the students of a free appropriate public education. A Virginia school district and its superintendent moved to dismiss on issues of venue and jurisdiction. The Southern

---

[83] Law Office of Carlos R. Perez v. Whittier Union High Sch. Dist., 303 Cal. Rptr. 3d 566, 411 Educ. L. Rep. 317 (Cal. Ct. App. 2023).
[84] Livingston Educ. Serv. Agency v. Becerra, 589 F. Supp. 3d 697, 408 Educ. L. Rep. 276 (E.D. Mich. 2022).

District of New York held that settling issues of venue should precede other considerations. Further, the Virginia county school district was improperly joined and was required to be severed, the venue (SDNY) was improper, and transfer to the District Court for the Eastern District of Virginia was warranted.[85]

A South Carolina Catholic corporation filed an action against the administrators of the governor's office concerning the allocation of federal funds designed to assist with extra expenses related to schools' response to the COVID-19 quarantine, the Coronavirus Aid, Relief, and Economic Security Act (CARES Act). A provision of the South Carolina constitution barred private schools and universities from accessing the special funds. The plaintiff corporation blamed the lack of access on "longstanding and pervasive" religious and racial bigotry, violating the Free Exercise Clause and the Equal Protection Clause. Both sides of the dispute filed motions in limine to exclude the organization's expert and a state memorandum and exhibit. The District of South Carolina, Charleston Division, found that the Catholic organization lacked standing to challenge the Governor's Emergency Education Relief (GEER) funds, and that it failed to establish proof of discriminatory intent. The plaintiff's motion for summary judgment was denied.[86]

A dispute in Wisconsin centered on a parent's speech during the participatory part of a school board meeting where she expressed her concerns about requirements for masks and social distancing. Part of her speech was addressed to criticism of the board member who was a physician and had been designated by the board as its medical liaison. She objected to him serving as the board's liaison, in part because he was also a "leader in the Islamic community." Her comments produced a backlash on social media, resulting in the district's condemnation of her remarks about the doctor, posting it on the district's website, and distributing it to an email list of over 7,000 people. She also was barred from attending board meetings or participating in events at her children's school without prior approval. Her comments were excised from the district's posted video recording of the board meeting, and the district's Facebook page was altered to remove her comments while retaining other comments in favor of the district's action and the

---

[85] U.S. *ex rel.* Donohue v. Carranza, 585 F. Supp. 3d 383, 407 Educ. L. Rep. 663 (S.D.N.Y. 2022).

[86] Bishop of Charleston v. Adams, 584 F. Supp. 3d 131, 407 Educ. L. Rep. 534 (D.S.C. 2022).

physician. After the ban was lifted, the school district moved for summary judgment because the complaining parent had failed to respond to district requests for admissions. The court's holding granted the district's motion by denying the parent compensatory damages for financial or economic harm. However, the district's motion was denied on the parent's request for mental or emotional harm, or on the merits of her claims involving the ban and the deletion of her Facebook comments. The parent's motion to withdraw or amend her admissions was denied.[87]

A Montana parent group filed two separate actions contesting mandatory masking rules during the COVID-19 epidemic. Specifically, the parent group requested injunctive relief for violations of constitutional privacy, constitutional individual dignity, and parental rights. Both district courts in which the original complaints were filed denied the parents' request for an injunction. The appellate court consolidated the complaints due to their factual similarity.[88] The court rejected the parents' assertion that the schools manifestly abused their discretion in violation of their rights because (a) refusing to wear a preventive mask was not akin to refusing medical treatment, and therefore did not restrict privacy decision; (b) the wearing of a mask was not so cruel or offensive as to deny a person's right to human dignity; and (c) wearing masks bore a rational relationship to the legitimate governmental purpose of controlling the spread of disease.

A California parent group filed multiple actions to petition for a writ of mandate when the school district required all students ages 16 or older to receive the COVID-19 vaccine before attending in-person classes or participating in sports or extracurricular activities. Those choosing not to vaccinate were placed in independent study; although medical exemptions were honored, the district refused to recognize religious exceptions or personal beliefs as a valid excuse. The trial court consolidated all claims and then ruled in favor of the school district. On appeal,[89] the court noted that all ten mandatory vaccinations were approved by the legislature, not an individual school district. Therefore, the

---

[87] Anderson v. Hansen, 583 F. Supp. 3d 1180, 407 Educ. L. Rep. 150 (E.D. Wis. 2022).

[88] Stand Up Montana v. Missoula Cnty. Pub. Schs., 514 P.3d 1062, 406 Educ. L. Rep. 976 (Mont. 2022).

[89] Let Them Choose v. San Diego Unified Sch. Dist., 301 Cal. Rptr. 3d 667, 410 Educ. L. Rep. 461 (Cal. Ct. App. 4th Dist. 2022).

district's plan for immunizing students conflicted with the state requirements to admit any student who has proof of immunization for the ten identified vaccinations, and the district could not unilaterally add to those requirements.

Like many states, Missouri requires all students enrolling in public schools to provide proof of immunizations required by law. Parents requesting a religious exemption from vaccination are required to complete a form where they acknowledge the risks of refusing vaccination. A family whose children attended a charter school alleged that their handwritten note requesting religious exemption from vaccination was accepted by the school in lieu of the state form. When the charter school changed policy after several years and demanded the form, the parents refused to provide it, stating that the health department required pro-vaccine videos or questionnaires before providing the form. The charter school subsequently disenrolled the children, and the family filed suit on multiple federal and state bases. After the federal district court dismissed all federal claims and declined supplemental jurisdiction, the parents pursued the remaining claims in state court. The state court granted dismissal for all defendants and the family appealed. The appellate court affirmed the lower court ruling,[90] noting that the defendants lacked standing to file claims against the health department because the department's role is to implement, not approve, the statute. Further, the parents suffered no adverse exposure to pro-vaccine information because they did not attempt to acquire the form from the health department. The court also stated that the use of the required form bore a rational relationship to the legitimate governmental interest of controlling the spread of disease, and the free exercise of religion did not prohibit a governmental entity from sharing truthful information. Finally, the court also opined that charter schools must comply with state health requirements.

Voters in a Washington school district filed petitions for the recall of three of the five members of their district's board. The claim was that the members had knowingly violated the Open Public Meetings Act as well as several other abuses of their office. The Supreme Court of Washington determined that the members had violated the Open Public Meetings Act and had violated the law in excess of the power of their office, despite warnings from the

---

[90] Baker v. Crossroads Acad.-Central St., 648 S.W.3d 790, 407 Educ. L. Rep. 318 (Mo. Ct. App. W.D. 2022).

state and legal counsel. Further, the members' violation of the district's policies and procedures was both legally and factually sufficient to support the recall effort.[91]

Conclusion

The volume of governance cases exceeded the previous year, a possible consequence of both COVID-related disputes and COVID-related delays in court proceedings. Elections and taxation issues were the largest sections. There are several cross-over issues, such as expression rights/board meetings and discrimination/taxation. Several charter school cases involved the same kinds of issues that occur in public schools. In addition, COVID-related disputes frequently included other issues.

As noted in previous years, property rights cases dominate the local governance issues litigation, with a total of twelve cases addressing some aspect of property rights. Similarly, the breach of contract cases were next in frequency and represented a mix of construction contracts and more general services contracts. Overall, decisions between plaintiffs and defendants were approximately evenly split.

---

[91] In re Recall of Misipati Semi Bird, Richland Sch. Bd., Position 3, 527 P.3d 1141, 414 Educ. L. Rep. 1060 (Wash. 2023).

Alphabetical List of Cases

A.V. *ex rel.* T.V. v. Bd. of Educ. of Fayette Cnty., Ky.

Anderson v. Hansen

Baker v. Crossroads Acad.-Central St.

Bates v. Poway Unified Sch. Dist.

Bd. of Educ. of Roxana Cmty. Unit Sch. Dist. No. 1, Madison Cnty. v. Regional Bd. of Sch. Trs. of Madison Cnty.

Bell v. Wilkinsburg Sch. Dist.

Bishop of Charleston v. Adams

Boerne to Bergheim Coal. for Clean Env't v. Tex. Comm'n on Env't Quality

Brinkley Sch. Dist. v. Terminix Int'l Co., L.P.

Brooks v. Francis Howell Sch. Dist.

Cantu v. Yakima Sch. Dist. No. 7

Cent. Dauphin Sch. Dist. v. Hawkins

Chabad Chayil, Inc. v. Sch. Bd. of Miami-Dade Cnty., Fla.

Choice Found. v. Law Indus., LLC

Coleman v. Winbigler

Collier Cnty. Pub. Schs. v. Mason Classical Acad.

Colorado State Bd. of Educ. v. Brannberg

Columbus City Schs. Bd. of Educ. v. Franklin Cnty. Bd. of Revision

Commonwealth *ex rel.* Cameron v. Johnson

Cypress Heights Acad. v. CHA Investors, LLC

Digital Media Solutions, LLC v. S. Univ. of Ohio, LLC

DP Fuller Family LP v. City of Canandaigua

Edgewood High Sch. of Sacred Heart, Inc. v. City of Madison

Educ. ReEnvisioned BOCES v. Colo. Springs Sch. Dist. 11

Eisenhauer v. Watertown City Sch. Dist.

Ex parte Jefferson Cnty. Bd. of Educ.

Fellowship of Christian Athletes v. San Jose Unified Sch. Dist. Bd. of Educ.

Fusion Learning, Inc. v. Andover Sch. Comm.

Gedney Ass'n, Inc. v. Common Council of City of White Plains

Gierl v. Mequon-Thiensville Sch. Dist.

GM Berkshire Hills LLC v. Berks Cnty. Bd. of Assessment

Hoke Cnty. Bd. of Educ. v. State

Huizenga v. Indep. Sch. Dist. Cnty. No. 11

In re Recall of Misipati Semi Bird, Richland Sch. Bd., Position 3

In re Stetson Renewables Holdings, LLC

Jackson Cnty. Bd. of Educ. v. City of Commerce Bd. of Educ.

Lake Ridge Sch. Corp. v. Holcomb

Landmark Grp., Inc. v. N.Y. City Sch. Const. Authority

Law Office of Carlos R. Perez v. Whittier Union High Sch. Dist.

Lehmann v. Bd. of Educ. of Fayette R3 Sch. Dist.

Let Them Choose v. San Diego Unified Sch. Dist.

Liddell v. Special Sch. Dist.

Livingston Educ. Serv. Agency v. Becerra

Lord v. Salt Lake Cnty. Clerk

McBreairty v. Sch. Bd. of RSU 22

Meinecke v. State

Meisman v. Hernandez

Menders v. Loudoun Cnty. Sch. Bd.

Miramonti v. Richland Cnty. Sch. Dist. One

Moms for Liberty Brevard Cnty., Fla. v. Brevard Pub. Schs.

Paul Terrault and Gary Cmty. Sch. Corp. v. Scheere

Pierce Coach Line, Inc. v. Port Wash. Union Free Sch. Dist.

Pleasant Grove Indep. Sch. Dist. V. FieldTurf USA Inc.

Rye Country Day Sch. v. Whitty

Save Our Saltsburg Schs. v. River Valley Sch. Dist.

Schooldev East, LLC v. Town of Wake Forest

Singleton v. E. Baton Rouge Parish Sch. Bd.

Souderton Charter Sch. Collaborative v. Souderton Area Sch. Dist.

Speight v. Gordon

Spiegel v. Bd. of Educ. of Howard Cnty.

Springboards to Education, Inc. v. McAllen Indep. Sch. Dist.

St. Ignatius Neighborhood Ass'n v. City & Cnty. of S.F.

Stand Up Montana v. Missoula Cnty. Pub. Schs.

State v. Alaska Legis. Council

State v. Edwards

State v. La. Land & Exploration Co.

State v. Richter

Suffern Educ. Ass'n v. Bd. of Educ. of Suffern Cent. Sch. Dist. (b)

Suffolk City Sch. Bd. v. Wahlstrom

Suffolk Constr. Co., Inc. v. L.A. Unified Sch. Dist.

Sumter Cnty. Bd. of Educ. v. Univ. of W. Ala.

Sunnyside Elgin Apartments, LLC v. Miller

Teays Valley Local Sch. Dist. Bd. of Educ. v. Struckman

Teblum v. City of Cape Coral Charter Sch. Auth.

Tex. Ass'n of Sch. Bds. Risk Mgmt. Fund v. Colo. Indep. Sch. Dist.

Texas Educ. Agency v. Houston Indep. Sch. Dist.

Thurber v. Finn Acad.: An Elmira Charter Sch.

Tucker v. City of N.Y.

U.S. *ex rel.* Donohue v. Carranza

UMB Bank, NA v. Parkview Sch., Inc.

Under the Rainbow Early Educ. Ctr. v. Cnty. of Goodhue

Vaughan v. Lewisville Ind. Sch. Dist.

Wayne Cnty. Sch. Dist. v. Quitman Sch. Dist.

West Bend Mut. Ins. Co. v. Community Unit Sch. Dist. 300

Western Hts. Indep. Sch. Dist. No. I-41 of Okla. Cnty. v. State *ex rel.* Okla. State Dep't of Educ.

Whitest v. Crisp Cnty. Sch. Dist.

Federal Cases

First Circuit

Maine
McBreairty v. Sch. Bd. of RSU 22

Massachusetts
Fusion Learning, Inc. v. Andover Sch. Comm.

Second Circuit

New York
Thurber v. Finn Acad.: An Elmira Charter Sch.
U.S. *ex rel.* Donohue v. Carranza

Fourth Circuit

South Carolina
Bishop of Charleston v. Adams

Virginia
Menders v. Loudoun Cnty. Sch. Bd.

Fifth Circuit

Springboards to Education, Inc. v. McAllen Indep. Sch. Dist.
Vaughan v. Lewisville Ind. Sch. Dist.

Louisiana
Singleton v. E. Baton Rouge Parish Sch. Bd.

Sixth Circuit

Kentucky
A.V. *ex rel.* T.V. v. Bd. Of Educ. of Fayette Cnty., Ky.
Coleman v. Winbigler

Ohio
Digital Media Solutions, LLC v. S. Univ. of Ohio

Michigan
Livingston Educ. Serv. Agency v. Becerra

Seventh Circuit

Wisconsin
Edgewood High Sch. of Sacred Heart, Inc. v. City of Madison
Anderson v. Hansen

Eighth Circuit

Huizenga v. Indep. Sch. Dist. No. 11
Liddell v. Special Sch. Dist.

Missouri
Brooks v. Francis Howell Sch. Dist.

Ninth Circuit

Fellowship of Christian Athletes v. San Jose Unified Sch. Dist. Bd. of Educ.

Tenth Circuit

Wyoming
Speight v. Gordon

Eleventh Circuit

Chabad Chayil, Inc. v. Sch. Bd. of Miami-Dade Cnty, Fla.

Florida
Moms for Liberty Brevard Cnty, Fla. v. Brevard Pub. Schs.
Teblum v. City of Cape Coral Charter Sch. Auth.

Georgia
Whitest v. Crisp Cnty Sch. Dist.

State and D.C. Cases

Alabama
Ex parte Jefferson Cnty. Bd. Of Educ.
Sumter Cnty. Bd. of Educ. v. Univ. of W. Ala.

Alaska
State v. Alaska Legis. Council

Arkansas
Brinkley Sch. Dist. v. Terminix Int'l Co.

Arizona
UMB Bank, NA v. Parkview Sch., Inc.

California
Bates v. Poway Unified Sch. Dist.
Law Office of Carlos R. Perez v. Whittier Union High Sch. Dist.
Let Them Choose v. San Diego Unified Sch. Dist.
St. Ignatius Neighborhood Ass'n v. City & Cnty. of S.F.
Suffolk Constr. Co., Inc. v. L.A. Unified Sch. Dist.

Colorado
Colorado State Bd. of Educ. v. Brannberg
Educ. ReEnvisioned BOCES v. Colo. Springs Sch. Dist. 11

Florida
Collier Cnty. Pub. Schs. v. Mason Classical Acad., Inc.
Meinecke v. State
Meisman v. Hernandez

Georgia
Jackson Cnty. Bd. of Educ. v. City of Commerce Bd. of Educ.

Illinois
Bd. of Educ. of Roxana Cmty. Unit Sch. Dist. No. 1, Madison Cnty. v. Regional Bd. of Sch. Trustees of Madison Cnty.
Sunnyside Elgin Apartments, LLC v. Miller
West Bend Mut. Ins. Co. v. Community Unit Sch. Dist. 300

Indiana
Lake Ridge Sch. Corp. v. Holcomb
Paul Terrault & Gary Cmty. Sch. Corp. v. Scheere

Iowa
Save Our Stadiums v. Des Moines Indep. Cmty. Sch. Dist.

Kentucky
Commonwealth *ex rel.* Cameron v. Johnson

Louisiana
Choice Found. v. Law Indus., LLC
Cypress Heights Acad. v. CHA Investors, LLC
Singleton v. E. Baton Rouge Parish Sch. Bd.
State v. La. Land & Exploration Co.

Minnesota
Under the Rainbow Early Educ. Ctr. v. Cnty. of Goodhue

Missouri
Baker v. Crossroads Acad.-Central St.
Brooks v. Francis Howell Sch. Dist.
Lehmann v. Bd. of Educ. of Fayette R3 Sch. Dist.

Maryland
Spiegel v. Bd. of Educ. of Howard Cnty.

Mississippi
Wayne Cnty. Sch. Dist. v. Quitman Sch. Dist.

Montana
Stand Up Montana v. Missoula Cnty. Pub. Schs.

New York
DP Fuller Family LP v. City of Canandaigua
Eisenhauer v. Watertown City Sch. Dist.
Gedney Ass'n, Inc. v. Common Council of City of White Plains
Landmark Grp., Inc. v. N.Y. City Sch. Const. Authority
Pierce Coach Line, Inc. v. Port Wash. Union Free Sch. Dist.
Rye Country Day Sch. v. Whitty
Suffern Educ. Ass'n v. Bd. of Educ. of Suffern Cent. Sch. Dist. (b)
Tucker v. City of N.Y.

North Carolina
Hoke Cnty. Bd. of Educ. v. State
Schooldev East, LLC v. Town of Wake Forest
State v. Edwards

Ohio
Columbus City Schs. Bd. of Educ. v. Franklin Cnty. Bd. of Revision
Teays Valley Local Sch. Dist. Bd. of Educ. v. Struckman

Oklahoma
Western Heights Indep. Sch. Dist. No. I-41 of Okla. Cnty. v. State *ex rel.* Okla. State Dep't of Educ.

Oregon
Scott-Schwalbach v. Rosenblum

Pennsylvania
Bell v. Wilkinsburg Sch. Dist.
Cent. Dauphin Sch. Dist. v. Hawkins
GM Berkshire Hills LLC v. Berks Cnty. Bd. of Assessment
Save Our Saltsburg Schs. v. River Valley Sch. Dist.
Souderton Charter Sch. Collaborative v. Souderton Area Sch. Dist.

South Carolina
Miramonti v. Richland Cnty. Sch. Dist. One

Texas
Boerne to Bergheim Coal. for Clean Env't v. Tex. Com'n on Env't Quality
In re Stetson Renewables Holdings, LLC
Pleasant Grove Indep. Sch. Dist. v. FieldTurf USA Inc.
Tex. Ass'n of Sch. Bds. Risk Mgmt. Fund v. Colo. Indep. Sch. Dist.
Texas Educ. Agency v. Houston Indep. Sch. Dist.

Utah
Lord v. Salt Lake Cnty. Clerk

Virginia
Suffolk City Sch. Bd. v. Wahlstrom

Washington
Cantu v. Yakima Sch. Dist. No. 7
In re Recall of Misipati Semi Bird, Richland Sch. Bd., Position 3
State v. Richter

Wisconsin
Gierl v. Mequon-Thiensville Sch. Dist.

CHAPTER 2

EMPLOYEES

Clarissa Bruton

Continued on the next page...

Introduction

The area of employment law covers a wide range of topics and areas of law. Employment law encompasses discrimination and retaliation, contracts, termination, demotions, workers' compensation, constitutional rights such as First Amendment and due process rights, and many other areas. Within the context of educational institution employers, there are additional issues that arise, such as tenure and, more recently, the impact of local, state, and federal regulations surrounding COVID-19.

The Equal Employment Opportunity Commission (EEOC) is the federal agency responsible for enforcing federal antidiscrimination laws in the workplace for covered employers. Some of these laws include Title VII of the Civil Rights Act of 1964, the Equal Pay Act of 1963, the Age Discrimination in Employment Act of 1967, Titles I and V of the Americans with Disabilities Act of 1990, Sections 501 and 505 of the Rehabilitation Act, and many others. Additionally, many, if not all, states have implemented state-specific protections for employees.

Employment law also protects employees from wrongful termination. Two major areas of wrongful termination are discrimination and retaliation. Termination based on discrimination occurs when an employer terminates employment with an employee for a discriminatory reason such as race, religion, sex, national origin, disability, or other legally protected class of people. Termination in retaliation is when an employer terminates an employee in retaliation for the employee engaging in certain protected activities including, but not limited to, filing a complaint with the EEOC, filing a workers' compensation claim, whistleblowing, or taking permitted medical leave. The key here is that the employee must show that they engaged in a protected activity and that their termination was in retaliation for them engaging in that activity.

Furthermore, all states have workers' compensation laws. These laws protect employees who sustain an injury during the course and scope of their employment. Workers' compensation claims are extremely fact driven. The likelihood of success on these claims depends strongly on where the injury occurred, what activity the claimant was engaged in during the injury, the scope of the claimant's job responsibilities, and often the terms of the contract between the employer and the insurer who covers the employer's workers' compensation claims. These claims can get particularly tricky in cases involving pre-existing conditions.

Finally, as the lasting effects from the COVID-19 pandemic continue to be uncovered, litigation surrounding the mandates and regulations passed by local, state, and the federal governments has continued. These regulations have generated a large amount of litigation surrounding an individual's rights to bodily autonomy, the practice of their religion and religious beliefs, and their employment interests. While courts have broadly acknowledged that individuals have a property interest in their salaries and benefits tied to their employment, the courts must balance the asserted individual interest against state and federal interests in protecting the health and safety of the public. As with most rights, courts have stated the right to work in a chosen job is not absolute and is subject to infringement based on a balancing of competing interests.

Discrimination

Race and National Origin

The Second Circuit, on appeal from a federal trial court in New York, affirmed in part and vacated and remanded in part the dismissal of a middle school principal's § 1983 claim for violations of the Equal Protection Clause and Title[1] The principal brought this claim against the school district, superintendent, and assistant superintendent alleging her failure to secure a summer position and termination were the result of discrimination based on her race and national origin. The dismissal of her claims against the superintendent and assistant superintendent was affirmed for failure to show proper service of process, but the dismissal of claims against the school district was vacated. The appellate court found that the school board's denial of the principal's applications for administrator and summer school positions and her termination as principal were sufficient to constitute adverse employment actions. Further, the court found that there was an issue of fact as to whether these decisions were motivated by discriminatory intent, as evidenced by the fact that the principal was qualified for each of the positions, and the positions were subsequently filled by a less-qualified individual of another racial or ethnic group.

---

[1] Buon v. Spindler, 65 F.4th 64, 414 Educ. L. Rep. 470 (2d Cir. 2023).

A group of Black current and former employees of the county board of education was selected for transfers and reassignments as part of a restructuring process.[2] The employees alleged these decisions were based on their race and brought suit in a federal trial court in Alabama for violations of Title VII, due process, and equal protection. The court granted summary judgment in favor of the board on all but one employee's claims, holding that a transfer or reassignment from administrative assistant for operations to assistant principal, guidance counselor to career tech counselor, counselor to counselor-teacher, special educator coordinator to teacher, and guidance counselor to kindergarten teacher did not constitute an adverse employment action. However, the court found that a transfer from career tech counselor to guidance counselor did constitute an adverse employment action based on a loss of prestige and lower skill and experience requirements; the employee was replaced by a white outside hire; a white counselor with performance issues was not transferred; and the board's inconsistent reasons for her transfer. Thus, this employee's claim survived summary judgment. An appeal to the Eleventh Circuit has been filed by the plaintiff employees in this case and is currently pending.

A federal trial court in Washington D.C. granted a motion to dismiss former employees' claims against an international school and the Embassy of the Kingdom of Saudi Arabia under § 1981.[3] The employees, who came from a mix of races, national origins, and religions, alleged that they were terminated based on their race. To succeed on their claims under § 1981, the employees must show that the alleged race discrimination was the "but for" cause for their termination. The employees offered several reasons relating to national origin and religion that plausibly contributed to their termination, but they failed to plausibly allege that race caused or contributed to their termination. The employees also alleged nondiscriminatory reasons for their termination, such as poor performance and financial concerns. Therefore, the former employees failed to state a claim for race-based discrimination under § 1981.

---

[2] West v. Butler Cnty. Bd. of Educ., 614 F. Supp.3d 1050, 412 Educ. L. Rep. 738 (M.D. Ala. 2022) [appeal filed].

[3] Adetoro v. King Abdullah Acad., 585 F. Supp.3d 78, 407 Educ. L. Rep. 586 (D.D.C. 2020).

Gender, Sexual Orientation, and Sexual Harassment

A former teacher successfully sued the county board of education in the Maryland federal trial court for hostile work environment, constructive discharge, and unlawful retaliation under Title VII, Title IX, state and local law, and the Fourteenth Amendment.[4] The teacher, a transgender woman, was transferred from a middle school to a high school, then back to another middle school, before ultimately resigning based on alleged harassment by coworkers, students, and parents that included insults, threats, and physical assaults. To succeed under Title VII, the teacher must show she experienced unwelcome conduct based on sex that was "sufficiently severe or pervasive to alter the conditions of employment" and there was "some basis for imposing liability on the employer." The defendants did not contest she was harassed based on sex. Further, her allegations of repeated complaints about harassment; treatment for PTSD related to the harassment; and continual harassment, threats, and physical assaults by coworkers, students, and parents at all three schools were sufficient to establish the harassment was severe or pervasive. Lastly, the court found reason to impose liability on the employer because the administration knew about the harassment and failed to take any reasonable action to resolve the issues.

A federal trial court in New York granted a Catholic school's motion for summary judgment on a former teacher's claims for discrimination under Title VII, state and city human rights laws, and state labor law.[5] The employee, who was gay, alleged that he was terminated from his teaching position because of his sexual orientation. Under the ministerial exception, Title VII cannot be applied "to claims concerning the employment relationship between a religious institution and its ministers." The Supreme Court has outlined six factors to consider in determining whether a ministerial exception applied: the school's stated missions, teachers' employment agreements, faculty handbooks, religious teaching, "catechist" status, and participation in prayer. Here, the job listing sought "a practicing Roman Catholic committed to the mission of Catholic education," the contract and handbook

---

[4] Eller v. Prince George's Cnty. Pub. Schs., 580 F. Supp.3d 154, 406 Educ. L. Rep. 657 (D. Md. 2022).
[5] Butler v. St. Stanislaus Kostka Cath. Acad., 609 F. Supp.3d 184, 412 Educ. L. Rep. 104 (E.D.N.Y. 2022).

referenced teaching and embodying Catholicism, and teachers were to incorporate religion and prayer in all subjects. Based on these considerations, the court found that the former employee's job did include ministerial duties, thus the ministerial exception applied and barred his Title VII claims.

Another federal trial court in New York heard an employee's case against the district, her supervisor, and administrators alleging gender- and disability-based discrimination in violation of Title VII, the Americans With Disabilities Act (ADA), and state human rights law.[6] The plaintiff, who was the only female maintenance mechanic in her department, alleged that she was unfairly scrutinized, harassed, disciplined, and ultimately demoted because of her gender. The plaintiff's membership to a protected class and qualifications were undisputed, and the fact that she, the only woman in her department, was singled out for conduct that male coworkers were not disciplined for gave rise to an inference of discrimination. Thus, the only issue before the court on her discrimination claim was whether she suffered an adverse employment action based on her gender. The defendants alleged that her demotion was due to taking regular, extended lunches. However, the plaintiff produced evidence that many of her male coworkers frequently took extended lunch breaks and were not disciplined. The court found this sufficient to survive the defendants' motion for summary judgment. However, her hostile work environment claim failed as oral reprimands were not sufficiently severe or pervasive to survive summary judgment.

The Supreme Court of Indiana affirmed as modified the appellate court's decision to reverse and remand the dismissal of a teacher's claims against the archdiocese for intentional interference with his contract and employment at a Catholic school.[7] The teacher was terminated after the archdiocese conditioned the school's Catholic identity on his termination due to his same-sex marriage. The archdiocese asserted the church-autonomy defense under the First Amendment in response to the teacher's claims. Under the church-autonomy doctrine, "a civil court may not (1) penalize via tort law (2) a communication or coordination among church officials or members (3) on a matter of

---

[6] Olin v. Rochester City Sch. Dist., 596 F. Supp.3d 475, 409 Educ. L. Rep. 854 (W.D.N.Y. 2022).

[7] Payne-Elliot v. Roman Cath. Archdiocese of Indianapolis, 193 N.E.3d 1009, 407 Educ. L. Rep. 265 (Ind. 2022).

internal church policy or administration that (4) does not culminate in a criminal act." Here, the claims involved were tort claims based on communications between church officials, specifically the archbishop, and members. Additionally, the question of whether the school could maintain its Catholic identity involved matters of church policy and administration. Finally, this case did not allege any criminal acts. Therefore, the church-autonomy defense barred the plaintiff's claims.

Age

The Supreme Court of Minnesota affirmed in part and reversed in part the grant of summary judgment in favor of the school district on a former employee's claims under state human rights law.[8] The plaintiff, a 57-year-old, was allegedly subjected to a hostile work environment and disparate treatment resulting in constructive discharge due to her age. She alleged she was singled out for discipline and placed on an unfeasible performance improvement plan (PIP). The court found these allegations insufficiently severe and pervasive to create a hostile work environment claim that could survive summary judgment. In support of her disparate treatment claim, the plaintiff alleged constructive discharge, which requires "(1) objectively intolerable working conditions that are (2) created by the employer with the intention of forcing the employee to quit." Here, the unfeasible PIP and communications expressing that termination was being considered based on exaggerated allegations in performance reviews could objectively cause a person to feel like they must resign. Additionally, an administrator testified that they were told to have the plaintiff "out by May" so they could rehire, which shows the board's intent to force the plaintiff to quit. Therefore, summary judgment was denied on her disparate treatment claim.

A former employer at a religious school brought suit against the school for age discrimination in violation of the California Fair Employment and Housing Act (FEHA), and the lower court granted summary judgment in favor of the school based on the ministerial exception.[9] The appellate court reversed and

---

[8] Henry v. Indep. Sch. Dist. #625, 988 N.W.2d 868, 414 Educ. L. Rep. 1015 (Minn. 2023).

[9] Atkins v. St. Cecilia Cath. Sch., 90 Cal. App.5th 1328, 415 Educ. L. Rep. 297 (Cal. Ct. App. 2023).

remanded, finding genuine issues of fact as to whether the ministerial exception applied to the former employee's position. The employee had been a part-time secretary for 40 years and a part-time art teacher for 19 years before her termination. On appeal, the employee argued that her job duties as a secretary and art teacher were secular, and, therefore, did not involve teaching religion to students as is required for the ministerial exception to apply. The court noted that in her role as a secretary, the employee performed solely secretarial or clerical tasks; in her role as an art teacher, she taught kindergarteners through eighth-graders art history and visual art. She did not, nor was she required to, teach the students about the Catholic faith. The employee leading an occasional end-of-day prayer and encouraging "Christ-like" behavior in class was not sufficient to grant summary judgment in favor of the school.

Religion

The Seventh Circuit, on appeal from Indiana, affirmed a federal trial court's grant of summary judgment in favor of the school corporation on a former teacher's claims under Title VII for discrimination and retaliation based on his religious beliefs.[10] The teacher was granted an accommodation to the school's requirement that he address transgender students by their chosen first names and pronouns that instead allowed him to address students by their last names only. However, the accommodation was later rescinded, and, after refusing to comply with the school's guidelines, he was terminated. The court held that the school's decision to rescind his accommodation did not violate Title VII, as the school presented evidence that the accommodation conflicted with its policy to affirm and respect all students, and there was no other suitable accommodation. Further, the teacher's retaliation claim failed because he failed to establish "but-for" causation between a protected activity and his termination. However, in light of a subsequent Supreme Court decision addressing the standard to be applied in religious accommodation claims under Title VII, the Seventh Circuit vacated and remanded this case for the clarified standard to be applied.

---

[10] Kluge v. Brownsburg Cmty. Sch. Corp., 64 F.4th 861, 413 Educ. L. Rep. 578 (7th Cir. 2023), *vacated*, No. 21-2475, 2023 WL 4842324 (7th Cir. July 28, 2023).

Disability

A school board rescinded a contingent offer to an individual who applied for a full-time instructional assistant position for special needs students after the applicant failed a physical examination and was deemed not medically suitable for the position.[11] The applicant sued the school district alleging retaliation and other disability-related claims under the Fair Employment and Housing Act (FEHA), which prohibits employers from refusing to hire an individual "based on the applicant's actual or perceived physical disability." Here, evidence supported the assertion that the board regarded the applicant as having or potentially having a disability, and whether she could perform the essential functions of the job without reasonable accommodation was a triable issue of fact. Additionally, the revocation of the applicant's job offer was an adverse employment action. However, the board was not obligated to engage in the interactive process before rescinding an offer under FEHA, and the applicant did not present evidence that the board rescinded her offer because she engaged in a protected activity. Therefore, a California appellate court held that the applicant's disability discrimination claim survived summary judgment, but the district was not liable for failure to engage in the interactive process for reasonable accommodations or retaliation.

Hostile Work Environment

A federal trial court in New York granted summary judgment in favor of the city department of education, principal, and superintendent on a former special education teacher's claim for religion- and race-based discrimination, but denied summary judgment on his hostile work environment and retaliation claims under Title VII and state and local human rights laws.[12] The teacher alleged that he was repeatedly subject to "racially and religiously charged slurs and epithets, combined with acts of violence and death threats" from a student, and his requests for help were ignored. There was also a genuine issue of fact as to

---

[11] Price v. Victor Valley Union High Sch. Dist., 85 Cal. App.5th 231, 409 Educ. L. Rep. 299 (Cal. Ct. App. 2022).

[12] Ringel v. N.Y. City Dep't of Educ., 616 F. Supp.3d 205, 413 Educ. L. Rep. 714 (E.D.N.Y. 2022).

whether the defendants adequately responded to the teacher's complaints. The court found this sufficient to create a hostile work environment due to the frequency and severity of the conduct, its escalation over time, and its interference with the teacher's job. Further, the teacher adequately pled that he engaged in a protected activity (i.e., filing a complaint and union grievances) and suffered an adverse employment action (i.e., his discontinuance and letters to file) that were causally connected because three of the letters to file were issued within weeks of him engaging in protected activities, thus stating a claim for retaliation.

Family and Medical Leave Act

The Seventh Circuit heard an appeal from Wisconsin involving a teacher who sued for Family and Medical Leave Act (FMLA) interference after her employer failed to return her to an equivalent position following FMLA leave.[13] The federal trial court found that the employer violated FMLA, and the teacher was awarded declaratory relief and attorney fees. The defendant, a governmental entity servicing 35 public school districts, appealed, arguing that allowing the plaintiff to return to her previous job would create an "unreasonable risk," instead placing her in a support position with the same salary and benefits but "significantly less responsibility, independence, discretion, and management." The appellate court held that, based on her reassignment to a position that was "below her professional capacity," the teacher suffered actual harm due to an FMLA violation, and she was entitled to declaratory relief and attorney fees.

The federal trial court in Connecticut denied the defendants' motion to dismiss a teacher's claims for retaliation under the FMLA.[14] Upon requesting FMLA leave for a mental health condition, the teacher was required by the board of education to submit to an additional "second opinion" medical exam. The court found that this requirement constituted an adverse employment action under FMLA, the additional required exams were the result of retaliatory intent, and the human resources director was an

---

[13] Simon v. Coop. Educ. Serv. Agency #5, 46 F.4th 602, 407 Educ. L. Rep. 100 (7th Cir. 2022).

[14] Larsen v. Berlin Bd. of Educ., 588 F. Supp.3d 247, 408 Educ. L. Rep. 219 (D. Conn. 2022).

"employer" for FMLA liability purposes. Thus, the teacher's claims for FMLA retaliation survived dismissal.

Procedural Issues

The Supreme Court of South Carolina reversed the trial court's order sanctioning an employee and her attorney.[15] The employee, who worked for the school district, was terminated after she pled guilty to "misconduct in office and misuse of public funds." After investigating, the employee's attorney filed suit in civil court. The respondents filed motions for sanctions, arguing that the complaint contradicted representations made by the employee when entering her guilty plea. The employee unsuccessfully sought to dismiss the suit within a month of filing, but the respondents resisted and requested roughly $250,000 in attorney fees. The trial court issued sanctions of $17,000 against the attorney and $48,000 against the employee. On appeal, the supreme court found that the sanction imposed on the employee constituted an abuse of discretion, as she was represented by an experienced attorney who conducted an independent investigation and determined, based on those findings, that the employee had a claim.

In the first of three appellate cases from California, the court denied a school district's petition for writ of mandate seeking review of the trial court's denial of its motion to disqualify the judge in a wrongful termination suit.[16] Following a multimillion-dollar verdict in favor of the employee, the presiding judge disclosed several interactions with another judge, who previously worked at the firm representing the employee, during the trial. The school argued that the presiding judge should be disqualified based on these interactions. Ultimately, the court found the allegations that the fellow judge entered the presiding judge's chambers was not supported by the evidence, the fellow judge's greeting of the employee's attorneys did not support the motion for disqualification, nor did any other interactions suggest an appearance of bias sufficient to warrant disqualification.

In a second appellate case from California, the court affirmed entry of a temporary restraining order (TRO) and preliminary injunction requiring the credentialing commission to suspend its

---

[15] Kovach v. Whitley, 878 S.E.2d 863, 409 Educ. L. Rep. 399 (S.C. 2022).
[16] Bassett Unified Sch. Dist. v. Super. Ct., 205 Cal. Rptr.3d 647, 412 Educ. L. Rep. 975 (Cal. Ct. App. 2023).

investigation into school administrators.[17] This case arose from the administrators' filing of a petition for writ of mandate or prohibition, arguing that the commission exceeded its jurisdiction when it commenced a review of the administrators' fitness to maintain their credentials. The primary issue on appeal was whether the commission had the jurisdiction to "'pick up the phone' and contact private citizens prior to commencing an initial review." The appellate court agreed with the trial court, holding that a teacher was not one of the agencies from which the commission was authorized to make inquiries; therefore, the commission lacked jurisdiction.

The final case from California arose after a teacher was served a Notice of Intent to Dismiss, including a suspension without pay, due to years of unsatisfactory performances.[18] Before proceedings resulting in dismissal, the teacher requested and was granted an immediate reversal of the suspension. The school district then brought this suit seeking a writ of administrative mandamus and to recover the salary payments made to the teacher while dismissal proceedings were pending. On appeal, the court affirmed the denial of the district's writ and entry of judgment in favor of the teacher because the statute governing dismissal proceedings did not allow for judicial review of the immediate reversal of suspension after the final decision dismissing the teacher was made.

In the first of two appellate cases from Louisiana, a teacher and her husband sued a parish school board for defamation and illegal termination after the teacher was terminated for allegedly falsifying test results.[19] The teacher sought judicial review of her termination, and a trial court ruled in favor of the school board at the summary proceeding. The plaintiffs then brought the current suit, and the school board argued that their claims were barred by res judicata. For res judicata to bar a claim, the first judgment must be valid and final, the parties must be the same, the cause(s) of action in the second suit must have existed at the time of the original judgment, and the cause(s) of action in the second suit must arise out of the same transaction or occurrence as the first

[17] Little v. Comm'n on Tchr. Credentialing, 300 Cal. Rptr.3d 296, 409 Educ. L. Rep. 221 (Cal. Ct. App. 2022).
[18] L.A. Unified Sch. Dist. v. Office of Admin. Hearings, 308 Cal. Rptr.3d 123, 415 Educ. L. Rep. 312 (Cal. Ct. App. 2023).
[19] Rogers v. Caddo Parish Sch. Bd., 342 So.3d 1151, 406 Educ. L. Rep. 561 (La. Ct. App. 2022).

suit. Here, the illegal termination claims were heard and adjudicated during the summary proceeding, but her defamation claims were not adjudicated. Therefore, the appellate court found that the plaintiffs' illegal termination claim was subject to res judicata due to the prior proceedings, but their defamation claims were not barred.

In the second case, a Louisiana appellate court heard the appeal of a former school district employee seeking a writ of mandamus to obtain documents through a public records request.[20] The employee requested access to his HR personnel file, documents related to an investigation involving him, and video surveillance footage. The school board denied the request, claiming the records were not subject to the Louisiana Public Records Act, but informed the employee he could access his personnel files anytime. The employee filed for a writ of mandamus to compel the board to release the documents. The board argued exceptions for insufficient service of process and no cause of action. The court found the board was properly served, though it ruled that the employee did not need to request his personnel file or investigation documents. Thus, the trial court's decision in favor of the board regarding these documents was upheld. Additionally, the board could not provide four of the five requested surveillance videos as they had been taped over. The court remanded the issue of the final video to the trial court for an in camera review to determine if it should be released.

An appellate court in New York denied a board of education's motion to dismiss and remitted the proceeding back to the trial court.[21] This case stems from an Article 78 proceeding brought by the board of education to annul the Public Employment Relation Board's (PERB) finding that the board committed an improper employer practice. PERB argued that the trial court erred because it transferred the proceeding to the appellate court before ruling on PERB's motion to dismiss. The appellate court denied the motion to dismiss, finding PERB improperly sought a merit-based determination in its pre-answer motion. Further, the court remitted the matter to the trial court to allow PERB an opportunity answer the petition.

---

[20] Lawrason v. St. Bernard Parish Pub. Sch. Dist., 351 So.3d 814, 410 Educ. L. Rep. 839 (La. Ct. App. 2022).
[21] Bd. of Educ. of Newburgh Enlarged City Sch. Dist. v. Pub. Emp. Relations Bd., 185 N.Y.S.3d 340, 414 Educ. L. Rep. 421 (N.Y. App. Div. 2023).

In a second appellate case from New York, a former employee filed an Article 78 proceeding and an amended petition to annul the department of education's denial of the request to withdraw her resignation.[22] The trial court dismissed the Article 78 proceeding and denied the amended petition, and the former employee brought this appeal. The court held that the employee's attempt to file an amended Article 78 petition two years after her initial filing was improper and untimely, and the decision of the trial court was affirmed.

Constitutional Rights

First Amendment Claims

The First Circuit affirmed a decision from Massachusetts granting summary judgment in favor of the defendant school officials, town, and school committee.[23] The suit was brought by a public school teacher who alleged First Amendment retaliation under § 1983, state law civil rights and whistleblower claims, and a defamation claim stemming from the response to her union advocacy efforts. Specifically, the teacher alleged she was subject to workplace harassment, disciplinary action, and transfer denial. Ultimately, the court found that school officials did not retaliate against the teacher in response to her union advocacy, and the actions and statements of officials did not rise to the level of retaliation, a civil rights violation, or defamation.

A former school bus driver and union official sued the school district for retaliation in violation of the First Amendment after he disputed the frequency of failed bus safety reports to the school's mechanic and school officials.[24] A federal trial court in New York dismissed the bus driver's claims, and the Second Circuit affirmed, finding that the bus driver was engaged in speech as an employee rather than as a private citizen. Further, the court held that the bus driver was not speaking on a matter of public concern. Therefore, First Amendment protections did not apply.

---

[22] Campbell-Lui v. N.Y.C. Dep't of Educ., 177 N.Y.S.3d 550, 409 Educ. L. Rep. 922 (N.Y. App. Div. 2022).

[23] Salmon v. Lang, 57 F.4th 296, 411 Educ. L. Rep. 55 (1st Cir. 2022).

[24] Shara v. Me.-Endwell Cent. Sch. Dist., 46 F.4th 77, 407 Educ. L. Rep. 48 (2d Cir. 2022).

The Ninth Circuit heard an appeal from Washington involving a middle school teacher's § 1983 action against the school's human resources (HR) officer and principal.[25] The teacher alleged retaliation in violation of his First Amendment rights to free speech based on him wearing a hat bearing the slogan of a presidential campaign to professional development sessions. The court found that the speech at issue did qualify for First Amendment protection, as the slogan addressed a matter of public concern, and the teacher was acting as a private citizen when wearing the hat. The court further found that there was an issue of fact as to whether the principal's statements toward the teacher constituted retaliation in violation of his First Amendment rights; thus, summary judgment was not appropriate.

In Florida, a federal trial court heard a case brought against the state Department of Education alleging First and Fourteenth Amendment violations through the enforcement of the state's Individual Freedom Act (IFA).[26] The IFA included training mandates that educational instruction and workplace training adhere to specific principles of individual freedom related to race and sex. Teachers, an incoming kindergarten student, and the president of a consulting firm sought a preliminary injunction to prevent enforcement of certain provisions of the IFA, which the court denied. The court found that the teachers were unable to demonstrate that their alleged injuries were linked to the DOE or how a preliminary injunction could address their injuries. Further, both the student and president failed to show any provable injury, and the president lacked standing.

A federal trial court in Indiana heard a bus driver's § 1983 claim stemming from First Amendment violations against a public school corporation and a school official.[27] The bus driver was suspended with pay for one week after making comments about a school realignment proposal. He was also prohibited from speaking negatively about the proposal moving forward. The court found that the bus driver's comments were protected under the First Amendment, and the corporation's ban on future statements amounted to an improper prior restraint on free speech. The claims

---

[25] Dodge v. Evergreen Sch. Dist. #114, 56 F.4th 767, 410 Educ. L. Rep. 589 (9th Cir. 2022).

[26] Falls v. DeSantis, 609 F. Supp.3d 1273, 412 Educ. L. Rep. 190 (N.D. Fla. 2022).

[27] Sizelove v. Madison-Grant United Sch. Corp., 597 F. Supp.3d 1246, 410 Educ. L. Rep. 262 (S.D. Ind. 2022).

against the school official in his official capacity were redundant due to the claims against the corporation itself, but claims against the official in an individual capacity were not. Finally, the bus driver was granted permanent injunctive relief, requiring the corporation to expunge, redact, or rescind the record of the unconstitutional disciplinary action.

A male employee in Virginia was terminated from his position as book fair field representative after the school board issued a no-trespass order barring him from all schools in the county following allegations that he behaved too personally with female librarians and made them uncomfortable.[28] The plaintiff sued his employer, the school board, and a board official for gender-based disparate treatment under Title VII and First and Fourteenth Amendment violations under §§ 1983 and 1985. The court dismissed his constitutional claims against the employer and school board, but his claims against the official survived. The court held that, due to the ban, the plaintiff lost his ability to solicit business at the school, thus violating his First Amendment right to commercial speech. Further, the plaintiff's equal protection claim survived dismissal as he identified a female comparator who was treated differently. Finally, regarding his due process claims, the plaintiff's allegations that his right to observe and influence his son's education and to vote on any school board property used as a polling place constituted a substantive due process right, and the plaintiff alleged a property interest and reputational injury sufficient to survive dismissal of his procedural due process claims.

A federal trial court in Wisconsin granted a school district's motion for summary judgment on a former teacher's claims for wrongful termination based on his religious beliefs and retaliation under the First Amendment.[29] Specifically, the teacher argued that he was retaliated against and ultimately terminated for sending an email to certain students expressing his opposition to same-sex marriage. The court found in favor of the district, holding that the email's effect on students was the cause of the teacher's termination, as opposed to his religious beliefs. Additionally, the court held that the teacher's free speech rights were not violated

---

[28] Rice v. Scholastic Book Fairs, 579 F. Supp.3d 786, 406 Educ. L. Rep. 252 (E.D. Va. 2022).

[29] Clay v. Greendale Sch. Dist., 602 F. Supp.3d 1110, 411 Educ. L. Rep. 276 (E.D. Wis. 2022).

under the First Amendment because the email he sent was in his capacity as a teacher and not as a private citizen.

Due Process Rights

In Illinois, a former employee brought suit against the school district under § 1983 for due process violations.[30] The employee failed to sign her contract for the upcoming year in a timely manner, so the school board posted her position as vacant. To establish a procedural due process claim, the plaintiff must show that "the defendants (1) engaged in conduct under color of state law, (2) that deprived the plaintiff of a protected property interest, (3) without due process of law." The court found that, because the employee never signed the contract, she never accepted the offer from the school board. Therefore, the employee did not have a protected property interest in her employment for the upcoming school year, and the Seventh Circuit affirmed the grant of summary judgment in favor of the school district.

A class of current and former school district employees brought suit against the school district and school board members under § 1983 and § 1988 alleging substantive due process violations.[31] The employees claimed that the defendants were aware of unsafe levels of asbestos and lead in schools for an extended period and failed to take appropriate action to address the issues or inform students, parents, employees, or independent contractors. The court found that the employees sufficiently alleged a foreseeable harm, but the employees failed to sufficiently assert that the harm was the direct result of acts by the defendants. Therefore, the plaintiffs' claims were dismissed.

Dismissal, Nonrenewal, Demotion, and Discipline

Dismissal and Nonrenewal

A federal trial court in California heard § 1983 claims for violations of the Fourteenth Amendment's Equal Protection and Due Process Clauses and the state's Fair Employment and Housing

---

[30] Bounds v. Country Club Hills Sch. Dist. 160, 64 F.4th 926, 413 Educ. L. Rep. 643 (7th Cir. 2023).

[31] O'Donnell v. Scranton Sch. Dist., 615 F. Supp.3d 262, 413 Educ. L. Rep. 181 (M.D. Pa. 2022).

Act (FEHA) brought by two former employees against the school board and individual members after their terminations.[32] The court first held that the board, as an arm of the state, was entitled to immunity under the Eleventh Amendment. Additionally, Plaintiff A failed to state an Equal Protection claim against board members because she failed to allege that her discipline or any differential treatment was motivated by discriminatory intent based on a protected class. However, Plaintiff B did state an equal protection claim based on sex discrimination sufficient to survive dismissal, as she alleged that the person hired to replace her was a white male with no relevant experience who was hired at a higher pay rate than hers. Both plaintiffs' due process claims failed; their procedural due process claims due to their not taking advantage of the adequate and available state law remedies, and, on the plaintiffs' substantive due process claims, the board members were entitled to qualified immunity.

In Kansas, a teacher and principal brought suit in the federal trial court against a public school district under the First Amendment and Title IX following their termination.[33] The employees alleged they were terminated in retaliation for reporting and pressing charges for the alleged student-on-student sexual assault of their daughter at school. The court held that the plaintiffs stated a plausible claim under Title IX because they engaged in protected actions based on conduct they reasonably believed violated Title IX, and they were terminated based on their protected conduct. Regarding their First Amendment claim, the plaintiffs alleged they were retaliated against for requesting that law enforcement pursue charges. First Amendment claims brought by government employees must establish that they were speaking as a private citizen on a matter of public concern, and that their free speech interests outweigh the government's interests. Here, the plaintiffs were not speaking pursuant to any official duties, their speech was on a matter of public concern as it was in the pursuit of criminal charges, and the plaintiffs' interest in prosecuting their daughter's assailants was not outweighed by the school's interest in efficiency. Thus, the plaintiffs stated a claim under the First Amendment.

---

[32] Garrett v. Governing Bd. of Oakland Unified Sch. Dist., 583 F. Supp.3d 1267, 407 Educ. L. Rep. 162 (N.D. Cal. 2022).

[33] Johnson v. Unified Sch. Dist. 507, Haskell Cnty., Kan., 580 F. Supp.3d 999, 406 Educ. L. Rep. 702 (D. Kan. 2022).

In the first of three state supreme court decisions, the Supreme Court of Iowa reversed and remanded the trial court's decision affirming the community school board's decision to terminate a teacher.[34] The teacher's contract was terminated based on her alleged failure to implement the recommended changes under an intensive assistance program she participated in to improve performance. Under the program's statutory requirements, teachers participating in the program were to be given a minimum of six months and a maximum of twelve months to complete the program. In this case, the teacher was placed in the program on April 25, 2021, and was terminated on October 11, 2021, for reasons that were not materially different than the reasons for which she was placed in the program. The court held that the statute and school district policy governing the intensive assistance program prohibited the board from terminating the teacher's contract for the performance reasons addressed in the program before the teacher was given a minimum of six months to participate in the program.

In a case involving a former principal's nonrenewal, the Supreme Court of Mississippi affirmed and remanded the chancery court's ruling that the principal's $200 bond was sufficient to perfect her appeal.[35] To perfect an appeal is to fully comply with the rules, procedures, and timelines of the court. Here, the school challenged the sufficiency of the bond posted by the former principal, arguing that it must be equal to the full cost of the hearing transcript, which was over $7,000. The court held that the section of the Education Employment Procedures Law that governed the appeal of a school board's final employment decision did not require the appeal bond to be set at an amount equal to the actual costs of the appeal or the cost of the transcript. Further, in determining that the $200 bond was sufficient, the chancellor considered "financial ability, cost of the transcript, court costs and costs of appeal." The court declined to disturb this ruling as the chancellor did not abuse his discretion or apply an erroneous legal standard, nor was he manifestly wrong or clearly erroneous.

In the final state supreme court case, the Supreme Court of Nebraska affirmed the lower court's decision affirming the

---

[34] Braaksma v. Bd. of Dirs. of Sibley-Ocheyedan Cmty. Sch. Dist., 981 N.W.2d 134, 409 Educ. L. Rep. 321 (Iowa 2022).

[35] Greenville Pub. Sch. Dist. v. Thomas, 352 So.3d 190, 411 Educ. L. Rep. 865 (Miss. 2022).

Department of Health and Human Services' (DHHS) termination of a former teacher's employment at a youth rehabilitation and treatment center.[36] The teacher argued on appeal that the lower court erred in its determination that he was a probationary employee who could be terminated without cause because he had not completed two calendar years of employment. Specifically, he argued that the two-year requirement referred to two school years, not calendar years, and he had completed two school years at the time of his termination so he could not be terminated without cause. However, based on the statute in question, the court held that the two-year probationary period for DHHS teachers referred to the first two calendar years of employment, so the teacher was still in the probationary period at the time of his termination and could be terminated without cause.

An assistant principal in Arkansas brought suit against the school district and superintendent under the state's Teacher Fair Dismissal Act (ATFDA) after her employment contract was not renewed.[37] Due to increasing salary requirements for staff, static enrollment, and the assistant principal's position not being required by state law, the board could not afford to renew her contract. Under the ATFDA, the board may decline to renew the contract of a licensed teacher employed for three or more years "when there is a reduction in force [RIF] created by districtwide reduction in licensed personnel...." Under the policy incorporated in the plaintiff's contract, a RIF may be necessary because of decreased enrollment or revenue shortage. The appellate court found that the plaintiff's nonrenewal did not substantially comply with the ATFDA and the school's policies, thus it was void as a matter of law and the claim survived summary judgment against the school district. However, the court held that the superintendent could not be held liable in his individual capacity.

An appellate court in Minnesota affirmed the school board's decision not to renew a school counselor's teaching contract.[38] The counselor argued that her due process rights were violated by the nonrenewal without a hearing because she was entitled to a

---

[36] Mollring v. Neb. Dep't of Health and Human Servs., 983 N.W.2d 536, 411 Educ. L. Rep. 358 (Neb. 2023).

[37] Digby-Branch v. Westside Consol. Sch. Dist. No. 5, 662 S.W.3d 723, 414 Educ. L. Rep. 745 (Ark. Ct. App. 2023).

[38] In re Termination and Nonrenewal of Teaching Cont. of a Probationary Tchr., 986 N.W.2d 251, 412 Educ. L. Rep. 1009 (Minn. Ct. App. 2023).

continuing contract after the one-year probationary period based on her previous three consecutive years of teaching at a charter school. Under the relevant law, a teacher's probationary period is the first three years of consecutive employment in a single district, after which the teacher is subject to a one-year probationary period when subsequently employed in another district. The issue here was whether prior employment at a charter school constituted teaching in a single district. The court found that the term "district" did not include charter schools, as charter schools were exempt from the statutory provisions that generally applied to schools, school boards, and school districts unless the rule explicitly stated otherwise. Therefore, because the counselor did not have a continuing contract, the school board did not violate her due process rights by failing to renew her contract without a hearing.

In the first of two cases from an appellate court in Mississippi, a former student support coordinator filed a complaint under the Education Employment Procedure Law (EEPL) after the school board declined to renew his contract.[39] The court affirmed the chancery court's dismissal for failure to exhaust administrative remedies and remand for a nonrenewal hearing. The school board argued that the coordinator was already under contract with another district for the school year following his termination, so, because he could not perform under two employment contracts at the same time, his request for a hearing was moot. However, the court agreed with the coordinator and held that under the EEPL, he was entitled to a hearing to clear his name from an adverse employment action that could affect future employment opportunities. Therefore, his due process rights had been violated. In the second case, both the school district and the former director of special education sought review of the chancery court's reversal of the board's decision to uphold the director's dismissal and to award him damages.[40] The board found that the director's contract was invalid and her dismissal proper, because she was not recommended by the superintendent and, as she did not hold an administrator's license, was unqualified to serve as director. However, the court found that this decision was not supported by substantial evidence and was arbitrary and capricious. First, the

---

[39] Laurel Sch. Dist. v. Lanier, 347 So.3d 210, 408 Educ. L. Rep. 1131 (Miss. Ct. App. 2022).
[40] Leland Sch. Dist. v. Brown, 342 So.3d 508, 406 Educ. L. Rep. 534 (Miss. Ct. App. 2022).

board failed to produce any evidence supporting its claim that the superintendent did not recommend the director. Additionally, the board did not provide any evidence of the necessary qualifications for the position or that the director failed to meet those qualifications. Therefore, because there was no substantial evidence supporting the finding that the director's contract was invalid, there was no substantial evidence supporting her termination. Further, the chancery court properly reduced the director's award of damages to account for her actual earnings as a teacher in other school districts during the years at issue, and it did not err in denying the director's request for attorney fees.

Two appellate cases involving dismissal and nonrenewal came from New York in 2023. In the first, a former business administrator for a school district brought an Article 78 proceeding against the district, board of education, and an official seeking to annul a determination eliminating her position and outsourcing her role.[41] In New York, public employers may eliminate a civil service position for economic or efficiency purposes, but they cannot act in bad faith when doing so. The court found that the defendants met this requirement because they established that outsourcing those roles would result in substantial savings, and that served as the sole basis for their decision. Additionally, the defendants did not act in bad faith in hiring an interim replacement employee for the administrator's position until the contract with the outside company was finalized. Therefore, the lower court's grant of summary judgment in favor of the defendants was affirmed.

In the second New York appellate case, the board of education alleged that a custodian threatened the safety of staff and students by failing to remove a hidden knife and pepper spray in a timely fashion, sending an inappropriate photograph to a fellow staff member, soliciting two students to play basketball and betting on the game, and violating the non-fraternization policy.[42] The employee brought an article 78 proceeding seeking review of the board of education's decision to terminate him after finding him guilty of incompetence, insubordination, and misconduct. In the court's limited review, it considered whether the board's

[41] Burdick v. Bath Cent. Sch. Dist., 182 N.Y.S.3d 435, 412 Educ. L. Rep. 282 (N.Y. App. Div. 2022).

[42] Kimble v. Yonkers Bd. of Educ., 186 N.Y.S.3d 247, 414 Educ. L. Rep. 966 (N.Y. App. Div. 2023).

determination was supported by substantial evidence. The court held that substantial evidence supported the board's finding of guilt, but, considering the employee's length of service and lack of prior discipline, termination was a disproportionate penalty. Thus, the matter was remitted to the board to impose a lesser penalty.

A former principal in Ohio appealed the board of education's decision to terminate her contract.[43] Specifically, the principal argued that the board failed to schedule a hearing within thirty days of her written demand, the treasurer did not sign the written notice of the board's intent to terminate her, and the referee and board departed from the grounds provided for her termination. The court did not find any errors regarding the timeliness and notice of the hearing, and the treasurer's typed signature on the notice was sufficient. Finally, the court found that the principal was given sufficient notice to prepare her defenses for the allegations against her, and the board was not required to give her an opportunity to change her conduct before termination. Thus, the principal's termination was affirmed.

In a second appellate case from Ohio, a teacher appealed the board of education's decision not to renew his limited teaching contract.[44] The teacher had faced prior disciplinary action due to several instances of leaving school without notifying the administration and failing to inform the administration when he would be absent. At his nonrenewal hearing, the teacher argued that, under the relevant statute, teachers under a limited contract were entitled to at least three formal observations before nonrenewal, but he was only present for two. Regardless, the board affirmed the nonrenewal of his contract, and the teacher sought judicial review. The court held that, because the statutory evaluation procedure could not be superseded by a collective bargaining agreement (CBA), the teacher was entitled to three formal observations, and the board failed to satisfy this requirement. Thus, the nonrenewal was reversed and remanded.

An appellate court in Washington affirmed a former teacher's dismissal and nonrenewal based on his off-campus conduct, which included several alcohol-related arrests, as well as his on-campus conduct, which included inappropriately touching students and

---

[43] DeVito v. Bd. of Educ. of Clear Fork Valley Loc. Schs., 199 N.E.3d 1049, 410 Educ. L. Rep. 788 (Ohio Ct. App. 2022).

[44] Jones v. Kent City Sch. Dist. Bd. of Educ., 207 N.E.3d 75, 414 Educ. L. Rep. 1004 (Ohio Ct. App. 2023).

colleagues and being intoxicated at work.[45] The teacher requested and was granted a hearing, and the hearing officer agreed with the school board, finding sufficient cause for dismissal and nonrenewal. The teacher then sought judicial review, arguing an inadequate notice of discharge, violation of the appearance of fairness doctrine, insufficient evidence, and insufficient cause for termination. The court affirmed that the notice of discharge complied with the statutory requirement; the hearing officer did not violate the basic fairness doctrine; the teacher's conduct was irremediable, materially affected his teaching performance; and these factors were legally sufficient to support his dismissal.

Demotion and Reassignment

In the only case addressing demotion and reassignment, a teacher in New Jersey brought suit after she was demoted from assistant principal to teacher.[46] On appeal, the teacher argued that the arbitrator did not have the authority to demote her and deny her back pay following her unpaid suspension. The court affirmed that the teacher was not entitled to back pay, but it reversed and remanded the demotion. Under state law, tenured employees of the public school system may only be dismissed or have their compensation reduced for "inefficiency, incapacity, unbecoming conduct, or other just cause." Thus, while the arbitrator had the authority to dismiss or reduce the teacher's compensation for the above-stated reasons, they did not have the authority to demote her. The Supreme Court of New Jersey subsequently reversed this decision, finding that the arbitrator did not exceed their authority by demoting the teacher.

Contractual Disputes

The Supreme Court of Iowa affirmed the lower court's findings in favor of a Catholic school on the former principal's claims for breach of contract arising from her termination.[47] When the principal was informed that her contract would not be renewed, she

---

[45] Cronin v. Cent. Valley Sch. Dist., 520 P.3d 999, 409 Educ. L. Rep. 981 (Wash. Ct. App. 2022).

[46] Sanjuan v. Sch. Dist. of W. N.Y., Hudson Cnty., 281 A.3d 270, 408 Educ. L. Rep. 358 (N.J. Super. Ct. App. Div. 2022), *rev'd* 309 A.3d 619 (N.J. 2024).

[47] Konchar v. Pins, 989 N.W.2d 150, 415 Educ. L. Rep. 334 (Iowa 2023).

was informed that she could finish the school year as long as she did not disclose the decision. However, the same day, she sent an email to parents and staff informing them of the decision not to renew her contract, and she was terminated accordingly. The principal argued that she entered into an agreement with the parish priest in which he stated that he wanted to help her fulfill her retirement plans and that this provided her with immunity from termination. The court disagreed, finding that the provision was not definite or certain enough to amount to an enforceable contract. Thus, her breach of contract claim failed.

In California, a teacher brought a breach of contract claim against a school after he was terminated based on a text exchange with a former student.[48] The trial court denied the school's motion to strike the breach of contract claims as a strategic lawsuit against public participation (SLAPP), and the school appealed. The Anti-SLAPP provision at issue here protects "any other conduct in furtherance of the constitutional right of petition or the constitutional right of free speech in connection with a public issue or an issue of interest." On appeal, the school agreed with the trial court's finding that the teacher's breach of contract claim arose from protected speech under the anti-SLAPP law but argued that he could not establish that the school breached his contract. The appellate court, however, found that the teacher's conduct was not based on speech but, instead, on his termination. Thus, he was not entitled to protection under California's Anti-SLAPP law.

In the first of two appellate cases from Georgia, a former public school teacher requested to revise a previous performance evaluation when applying for reemployment and was denied.[49] The trial court dismissed her claim, and the teacher appealed. On appeal, the court reversed the dismissal of the teacher's breach of contract claim, finding that she was not required to exhaust administrative remedies prior to filing suit because she was not presently a tenured teacher, and the statute codifying the requirement to exhaust administrative remedies specifies that it applies to tenured teachers.

In the second case, the appellate court in Georgia reversed the lower court's grant of summary judgment in favor of the school

---

[48] Bishop v. The Bishop's Sch., 302 Cal. Rptr.3d 594, 410 Educ. L. Rep. 731 (Cal. Ct. App. 2022).

[49] Sigmon v. DeKalb Cnty. Sch. Dist., 881 S.E.2d 695, 411 Educ. L. Rep. 389 (Ga. Ct. App. 2022).

district based on sovereign immunity.[50] In this case, the teacher brought a breach of contract claim against the school board after it decided not to reinstate him the following school year because the teacher failed to properly execute the renewal agreement he was electronically sent. Sovereign immunity prohibits "any suit against the [s]tate to which it has not given its consent," with county-wide school districts included in the definition of state. However, the state constitution provides that sovereign immunity is waived for any action arising from the breach of a written contract. Thus, because the contract at issue here was a written contract, sovereign immunity was waived as to the school district. Further, under state law, teaching contracts are automatically renewed unless the board or the teacher notifies the other that it does not intend to renew. Because the board failed to provide written notice of an intent not to renew by the statutorily specified date, the teacher's contract was automatically renewed.

Discipline

In the first of two cases involving employee discipline in 2023, an appellate court in California affirmed the lower court's grant of a former high school principal's petition for writ of mandate to set aside the disciplinary recommendation.[51] The Committee of Credentials revoked the principal's teaching credentials after he investigated, found no improper conduct, and took no further action in response to allegations that a coach was sexually involved with students. The primary issue on appeal was whether the Committee had jurisdiction to conduct a formal review. Under the relevant statute, jurisdiction to hold a formal review is granted to the Committee when it receives notice from an employer that a credential holder's employment status has changed due to an allegation of misconduct. However, here, the school board expressly stated in its letter that it did not take adverse employment action against the principal due to alleged misconduct, but because he did not adequately perform his job. Thus, the Committee lacked jurisdiction to conduct a formal review, and its findings were not enforceable.

---

[50] Tibbets v. Worth Cnty. Sch. Dist., 885 S.E.2d 291, 414 Educ. L. Rep. 739 (Ga. Ct. App. 2023).

[51] Earnest v. Comm'n on Tchr. Credentialing, 306 Cal. Rptr.3d 801, 414 Educ. L. Rep. 662 (Cal. Ct. App. 2023).

The second disciplinary case involved a public school teacher in Wisconsin who was banned from school district property due to alleged physical contact with students.[52] The teacher then brought suit arguing that it was unlawful for the board to ban him without express permission from the human resources director or superintendent, as well as for his ban to be maintained after he resigned. The trial court granted summary judgment in favor of the school district, and the teacher appealed. On appeal, the court found that a public school board has the authority to ban an individual from school district property if that individual's presence "would unnecessarily expose students to potentially dangerous behavior." Further, the board had reasonable grounds to ban the teacher from school district property based on his conduct with students. Thus, the grant of summary judgment was affirmed.

Tenure

In New York, tenured employees of the city department of education brought an Article 78 proceeding to challenge the department's decision to place employees on leave without pay and their subsequent reassignment.[53] The employees were placed on leave and then reassigned pending the outcome of an investigation into allegations that they provided fraudulent proof of COVID-19 vaccinations. In an Article 78 proceeding, courts only consider whether the decision violated lawful procedure or was an error of law, arbitrary and capricious, or an abuse of discretion. The employees argued that the department's actions were arbitrary and capricious, and contrary to the law, as they constituted disciplinary action without due process. The court found that the employees' allegedly fraudulent proof of vaccination constituted misconduct rather than failure to meet a condition of employment because the issue was not that the employees failed or refused to comply with the vaccine mandate, it was that the vaccine cards provided by the employees may have been fraudulent. Therefore, the department was required to commence the statutorily

---

[52] Klosterman v. Sch. Dist. of Omro, 981 N.W.2d 424, 409 Educ. L. Rep. 354 (Wis. Ct. App. 2022).

[53] Kambouris v. N.Y.C. Dep't of Educ. of City of N.Y., 184 N.Y.S.3d 515, 413 Educ. L. Rep. 402 (Sup. Ct. N.Y. 2022).

mandated disciplinary proceedings before reassignment to a lesser position.

COVID-19

A federal trial court in New York denied motions for a preliminary injunction and temporary restraining order brought by city department of education employees who failed to comply with the city's COVID-19 vaccine mandate.[54] The preliminary injunction would prevent the department from terminating unvaccinated employees without due process. In denying the injunction, the court held that the processes employees were afforded before and after losing their employment were adequate, the vaccine mandate was lawful and did not violate their civil rights, and the employees failed to show a likelihood of success on the merits of their claims.

A group of nonprofit organizations, healthcare providers and staff, teachers, school staff and volunteers, and state government and bar employees brought suit against the governor of Oregon, along with other state officials, to challenge executive orders requiring "executive branch employees, teachers, school staff, volunteers, and healthcare providers and their staff be vaccinated against COVID-19."[55] The federal trial court granted the defendants' motion to dismiss, finding that the employees' claims were moot because the governor rescinded the executive orders at issue. Additionally, the court found that the plaintiffs failed to show that the orders were not "rationally related to legitimate state interest or shocked the conscience," and the Supremacy Clause did not provide an independent cause of action. This decision was subsequently affirmed in part and vacated in part by the Ninth Circuit.

In Rhode Island, an employee brought suit against her employer for interference and retaliation under the FMLA, Emergency Family and Medical Leave Expansion Act (EFMLEA), and the state Healthy and Safe Families and Workplaces Act

---

[54] Broecker v. N.Y.C. Dep't of Educ., 585 F. Supp.3d 299, 407 Educ. L. Rep. 638 (E.D.N.Y. 2022).

[55] Johnson v. Brown, 614 F. Supp.3d 776, 412 Educ. L. Rep. 714 (D. Or. 2022), *aff'd in part, vacated in part* Johnson v. Kotek, No. 22-35624, 2024 WL 747022 (9th Cir. Feb. 23, 2024).

(HSFWA).[56] The employee filed suit after her termination following repeated requests to work remotely during the COVID-19 pandemic due to her son's hybrid schooling and a lack of childcare options. While the employee's FMLA claim failed, her EFMLEA and HSFWA claims survived dismissal. The federal trial court held that, because the employee's EFMLEA complaint stemmed from the failure to notify her of her rights, she stated a plausible claim at the dismissal stage. Additionally, the employer's failure to notify the employee of her HSFWA rights and the subsequent harm constituted interference.

A Labor and Industrial Relations Commission in Missouri found that a bus driver was entitled to unemployment benefits during summer break as the school had switched from in-person to virtual learning due to the COVID-19 pandemic, so the bus driver did not have a reasonable assurance of returning to work the following school year.[57] The school district appealed, and an appellate court affirmed the Commission's decision. The court held that due to the pandemic, the bus driver did not have reasonable assurance that she would be able to return to work the following school year, so she was qualified to receive unemployment benefits during the summer.

An appellate court in New York affirmed the denial of three teachers' petitions to annul the decision placing them on unpaid leave due to their failure to comply with the department of education's COVID-19 vaccine mandate.[58] The teachers brought claims under Articles 75 and 78. The court first found that the teachers lacked standing to bring claims under Article 75. Further, the court found that the statutes governing teacher discipline were inapplicable; therefore, the department did not act unlawfully or irrationally when it implemented an arbitration award without a disciplinary hearing. Finally, the teachers' due process rights were not violated in regard to the arbitration award.

A second appellate case in New York involved a bus driver, the claimant, appealing the Unemployment Insurance Appeal Board's determination that she was ineligible for unemployment benefits

---

[56] Jarry v. ECC Corp., 581 F. Supp.3d 376, 406 Educ. L. Rep. 794 (D.R.I. 2022).
[57] Thiemann v. Parkway Sch. Dist., 655 S.W.3d 460, 410 Educ. L. Rep. 545 (Mo. Ct. App. 2022).
[58] O'Reilly v. Bd. of Educ. City Sch. Dist. of City of N.Y., 185 N.Y.S.3d 14, 413 Educ. L. Rep. 938 (N.Y. App. Div. 2023).

as she was not totally unemployed.[59] The claimant's work was ended early the prior school year due to the COVID-19 pandemic, but she continued to receive her usual salary until the end of the school year and signed a letter from the school district indicating its intent to rehire her for the upcoming school year. The appellate court affirmed the Board's decision, finding that it was supported by substantial evidence that the bus driver had reasonable assurance of continued employment the following school year.

In Pennsylvania, the Unemployment Compensation Board of Review determined that a full-time bus driver was eligible for unemployment benefits during the summer he had no work due to the COVID-19 pandemic.[60] The employer petitioned the court for a review of this decision. An appellate court reversed the board's finding, instead overruling a prior decision to hold that the bus driver was disqualified from receiving unemployment benefits during the summer because he had received reasonable assurance that he would return to work for the upcoming school year.

Workers' Compensation

The Supreme Court of Alaska affirmed the denial of a school nurse's claim for benefits after suffering mental health injuries following an unsuccessful attempt to resuscitate a student who was choking and related physical injuries from exposure to the student's bodily fluids.[61] In its opinion, the court affirmed the Workers' Compensation Appeals Commission's conclusion that the claimant's injury was due to a pre-existing mental health condition not primarily caused by work-related stress. Further, while the Commission failed to adequately consider the nature of the underlying incident, no harm resulted.

In Louisiana, a claimant was awarded roughly two extra years of temporary, total disability benefits along with penalties and attorney fees due to the school board's arbitrary and capricious conduct.[62] The claimant, a teacher, suffered injuries after being

---

[59] Overacker v. Churchville-Chili Cent. Sch. Dist., 184 N.Y.S.3d 845, 413 Educ. L. Rep. 930 (N.Y. App. Div. 2023).

[60] Rose Tree Media Sch. Dist. v. Unemp. Comp. Bd. of Rev., 280 A.3d 1125, 407 Educ. L. Rep. 858 (Commw. Ct. Pa. 2022).

[61] Patterson v. Matanuska-Susitna Borough Sch. Dist., 523 P.3d 945, 411 Educ. L. Rep. 1170 (Alaska 2022).

[62] Mayes v. Morehouse Parish Sch. Bd., 355 So.3d 750, 412 Educ. L. Rep. 874 (La. Ct. App. 2023).

struck by a broken door while trying to separate fighting students. The school board and its insurer appealed this decision, arguing that the claimant's testimony was contradicted by witness testimony and physical evidence. The court agreed, holding that the award of temporary, total disability in this case was plainly wrong.

A workers' compensation claimant in Nevada petitioned for judicial review after an appeals officer affirmed the denial of his request for additional medical treatment and to reopen his claim.[63] The claimant sustained injuries while defusing an altercation between students. The appellate court reversed and remanded with instructions, holding that the acceptance letter from the insurer did not equate to a denial of coverage for the claimant's spinal injury. Thus, the claimant was not obligated to appeal the coverage decision in order to reopen the claim for the spinal treatment.

A school district in Pennsylvania sought review of the Workers' Compensation Appeal Board's decision granting the claimant's petitions for review and reinstatement and denying the board's petition for termination.[64] On appeal, the board argued that a doctor's opinion contradicted the established facts of the case and that, according to the medical evidence, the claimant had fully recovered from their work-related injuries. The appellate court affirmed the Board's decision, finding no error in the Board allowing an amendment to the description of the claimant's injuries or in concluding that the claimant's disability from those injuries was ongoing.

An appellate court in Texas affirmed a jury's finding that the claimant suffered from permanent cognitive impairment arising from his accident, entitling him to lifetime income benefits (LIBs).[65] The claimant, who suffered a work-related traumatic brain injury as an HVAC technician for the school district, was originally denied LIBs by the Department of Insurance-Division of Workers' Compensation before a jury found in his favor. In affirming the jury's decision, the court noted that the trial court

---

[63] Gilman v. Clark Cnty. Sch. Dist., 527 P.3d 624, 414 Educ. L. Rep. 724 (Ct. App. Nev. 2023).
[64] Pocono Mountain Sch. Dist. v. Kojeszewski, 280 A.3d 12, 407 Educ. L. Rep. 178 (Commw. Ct. Pa. 2022).
[65] El Paso Indep. Sch. Dist. v. Portillo, 661 S.W.3d 512, 413 Educ. L. Rep. 484 (Tex. App. 2023).

sufficiently and properly instructed the jury on the legal definition of "uncurable imbecility," and the evidence was legally sufficient to establish the nature of the injury and the resulting permanent disability.

Crime

In 2023, there were nine criminal cases involving K-12 school employees. A federal trial court in Alabama denied the defendant's motion for a new trial after he was convicted of conspiracy to commit offenses against the United States, wire fraud, and aggravated identity theft.[66] These charges arose from fraud through the state's system of funding for public education through the enrollment of private school students as full-time public school virtual students. The court first affirmed that the defendant's co-conspirators' statements were admissible because a conspiracy existed that included both the declarants and the defendant, and the statement was made during and in furtherance of the conspiracy. In support of his motion for a new trial, the defendant argued that the codefendants who testified against him could not be reasonably credited, and the evidence at trial was as consistent with the interpretation that the defendant was innocent and lacked the required intent to defraud as it was that he was guilty. However, the court found that the evidence proved beyond a reasonable doubt that the defendant willingly joined the conspiracy, and there were no substantial credibility concerns with his codefendants.

The Supreme Judicial Court of Maine affirmed the lower court's denial of the defendant's motion for a new trial after the defendant was convicted of two counts of gross sexual assault.[67] The conviction was the result of the defendant, who owned a driver's education business, engaging in sexual acts with a high school student taking his class for credit. The governing statute provides that an individual is guilty of gross sexual assault if they engage "in a sexual act with a student at an educational institution and is 'a teacher, employee or other official having instructional ... authority over the student.'" The issue on appeal was whether the defendant was an "other official" under the statute, as he was not

---

[66] U.S. v. Carter, 614 F. Supp.3d 1081, 412 Educ. L. Rep. 769 (M.D. Ala. 2022).
[67] State v. Marquis, 290 A.3d 96, 413 Educ. L. Rep. 354 (Me. 2023).

an employee of the school. The court found that "other official" referred to someone the school had authorized to exercise disciplinary, supervisory, or instructional authority over students. Further, the court found that the defendant fell under the definition of "other official" as he taught the driver's education class at the high school.

After the defendant was convicted in a trial court of sexual abuse of a minor, the appellate court reversed.[68] However, the Supreme Court of Maryland affirmed the conviction by the trial court and remanded with instruction. The defendant, a substitute teacher, engaged in a sexually exploitative relationship with a 12-year-old middle school student in one of the classes he subbed for. To be convicted under the relevant statute, the defendant must have care, custody, or responsibility of the minor at the time they engage in the sexual abuse. The primary issue on appeal was whether electronic communications that took place outside of school were sufficient to meet the statutory requirements. The state supreme court found that electronic communications outside school are sufficient when the defendant engaged in an act related to the out-of-school sexual exploitation when the minor was in their care, custody, or responsibility. Here, because the defendant kept the minor after class to discuss his anger and jealousy over her feelings for another man, followed by more sexually exploitative communications after school, the court found sufficient evidence to support the conviction.

The Supreme Court of Ohio affirmed the appellate court's reversal of summary judgment against the CEO of a community school for misappropriation of public funds.[69] The court found that, because the CEO did not receive or collect the public funds at issue, he could not be held liable for the alleged misappropriation of those funds.

In Illinois, an elementary school principal was found guilty of failing to report child abuse despite having reasonable cause to believe a student was being abused by a social worker at the school.[70] On appeal, the principal first argued that the trial court erred in treating the failure to report child abuse as a strict liability offense. Instead, he argued that it required a "willful" failure to report. The appellate court agreed with the defendant, holding that

---

[68] State v. Krikstan, 290 A.3d 974, 414 Educ. L. Rep. 537 (Md. 2023).
[69] State *ex rel.* Yost v. Burns, 200 N.E.3d 183, 410 Educ. L. Rep. 800 (Ohio 2022).
[70] People v. Willigman, 192 N.E.3d 861, 407 Educ. L. Rep. 223 (Ill. App. Ct. 2021).

failure to report child abuse was not a strict liability offense. Next, the court addressed the issue of double jeopardy, which prohibits the state from retrying a case unless it presented sufficient evidence to prove the defendant guilty beyond a reasonable doubt in the first trial. Ultimately, the court found that double jeopardy was not an issue in this case, as the state provided sufficient evidence in the first trial to convict the principal of failure to report child abuse beyond a reasonable doubt. Thus, the defendant's conviction was reversed, and the case was remanded to the trial court.

An appellate court in Kansas affirmed the defendant's conviction for reckless stalking.[71] The defendant, a fourth-grade teacher, admitted to taking hundreds of photos and videos of a fourth-grade student's buttocks. On appeal, the defendant argued that, under the relevant statute, the victim must fear for their safety or a family member's safety at the time the conduct occurs despite no precedent supporting his position. The court disagreed with this interpretation, holding that the victim must fear for their own or their family's safety at some point, but it does not have to be while the defendant is actively engaged in stalking. Thus, the conviction was upheld.

A teacher in Louisiana was convicted of simple battery and sentenced to three days imprisonment with 57 days suspended and six months of probation; she was also required to complete anger management counseling, community service, and drug testing as part of her sentence.[72] The charges arose from an incident at school where a 9-year-old student with special needs accidentally hit the defendant with his backpack, and the defendant responded by grabbing the student by his backpack strap. On appeal, the defendant argued that the evidence presented was insufficient to convict her of simple battery, and, regardless, her sentence was excessive. Specifically, she argued that she lacked the requisite criminal intent, did not use force or violence, and any force used was justified. However, the appellate court found sufficient evidence to establish that the student did not consent to the use of force and the defendant used force against the student; thus, the elements for simple battery were sufficiently proven. Additionally, the defendant's

---

[71] State v. Loganbill, 518 P.3d 437, 408 Educ. L. Rep. 1032 (Kan. Ct. App. 2022).
[72] State v. Freeman, 357 So.3d 880, 414 Educ. L. Rep. 761 (La. Ct. App. 2023).

sentence was within the statutory range, and the court found that the trial court did not abuse its discretion in its sentencing.

In Michigan, an appellate court reversed and remanded the lower court's denial of the defendant's motion to dismiss the charge of first-degree criminal sexual conduct.[73] The charges arose from an alleged sexual relationship between the defendant, a substitute teacher, and a student at the school where she worked. The defendant argued that the trial court erred in denying her motion to dismiss because she was no longer a substitute teacher at that school at the time of the alleged sexual conduct, as the statute required. The court agreed and remanded the case with instructions to dismiss.

In the final criminal case, the defendant, a high school vo-tech principal, was convicted of fondling based on two incidents with a twelfth-grade student.[74] The issues on appeal involved a jury instruction regarding the victim's testimony and the admissibility of an expert witness's testimony and other evidence. The appellate court in Mississippi affirmed the conviction, finding no issue with the disputed jury instruction or with the evidence admitted.

Whistleblower

The Seventh Circuit, on appeal from Illinois, vacated the decision of the Department of Education's Office of Hearings and Appeals finding that a regional office of education violated the National Defense Authorization Act by retaliating against a former employee for making protected disclosures.[75] The appellate court ordered the case be remanded based on the judge's failure to address the significance of the state university being a separate entity from the regional office. Further, the judge arbitrarily found that the regional office's decision to lessen the employee's work-related duties and ultimately terminate the employee for poor performance was in retaliation. Thus, the case was remanded for further consideration.

---

[73] People v. Hofman, 981 N.W.2d 112, 408 Educ. L. Rep. 1028 (Mich. Ct. App. 2021).
[74] Barnes v. State, 348 So.3d 974, 409 Educ. L. Rep. 577 (Miss. Ct. App. 2022).
[75] DuPage Reg'l Office of Educ. v. U.S. Dep't of Educ., 58 F.4th 326, 411 Educ. L. Rep. 200 (7th Cir. 2023).

Professional Licensing

In Minnesota, the Professional Educator Licensing and Standards Board denied a former peace officer's application for a substitute teacher license.[76] While working as a peace officer, the applicant fatally shot an employee of the local school district during a traffic stop, which the Board considered "immoral character or conduct" under the relevant statute. On appeal, the court held that the statutory language identifying the potential grounds on which to deny a state teaching license, "immoral character or conduct," was impermissibly vague. Because the language was impermissibly vague, it must be narrowly construed to pertain only to professional ethics in the teaching profession, and the character or conduct must demonstrate an unsuitability for the role of teaching.

Compensation and Benefits

The Supreme Court of Alabama reversed and remanded the trial court's entry of summary judgment in favor of individuals participating in the Public Education Employees' Health Insurance Plan (PEEHIP).[77] The individuals brought a putative class action against the secretary-treasurer and individual board members of PEEHIP, arguing violations of equal protection and due process. Specifically, the individuals took issue with a new rate structure requiring spouses who both work in public education to pay the same monthly premiums for family hospital-medical coverage that other PEEHIP participants were paying. Because this issue does not involve a fundamental right protected by the Constitution nor a suspected class, the court applied rational basis review. There are two considerations using rational basis review: "(a) Whether the classification furthers a proper governmental purpose, and (b) whether the classification is rationally related to that purpose." Here, the court found that the new rate structure survived rational basis review.

An appellate court in California reversed the trial court's decision, with instructions, after the trial court held that forfeiture did not bar retired teachers from asserting equitable estoppel and

---

[76] Matter of Yanez, 983 N.W.2d 89, 410 Educ. L. Rep. 807 (Minn. Ct. App. 2022).
[77] Bronner v. Barlow, 354 So.3d 991, 412 Educ. L. Rep. 399 (Ala. 2021).

laches claims, instead holding that both defenses applied.[78] The teachers received overpayment of their retirement benefits and challenged the monthly reductions that were made to recover the excess paid as well as the adjustment to reduce their monthly payments to the proper amount. On appeal, the court noted that the teachers were asserting legal, as opposed to equitable, claims. The court held that the state retirement system could not be equitably estopped from reducing and adjusting benefits to the proper amounts as was otherwise permitted by the statute of limitations. Further, the defense of laches would not preclude the state retirement system from adjusting benefits so long as the adjustments only affected payments within the three-year statute of limitations.

In Mississippi, an appellate court affirmed the decision of a retirement system board adopting the Appeals Committee's recommendation to deny a school bus aide's request for disability benefits after an alleged fall at work resulted in injury.[79] While the Committee found that the aide fell "in the course of her employment," she did not adequately prove with medical evidence that the fall directly resulted in disability. The court agreed with this finding and further held that the Committee's failure to request the aide's Social Security file did not constitute arbitrary or capricious behavior.

An appellate court in Missouri dismissed a bus driver's appeal after the Labor and Industrial Relations Commission affirmed that the driver lacked adequate cause for his untimely appeal.[80] The bus driver, who received his regular salary while off work due to the COVID-19 pandemic, as well as notice of the school's intent to employ him the following school year, sought unemployment benefits on May 3, 2020. He was denied unemployment due to his assurance of employment the following school year and informed of his right to appeal by October 13, 2020, but the driver did not file his appeal until January 23, 2021. At the hearing to determine whether the driver had good cause for the late filing, the driver claimed to be unaware of whether he saw the original decision

---

78 Blaser v. State Tchr.'s Ret. Sys., 302 Cal. Rptr.3d 428, 410 Educ. L. Rep. 697 (Cal. Ct. App. 2022).

79 Thomas v. Pub. Emps.' Ret. Sys. of Miss., 346 So.3d 921, 408 Educ. L. Rep. 630 (Miss. Ct. App. 2022).

80 Thompson v. Special Sch. Dist. of St. Louis Cnty., 663 S.W.3d 493, 414 Educ. L. Rep. 1076 (Mo. Ct. App. 2023).

because the division sent "a lot of stuff" and did not offer any further explanation for the delay. As a result, the court found that driver failed to comply with the applicable rules, and his appeal was dismissed.

In the first of three appellate cases from New York, a teacher's designated beneficiary filed a petition to annul the retirement system's denial of the beneficiary's application for ordinary death benefits and of the request for recalculation of accidental death benefits.[81] The trial court granted the petition, and the appellate court reversed. In reaching this decision, the court noted that the beneficiary was not eligible for ordinary death benefits under the relevant statute, but they were entitled to unreduced accidental death benefits.

In another case, the appellate court dismissed a former custodian's Article 78 proceeding seeking review of the State Comptroller's decision to deny the custodian's application for disability retirement benefits.[82] Specifically, the custodian alleged that the was permanently disabled due to breathing problems caused by chemical exposure at work. The Comptroller denied her application, finding that the custodian failed to meet her burden of proving a permanent incapacitation, and the appellate court agreed.

In the third appellate case from New York, the court reversed and remitted the trial court's denial and dismissal of a retired teacher's Article 78 proceeding and request for declaratory relief and damages.[83] The teacher brought this claim in response to the school board diminishing the health insurance contribution rate for some retirees, which she alleged was in violation of the Retiree Health Insurance Moratorium Act. Under the Act, an employer covered by the statute may not "provide retirees with lesser health insurance benefits than active employees." Because there was no evidence that the board made the same reductions in health insurance benefits for active employees, the appellate court found that the board violated the Act. Thus, the trial court's decision was reversed and the case remitted for further proceedings.

---

[81] Colon v. Tchrs.' Ret. Sys. of City of N.Y., 177 N.Y.S.3d 228, 409 Educ. L. Rep. 905 (N.Y. App. Div. 2022).
[82] DeFazio v. DiNapoli, 180 N.Y.S.3d 331, 411 Educ. L. Rep. 724 (N.Y. App. Div. 2022).
[83] Perrotta v. Syosset Cent. Sch. Dist., 179 N.Y.S.3d 265, 410 Educ. L. Rep. 767 (N.Y. App. Div. 2022).

A preschool and childcare teacher in Washington was denied unemployment benefits because the commissioner found that she voluntarily left her position without adequate cause and was not available to accept alternative work while seeking unemployment.[84] The trial court disagreed with the finding that the teacher voluntarily quit and was unavailable for other work but affirmed the denial, finding that the teacher was ineligible for unemployment because she was discharged for misconduct. Both parties appealed. On appeal, the court found that substantial evidence supported the commissioner's findings that the facility's owner informed the teacher that she must quit vaping to keep her job, that the facility terminated the claimant based on its policy that all employees must be nonsmoking, and that the facility's owner could not subject children to the risks associated with third-hand nicotine exposure. Based on these findings, the court affirmed that the claimant voluntarily quit. However, the court disagreed with the ruling that the teacher was not available for other work as it was not supported by sufficient evidence.

Miscellaneous

The Fourth Circuit heard an appeal from a federal trial court in North Carolina involving a middle school teacher who allegedly was physically attacked by a special education student in her class.[85] The teacher brought suit against the county board of education and individual administrators, one of whom moved to dismiss on the grounds of qualified immunity. The trial court denied the motion to dismiss, and the administrator appealed. To determine if qualified immunity applies, the court asks whether "the plaintiff alleged a violation of a federal right" and "[w]as the right at issue clearly established at the time of the alleged violation?" Here, the teacher failed to show that the administrator violated her constitutional liberty interest in bodily integrity through a state-created danger, nor was it clearly established at the time that a defendant's failure to act could trigger a state-created danger claim. Thus, the administrator's motion to dismiss should have been granted.

---

[84] Whitehall v. Wash. State Emp't Sec. Dep't, 523 P.3d 835, 411 Educ. L. Rep. 1158 (Wash. Ct. App. 2023).

[85] Burns-Fisher v. Romero-Lehrer, 57 F.4th 421, 411 Educ. L. Rep. 87 (4th Cir. 2023).

An appellate court in Washington reversed the trial court's dismissal of the plaintiffs' claims under the Consumer Protection Act (CPA).[86] The plaintiffs here were members of a teachers' credit union who brought a putative class action against the credit union alleging unfair or deceptive acts when imposing overdraft fees on the use of a debit card despite the member not overdrawing her account. To successfully state a claim under the CPA, a party must prove five elements: "(1) unfair or deceptive act or practice (2) occurring in trade or commerce, (3) public interest impact, (4) injury to plaintiff in his or her business or property, and (5) causation." There is no requirement that the act or practice must be intentionally deceptive, only that it had "the capacity to deceive a substantial portion of the public." The court found that the plaintiffs alleged facts sufficient to establish all elements of a CPA violation, and the credit union did not dispute that its acts took place in trade or commerce and impacted the public interest. Thus, the CPA claim survived dismissal.

Conclusion

In 2023, the number of cases involving primary and secondary school employees increased slightly, from 84 in 2022 to 87 in 2023. The issues that arose were similar to those last year, ranging from civil rights issues like discrimination to constitutional violations, termination, workers' compensation, compensation and benefits, and crime-related concerns, among many others. These cases were brought in both state and federal courts, but most issues were decided by state courts and involved primarily state law. Additionally, the cases presented in this chapter displayed tensions between employees and a variety of opposing parties, including fellow employees, employers, state retirement boards, and state departments of education.

---

[86] Feyen v. Spokane Tchrs. Credit Union, 515 P.3d 996, 407 Educ. L. Rep. 301 (Wash. Ct. App. 2022).

Alphabetical List of Cases

Adetoro v. King Abdullah Acad.

Atkins v. St. Cecilia Cath. Sch.

Barnes v. State

Bassett Unified Sch. Dist. v. Super. Ct. of L.A. Cnty.

Bd. of Educ. of Newburgh Enlarged City Sch. Dist. v. Pub. Emp. Rel. Bd.

Bishop v. Bishop's Sch.

Blaser v. Cal. St. Teachers' Ret. Sys.

Bounds v. Country Club Hills Sch. Dist.

Braaksma v. Bd. of Dirs. of Sibley-Ocheyedan Cmty. Sch. Dist.

Broecker v. N.Y. City Dep't of Educ.

Bronner v. Barlow

Buon v. Spindler

Burdick *ex rel.* Bath Cent. Sch. Dist.

Burns-Fisher v. Romero-Lehrer

Butler v. St. Stanislaus Kostka Catholic Acad.

Campbell-Lui v. New York City Dept. of Educ.

Clay v. Greendale Sch. Dist.

Colon v. Teachers' Ret. Sys. of City of N.Y.

Cronin v. Cent. Valley Sch. Dist.

DeFazio v. DiNapoli

DeVito v. Bd. of Educ. of Clear Fork Valley Local Sch.

Digby-Branch v. Westside Consol. Sch. Dist. No. 5

Dodge v. Evergreen Sch. Dist. #114

DuPage Reg'l Office of Educ. v. U.S. Dept. of Educ.

Earnest v. Comm'n on Teacher Credentialing

El Paso Indep. Sch. Dist. v. Portillo

Eller v. Prince George's Cnty. Pub. Schs.

Falls v. DeSantis

Feyen v. Spokane Teachers Credit Union

Foster v. Bias

Garrett v. Governing Bd. of Oakland Unified Sch. Dist.

Gilman v. Clark Cnty. Sch. Dist.

Greenville Pub. Sch. Dist. v. Thomas

Henry v. Indep. Sch. Dist. #625

Jarry v. ECC Corp.

Johnson v. Brown

Johnson v. Unified Sch. Dist. 507, Haskell Cnty., Kan.

Jones v. Kent City Sch. Dist. Bd. of Educ.

Kambouris v. N.Y. City Dep't of Educ.

Kimble v. Yonkers Bd. of Educ.

Klosterman v. Sch. Dist. of Omro

Kluge v. Brownsburg Cmty. Sch. Corp.

Konchar v. Pins

Kovach v. Whitley

L.A. Unified Sch. Dist. v. Office of Admin. Hearings

Larsen v. Berlin Bd. of Educ.

Laurel Sch. Dist. v. Lanier

Lawrason v. St. Bernard Parish Pub. Sch. Dist.

Leland Sch. Dist. v. Brown

Little v. Comm'n on Teacher Credentialing

Mayes v. Morehouse Parish Sch. Bd.

Mollring v. Neb. Dept. of Health and Human Servs.

O'Donnell v. Scranton Sch. Dist.

O'Reilly v. Bd. of Educ. of City Sch. Dist. of City of N.Y.

Olin v. Rochester City Sch. Dist.

Overacker v. Churchville-Chili Cent. Sch. Dist.

Patterson v. Matanuska-Susitna Borough Sch. Dist.

Payne-Elliott v. Roman Catholic Archdiocese of Indianapolis, Inc.

People v. Hofman

People v. Willigman

Perrotta v. Syosset Cent. Sch. Dist.

Pocono Mountain Sch. Dist. v. Kojeszewski

Price v. Victor Valley Union High Sch. Dist.

Rice v. Scholastic Book Fairs, Inc.

Ringel v. NY City Dep't of Educ.

Rogers v. Caddo Parish Sch. Bd.

Rose Tree Media Sch. Dist. v. Unemp. Comp. Bd. of Review

Salmon v. Lang

Sanjuan v. Sch. Dist. of W. New York, Hudson Cnty.

Shara v. Maine-Endwell Cent. Sch. Dist.

Sigmon v. DeKalb Cnty. Sch. Dist.

Simon v. Coop. Educ. Serv. Agency #5

Sizelove v. Madison-Grant United Sch. Corp.

State *ex rel.* Yost v. Burns

State v. Freeman

State v. Krikstan

State v. Loganbill

State v. Marquis

Termination and Nonrenewal of Teaching Contract of a Probationary Teacher, In re

Thiemann v. Parkway Sch. Dist.

Thomas v. Pub. Emps.' Ret. Sys. of Miss.

Thompson v. Special Sch. Dist. of St. Louis Cnty.

Tibbetts v. Worth Cnty. Sch. Dist.

U.S. v. Carter

Federal Cases

First Circuit

Salmon v. Lang

Rhode Island
Jarry v. ECC Corp.

Second Circuit

Shara v. Maine-Endwell Cent. Sch. Dist.
Buon v. Spindler

Connecticut
Larsen v. Berlin Bd. of Educ.

New York
Broecker v. N.Y. City Dep't of Educ.
Butler v. St. Stanislaus Kostka Catholic Acad.
Ringel v. N.Y. City Dep't of Educ.
Olin v. Rochester City Sch. Dist.

Third Circuit

Pennsylvania
O'Donnell v. Scranton Sch. Dist.

Fourth Circuit

Burns-Fisher v. Romero-Lehrer

Maryland
Eller v. Prince George's Cnty. Pub. Schs.

Virginia
Rice v. Scholastic Book Fairs, Inc.

Seventh Circuit

Simon v. Coop. Educ. Serv. Agency #5
DuPage Reg'l Office of Educ. v. U.S. Dept. of Educ.
Kluge v. Brownsburg Cmty. Sch. Corp.

Bounds v. Country Club Hills Sch. Dist.

Indiana
Sizelove v. Madison-Grant United Sch. Corp.

Wisconsin
Clay v. Greendale Sch. Dist.

Ninth Circuit

Dodge v. Evergreen Sch. Dist. #114

California
Garrett v. Governing Bd. of Oakland Unified Sch. Dist.

Oregon
Johnson v. Brown

Tenth Circuit

Kansas
Johnson v. Unified Sch. Dist. 507, Haskell Cnty., Kan.

Eleventh Circuit

Alabama
U.S. v. Carter
West v. Butler Cnty Bd. of Educ.

Florida
Falls v. DeSantis

D.C. Circuit

D.C.
Adetoro v. King Abdullah Acad.

State and D.C. Cases

Alabama
Bronner v. Barlow

Alaska
Patterson v. Matanuska-Susitna Borough Sch. Dist.

Arkansas
Digby-Branch v. Westside Consol. Sch. Dist. No. 5

California
Price v. Victor Valley Union High Sch. Dist.
Little v. Comm'n on Teacher Credentialing
Blaser v. Cal. St. Teachers' Ret. Sys.
Bishop v. Bishop's Sch.
Bassett Unified Sch. Dist. v. Super. Ct. of L.A. Cnty.
Earnest v. Comm'n on Teacher Credentialing
Atkins v. St. Cecilia Cath. Sch.
LA Unified Sch. Dist. v. Office of Admin. Hearings

Georgia
Sigmon v. DeKalb Cnty. Sch. Dist.
Tibbetts v. Worth Cnty. Sch. Dist.

Illinois
People v. Willigman

Indiana
Payne-Elliott v. Roman Catholic Archdiocese of Indianapolis, Inc.

Iowa
Braaksma v. Bd. of Directors of Sibley-Ocheyedan Cmty. Sch. Dist.
Konchar v. Pins

Kansas
State v. Loganbill

Louisiana
Rogers v. Caddo Parish Sch. Bd.
Lawrason v. St. Bernard Parish Pub. Sch. Dist.
Mayes v. Morehouse Parish Sch. Bd.
State v. Freeman

Foster v. Bias

Maine
State v. Marquis

Maryland
State v. Krikstan

Michigan
People v. Hofman

Minnesota
Henry v. Indep. Sch. Dist. #625
Termination and Nonrenewal of Teaching Contract of a Probationary Tchr., In re
Yanez, In re

Mississippi
Greenville Pub. Sch. Dist. v. Thomas
Leland Sch. Dist. v. Brown
Thomas v. Pub. Emps.' Ret. Sys. of Miss.
Laurel Sch. Dist. v. Lanier
Barnes v. State

Missouri
Thiemann v. Parkway Sch. Dist.
Thompson v. Special Sch. Dist. of St. Louis Cnty.

New Jersey
Sanjuan v. Sch. Dist. of W. New York, Hudson Cnty.

New York
Colon v. Teachers' Ret. Sys. of City of N.Y.
Campbell-Lui v. N.Y. City Dept. of Educ.
Perrotta v. Syosset Cent. Sch. Dist.
DeFazio v. DiNapoli
Burdick *ex rel.* Bath Cent. Sch. Dist.
O'Reilly v. Bd. of Educ. of City Sch. Dist. of City of N.Y.
Overacker v. Churchville-Chili Cent. Sch. Dist.
Bd. of Educ. of Newburgh Enlarged City Sch. Dist. v. Pub. Emp. Rel. Bd.
Kimble v. Yonkers Bd. of Educ.
Kambouris v. N.Y. City Dep't of Educ.

Nebraska
Mollring v. Neb. Dept. of Health and Human Servs.

Nevada
Gilman v. Clark Cnty. Sch. Dist.

Ohio
State *ex rel.* Yost v. Burns
DeVito v. Bd. of Educ. of Clear Fork Valley Local Sch.
Jones v. Kent City Sch. Dist. Bd. of Educ.

Pennsylvania
Pocono Mountain Sch. Dist. v. Kojeszewski
Rose Tree Media Sch. Dist. v. Unemp. Comp. Bd. of Review

South Carolina
Kovach v. Whitley

Texas
El Paso Indep. Sch. Dist. v. Portillo

Washington
Feyen v. Spokane Teachers Credit Union
Cronin v. Cent. Valley Sch. Dist.
Whitehall v. Wash. State Emp. Sec. Dep't

Wisconsin
Klosterman v. Sch. Dist. of Omro

CHAPTER 3

STUDENTS

Christine Collins-Otto and Brian Boggs

Continued on the next page...

Introduction

All 80 of the student cases this year appeared in West's *Education Law Reporter,* volumes 406-416. In reviewing these cases, this chapter begins where it began last year with cases addressing COVID-19 mitigation and other health orders. It then dives into First Amendment rights and Fourth Amendment search and seizure before detailing an alarming number of cases centered on abuse, harassment, and discrimination. Next, cases related to discipline, including several touching on off-campus behavior, criminal conduct, and due process are detailed. Rounding out the chapter are emergency protective orders, issues involving school enrollment, data privacy, wrongful death, and transgender rights.

While COVID-19 topics dominated the dockets last year with one in four cases addressing mitigation efforts, many of those cases have since become moot due to the dynamic nature of the pandemic. For example, in most of the cases before the courts this year, by the time the claim was reviewed, the mitigation effort had ceased to be in place. As one judge recognized, in a rebuttal to dismissing a mask mandate case, the decision "may be viewed as anticlimactic given the passions brought to the public controversy that led to what was once a live, legal dispute, as well as the resources devoted to prosecuting and defending this action" but "disappointment in this outcome"[1] does not justify reigniting the debate when it is moot.

In contrast to the COVID-19 focus last year, this year included a disturbing number of cases involving racial harassment and racial discrimination. Perhaps as a byproduct of our digital world, many of these cases went viral, with community members and social media campaigns weighing in on the controversies. In almost every case the harassment and discrimination involved Black/African American youth, and in many cases there was video evidence of it. These cases raised questions about the influence of social media campaigns on school discipline and whether events captured on video outside of school, but distributed among students, were sufficient grounds for discipline.

As a further indication of our increasingly digital and diverse world, this year also saw a case where artificial intelligence and

---

[1] CT Freedom All., LLC v. Dep't of Educ., 287 A.3d 569, 411 Educ. L. Rep. 1128 (Conn. 2023).

Google biodata highlighted the potential new frontier of case controversy. Questions about the rights of transgender and gender-diverse youth were also addressed. Additionally, cases centered on the responsibilities of schools for student mental health were brought forth as families and schools grappled with the needs of students in our changing world. However, before looking at the cases that point toward ongoing future controversy, this chapter begins by revisiting COVID-19.

COVID-19 and Health Orders

Masks

After the Oklahoma legislature passed Senate Bill 658 in 2021, which forbade public schools from requiring masks or COVID-19 vaccinations except in cases when the governor had declared a state of an emergency *and* the local county health department advised it, a group of Oklahoma parents,[2] some of whom were doctors, along with the Oklahoma Medical Association sought an injunction to prevent the law from taking effect. They contested the law as a violation of Oklahoma Equal Protection and due process guarantees, as it applied only to public schools. They also argued that the legislation violated students' rights to an education in a safe environment, and school districts' legal rights to local control of educational decisions. The Oklahoma Supreme Court agreed with the plaintiffs, striking the language that required the governor's declaration of a state of emergency and reinstating local control over vaccine and masking decisions.

The Arkansas legislature also weighed in on the COVID-19 mitigation protocols in April 2021, prohibiting state and local government officials and agencies from mandating masks or other face coverings. When a number of parents[3] brought action against the state asking for an injunction barring the law from taking effect, the circuit court found on behalf of the parents. Yet, upon review, the Arkansas Supreme Court found that the circuit court lacked jurisdiction in the matter and vacated the decision, allowing the law to take effect.

---

[2] Ritter v. State, 520 P.3d 370, 409 Educ. L. Rep. 967 (Okla. 2022).

[3] State *ex rel.* 93rd Gen. Assembly v. McClane, 657 S.W.3d 872, 411 Educ. L. Rep. 1214 (Ark. 2023).

Another group of parents,[4] this time in Pennsylvania, brought action under Section 1983 after masks were made optional in their local district during an August 2021 school board meeting. The parents argued that the board violated public notice laws and sought a temporary restraining order from the mask mandate being dropped, which the court granted. When the board revisited the mask policy again in December after plentiful notice, it upheld the mask mandate but then revoked it again in January. In reviewing the case, the federal district court dismissed the parents' claims of injury and noted that the board had listened to hours of comment before deciding to lift the mask mandates, which demonstrated that they were not doing so with willful disregard to student safety. Additionally, the board members, acting as publicly elected officials, had qualified immunity.

In contrast to the cases in Oklahoma, Arkansas, and Pennsylvania, a group of parents and a local organization in Connecticut[5] sought to prevent a mask mandate from taking effect. In their 2020 lawsuit against the Department of Education, Commissioner of Education, and governor, they contested the recently issued Executive Order No. 9, which mandated masking in schools. After a trial, the Superior Court granted the defendants a summary judgment, dismissing the complaint. The plaintiffs then appealed the decision, but while the appeal was in progress, the state removed the mask mandate. After the mandate was lifted, the defendants sought to dismiss the appeal as moot. In reviewing the case, the Connecticut Supreme Court agreed to dismiss the appeal because it was now a moot issue.

Parents in Nevada also sought to remove mask mandates. After the district court in Nevada dismissed a case against Clark County School District[6] by two parents who alleged that mandatory masking as part of the COVID-19 pandemic mitigation efforts infringed upon their Ninth and Fourteenth Amendment rights, the school district filed a motion for the parents to pay the district's attorney fees. The district had hired outside counsel as part of their defense, which cost the district $57,416. The parent

---

[4] B.P. *ex rel.* L.P. v. N. Allegheny Sch. Dist., 579 F. Supp. 3d 713, 406 Educ. L. Rep. 232 (W.D. Pa. 2022).
[5] CT Freedom All., LLC v. Dep't of Educ., 287 A.3d 557, 411 Educ. L. Rep. 1128 (Conn. 2023).
[6] Branch-Noto v. Sisolak, 618 F.Supp.3d 990, 414 Educ. L. Rep. 188 (D. Nev. 2022).

plaintiffs contested this request noting that the school district had inside counsel and did not need to hire outside counsel. However, the district court sided with the school district, commenting on the frivolous nature of the original lawsuit and the reasonableness of the fees, and awarded the defendants attorney fees.

Mootness was also at the center of a case in Maine filed by a parent in August 2021. After his child's district issued a mask mandate, he filed suit against Winslow Public Schools alleging violations of his substantive due process rights under Section 1983 and seeking declaratory, injunctive, and other relief. The plaintiff argued that mask policy interfered with his parental rights. When the district shifted to making masks optional in March 2022, the district filed for dismissal, which the parent contested because there was still a potential the mandate would return. Using the Jacobson[7] standard, the District Court reviewed the amended complaint to determine whether the mask policies, based on state guidance, infringed the parent's rights, and found that the mandate was reasonable and necessary as it addressed the need for COVID-19 mitigation actions.

Vaccines

Masks were not the only area of contention connected to COVID-19 mitigation efforts. Frustrated by frequent quarantining, parents of children[8] who had not received the COVID-19 vaccine sued their Virginia school district and local public health authorities in January 2022 to prevent further quarantines. The local policies required unvaccinated people to quarantine longer than unvaccinated people after exposure to COVID-19. In their complaint, the parents alleged that the district's policies violated the Equal Protection Clause because it created two classes of people (vaccinated and unvaccinated), as well as their children's rights to an education under the Virginia Constitution, their parental rights, and substantive and procedural due process rights. However, by March 2022, the district had removed that policy. Upon review, the district court found that the parents lacked standing to challenge the policy because their children were not quarantined under it. Even if the

---

[7] Jacobson v. Massachusetts, 197 U.S. 11, 25 S.Ct. 358, 49 L.Ed. 643 (1905).
[8] McArthur v. Brabrand, 610 F.Supp.3d 822, 412 Educ. L. Rep. 219 (E.D. Va. 2022).

parents had standing, the court opined that the quarantine orders were defensible because they were based on legitimate public health measures. Additionally, the court found that students were not deprived of an education because the school provided a virtual education option for students being quarantined.

COVID-19 mitigation efforts were not the only health-related controversy this past year. As a carryover from pre-pandemic times, one of the cases on the dockets this year began in 2018 when the Rockland County Department of Health[9] barred unvaccinated students from attending school in areas located with higher concentrations of measles cases. The orders allowed for medical exemptions, but not religious exemptions. When the parents of several impacted students sought an injunction from the continued enforcement of the exclusion, citing a First Amendment free exercise right, the county executive made disparaging comments to the court about the parents being anti-vaxxers and religious extremists. Later, the district court dismissed all of the parents' claims in a summary judgment; however, when reviewing the case, the Second Circuit found that there were factual disputes and indications of potential religious animus on the part of the County Department of Health. Consequently, the Second Circuit vacated the lower court's decision and remanded it for a trial.

Religious exemptions were also a concern in a 2021 case after Connecticut updated its mandatory vaccination law for students attending public schools, removing the option for a religious exemption for all new exemption cases, but still permitting medical exemptions. Several non-profits and parents[10] filed suit alleging violations of their First Amendment rights to free exercise, First, Fourth, Fifth and Fourteenth Amendment rights to medical privacy and medical freedom, Fourteenth Amendment Equal Protection guarantees, and their child's rights under IDEA to a free and appropriate public education in the least restrictive environment. The plaintiffs expressed concerns that taking certain vaccines, which often included human fetal cells and animal and pork derivatives, violated their religious beliefs. In reviewing the case, the U.S. District Court in Connecticut dismissed all five claims, noting that the plaintiff organization lacked standing, and

---

[9] M.A. *ex rel.* H.R. v. Rockland Cnty. Dep't of Health, 53 F.4th 29, 408 Educ. L. Rep. 731 (2d Cir. 2022).

[10] We the Patriots USA, Inc. v. Conn. Office of Early Childhood Development, 579 F. Supp. 3d 290, 406 Educ. L. Rep. 189 (D. Conn. 2022).

the law was religiously neutral. Citing the Jacobson[11] precedent, the court found that there was no conflict between having secular exemptions while forbidding religious ones, because "medical exemptions further the state's interest in health and safety while religious exemptions undercut that same interest."[12]

First Amendment free exercise was again in question in a case involving four parents[13] in D.C. who filed suit and sought a preliminary injunction after the D.C. council passed the Minor Consent for Vaccinations Act Amendment of 2020 (MCA). The MCA lowered the age that children could consent for a vaccination without parental consent or notification to 11and allowed the minor children to overrule any religious exemptions that their parent(s) may have filed on their behalf. The act went further, allowing medical providers to conceal the change in vaccine status and the exemption removal from parents. The parents, who all had religious objections to vaccinations, expressed concerns that MCA violated the Religious Freedom and Restoration Act of 1993 (RFRA), infringed on their First Amendment free exercise right, and conflicted with federal law. They also alleged that it violated their rights as parents, including their procedural due process rights. The D.C. District Court agreed that the parents' argument, including the violations of their First Amendment rights, was compelling, and granted the injunction.

First Amendment

While many of the COVID-19 related challenges involved concerns about First Amendment violations, COVID-19 related issues were not the only area where plaintiffs brought First Amendment challenges, as a Ninth Circuit case highlights. In 2019, A Native American student[14] was barred from participating in her Arizona high school graduation ceremony when she arrived with a feather attached to her graduation cap, which was in violation of the district's graduation dress code policy. However, on that same day, although not at the same ceremony, another student wore a breast cancer awareness sticker on his cap at a graduation ceremony. The student filed a Section 1983 claim

---

[11] Jacobson v. Massachusetts, 197 U.S. 11 (1905).

[12] *Supra,* note 10 at 307.

[13] Booth v. Bowser, 597 F. Supp. 3d 1, 410 Educ. L. Rep. 150 (D.C. Cir. 2022).

[14] Waln v. Dysart Sch. Dist., 54 F.4th 1152, 410 Educ. L. Rep. 16 (9th Cir. 2022).

alleging violations of her First Amendment free speech and free exercise rights, but the district court dismissed the case. Upon appeal, the Ninth Circuit found sufficient evidence that the claims had weight and remanded the case back to the district court. Since then, the student and the district have settled out of court.[15]

In a different dress code-related case, a Tennessee student[16] was disciplined for wearing a shirt that said homosexuality is a sin. The student's father filed a claim because of that discipline, on his own behalf and on his daughter's behalf. The Section 1983 claim against the teacher, principal, and school board asserted that they violated her First Amendment free speech and free exercise rights, her Fifth and Fourteenth Amendment due process, and her Fourteenth Amendment equal protection rights. The defendants filed for dismissal on the basis that the student failed to state a claim, and they had qualified immunity. In reviewing the facts, the court found that the father lacked standing on his own, but his daughter's First Amendment claims were potentially valid since there was no evidence of foreseeable disruption from her attire.

Free speech rights were also a factor in a Loudoun County, Virginia case when several parents[17] filed suit on behalf of their children alleging that the district's equity ambassador program and bias-reporting system violated the students' equal protection and First Amendment rights. Upon review, the district court dismissed these claims for failing to establish injury under Article III. The Fourth Circuit, hearing the parents' appeal, held that the district court was correct in dismissing the claims directed at the ambassador program, observing that even if the program was in fact discriminatory, the parents failed to show that their children would have wanted to participate in it and were injured by the policy. On the second account, however, the Fourth Circuit found the bias reporting policy did plausibly chill their children's First Amendment free speech, as there was indication the children did want to speak but were fearful of the effects of the policy. The court

---

[15] Shondiin Silversmith, *Indigenous Student Settles Lawsuit Against Arizona School District*, AZMirror, https://azmirror.com/2023/04/28/indigenous-student-settles-lawsuit-against-arizona-school-district/, (April 28, 2023).

[16] B.A.P. v. Overton Cnty Bd. of Educ., 600 F.Supp.3d 839, 410 Educ. L. Rep. 924 (M.D. Tenn. 2022).

[17] Menders v. Loudoun Cnty Sch. Bd., 65 F.4th 157, 414 Educ. L. Rep. 499 (4th Cir. 2023).

vacated the lower court's dismissal of this second claim and remanded it back for review.

A Missouri parent was less successful in a First Amendment challenge to prohibit an adopted book review policy from taking effect in the local school district.[18] On behalf of her minor student, the parent sought a preliminary injunction to enjoin the school district from following its adopted policy that provided a mechanism for parents, guardians, and students to initiate challenges to materials in the school library. She also sought to restore access to any materials that had been removed from the library recently. In her action, the complainant alleged that the removal of books and other materials violated her child's First Amendment rights and improperly restricted access to ideas and information. The federal District Court of Missouri denied the motion, holding that the student was unlikely to prevail on the challenge to the book removal policy, nor was the student irreparably harmed by the removal of the books. Finally, the court observed that the preliminary injunction would be unfairly against the public interest of the district because "it is not the function of the courts to make the decisions that have been properly relegated to the elected members of school boards."[19]

Fourth Amendment

Search and Seizure

The powers of other public officials were challenged in a search and seizure case brought forth by two infant children by and through their father, who filed claims against the local school district, the county policy, and a medical center.[20] The allegations include that the defendants violated the Fourth Amendment rights of the infants by searching and seizing the father's cell phone. However, the U.S. District Court of New York heard this case not on Fourth Amendment issue, but as a request to reopen discovery because the medical expert had not submitted the final version of a report and, thereby, extended discovery. The court held that the

---

[18] C.K.-W. *ex rel.* T.K. v. Wentzville R-IV Sch. Dist., 619 F.Supp.3d 906, 414 Educ. L. Rep. 398 (E.D. Mo. 2022).
[19] *Id.* at 920.
[20] Singh v. Sachem Cent. Sch. Dist., 342 F.R.D. 367, 410 Educ. L. Rep. 685 (E.D.N.Y. 2022).

plaintiff did not demonstrate a good cause argument to reopen the discovery and allow for the correct expert disclosure or extend the discovery period.

Another search and seizure related claim came after an incident with a firearm. Prior to the return of a student who had been out of school due to weapons charges, the school had instituted a safety plan which allowed for random and regular backpack searches. When he returned and school personnel found a gun in his backpack, they alerted law enforcement, who then arrested him. The student[21] later contested his adjudication for this second offense, claiming the search was illegal because it was without warrant. The Colorado Court of Appeals disagreed, upholding the original adjudication on the grounds that the school was justified in its search and notification of the police.

Items in a backpack also played a role in a Maryland case involving a high school student.[22] After a fight with another student at school was broken up, the student dropped his backpack and ran. All of the contents in the backpack spilled to the ground, including a gun, multiple cell phones, and his ID. Upon inspection, the cell phones tied him to a recent armed robbery. In a motion to suppress the evidence after arrest, the student claimed that his bag was illegally searched at school and the review of the evidence from the cellphone was obtained illegally. However, the trial court denied his request to suppress the evidence, which the Maryland Appellate Court upheld, finding that his bag was dropped and abandoned, not illegally searched, and the officers acted in good faith.

Excessive Force

Other Fourth Amendment cases involved excessive force. For instance, while attending an evening basketball game, a Madisonville, Texas student[23] had a physical altercation with the vice principal after being asked to leave the game, which led to her arrest. During the arrest, the student was injured and ended up going to the hospital later to seek medical treatment. In the aftermath of the event, the student, who was expelled for assaulting the vice principal and the two police officers, filed a

---

[21] People *ex rel.* J.G., 517 P.3d 1267, 408 Educ. L. Rep. 560 (Colo. App. 2022).
[22] Richardson v. State, 282 A.3d 98, 408 Educ. L. Rep. 430 (Md. 2022).
[23] Byrd v. Cornelius, 52 F.4th 265, 408 Educ. L. Rep. 711 (5th Cir. 2022).

Section 1983 claim against the district and the police officers for excessive force during the arrest. In response, the school district sought a summary judgment dismissal. However, the district court found a dispute in the facts which prevented a summary judgment. The two officers then filed an appeal seeking immunity, but the Fifth Circuit lacked jurisdiction in the case and returned it to the district court.

Excessive force was also a consideration in a case involving a school resource officer who intervened after a student[24] pushed his own mother at school. After witnessing the student's behavior, the officer reacted by pushing the student to the floor and holding him for over three minutes. The whole encounter was captured on video. Afterward, the officer lost his job and was prosecuted for child abuse and battery. Later, the student pressed charges including Section 1983 claims of false arrest and battery. The officer responded seeking qualified immunity and statutory immunity, which the distinct court granted. Upon appeal, the Eleventh Circuit upheld the finding that the officer was acting within the scope of his job and, therefore, had qualified immunity. However, in a split decision, the court found that the officer clearly used excessive force and that the lower court's finding of statutory immunity was misguided. As a result, the district court remanded it back for further proceedings.

Data Privacy

While the Fourth Amendment provides some guarantees to privacy, the privacy rights sought in the next two cases did not assert those rights. Instead, they relied on state protections and were heard in state courts. In the first of these state claims, several elementary and middle school students, by and through their parents and legal guardians, brought a state class action lawsuit against Google.[25] The case alleged that Google provided schools with laptops, both in their district and across the country, that were already pre-installed with "G Suite for Education," a cloud-based education platform. While Google promised that it did not data mine or collect information that was not educationally relevant, the students alleged that the voice and visual recording

---

[24] Richmond v. Badia, 47 F.4th 1172, 407 Educ. L. Rep. 479 (11th Cir. 2022).
[25] H.K. *ex rel.* Farwell v. Google LLC, 595 F. Supp. 3d 702, 409 Educ. L. Rep. 825 (C.D. Ill. 2022).

software collected their information without written permission of parents or legal guardians and was used by the company in violation of the Illinois Biometric Information Privacy Act (BIPA). Google then removed the case to federal district court in Illinois and filed a motion to dismiss. The court held that the allegations that Google recorded voice details to be used as part of a stored catalog of voiceprints in the company's database may have implicated the provisions of the BIPA, but this could not be proven during a motion to dismiss and thus survived to move forward. However, the Children's Online Privacy Protection Act preempted claims for students under 13 years old and was dismissed.

In a separate Illinois case concerning data privacy, a student brought a class action lawsuit against an online test proctoring company alleging that it violated the Illinois Biometric Information Privacy Act (BIPA).[26] The company serves over one million test-takers through its cloud-based system that monitors remote administration of testing. Specifically, students use their own computers, and the software collects information on the student, including their IP address, web activity, cookies; it also surveils the students through the webcam and microphone, as well as facial geometry, to verify the students' identities based on photo identification and behaviors while on camera. Beginning in the spring of 2020, many Illinois students were required to take their exams using this software because of C-19 and had no choice but to agree to the terms of service. The testing company moved to enforce arbitration in the federal district court or have the case dismissed. The court denied the motion to dismiss, but granted the motion for arbitration stating that the arbitrator would make the determination about agreeing to the terms under duress.

Sexual Abuse and Harassment

Employee-on-Student

Several cases this year involved the New York Child Victims Act, a state claims-revival statute, beginning with a former student at a New York private preparatory school who brought an action against the school and members of the former school

---

[26] Healy v. Honorlock Inc., 609 F.Supp.3d 1294, 412 Educ. L. Rep. 205 (S.D. Fla. 2022).

administration.[27] The student claimed that he was sexually abused in the late 1970s by a gym teacher and coach, who was still alive when he brought the motion. The school moved to dismiss the case on the plaintiff's failure to state a claim and because the revival language of the Child Victims Act violated the due process clause of the state constitution. The federal district court in New York was not persuaded, holding that the New York Child Victims Act and, in particular, the claim-revival statute, were constitutional. Further, the court held that the student did state a valid claim for adjudication on negligent hiring, retention, supervision, and direction, as well as negligence, gross negligence, and willful misconduct. However, the court did side with the school in one area when it dismissed the claim of negligent infliction of emotional distress because it was duplicative of other charges.

A former Catholic school student in New York also brought an action under the Child Victims Act against the diocese, local church, priest, and various employees of the school.[28] The student alleged that he was sexually abused while attending the school and local parish. As part of the case, Belcastro made allegations of negligent hiring, supervision, as well as negligence and gross negligence. The diocese, church, and school moved to dismiss, and the local court denied the motion. Upon appeal to the New York appellate court, the court affirmed the lower court's decision stating that the student had provided sufficient facts for the proceedings to continue.

A third case involving the Child Victims Act was initiated by a former Niagara Falls City School District (NFCSD) student. The student alleged that he had been sexually abused while attending junior high in the district.[29] NFCSD moved to dismiss the complaint because of the statute of limitations, but the lower court denied this motion. On appeal, an appellate court in New York wrestled with the question of whether the Child Victims Act's revival clause affected the statute of limitations and whether it violated the due process clause of the New York State Constitution.

---

[27] PC-41 Doe v. Poly Prep Cntry. Day Sch., 590 F.Supp.3d 551, 408 Educ. L. Rep. 770 (E.D.N.Y. 2021).
[28] Belcastro v. Roman Catholic Diocese of Brooklyn, 184 N.Y.S.3d 367, 413 Educ. L. Rep. 389 (N.Y. App. Div. 2023).
[29] PB-36 Doe *ex rel.* Niagara Falls City Sch. Dist., 182 N.Y.S.3d 850, 412 Educ. L. Rep. 286 (N.Y. App. Div. 2023).

As with *PC-41 Doe v. Poly Prep County*,[30] the appellate court held that it did not.

After the statute of limitations was removed, a New York school district[31] was found liable when a former student brought charges against the district for not reporting suspected child abuse while she was a student in the mid-1970s. The former student's teacher knew that she was being abused by her stepfather and used that knowledge to groom her for abuse as well. While the district was unaware of the abuse by her stepfather, they were aware of her abuse by the teacher and failed to report it. At the initial hearing, the district filed multiple motions to dismiss, which were denied. When the district appealed this decision, the appellate division granted motions to dismiss two elements of the charges, as well as the punitive damages associated with those branches.

In contrast to the New York state cases, the statute of limitations did affect the case of a former Washington, D.C. charter school student who brought suit under a civil rights claim of Section 1983 and Title IX against her former school and an additional charter school.[32] The plaintiff alleged that her former teacher sexually abused her, claiming that her relationship with that teacher began when she was in middle school, continued for several years, and even involved living with him after attending school. When she first brought the case before the federal district court, it was dismissed as having been time-barred by the statute of limitations. Shortly after that ruling, the D.C. Sexual Abuse Statute of Limitations Amendment Act came into effect, and so she brought the case again, arguing the new tolling statute. However, the court had already heard and ruled on the first case, which barred this case from returning because the Sexual Abuse Statute of Limitations Amendment Act of 2018 did not apply to previously adjudicated cases.

In a case that was not subject to the statute of limitations, two female middle school students brought action against the local

---

30 *Supra,* note 23.

31 Hanson v. Hicksville Union Free Sch. Dist., 175 N.Y.S.3d 327, 408 Educ. L. Rep. 972 (N.Y. App. Div. 2022).

32 Perez v. KIPP DC Supporting Corp., 590 F.Supp.3d 150, 408 Educ. L. Rep. 330 (D.C. Cir. 2022). [reversed and remanded by 70 F.4th 570, 416 Educ. L. Rep. 275 (D.C. 2023)].

public school district and a former male teacher.[33] Specifically, they brought civil rights charges under Section 1983 for violations of due process; deprivation of their rights for safety, security, and bodily integrity; as well as violations of the Equal Protection Clause, Title IX, and sexual abuse. In addition to the experiences of these students, they alleged that the district had a "pass the trash" policy where teachers were hired without proper screening for sexual and criminal misconduct, and when they were accused of sexual abuse, the district would transfer the employee to another school. The school district moved for dismissal in the federal district court in Texas. The court held that allegations were sufficiently presented, the irreparable harm was the result of the district's policy, and a nexus existed between the policy and results. The case survived the challenge.

Also in Texas, the parents of sexually abused students who attended an open-enrollment charter school sued the school's operator for assault and negligence.[34] A school counselor, who had already pleaded guilty to several sex crimes including these, had abused the students. Yet, the operator asserted a plea of immunity from the suit and liability under the state constitution, which the circuit court denied. The school appealed this decision and contended that as an open-enrollment charter school, they had governmental immunity to the same degree as traditional public schools. The Texas appellate court reversed the lower court's ruling and dismissed the suit holding that the charter school did have governmental immunity because of their open-enrollment status.

Questions about immunity were also addressed when a former Georgia public high school student brought an action against several school administrators for alleged sexual abuse from a teacher during an extracurricular club meeting.[35] He argued that the administrators were not eligible for official immunity as school personnel. The lower court held that the administrators were eligible for immunity despite performing their duties poorly. The student appealed this decision, and a Georgia appellate court affirmed the decision that the administrators were entitled to

[33] Doe v. Beaumont Indep. Sch. Dist., 615 F. Supp. 3d 471, 413 Educ. L. Rep. 209 (E.D. Tex. 2022).
[34] KIPP Texas, Inc. v. Doe #1, 649 S.W.3d 850, 407 Educ. L. Rep. 367 (Tex. App. 2022).
[35] R.H. v. Wagner, 879 S.E.2d 653, 409 Educ. L. Rep. 543 (Ga. Ct. App. 2022).

official immunity, but the court held that approving clubs was not part of their position or official duties.

In a neighboring state, a former JROTC was convicted in a local Florida circuit court of sexual battery of a 17-year-old student in his custodial authority, which the defendant teacher appealed.[36] The teacher had spent unsupervised time with the student and had, on several occasions, been granted permission to drive the student home and be in her house. However, during the time in question, he did not have permission to drive the victim home, enter, or remain in the residence, and the offense did not occur on school property or in connection with any extracurricular activity, which meant that the girl was not in his custodial authority. The state argued that there was a nexus because the events happened during the school year. An appeals court for Florida focused on whether there was sufficient evidence to prove that the teacher was in a position of custodial authority at the time of the alleged sexual intercourse. Upon review, the court held the evidence was insufficient; therefore, the teacher was not acting *in loco parentis* at the time. Because this was a necessary element of the crime, the case was reversed.

Student-on-Student

While there were a number of employee-on-student abuse instances, there were also a number of student-on-student incidents that went before the court beginning with the mother of a female middle school student, who brought a Section 1983 civil rights action against several local school officials.[37] She alleged that the school officials violated the student's due process right under a state-created danger theory. The student was allowed to wander the hallways of a school with another student that had previously sexually assaulted her and was assaulted again. Both students were required to be supervised based on their individualized education plans (IEP). The state-created danger doctrine is an exception to the rule that the government has no duty under the due process clause to protect people from privately inflicted harms. However, the school sought to dismiss the claims based on qualified immunity because the state-created danger

[36] Teet v. State, 343 So. 3d 117, 406 Educ. L. Rep. 22 (Fla. Ct. App. 2022).

[37] Fisher v. Moore, 62 F.4th 912, 413 Educ. L. Rep. 49 (5th Cir. 2023). [withdrawn and superseded on denial of rehearing en banc by 73 F.4th 367 (5th Cir. 2023)]

doctrine had not been clearly established in this circuit. The federal district court denied the school's motion, but the Fifth Circuit Court reversed it, agreeing with the school that the state-created danger doctrine had not been clearly established in the Fifth Circuit, thus, the school was entitled to qualified immunity.

The Fifth Circuit also heard the case involving a former Texas student, Roe, who brought action against her local district under Title IX.[38] Roe alleged that when she was 14 years old, another student sexually assaulted her. The student, with whom she had an abusive relationship, assaulted her in the stairwell of the high school and she suffered severe injuries as a result. Roe claimed the school did not provide her any support, but rather encouraged her to drop out, which she did. She also alleged that the school acted with deliberate indifference both in the risk of sexual assault and in response to the abusive relationship, sexual assault, and harassment that occurred at school. When the federal district court reviewed the case, it granted the district's motion for summary judgment. At appeal, the Fifth Circuit affirmed the lower court decision in part and reversed it in part. Specifically, the court said the district court ruled correctly on the issue that the school was not deliberately indifferent to the risk of sexual assault. However, because a reasonable jury could find that the school was deliberately indifferent on the sexual harassment issue, the court reversed for further proceedings.

When a former public high school student from New York brought action against her local school district, board of education, and several members of the administration[39] with claims of retaliation related to her First Amendment rights, Title IX violations, Equal Protection Clause violations, as well as Due Process Clause violations, she also found some success in the courts. Her claims were the result of sexual harassment from a male student and the school's response to that harassment. Rebutting the action, the school district sought a motion for dismissal. However, a federal district court in New York rejected the motion and held that several of the claims were plausible. Specifically, the court found the complaint's allegation that the

---

[38] Roe v. Cypress-Fairbanks Indep. Sch. Dist., 53 F.4th 334, 409 Educ. L. Rep. 20 (5th Cir. 2022). [petition for certiorari filed Sept. 29, 2023]
[39] A.S. v. City Sch. Dist. of Albany, 585 F. Supp. 3d 246, 407 Educ. L. Rep. 595 (N.D.N.Y. 2022).

district had knowledge of harassment and acted with indifference to be plausible.

Deliberate indifference was also cited in a case involving a former Tennessee female high school student who filed claims against her district under Title IX and Section 1983 based on the district's actions before and after a video recording of her being raped on school grounds. Several other female students brought similar claims that were consolidated with S.C.'s claim on the matter of law. The federal district court held a bench trial on the claims brought forth by the now-adult students, entering a verdict in favor of the student on the Title IX issue and for the district on the civil rights issue. The court held that this incident did implicate the district's Title IX duties because the threats the student received amounted to sexual harassment and the district had knowledge. The court also held that the district acted with deliberate indifference related to the harassment when it became aware, but the students were unable to connect the indifference to specific sanctioned policies.

In another case where the court found potential merit, several female high school students[40] brought an action against their North Carolina private school alleging sex discrimination as well as retaliation in violation of Title IX, intentional infliction of emotional distress (IIED), negligent infliction of emotional distress (NIED), and breach of contract. The students felt that classmates harassed them during class, and when they brought it to the attention of school personnel, the students alleged nothing resulted from it. When they tried to take action against a student who they believed was harassing them, by circulating a petition to have him removed as a graduation speaker, they were forced to remove the petition by the school. A federal district court in North Carolina held that because the private school received federal assistance through the federal Paycheck Protection Program (PPP), the school was subject to the requirements of Title IX. Further, the court held that the students sufficiently alleged claims to survive dismissal for all of the causes except intentional infliction of emotional distress.

In the last student-on-student case, grandparents, who were also the legal guardians of a developmentally disabled student in

[40] Karanik v. Cape Fear Acad., Inc., 608 F. Supp. 3d 268, 411 Educ. L. Rep. 1048 (E.D.N.C. 2022).

New York, brought suit against a local school district alleging that the student was raped several times by another student on school grounds.[41] Two of the incidents had been brought as part of the case, but during testimony, it came to light that there were additional incidents. The grandparents requested permission to file a late notice of claim. The appellate court heard this appeal and granted it. The court held that because the school district already had knowledge of some of the acts that were included in the late notice of claim, and because the court concluded that the grandparents had a reasonable excuse for the delay due to the student's disabilities, the school district was not unfairly prejudiced by this late notice.

Child Abuse

Even when the abuse or harassment did not occur on school grounds, the school still has some obligations, depending on the circumstances of the school's awareness. This is particularly true when it involves child abuse. While each of these cases is quite different, the school's obligations for reporting child abuse are at the center of the next few cases.

The first case began when the State of Missouri, through its Attorney General, filed a petition against a private boarding school.[42] The petition asked the school to cease operations because of alleged child abuse and neglect by employees. However, the boarding school asked each parent to be joined, which was granted. In response to the joining, the attorney general requested a writ of prohibition to prevent the local circuit court from joining all parents as parties to the suit and assigning each of them a guardian ad litem. An appellate court for Missouri held that the parents were not necessarily mandated parties to the case, and that because the students were not in a residential care facility, the circuit court did have authority to require a guardian ad litem for each child.

A Connecticut student filed a civil rights action against the local police department and its officers for allegedly violating her

---

[41] Doe v. Elmira City Sch. Dist., 177 N.Y.S.3d 749, 410 Educ. L. Rep. 485 (N.Y. App. Div. 2022).

[42] State *ex rel.* Schmitt v. Pyle, 657 S.W.3d 260, 411 Educ. L. Rep. 809 (Mo. Ct. App. S.D. 2022).

right to equal protection.[43] Specifically, she told a school counselor that a student who attended a different school sexually assaulted her at a pool party. This assault was reported to the police. The student accused the police of working with the school district to do a "sham" investigation and shield the assailant-student from prosecution. After years of discovery and litigation, both parties filed motions for summary judgment. The federal district court held that the student failed to support her claims with facts; thus, the defendant's facts were deemed admitted. As a result, the defendant's motion of summary judgment was granted.

In a Washington state case, the school district notified the Department of Children, Youth & Families[44] of suspected child abuse, which then led to the children being removed from school for an examination at the local hospital. Ultimately, the parents pled guilty to multiple charges of assault and abuse; however, they then filed suit against the hospital and several state and hospital employees who participated in the examination, claiming violations of the children's Fourteenth Amendment right to familial association and asserting Washington state law tort claims for multiple instances of negligence. In the process of the suit, the parents alleged that the defendants conspired with the school and among themselves and were motivated by racial animus. After reviewing the claims, the United States District Court, W.D. Washington dismissed the case with prejudice, noting the lack of substance to the claims. Even so, while racial animus had no bearing in this case, it did in many of the cases involving discrimination.

Discrimination

Racial

After multiple instances of student-to-student racial harassment, a Black student[45] sued Austin Independent School District claiming that the Texas district acted with indifference to

---

[43] Scanlon v. Twp. of Greenwich, 605 F. Supp. 3d 344, 411 Educ. L. Rep. 567 (D. Conn. 2022).
[44] Grae-El v. City of Seattle, 618 F.Supp.3d 1080, 414 Educ. L. Rep. 194 (W.D. Wash. 2022).
[45] Sneed v. Austin Indep. Sch. Dist., 50 F.4th 483, 408 Educ. L. Rep. 158 (5th Cir. 2022).

racial incidents and violated her rights under Title VI of the Civil Rights Act of 1964. Upon review, the magistrate moved to dismiss 12 of the charges as part of a summary judgment. The plaintiff was given the opportunity to object, but did not, thus forfeiting her right to further appeals on these claims. The remaining three claims were reviewed during a bench trial, in which the court found in favor of the district. She appealed to the Fifth Circuit, which affirmed the lower court decision, remarking that a "Title VI defendant is not deliberately indifferent where it actively responds to harassment, provided that its response is not pretextual or knowingly ineffective. An adequate response need not put an end to harassment, nor be the most effective measure available. Administrators are entitled to make these decisions without second-guessing from courts."[46]

The Fifth Circuit again found in favor of the Austin Independent Schools[47] in a different Title VI case and Section 1983 claim. The parent of a recent immigrant from Cameroon alleged that the student was subject to harassment, which included physical violence and verbal bullying by her peers on the basis of her race and national origin, and the district failed to take reasonable corrective measures, including failing to train staff. As a result, the student experienced disciplinary action after confronting her harassers and needed treatment for depression and suicidal ideation. In review of the case, the district court granted the district summary judgment and dismissed the allegations, which the Fifth Circuit affirmed.

In a separate Texas case, the United States District Court issued a temporary restraining order (TRO) preventing the Needville Independent School District[48] from enforcing its dress code policy, which required a Black student to cut his hair in order to attend class and participate in extracurricular activities and graduation. The student alleged that the policy violated prohibitions against racial discrimination in the Fourteenth Amendment's Equal Protection Clause, and Title VI of the Civil Rights Act of 1964, as well as prohibitions against sex discrimination under the Fourteenth Amendment's Equal

---

[46] *Id.*, at 492.

[47] Menzia v. Austin Indep. Sch. Dist., 47 F.4th 354, 407 Educ. L. Rep. 468 (5th Cir. 2022).

[48] Gray v. Needville Indep. Sch. Dist., 601 F.Supp.3d 188, 410 Educ. L. Rep. 991 (S.D. Tex. 2022).

Protection Clause, Title IX, and multiple Texas state statutes. The district policy also violated the student's First Amendment free speech right. The court granted the TRO based on the Fourteenth Amendment's equal protection from sex discrimination.

Further north along I-35, concerns about racial discrimination, harassment, and disproportionate discipline led a group of Black parents, on behalf of their minor children, to file suit against a Minnesota district in *K.R. ex rel. Proctor v. Duluth Public School Academy*.[49] In turn, the district filed for summary judgment, which, in review of the facts, the court dismissed on all counts. The court found that there was enough evidence to demonstrate that the district allowed for a racially hostile environment. Evidence cited included staff making comments to just ignore the use of the "N word," dismissing family surveys that indicated concerns about harassment, and appearing to discipline Black and white students differently for similar infractions; all of these instances highlighted a pattern of action that violated Title VI, the Minnesota Human Rights Act, and the Fourteenth Amendment Equal Protection Clause. In denying the request, the district court cautioned that the case still needed to be tried for a conclusive judgment.

Six Minnesota families, on behalf of their children, made similar claims in another Minnesota district. Of those the claims, four were settled or dismissed and two[50] remained, alleging violations of Title VI of the Civil Rights Act of 1964, the Minnesota Human Rights Act, and the Equal Protection Clause of the Fourteenth Amendment, and seeking relief under Section 1983 for those violations. Their claims arose from several years of racially charged practices, which created a hostile environment for the African American students. These incidents included countless instances of white students regularly using racial slurs and even appearing in blackface in the yearbook, and district inaction when bullying and harassment were reported. In response to this suit, as in *K.R. ex rel. Proctor*,[51] the district filed for summary judgment. This the federal district court dismissed, finding that there were sufficient facts that the district had knowledge of the incidents, had the authority to address them, and instead, acted with indifference. After rejecting the district's summary judgment request, both

---

[49] 591 F.Supp.3d 418, 408 Educ. L. Rep. 813 (D. Minn. 2022).
[50] T.B. *ex rel.* Bursch v. Independent Sch. Dist. 112 (b), 620 F.Supp.3d 818, 414 Educ. L. Rep. 857 (D. Minn. 2022).
[51] *Supra*, note 45.

parties[52] sought to exclude expert witnesses that the other party wished to have testify once the case went to trial. Pleas for exclusion by both sides were denied, as the court found that all of the suspect witnesses had relevant expertise.

A Wisconsin case[53] also addressed the inclusion of expert witnesses, as well as violations of the Fourteenth Amendment, the Establishment Clause, Title VI, the Americans with Disabilities Act, and state tort laws after incidents of alleged racism. In a highly publicized incident during Black History Month, three middle school social studies teachers asked students to determine just punishment for a defiant slave under Hammurabi's Code. The parents of two students in these classes as well as another student not in the class, filed suit on behalf of the students and themselves based on the impact of the event on the students afterward. In reviewing the case, the district court found that one expert witness on behalf of the plaintiffs was unreliable and unhelpful, therefore, upholding the district's appeal to remove the witness. The court also found that the parents lacked standing on their own claims; that the claims regarding the children lacked evidentiary support that the youth were subjected to a racially hostile learning environment; or that teaching Hammurabi's Code was a lesson in religion, violating the Establishment Clause. While the court dismissed all federal claims, it remanded the state violations to the state courts.

In a continuation of a case whereby the Association for Educational Fairness[54] challenged the Montgomery County policies to diversify the student body at a prestigious magnet school, the Association's amended complaint again alleged disparate and discriminatory impact on Asian American students. Since the most recent complaint, the district adjusted its admissions policy as part of its response to the COVID-19 pandemic. Under the Pandemic Plan, which the district adopted as permanent, Asian American students are again disproportionately represented in the student population, invalidating claims of

---

[52] T.B. *ex rel.* Bursch v. Indep. Sch. Dist. 112 (a), 619 F.Supp.3d 886, 414 Educ. L. Rep. 389 (D. Minn. 2022).

[53] Ervins v. Sun Prairie Area Sch. Dist., 609 F.Supp.3d 709, 412 Educ. L. Rep. 137 (W.D. Wis. 2022).

[54] Ass'n for Educ. Fairness v. Montgomery Cnty Bd. of Educ., 617 F.Supp.3d 358, 414 Educ. L. Rep. 42 (D. Md. 2022).

discriminatory impact. As a result, the federal district court in Maryland dismissed the case as moot.

Disability

Racial discrimination was not the only form of discrimination addressed in the cases this year. A student with developmental disabilities[55] alleged that during his time as a student he was sexually assaulted repeatedly by other students and by a school district staff member. In 2016, his guardian brought suit claiming that the district had violated California's 1959 Unruh Civil Rights Act, which prohibits businesses from engaging in unlawful discrimination. In particular, the case alleged disability discrimination. On petition of a writ of mandamus, the Supreme Court of California heard the case and sought to answer the question of whether a school district was liable under the Unruh Civil Rights Act, in which case the plaintiff could avail himself of the enhanced remedies of the statute. The court held that the Unruh Civil Rights Act applied to business establishments under the law, that the school district was not a business establishment, and any violation under the federal Americans with Disabilities Act was not a violation of the Unruh Act. Even though the court did not find discrimination in this case, discrimination, of all kinds, can play a role in discipline as some of the cases in the next section demonstrate.

Discipline

Off-Campus Behavior

Racially charged Instagram posts, which "dehumanized African American students through imagery and verbiage harkening back to the days of slavery and the discredited language of eugenics,"[56] created and shared off-campus by several California high school students,[57] resulted in widespread concerns for student

---

[55] Brennon B. v. Super. Ct. of Contra Costa Cnty., 513 P.3d 971, 406 Educ. L. Rep. 474 (Cal. 2022).
[56] Chen v. Albany Unified Sch. Dist., 56 F.4th 726, 410 Educ. L. Rep. 566 (9th Cir. 2022).
[57] Chen v. Albany Unified Sch. Dist., 56 F.4th 708, 410 Educ. L. Rep. 566 (9th Cir. 2022).

safety, disruptions at school, protests, and many students experiencing negative mental health impacts. In an attempt to address the situation, the school disciplined a number of students who participated in or disseminated the posts, and the main instigators were expelled. Several of the disciplined students brought action against the school alleging violations of their First Amendment free speech and Fourteenth Amendment due process rights, and complementary California constitutional rights. After the district court dismissed their claims in a summary judgment, two of the students appealed the decision, noting that the posts occurred off school grounds and arguing that the students' behavior should not be judged by how people reacted to the posts, since that was tantamount to a heckler's veto. A student also argued that one of the school board members had a conflict of interest when voting to expel him, thus depriving him of due process. The Ninth Circuit disagreed with the students' claims on all accounts and upheld the lower court's ruling. In a concurring decision, Circuit Judge Gould emphasized that "just as a school cannot be forced to teach hate speech, neither should it be forced to entertain and tolerate within its walls hate speech promulgated by arrantly misguided students."[58]

A Texas parent, unhappy with the school's response to a video of her Black son being bullied off-campus at a sleepover, turned to social media to accuse the school of turning a blind eye to racial slurs and bullying on the basis of race. Her video went viral, leading to mass protests and multiple death threats against one of the alleged bullies and the district administrators. The school responded by revisiting the incident and extending disciplinary action to one of the accused students, placing him in alternative school and taking away his ability to participate in the school's football program. In response, that student's parent appealed the discipline, but got no relief from that administrative action and so turned to the courts.[59] In seeking relief, the parent alleged a violation of his Fourteenth Amendment substantive due process rights, but the court found no such infraction on his ability to direct the upbringing of his child. He also sought injunction from the extended discipline, stating that the student was deprived of his Fourteenth Amendment due process rights through the

---

[58] *Id.* at 726.

[59] A.V. v. Plano Indep. Sch. Dist., 585 F. Supp. 3d 881, 407 Educ. L. Rep. 735 (E.D. Tex. 2022).

disciplinary action. At trial, the district court found that the district misinterpreted the definition of cyberbullying as any bullying captured on video, and that there was no evidence that the disciplined student even knew about the incident, which occurred in his home while being captured on video. Consequently, it found that the district, perhaps caving to massive public pressure, violated the student's substantive due process rights, as the disciplinary action was "arbitrary and capricious, and unreasonable under the law and facts of this case."[60]

Video evidence featured in another case after the captain of the Katy High School football team[61] was captured using the "N word" toward a rival football player at a post-game, off-campus Whataburger meet-up. A Black student, who was not the recipient of the slur or even present during the event, but did see the video on social media, then shared this video. The incident went viral. When the team captain's school met with him over the matter, he was given a two-game suspension and lost his role as team captain. However, after he apologized for his actions on Twitter and shared his consequences, his principal and his football coach asked him to take it down for fear it would look like they were not taking his actions seriously. The district then followed up with a separate announcement on social media implying that the football player's actions were directed toward a Black student, which harmed his NCAA recruitment prospects, and so he sued. Shortly after he filed suit, his vehicle, which he shared with another student, was searched by school officials and marijuana was found in it. The plaintiff was suspended and ultimately reassigned to an alternative school placement. When his Section 1983 claims alleging First Amendment free speech and Fourteenth Amendment due process violations were brought before the court, the school district sought a summary judgment dismissal, which the court granted. Upon appeal, the Fifth Circuit upheld the lower court's ruling in its entirety.

Criminal Behavior

Social media also played a role in a case that began one day before the shooting at Marjory Stoneman Douglas High School in

---

[60] *Id.* at 904.

[61] McClelland v. Katy Indep. Sch. Dist., 63 F.4th 996, 413 Educ. L. Rep. 121 (5th Cir. 2023).

2018, when an eighth-grade Florida student[62] posted a meme on his Instagram account showing someone intent on shooting up a school. The meme was then shared around the school until a parent reported it to the boy's school a couple of days later. After the report, the principal contacted the school board and was advised to report it to law enforcement. Later that day, the school was placed into lockdown until the police arrived and arrested the student. While criminal charges were in progress, the school district reassigned the youth to an alternative school in the district. Meanwhile, the student filed claims of false arrest, battery, and Section 1983 violations of his First, Fourth, and Fourteenth Amendment rights. However, in review of the facts, the district court granted the defendant's motions to dismiss all allegations on the grounds that there was probable cause, and all of the defendants were acting within the scope of their job duties in good faith.

Replicating the "TikTok penny challenge," a Plymouth high school student[63] repeatedly attempted to create electrical sparks in class, which resulted in burnt outlets. After being tried and found guilty of attempted arson, he appealed his adjudication, arguing that he did not intend to set fire to the school. Nonetheless, upon appeal the Massachusetts Supreme Court opined that his intention to create sparks was sufficient to meet the definition of attempted arson and upheld the court's verdict.

A dispute on social media led to a physical altercation between two girls, one white and one Black. Afterward, the Black student[64] was arrested for disorderly conduct, a misdemeanor. Prior to her arrest, the student's mother offered to take her to the police station, but the officer refused that request and placed her in handcuffs while still at school. The student later filed a Section 1983 claim alleging unreasonable and excessive force, and racially selective enforcement of the law. Claims against the principal, as well as claims alleging unreasonable and excessive force, were dismissed, but claims of racially discriminatory actions were

---

[62] Alvoid *ex rel.* A.R.A. v. Sch. Dist. of Escambia Cnty., 582 F. Supp. 3d 1140, 406 Educ. L. Rep. 22 (N.D. Fla. 2021).

[63] Commonwealth v. Qasim Q., 205 N.E.3d 1077, 413 Educ. L. Rep. 964 (Mass. 2023).

[64] T.J. *ex rel.* Johnson v. Rose, 615 F. Supp. 3d 115, 413 Educ. L. Rep. 170 (D.R.I. 2022).

brought forth for further review pending discovery evidence requested from the school district.

Due Process

Just before graduation, a California senior[65] posted an image of a Black classmate and used a racial slur about the student, while at school. When his principal learned of this, she barred him from attending the graduation ceremony. Afterward, he brought action against his school district for violating his First Amendment free speech right, his Fourteenth Amendment due process right, and similar rights under the California Constitution and California Education Code. However, citing *Tinker,* the district court rejected his arguments, finding that the school district acted appropriately to protect the rights of others given that the incident occurred on school grounds and that the district did provide him with adequate notice and due process.

In another case where race was alleged to be a factor, an elementary-aged African American male[66] was suspended from his school without due process for allegedly disseminating nude pictures on his cell phone. While the Department of Elementary and Secondary Education overturned his suspension, he experienced anxiety, post-traumatic stress disorder, and sleep deprivation stemming from his experience. As a result, he filed a claim under the Massachusetts Tort Claims Act for negligent infliction of emotional distress, race and sex discrimination, and denial of due process. However, in doing so, he sent his notice to the superintendent but failed to send notice to the correct city executive officer, a requirement of the tort laws. The notice should have gone to the mayor. Noting this discrepancy, the school district sought a dismissal of the complaint, but the court rejected this argument. Upon appeal, the Massachusetts appellate court sided with the school district, dismissing the claim on a technicality, but not without a dissenting argument by one appellant judge who argued that the proper authority for the notice was the superintendent.

---

[65] Castro v. Clovis Unified Sch. Dist., 604 F. Supp. 3d 944, 411 Educ. L. Rep. 494 (E.D. Cal. 2022).

[66] Doe v. Cambridge Pub. Schs., 194 N.E.3d 217, 407 Educ. L. Rep. 905 (Mass. App. Ct. 2022).

Not all cases involved videos and social media as the next several cases illustrate. In one South Carolina case, the state attorney general contested[67] a district court ruling that permanently enjoined the state from enforcing two state statutes which made disorderly conduct and profane language in public spaces, including in schools, a misdemeanor, and required the state to expunge the records of students punished under the law. The statutes had been challenged in a class action lawsuit as excessively vague, thus denying the accused of due process. As a result of the statutes, an alarming number of youth were being prosecuted in juvenile courts for school incidents, with over 13,000 referrals in a six-month period for youth ages 7 to 18; of those, Black youth were seven times more likely to be charged. Affirming the lower court's decision, the Fourth Circuit questioned how "this statute objectively distinguishes criminally disorderly, boisterous, obscene, or profane childhood misbehavior from garden-variety disorderly, boisterous, obscene, or profane childhood misbehavior…[given] elementary and secondary school students ' are in many ways disorderly or boisterous by nature,'"[68] ultimately determining that it did not distinguish between the two. The Fourth Circuit decision was not unanimous, as one judge noted that the statutes had been enforced for many years without concerns about their specificity.

The disproportionate consequences of behavior were also contested in Washington after an incident at school involving a gang clash. One of the students involved[69] was expelled under a Washington law allowing for a 10-day emergency expulsion. However, as the end of the 10 days approached, his district changed his removal to a suspension and extended his suspension multiple times, eventually reassigning him to another school. The student repeatedly sought other educational options, but was barred from doing so, leading him to seek relief from the courts, which included compensatory education so he could earn his diploma or GED. In reviewing his case, the lower court initially dismissed it, but upon appeal, the Washington Court of Appeals

---

[67] Carolina Youth Action Project; D.S. *ex rel.* Ford v. Wilson, 60 F.4th 770, 412 Educ. L. Rep. 44 (4th Cir. 2023).
[68] *Id.* at 424.
[69] M.G. *ex rel.* Priscilla G. v. Yakima Sch. Dist. No. 7, 524 P.3d 670, 412 Educ. L. Rep. 354 (Wash. Ct. App. 2022).

overturned the dismissal and remanded it back for further proceedings.

The final due process case involved an 11-year-old student[70] who brought two orange-tipped plastic BB guns and plastic BBs to school with the intention of playing with them at a park after school. However, while at school he showed them off to friends and at one point fired one of the unloaded guns at the ground. Witnesses reported his actions, and a threat assessment was conducted with the finding that he did not pose a threat. At the same time as the threat assessment, he was recommended for expulsion. At the expulsion hearing, new charges of witness intimidation were brought against him by the district. Ultimately, the student received a suspended expulsion order, based on the weapons and the witness intimidation charges, which he then appealed to the Sacramento County Board of Education (County Board). The County Board found in the boy's favor and ordered his expulsion be expunged, which led to the district filing a writ of administrative mandamus and civil complaint asking for an immediate injunction on the repeal. When the trial court refused the injunction, the district asked for the trial to move to a different county, believing the Sacramento County court had a conflict of interest. When the Placer County court reviewed the case, they found that the County Board overstepped its authority and awarded the district $150,000 in attorney fees. Upon appeal by the County Board and the student, the California Appellate Court found that the County Board was justified in their ruling, the district had abused its discretion in disciplining the boy, and overruled the lower court decision and associated award amount. While the school ultimately lost that case, this was not the only weapons case that caused school officials to be alarmed.

Emergency Protection Orders

In one weapons-related case, where a minor student had made threats to harm himself and others, school officials and local police in New York filed petitions seeking an extreme risk protection order (ERPO) against him that would prohibit the student from

---

[70] Natomas Unified Sch. Dist. v. Sacramento Cnty. Bd. of Educ., 302 Cal.Rptr.3d 771, 410 Educ. L. Rep. 746 (Cal. Ct. App. 2022).

purchasing or possessing a firearm for one year.[71] The petitions argued the student was likely to engage in conduct that would result in serious harm to himself or others, and his threats included acts he wanted to commit during the graduation ceremony. The Supreme Court in New York heard the case and considered that the "red flag" laws were drafted with adult respondents in mind rather than addressing the special circumstances of minors. However, the court agreed that the red flag law applied to an underage youth even if the youth was already prohibited from owning a firearm based on age. The court also found that the petitioners had sufficiently met their burden of proof with clear and compelling evidence, and it granted the petition. While this case saw school officials trying to keep students safe both in and out of school, the next cases shift from protecting students to deciding who is allowed at school and under what circumstances.

School Enrollment

Segregation

When a Mississippi student's local school district consolidated with another school district as part of a longstanding desegregation decree, she brought a federal case alleging that her district denied her due process rights under the Fourteenth Amendment.[72] She was concerned about the impact that the consolidation had on her academic rankings, because her class ranking slipped from second to third when adjusted with the larger class. The student alleged a property interest in her class ranking, the federal district court dismissed the claim, and she appealed. The Fifth Circuit then heard the case and held that she did not have any property interest, rejecting her procedural and substantive due process claims.

Also related to desegregation, a case[73] originating from 1965 was again before the courts. The case began when the St. Martin

---

[71] Anonymous Sch. v. Anonymous Student, 174 N.Y.S.3d 812, 408 Educ. L. Rep. 501 (N.Y. Sup. Ct. 2022).

[72] James v. Cleveland Sch. Dist., 45 F.4th 860, 406 Educ. L. Rep. 22 (5th Cir. 2022).

[73] Borel *ex rel.* AL v. Sch. Bd. St. Martin Parish, 44 F.4th 307, 406 Educ. L. Rep. 157 (5th Cir. 2022).

Parish School Board was found to be in violation of the Fourteenth Amendment Equal Protection Clause because it engaged in intentional racial discrimination. This time the district sought to reverse a desegregation remedial order to close a racially homogeneous elementary school and to regain unitary status. When reviewing the school closure, the Fifth Circuit found that the district court overstepped its authority in ordering the closure. However, the court affirmed the decision of the lower court to deny the district unitary status because St Martin Parish must first demonstrate that it complied with desegregation orders and had removed the "vestiges of prior de jure segregation,"[74] which the district had not yet done.

Concern about racial segregation also occurred in Minnesota where a group of parents[75] from Minneapolis and St. Paul filed a class action lawsuit against the state. The parents alleged that many schools in their district were segregated by race and socioeconomics, a violation of the Education Clause of the Minnesota Constitution. The district court dismissed this claim, but did support an interlocutory appeal focused on the certified question of "Is the Education Clause of the Minnesota Constitution violated by a racially imbalanced school system, regardless of the presence of de jure segregation or proof of a causal link between the racial imbalance and the actions of the state?"[76] The Minnesota Court of Appeals found the question both important and doubtful, but upon review determined that the answer was no. Unless the imbalance was caused by intentional, de jure segregation, it was not a violation of the Minnesota Constitution.

Adequate Education and Standing

In New Jersey, concerns about the application of state education law came from a different angle than those in Minnesota when parents filed a petition alleging that a local New Jersey school district was not providing students a thorough and efficient education as required by the state constitution.[77] The parents

---

[74] *Id,* at 314.
[75] Cruz-Guzman v. State, 980 N.W.2d 816, 408 Educ. L. Rep. 1016 (Minn. Ct. App. 2022).
[76] *Id.* at 822.
[77] Alcantara v. Allen-McMillan, 291 A.3d 288, 414 Educ. L. Rep. 604 (N.J. Super. Ct. App. Div. 2023).

argued that this was due to the failure of the New Jersey Department of Education to properly fund the district in light of their special circumstances, and that the state School Funding Reform Act was unconstitutional as applied to the local district. A majority of the 37,000 students in this district (84%) attended a private religious school, leaving 6,000 enrolled in the public school. However, the public school provided special education and transportation support for the privately enrolled students. A state administrative law judge determined that the district was failing to provide a thorough and efficient education, but this failure was due to mismanagement and not a constitutional defect in the funding law. The parents appealed this to the New Jersey Education Commissioner, and the Commissioner rejected the administrative law judge's conclusion that the district was not providing a thorough and efficient education. An appellate court in New Jersey reviewed the record and held that it did not support the commissioner's finding, remanding the case back for re-examination.

Shifting gears from concerns about public school compliance, a New York mother filed a petition requesting that the New York Education Commissioner issue an order requiring the city's department of education to ensure that the private religious school attended by her son complied with the state's educational law. The mother's concern was that New York's educational law required that private, nonpublic schools provide an education that was substantially equivalent to public schools. After her petition was dismissed, she brought proceedings under Article 78 of the state's education law against the New York State Education Department and its commissioner for the dismissal.[78] Her attorney also brought a challenge under the Freedom of Information Law to obtain records held by the city department of education. The Supreme Court of New York held that the information requested was not material or necessary, but that the mother did have standing to bring her complaint against the commissioner. Further, this was a matter of first impression related to whether the court had subject matter jurisdiction to hear the mother's claim under New York Education law, in which the court ruled it did. Finally, the court concluded an order was necessary to compel the commissioner to

[78] Weber v. N.Y. State Educ. Dep't, 174 N.Y.S.3d 791, 408 Educ. L. Rep. 480 (N.Y. Sup. Ct. 2022).

make a determination on the merits of the petition filed by the mother.

School Selection

Also making an Article 78 claim, New York parents whose children had been denied admission to specialized public high schools brought proceedings against the state department of education and its education commissioner.[79] The parents challenged the admission test cut-off scores, as well as the rules that allowed students admissions even if their scores fell below the cut scores if they were considered "disadvantaged" under state criteria. However, the contesting parents did not meet the new or previously used state definition of disadvantaged, and so they did not have standing for a judicial review of the definition. Still, the New York Supreme Court held that the parents could challenge the program's expanded enrollment process, as well as the practice of using admissions test cut-off scores for program admission.

Not all school selection cases involved decisions made by school officials, as the next two cases demonstrate. In a case initiated as part of post-divorce proceedings pursuant to the property settlement agreement, a mother[80] requested that her three children attend public school where both parents and the children lived. Her ex-husband, the father, wanted the children to attend a private school or a public school where his new wife was a teacher. According to the Property, Child Support, and Child Custody Agreement, the father had final say if the two parents could not agree. However, there was a clause allowing the chancery court to approve or disapprove any agreement. The chancery court ruled that the children would attend public school where the children lived unless the father could pay to send them to private school. The father appealed, and the Supreme Court in Mississippi agreed with the chancery court stating the agreement could not deprive the court of its authority to reevaluate the issue and that the decision was in the children's best interests.

Following a divorce, and as part of a post-divorce marriage, a mother filed a motion to modify her child's custody order.[81]

---

[79] C.K. v. Tahoe, 177 N.Y.S.3d 364, 409 Educ. L. Rep. 910 (N.Y. App. Div. 2022).
[80] Bryant v. Bryant, 348 So.3d 309, 408 Educ. L. Rep. 1164 (Miss. 2022).
[81] Sendlein v. Sendlein, 655 S.W.3d 422, 410 Educ. L. Rep. 533 (Mo. Ct. App. E.D. 2022).

Specifically, she sought to change the child's legal address for mailing and educational purposes. She stated that the father had unilaterally changed the child's address as well as the child's school. The court granted her request, and the father appealed. When the appellate court considered the case, it focused on two important questions: What happens when joint legal and physical custodians cannot agree where a child should go to school, and does the circuit court have the ability to decide upon which school a minor child should attend when the custodial parents cannot? Citing the Missouri Supreme Court best interest of the child standard in custody issues, the appellate court held that the circuit did have the power to determine the address and the school by applying that standard. Thus, the court upheld the lower court decision and rejected the father's appeal. Sometimes though, school selection has less to do with what opposing parents want and more to do with the needs of the school.

Charitable Gifts

Parents did not have much say when the Archdiocese of Hartford announced that it would be closing two Catholic schools and opening a new Catholic school for local students.[82] Students from the closed schools were allowed to attend the new school, but the parents and former students were less concerned with who could attend and more concerned about a large charitable bequest that had been made to one of the schools now closing. Former students, as well as parents, formed a separate corporation to open a similar school to the one closing. They filed suit arguing they were the putative beneficiaries of the testamentary bequest and sought the court to award them, or the deceased benefactor's estate, residue of the original gift. Having been dismissed by lower state courts, the Supreme Court of Connecticut took up the case on appeal. Based on the facts, the court concluded that the bequest to the now-defunct school was an unrestricted gift and thus was able to be incorporated into the new school. Furthermore, the court explained that the plaintiffs did not have standing to bring the case.

---

[82] Derblom v. Archdiocese of Hartford, 289 A.3d 1187, 413 Educ. L. Rep. 336 (Conn. 2023).

Student Records

In a post-divorce proceeding, a mother filed a motion to restrict the father's parenting time with a minor child, arguing that the father's engagement would continue to interfere with necessary services provided to the child related to mental health.[83] A circuit court denied the father his request for the child's medical records, but granted the father leave to file an interlocutory appeal based on this denial. An appellate court in Illinois heard the argument and concluded that the Illinois Mental Health and Developmental Disabilities Confidentiality Act applied to the issue; thus, the father was entitled to request the records from the trial court, but the trial court could deny access if it was in the best interests of the child. However, the trial court could not deny the father nonprivileged records, such as school records, under the confidentiality act.

An Arkansas circuit court also heard a post-divorce motion, but this motion was filed by a father[84] who sought to modify a child custody order, citing evidence found in his children's school and medical records indicating that their mother's mental health was negatively affecting them. As a result, the court found there was a material change of circumstance that would warrant a modification of custody. In particular, the court changed the custody from the mother to the father. The mother appealed the court's ruling, arguing that the judge erred in prohibiting testimony made by the father's adult son to his counselor that predated the original order now being modified. An appellate court in Arkansas heard the case and held that the trial court did not abuse its discretion concerning evidence or events that took place before the entry of the child support and custody order. Further, the court concluded the changes in circumstances warranted a change in custody.

Wrongful Death

Parents of two students who attended a private Christian school sued when their children, who were driving themselves, died

---

[83] In re Marriage of Wendy W. and James W., 202 N.E.3d 1034, 412 Educ. L. Rep. 301 (Ill. App. Ct. 2022).

[84] Morris v. Morris, 653 S.W.3d 533, 408 Educ. L. Rep. 1102 (Ark. Ct. App. 2022).

in a car accident on their way to a basketball tournament.[85] The parents filed federal civil rights claims under Section 1983 and Section 1985 alleging the school, police, and the state of Minnesota engaged in a conspiracy to interfere with the administration of justice and deny equal protection under the law. Specifically, the parents alleged that the police sergeant violated their constitutional rights and the laws of Minnesota because he had a personal relationship with school officials and thus had a bias toward the school that corrupted his investigation. The state court denied these claims, after which the parents filed similar claims in federal court. The Eighth Circuit held that collateral estoppel barred the claims because issues presented had already been litigated, and that minority students that paid tuition were not a protected class.

In another private school case, a Florida parent brought suit against the school after a student, who had been asked to withdraw from the school for selling a vape pen to a fellow student, died by suicide.[86] The case alleged wrongful death, as well as negligence claims asserting that the school had violated its common law duty to the student and failed to assess the student for suicide and crisis support as part of its policies and procedures. The school brought a motion to dismiss or compel arbitration in accordance with the signed school enrollment contract and handbook. The local circuit court denied these motions, and the school appealed. A court of appeals in Florida held that the arbitration clause applied in this case as written, and the wrongful death issue was related to the contract. The case was reversed and remanded.

The death by suicide of an Alabama minor student also led the mother to file suit against the local school system, its superintendent, elementary school principal and assistant principal, and a teacher.[87] The mother alleged that there were Section 1983 civil rights claims for violations of Fourteenth Amendment equal protection and substantive due process rights, a violation of Title IX, as well as several wrongful death claims under state law governing the wrongful death of a minor. The U.S.

---

[85] Kvalvog v. Park Christian Sch., Inc., 66 F.4th 1147, 415 Educ. L. Rep. 6 (8th Cir. 2023).
[86] Calvary Chapel Church, Inc. v. Happ, 353 So. 3d 649, 411 Educ. L. Rep. 1265 (Fla. Dist. Ct. App. 2023).
[87] Adams v. Demopolis City Sch., 592 F.Supp.3d 1049, 408 Educ. L. Rep. 879 (S.D. Ala. 2022).

District Court in Alabama heard the case and held that the school and its personnel were not deliberately indifferent to any known harassment, which precluded an Equal Protection Clause violation, and the actions of the school did not shock the conscience, thus precluding due process claims. Finally, the court held that there was governmental immunity for a state-agent. The case was dismissed.

The parents of a Tennessee high school student who died by suicide brought action in state and federal courts against the local school district and its administration.[88] The action began in state court with allegations of a due process violation claim, as well as claim for negligent infliction of emotional distress under state law. The case asserted that the school and its administrators engaged in discriminatory discipline against the student because of his appearance, speech, and perceived sexual orientation, and all of this led to the student's suicide. The action was removed to federal court and, several years later, the complaint was amended to include federal constitutional claims. The Sixth Circuit Court of Appeals heard this case on appeal of its dismissal. The court held that the parents had waived their procedural due process claims and forfeited their substantive due process claims, as well as their Title IX claims, because of the delays by the parents' attorney in the case and changing claims. While the plaintiffs in this case were not able to assert rights in court, other youth who identify as LGBTQ+ were able to find solace in the court proceedings for their cases.

Transgender Rights

Restrooms

A 13-year-old transgender boy from Indiana, designated female at birth, brought an action against a local school district as well as the principal seeking declaratory relief and a preliminary injunction,[89] claiming that the school violated his Title IX and the Equal Protection Clause. Further, he asked the court to enjoin the district from restricting his use of male restrooms and require that

---

[88] Bannister v. Knox Cnty Bd. of Educ., 49 F.4th 1000, 408 Educ. L. Rep. 97 (6th Cir. 2022).

[89] A.C. *ex rel.* M.C. v. Metro. Sch. Dist. of Martinsville, 601 F.Supp.3d 345, 410 Educ. L. Rep. 993 (S.D. Ind. 2022).

the school treat him like a male for all purposes. Prior to this action, the school had granted the student an accommodation to use a family restroom, but the restroom was far away, causing him to be tardy as well as singling him out for using it. His parents asked the school to allow him to use the male restrooms, but the school refused the request. The federal district court granted the injunction and the motion, stating that A.C. was likely to succeed based on the merits and that he would likely suffer irreparable harm if it were not granted. The court concluded that most federal courts, including the Seventh Circuit where this district court is located, have held that Title IX covers transgender education-discrimination claims, and that preventing the student from using the restroom would violate Title IX.

In a similar case, a transgender boy student, born biologically female, filed suit under a Section 1983 action against his local county school board.[90] Specifically, he alleged his rights were violated under the Equal Protection Clause and Title IX because of the district's restroom policy. His district's policy allowed students to be addressed by their preferred pronouns and provided students with access to gender-neutral restrooms instead of requiring students to use restrooms that corresponded to their biological sex. The school argued that this kept the longstanding separation of restrooms based on biological sex but also provided sex-neutral restrooms in accordance with Best Practice Guidelines. Further, it allowed for gender fluidity. The federal district court ruled in favor of the student, and the school district appealed. The Eleventh Circuit said the case "involves the unremarkable—and nearly universal—practice of separating school restrooms based on biological sex."[91] The court focused on two issues: Did the district policy of assigning restrooms based on sex violate the Equal Protection Clause, and did this policy violate Title IX? The court held that it did not on either issue; separate school restrooms pass constitutional muster and comport with Title IX.

Two Indiana transgender male students, born female, sought a preliminary injunction against their local county school for refusal to allow them to use male restroom and locker room

---

[90] Adams *ex rel.* Kasper v. Sch. Bd. of St. Johns Cnty, 57 F.4th 791, 411 Educ. L. Rep. 99 (11th Cir. 2022).
[91] *Id.* at 796.

facilities.[92] Specifically, the students brought this claim under Title IX and the Equal Protection Clause. The students, now in high school, had identified as male since they were 11 and 15, had both already begun gender-affirming testosterone therapy, had changed their names, and updated their birth certificates. A federal district court in Indiana ruled in favor of the students because they were likely to succeed on the merits of the claim, they would suffer irreparable harm, there was no adequate remedy of law, and balancing public interest weighed in favor of the injunction.

Bullying

A parent on behalf of his child, a minor with disabilities, brought action against the New York City Department of Education, the Board of Education of New York, and various teachers and administrators of the district.[93] Included in the claims were Title IX violations and Section 504 of the Rehabilitation Act of 1973 violations, as well as claims under New York Civil Rights Law and the New York State Human Rights Law. The student faced bullying from other students while in school based on his sexuality and gender expression, and alleged the school failed to meaningfully address it, which denied the student a free and appropriate public education. The school district filed for a motion to dismiss, but a federal district court in New York denied the motion, stating that the parent sufficiently pleaded allegations to advance the case.

School Gender Identity Policy

Several Maryland parents of public school students brought action in state court, later removed by the school to federal court, against the county board of education.[94] The parents alleged that the school's guidelines on student gender identity, confidentiality, and support violated their parental rights under both the state and

---

[92] B.E. v. Vigo Cnty Sch. Corp., 608 F. Supp. 3d 725, 411 Educ. L. Rep. 1075 (S.D. Ind. 2022).

[93] Cianciotto *ex rel.* D.S. v. N.Y. City Dept. of Educ., 600 F.Supp.3d 434, 410 Educ. L. Rep. 858 (S.D.N.Y. 2022).

[94] John and Jane Parents 1 v. Montgomery Cnty. Bd. of Educ., 622 F. Supp. 3d 118, 415 Educ. L. Rep. 116 (D. Md. 2022);vacated and remanded by 78 F.4th 622 (4th Cir. 2023) (petition for certiorari filed)

federal constitution. The parents felt this policy shut them out of the process of engaging on gender identity issues and encouraged the school to keep this information from parents. A federal district court in Maryland held that this was not the case when read in totality. Specifically, the court said there was not a fundamental right under the Due Process Clause to be promptly informed of their child's gender identity choices when they differed from their assigned gender, and the school guidelines satisfied rational basis review.

Conclusion

This chapter began with COVID-19 mitigation cases, a hot topic from the previous year, and ended on a topic predicted to be a hot topic this year, parental rights. While COVID-19 issues waned, the prevalence of parental rights cases never took hold as suspected. Instead, the cases this year highlighted the shifting concerns of an increasingly diverse and digital world with a specific focus on student rights.

Social media and videos were at the forefront of many of the cases, raising questions about the reach and necessity of schools to address off-campus behavior. In almost every social media-related case, the viral nature of the behavior created substantial disruption to the schools and even led to death threats against school personnel[95] in at least one instance because of the school's perceived lack of response. In *Chen v. Albany Unified School District*,[96] the student involved in creating off-campus memes on a private Instagram account shared with only a few friends argued that he had no intention of his memes going beyond his friend group and so should not suffer the consequences of the massive disruption the eventual leaking of the images cause. But, as the court found, "whether it was reasonably foreseeable that the speech would reach and impact the school…[the plaintiff] failed in his effort to keep the posts private….Given the ease with which electronic communications may be copied or shown to other persons, it was plainly foreseeable that Epple's posts would ultimately hit their targets, with resulting significant impacts to those individual students and to the school as a whole."[97]

---

[95] *Supra,* note 57.
[96] *Supra,* note 54.
[97] *Id.* at 720.

Many of the social media cases also included an element of racial discrimination. Race was a factor in at least 15 of the cases, and, in nearly all of the cases where race was in play, it involved those who identified as Black/African American. These cases ranged from disproportionate discipline to disparate impact to outright racism, and implicated students, school staff, medical staff, and law enforcement. While not all of the cases had merit in the eyes of the court, the mere magnitude this year indicated a troubling pattern that we hope does not continue into the future. However, given the facts in many of the cases and the community response to them, race is likely to remain a factor in future years.

Looking ahead, the rights of transgender youth also remain unsettled. This year, two different circuits concluded two similar cases very differently. Specifically, one of the cases relied heavily on what had been previously decided in the Sixth Circuit. The case focused on Title IX and the Equal Protection Clause violations because the school provided students with accommodations to use gender-neutral restrooms instead of using the restrooms that aligned with the student's identity.[98] The court concluded that not allowing students to use the restrooms of their choice was a violation of their rights. However, a case decided in the Eleventh Circuit had an opposite ruling,[99] finding that having gender-neutral restrooms was not a violation of Title IX and the Equal Protection Clause. With circuits diverging on this issue, it is only a matter of time before it comes before the U.S. Supreme Court.

Finally, two cases this year—one concerning a charter school[100] granted governmental immunity and the other a private school[101] subject to federal law after taking federal money—further complicated the question about the conditions in which a charter school (or a private school) may be considered a state actor. Raised last year in the review of the *Peltier* case,[102] the answer to this question has the potential to affect the educational experiences of students across the country, many of whom are enrolled in these nontraditional schools. As more and more states

---

[98] *Supra*, note 88.
[99] *Supra*, note 90.
[100] *Supra*, note 34.
[101] *Supra*, note 40.
[102] Peltier v. Charter Day Sch., 37 F.4th 104, 120, 403 Educ. L. Rep. 436 (4th Cir. 2022).

adopt school choice policies[103] the rights of students in this new educational frontier may look very different in years to come.

[103]Samuel Wonacott, Five States Have Enacted Education Savings Account Programs This Year, Most Since 2021, Ballotpedia (Nov. 1, 2023), https://news.ballotpedia.org/2023/11/01/five-states-have-enacted-education-savings-account-programs-this-year-most-since-2021/.

Alphabetical List of Cases

A.C. *ex rel.* M.C. v. Metro. Sch. Dist. of Martinsville

A.S. v. City Sch. Dist. of Albany

A.V. v. Plano Indep. Sch. Dist.

Adams *ex rel.* Kasper v. Sch. Bd. of St. Johns Cnty

Adams v. Demopolis City Sch.

Alcantara v. Allen-McMillan

Alvoid *ex rel.* A.R.A. v. Sch. Dist. of Escambia Cnty.

Anonymous Sch. v. Anonymous Student

Ass' n for Educ. Fairness v. Montgomery Cnty Bd. of Educ.

B.A.P. v. Overton Cnty Bd. of Educ.

B.E. v. Vigo Cnty Sch. Corp.

B.P. *ex rel.* L.P. v. N. Allegheny Sch. Dist.

Bannister v. Knox Cnty Bd. of Educ.

Belcastro v. Roman Catholic Diocese of Brooklyn

Booth v. Bowser

Borel *ex rel.* AL v. Sch. Bd. St. Martin Parish

Branch-Noto v. Sisolak

Brennon B. v. Super. Ct. of Contra Costa Cnty.

Bryant v. Bryant

Byrd v. Cornelius

C.K. v. Tahoe

C.K.-W. *ex rel.* T.K. v. Wentzville R-IV Sch. Dist.

Calvary Chapel Church, Inc. v. Happ

Carolina Youth Action Project; D.S. *ex rel.* Ford v. Wilson

Castro v. Clovis Unified Sch. Dist.

Chen v. Albany Unified Sch. Dist.

Cianciotto *ex rel.* D.S. v. NY City Dept. of Educ.

Commonwealth v. Qasim Q.

Cruz-Guzman v. State

CT Freedom All., LLC v. Dep' t of Educ.

Derblom v. Archdiocese of Hartford

Doe v. Beaumont Indep. Sch. Dist.

Doe v. Cambridge Pub. Schs.

Doe v. Elmira City Sch. Dist.

Ervins v. Sun Prairie Area Sch. Dist.

Fisher v. Moore

Fortuna v. Twp. of Winslow

Grae-El v. City of Seattle

Gray v. Needville Indep. Sch. Dist.

H.K. *ex rel.* Farwell v. Google LLC

Hanson v. Hicksville Union Free Sch. Dist.

Healy v. Honorlock Inc.

James v. Cleveland Sch. Dist.

John and Jane Parents 1 v. Montgomery Cnty. Bd. of Educ.

K.R. *ex rel.* Proctor v. Duluth Pub. Sch. Acad.

Karanik v. Cape Fear Acad.

KIPP Texas, Inc. v. Doe #1

Kvalvog v. Park Christian Sch., Inc.

M.A. *ex rel.* H.R. v. Rockland Cnty. Dep' t of Health

M.G. *ex rel.* Priscilla G. v. Yakima Sch. Dist. No. 7

Marriage of Wendy W. and James W., In re

McArthur v. Brabrand

McClelland v. Katy Indep. Sch. Dist.

Menders v. Loudoun Cnty Sch. Bd.

Menzia v. Austin Indep. Sch. Dist.

Morris v. Morris

Natomas Unified Sch. Dist. v. Sacramento Cnty. Bd. of Educ.

PB-36 Doe *ex rel.* Niagara Falls City Sch. Dist.

PC-41 Doe v. Poly Prep Cntry. Day Sch.

People In Interest of J.G.

Perez v. KIPP DC Supporting Corp.

R.H. v. Wagner

Richardson v. State

Richmond v. Badia

Ritter v. State

Roe v. Cypress-Fairbanks Indep. Sch. Dist.

S.C. v. Metropolitan Gov' t of Nashville & Davidson Cnty., Tenn.

Scanlon v. Twp. of Greenwich

Sendlein v. Sendlein

Singh v. Sachem Cent. Sch. Dist.

Sneed v. Austin Indep. Sch. Dist.

State *ex rel.* 93rd Gen. Assembly v. McClane

State *ex rel.* Schmitt v. Pyle

T.B. *ex rel.* Bursch v. Indep. Sch. Dist. 112 (a)

T.B. *ex rel.* Bursch v. Independent Sch. Dist. 112 (b)

T.J. *ex rel.* Johnson v. Rose

Teet v. State

Waln v. Dysart Sch. Dist.

We the Patriots USA, Inc. v. Conn. Office of Early Childhood Development

Weber v. N.Y. State Educ. Dep't

Federal Cases

First Circuit

Maine
Fortuna v. Twp. of Winslow
Rhode Island
T.J. *ex rel.* Johnson v. Rose

Second Circuit

M.A. *ex rel.* H.R. v. Rockland Cnty. Dep't of Health

Connecticut
Scanlon v. Twp. of Greenwich
We the Patriots USA, Inc. v. Conn. Office of Early Childhood Development

New York
A.S. v. City Sch. Dist. of Albany
Cianciotto ex rel. D.S. v. N.Y. City Dept. of Educ.
PC-41 Doe v. Poly Prep Cntry. Day Sch.
Singh v. Sachem Cent. Sch. Dist.

Third Circuit

Maryland
Ass'n for Educ. Fairness v. Montgomery Cnty. Bd. of Educ.

Pennsylvania
B.P. *ex rel.* L.P. v. N. Allegheny Sch. Dist.

Fourth Circuit

Carolina Youth Action Project; D.S. ex rel. Ford v. Wilson
John and Jane Parents 1 v. Montgomery Cnty. Bd. of Educ.
Menders v. Loudoun Cnty. Sch. Bd.

North Carolina
Karanik v. Cape Fear Acad.

Virginia
McArthur v. Brabrand

Fifth Circuit

Borel *ex rel.* AL v. Sch. Bd. St. Martin Parish
Byrd v. Cornelius
Fisher v. Moore
James v. Cleveland Sch. Dist.
McClelland v. Katy Indep. Sch. Dist.
Menzia v. Austin Indep. Sch. Dist.
Roe v. Cypress-Fairbanks Indep. Sch. Dist.
Sneed v. Austin Indep. Sch. Dist.

Texas
A.V. v. Plano Indep. Sch. Dist.
Doe v. Beaumont Indep. Sch. Dist.
Gray v. Needville Indep. Sch. Dist.

Sixth Circuit

Bannister v. Knox Cnty Bd. of Educ.

Tennessee
B.A.P. v. Overton Cnty Bd. of Educ.
S.C. v. Metropolitan Gov't of Nashville & Davidson Cnty., Tenn.

Seventh Circuit

Illinois
H.K. *ex rel.* Farwell v. Google LLC

Indiana
A.C. *ex rel.* M.C. v. Metro. Sch. Dist. of Martinsville
B.E. v. Vigo Cnty. Sch. Corp.

Wisconsin
Ervins v. Sun Prairie Area Sch. Dist.

Eighth Circuit

Kvalvog v. Park Christian Sch.

Minnesota
K.R. *ex rel.* Proctor v. Duluth Pub. Sch. Acad.
T.B. *ex rel.* Bursch v. Indep. Sch. Dist. 112 (a)
T.B. *ex rel.* Bursch v. Independent Sch. Dist. 112 (b)

Missouri
C.K.-W. *ex rel.* T.K. v. Wentzville R-IV Sch. Dist.

Ninth Circuit

Chen v. Albany Unified Sch. Dist.
Waln v. Dysart Sch. Dist.

California
Castro v. Clovis Unified Sch. Dist.

Nevada
Branch-Noto v. Sisolak

Washington
Grae-El v. City of Seattle

Eleventh Circuit

Adams *ex rel.* Kasper v. Sch. Bd. of St. Johns Cnty.
Richmond v. Badia

Alabama
Adams v. Demopolis City Sch.

Florida
Alvoid *ex rel.* A.R.A. v. Sch. Dist. of Escambia Cnty.
Healy v. Honorlock Inc.

State and D.C. Cases

D.C.
Booth v. Bowser
Perez v. KIPP DC Supporting Corp.

Arkansas
State *ex rel.* 93rd Gen. Assembly v. McClane
Morris v. Morris

California
Brennon B. v. Super. Ct. of Contra Costa Cnty.
Natomas Unified Sch. Dist. v. Sacramento Cnty. Bd. of Educ.

Colorado
People In Interest of J.G.

Connecticut
CT Freedom All., LLC v. Dep't of Educ.
Derblom v. Archdiocese of Hartford

Florida
Calvary Chapel Church, Inc. v. Happ
Teet v. State

Georgia
R.H. v. Wagner

Illinois
Marriage of Wendy W. and James W., In re

Maryland
Richardson v. State

Massachusetts
Commonwealth v. Qasim Q.
Doe v. Cambridge Pub. Schs.

Minnesota
Cruz-Guzman v. State

Mississippi
Bryant v. Bryant

Missouri
Sendlein v. Sendlein
State *ex rel.* Schmitt v. Pyle

New Jersey
Alcantara v. Allen-McMillan

New York
Anonymous Sch. v. Anonymous Student
Belcastro v. Roman Catholic Diocese of Brooklyn
C.K. v. Tahoe
Doe v. Elmira City Sch. Dist.
Hanson v. Hicksville Union Free Sch. Dist.
PB-36 Doe *ex rel.* Niagara Falls City Sch. Dist.
Weber v. N.Y. State Educ. Dep't

Oklahoma
Ritter v. State

Texas
KIPP Texas, Inc. v. Doe #1

Washington
M.G. *ex rel.* Priscilla G. v. Yakima Sch. Dist. No. 7

CHAPTER 4

BARGAINING

Jeffrey S. Greenly

Introduction

This chapter will review K-12 collective bargaining cases published during the year 2023. The cases come from both state and federal courts and provide a glimpse of the current state of the ever-changing collective bargaining process. The chapter is divided by subject matter to better organize the various cases and their holdings.

Arbitration

Only the parties involved in an arbitration have standing to appeal a decision. A New York Supreme Court affirmed the dismissal of several hybrid proceedings brought by individual teachers challenging their placement on leave without pay due to noncompliance with a COVID-19 vaccine mandate.[1] The court found that the individual petitioners lacked standing to challenge the arbitration award resulting from the mandate's implementation because such a challenge could only be brought by the union as an organization.

Ohio reached a related conclusion in another case involving COVID-19 employment actions. A group of Ohio educators laid off during the COVID-19 pandemic sought to circumvent their layoff, citing a state statute purporting to prevent such actions during a pandemic. The Ohio Court of Appeals reversed a lower court decision and held that the trial court lacked subject matter jurisdiction to review the union's complaint because the collective bargaining agreements (CBAs) between the parties contained provisions mirroring the statutory rights at issue in the dispute.[2] The court emphasized that when a CBA addresses the same matter as a statute, the CBA's grievance and arbitration procedures provide the exclusive means of resolving disputes, even when those disputes involve statutory rights.

Filing an arbitration may not toll the statute of limitation for redress under a state-level statute. A New York teacher brought a challenge against the City of New York and others' denial of a retirement incentive. The New York Supreme Court, Appellate

---

[1] Clarke v. Bd. of Educ. of City Sch., 185 N.Y.S.3d 8, 413 Educ. L. Rep. 934 (N.Y. App. Div. 2023).

[2] State *ex rel.* Ohio Ass'n of Pub. Sch. Emp. v. Willoughby-Eastlake City Sch. Dist., 202 N.E.3d 111, 412 Educ. L. Rep. 293 (Ohio Ct. App. 2022).

Division, affirmed the dismissal of her petition.[3] The court held that the four-month statute of limitations to commence a proceeding challenging the decision began when the teacher was informed of the denial three-and-a-half years earlier, as there was no further administrative review available within the Department of Education at that time. Although the teacher pursued a grievance procedure under the collective bargaining agreement, the court found that this did not toll the statute of limitations for the underlying denial of the retirement incentive.

Duty of Fair Representation

The duty of fair representation by a union only extends to employees who are eligible for union membership. A California substitute teacher brought an action against a union and the state employee relations board for a specialty writ certifying her as a member of the union. After the board ruled against her, the substitute appealed, and its decision was upheld by the California Court of Appeals. [4] The court held that the substitute teacher did not have a constitutional or statutory right to union representation as an alleged misclassified employee or as a substitute teacher. The court deferred to the Board's interpretation of the relevant statute, finding that it was not an erroneous construction to conclude that substitute teachers could be excluded from bargaining units representing classroom teachers.

Fair Share Fees and Union Dues

An Illinois teacher mistakenly joined her local teachers' union believing that membership was mandatory. After realizing her error, she sought to resign and revoke her dues deduction authorization. Despite initially indicating that dues would still be required, the union eventually acknowledged her resignation and provided a full refund. The teacher filed a lawsuit alleging a violation of her First Amendment rights under *Janus v. AFSCME*, but the U.S. District Court for the Northern District of Illinois

---

[3] Dourdounas v. City of N.Y., 180 N.Y.S.3d 137, 411 Educ. L. Rep. 711 (N.Y. App. Div. 2022).

[4] Wu v. Pub. Emp. Relations Bd., 303 Cal.Rptr.3d 693, 411 Educ. L. Rep. 687 (Cal. Ct. App. 2022).

dismissed the case.[5] The court held that the teacher's voluntary union membership, even if based on a misunderstanding, meant she was bound by the terms of the membership agreement and had not suffered a First Amendment violation. The court distinguished this case from *Janus*, which dealt with the rights of non-union members, and emphasized that the teacher had affirmatively consented to pay dues.

A school custodian challenged the continued deduction of dues after her resignation, arguing (1) that the prior system of offering a choice between full membership and fair-share fees was unconstitutional and (2) that the union violated her individual and free speech rights by speaking on her behalf without her will. The U.S. District Court for the Central District of Illinois upheld the legality of union dues deductions and exclusive representation under the Illinois Educational Labor Relations Act (IELRA), even in light of the Janus v. AFSCME decision.[6] The court held that Janus did not invalidate her contractual duty to pay dues and reaffirmed the union's exclusive representation of union members as a bedrock principle of labor law.

Unions are not liable for their good faith reliance on prior case law even if it is overturned. A former teacher brought an action against her former union seeking the reimbursement of many years of dues she had paid to her union before the Janus decision as well as some paid after. The U.S. District Court for the District of Hawaii determined that the union's reliance on prior Supreme Court precedent shielded it from pre-Janus liability.[7] The court also held that the plaintiff's post-Janus claims were moot due to a full refund and her current non-member status.

A case from California has a similar result. A teacher's lawsuit against his union and his school district was similarly dismissed by the U.S. District Court for the Central District of California.[8] The court held that the plaintiff's claim for pre-Janus damages was barred by the good faith defense, as the union had relied on then-binding Supreme Court precedent in collecting dues. The court further dismissed the

---

[5] Baro v. Lake Cnty. Fed'n of Teachers Local 504, 594 F. Supp. 3d 1012, 409 Educ. L. Rep. 706 (N.D. Ill. 2022).

[6] Bennett v. Am. Fed'n of State, Cnty, and Mun. Emps., Council 31, AFL-CIO, 612 F.Supp.3d 821, 412 Educ. L. Rep. 637 (C.D. Ill. 2020).

[7] Grossman v. Haw. Gov't Emps. Ass'n/AFSCME Local 152, 611 F.Supp.3d 1033, 412 Educ. L. Rep. 568 (D. Haw. 2020).

[8] Laird v. United Teachers L.A., 615 F. Supp. 3d 1171, 413 Educ. L. Rep. 307 (C.D. Cal. 2022).

plaintiff's post-Janus claims for damages and prospective relief as moot, since he had received a full refund of dues and was no longer a union member subject to the challenged opt-out window. Finally, the court dismissed claims against the school district based on sovereign immunity and against the union for lack of state action.

Similarly, the Seventh Circuit Court of Appeals recently reached the same conclusion in a case on appeal that was reviewed at the trial-court level earlier in this chapter.[9] The Seventh Circuit Court of Appeals affirmed the dismissal of a teacher's lawsuit seeking a refund of union dues paid after signing a union membership agreement. The court held that the Supreme Court's decision in Janus did not apply to the teacher who had voluntarily signed a membership agreement. The court reasoned that the plaintiff's voluntary agreement to pay dues, even if based on a misunderstanding of the optional nature of union membership, constituted a waiver of her First Amendment right not to associate with the union.

Unfair Labor Practice

A union's ability to strike is limited, even in the face of safety concerns. A New York teacher's union sought to invalidate the decision of a state labor relations board that its members had engaged in an unlawful strike in response to a safety threat at their school. Following a violent incident involving a threat to "shoot up" the school, a teacher and union representative at the school called a meeting and announced her intention to be absent the next day. She advised other teachers to do the same. Subsequently, 23 teachers called in sick. The state agency found that 16 of the teachers engaged in an unlawful strike and that the union caused, instigated, encouraged, or condoned the strike. The New York Supreme Court, Appellate Division, upheld the agency's determination that a union representative's encouragement of teachers to call in sick constituted a concerted stoppage of work, or strike, under the New York law.[10] The court also found that the union itself condoned the strike by failing to take affirmative steps to distance itself from the representative's actions.

---

[9] Ramon Baro v. Lake Cnty. Fed'n of Teachers Local 504, IFT-AFT/AFL-CIO, 57 F.4th 582, 411 Educ. L. Rep. 93 (7th Cir. 2023).
[10] Buffalo Teachers Fed'n, Inc. v. N.Y. State Pub. Empl. Relations Bd., 173 N.Y.S.3d 83, 407 Educ. L. Rep. 218 (N.Y. App. Div. 2022).

Interpretation of CBAs and Statutes

To the extent possible, CBAs should have a clear and unambiguous contract. If not, past practice can be used by courts to aid in the interpretation of ambiguous provisions. A group of Ohio teachers grieved their district's decision to unilaterally no longer pay them a stipend for teaching eight periods during a student instructional day, regardless of whether a planning period occurred outside of those hours. The trial court found that the CBA language was ambiguous and, given that the district had been playing the stipend for many years, sided with the union. The Ohio Eleventh District Court of Appeals affirmed the decision.[11]

Each CBA provision is interpreted according to its own plain language. An Illinois union for support staff employees brought two unfair labor practice charges against a district for an allegedly unlawful termination of a custodian. The district demurred, arguing that the union could not bring such an action but must instead utilize the arbitration provision of the contract. The trial court, reviewing the plain language of the provision, found that the mandatory arbitration language only applied to individual members of the union, not the union as a whole. After reviewing the merits of the case, the court found in the union's favor (and reversed the termination) because of the trivial value of the items taken, the employee's prompt replacement of the bags, the fact that she used them for school-related purposes, and alleged disparate treatment of the custodian who received a harsher penalty than another custodian for a similar offense. Importantly, the court further considered a supervisor's anti-union statement as evidence of discriminatory motive. The Illinois Appellate Court upheld the decision.[12] The court rejected the district's argument that allowing the dispute to proceed in two forums was absurd, stating that parties must be held to the language they agreed upon in their contract.

Grievances must be filed in a timely manner in order to be heard. A Nebraska school teacher discovered that she had been underpaid for several school years. The district, citing a specific CBA provision limiting back pay for such errors to just one school year, only provided reimbursement for the most recent year the error

---

[11] Career & Technical Ass'n v. Auburn Vocational Sch. Dist. Bd. of Educ., 194 N.E.3d 782, 407 Educ. L. Rep. 917 (Ohio Ct. App. 2022).

[12] Cook Cnty. Sch. Dist. 130 v. Ill. Educ. Lab. Rels. Bd., 200 N.E.3d 852, 411 Educ. L. Rep. 736 (Ill. App. Ct. 2021).

occurred. The teacher brought suit attempting to gain back pay for all of the previous years. The Nebraska Supreme Court affirmed the lower court's judgment in favor of the school district, denying the teacher's claim for retroactive pay for salary errors made in prior years.[13] The court held that the teacher's claim was not for "wages" subject to the Nebraska statute because the collective bargaining agreement unambiguously limited retroactive pay to the year in which the error was discovered and the teacher had failed to timely grieve the issue within the contractual timeframe. Additionally, the court determined that the contract's limitation on retroactive pay was not inconsistent with public policy or Nebraska law, which does not create an independent right to compensation beyond the terms of the employment agreement.

A group of current and retired superintendents and administrators challenged the Office of Retirement Services (ORS) authority to create and implement a Normal Salary Increase (NSI) schedule, arguing that they violated the Retirement Act and other laws. The Michigan Court of Appeals determined that ORS lacked the authority to create and implement NSI schedules to calculate reportable compensation for public school superintendents and administrators working under personal employment contracts.[14] The court held that the plain language of the Public School Employees Retirement Act only applied to existing salary schedules in collective bargaining agreements, not to employees working under individual contracts. Therefore, the NSI schedules were invalidated, and the case was remanded for entry of judgment in favor of the plaintiffs.

Conclusion

Although there were still a few case in this year's chapter related to the pandemic, there were more cases to review this year that related to the day-to-day operation of the school year. The landmark U.S. Supreme Court case *Janus*, decided way back in 2018, continues to cast a long shadow, with many cases still present in this year's chapter to test and/or clarify that holding. This year marks my 12th year writing this chapter and, after all

---

[13] Hoagbin v. Sch. Dist. No. 28-0017 of Douglas Cnty., 984 N.W.2d 305, 411 Educ. L. Rep. 787 (Neb. 2023).

[14] Batista v. Office of Ret. Servs., 980 N.W.2d 107, 408 Educ. L. Rep. 547 (Mich. Ct. App. 2021), aff'd in part, vacated in part, rev'd in part, 511 Mich. 973 (2023).

these years reviewing cases and practicing in the field, my best piece of advice remains: Administration and unions are better off hammering out their disagreements together, behind closed doors, than relying on our judicial system for them.

Alphabetical List of Cases

Baro v. Lake Cnty. Fed'n of Teachers Local 504

Ramon Baro v. Lake Cnty. Fed'n of Teachers Local 504

Batista v. Office of Ret. Servs.

Bennett v. Am. Fed'n of State, Cnty, and Mun. Emps.

Buffalo Teachers Fed'n, Inc. v. N.Y. State Pub. Empl. Relations Bd.

Career & Technical Ass'n v. Auburn Vocational Sch. Dist. Bd. of Educ.

Clarke v. Bd. of Educ. of City Sch.

Cook Cnty. Sch. Dist. 130 v. Ill. Educ. Lab. Rels. Bd.

Dourdounas v. City of NY

Grossman v. Haw. Gov't Emps. Ass'n/AFSCME Local 152

Hoagbin v. Sch. Dist. No. 28-0017

Laird v. United Teachers L.A.

State *ex rel.* Ohio Ass'n of Pub. Sch. Emp. v. Willoughby-Eastlake City Sch. Dist.

Wu v. Pub. Emp. Relations Bd.

Federal Cases

7th Circuit

Ramon Baro v. Lake Cnty. Fed'n of Teachers Local 504

District Courts

Baro v. Lake Cnty. Fed'n of Teachers Local 50

Bennett v. Am. Fed'n of State, Cnty, and Mun. Emps.

Grossman v. Haw. Gov't Emps. Ass'n/AFSCME Local 152

Laird v. United Teachers L.A.

State and D.C. Cases

California
Wu v. Pub. Emp. Relations Bd.

Illinois
Cook Cnty. Sch. Dist. 130 v. Ill. Educ. Lab. Rels. Bd.

Michigan
Batista v. Office of Ret. Servs.

Nebraska
Hoagbin v. Sch. Dist. No. 28-0017

New York
Buffalo Teachers Fed'n, Inc. v. N.Y. State Pub. Empl. Rels. Bd.
Clarke v. Bd. of Educ. of City Sch.
Dourdounas v. City of NY

Ohio
Career & Technical Ass'n v. Auburn Vocational Sch. Dist. Bd. of Educ.
State *ex rel.* Ohio Ass'n of Pub. Sch. Emp. v. Willoughby-Eastlake City Sch. Dist.

This page is intentionally left blank.

CHAPTER 5

STUDENTS WITH DISABILITIES

Allan G. Osborne, Jr. and Susan Bon

Continued on the next page...

Introduction

When enacted by Congress in 1975, what is now known as the Individuals with Disabilities Education Act (IDEA)[1] altered the way public schools deliver educational services. Spurred in part by litigation,[2] this landmark legislation requires states to guarantee students with disabilities a free appropriate public education (FAPE) in the least restrictive environment. Today, school boards are charged with providing necessary educational services and programs for students with a wide array of disabilities in the face of many parental challenges to the services offered.

In the decades since the law took effect in 1977, much of the litigation has focused on parental challenges to placement decisions. While the underlying issue in most of the litigation is whether school boards offered students FAPEs, courts are asked to adjudicate myriad procedural questions. In addition, hearing officers and judges often must fashion equitable remedies when boards fail to live up to their statutory responsibilities. In this respect, tuition reimbursement, compensatory educational services, and attorney fees remain oft-litigated topics.

The IDEA defines a FAPE as a program consisting of any needed special education and related services.[3] Even so, given the emphasis on individualization, the statute does not establish any clear-cut substantive standards by which the adequacy of those services can be easily measured. The IDEA stipulates that students must be given specially designed instruction[4] as outlined in their individualized education programs (IEPs).[5] The Supreme Court has stated that the IDEA obliges school boards to furnish students with disabilities with personalized instruction and support services sufficient for them to benefit from the education provided,[6] consistent with their unique circumstances.[7] Conversely, the Court cautioned lower courts not to impose their

---

[1] 20 U.S.C. §§ 1400-1485 (2018).
[2] *See, e.g.,* Pa. Ass'n for Retarded Children (PARC) v. Pa., 343 F. Supp. 279 (E.D. Pa. 1972); Mills v. Bd. of Educ. of Dist. of Columbia, 348 F. Supp. 866 (D.D.C. 1972).
[3] 20 U.S.C. §§ 1401(9), 1412(a)(1)(A)
[4] 20 U.S.C. § 1401(29).
[5] 20 U.S.C. §§ 1401(14), 1414(d).
[6] Bd. of Educ. of Hendrick Hudson Cent. Sch. Dist. v. Rowley, 458 U.S. 176, 5 Educ. L. Rep. 34 (1982).
[7] Endrew F. *ex rel.* Joseph F. v. Douglas Cnty. School Dist. RE-1, 580 U.S. 386 (2017).

views of preferable educational methods on school personnel.[8] Nevertheless, hearing officers and judges must determine the level of services required to meet the IDEA's minimum standards.

Although most of the litigation covered in this chapter focuses on the IDEA, consistent with previous years, lawsuits were filed on behalf of students with disabilities under Section 504 of the Rehabilitation Act (Section 504)[9] and the Americans with Disabilities Act (ADA).[10] The plaintiffs in these actions by and large alleged that students were subjected to discriminatory treatment based on their disabilities. Quite frequently, parents coupled their discrimination claims with related IDEA complaints.

Entitlement to Services

As a condition of receiving federal funds under the IDEA, states must ensure that a FAPE is available to each resident child with disabilities between the ages of three and twenty-one, inclusive.[11] The statute does, however, contain two significant limitations to that requirement. First, states do not have to provide services to students between the ages of three through five and eighteen through twenty-one if doing so would be inconsistent with state law, practice, or a court order concerning the provision of public education to children in those age ranges.[12] Second, states are not mandated to provide special education to youth between the ages of eighteen through twenty-one who are incarcerated in adult facilities if they had not previously been identified as having disabilities and did not have IEPs at the time of their incarceration.[13] Further, students who have graduated from high school with a regular diploma are no longer eligible under the IDEA.[14]

The federal trial court in Kentucky declared that a high school student who attended a dual-enrollment, dual-credit program offered on a college campus was not entitled to special education and related services.[15] The court wrote that state regulations

---

[8] Rowley, *supra* n. 6.
[9] 29 U.S.C. § 794.
[10] 42 U.S.C. §§ 12101 - 12213.
[11] 20 U.S.C. § 1412(a)(1)(A).
[12] 20 U.S.C. § 1412(a)(1)(B)(i).
[13] 20 U.S.C. § 1412(a)(1)(B)(ii).
[14] 34 C.F.R. § 300.102(a)(2)(B).
[15] Bradley v. Jefferson Cnty. Pub. Schs., 598 F. Supp. 3d 552, 410 Educ. L. Rep. 352 (W.D. Ky. 2022).

classified the program as postsecondary education. Thus, as a matter of law, the IDEA's obligation to provide the student with a FAPE did not apply to his enrollment in the program.

Procedural Safeguards

The IDEA includes a system of due process safeguards to make sure that students with disabilities are properly identified, evaluated, and placed according to the law's requirements.[16] The statute mandates that school boards allow parents or guardians of children with disabilities to participate in the development of the IEPs for and placement of their children.[17] The IDEA further requires school boards to provide written notice and obtain parental consent before evaluating any children[18] or making any initial placements.[19] Once students have been placed in special education, school boards need to provide parents with proper notice before initiating any changes in placement.[20] At the same time, while administrative or judicial actions are pending, school boards may not change students' placements without parental consent,[21] hearing officers' orders,[22] or court decrees.[23]

The IDEA gives school boards an affirmative obligation to identify, locate, and evaluate all children with disabilities who reside within the school district.[24] This includes children who have been placed in nonpublic schools by their parents.[25] Regarding nonpublic school students, the IDEA's regulations place the child-find obligation on the boards in the districts where the nonpublic schools are located.[26]

School personnel must conduct initial evaluations before they place students in special education programs.[27] Evaluators need to complete all assessments within 60 days of the date when parents

---

[16] 20 U.S.C. § 1415.
[17] 20 U.S.C. §§ 1414(d)(1)(B)(i), 1414(f).
[18] 20 U.S.C. § 1414(a)(1)(D).
[19] 20 U.S.C. § 1415(b)(3).
[20] 20 U.S.C. § 1415(b)(3)(A).
[21] 20 U.S.C. § 1415(j).
[22] 20 U.S.C. § 1415(k)(3)(B)(ii).
[23] Honig v. Doe, 484 U.S. 305, 43 Educ. L. Rep. 857 (1988).
[24] 20 U.S.C. § 1412(a)(3).
[25] 20 U.S.C. § 1412(a)(10)(A)(ii)(I).
[26] 34 C.F.R. § 300.131.
[27] 20 U.S.C. § 1414(a)(1)(A).

gave consent to conduct the evaluations.[28] All evaluations must be multidisciplinary, meaning that they should consist of a variety of assessment tools and strategies to obtain relevant information in the suspected areas of disability.[29] Students with disabilities may be entitled to independent evaluations at public expense if their parents disagree with school boards' evaluations.[30] However, school boards can challenge requests for independent evaluations via administrative hearings, and parents are not entitled to obtain independent evaluations at public expense if the school boards' evaluations are shown to be appropriate.[31]

The IDEA stipulates that all IEPs ought to contain statements of students' current educational performance, annual goals, short-term objectives, specific educational services to be provided, the extent to which each child can participate in general education, the dates of initiation and duration of services, and evaluation criteria to determine if the objectives are being met.[32] IEPs must include statements concerning how students' impairments affect their abilities to be involved in and progress in the general education curriculum along with statements regarding any modifications they may need to allow them to participate in the general education program. IEP teams should review the situations of all students who have IEPs at least annually[33] and reevaluate them at least every three years unless the parents and school officials feel that a reevaluation is unnecessary.[34]

Child Find

In an appeal from North Carolina, the Fourth Circuit affirmed that a school board had not violated its child-find obligation when it determined that a child who had been diagnosed as having autism by a private psychologist was not eligible for special education services.[35] The court explained that a parent's disagreement with the outcome of a comprehensive evaluation did

---

[28] 20 U.S.C. § 1414(a)(1)(C)(i)(I).
[29] 20 U.S.C. § 1414(b)(2), (3).
[30] 20 U.S.C. § 1415(b)(1).
[31] 34 C.F.R. § 300.502(b).
[32] 20 U.S.C. § 1414(d)(1)(A).
[33] 20 U.S.C. § 1414(d)(4)(A).
[34] 20 U.S.C. § 1414(a)(2).
[35] Miller *ex rel.* JM v. Charlotte-Mecklenburg Schs. Bd. of Educ., 64 F.4th 569, 413 Educ. L. Rep. 550 (4th Cir. 2023).

not amount to a failure to conduct an evaluation. Noting that the IDEA does not cover every student who is struggling, the court commented that its protections extend only to those with a qualifying disability who require special education.

School personnel in Tennessee developed a Section 504 accommodation plan for a middle school student who was experiencing disciplinary problems. After he received additional disciplinary referrals, his parents removed him from his school, enrolled him in a private school, and filed a due process complaint. The Sixth Circuit affirmed that the school board had not violated their child-find obligation because school personnel had taken steps to support him and address the problem during the period in question.[36] The court acknowledged that a school does not violate its child-find duty by first attempting other interventions for a student instead of immediately referring him for a special education evaluation.

The Tenth Circuit was satisfied that because a Colorado student's emotional dysfunction had not manifested itself in the school environment and his struggles were readily explainable by acute, nonacademic stressors, his IEP team should not necessarily have identified him as having a disability earlier than it did.[37] The court stated that although the child struggled to regulate his emotions within his family, his behavioral problems did not emerge in school or interfere with his ability to benefit from general education so the school had no reason to suspect that its general education supports were insufficient.

Evaluation

The Fourth Circuit, in a suit from North Carolina, affirmed that a school board did not fail to evaluate a child in all areas of suspected disability.[38] The court found that, based on the comprehensive assessments school personnel conducted, they were able to conclude that the child did not meet the criteria for eligibility under the specific learning disability category. Further,

---

[36] Ja. B. v. Wilson Cnty. Bd. of Educ., 61 F.4th 494, 412 Educ. L. Rep. 494 (6th Cir. 2023).

[37] D.T. *ex rel.* Yasiris T. v. Cherry Creek Sch. Dist., 55 F.4th 1268, 410 Educ. L. Rep. 131 (10th Cir. 2022).

[38] Miller *ex rel.* JM v. Charlotte-Mecklenburg Schs. Bd. of Educ., 64 F.4th 569, 413 Educ. L. Rep. 550 (4th Cir. 2023).

the court agreed that the school board did not deny the child a FAPE by not completing the evaluation within the required time, because he was not entitled to a FAPE.

The Ninth Circuit ruled that an IEP team's delay in evaluating a child from California was not a violation of the IDEA.[39] The child's parent had informed the school that a private psychologist had diagnosed him as having autism but never requested an assessment and failed to provide the team with the psychologist's report. The court found that the IEP team needed that report to develop its assessment plan and to not repeat assessments which would render the evaluation invalid due to the test-retest effect.

A federal trial court in Tennessee was satisfied that a school board had evaluated a child in all areas of suspected disability.[40] The court found that board personnel evaluated the child in all of his deficit areas but were not able to complete all assessments in a timely manner because the child's parent had not provided consent.

Rights of Parents or Guardians

A federal trial court in Tennessee maintained that a school board did not violate parents' procedural rights.[41] The court discovered that the child's mother effectively advocated for him at IEP meetings, was given opportunities to meaningfully participate in drafting her son's IEP, and that the team made changes based on her suggestions. In the court's view, there was give and take throughout the process.

Developing Individualized Education Programs

The mother of a child who attended a nonpublic school requested that public school personnel evaluate the child and prepare an IEP. The parent rejected the resultant IEP and filed a due process complaint alleging several procedural and substantive violations of the IDEA. A federal trial court in Tennessee held that the IEP team had not predetermined the child's placement, finding that school

---

[39] D.O. *ex rel.* Walker v. Escondido Union Sch. Dist., 59 F.4th 394, 411 Educ. L. Rep. 922 (9th Cir. 2023).

[40] G.A. and W.A. v. Williamson Cnty. Bd. of Educ., 594 F. Supp. 3d 979, 409 Educ. L. Rep. 691 (M.D. Tenn. 2022).

[41] C.M. *ex rel.* B.M. v. Rutherford Cnty. Schs., 595 F. Supp. 3d 630, 409 Educ. L. Rep. 809 (M.D. Tenn. 2022).

personnel came to the IEP meeting with open minds and were willing to listen to the parent's preferences.[42] In a separate case, that same court ascertained that a child's IEP team did not predetermine his reading program, while acknowledging that parents are not entitled to prescribe or mandate a specific methodology.[43]

Limited English-proficient parents in Texas filed suit alleging that they were denied appropriate translation and interpretation services, depriving them of the information needed to make fully informed decisions and meaningfully participate in the IEP process. Specifically, they challenged a state regulation that limited these services in violation of the IDEA. A magistrate judge determined that the parents stated a plausible claim that the state regulation in question was preempted by the IDEA.[44]

Change in Placement

Parents of five students with disabilities from New York filed administrative complaints challenging the adequacy of their children's IEPs and successfully obtained pendency orders requiring the school board to fund their private school placements until the completion of proceedings. The parents then filed suit seeking an order for the board to implement the pendency orders immediately. The Second Circuit upheld the federal trial court's dismissal, commenting that the IDEA's stay-put provision does not create an entitlement to immediate payment.[45] Absent a showing that a delay or failure to pay jeopardized the children's placements, the court was unwilling to require the board to deviate from its usual payment procedures.

The federal trial court in Massachusetts held that the state's switch to remote learning during the COVID-19 pandemic did not violate the IDEA's stay-put provision.[46] The court opined that the IDEA's stay-put provision is not implicated under the unusual and unprecedented circumstances that existed during the pandemic. The court added that students were not singled out during the

---

[42] G.A. and W.A. v. Williamson Cnty. Bd. of Educ., 594 F. Supp. 3d 979, 409 Educ. L. Rep. 691 (M.D. Tenn. 2022).

[43] C.M. *ex rel.* B.M. v. Rutherford Cnty. Schs., 595 F. Supp. 3d 630, 409 Educ. L. Rep. 809 (M.D. Tenn. 2022).

[44] Garcia v. Morath, 624 F. Supp. 3d 690, 415 Educ. L. Rep. 651 (W.D. Tex. 2022).

[45] Mendez *ex rel.* A.C. v. Banks, 64 F.4th 56, 414 Educ. L. Rep. 462 (2d Cir. 2023).

[46] Roe v. Baker, 624 F. Supp. 3d 52, 415 Educ. L. Rep. 587 (D. Mass. 2022).

pandemic and school closings and remote instruction affected all public schools and all students in the state. In the court's view, Congress did not intend for the IDEA to apply to system-wide administrative decisions.

Dispute Resolution

Even though Congress envisioned collaborative efforts in developing IEPs, it recognized that disagreements between school officials and parents were inevitable and incorporated into the IDEA a detailed mechanism to resolve disputes between the parties. That process includes resolution meetings,[47] mediation,[48] administrative due process hearings,[49] and, as a final resort, appeals to the courts.[50] The statute stipulates that school officials must schedule a resolution session with the parents within 15 days of the receipt of a complaint. While resolution sessions are mandatory unless waived by mutual consent, mediation is a voluntary next step and may not be used to deny or delay parents' rights to administrative hearings.

Parents may request impartial due process hearings if they disagree with any recommendations or decisions made by school personnel regarding proposed IEPs or any aspect of a FAPE. Parties must request hearings within two years of the date they knew or should have known about the actions upon which the complaints are based.[51] Even so, parents can be excused from meeting this timeline if they can show that school officials misrepresented that the problems complained of had been resolved or withheld required information from the parents.[52] Any party not satisfied with the final decision of the administrative proceedings has the right to appeal to state or federal courts; however, all administrative remedies must be exhausted before parties resort to the courts unless it is futile to do so. The IDEA requires aggrieved parties to file judicial appeals within 90 days of final administrative decisions.[53]

---

[47] 20 U.S.C. § 1415(f)(1)(B).
[48] 20 U.S.C. § 1415(e).
[49] 20 U.S.C. §§ 1415(f), (g).
[50] 20 U.S.C. § 1415(i)(2)(A).
[51] 20 U.S.C. § 1415(f)(3)(C).
[52] 20 U.S.C. § 1415(f)(3)(D).
[53] 20 U.S.C. § 1415(i)(2)(B).

The U.S. Supreme Court, in *Schaffer ex rel. Schaffer v. Weast* (*Schaffer*),[54] placed the burden of proof in administrative proceedings on the parties challenging the IEPs. This ruling effectively puts the burden of proof on parents in most due process hearings since they are the ones who typically challenge IEPs. The IDEA empowers the courts to review the record of the administrative proceedings, hear additional evidence, and "grant such relief as the court determines is appropriate" based on the preponderance of evidence standard.[55] In this regard, the Court has cautioned judges not to substitute their views of proper educational methodology for that of competent school authorities.[56] Parties appealing final administrative decisions have 90 days to do so unless state law dictates otherwise.

Administrative Hearings

Complaints Brought under the IDEA

The Fourth Circuit, in a dispute from North Carolina, affirmed that the federal trial court did not err by deciding that parents had not met their burden of showing that appealing an ALJ's decision would have been futile.[57] The parents had failed to timely file an appeal that complied with the state's due process statute and instead proceeded directly to federal court. In another case from North Carolina, that same court affirmed that parents did not have to exhaust administrative remedies before filing a counterclaim in an appeal brought by the school board.[58] The court explained that the father's counterclaim was compulsory, and thus not subject to the exhaustion requirement.

A federal trial court in Massachusetts determined that parents who contended that their children had been denied FAPEs when the commonwealth suspended in-person learning and offered virtual instruction in response to the COVID-19 pandemic were

---

[54] 546 U.S. 49, 203 Educ. L. Rep. 49 (2005).
[55] 20 U.S.C. § 1415(i)(2)(C)(iii).
[56] Bd. of Educ. of Hendrick Hudson Cent. Sch. Dist. v. Rowley, 458 U.S. 176, 5 Educ. L. Rep. 34 (1982).
[57] K.L., J.L. v. Durham Pub. Schs. Bd. of Educ., 54 F.4th 779, 409 Educ. L. Rep. 632 (4th Cir. 2022).
[58] Charlotte-Mecklenburg Cnty. Bd. of Educ. v. Brady, 66 F.4th 205, 414 Educ. L. Rep. 799 (4th Cir. 2023).

required to exhaust their administrative remedies.[59] The court discerned that the parents had not identified a basis for exemption from the requirement and that the issues were best addressed via the administrative process.

Similarly, a federal trial court in Virginia asserted that parents who alleged that their school boards had failed to provide their children with FAPEs during the pandemic had to first exhaust administrative remedies.[60] The court ascertained that the parents had not offered any support for their proposition that exhaustion would be futile, because their request for relief was outside the authority of a hearing officer. The court also ruled that their argument that exhaustion was not required for alleged stay-put violations lacked merit, because it was not an excuse for failure to exhaust where all students were moved to remote learning and the change was system-wide.

A parent from Puerto Rico appealed an ALJ's decision to not award reimbursement for private school costs after ruling that her son had been denied a FAPE. The federal trial court ruled that she had exhausted her administrative remedies because the ALJ had issued a final resolution.[61]

A federal trial court was satisfied that limited English-proficient parents from Texas, who filed suit alleging that they were denied appropriate translation and interpretation services, were not required to exhaust administrative remedies because it would have been futile.[62] The court pointed out that a hearing officer would have been bound by the state regulation the parents were challenging.

Complaints Brought Under Other Statutes

Parents have sometimes attempted to sidestep the IDEA's exhaustion rule by suing under statutes such as Section 504 or the ADA that do not have an analogous requirement. In *Fry v. Napoleon Community Schools* (*Fry*)[63] the Supreme Court ruled that

---

[59] Roe v. Baker, 624 F. Supp. 3d 52, 415 Educ. L. Rep. 587 (D. Mass. 2022).
[60] Bills. v. Va. Dept. of Educ., 605 F. Supp. 3d 744, 411 Educ. L. Rep. 596 (W.D. Va. 2002).
[61] Navarro-Villanueva *ex rel.* D.A.V.N. v. Commw. of Puerto Rico, 628 F. Supp. 3d 386, 416 Educ. L. Rep. 502 (D.P.R. 2022).
[62] Garcia v. Morath, 624 F. Supp. 3d 690, 415 Educ. L. Rep. 651 (W.D. Tex. 2022).
[63] 580 U.S. 154, 340 Educ. L. Rep. 19] (2017).

exhaustion is not required when the crux of the suit is something other than a denial of a FAPE but is required if relief is available under the IDEA. Thus, if the gravamen of the complaint seeks relief for the denial of a FAPE, the parties must first exhaust the IDEA's administrative remedies. Despite its ruling, litigation continued, and the Court revisited the issue in 2023.

In *Perez v. Sturgis Public Schools* (*Perez*),[64] the Supreme Court clarified that the IDEA's administrative exhaustion requirement applies only to suits seeking relief that is available under that statute. Thus, the Court ruled that when parents seek relief, such as compensatory damages that are not available under the IDEA, they are not required to first exhaust the IDEA's administrative remedies.

In the first of two cases, the Fourth Circuit affirmed that parents from North Carolina, who challenged their school board's decision that their daughter was ineligible for special education and instead developed a Section 504 accommodation plan, were required to exhaust the IDEA's administrative remedies.[65] The court agreed that their Section 504 and ADA claims sought relief for the board's failure to provide a FAPE. In the second decision, the Fourth Circuit determined that parents who alleged that a school board's denial of their request for their son's privately funded therapist to accompany him to school violated Section 504 and the ADA did not need to exhaust administrative remedies.[66] In reversing a contrary decision of a federal trial court in South Carolina, the appeals court stated that the parents could bring the same claim against a library and a nonstudent could bring a similar one against the board. Further, the court opined that because the parents' request did not involve public funding, it did not concern the denial of a FAPE.

The Sixth Circuit stipulated that parents from Tennessee whose daughter suffered from hypersensitivity to the everyday sounds of people eating food and chewing gum did not need to exhaust the IDEA's administrative remedies to challenge her school's denial of their request to ban students from eating or

---

[64] 598 U.S. ___, 143 S. Ct. 859, 412 Educ. L. Rep. 423 (2023).
[65] K.L., J.L. v. Durham Pub. Schs. Bd. of Educ., 54 F.4th 779, 409 Educ. L. Rep. 632 (4th Cir. 2022).
[66] Z.W. *ex rel.* Warner v. Horry Cnty. Sch. Dist., 68 F.4th 915, 416 Educ. L. Rep. 157 (4th Cir. 2023).

chewing in class.[67] The court acknowledged that the parents' request did not relate to a FAPE because they had not requested any instructional changes.

The Ninth Circuit affirmed that parents who claimed that their children's schools had failed to update the students' IEPs and provide sufficient accommodations during the COVID-19 pandemic were required to exhaust the IDEA's administrative remedies, even though some of their claims were based on the Fourteenth Amendment.[68] The court pointed out that the parents were seeking relief for the denial of FAPEs and sought remedies to compensate for that denial.

Three cases brought by parents in Pennsylvania challenging their school boards' decision to make wearing masks optional during the COVID-19 pandemic reached mixed results. In the first, a federal trial court averred that the parents were not required to exhaust the IDEA's administrative remedies.[69] In the court's view, the parents' claim that the lack of a universal mask mandate put immunocompromised students in the position of not having access to the school building was non-FAPE-based because it involved access to a facility rather than access to the curriculum. Four days later, a different judge in that same court ruled that parents challenging a similar optional mask policy were required to exhaust administrative remedies.[70] That judge rationalized that the complaint focused on the denial of access to school buildings and the educational experience inherent in in-person instruction, and that availing themselves of the administrative process could result in satisfactory relief. In the final case, a different federal trial court decided that the parents were not required to exhaust administrative remedies because their claims did not center on the quality of the children's education.[71] Like the court in the first case, this judge felt that the issue involved access to facilities rather than curriculum.

A federal trial court in Virginia held that parents of students with health risks, who were challenging the governor's executive

---

[67] Doe *ex rel.* K.M. v. Knox Cnty. Bd. of Educ., 56 F.4th 1076, 411 Educ. L. Rep. 22 (6th Cir. 2022).

[68] Martinez v. Newsom, 46 F.4th 965, 407 Educ. L. Rep. 113 (9th Cir. 2022).

[69] Doe 1 v. N. Allegheny Sch. Bd., 580 F. Supp. 3d 140, 406 Educ. L. Rep. 643 (W.D. Pa. 2022).

[70] Doe 1 v. Upper Saint Clair Sch. Dist., 581 F. Supp. 3d 711, 406 Educ. L. Rep. 823 (W.D. Pa. 2022).

[71] Doe 1 v. Perkiomen Valley Sch. Dist., 585 F. Supp. 3d 668, 407 Educ. L. Rep. 695 (E.D. Pa. 2022).

order providing that parents could opt out their children from mask requirements, did not need to exhaust the IDEA's administrative remedies.[72] The court surmised that the complaint did not allege any insufficiency of special education or related services, but alleged only disability-based discrimination. The court likened the students' situation to that of a wheelchair-bound student who could not access a school because it lacked ramps.

The parents of a student with autism and intellectual disabilities filed suit, alleging that a paraprofessional subjected their daughter to ongoing physical and psychological abuse. A federal trial court in California held that they were not required to exhaust administrative remedies because their allegations involved a disability discrimination claim and did not equate to a denial of a FAPE.[73] Similarly, a federal trial court in Georgia was satisfied that parents who alleged that their child had been physically and verbally abused by his special education teacher and paraprofessional did not have to exhaust administrative remedies.[74] As in the California case, the court saw the issue as one of unlawful intentional discrimination.

In Connecticut, the father of a child with disabilities filed a complaint alleging that the local school board discriminated against the child by unilaterally withdrawing him from school. The state's highest court affirmed that the parent was not required to exhaust administrative remedies because the parent's complaint did not allege a violation of rights under the IDEA or even make any reference to the statute or a FAPE.[75]

Other Hearing Issues

A hearing officer in North Carolina, although overall finding in favor of a school board, found fault with an IEP team's failure to establish any requirements or benchmarks for a child with severe autism to be considered for placement in a less restrictive environment. The Fourth Circuit affirmed that the administrative

---

[72] Seaman v. Virginia, 593 F. Supp. 3d 293, 409 Educ. L. Rep. 69 (W.D. Va. 2022).
[73] R.N. *ex rel.* Neff v. Travis Unified Sch. Dist., 599 F. Supp. 3d 973, 410 Educ. L. Rep. 674 (E.D. Cal. 2022).
[74] D.D.T. v. Rockdale Cnty. Sch. Pub. Schs., 580 F. Supp. 3d 1314, 406 Educ. L. Rep. 1314 (N.D. Ga. 2021).
[75] Bd. of Educ. of New Haven v. Comm. on Human Rights and Opportunities, 344 Conn. 603, 280 A.3d 424, 407 Educ. L. Rep. 824 (Conn. 2022).

law judge (ALJ) did not err by directing school personnel to establish those benchmarks.[76] The court maintained that the ALJ reasonably turned to the IEP team to correct errors in the child's IEP.

Court Procedures

A case is moot when there is no longer a live controversy. The Ninth Circuit declared that a suit alleging that school boards failed to determine what changes needed to be made by IEP teams in California because of the transition to remote learning during the COVID-19 pandemic was not moot.[77] The court wrote that the plaintiffs' request for compensatory education and attorney fees kept the dispute alive even though schools had returned to in-person learning.

The Eleventh Circuit, in a dispute from Georgia, ascertained that it did not have jurisdiction to hear a school board appeal of the lower court's decision to remand the case back to an ALJ.[78] The court discerned that the remand order was not a final and appealable decision, explaining that the trial court did not decide the merits of the dispute or address whether the school district failed to provide a FAPE.

A federal trial court in Virginia denied a school board's motion to dismiss for failure to state a claim in a suit in which the parents sought reimbursement after having unilaterally placed their child in a private school.[79] The court commented that at this stage in the litigation, the parents did not need to prove that they were entitled to relief but only needed to show that their claim was plausible. The court added that the school board had been given fair notice of their claims.

Standing to Sue

The Ninth Circuit avowed that parents did not have standing to file a class action suit against their school boards alleging that

---

[76] Bouabid *ex rel.* A.C. v. Charlotte-Mecklenburg Schs. Bd. of Educ., 62 F.4th 851, 413 Educ. L. Rep. 37 (4th Cir. 2023).

[77] Martinez v. Newsom, 46 F.4th 965, 407 Educ. L. Rep. 113 (9th Cir. 2022).

[78] S.S. *ex rel.* A.S. v. Cobb Cnty. Sch. Bd., 43 F.4th 1165, 406 Educ. L. Rep. 111 (11th Cir. 2022).

[79] A.C. *ex rel.* R.C. v. Henrico Cnty. Sch. Bd., 610 F. Supp. 3d 857, 412 Educ. L. Rep. 246 (E.D. Va. 2022),

schools in California were not updating their children's IEPs and that students with disabilities were not offered sufficient accommodations.[80] The court stated that plaintiffs in a class action suit lacked standing to sue defendants who had not injured them personally. In the present cases, the court noted that the parents had not claimed that the school boards of the districts in which their children were not enrolled had injured them personally, and therefore they did not have standing to sue.

In a case from Connecticut, the federal district court ruled that parents did not have standing to bring an IDEA complaint on behalf of their 18-year-old daughter.[81] The court explained that state law transferred IDEA rights from the parents to the child when the student turned 18. Thus, the court found that the hearing officer correctly determined that the parents no longer had the statutory right to seek reimbursement for private school costs.

Parents in Pennsylvania whose children had medical conditions had standing to sue their school board to challenge its decision to make masking optional during the COVID-19 pandemic according to a ruling of a federal trial court.[82] The court commented that their injuries were not speculative because they had shown that the optional mask policy increased the likelihood that their children would be infected.

A federal magistrate judge in Texas decided that parents who challenged a state regulation had standing to sue.[83] The judge was convinced that the parents had sufficiently alleged that their injuries were traceable to the state, and because the parents had shown sufficient facts to demonstrate redressability.

A federal trial court dismissed a class action suit alleging that a school board in Michigan violated parental rights under the IDEA when it closed schools due to the COVID-19 pandemic.[84] The court stated that the parents had not alleged a real or immediate threat that the school board would repeat, or an ongoing or continuous harm.

---

[80] Martinez v. Newsom, 46 F.4th 965, 407 Educ. L. Rep. 113 (9th Cir. 2022).
[81] Doe v. Westport Bd. of Educ., 609 F. Supp. 3d 75, 412 Educ. L. Rep. 93 (D. Conn. 2020).
[82] Doe 1 v. Perkiomen Valley Sch. Dist., 585 F. Supp. 3d 668, 407 Educ. L. Rep. 695 (E.D. Pa. 2022).
[83] Garcia v. Morath, 624 F. Supp. 3d 690, 415 Educ. L. Rep. 651 (W.D. Tex. 2022).
[84] Simpson-Vlach v. Mich. Dept. of Educ., 616 F. Supp. 3d 711, 413 Educ. L. Rep. 756 (E.D. Mich. 2022).

Statute of Limitations

As indicated above, the IDEA establishes two separate limitation periods: Two years for requesting an administrative hearing[85] and 90 days to appeal a final administrative decision.[86] Even so, if state law provides for an alternative limitations period, the state law prevails. The IDEA does not have a statute of limitations for attorney fee claims, so one must be borrowed from state law.

Limitations Period for Requesting a Hearing

The Fourth Circuit held that a father's claim that the school board had failed to provide his child with a FAPE was not time-barred because he was prevented from filing a timely administrative complaint.[87] The court pointed out that an email the father sent to school personnel constituted a request for an evaluation. School officials were required to provide him with a copy of the procedural safeguards notice, but their failure to do so prevented him from filing a timely complaint. Similarly, a federal trial court in Illinois ascertained that a complaint was not time-barred because the parent's allegations that the school board continually refused to hold IEP meetings or make school referrals raised the possibility of a continuing violation.[88]

Limitations Period for Seeking Attorney Fees

The Fourth Circuit affirmed that a suit seeking attorney fees almost two years after the parents received a partially favorable hearing decision was time-barred.[89] A federal trial court had determined that a Virginia statute giving parents 180 days to file for judicial review of administrative decisions was applicable,

---

[85] 20 U.S.C. § 1415(f)(3)(C). This limitations period may be tolled if parents can show that school officials misrepresented that the problem had been resolved or withheld required information. 20 U.S.C. § 1415(f)(3)(D).

[86] 20 U.S.C. § 1415(i)(2)(B).

[87] Charlotte-Mecklenburg Cnty. Bd. of Educ. v. Brady, 66 F.4th 205, 414 Educ. L. Rep. 799 (4th Cir. 2023).

[88] C.B. v. Bd. of Educ. of City of Chi. Dist., 624 F. Supp. 3d 898, 415 Educ. L. Rep. 667 (N.D. Ill. 2022).

[89] Sanchez v. Arlington Cnty. Sch. Bd., 58 F.4th 130, 411 Educ. L. Rep. 187 (4th Cir. 2023), *aff'g* 563 F. Supp. 3d 484, 402 Educ. L. Rep. 235 (E.D. Va. 2021).

rendering the parents' claim untimely. The appeals court agreed, noting that the limitations period did not begin to run until the end of the aggrieved party's time to seek substantive review. This would effectively give a party 360 days from the date of the hearing decision to file a claim for attorney fees.

Placement

The IDEA regulations expect school boards to ensure that a "continuum of alternative placements" exists to meet the needs of students with disabilities for special education and related services.[90] That continuum ranges from placements in general education to private residential facilities and includes homebound services. Still, the placements chosen for all students have to be in the least restrictive environment (LRE) for each child, and removal from general education can occur only to the extent necessary to provide special education and related services.[91] All placements must be made at public expense and meet state educational standards.[92] IEP teams ought to review all placements at least annually and revise them when necessary.[93] The Supreme Court, in *Rowley*, defined an appropriate education as one that is developed in compliance with the IDEA's procedures and is reasonably calculated to enable the child to receive educational benefits.[94] In *Endrew F.* the Court clarified that children's programs should be appropriately ambitious in light of their circumstances.[95] Although states, at a minimum, must adopt policies and procedures that are consistent with the IDEA, they may provide greater benefits than those required by the federal law. If states do establish higher standards, courts will consider those standards along with the IDEA when evaluating the appropriateness of IEPs.[96]

---

[90] 34 C.F.R. § 300.115.
[91] 20 U.S.C. § 1412(a)(5).
[92] 20 U.S.C. § 1401(9).
[93] 20 U.S.C. § 1414(d)(4).
[94] Bd. of Educ. of Hendrick Hudson Cent. Sch. Dist. v. Rowley, 458 U.S. 176, 5 Educ. L. Rep. 34 (1982).
[95] Endrew F. *ex rel.* Joseph F. v. Douglas Cnty. Sch. Dist. RE-1, ___ U.S. ___, 137 S. Ct. 988 (2017).
[96] *See, e.g.*, David D. v. Dartmouth Sch. Comm., 775 F.2d 411, 28 Educ. L. Rep. 70 (1st Cir. 1985); Geis v. Bd. of Educ. of Parsippany-Troy Hills, 774 F.2d 575, 27 Educ. L. Rep. 1093 (3d Cir. 1985).

Appropriate Educational Placement

In the first of two appeals, the First Circuit affirmed a lower court's decision that a school board in Maine denied a FAPE to a child with disabilities because it failed to take meaningful steps to address his unique circumstances and challenges.[97] The appeals court was satisfied that the trial court accounted for the fact that the student was a slow learner in concluding that his IEPs were inadequate because they did not address the child's deficits.

In a separate case, that same court affirmed that IEPs for a student with autism's junior and senior years were inappropriate.[98] The court agreed with the trial court in Massachusetts that there was sufficient evidence that the IEPs were not reasonably calculated to provide a FAPE, noting that the student's treating clinicians had specifically recommended placement in a therapeutic school. The court commented that the professionals who had made that recommendation were the ones who had conducted the most recent evaluations.

In an appeal from California, the Ninth Circuit ascertained that a school board's delay in evaluating a child did not deny him a FAPE.[99] In reversing the lower court, the appeals panel pointed out that the child had not been denied any educational benefits. Since his educational placement had remained the same, any delay in assessments was of no consequence.

A federal trial court affirmed a Pennsylvania hearing officer's decision that a school board provided a gifted student with learning disabilities with an appropriate education.[100] The court agreed that the school board offered the student an education that was appropriately ambitious given his unique circumstances, noting that his progress was close to grade level. The court commented that the repetition of goals in his IEP did not indicate a lack of progress because those goals were applied to new and additional situations.

---

[97] Falmouth Sch. Dept. v. Doe, 44 F.4th 23, 406 Educ. L. Rep. 131 (1st Cir. 2022).
[98] Doe v. Newton Pub. Schs., 48 F.4th 42, 407 Educ. L. Rep. 499 (1st Cir. 2022), *aff'g* 537 F. Supp. 3d 56, 397 Educ. L. Rep. 111 (D. Mass. 2021).
[99] D.O. *ex rel.* Walker v. Escondido Union Sch. Dist., 59 F.4th 394, 411 Educ. L. Rep. 922 (9th Cir. 2023).
[100] A.M. v. Wallingford-Swarthmore Sch. Dist., 629 F. Supp. 3d 285, 416 Educ. L. Rep. 796 (E.D. Pa. 2022).

In a case from Tennessee, the federal trial court ascertained that the school board offered an appropriate IEP to a student with several disabilities including autism, motor difficulties, and hearing loss.[101] In the court's opinion, the proposed IEP included goals, which were developed based on objective data, that were reasonably calculated to enable the child to progress.

In a dispute challenging a school board's delivery of special education services during the COVID-19 pandemic, a state appellate court in Minnesota found that a school board met its obligations under state and federal regulations.[102] In reversing a decision by the state's education department, the court explained that a board must offer or make available services to eligible children, but does not deny a FAPE when the children's parents reject appropriate services and do not cooperate in developing a new IEP.

Least Restrictive Environment

The Sixth Circuit affirmed that a proposed placement for a kindergarten child with autism from Tennessee was not his least restrictive environment.[103] The child's parents preferred a full-time general education placement with aids and services, but his IEP team proposed that he attend a self-contained classroom for all academic subjects. The court sided with the parents, finding that many of the supports the child needed could be provided in the general education setting. The court commented that the school board's placement recommendation appeared to stem from an unwillingness to mainstream the child because it would be difficult to do so.

In a dispute from California, the Ninth Circuit determined that an IEP team's proposal for a fifth grader with autism to spend approximately half of his school day out of general education was too restrictive.[104] In reaching its decision, the court found that the student had derived significant nonacademic benefits from prior

---

[101] G.A. and W.A. v. Williamson Cnty. Bd. of Educ., 594 F. Supp. 3d 979, 409 Educ. L. Rep. 691 (M.D. Tenn. 2022).

[102] Special Educ. Complaint *ex rel.* V.S., 981 N.W.2d 201, 409 Educ. L. Rep. 329 (Minn. Ct. App. 2022).

[103] Knox Cnty, Tenn. v. M.Q., 62 F.4th 978, 413 Educ. L. Rep. 57 (6th Cir. 2023).

[104] D.R. *ex rel.* R.R. v. Redondo Beach Unified Sch. Dist., 56 F.4th 636, 410 Educ. L. Rep. 553 (9th Cir. 2022).

placement in general education and his presence there did not impede his teachers' ability to instruct other students. Further, according to the court, evidence showed that he made substantial progress toward meeting his IEP goals and received benefits from placement therein. The court made it clear that school personnel cannot remove a child from general education solely because of the need for curricular modifications.

Private Facilities

The First Circuit agreed with the conclusions of the federal trial court in Massachusetts that a student with autism required a therapeutic placement as recommended by his treating clinicians.[105] In reaching this decision, the lower court had posited that the IEP proposed by the child's IEP team for his junior year calling for placement in an unspecified school was not adequate, because it did not account for his severe mental health needs or the crisis he experienced during the previous summer. As far as his senior year was concerned, the court felt that the IEP team's failure to offer an appropriate placement the previous year rendered an IEP calling for a transfer to another school inappropriate, inasmuch as removing him from a supportive environment could pose emotional and social disruption.

Discipline

The IDEA has specific provisions outlining disciplinary requirements for students with disabilities.[106] Before these requirements were added to the statute, courts applied the IDEA's change in placement and status quo provisions to the disciplinary process. The Supreme Court even emphasized that special education students could not be expelled for disciplinary reasons where their infractions were manifestations of, or caused by, their disabilities.[107] The IDEA's current provision allows school administrators to transfer students to interim alternative settings for up to 45 days for possession of weapons or drugs, or infliction of

---

[105] Doe v. Newton Pub. Schs., 48 F.4th 42, 407 Educ. L. Rep. 499 (1st Cir. 2022), *aff'g* 537 F. Supp. 3d 56, 397 Educ. L. Rep. 111 (D. Mass. 2021).
[106] 20 U.S.C. § 1415(k).
[107] Honig v. Doe, 484 U.S. 305, 43 Educ. L. Rep. 857 (1988).

serious bodily injury.[108] The statute also makes it clear that educational services must continue during expulsion periods.[109] Another important section requires school boards to conduct functional behavioral assessments (FBAs) and develop behavior intervention plans (BIPs) under specified circumstances.[110]

Nevertheless, the Supreme Court decision and the current language of the IDEA have not left school authorities without the ability to impose discipline. Special education students may be suspended temporarily and are subject to other normal disciplinary sanctions that do not result in changes in placement. If necessary, school boards may seek hearing officer or court intervention pending completion of administrative due process hearings in situations where it can be shown that students are dangerous, and school officials cannot reach an agreement with their parents concerning proper placements. In one such instance, the federal trial court in Maine agreed with a hearing officer that school administrators were justified in requesting an expedited hearing to exclude a student who had assaulted a staff member, because they believed that maintaining the child in his then-current placement was likely to result in injury to the child or others.[111] The court added that the child's IEP team had the authority to determine the appropriate alternative placement.

Remedies

When school boards fail to provide FAPEs for students with disabilities, the courts are empowered to grant such relief as they determine to be appropriate.[112] In addition to prospective relief, courts frequently award reimbursement of costs borne by parents in unilaterally obtaining appropriate services for their children. The Supreme Court explained that school boards may be required to reimburse parents for costs incurred in providing their children with special education and related services if they prevail in having their chosen placements deemed appropriate.[113] Although those

---

[108] 20 U.S.C. § 1415(k)(1)(G).
[109] 20 U.S.C. § 1415(k)(1)(D).
[110] 20 U.S.C. § 1415(k)(1)(D), (E).
[111] K.C. *ex rel.* M.D. v. Reg. Sch. Unit 73, 616 F. Supp. 3d 63, 413 Educ. L. Rep. 658 (D. Me. 2022).
[112] 20 U.S.C. § 1415(i)(2)(C)(iii).
[113] Burlington Sch. Comm. v. Dep't of Educ., Commw. of Mass., 471 U.S. 359, 23 Educ. L. Rep. 1189 (1985).

rulings have now been codified, reimbursement awards may be limited when parents do not provide school boards with prior notice of their dissatisfaction with their children's placements and their intent to enroll them in private schools.[114] Reimbursement is allowed even if the parents' chosen facilities are not state-approved, as long as they offer otherwise appropriate programs,[115] and even where the students had not previously received services from the public schools.[116]

In 1986, Congress passed the Handicapped Children's Protection Act to allow parents who prevail in lawsuits under the IDEA to recover their legal expenses.[117] This amendment to the federal special education law was enacted in response to a Supreme Court opinion that the original act did not allow for recovery of attorney fees by prevailing parents.[118] Another Court decision in a non-education case, *Buckhannon Board and Care Home, Inc. v. West Virginia Department of Health and Human Resources* (*Buckhannon*),[119] generated a new line of attorney fees litigation under the IDEA. In *Buckhannon,* the Court struck down the catalyst theory as a means for recovering attorney fees by holding that to be reimbursed for legal expenses a plaintiff must either receive an enforceable judgment on the merits or a court-ordered consent decree. The Court further ascertained, in *Arlington Central School District Board of Education v. Murphy* (*Arlington*)[120] that expert witness fees were not reimbursable under the IDEA's attorney fees provision. In 2004, Congress again amended the attorney fees section of the IDEA to give school boards the option of seeking reimbursement of their legal expenses when parental complaints are later found to be frivolous, unreasonable, or without foundation, or when the litigation was continued after it clearly became frivolous, unreasonable, or without foundation. School boards may also seek awards when parents' actions are brought for improper purposes, cause unnecessary delays, or needlessly increase the cost of litigation.[121]

---

[114] 20 U.S.C. § 1412(a)(10)(C)(iii).
[115] Florence Cnty. Sch. Dist. Four v. Carter, 510 U.S. 7, 86 Educ. L. Rep. 41 (1993).
[116] Forest Grove Sch. Dist. v. T.A., 557 U.S. 230 (2009).
[117] 20 U.S.C. § 1415(i)(3)(B)-(G).
[118] Smith v. Robinson, 468 U.S. 992, 18 Educ. L. Rep. 148 (1984).
[119] 532 U.S. 598 (2001).
[120] 548 U.S. 291 (2006).
[121] 20 U.S.C. § 1415(i)(3)(B)(i)(II), (III).

It should be noted that under this provision, awards are levied against the parents' attorneys, not the parents themselves.

Tuition Reimbursement

The First Circuit affirmed that parents who had placed their child with autism in a private residential program were entitled to reimbursement for the day portion, but not the residential component, of the placement.[122] The federal trial court in Massachusetts previously ruled that the school system had denied the child a FAPE, but the residential placement was not warranted as it was not the least restrictive environment. Similarly, the Ninth Circuit affirmed that parents from California who had removed their child from a public school placement during an IEP dispute and had him tutored at home were not entitled to reimbursement for the costs of the tutor.[123] The court commented that the parents should not have unilaterally withdrawn the child from school, but instead could have invoked the IDEA's stay-put provision to maintain his existing program during the pendency of the dispute. In the court's view, the tutoring placed the child in a more restrictive setting than that proposed by the school board.

The federal trial court in Puerto Rico, after finding that a parent had credibly alleged that the education department had not prepared proper IEPs for her son, held that she could sue for reimbursement.[124] The court also found her claims that the private sectarian school she enrolled him in provided educational benefits were plausible.

Parents in New York City were not entitled to reimbursement, according to a federal trial court, because they had not properly put the school board on notice of their concerns.[125] Although the parents had communicated their intent to place the child in a private school, they never asked the public schools to develop an IEP for him instead of a service plan. In the court's view, they

---

[122] Doe v. Newton Pub. Schs., 48 F.4th 42, 407 Educ. L. Rep. 499 (1st Cir. 2022), *aff'g* 537 F. Supp.3d 56, 397 Educ. L. Rep. 111 (D. Mass. 2021).

[123] D.R. *ex rel.* R.R. v. Redondo Beach Unified Sch. Dist., 56 F.4th 636, 410 Educ. L. Rep. 553 (9th Cir. 2022).

[124] Navarro-Villanueva *ex rel.* D.A.V.N. v. Commw. of Puerto Rico, 628 F. Supp. 3d 386, 416 Educ. L. Rep. 502 (D.P.R. 2022).

[125] R.G. *ex. rel.* E.G. v. N.Y.C. Dep't of Educ., 585 F. Supp. 3d 524, 407 Educ. L. Rep. 672 (S.D.N.Y. 2022).

denied the school board the opportunity to address and remedy their concerns.

Attorney Fees

A federal trial court in Pennsylvania ascertained that parents who had prevailed in having their child determined to be eligible under the IDEA were entitled to attorney fees.[126] However, the court reduced the requested fee award due to excessive or unwarranted billing, invoices with insufficient detail, and the limited success of the litigation. A federal trial court in California also reduced a requested fee award, noting that entries for work that was clerical are not compensable.[127] The court granted the rest of the requested fee award, rejecting the school board's argument that an award was improper because the parents had no obligation to pay their counsel's fees.

A federal trial court in Florida awarded fees to a student who had filed suit to enforce an agreement made during mediation.[128] The court was satisfied that such a suit constituted an action or proceeding under the terms of the IDEA's attorney fees provision. Because the student received a consent decree that provided more services than the school board initially agreed to provide, the court opined that she was the prevailing party.

Discrimination Under Section 504 of the Rehabilitation Act and the Americans with Disabilities Act

Section 504 of the Rehabilitation Act of 1973 (Section 504), as amended, provides that "[n]o otherwise qualified individual with a disability [...] shall, solely by reason of her or his disability, be excluded from participation in, be denied the benefits of, or be subjected to discrimination under any program or activity receiving [f]ederal financial assistance [...]."[129] Section 504 effectively prohibits any recipient of federal funds from

---

[126] Pocono Mtn. Sch. Dist. v. T.D., 597 F. Supp. 3d 709, 410 Educ. L. Rep. 184 (M.D. Pa. 2022).
[127] Bellflower Unified Sch. Dist. v. Arnold, 586 F. Supp. 3d 1010, 407 Educ. L. Rep. 778 (C.D. Cal. 2022).
[128] Johnson v. Flagler Cnty. Sch. Dist., 658 F. Supp. 3d 1167, 416 Educ. L. Rep. 570 (M.D. Fla. 2022).
[129] 29 U.S.C. § 794.

discriminating against individuals with disabilities in the provision of services or employment. Section 504 applies to any agency that receives federal funds, not just the schools.

The Americans with Disabilities Act (ADA),[130] which was enacted in 1990, is designed to prohibit discrimination against persons with disabilities in a wide range of activities sponsored by private as well as public entities. The ADA's greatest impact is on the private sector; even so, since many of its provisions apply to public entities and are similar in scope to those of Section 504, lawsuits filed under the ADA should interest consumers of education law. Generally, compliance with Section 504 will result in compliance with the ADA; however, several provisions of the ADA addressed loopholes in Section 504 and codified judicial interpretations of the Rehabilitation Act. Many of the lawsuits that arise in the public sector are now based on the ADA as well as Section 504. In most cases, the disposition for both laws is identical.

Individuals are considered to have disabilities under Section 504 and the ADA if they have physical or mental impairments that substantially limit one or more of their major life activities, have a record of such impairments, or are regarded as having such impairments.[131] Major life activities are "functions such as caring for oneself, performing manual tasks, walking, seeing, hearing, speaking, breathing, learning, and working."[132] The Supreme Court has noted that individuals are otherwise qualified for purposes of Section 504 if they are capable of meeting all of a program's requirements despite their disabilities.[133] When individuals are otherwise qualified, recipients of federal funds are expected to make reasonable accommodations for their disabilities unless doing so would create an undue hardship.[134] Similarly, under the ADA, private entities may also be required to make reasonable accommodations.

Congress amended the ADA in 2008 to clarify its intent regarding the definition of individuals with disabilities.[135] The

---

[130] 42 U.S.C. § 12101-12213.
[131] 29 U.S.C. § 706(7)(B).
[132] 34 C.F.R. § 104.3(j)(2)(ii).
[133] Sch. Bd. of Nassau Cnty. v. Arline, 480 U.S. 273, 37 Educ. L. Rep. 448 (1987); Southeastern Cmty. Coll. v. Davis, 442 U.S. 397 (1979).
[134] 34 C.F.R. § 104.12(a).
[135] The ADA Amendments Act of 2008, P.L. 110-325, 122 Stat. 3553 (2008).

amendment effectively expanded the definition of individuals with disabilities to exclude the effect mitigating measures had on the classification of persons as having disabilities.[136] The amendment also revised Section 504's definition of individuals with disabilities to make the meaning of both laws consistent.

Students at the Elementary and Secondary Levels

Students with disabilities attending elementary and secondary schools have rights under Section 504 and the ADA, as well as the IDEA. Often students and their parents file lawsuits that state claims under all three statutes. Frequently the claims stated under one statute are identical or similar to the claims stated under the other laws; however, sometimes distinct claims are brought under Section 504 and/or the ADA.

Other Section 504 and ADA Issues

Parents continued to seek relief for disability discrimination pursuant to the IDEA, Section 504, and the ADA. In several cases, the parents sought relief under Section 504 and the ADA based on failure to reasonably accommodate their children's disability needs. Parents also sought relief pursuant to Section 504 and the ADA for alleged verbal and physical abuse of their children with disabilities by special education teachers and paraprofessionals. Disputes over the adoption of optional masking provisions and mandatory mask bans were a prevailing focus of litigation by parents of medically vulnerable students across several states.

The mother of a student with autism filed suit alleging violations of Section 504 and the ADA by a school resource officer (SRO) who failed to reasonably accommodate her child's disability when responding to an incident during which the student stabbed

---

[136] Sutton v. United Air Lines, 527 U.S. 471 (1999); Murphy v. United Parcel Service, 527 U.S. 516 (1999); Albertson's, Inc. v. Kirkingburg, 527 U.S. 555 (1999). Taken together these decisions indicated that individuals whose physical or mental impairments were corrected through medication or other measures did not have impairments that limited major life activities. Thus, under these decisions, employers could consider the effect of mitigating measures when determining if a person's major life activities were substantially limited. In a later decision, *Toyota Motor Mfg. v. Williams*, 534 U.S. 184 (2002), the Court stipulated that an impairment must be permanent or long-term to constitute a disability under the ADA.

a classmate with a pencil. The Colorado federal district court denied the school district's motion to dismiss, finding the parent's claims could plausibly reveal that the SROs acted with deliberate indifference to the student's rights when he ignored the stepfather's request for the child to be taken to the hospital and instead took him to a juvenile detention center, where he was charged with misdemeanor assault.[137]

Parents and advocacy agencies filed a class action lawsuit alleging concerns about the school district's failure to reasonably accommodate students with disabilities. They claimed that the school district did not provide nurses to administer insulin to students who cannot self-administer insulin during field trips or on school buses. The New York federal district court declared that the school district discriminated against students with diabetes by not reasonably accommodating their medical needs on field trips and school buses. As the court explained, the school district's policy of having bus drivers call 911 when students suffer hypoglycemia is not reasonable.[138]

In a suit from Arkansas, the Eighth Circuit Court affirmed that the school district provided reasonable accommodations for a student who had a visual impairment but was not diagnosed as legally blind.[139] Contrary to the parents' assertions, the school district revised multiple Section 504 plans and demonstrated consistent efforts to accommodate the student's vision issues and ensure her safety in school. No reasonable factfinder could conclude that the school district failed to implement safety accommodations for the child's vision issues.

Following an autism-related outburst, a fifth-grade student with noncommunicative autism was removed from his classroom and placed in seclusion. Subsequently, the student was handcuffed by sheriff's office personnel and transported to a mental health facility, where he was involuntarily committed. The student's parents brought suit alleging disability-based discrimination under the ADA and asserting that a reasonable modification was necessary under the ADA. The Florida federal district court denied

---

[137] A.V. *ex rel.* Hanson v. Douglas Cnty. Sch. Dist. RE-1, 586 F. Supp. 3d 1053, 407 Educ. L. Rep. 788 (C. Colo. 2022).
[138] M.F. *ex rel.* Ferrer v. New York City Dept. of Educ., 582 F. Supp.3d 49, 406 Educ. L. Rep. 848 (E.D.N.Y. 2022).
[139] Baker v. Bentonville Sch. Dist. 610 F. Supp. 3d 1157, 412 Educ. L. Rep. 255 (W.D. Ark. 2022), *aff'd* 75 F.4th 810, 418 Educ. L. Rep. 691 (8th Cir. 2023).

the motion to dismiss, noting that additional fact-finding was needed to determine if the deputy knew of about the disabilities and if the parents had requested any modifications.[140]

Section 504 claims are unlikely to succeed when parents merely repeat IDEA claims based on a denial of a FAPE. Courts continue to require more than a basic denial of FAPE in Section 504 cases. The federal district court in Illinois affirmed this point in their dismissal of a parent's claim which failed to allege bad faith or gross misjudgment.[141] Similarly, a federal trial court in Tennessee agreed with the ALJ's finding that the parents' Section 504 and ADA claims were duplicative, given the success of their IDEA complaint asserting that the proposed placement was not the least restrictive environment.[142] The court declared that the parents failed to show that the school district discriminated against the child in developing his IEP.

The parents of a nonverbal, developmentally disabled child alleged physical and verbal abuse by his teacher in their disability discrimination lawsuit against the school board. According to the Florida district court, there was no evidence that the school board acted, or failed to act, based on their child's disability, as required to demonstrate a violation of Section 504 and the ADA.[143]

In a similar case from Georgia, a federal trial court asserted that an inference was reasonable that school administrators were aware a student's federally protected rights were being violated by a special education teacher and paraprofessional.[144] The alleged abuse had been reported to school administrators on several occasions by another paraprofessional, but the perpetrators had not been reprimanded or disciplined until the child's mother and local police contacted the school officials. As such, the court determined it was sufficient to allege that school officials were deliberately indifferent to disability-based discrimination.

---

[140] D.L. *ex rel.* S.L. and R.L. v. Hernando Cnty. Sheriff's Office, 620 F. Supp. 3d 1182, 414 Educ. L. Rep. 895 (M.D. Fla. 2022).

[141] C.B. v. Bd. of Educ. of City of Chicago Dist., 624 F. Supp. 3d 898, 415 Educ. L. Rep. 667 (N.D. Ill. 2022).

[142] Knox County, Tennessee v. M.Q., 62 F.4th 978, 413 Educ. L. Rep. 57 (6th Cir. 2023).

[143] C. H. *ex rel.* Hilligoss v. Sch. Bd. of Okaloosa Cnty., 606 F. Supp. 3d 1186, 411 Educ. L. Rep. 642 (N.D. Fla. 2022).

[144] D.D.T. v. Rockdale Cnty. Public Schs., 580 F. Supp.3d 1314, 406 Educ. L. Rep. 756 (N.D. Ga. 2021).

A federal district court in Illinois dismissed a deliberate indifference claim under Section 504 by parents who alleged that a teaching assistant had inappropriately touched the student's genitals during a shower, and that another assistant failed to intervene.[145] As the court observed, the facts did not indicate that school officials had any knowledge of the alleged abuse of the student at the time it was happening, nor was there any evidence that the assistant had a history of sexual misconduct, and there was no actual notice a school official was deliberately indifferent to the teaching assistant's inappropriate touching.

In response to the COVID-19 pandemic, many school boards closed schools and students were provided education in virtual learning environments. When many of these schools reopened, they employed universal masking mandates but subsequently adopted optional masking mandates. Parents in three Pennsylvania school districts sought preliminary restraining orders and temporary restraining orders.[146]

According to Pennsylvania federal district courts in two of the cases, parents sufficiently demonstrated that the school districts failed to provide reasonable accommodations and placed medically vulnerable students at an increased risk of physical harm.[147] As alleged in the parents' Section 504 and ADA claims, the optional masking policies put them in the position of either keeping their children at home or sending them into an environment that presented a serious risk to their health and safety. Further, the parents demonstrated a likelihood of success on the merits of their Section 504 and ADA discrimination claims. In both cases, the court found that denying medically vulnerable students the opportunity to access educational services would cause them to suffer irreparable harm. School districts would not suffer an undue hardship by requiring universal masking, and the public interest weighed in favor of removing barriers to access for students with disabilities.

---

[145] Doe v. Bd. of Educ. of the City of Chicago, 611 F. Supp. 3d 516, 412 Educ. L. Rep. 521 (N.D. Ill. 2020).

[146] Doe 1 v. North Allegheny Sch. Dist., 580 F. Supp.3d 140, 406 Educ. L. Rep. 643 (W.D. Pa. 2022). Doe 1 v. Perkiomen Valley Sch. Dist., 585 F. Supp.3d 668, 407 Educ. L. Rep. 695 (E.D. Pa. 2022). Doe 1 v. Upper Saint Clair Sch. Dist., 581 F. Supp.3d 711, 406 Educ. L. Rep. 823 (W.D. Pa. 2022).

[147] *Id.*

In another nearly identical case from Pennsylvania, however, the federal district court denied the temporary restraining order requests by parents of several medically fragile students with disabilities.[148] After the school board enacted an optional face mask policy, the parents filed suit alleging that the new policy subjected the children to an increased risk of harm. As the Pennsylvania federal district court averred, the parents' arguments were purely speculative, and they could not prove that the children would contract COVID-19 in the absence of universal masking or that they would not contract the virus even with universal masking. Further, the court found that the accommodation request was unreasonable and would impose an unprecedented requirement on the school district to mandate universal masking for all students and staff.

Georgia school districts adopted similar optional masking policies which led parents of medically vulnerable students with disabilities to seek a temporary restraining order and preliminary injunction. As in the prior cases, the parents claimed that optional masking policies presented a serious risk to their children's health and safety. Further, the parents asserted the school district failed to reasonably accommodate their disabilities and denied access to in-person education for the medically vulnerable students with disabilities.

A federal trial court in Georgia denied the parents' motion for a temporary restraining order, noting that the school district's COVID policies were facially neutral and applied to all students.[149] On appeal, the school district claimed that the case was moot because CDC guidelines no longer recommended mandatory masking. The Eleventh Circuit reversed and remanded to the district court, indicating the court erred by misconstruing the parents' argument as a right to education generally, rather than a denial of access to in-person education that the school district provides to all students.[150] On remand, the district court was

---

[148] Doe 1 v. Upper Saint Clair Sch. Dist., 581 F. Supp.3d 711, 406 Educ. L. Rep. 823 (W.D. Pa. 2022).

[149] L.E. *ex rel.* Cavorley v. Supt. of Cobb Cnty. Sch. Dist., 55 F.4th 1296, 410 Educ. L. Rep. 141 (11th Cir. 2022). *Sub nom.* L.E. v. Ragsdale, 568 F. Supp. 3d 1364, 403 Educ. L. Rep. 664 (N.D. Ga. 2021).

[150] L.E. *ex rel.* Cavorley v. Supt. of Cobb Cnty. Sch. Dist., 55 F.4th 1296, 410 Educ. L. Rep. 141 (11th Cir. 2022). *Sub nom.* L.E. v. Ragsdale, 568 F. Supp. 3d 1364, 403 Educ. L. Rep. 664 (N.D. Ga. 2021).

charged to determine if virtual schooling was a reasonable accommodation for in-person schooling, not education in general.

Optional masking mandates and mask mandate bans in response to the COVID-19 pandemic in Tennessee and Virginia, were similarly challenged by parents who claimed that exposure to COVID-19 placed their children at a heightened risk of severe illness and death. The Sixth Circuit court vacated and remanded a Tennessee federal trial court's determination that parents demonstrated more than a mere probability of success on the merits of their Section 504 and ADA claims.[151] Although the federal trial court agreed that the Tennessee state law impeded reasonable accommodations under both Section 504 and the ADA. The Sixth Circuit found that the parents lacked standing and did demonstrate that they suffered an injury in fact. The court added that the parents filed suit before testing the practical effect of the state law on their accommodation requests. Further, the court observed, the parents failed to support their claim that universal masking and quarantining would be the only reasonable accommodations under the ADA.

On the other hand, a federal trial court in Virginia granted a preliminary injunction to enjoin the state from enforcing opt-out provisions, which parents alleged put their children with disabilities at significant health risk if they contracted the virus.[152] According to the parents, the ban on mask requirements had forced students to forego critical educational opportunities, including in-person learning. Furthermore, their injuries were the foreseeable result of the state's enforcement of the executive order and legislation which violated their rights under Section 504 and the ADA.

Conclusion

Litigation over provisions of the IDEA, Section 504, and the ADA continues, but at a slower pace than in previous years. Even so, parents continue to challenge the educational services offered to their children. In this respect, parents brought several cases contesting school board decisions regarding the educational

---

[151] R.K. *ex rel.* J.K. v. Lee, 53 F.4th 995, 409 Educ. L. Rep. 57 (6th Cir. 2022). 575 F. Supp. 3d 957, 405 Educ. L. Rep. 214 (M.D. Tenn. 2021).

[152] Seaman v. Virginia, 593 F. Supp.3d 293, 409 Educ. L. Rep. 69 (W.D. Va. 2022).

arrangements for students with disabilities during the COVID-19 pandemic.

Despite the Supreme Court's decision in *Fry*, litigation over when parents asserting claims under other statutes such as Section 504 and the ADA must exhaust the IDEA's administrative remedies before filing suit has continued, resulting in the Supreme Court clarifying its orders. In *Perez v. Sturgis*, the Court explained that the IDEA's administrative exhaustion requirement applies only to suits seeking relief that is available under that statute.

Parents continued to seek remedies for school boards' failures to provide FAPEs in the form of tuition reimbursement, compensatory education awards, and attorney fees. Although litigation in this area continued, it was not as prevalent as in past years.

Students with disabilities have rights and protections under Section 504 and the ADA, in addition to the IDEA, so parents continue to file suits under all three statutes. As in the past, courts are reluctant to find discrimination absent evidence of bad faith or gross negligence on the part of school officials.

Alphabetical List of Cases

A.C. *ex rel.* R.C. v. Henrico Cnty. Sch. Bd.

A.M. v. Wallingford-Swarthmore Sch. Dist.

A.V. *ex rel.* Hanson v. Douglas Cnty. Sch. Dist. Re-1

Bd. of Educ. of Hendrick Hudson Cent. Sch. Dist. v. Rowley

Bd. of Educ. of New Haven v. Comm. on Human Rights and Opportunities

Bellflower Unified Sch. Dist. v. Arnold

Bills. v. Va. Dept. of Educ.

Bouabid *ex rel.* A.C. v. Charlotte-Mecklenburg Schs. Bd. of Educ.

Bradley v. Jefferson Cnty. Pub. Schs.

Burlington Sch. Comm. v. Dep't of Educ., Commw. of Mass.

C.B. v. Bd. of Educ. of City of Chi. Dist.

C.H. *ex rel.* Hilligoss v. Sch. Bd. of Okaloosa Cnty.

C.M. *ex rel.* B.M. v. Rutherford Cnty. Schs.

Cedar Rapids Cmty. Sch. Dist. v. Garret F.

D.O. *ex rel.* Walker v. Escondido Union Sch. Dist.

D.D.T. v. Rockdale Cnty. Sch. Pub. Schs.

D.L. *ex rel.* S.L. and R.L. v. Hernando Cnty. Sheriff's Off.

D.R. *ex rel.* R.R. v. Redondo Beach Unified Sch. Dist.

D.T. *ex rel.* Yasiris T. v. Cherry Creek Sch. Dist.

David D. v. Dartmouth Sch. Comm.

Doe *ex rel.* K.M. v. Knox Cnty. Bd. of Educ.

Doe v. Bd. of Educ. of the City of Chi.

Doe v. Newton Pub. Schs.

Doe v. Westport Bd. of Educ.

Doe 1 v. N. Allegheny Sch. Bd.

Doe 1 v. Perkiomen Valley Sch. Dist.

Doe 1 v. Upper Saint Clair Sch. Dist.

Endrew F. *ex rel.* Joseph F. v. Douglas Cnty. Sch. Dist. RE-1

Falmouth Sch. Dept. v. Doe

Florence County Sch. Dist. Four v. Carter

Forest Grove Sch. Dist. v. T.A.

Fry v. Napoleon Cmty. Schs.

G.A. and W.A. v. Williamson Cnty. Bd. of Educ.

Garcia v. Morath

Geis v. Bd. of Educ. of Parsippany-Troy Hills, Morris Cnty.

Honig v. Doe

Irving Indep. Sch. Dist. v. Tatro

Ja. B. v. Wilson Cnty. Bd. of Educ.

Johnson v. Flagler Cnty. Sch. Dist.

K.C. *ex rel.* M.D. v. Reg. Sch. Unit 73

K.L., J.L. v. Durham Pub. Schs. Bd. of Educ.

Knox Cnty., Tenn. v. M.Q.

L.E. *ex rel.* Cavorley v. Supt. of Cobb Cnty. Sch. Dist.

M.F. *ex rel.* Ferrer v. N.Y.C. Dept. of Educ.

Martinez v. Newsom

Mendez *ex rel.* A.C. v. Banks

Miller *ex rel.* JM v. Charlotte-Mecklenburg Schs. Bd. of Educ.

Mills v. Bd. of Educ. of Dist. of Columbia

Navarro-Villanueva *ex rel.* D.A.V.N. v. Commw. of Puerto Rico

Pa. Ass'n for Retarded Children (PARC) v. Pa.

Perez v. Sturgis Pub. Schs.

Pocono Mtn. Sch. Dist. v. T.D.

R.G. *ex. rel.* E.G. v. N.Y.C. Dep't of Educ.

R.K. *ex rel.* J.K. v. Lee

R.N. *ex rel.* Neff v. Travis Unified Sch. Dist.

Roe v. Baker

S.S. *ex rel.* A.S. v. Cobb Cnty. Sch. Bd.

Sanchez v. Arlington Cnty. Sch. Bd.

Schaffer *ex rel.* Schaffer v. Weast

Sch. Bd. of Nassau Cnty. v. Arline

Seaman v. Virginia

Simpson-Vlach v. Mich. Dept. of Educ.

Southeastern Cmty. Coll. v. Davis

Special Educ. Complaint *ex rel.* V.S.

Z.W. *ex rel.* Warner v. Horry Cnty. Sch. Dist.

Federal Cases

United States Supreme Court

Bd. of Educ. of Hendrick Hudson Cent. Sch. Dist. v. Rowley
Burlington Sch. Comm. v. Dep't of Educ., Commw. of Mass.
Cedar Rapids Cmty. Sch. Dist. v. Garret F.
Endrew F. *ex rel.* Joseph F. v. Douglas Cnty. Sch. Dist. RE-1
Florence Cnty. Sch. Dist. Four v. Carter
Forest Grove Sch. Dist. v. T.A.
Fry v. Napoleon Cmty. Schs.
Honig v. Doe
Irving Indep. Sch. Dist. v. Tatro
Perez v. Sturgis Pub. Schs.
Schaffer *ex rel.* Schaffer v. Weast
Sch. Bd. of Nassau Cnty. v. Arline
Southeastern Cmty. Coll. v. Davis

First Circuit

David D. v. Dartmouth Sch. Comm.
Doe v. Newton Pub. Schs.
Falmouth Sch. Dept. v. Doe

Maine
K.C. *ex rel.* M.D. v. Reg. Sch. Unit 73

Massachusetts
Roe v. Baker

Puerto Rico
Navarro-Villanueva *ex rel.* D.A.V.N. v. Commw. of Puerto Rico

Second Circuit

Mendez *ex rel.* A.C. v. Banks

Connecticut
Doe v. Westport Bd. of Educ.

New York
M.F. *ex rel.* Ferrer v. N.Y.C. Dept. of Educ.
R.G. *ex. rel.* E.G. v. N.Y.C. Dep't of Educ.

Third Circuit

Geis v. Bd. of Educ. of Parsippany-Troy Hills, Morris Cnty.

Pennsylvania
A.M. v. Wallingford-Swarthmore Sch. Dist.
Doe 1 v. N. Allegheny Sch. Bd.
Doe 1 v. Perkiomen Valley Sch. Dist.
Doe 1 v. Upper Saint Clair Sch. Dist.
Pa. Ass'n for Retarded Children (PARC) v. Pa.
Pocono Mtn. Sch. Dist. v. T.D.

Fourth Circuit

K.L., J.L. v. Durham Pub. Schs. Bd. of Educ.
Bouabid *ex rel.* A.C. v. Charlotte-Mecklenburg Schs. Bd. of Educ.
Miller *ex rel.* JM v. Charlotte-Mecklenburg Schs. Bd. of Educ.
Z.W. *ex rel.* Warner v. Horry Cnty. Sch. Dist.

Virginia
A.C. *ex rel.* R.C. v. Henrico Cnty. Sch. Bd.
Bills. v. Va. Dept. of Educ.
Sanchez v. Arlington Cnty. Sch. Bd.
Seaman v. Virginia

Fifth Circuit

Texas
Garcia v. Morath

Sixth Circuit

Doe *ex rel.* K.M. v. Knox Cnty. Bd. of Educ.
Ja. B. v. Wilson Cnty. Bd. of Educ.
Knox Cnty, Tenn. v. M.Q.

Kentucky
Bradley v. Jefferson Cnty. Pub. Schs.

Michigan
Simpson-Vlach v. Mich. Dept. of Educ.

Tennessee
C.M. *ex rel.* B.M. v. Rutherford Cnty. Schs.
G.A. and W.A. v. Williamson Cnty. Bd. of Educ.

Seventh Circuit

Illinois
C.B. v. Bd. of Educ. of City of Chi. Dist.
Doe v. Bd. of Educ. of the City of Chi.

Eighth Circuit

Baker v. Bentonville Sch. Dist.

Ninth Circuit

D.O. *ex rel.* Walker v. Escondido Union Sch. Dist.
D.R. *ex rel.* R.R. v. Redondo Beach Unified Sch. Dist.
Martinez v. Newsom

California
Bellflower Unified Sch. Dist. v. Arnold
R.N. *ex rel.* Neff v. Travis Unified Sch. Dist.

Tenth Circuit

D.T. *ex rel.* Yasiris T. v. Cherry Creek Sch. Dist

Colorado
A.V. *ex rel.* Hanson v. Douglas Cnty. Sch. Dist. Re-1

Eleventh Circuit

L.E. *ex rel.* Cavorley v. Supt. of Cobb Cnty. Sch. Dist.
S.S. *ex rel.* A.S. v. Cobb Cnty. Sch. Bd.

Florida
C.H. *ex rel.* Hilligoss v. Sch. Bd. of Okaloosa Cnty.
D.L. *ex rel.* S.L. and R.L. v. Hernando Cnty. Sheriff's Off.
Johnson v. Flagler Cnty. Sch. Dist.

Georgia
D.D.T. v. Rockdale Cnty. Sch. Pub. Schs.

D.C. Circuit

District of Columbia
Mills v. Bd. of Educ. of Dist. of Columbia

State and D.C. Cases

Connecticut

Bd. of Educ. of New Haven v. Comm. on Human Rights and Opportunities

Minnesota

Special Educ. Complaint *ex rel.* V.S.

CHAPTER 6

TORTS

Beth Godett and Elizabeth Zagata

Continued on the next page...

Introduction

This chapter provides summaries of tort cases from 2022 and 2023 involving K-12 schools and institutions of higher education. For the elementary- and secondary school-related cases, there were claims by students regarding assault, sexual assault, vehicular accidents, sporting events and school activities, violations of school policy, dangerous or faulty conditions on school premises, wrongful death and statute of limitations defense. In some of these cases, family members initiated litigation on behalf of their minor children. Additionally, there were claims by school employees related to work-related injuries, claims by other injured parties, and defamation. For the cases involving institutions of higher education, claims addressed harms involving institutional officials or others, defamation, dangerous conditions on campuses, and sexual assault.

Many of the cases involved allegations of negligence against schools, school districts, or universities. In order to succeed in negligence claims, plaintiffs must prove by a preponderance of the evidence that defendants owed them duties of care to protect them from foreseeable harms and that defendants breached their duties by acting unreasonably, resulting in their being the proximate case of the harms the plaintiffs experienced. In attempting to limit or eliminate liability, defendants can contest any of the legal elements of the negligence claims by denying that they had duties, by raising other defenses such as immunity, or by relying on procedural defenses to prevent plaintiffs from moving forward with their claims.

Elementary and Secondary Education

Student Claims

Assault

The nine assault cases included five cases of student-on-student assault, and two cases of assault related to school staff involved in student restraint. The student-on-student assault cases often included allegations of bullying. One case involved what could be considered an assault on a student via his social media account, which ended in the student's death by suicide. Another case involved harassment and assault on the basis of a student's religious beliefs.

An assistant principal intervened to separate two high school students in a physical altercation, resulting in one student being restrained on the floor and alleging that the assistant principal kicked him while he was subdued. The student's mother brought action against the administrator and the board of education for assault and battery. The trial court granted summary judgment to the district and the administrator, citing immunity grounds. On appeal, an appellate court reversed the decision, prompting the defendants to seek discretionary review from the Supreme Court of Kentucky. The Supreme Court, after considering the issue of immunity, found that while the district was not entitled to sovereign immunity, it was protected by governmental immunity. Therefore, the supreme court reversed the appellate court's decision, reinstating the trial court's dismissal of the claims against the administrator. However, this decision did not affect the reversal of summary judgment granted in favor of the administrator.[1]

A student sought to serve a late notice of claim against a district regarding a tort claim stemming from an injury sustained at school. The student alleged another student struck him during a flag football game, causing injuries. The New York Supreme Court denied the petition, and the student appealed. The Appellate Division affirmed the denial, ruling that the district did not obtain actual knowledge of the essential facts of the claim within the required time frame, and the student failed to provide a reasonable excuse for the delay in serving the notice of claim. The court also found no evidence that the delay prejudiced the respondents' defense. Therefore, the Supreme Court's denial of the petition was upheld.[2]

The mother of a student who died by suicide brought a suit against the student's teacher, school district, and other school staff, alleging negligence and negligent hiring and retention. The day before the student died, a fellow student alerted the teacher about the student's post threatening to die by suicide. The student's post came after he had allegedly been the subject of ridicule on his Instagram account. The teacher had intended to report the incident to the school psychologist, but the student died prior to her doing so. The New York Supreme Court granted the defendants' motion for summary judgement, finding no duty owed to the student or his

---

[1] Jefferson Cnty. Pub. Schs. v. Tudor, Next Friend of J.T., 664 S.W.3d 600, 415 Educ. L. Rep. 413 (Ky. 2023).

[2] C.N. v. City of New York, 174 N.Y.S.3d 97, 408 Educ. L. Rep. 471 (N.Y. App. Div. 2022).

mother to prevent the suicide. The mother appealed, arguing that the defendants had a special relationship which created a duty to prevent harm. The appellate court affirmed the lower court's decision, stating that a defendant's duty to provide adequate supervision ends when students leave school premises.[3]

A sixth-grade student, represented by her mother, filed a claim of negligence against the school district by alleging that the district failed to protect her from being physically attacked by a fellow student. The fellow student began yelling at the plaintiff and cursing at the teacher during an award ceremony and was subsequently asked to leave. After being allowed to return a short time later, the student attacked the plaintiff, causing severe injuries. The plaintiff argued that the district was liable for damages because it failed to provide a safe school environment, specifically through a lack of proper supervision and discipline. The district filed a motion to appeal, which was granted. The Mississippi Court of Appeals considered the dismissal and found that the plaintiff had adequately stated a claim of negligence against the school; the court also rejected the district's claim of immunity under the Mississippi Torts Claims Act. The case was remanded for further proceedings.

A ninth-grade student claimed she was harassed and assaulted due to her religious beliefs and practices, including modest appearance. While a claim against the perpetrating peer and his father was settled, this case also concerned allegations of gross negligence against an administrator for failing to protect the plaintiff from bullying and abuse. The administrator had held investigations and interventions after the student's complaints, but the student withdrew from the school and issued claims of violations to her constitutional rights and gross negligence. Based on the administrator's efforts to address the bullying, the court found insufficient support for the student's due process claim, equal protection claim, Free Exercise Clause violation, and gross negligence claim, and granted the administrator's motion for summary judgment.[4]

The parents of a middle school student brought a negligence claim against the teachers and administrators at their daughter's

---

[3] Hauburger v. McMane, 179 N.Y.S.3d 710, 411 Educ. L. Rep. 325 (N.Y. App. Div. 2022).

[4] A.P. *ex rel.* Pyscher v. A.P., 598 F. Supp. 3d 598, 410 Educ. L. Rep. 369 (E.D. Mich. 2022).

school due to injuries she sustained from alleged bullying and physical assaults from other students. The school staff sought summary judgment, claiming immunity under the Coverdell Act. Further, school staff argued that the negligence claims fell under the educational malpractice doctrine, which prevents claims related to quality of education. The circuit court granted the defendants' request for summary judgment, and the Court of Special Appeals affirmed this decision. The Court of Appeals of Maryland reversed the lower court's decision, arguing that the Coverdell Act does not provide immunity from liability for school personnel, nor does it preempt Maryland law. The appellate court further argued that the negligence claims addressing supervision and safety did not fall under the educational malpractice doctrine. The case was remanded to the circuit court.[5]

A student alleged he was subject to bullying in the form of verbal and physical abuse over a period of three years and subsequently filed a negligence claim against the school district. The circuit court dismissed this claim due to insufficient support for the required duty and causation elements. The West Virginia Supreme Court of Appeals reversed this decision, finding the student's claim had sufficient information about the nature of the bullying and the district's alleged knowledge, which could support the negligence claim. Specifically, the Supreme Court of Appeals addressed the district's responsibility under the consideration of the duty standards of the Tort Claims Act and if their actions or inactions could be determined a proximate cause of the student's injuries. The case was remanded to the circuit court for further consideration.[6]

When a 16-year-old student expressed frustration with her teacher's decision, her teacher ordered her to step into the hallway and called security. After the student refused to leave, the security officer restrained her, put her in handcuffs, and pepper-sprayed her in the face. The student "begged" for help washing her face, but the officer did not provide immediate decontamination. The student filed suit against the officer with claims of excessive force, negligence, assault and battery, and intentional infliction of emotional distress. The trial court granted the officer's motion for

---

[5] Gambrill v. Bd. of Educ. of Dorchester Cnty, 281 A.3d 876, 408 Educ. L. Rep. 400 (Md. 2022).

[6] Jones v. Logan Cnty. Bd. of Educ., 881 S.E.2d 374, 410 Educ. L. Rep. 516 (W. Va. 2022).

summary judgment based on his claims that he was entitled to official immunity and that the student failed to present evidence of actual malice or intent to injure. The student appealed, and the Georgia Court of Appeals ruled that the officer's failure to wash the pepper spray was a violation of ministerial duty based on a school policy explicitly mandating that officers must flush the eyes and face of affected subjects with clean water after using pepper spray. The Court of Appeals rejected the student's argument that the officer acted with actual malice and upheld the trial court's grant of official immunity for the officer's other alleged acts.[7]

The parents of a minor filed suit against a school, teacher, and student to seek damages for personal injuries on behalf of their child. The case was voluntarily dismissed without prejudice on September 6, 2019, and the parents attempted to renew the action electronically on March 5, 2020, the day before the six-month renewal period expired. It was not accepted for docketing until March 11, 2020, due to a payment error. The parents filed a motion to revert the filing date of March 5, clarifying the payment error. The defendants' motion to dismiss the renewal action due to untimely filing was denied, and they appealed. The Georgia Court of Appeals affirmed the lower court's decision, citing the trial court's broad discretion to correct clerical errors and stating that the actual date of filing is when the paper is handed to the clerk (March 5). Further, the plaintiffs promptly addressed the payment issue when notified by the clerk's office.[8]

A sixth-grade student, represented by her mother, filed a claim of negligence against the school district by alleging that the district failed to protect her from being physically attacked by a fellow student. The fellow student began yelling at the plaintiff and cursing at the teacher during an award ceremony and was subsequently asked to leave. After being allowed to return a short time later, the student attacked the plaintiff, causing severe injuries. The plaintiff. argued that the district was liable for damages because it failed to provide a safe school environment, specifically through a lack of proper supervision and discipline. The district filed a motion to appeal, which was granted. The Mississippi Court of Appeals considered the dismissal and found

---

[7] Hall v. Acker, 885 S.E.2d 266, 414 Educ. L. Rep. 731 (Ga. Ct. App. 2023).

[8] Dannenfelser v. Squires, 879 S.E.2d 506, 409 Educ. L. Rep. 538 (Ga. Ct. App. 2022).

that the plaintiff had adequately stated a claim of negligence against the school and also rejected the district's claim of immunity under the Mississippi Torts Claims Act. The case was remanded for further proceedings.[9]

Sexual Assault

Of the eighteen cases in this section, three involve student-on-student sexual assault, fourteen involved educator-on-student sexual assault, and one involved a non-school party.

Student-on-Student Sexual Assault. A student identified as having special needs and her father filed a negligence claim against a private busing contractor and the driver after the student was sexually assaulted by another student while riding on the bus. The district court denied the defendants' motion for summary judgment based on noncompliance with pre-suit notice requirements of the Kansas Tort Claims Act (KTCA), and the defendants appealed. The Court of Appeals of Kansas affirmed the decision of the district court, which ruled that a private company providing busing services under contract with a school district does not qualify as a governmental entity under the KTCA. Specifically, the court deemed that as a for-profit private corporation operating independently from the district, the busing company did not qualify as an instrumentality under the KTCA.[10]

A high school student, by and through his guardian ad litem and parents, sued his school district for negligence, sexual harassment, and negligent infliction of emotional distress after alleging that he was sexually assaulted by two other students in a school bathroom. During legal proceedings, the student learned that the video evidence in the case had been erased, and subsequently the student sought sanctions against the district for the loss of evidence. The trial court denied terminating sanctions but granted issue, evidence, and monetary sanctions on the district. The district challenged this decision, arguing that they were protected under the safe-harbor provision of Cal. Civ. Proc. Code 2023.030(f). The California Court of Appeals agreed that the

---

[9] J.D. *ex rel.* Mingo v. McComb Sch. Dist., 347 So.3d 199, 408 Educ. L. Rep. 1123 (Miss. Ct. App. 2022).

[10] R.P. v. First Student Inc., 515 P.3d 283, 406 Educ. L. Rep. 1001 (Kan. Ct. App. 2022).

trial court had misapplied the legal standard for determining the duty to preserve evidence and vacated the sanctions order.[11]

A former student alleged she was sexually assaulted starting at the age of 14 by a fellow student at the high school. She brought action against the school, district, board of education, school staff, and the alleged assailant, under the Child Victims Act (CVA), asserting claims against the school defendants for negligence, gross negligence, and negligent hiring, retention and supervision. She also alleged that the school defendants failed to protect her when the assailant committed sexual assault against her at school. The court denied the defendants' motion to dismiss, and they appealed. The appellate court upheld the denial of dismissal, concluding that reviving claims under NY CPLR 214-g is consistent with the legislative intent of the CVA in providing options for justice for survivors of child sexual abuse.[12]

Educator-on-Student Sexual Assault. While a student at a New Hampshire religious boarding school, the plaintiff alleged sexual abuse by a school staff member, his superior and supervisor. Suffering psychological and emotional injuries, the plaintiff brought claims including recklessness on the part of the defendant school, as well as breach of fiduciary duty to care for him. The plaintiff alleged the staff member provided him with special attention and interaction, expecting him to neither challenge nor report the abuse, with the understanding that doing so would be considered a sin. The plaintiff also alleged the defendant was not only aware of sexual abuse coming from the clergy but took no steps to protect students. Despite the plaintiff's residing in Connecticut, the United States District Court for the district of Connecticut determined the venue to be New Hampshire where, at the time of the abuse, the plaintiff resided and where the alleged abuse took place. This was critical to the case, as New Hampshire law does not acknowledge a breach of fiduciary claim at secondary schools; neither does it recognize an independent cause of action for

---

[11] Victor Valley Union High Sch. Dist. v. Super. Ct. of San Bernardino Cnty., 305 Cal. Rptr. 3d 442, 412 Educ. L. Rep. 942 (Cal. Ct. App. 2022), vacated by 309 Cal. Rptr. 3d 258, 416 Educ. L. Rep. 1111 (Cal. Ct. App. 2023).

[12] Anonymous v. Castagnola, 178 N.Y.S.3d 587, 410 Educ. L. Rep. 499 (N.Y. App. Div. 2022).

recklessness as an intentional tort. The court ruled in favor of the defendants, granting their motion to dismiss.[13]

A student alleged he sustained injuries resulting from sexual abuse by a former teacher, and he brought negligence action against the board of education and principal. The Superior Court, Judicial District of New Haven, granted summary judgment for the defendants, citing governmental immunity, and the student appealed. The appeal was dismissed as the appellate court found that the principal did not breach ministerial duties, and neither he nor the board had prior knowledge of the teacher's misconduct because the student did not report it. Additionally, the appellate court affirmed the trial court's conclusion that the plaintiff did meet the standard for the identifiable personal-imminent harm exemption to governmental immunity.[14]

An adult female student with an intellectual disability, by and through her parents, filed a complaint against her teacher alleging that the teacher had failed to prevent another student from touching her inappropriately when the students were being transported to submit job applications. The teacher argued that she was entitled to state-agent immunity because she was engaged in a discretionary function at the time of the incident. Her motion for summary motion was denied, and she petitioned for a writ of mandamus. The Supreme Court of Alabama granted this petition and directed the trial court to enter summary judgment in her favor based on state-agent immunity. The court found the plaintiff did not provide evidence showing that the teacher had acted willfully, maliciously, fraudulently, in bad faith, or beyond her authority, and that the teacher's actions were not a violation of a clear, established policy.[15]

A former student filed suit against the board of education and other school defendants under the Child Victims Act (CVA), alleging negligence and intentional infliction of emotional distress resulting from her teacher's alleged sexual abuse when she was a student in 1991. The defendants moved for summary judgment under the argument that the CVA did not revise the former student's claims because the alleged abuse occurred before she

---

[13] Doe #2 v. Legion of Christ, Inc., 588 F. Supp. 3d 240, 408 Educ. L. Rep. 212 (D. Conn. 2022).
[14] Doe v. City of New Haven, 281 A.3d 480, 408 Educ. L. Rep. 367 (Conn. App. Ct. 2022).
[15] *Ex parte* Williamson, 348 So. 3d 1089, 409 Educ. L. Rep. 597 (Ala. 2021).

reached the age of consent. The court rejected this argument under a broader interpretation of the CVA which did not time-bar the former student's claims. The court allowed the negligence claim to proceed and also granted the defendants' motion to dismiss the claim for intentional infliction of emotional distress and punitive damages.[16]

In the course of filing action under the Child Victims Act to recover damages for negligence and negligent supervision due to alleged sexual abuse by a middle school music teacher, the plaintiff filed a motion seeking permission to use a pseudonym. The court allowed for the use of the pseudonym and the defendants moved for leave to reargue their opposition. The court affirmed its decision, and the defendants appealed. The appellate court affirmed the lower court's decision, finding that the plaintiff provided sufficient support for proceeding anonymously. This justification included a submitted affidavit stating the disclosure of their identity would cause additional emotional stress, embarrassment and loss of self-esteem. The defendants did not demonstrate any prejudice that would result if they were unable to use the plaintiff's name.[17]

A former high school student alleged that he was physically and sexually assaulted by a teacher while attending a party at that teacher's home. The student filed suit against the school district, claiming negligent supervision, hiring, and retention, and seeking damages for the assault. The district argued that the complaint failed to state a cause of action and filed a motion to dismiss, which was granted. The student appealed. The Appellate Division upheld the decision, clarifying the limitations on a school district's liability in cases of misconduct by employees off school grounds.[18]

A former student at a New York Roman Catholic parish school appealed after a lower court dismissed his allegations of sexual abuse by a priest who was an employee of the defendant. An appellate court reversed the lower court ruling to allow that the plaintiff successfully pleaded causes of action alleging both negligence and intentional infliction of emotional distress (IIED).

---

[16] SR v. Gates Chili Bd. of Educ., 185 N.Y.S.3d 912, 414 Educ. L. Rep. 678 (N.Y. Sup. Ct. 2023).
[17] Roe *ex rel.* Harborfields Cent. Sch. Dist., 182 N.Y.S.3d 232, 412 Educ. L. Rep. 278 (N.Y. App. Div. 2023).
[18] Doe *ex rel.* Hauppauge Union Free Sch. Dist. v. Hauppauge Union Free Sch. Dist., 184 N.Y.S.3d 150, 412 Educ. L. Rep. 1004 (N.Y. App. Div. 2023).

The appellate court based its decision on finding that the priest was an agent of the defendant; that the defendant had previous knowledge of the priest's propensity to abuse students, including the plaintiff; and that the abuse occurred during times when "the plaintiff was under the Defendant's supervision and care, custody, and control."[19] The court also found the complaint to be "sufficiently outrageous in character and extreme in degree" to support a cause of action for IIED. The court's ruling clears the path for the parties to proceed with discovery and places the burden on the plaintiff to prove the allegations true.[20]

A parent filed suit against the school board on her own behalf and on behalf of her minor child, alleging claims of negligence, negligent hiring, negligent retention, negligent supervision, and loss of filial consortium due to alleged sexual abuse of her child at an aftercare program more than four years prior. The school board moved for summary judgment, arguing that the suit was time-barred under the four-year statute of limitations applicable to defendants with sovereign immunity. The circuit court granted the motion for summary judgment, and the parents appealed, arguing that the case should be subject to the limitations period applicable to sexual battery offenses on victims under age 16. The court considered that both statuses were implicated but ultimately concluded that the four-year limitation period for claims against defendants with sovereign immunity as per section 768.28(14) should apply. The summary judgment was affirmed.[21]

A group of former elementary school students brought actions against a school district asserting tort claims based on allegations of sexual abuse by a school counselor. Previous action for the same case had been dismissed on summary judgment, but the students filed a new claim based on the extended statute of limitations for child sexual assault claims under Assembly Bill 218. The trial court dismissed their claims, and the students appealed. The Court of Appeals affirmed the dismissal, stating that Assembly Bill 218 only revived claims that had not been fully adjudicated, and in this case, the students' claims had been litigated to finality. Further,

---

[19] Novak v. Sisters of Heart of Mary, 180 N.Y.S.3d 187, 189, 411 Ed L. Rep. 720, (N.Y. App. Div. 2022).
[20] Novak v. Sisters of Heart of Mary, 180 N.Y.S.3d 187, 411 Ed L. Rep. 720, (N.Y. App. Div. 2022).
[21] S.S. v. Sch. Bd. of Sarasota Cnty., 357 So.3d 802, 414 Educ. L. Rep. 751 (Fla. Dist. Ct. App. 2023).

the distinction between litigated and not litigated claims did not violate equal protection.[22]

Three students filed claims against a district for negligence and sexual harassment due to alleged sexual abuse by a high school drama teacher. A jury assigned fault to the teacher and the district, and both sides appealed. The students argued that they should be allowed to seek retroactive treble damages under Assembly Bill 218. The court rejected this argument, stating that the treble damages provision in Section 340.1 is not retroactive and does not apply to schools. The court upheld the original judgment and denied the district's appeal regarding costs due to invalid Section 998 offers in the prior settlement agreement.[23]

A group of elementary school students alleged that they had been sexually abused by the school janitor when they were in first grade. They subsequently brought action against the district alleging negligence in supervising students and the janitor; failing to maintain professional boundaries between staff and students, and in monitoring classroom usage during breaks and lunch; negligent hiring and retention of the janitor; negligence per se; violation of the Unruh Civil Rights Act; violation of Title IX; failure to perform mandated duties under the Child Abuse and Neglect Reporting act (CANRA); and sex discrimination. The trial court sustained the district's demurrer to several causes of action, stating that the students did not provide sufficient evidence that the district had knowledge of the abuse or failed to act upon it. The students appealed, and the appellate court affirmed in part and reversed in part the decision. The court found that the students had adequately pleaded negligence, negligent hiring and retention, negligent supervision, and other claims against the district, but the appellate court concluded that the lower court did not abuse its discretion in denying leave to amend certain causes of action.[24]

A former student alleged that he was sexually assaulted by his teacher when he was in sixth grade in the 1997-1997 school year. The former student's claim accrued in 2016, but he filed a lawsuit in January 2020 against the school district, elementary school, and

---

[22] Doe v. Marysville Joint Unified Sch. Dist., 306 Cal. Rptr. 3d 105, 413 Educ. L. Rep. 920 (Cal. Ct. App. 2023).
[23] K.M. v. Grossmont Union High Sch. Dist., 300 Cal. Rptr. 3d 598, 409 Educ. L. Rep. 253 (Cal. Ct. App. 2022).
[24] Roe v. Hesperia Unified Sch. Dist., 300 Cal. Rptr. 3d 340, 409 Educ. L. Rep. 233 (Cal. Ct. App. 2022).

school personnel. The defendants moved to dismiss the complaint for failure to file a timely notice of claim under the 90-day requirement of the Torts Claims Act (TCA). However, amendments to the TCA effective December 1, 2019, extended the statute of limitations for child sexual abuse survivors and removed the TCA's notice of claim requirements for such cases against public entities. The defendants' motion to dismiss was denied; upon appeal, the appellate court and Supreme Court both affirmed the decision, confirming that the amendments applied retroactively.[25]

A former student filed claims of intentional infliction of emotional distress (IIED), negligence, and negligent infliction of emotional distress against the board of education due to allegations that he was sexually abused by a teacher. The IIED claim was dismissed under the board's motion for summary judgment, and the court also found that the former student failed to meet the monetary threshold under the Tort Claims Act (TCA). The former student appealed. The appellate court rejected his argument that child sexual abuse cases should be exempt from the medical expense threshold and subsequently upheld the dismissal because he had failed to demonstrate past, present or future medical expenses exceeding $3,600, thus precluding him from seeking pain and suffering damages under the TCA.[26]

A student reported to his mother that he had been sexually assaulted by his teacher on multiple occasions. His mother, as the student's tutrix, filed suit against the teacher, school, and schools' insurer. The teacher filed a motion for summary judgment, arguing a lack of physical evidence supporting the student's claims along with inconsistencies in the student's accounts. The trial court granted summary judgment, and the mother appealed, citing genuine issues of material fact that precluded summary judgment. The Court of Appeals reversed judgment, and the case was remanded for further proceedings so that credibility of all parties and evidence could be further assessed.[27]

Sexual Assault Involving Non-School Parties. A former student at a Scranton, Pennsylvania, Catholic school filed suit under the Child Victims Act for negligent supervision, failure to

---

[25] W.S. v. Hildreth, 287 A.3d 421, 411 Educ. L. Rep. 1116 (N.J. 2023).
[26] C.W. v. Roselle Bd. of Educ., 290 A.3d 229, 413 Educ. L. Rep. 894 (N.J. Super. Ct. 2023).
[27] Henderson v. Capdeville, 358 So.3d 1021, 415 Educ. L. Rep. 419 (La. Ct. App. 2023).

warn, failure to provide a safe and secure environment, and failure to train, alleging he was repeatedly molested by a priest to whom he had been referred for discipline as the result of his misbehavior. The lower court granted the defendant's motion to dismiss. On appeal, an appellate court affirmed the decision of the lower court, modified to reflect that the parish church should have been aware of the priest's inclination to molest children, and that the student's claims of failure to warn did not duplicate his cause of action for negligent supervision. The appellate court did, however, affirm the lower court's ruling in dismissing failure to train as a cause of action on the basis that the priest was not alleged to be an employee of the school and, thus, no nexus existed between the abuse and the breach of a duty to train.[28]

Vehicular Accidents and Other Related Issues

Students were injured in accidents involving school vehicles including school buses and vans.

Parents of a 17-year old Nebraska student filed suit for negligence after their son was injured when a school district van in which he was riding was hit head-on by a truck. The district court issued a verdict in favor of the school district. The parents appealed, as did the estate of the deceased truck driver against which suit was also filed. The Supreme Court of Nebraska affirmed the decision of the lower court in favor of the school district and dismissed cross-appeals filed by the district and the truck driver's estate as moot or without merit. The court's decision was based upon the interpretation of two Nebraska statutes, one requiring that drivers ensure children use seatbelts when being transported and another that prohibits evidence that someone was not wearing a seatbelt to be used to establish proximate cause in a negligence suit. The court emphasized that violation of the statute was not enough, noting causation as only one element proving negligence. Its analysis revealed a lack of evidence supporting that the seatbelt violation caused the student's injury.[29]

A school bus driver in Kentucky filed suit against a police officer and the school's superintendent after the driver was

---

[28] Sullivan v. St. Ephrem Roman Catholic Par. Church, 186 N.Y.S. 3d 226, 414 Educ. L. Rep. 962 (N.Y. App. Div. 2023).

[29] Christensen v. Broken Bow Pub. Schs., 981 N.W.2d 234, 409 Educ. L. Rep. 345 (Neb. 2022).

suspended pending an investigation into his alleged assault of a student who was causing a disturbance on the bus he was driving. After an investigation by the police officer, the driver was arrested and terminated from his job. At the arraignment, the charge of assault was changed to harassment, to which the driver pleaded not guilty. At that point the driver brought a cause of action against the officer and the superintendent for malicious prosecution, abuse of process, and defamation. The trial court granted summary judgment to the officer based on qualified immunity, but the appellate court concluded the officer was not entitled to summary judgment on this basis. The Supreme Court of Kentucky, noting that the officer's asserting a claim of qualified official immunity had deprived the driver of an opportunity to establish a record supporting his claim, remanded the case for further proceedings on the basis that the driver should not be penalized for a lack of discovery that he had been prevented from developing.[30]

The parent of a child using a wheelchair, whose IEP required transportation in a special services school bus equipped with a wheelchair lift, filed suit against the school board for injuries she and her child sustained after she transported him to school and fell in the school parking lot while transitioning him from her car to his wheelchair. The mother had elected to drive him to school on a day when the wheelchair lift was not operational, and the district was unable to meet its duty to transport. An appellate court affirmed the ruling of the trial court that, in the absence of any parking lot defect or other reason for her fall, the school board owed no duty to the mother and that the injury she sustained was too far removed from the school board's duty to provide transportation required under the child's IEP. Facts revealed that the parent voluntarily and often drove her children to school, had permission to park at the school's entrance to facilitate her son's car to wheelchair transition, and had requested neither assistance from school personnel nor available homebound instruction on the day the school was unable to transport.[31]

The mother of a motorist who was left in a vegetative state after sustaining injuries in a collision with a school bus filed suit to prevent the defendants from obtaining her son's cellular phone. An appellate court reversed the decision of the lower court

---

[30] Martin v. Wallace, 651 S.W.3d 753, 408 Educ. L. Rep. 573 (Ky. 2022).

[31] Green v. E. Carroll Par. Sch. Dist./Bd., 357 So.3d 541, 413 Educ. L. Rep. 994 (La. Ct. App. 2023) [writ granted, reversed by 360 So.3d 833 (Mem) (La. 2023)].

permitting disclosure of the phone on the basis that such disclosure was "sought in good faith"[32] and could provide information material to the cause of action. Although the defendant had previously been granted access to the plaintiff's cell phone records through his service provider, the appellate court noted that critical information—such as whether the plaintiff had been using social media or messaging while driving—would not be included in those records and could be relevant to determining whether the driver plaintiff had been distracted in this negligence action.[33]

A North Carolina KinderCare center attempted to enjoin the local school district in a negligence lawsuit filed on behalf of a child who, after having been dropped off by a school district bus, was struck by an SUV while crossing the street to the center. An appellate court reversed and remanded the trial court's order dismissing the school board's motion to dismiss on grounds of governmental immunity from third-party claims. The dismissal was on the basis that school boards are governmental agencies and that even the purchase of insurance by the school board would not waive its governmental immunity for claims alleging school bus negligence. The appellate court ruled that waiver of governmental immunity against local school boards could apply to claims brought to the Industrial Commission, but not to court claims against third parties.[34]

A North Carolina school district was sued by an injured passenger's guardian and the administrators of a passenger's estate when the driver of a district school bus collided head-on with a car. The driver of the car was found to be driving recklessly while under the influence of a mixture of marijuana and Xanax. An appellate court affirmed the decision of the Industrial Commission, which denied the claims of the administrators and the guardian in this action brought under the Tort Claims Act. The bus driver was found not to be liable under the Doctrine of Sudden Emergency, as the driver of the car was traveling in the wrong lane and the bus driver was forced to act instantly in a manner consistent with her

---

[32] Tousant v. Aragona, 172 N.Y.S.3d 789, 792, 406 Educ. L. Rep. 954 (N.Y. App. Div. 2022).

[33] Tousant v. Aragona, 172 N.Y.S.3d 789, 406 Educ. L. Rep. 954 (N.Y. App. Div. 2022).

[34] Devore for Horton v. Samuel, 882 S.E.2d 389, 411 Educ. L. Rep. 802 (N.C. Ct. App. 2022).

training, experience, and as a reasonable person would act in a similar situation.[35]

Sporting Events and School Activities

A mother brought personal injury action against the school district after her son, a varsity football player, was injured during an off-season weightlifting exercise supervised by the football coach. The player's finger was crushed, and the suit alleged negligence in supervision. The district filed a motion for summary judgment, arguing that the doctrine of primary assumption of risk absolved them of liability because the player participated voluntarily and thus consented to inherent risks. The Supreme Court granted this motion, and the mother appealed. The Appellate Division reversed the judgment, clarifying that the doctrine of primary assumption of risk did not apply since the player's injury resulted not from playing football but from weightlifting, a separate activity. Further, the district did not provide sufficient evidence regarding the adequacy of supervision.[36]

Violations of School Policy

The estate of a deceased high school student, who died by suicide after being suspended and discharged from school, sued a New York school district for breach of its *in loco parentis* duty that the plaintiffs claimed resulted in wrongful death. The estate alleged the district did not assume its responsibility for the proper supervision of students, including failing to address purported bullying suffered by the decedent. Finding that the suicide occurred off school grounds, after the decedent had been released into the custody of his parents, into a situation that was not foreseeably hazardous or that the district had involvement in creating, an appellate court affirmed the decision of the lower court granting summary judgment for the school district.[37]

---

[35] Estate of Johnson *ex rel.* Johnson v. Guilford Cnty. Bd. of Educ., 877 S.E.2d 322, 407 Educ. L. Rep. 957 (N.C. Ct. App. 2022).

[36] Annitto v. Smithtown Cent. Sch. Dist., 177 N.Y.S.3d 620, 410 Educ. L. Rep. 473 (N.Y. App. Div. 2022).

[37] Boyle v. Brewster Cent. Sch. Dist., 175 N.Y.S.3d 343, 408 Educ. L. Rep. 975 (N.Y. App. Div. 2022).

Dangerous or Faulty Conditions on School Premises

Ten cases involved students who suffered injuries related to allegedly faulty school property and lack of supervision. One case involved allegations of how school policy could have contributed to creating unsafe conditions on school premises.

After the estranged husband of a California elementary teacher entered her classroom, shooting and killing the teacher, a student, and himself, students filed suit against the district and the building principal alleging negligence and dangerous condition of property. The trial court granted summary judgment for the defendants. An appellate court affirmed on the basis that the shooting was unforeseeable as, without a duty to disclose, the teacher had not shared that she and her husband were estranged, nor did she fear for her safety; that the assailant and school personnel had properly followed district procedures for admitting visitors to the building; that the assailant had previously visited his wife at the school without incident; that it was common for spouses to visit at the school; and that the conditions of the building did not facilitate the harm caused by the attack. Further, the appellate court reasoned that on the basis of public policy, the burden for schools to anticipate any intentional harm, even unexpected, would be overwhelming in both the costs of protection, including insurance, and the impact on the school culture imposing an almost prison-like environment for learning.[38]

Parents of a student in an El Paso, Texas, elementary school filed suit against the school district under the Texas Tort Claims Act (the Act) for premises defect, negligence, and infliction of emotional distress after a ceiling light at school fell on their son, hitting and injuring his arm. The lower court denied the school district's plea to the jurisdiction which called into question the court's subject matter jurisdiction. An appellate court reversed the lower court's decision and dismissed the plaintiff's claims against the school district on the basis that, under the Act, school districts are provided a limited waiver of sovereign immunity which provides tort liability only applies if the claimant's injury arises from the "operation or use of a motor vehicle."[39] As the personal

---

[38] C.I. v. San Bernardino City Unified Sch. Dist., 298 Cal. Rptr. 3d 651, 407 Educ. L. Rep. 867 (Cal. Ct. App. 2022).

[39] El Paso Ind. Sch. Dist. v. De La Rosa, 656 S.W.3d 586, 587, 411 Educ. L. Rep. 394 (Tex. App. 2022).

injury alleged in this case was unrelated to the operation or use of a motor vehicle, the appellate court ruled the school district immune from the suit.[40]

An elementary school student in New York fell off the monkey bars on his school's playground during recess, allegedly sustaining injuries. A suit was filed on his behalf contending the playground surface was "dangerous and defective," and the District filed a motion for summary judgment. While the plaintiff's expert demonstrated that the playground's surface of engineered wood chips met "good and accepted safety standards" and was "maintained in a reasonably safe condition," the defendant's expert opined otherwise, citing "insufficient depth of the wood chips and the absence of rubber mats below that surface."[41] Noting that challenges from both the plaintiff and the defendant regarding the credibility of each other's expert opinion could not be resolved on a summary judgment motion, an appellate court affirmed the Supreme Court of Nassau County's decision to deny the school district's motion.[42]

Plaintiffs alleged personal injuries stemming from incidents at their school between June 13, 2016, and November 2017. An untimely notice of claim was served on the district on May 16, 2018, and the plaintiffs commenced an action against the district. The New York Supreme Court Appellate Division granted the motion only with respect to incidents occurring after May 31, 2017, and denied the motion regarding incidents from June 13, 2016, to May 31, 2017, because they were time-barred. The plaintiffs appealed. The Supreme Court found that the district had actual knowledge of the claim and would not be prejudiced by the delay. Further, the lower court was wrong in concluding the claims based on incidents prior to May 31, 2017, would be time-barred. Thus, the plaintiffs were granted leave to serve a late notice of claim for these incidents.[43]

While in kindergarten, a student was being chased by classmates during recess and fell head-first into a metal pole. The student and his mother filed a petition seeking leave to serve a late

---

[40] El Paso Ind. Sch. Dist. v. De La Rosa, 656 S.W.3d 586, 411 Educ. L. Rep. 394 (Tex. App. 2022).

[41] J.H.V. v. Locust Valley Cent. Sch. Dist., 183 N.Y.S.3d 469, 470, 412 Educ. L. Rep. 865 (N.Y. App. Div. 2023).

[42] J.H.V. v. Locust Valley Cent. Sch. Dist., 183 N.Y.S.3d 469, 412 Educ. L. Rep. 865 (N.Y. App. Div. 2023).

[43] M.S. *ex rel.* Rye Neck Union Free Sch. Dist., 182 N.Y.S.3d 222, 412 Educ. L. Rep. 274 (N.Y. App. Div. 2023).

notice of claim upon the board of education. The claim asserted negligence due to inadequate supervision, failure to instruct students about playground safety, and failure to provide safe equipment. The court granted the petition, and the school board appealed. The appellate court agreed with the district's argument and emphasized that schools cannot be expected to continuously supervise all student movement and activities. Further, the accident claim form was insufficient evidence for the negligence claim.[44]

A child allegedly sustained chemical burns after kicking a "foggy" plastic water bottle containing Drano. The child and her mother brought personal injury action against the operator of the after-school care program, alleging negligent supervision. The program operator was granted summary judgment, and the plaintiffs appealed. The appellate court affirmed the decision that the program staff did not have notice of the dangerous condition that led to the injury. Further, the program staff did not have control over the "impulsive" and "unanticipated" actions that led to the injuring incident.[45]

A kindergarten student alleged he was injured when another student climbed onto a playground apparatus, a prohibited behavior, and then jumped off and landed on him. The student brought action against the city's department of education, claiming negligence. The department's motion for summary judgment was denied, and the department appealed. The amount of supervision present during the incident was unclear due to contradicting testimonies from school staff. The appellate court upheld the denial of summary judgment, due to material issues of fact regarding supervision and the subsequent impact on the student's injuries.[46]

An eighth-grade student in New York allegedly sustained injuries after shattering a glass panel on a wall-mounted display case when, pretending to play basketball in the entranceway to his school, he accidentally slapped the panel. Evidence revealed that the display case had two shatterproof plexiglass panes as well as the shattered glass panel; that a glass panel in a similar display case in the school had shattered previously; and that it was unclear

---

[44] R.M. *ex rel.* Bd. of Educ. of Long Beach City Sch. Dist., 182 N.Y.S.3d 213, 412 Educ. L. Rep. 270 (N.Y. App. Div. 2023).

[45] S.G. v. Harlem Village Acad. Charter Sch., 184 N.Y.S.3d 334, 413 Educ. L. Rep. 385 (N.Y. App. Div. 2023).

[46] A.M. v. N.Y. City Dept. of Educ., 183 N.Y.S.3d 19, 412 Educ. L. Rep. 290 (N.Y. App. Div. 2023).

as to whether the glass panel in the display case in the entranceway was obviously open and not an inherent danger. These facts, leaving in question the issue of whether the defendant had notice of the defect, led the appellate court to modify the lower court's granting of summary judgment to the district on the allegation of premises liability, reinstating that cause of action. The appellate court affirmed the lower court's ruling that alleged lack of supervision by the district was not the proximate cause of the student's injuries, on the basis that the district "lacked specific notice of the allegedly dangerous conduct"[47] and that the accident occurred almost instantly, resulting from the plaintiff's spontaneous act of pretending to play basketball.[48]

A kindergarten student allegedly was injured after a wooden cubby unit in the hallway outside of her classroom fell on top of her. The student and her mother brought personal injury action and inadequate supervision claims against the department of education. The court denied the plaintiffs' summary judgment, and they appealed. The appellate court upheld this decision, citing that the insufficiency of the plaintiffs' affidavit in establishing both that the cubby unit created a dangerous condition and the inadequacy of supervision.[49]

A substitute bus driver was unable to start a bus, leaving students to play an unsupervised game of tag in which one student was injured. The student's mother filed suit to recover damages for the student's injuries resulting from the alleged negligent supervision. The trial court ruled in favor of the parent, and the district appealed on three grounds: denial of the motion for involuntary dismissal, absence of supporting evidence for judgment, and rendering judgment on a claim not presented. The court of appeals ruled in favor of the district, citing a lack of evidence supporting the district's liability for the student's injury. In particular, both the student's testimony about the incident and subsequent medical records had inconsistencies, and the plaintiffs

---

[47] R.B. v. Sewanhaka Cent. High Sch. Dist., 172 N.Y.S.3d 686, 689, 406 Educ. L. Rep. 949 (N.Y. App. Div. 2022).
[48] R.B. v. Sewanhaka Cent. High Sch. Dist., 172 N.Y.S.3d 686, 406 Educ. L. Rep. 949 (N.Y. App. Div. 2022).
[49] M.O. *ex rel.* Lopez v. City of New York, 181 N.Y.S.3d 28, 411 Educ. L. Rep. 731 (N.Y. App. Div. 2022).

failed to establish proximate cause for either negligent supervision or failure to render aid.[50]

Wrongful Death/Conscious Pain and Suffering

More than one year after the shooting death of a New York public charter high school student, the student's mother, who was also the administrator of the student's estate, petitioned to file a late notice of claims for wrongful death and conscious pain and suffering against the school, the city, and the city's department of education. The New York Supreme Court, Kings County, granted leave for the petitioner to file late notice of a wrongful death claim on the basis that the claim, under General Municipal Law, was filed within 90 days of the appointment of an estate administrator. As it was established that the school had knowledge of key details, including prior knowledge of concerns regarding the student's safety and evidence of communication between the student's coach and the petitioner after the shooting, the court also granted leave to file late notice for pain and suffering. Additionally, based on the school's status as "an independent and autonomous public school,"[51] the court ruled the City of New York and the New York City Department of Education as improper parties to the suit, not to be held liable for any allegations of negligence.[52]

Statute of Limitations Defense

The mother of a student who sustained the loss of two fingers in a bicycle chain accident after he was allegedly ordered off the school bus, told to walk home, and accepted a bicycle ride from another student, filed suit against the school district and district officials. Seeking damages for her son's injury, the plaintiff filed suit three times. The first action was voluntarily dismissed for defective service of process. The second action was also voluntarily dismissed. The third action resulted in the parties' engaging in several months of discovery, after which the defendants filed a

---

[50] Simpson Cnty. Sch. Dist. *ex rel.* Wigley v. Wigley as Next Friend of J.L.H., 356 So.3d 147, 412 Educ. L. Rep. 1032 (Miss. Ct. App. 2022).
[51] Watt v. Urban Dove Team Charter Sch., 185 N.Y.S.3d 606, 613, 414 Educ. L. Rep. 425 (N.Y. Super. Ct. 2023).
[52] Watt v. Urban Dove Team Charter Sch., 185 N.Y.S.3d 606, 414 Educ. L. Rep. 425 (N.Y. Super. Ct. 2023).

motion to dismiss on grounds that the statute of limitations had expired. The Mississippi Supreme Court ruled in favor of the plaintiff mother on the basis that the district defendants had waived the statute of limitations defense by failing to plead it in accordance with Mississippi Rule of Civil Procedure and without providing a reasonable explanation for such failure.[53]

Employee Claims

Work-related Injuries

A school psychologist sought damages for personal injuries after an alleged assault by a student with autism during her employment at a school. She brought an action for negligence and assault against the student and a claim for negligent parental supervision against the student's parents. The New York Supreme Court granted summary judgment dismissing the complaint against the student's parents but denied it against the student. On appeal, the court affirmed the dismissal of the complaint against the parents but reversed the denial of summary judgment against the student. The court held that the parents failed to demonstrate their entitlement to judgment as a matter of law as parents can be held liable if they negligently fail to prevent the child from engaging in dangerous behavior known to them. Regarding the student's liability, the court found that the argument of immunity due to a developmental disability consisted of inadmissible hearsay, and thus did not establish the student's immunity from liability.[54]

A school bus matron alleged she was injured when the school bus in which she was a passenger collided with another vehicle. She filed a personal injury action against the bus company and the bus driver, and the defendants moved for summary judgment based on the exclusivity provisions of the Workers' Compensation Law. Summary judgment was denied, and the Defendants appealed citing that the doctrine of collateral estoppel precluded them from disputing the matron's employer. The court affirmed the denial of summary judgment because the burden of proof had not

---

[53] Pruitt *ex rel.* Brooks v. Sargent, 349 So.3d 729, 409 Educ. L. Rep. 1016 (Miss. 2022).

[54] Levine v. George, 174 N.Y.S.3d 699, 408 Educ. L. Rep. 476 (N.Y. App. Div. 2022).

been met due to conflicting evidence regarding the matron's employer at the time of the accident.[55]

A pedestrian alleged she sustained personal injuries on a step located outside of a public school building in Queens, and she subsequently brought personal injury action against the city. The city was granted its motion for summary judgment, in which it argued that it does not operate, maintain, or control the school. The pedestrian appealed but failed to show that the city created the alleged defect or retained control over the premises to impose liability for any violation of the Administrative Code. The appellate court upheld the summary judgment in favor of the city.[56]

Claims by Other Injured Parties

While attending a school event in a commercial building, the plaintiff slipped and fell on a puddle of water created by a defective water cooler and sued the school, the commercial owner of the building, and the board of education for negligence. The school was granted a motion to dismiss two counts of the complaint, claiming immunity under section 2-105 of the Tort Immunity Act which provides immunity to local public entities for injuries caused by failure to inspect property they do not own. The plaintiff appealed, arguing the school's use of a defective water cooler created a dangerous condition. The appellate court reversed the dismissal, reinstated the two counts, and remanded the case for further proceedings.[57]

Defamation

A public high school principal in Georgia sued the school's assistant principal for libel and slander, among other torts, regarding what she viewed as defamatory statements he made about her alleged criminal arrest record and falsification of employment applications. A court of appeals affirmed the decision of the lower court on the basis that he was entitled to official immunity absent evidence he had either "negligently performed a ministerial act or had performed a

---

[55] Calixte v. City of New York, 172 N.Y.S.3d 50, 406 Educ. L. Rep. 338 (N.Y. App. Div. 2022).
[56] Giannikas v. City of New York, 178 N.Y.S.3d 138, 410 Educ. L. Rep. 489 (N.Y. App. Div. 2022).
[57] Williams v. Miracle Ctr., Inc., 206 N.E.3d 1088, 414 Educ. L. Rep. 974 (Ill. App. Div. 2022).

discretionary act with malice."[58] The assistant principal's complaint alleged the principal had failed to disclose a record of her criminal history. However, a previous appeal by the principal to an administrative law judge deemed her omission an honest mistake, as the previous criminal case against her had been expunged, and she believed it was, as a result, unnecessary to report it.[59]

Claims for defamation and tortious interference with prospective business relations were brought by an Irish Dance company and its owner from the United Kingdom against an Irish Dance teacher and members of the regional chapter of the Irish Dancing teachers' association after the teacher's students received an obscene video allegedly sent by the company, and the chapter subsequently withdrew approval it had previously granted for the U.K. company's owner to host a dance camp in the United States. The United States District Court for the Southern District of New York granted the defendants' motion to dismiss for failure to state claims. The court issued its ruling attributing common interest privilege to conversations and other communications taking place between the parties and stating the plaintiff's allegations for malice were insufficient to overcome privilege. The court also ruled that the defendants' withdrawal of approval to host the dance camp did not support the claim for tortious interference.[60]

A former teacher sued his former student and the student's attorney for defamation, alleging the student and his attorney sent letters to a private Pennsylvania school claiming the teacher had sexually abused the student when the student attended the school in the mid-1990s. After a two-week bench trial, but before conclusions could be drawn from the findings of fact, the student died in Wisconsin, where he resided. The United States District Court for the Eastern District of Pennsylvania held that under the Pennsylvania survival statute, the teacher's claim was not extinguished by the death of the former student. The court would stay the issuance of a judgment in the case, allowing time for the teacher to serve notice of death and to substitute a proper party for the student against whom he filed the suit.[61]

---

[58] Griffith v. Robinson, 884 S.E.2d 532, 534, 413 Educ. L. Rep. 978 (Ga. Ct. App. 2023).
[59] Griffith v. Robinson, 884 S.E.2d 532, 413 Educ. L. Rep. 978 (Ga. Ct. App. 2023).
[60] Hodges v. Lutwin, 595 F. Supp. 3d 12, 409 Educ. L. Rep. 752 (S.D.N.Y. 2022).
[61] Ralston v. Garabedian, 603 F. Supp. 3d 208, 411 Educ. L. Rep. 476 (E.D. Pa. 2022).

A piano tuner accused an Oregon school district theater technician, the technician's supervisor, and a district support services assistant for defamation in alleging that he "smelled of alcohol" and "appeared to be intoxicated"[62] at a time when he was assisting in the production of a school concert. The circuit court judge allowed the school district to be substituted for the individually named plaintiffs on the basis that the individuals were communicating about their concerns regarding the piano tuner within the scope of their employment. The court ruled in favor of the district, and the summary judgment was affirmed by the court of appeals. The Oregon Supreme Court reversed and remanded the decision, holding the district was not entitled to claim absolute privilege as this affirmative defense only applies when effective governance is threatened. In this case it did not apply, as the individual defendants were not "officers" or did not assume leadership positions in their roles as public employees.[63]

The Massachusetts state teachers' union (MTA) was accused of defamation by the former chief operating officer (COO) of a nonprofit conservative media outlet after the union posted a "look book" on its website revealing names and pictures of individuals associated with the media outlet. The United States District Court for the District of Massachusetts found the MTA was entitled to summary judgment on the basis that the union had no reason to question the veracity of the "look book," having received it from the national labor union. The court also reasoned that the statements made by the union in posting the material on its website were either not false statements or did not concern the former COO.[64]

Higher Education

Harms Involving Institutional Officials or Others

Six higher education cases involved harms to institutional officials or others. Two cases concerned medical care provided at

---

[62] Lowell v. Medford Sch. Dist. 549C, 515 P.3d 359, 360, 407 Educ. Law Rep. 291 (Or. 2022).

[63] Lowell v. Medford Sch. Dist. 549C, 515 P.3d 359, 407 Educ. Law Rep. 291 (Or. 2022).

[64] Landino v. Mass. Teachers Ass'n, 621 F. Supp. 3d 185, 415 Educ. L. Rep. 15 (D. Mass. 2022) [appeal filed].

university hospitals and two involved motor vehicles. Hazing at a university sorority was the subject of another.

Alleging that a government-employed physician failed to properly diagnose and treat a patient for concussion after she sustained injuries playing field hockey at a D.C. university, the patient and former student filed suit against the United States for negligence and medical malpractice. The district court found in the patient's favor, awarding her $1,037,047 in economic damages and $800,000 in non-economic damages, the latter reduced by 5% in light of her suffering a subsequent concussion. The court found that the physician was neither an agent of the university nor the university's borrowed servant at the time he treated the patient and, thus, not covered under the university's waiver of liability. Rather, the court held that the physician did have a duty of care to the patient and that he breached the applicable standard of care by not properly diagnosing her concussion, which resulted in life-impacting, permanent symptoms and conditions extensively documented in this case.[65]

After an emergency room patient complaining of chest and neck pain died of an aortic dissection the day following his discharge from a university hospital in West Virginia (WVUH), his estate filed suit against the supervising faculty physician and resident physician for negligence, saying the doctors should have recognized the condition, ordered imaging to confirm, and intervened with a surgical procedure that would have prevented death. The court of appeals reversed the circuit court's denial of the university hospital's motion to dismiss, which was converted into summary judgment. This case distinguished between the Board of Risk and Insurance Management (BRIM) statutes and the general West Virginia state statutes in providing appropriate liability insurance coverage for state medical and dental schools and those employed by and associated with them. Under BRIM, coverage is provided to physicians per occurrence rather than per defendant physician, thus insulating WVUH from ostensible agency liability.[66]

Along with their relatives, subjects of federally funded experiments conducted in Guatemala that allegedly infected

---

[65] Bradley v. United States, 619 F. Supp. 3d 36, 414 Educ. L. Rep. 311 (D.C. Cir. 2022).

[66] State *ex rel.* W. Va. Univ. Hosps., Inc. v. Gaujot, 886 S.E.2d 346, 415 Educ. L. Rep. 372 (W. Va. 2023).

prisoners and psychiatric patients with syphilis without their consent filed suit under the Alien Tort Statute against various divisions of Johns Hopkins University and individuals associated with the University. The district court granted the defendants' motion for summary judgment and dismissed the plaintiffs' cross-motion. In a lengthy case, the court assessed various doctors' roles as to whether the evidence presented was sufficient to show a violation of the law of nations for their role in funding the experiments as the funding recommendation for the Guatemala Experiments was the basis of the plaintiffs' cause of action. Issues of consent and agency were examined. Ultimately, the court expressed frustration in its judgment in favor of the defendants, noting that "rulings in a court of law, as opposed to the reasoned judgments of historians, must be grounded in admissible evidence" which the court finds, in this case, is insufficient.[67] The court further cited moral concerns regarding the experiments, but lamented this case as an "illustrat[ion of] the limits of the court system to provide justice for every injustice."[68]

In a case that largely focused on the statute of limitations regarding the filing of a new complaint after the plaintiff unilaterally dismissed her previous complaint without prejudice, an invitee sought damages from a Mississippi university after she was injured when forced off the road as she walked back to her car after attending a university baseball game. Jumping out of the way to avoid being hit by an ATV driven by a university employee, she tripped and fell, breaking her arm. The circuit court dismissed the case on the basis that the plaintiff's complaint had exceeded the statute of limitations. However, the court of appeals reversed the circuit court's decision, reasoning that the plaintiff's dismissal of her first complaint did not stop tolling the statute of limitations under the Mississippi Tort Claims Act. The appeals court also held that the defendants were not entitled to immunity and that the plaintiff stated a viable claim for relief. The case was remanded so that issues regarding negligence on the part of the university could either be brought to trial or raised in a motion for summary judgment.[69]

---

[67] Estate of Alvarez v. Johns Hopkins Univ., 598 F. Supp. 3d 301, 410 Educ. L. Rep. 304 (D. Md. 2022), appeal filed.

[68] Id. at 347.

[69] Keever v. Bd. of Trs. for Miss. Insts. Of Higher Learning, 343 So.3d 400, 406 Educ. L. Rep. 1063 (Miss. Ct. App. 2022).

When a sorority member died by suicide after initiation-related hazing at an Illinois university, her mother brought suit on behalf of her estate against the sorority under the Illinois Wrongful Death Act and the Illinois Survival Act, arguing that she was entitled to receive the sorority's investigative report regarding her daughter's death. While the sorority claimed the report was protected under attorney-client privilege and as work product, the district court disagreed, finding in favor of the plaintiff. Through an *in camera* review, the court determined the document had not been prepared to provide legal assistance and that, even absent litigation, the document would have been prepared anyway as its purpose was to investigate allegations of hazing at the university. Having determined this, the court found it unnecessary to address the defendants' claim that the document was protected as a work product.[70]

When the plaintiff, a passenger in a car rear-ended by the defendant, filed a negligence action against the defendant, the issue became whether the statute of limitations had tolled against the defendant, with her residence in question between her home in Texas and her enrollment as a student at Harvard University in Massachusetts. Also in question was the plaintiff's failure to initially name the other motorist as a defendant and whether the other named defendants bore any responsibility to reveal the omission. The trial court rejected the plaintiff's allegation of fraudulent concealment against the defendant and overruled the plaintiff's claim that the statute of limitations was tolled against the defendant driver. A court of appeals affirmed.[71]

Defamation

Four higher education cases focused on defamation. Two of the cases involved alleged insensitive speech from university administrators.

Alumni fraternity members brought a claim for defamation against the president of a private university and *The Washington Post* after the president remarked that members of the fraternity

---

[70] Hankins v. Alpha Kappa Alpha Sorority, Inc., 619 F. Supp. 3d 828, 414 Educ. L. Rep. 364 (N.D. Ill. 2021).
[71] Ferrer v. Almanza, 647 S.W.3d 726, 406 Educ. L. Rep. 529 (Tex. App. 2021).

had "become the face of systemic racism in our community."[72] This referred both to a photo that surfaced of members wearing robes reminiscent of the Ku Klux Klan, offering a "Bellamy salute" which evoked similarities to Nazis and Fascists. Determining that the president, in her speech, spoke only to a group and did not name individuals, and that two plaintiffs were not even among those fraternity members in the photograph, the D.C. district court found that neither the president's statements nor *The Washington Post* article could be interpreted by any reasonable person as defamatory against any individual. The court went on to cite the speech as opinion based upon true facts either already known by readers or revealed to them. On this basis the court found in favor of the defendants and granted a motion to dismiss the case. with prejudice.[73]

A letter was submitted to a university's dean and provost by faculty members in New York alleging a fellow faculty member allegedly used intimidation tactics and hate speech in his class. The faculty member who was the subject of the letter brought an action for defamation against his colleagues. The defendants requested dismissal for failure to state a claim, alleging the suit was "a strategic lawsuit against public participation (SLAPP) brought in retaliation for exercising their free speech rights on issues of public interest."[74] The state supreme court dismissed the complaint for failure to state a claim, but denied dismissal under SLAPP. The appellate court deemed the letter an internal complaint rather than one about a topic of public interest, affirming the suit was not a SLAPP suit and saying the letter was not actionable. [75]

The former dean at a public college in New York City brought a cause of action for defamation against the college and its president in regard to a letter published responding to community concerns about allegedly culturally insensitive accessories that appeared as part of a college-sponsored fashion show. An appellate court, affirming the lower court's granting the president and

---

[72] Florio v. Gallaudet Univ., 619 F. Supp. 3d 36, 40, 414 Educ. L. Rep. 298 (D.C. Cir. 2022). [appeal filed].
[73] Florio v. Gallaudet Univ., 619 F. Supp. 3d 36, 414 Educ. L. Rep. 298 (D.C. Cir. 2022). [appeal filed].
[74] Miller v. Appadurai, 185 N.Y.S.3d 93, 93, 414 Educ. L. Rep. 413 (N.Y. App. Div. 2023).
[75] Miller v. Appadurai, 185 N.Y.S.3d 93, 414 Educ. L. Rep. 413 (N.Y. App. Div. 2023).

college's motion to dismiss for failure to state a claim, held that while the letter was not defamatory on its face, it was susceptible to defamatory connotation, which precluded its dismissal. The court reasoned that the letter implied that the plaintiff had responsibility for the show, despite the fact she did not participate in either its production, direction, or management, nor was she aware of the accessories selected by the show's designers. The letter also neglected to mention either the college's policy disallowing academic deans from vetting the work of students or alumni, or the plaintiff's speedy response to addressing concerns that arose regarding the event.[76]

After the suicide of his son, a father filed suit for defamation against his son's university classmate in Texas based upon the classmate's Facebook posts and for statements the classmate allegedly made in response to what was perceived as threats made by the deceased. These statements, shared by the classmate with the university administration, allegedly caused the classmate to feel unsafe attending class with the decedent, leading the administration to remove the decedent from class. The plaintiff believed the statements and action taken to remove his son from class led to his son's suicide, on the basis that the statements damaged his son's reputation and caused him mental anguish. The district court ruled in favor of the defendant, finding the plaintiff had not established any indication of falsity in the defendant's social media posts, had not defamed the deceased, and had established truth as an affirmative defense.[77]

Dangerous Conditions on Campuses

Five higher education cases involved dangerous conditions on campus. One involved campus maintenance and university design of roadways. Four cases involved falls, with plaintiffs alleging failure on the part of the universities to warn of hazardous conditions or to provide lighting that would mitigate the possibility of danger.

After a motorist sustained injuries in a one-car crash at an intersection maintained by a public Texas university, he filed suit against the university for premises-defect. The motorist alleged that the university, which had changed the intersection from a

---

[76] Davis v. Brown, 181 N.Y.S.3d 34, 411 Educ. L. Rep. 734 (N.Y. App. Div. 2022).
[77] Klocke v. Watson, 597 F. Supp. 3d 1019, 410 Educ. L. Rep. 214 (N.D. Tex. 2022).

four-way intersection to a T-intersection, needed to have provided a better design for the intersection and included warning signs and better lighting to ensure drivers would not land in a ditch. The plaintiff, after having the opportunity to inspect design plans for the intersection, did not allege the work was subpar, the materials defective, or that the university failed to maintain proper safety measures. The Texas Supreme Court affirmed the decision of the court of appeals ordering the case dismissed, saying that, as the omission of signage or lighting is discretionary on the part of the government agency, and that the ditch into which the motorist drove his car was not a "special defect," the decision of the university was subject to immunity under the Tort Claims Act.[78]

A university student in Colorado filed a claim for premises liability against the university after he slipped on imperceptibly wet dormitory stairs, suffering a dislocated shoulder needing two surgeries to repair. The appellate court ruled for the student, finding the district court erred in its decision in favor of the university on the basis of immunity under the Colorado Governmental Immunity Act (CGIA). The appellate court's analysis revealed that, in accordance with the student's claim that danger posed by the wet dormitory steps was difficult to discern on account of their black color and the fact that the university had failed to post any warning of the potential for a slip-and-fall accident to take place, in fact created a "dangerous condition" per the CGIA, based upon the university's duty of maintenance rather than faulty design of the facility.[79]

The third-party defendant, a Louisiana charter school association, sought review of a trial court decision granting no cause of action in a slip-and-fall injury that occurred at a graduation ceremony held at a university arena rented out to a school owned and operated by the association. The woman sustaining the injury alleged it was caused by negligence on the part of the association, the university where the graduation took place, and the association's insurer in failing to properly light the arena and warn guests of hazardous conditions. In a de novo review, an appellate court reversed the decision of the district court, saying that the university adequately pled facts to establish the existence of its contract with the association and a cause of

---

[78] Fraley v. Tex. A&M Univ. Sys., 664 S.W.3d 91, 415 Educ. L. Rep. 387 (Tex. 2023).
[79] Galef v. Univ. of Colo., 520 P.3d 184, 409 Educ. L. Rep. 957 (Colo. App. 2022).

action alleging a breach of that contract regarding the provision of, among other things, indemnification of the university and proof of insurance.[80]

Injured in a slip-and-fall incident during a preparatory school graduation that took place at a public university arena, the plaintiff filed a cause of action against the state through the state university system alleging negligence on the part of the university to properly light the facility. The plaintiff claimed that that failure to do so created "an unreasonable risk of harm," with her fall as the "foreseeable outcome of this failure," causing her to undergo various surgeries.[81] The state filed a third-party demand against the charter school association (that owned and operated the preparatory school) and its insurer for breach of contract in denying coverage to the state under the charter school's policy for general liability. The district court granted the insurer's peremptory exception of no cause, and the appellate court reversed the district court's ruling in a de novo review, saying the state had a valid cause of action for breach of contract against the insurer of the charter school association. Whether the state was additionally afforded coverage was deemed by the appellate court as not ripe for review.[82]

While attending a funeral repast at a university facility, a woman fell and broke her ankle when she became dizzy from excessive heat in the facility due to the failure of the AC/HVAC system. She and her husband brought claims for negligence and premises liability against the university, later amending their suit to include the Board of Supervisors, the University System, and the State of Louisiana. The district court granted the university defendants the exception of no cause of action and dismissed claims against them with prejudice. Ruling that the issue of whether or not the temperature in the building was a dangerous condition "open and obvious to all who encountered it" (cite to case at 455), the appellate court, hearing the case *de novo* as it raised a question of law, determined that "whether or not the high temperature in the [...] building was open and obvious to everyone is arguably an

---

[80] Ross v. State *ex rel.* Univ. of La. Sys. (b), 358 So.3d 162, 414 Educ. L. Rep. 768 (La. Ct. App. 2023).

[81] Ross v. State *ex rel.* Univ. of La. Sys. (a), 352 So.3d 90, 92, 411 Educ. L. Rep. 858 (La. Ct. App. 2022).

[82] Ross v. State *ex rel.* Univ. of La. Sys. (a), 352 So.3d 90, 411 Educ. L. Rep. 858 (La. Ct. App. 2022).

issue for the trier of fact to decide,"[83] reversing the action of the trial court and remanding it to the trial court for further action.[84]

Sexual Assault

The victim of alleged sexual assault appealed the decision of the lower court which granted the defendants' motion to dismiss charges of negligence in failing to prevent members of a university fraternity from sexually assaulting her. An appellate court dismissed the appeal on the grounds that it was time-barred and that the court lacked personal jurisdiction over the matter. The court held the victim's appeal was moot on the basis that she had failed to challenge the specific grounds on which the lower court based their adverse ruling on her claim.[85]

A visitor to a fraternity Halloween party in Missouri brought charges for negligence and premises liability against the fraternity and the association which owned the fraternity house after she allegedly was sexually assaulted while at the party. An appellate court affirmed the decision of the circuit court granting summary judgment for the defendants on the basis that the visitor was a licensee at the party, not an invitee. In Missouri, a social guest receiving an invitation is considered a licensee, and the plaintiff's argument that she was an invitee as the fraternity was recruiting new members and the party was a way to "aid men in their social development"[86] failed. The appellate court also ruled that the association had no prior knowledge of the alleged assailant that would have precipitated an obligation to protect the visitor, and that neither the international fraternity nor the association had either premises liability duty to a visitor nor a duty to supervise a fraternity member. The court reasoned that, in general in Missouri, there is "no legal duty in negligence to protect someone from a third-party criminal attack."[87]

---

[83] George v. ABC Ins. Co., 351 So.3d 447, 456, 410 Educ. L. Rep. 820 (La. Ct. App. 2022).

[84] George v. ABC Ins. Co., 351 So.3d 447, 410 Educ. L. Rep. 820 (La. Ct. App. 2022).

[85] Doe v. Quinnipiac Univ., 291 A.3d 153, 414 Educ. L. Rep. 598 (Conn. App. Ct. 2023).

[86] A.R.R. v. Tau Kappa Epsilon Fraternity, Inc., 649 S.W.3d 1, 12, 407 Educ. L. Rep. 228 (Mo. Ct. App. W.D. 2022).

[87] A.R.R. v. Tau Kappa Epsilon Fraternity, Inc., 649 S.W.3d 1, 6, 407 Educ. L. Rep. 228 (Mo. Ct. App. W.D. 2022).

Conclusion

The vast majority of the tort cases this year were state cases, with a large number coming from New York. Many addressed issues alleging negligence, and often school districts and their employees filed motions for summary judgment due to claims of immunity or missed timelines. A number of cases also involved de novo review by appellate courts, cases that had been amended and/or refiled, and courts seeking to determine insurer liability. Regardless of the ruling, many claims were subsequently appealed to a higher court.

Based upon the wide variety of complaints, it was difficult to clearly determine whether schools/universities were more successful in these causes of action or those filing suit against them, yet some patterns did emerge in the decisions of the courts. In the area of defamation, the courts consistently ruled in favor of the defendants in higher education but were split in elementary and secondary education. In cases having to do with dangerous conditions on either school premises or campuses, the courts almost always found in favor of the defendants. And finally, in filings for assault and sexual assault, the largest classification of torts cases summarized this year, decisions were split evenly among plaintiffs and defendants in elementary and secondary education. The two sexual assault cases in higher education resulted in rulings for the defendant universities.

Alphabetical List of Cases

A.M. v. N.Y. City Dept. of Educ.

A.P. *ex rel.* Pyscher v. A.P.

A.R.R. v. Tau Kappa Epsilon Fraternity, Inc.

Annitto v. Smithtown Cent. Sch. Dist.

Anonymous v. Castagnola

Boyle v. Brewster Cent. Sch. Dist.

Bradley v. United States

C.I. v. San Bernardino City Unified Sch. Dist.

C.N. v. City of New York

C.W. v. Roselle Bd. of Educ.

Calixte v. City of New York

Christensen v. Broken Bow Pub. Schs.

Dannenfelser v. Squires

Davis v. Brown

Devore for Horton v. Samuel

Doe #2 v. Legion of Christ, Inc.

Doe v. City of New Haven

Doe v. Marysville Joint Unified Sch. Dist.

Doe v. Quinnipiac Univ.

Doe *ex rel.* Hauppauge Union Free Sch. Dist. v. Hauppauge Union Free Sch. Dist.

El Paso Indep. Sch. Dist. v. De La Rosa

Estate of Alvarez v. Johns Hopkins Univ.

Estate of Johnson *ex rel.* Johnson v. Guilford Cnty. Bd. of Educ.

Ex parte Williamson

Ferrer v. Almanza

Florio v. Gallaudet Univ.

Fraley v. Texas A&M Univ. Sys.

Galef v. Univ. of Colo.

Gambrill v. Bd. of Educ. of Dorchester Cnty.

George v. ABC Ins. Co.

Giannikas v. City of New York

Green v. E. Carroll Par. Sch. Dist./Bd.

Griffith v. Robinson

Hall v. Acker

Hankins v. Alpha Kappa Alpha Sorority, Inc.

Hauburger v. McMane

Henderson v. Capdeville

Hodges v. Lutwin

J.D. *ex rel.* Mingo v. McComb Sch. Dist.

J.H.V. *ex rel.* Locust Valley Cent. Sch. Dist.

Jefferson Cnty. Pub. Schs. v. Tudor, Next Friend of J.T.

Jones v. Logan Cnty. Bd. of Educ.

K.M. v. Grossmont Union High Sch. Dist.

Keever v. Bd. of Trs. for Miss. Insts. of Higher Learning

Klocke v. Watson

Landino v. Mass. Teachers Ass'n

Levine v. George

Lowell v. Medford Sch. Dist.

M.O. *ex rel.* Lopez v. City of New York

M.S. *ex rel.* v. Rye Neck Union Free Sch. Dist.

Martin v. Wallace

Miller v. Appadurai

Novak v. Sisters of the Heart of Mary

Pruitt *ex rel.* Brooks v. Sargent

R.B. v. Sewanhaka Cent. High Sch. Dist.

R.M. *ex rel.* Bd. of Educ. of Long Beach City Sch. Dist.

R.P. v. First Student Inc.

Ralston v. Garabedian

Roe v. Hesperia Unified Sch. Dist.

Roe *ex rel.* Harborfields Cent. Sch. Dist.

Ross v. State *ex rel.* Univ. of La. Sys. (a)

Ross v. State *ex rel.* Univ. of La. Sys. (b)

S.G. v. Harlem Village Acad. Charter Sch.

S.S. v. Sch. Bd. of Sarasota Cnty.

Simpson Cnty. Sch. Dist. *ex rel.* Wigley v. Wigley as Next Friend of J.L.H.

SR v. Gates Chili Bd. of Educ.

State *ex rel.* W.V. Univ. Hosps., Inc. v. Gaujot

Sullivan v. St. Ephrem Roman Catholic Par. Church

Tousant v. Aragona

Victor Valley Union High Sch. Dist. v. Super. Ct. of San Bernardino Cnty.

W.S. v. Hildreth

Watt v. Urban Dove Team Charter Sch.

Williams v. Miracle Ctr., Inc.

Federal Cases

First Circuit

Massachusetts
Landino v. Mass. Teachers Ass'n

Second Circuit

Connecticut
Doe #2 v. Legion of Christ, Inc.

New York
Hodges v. Lutwin

Third Circuit

Pennsylvania
Ralston v. Garabedian

Fourth Circuit

Maryland
Estate of Alvarez v. Johns Hopkins Univ.

Fifth Circuit

Texas
Klocke v. Watson

Sixth Circuit

Michigan
A.P. *ex rel.* Pyscher v. A.P.

Seventh Circuit

Illinois
Hankins v. Alpha Kappa Alpha Sorority, Inc.

D.C. Circuit

Bradley v. United States
Florio v. Gallaudet Univ.

State and D.C. Cases

Alabama
Ex parte Williamson

California
C.I. v. San Bernardino City Unified Sch. Dist.
Doe v. Marysville Joint Unified Sch. Dist.
K.M. v. Grossmont Union High Sch. Dist.
Roe v. Hesperia Unified Sch. Dist.
Victor Valley Union High Sch. Dist. v. Super. Ct. of San Bernardino Cnty.

Colorado
Galef v. Univ. of Colo.

Connecticut
Doe v. City of New Haven
Doe v. Quinnipiac Univ.

Florida
S.S. v. Sch. Bd. of Sarasota Cnty.

Georgia
Dannenfelser v. Squires
Griffith v. Robinson
Hall v. Acker

Illinois
Williams v. Miracle Ctr., Inc.

Kansas
R.P. v. First Student Inc.

Kentucky
Jefferson Cnty. Pub. Schs. v. Tudor, Next Friend of J.T.
Martin v. Wallace

Louisiana
George v. ABC Ins. Co.
Green v. E. Carroll Par. Sch. Dist./Bd.
Henderson v. Capdeville
Ross v. State *ex rel.* Univ. of La. Sys. (a)

Ross v. State *ex rel.* Univ. of La. Sys. (b)

Maryland
Gambrill v. Bd. of Educ. of Dorchester Cnty.

Mississippi
J.D. *ex rel.* Mingo v. McComb Sch. Dist.
Keever v. Bd. of Trs. for Miss. Insts. Of Higher Learning
Pruitt *ex rel.* Brooks v. Sargent
Simpson Cnty. Sch. Dist. *ex rel.* Wigley v. Wigley as Next Friend of J.L.H.

Missouri
A.R.R. v. Tau Kappa Epsilon Fraternity, Inc.

Nebraska
Christensen v. Broken Bow Pub. Schs.

New Jersey
C.W. v. Roselle Bd. of Educ.
W.S. v. Hildreth

New York
A.M. v. N.Y. City Dept. of Educ.
Annitto v. Smithtown Cent. Sch. Dist.
Anonymous v. Castagnola
Boyle v. Brewster Cent. Sch. Dist.
C.N. v. City of New York
Calixte v. City of New York
Davis v. Brown
Doe *ex rel.* Hauppauge Union Free Sch. Dist. v. Hauppauge Union Free Sch. Dist.
Giannikas v. City of New York
Hauburger v. McMane
J.H.V. v. Locust Valley Cent. Sch. Dist.
Levine v. George
M.O. *ex rel.* Lopez v. City of New York
M.S. *ex rel.* Rye Neck Union Free Sch. Dist.
Miller v. Appadurai
Novak v. Sisters of Heart of Mary
R.B. v. Sewanhaka Cent. High Sch. Dist.
R.M. *ex rel.* Bd. of Educ. of Long Beach City Sch. Dist.
Roe *ex rel.* Harborfields Cent. Sch. Dist.

S.G. v. Harlem Village Acad. Charter Sch.
SR v. Gates Chili Bd. of Educ.
Sullivan v. St. Ephrem Roman Catholic Par. Church
Tousant v. Aragona
Watt v. Urban Dove Team Charter Sch.

North Carolina
Devore for Horton v. Samuel
Estate of Johnson *ex rel.* Johnson v. Guilford Cnty. Bd. of Educ.

Oregon
Lowell v. Medford Sch. Dist. 549C

Texas
El Paso Ind. Sch. Dist. v. De La Rosa
Ferrer v. Almanza
Fraley v. Tex. A&M Univ. Sys.

West Virginia
Jones v. Logan Cnty. Bd. of Educ.
State *ex rel.* W. Va. Univ. Hosps., Inc. v. Gaujot

This page is intentionally left blank.

CHAPTER 7

SPORTS

Gillian P. Foss and Joy Blanchard

Introduction

This chapter reviews litigation from 2023 addressing issues in sports in K–12 schools and higher education. The legal issues of both sectors were reflective of athlete injury negligence claims, Title IX equity and sex discrimination suits from marginalized student-athletes, and employment-related incidents on myriad fronts, among other topics. Some cases may also appear in other chapters due to intersecting topics (e.g., student rights in higher education, employees, and torts).

Discrimination

Title IX and Equity

An Ohio district court granted all motions for dismissal in favor of the defendants—comprised of a Cincinnati school district, youth volleyball league, and youth sports organization—after a disgruntled parent filed suit on the basis of a Title IX equity violation, breach of contract, and intentional infliction of emotional distress.[1] The parent, and subsequently his student-athlete, had been banned from participation in the youth volleyball league for ambiguous reasons following a previous incident where the parent had filed a police report against a league referee who was making explicit sexual remarks toward the female athletes. Despite the court's finding that the reasons for the plaintiff's ban stemmed from rather unspecific violations of the league's code of conduct, they held the plaintiff's Title IX and intentional infliction of emotional distress claims to be without merit due to their inability to show concerted harm.[2]

A group of female student-athletes sought a preliminary injunction after the public university, citing budget constraints, announced it would discontinue its men's and women's varsity swimming and diving programs. After an initial denial, on appeal a federal district court granted the motion for an injunction while the plaintiffs pursued their Title IX gender equity claims. The

---

[1] Doe v. BMG Sports, 584 F. Supp. 3d 497, 407 Educ. L. Rep. 556 (S.D. Ohio 2022).
[2] *Id.* at 509.

court also required the university to submit to the court a Title IX compliance plan.[3]

The Eighth Circuit upheld a trial court's decision not to grant an injunction after a public university eliminated its men's gymnastics team. The court affirmed the prior court's finding that the claim failed to meet the "irreparable harm" standard in order to grant the injunction. The court noted that because the team staff had been laid off and only five players remained at the university, it was questionable if the plaintiffs could even compete. The court also found it unreasonable that plaintiffs waited 13 months to file their initial complaint. [4]

A former coach sued for retaliation after his contract was not renewed after complaining to the university's athletic department administrators about a lack of gender equity. The district court dismissed the claims, finding that he had not demonstrated how nonrenewal of his term-limited contract was an adverse employment decision. On appeal, the Ninth Circuit reversed that decision and remanded for further proceedings.[5]

Title IX and Sex Discrimination

In Indiana, a 10-year-old transgender student and the student's mother filed suit after Indianapolis Public Schools officials informed the student that a 2022 Indiana state statute[6] would prevent her from being able to play on the girls' softball team. The student, who had identified as female for years and whose record of gender dysphoria made the prospect of playing on the boy's baseball team traumatic, argued successfully alongside five other transgender student-athletes to the district court that being prohibited from participating on the girls' softball team would constitute a Title IX violation on the basis of sex.[7] Upon finding a flaw in district officials' interpretation of the state statute, namely the lack of legal recourse for the student-athlete to participate in sports, the court held that the plaintiff's Title IX

---

[3] Balow v. Mich. State Univ., 620 F. Supp. 3d 694, 414 Educ. L. Rep. 827 (W.D. Mich. 2022).

[4] Ng v. Bd. of Regents of Univ. of Minn., 64 F.4th 992, 413 Educ. L. Rep. 650 (8th Cir. 2023).

[5] MacIntyre v. Carroll Coll., 48 F.4th 950, 408 Educ. L. Rep. 62 (9th Cir. 2022).

[6] see Ind. Code § 20-33-13-4 (2024).

[7] A.M. by E.M. v. Indianapolis Pub. Sch., 617 F. Supp. 3d 950 (2022).

argument had merit, granting their motion for a preliminary injunction and denying the defendant's motion to dismiss the suit.

In another suit pertaining to transgender student athletes, the U.S. Court of Appeals for the Second Circuit presided over a case brought about by four cisgender track-and-field athletes, who argued the Connecticut Interscholastic Athletic Conference's policy regarding transgender student-athletes was in violation of Title IX.[8] The court of appeals affirmed the trial court's dismissal of the plaintiff's claims, which sought to both render the conference's transgender policy unenforceable and retroactively adjust all athletic records to reflect this change. As with the trial court and other court of appeals, the plaintiff's Title IX complaint was dismissed on the mere notion that there was no sufficient evidence that the conference's transgender participation policy was wielded to intentionally harm cisgender athletes.[9]

A male wrestler who had been held down by his coaches and teammates to forcibly cut his hair before a match appealed the trial court's granting of summary judgment toward the school district defendants, tailoring his argument specifically to a gender-based violation of the Missouri Human Rights Act.[10] Specifically, he argued that he was subject to the emotionally distressing haircut as a male athlete, when in fact he could have opted to wear a hair covering in the same manner as the female wrestler on his team. On this appeal, the court found merit, reversing and remanding the claim of sex discrimination for further deliberation under Missouri Human Rights Act parameters.[11]

In California, a female student-athlete had enjoyed success as a starting wide receiver on her high school's football team until—after a scrimmage against a competing Christian school during which she only revealed her gender by taking off her helmet after the game—the opposing school officials informed her that she would not be allowed to compete in subsequent games against their

---

[8] Soule *ex rel.* Stanescu v. Conn. Ass'n of Schs., Inc., 57 F.4th 43, 411 Educ. L. Rep. 41 (2d Cir. 2022).

[9] *Id.* at 56.

[10] J.H. *ex rel.* Meudt-Antele v. Jefferson City Pub. Sch. Dist., 661 S.W.3d 353, 413 Educ. L. Rep. 477 (Mo. Ct. App. 2023).

[11] *Id.* at 359 ("We conclude that the inconsistencies in Coach Werdehausen's deposition testimony, coupled with the deposition testimony of Coach Whelan and J.H. himself create a genuine factual issue as to whether male wrestlers with long hair were provided the same accommodations as female wrestlers.")

team.[12] The school argued its decision came in its effort to "respect the 'guiding principles of the Bible regarding the care of a woman.'"[13] The plaintiff's resulting Title IX argument was successful and resulted in a dismissal of the defendant's request for summary judgment, as the court agreed with her arguments that (a) the defending school had benefited from federal funds in the form of paycheck protection program (PPP) loans, negating its religious exemption; (b) the conduct fell within Title IX constraints after occurring on the defendant's grounds; and (c) the "Title IX clearly does apply to contact sports"[14] and would hence apply to the female student's participation in football.

The Sixth Circuit ruled in two separate proceedings against a state university that had employed for decades a doctor who allegedly abused hundreds of student-athletes while serving as team doctor. The plaintiffs in the various lawsuits alleged that the university knew of the abuse yet failed to act appropriately, in violation of Title IX reporting provisions. A district court had ruled that the claims were time-barred, but on appeal the court found that the time for the claim did not accrue until plaintiffs knew or reasonably should have known that the defendant university caused injury—which would have been when administrators with authority to take corrective action knew of the physician's action. The plaintiffs were teenagers and young adults at the time of the abuse, and did not know to question what was medically appropriate or not. They also could not have known that other victims had complained to the university, nor how the university responded, until the report from an independent investigation was released in 2018.[15]

A federal district court dismissed claims against a public university when the survivors of sexual abuse by a former hockey coach filed suit. The court opinion traced a lengthy history of abuse on the part of the coach across several institutions and organizations. The court dismissed the federal claims (Section 1983 and Title IX) for lack of jurisdiction, noting the alleged abuse of the plaintiffs occurred years after the defendant university had

---

[12] E.H. *ex rel.* Herrera v. Valley Christian Acad., 616 F. Supp. 3d 1040, 413 Educ. L. Rep. 852 (C.D. Cal. 2022).
[13] *Id.* at 1044.
[14] *Id.* at 1054.
[15] Garrett v. Ohio State Univ., 60 F.4th 359, 411 Educ. L. Rep. 1002 (6th Cir. 2023) and Snyder-Hill v. Ohio State Univ., 48 F.4th 686, 408 Educ. L. Rep. 26 (6th Cir. 2022).

terminated the coach's employment. The court referred the 28 state law claims to the appropriate venue.[16]

Race-Based Discrimination

An eastern Pennsylvania district court denied a plaintiff's further pursual of sanctions against school district officials following the district's failure to produce a final version of a reprimand letter toward key personnel accused of racial discrimination during the initial proceedings.[17] The litigation had come about after a Black wrestling coach filed suit for racial discrimination under Title VII of the Civil Rights Act of 1964, arguing the school's athletic director and principal, among others, engaged in hostile workplace behaviors that reflected undue retaliation and treatment toward him on the basis of race. The plaintiff had been successful in his claims and received compensatory damages after the trial; given the prior ruling and the plaintiff's inability to argue that the district officials withheld the reprimand letter in bad faith, the court determined this subsequent motion for sanctions to be moot.[18]

An embattled former junior varsity basketball coach in New York pursued claims of race and gender discrimination, in addition to deprivation of due process under the Fourth and Fourteenth Amendments,[19] after a school and law enforcement investigation of accusations that he had groomed and sexually assaulted one of his student-athletes. The plaintiff argued the investigation arose not from actual allegations of misbehavior, but from the then-school superintendent's personal agenda, as he was dating the same colleague as the coach at the time. Though the plaintiff was found not guilty on all charges, he argued the multi-year investigation caused irreparable harm to his well-being and reputation, especially as one of the few Black men in the community. Although the court dismissed most of the plaintiff's claims, where he did have

---

[16] Sacks v. Univ. of Minn., 600 F. Supp. 3d 915, 410 Educ. L. Rep. 938 (D. Minn. 2022).
[17] Billman v. Easton Area School District, 620 F. Supp. 3d 215 (2022).
[18] *Id.* at 223.
[19] Watkins v. Town of Webster, 592 F. Supp. 3d 96, 408 Educ. L. Rep. 828 (W.D.N.Y. 2022).

some success concerned the equal protection claim after arguing differential treatment from the White colleagues.[20]

The U.S. Court of Appeals for the Seventh Circuit upheld a lower court ruling that the plaintiff, a White man, was insufficiently persuasive in his pursuit of a reverse race discrimination claim after falling short on two prospective athletic administration job opportunities in South Bend, Indiana.[21] Both positions were eventually filled by Black applicants, and the plaintiff argued his professional experience in the field and lack of any prior misconduct made clear that these hiring decisions were based on race alone. The court of appeals, echoing the lower court's decision, found no indication that the school district's hiring pattern was based on race, nor did they find that the plaintiff's experience was more substantive than the other candidates—in fact, the hiring committee's concerns about the plaintiff's candidacy came twice from problematic responses to interview questions, further removing the factor of race from the decision-making process.[22]

Negligence

Athlete Injury

Following an on-field skirmish between two high school football players during which one player in particular sustained serious injuries, an appellate court in Louisiana affirmed the earlier trial court ruling granting summary judgment on behalf of the defendant, the opposing school.[23] The court held that school officials had provided reasonable supervision of players during the game, in addition to having a record of emphasizing values of player safety and sportsmanship during practices; as such, the physical altercation initiated by their player was unforeseeable

---

[20] *Id.* at 126 ("Whether Plaintiff can provide evidence supporting his claim that Principal Benz and AP Goodwine were involved in violations of his right to equal protection remains to be seen but, at this stage of the litigation, his claim against them may proceed to discovery.").

[21] Groves v. S. Bend Cmty. Sch. Corp., 51 F.4th 766, 408 Educ. L. Rep. 705 (7th Cir. 2022).

[22] *Id.* at 771.

[23] Slack *ex rel.* C.S. v. Copeland, 343 So.3d 346, 406 Educ. L. Rep. 1053 (La. Ct. App. 2022).

and precluded the school from the prongs needed to satisfy a negligence claim.

Another appellate court, this time in Ohio, affirmed a trial court's earlier granting of summary judgment in favor of the defendant school district and baseball coach accused of negligent behavior that resulted in a student-athlete's injury. The player sustained a serious eye injury during an indoor batting practice to the extent that his eye needed to be removed. The basis of the plaintiff's appeal rested on the trial court erring in two areas: (a) excluding the statement of an expert witness, which the plaintiff felt was relevant in arguing that the coach knowingly put the players at risk with faulty equipment; and (b) holding that the defendants were entitled to the protection of sovereign immunity.[24] The appellate court ruled that the facts of the case showed the coach to have clearly neglected to consider safety during their equipment decisions, and subsequently the expert testimony would not have made a difference. However, despite the coach's mistakes, the court held that "for Allison [the coach] to be subject to personal liability, his conduct had to be more than negligent,"[25] a threshold that was not met in this instance. As a result, the sovereign immunity standard was appropriate.

In a ruling more successful for a student plaintiff, the Supreme Court of New Jersey affirmed an appellate court ruling that presided over which negligence standard to employ when in the context of informal athletic situations.[26] In this case, a former high school field hockey player filed a negligence suit after her coach, who began practice informally 45 minutes earlier than scheduled, had the players warm up in an area of the school's athletics complex that was subject to errant soccer balls being kicked from the then-scheduled soccer team practice across the field. The plaintiff sustained a neck injury after being hit with one of these soccer balls before her official practice commenced. The trial court employed the standard of *Crawn v. Campo*[27] for their initial holding that the coach's decision to begin an informal practice early

---

[24] Conley v. Wapakoneta City Sch. Dist. Bd. of Educ., 195 N.E.3d 1061, 408 Educ. L. Rep. 524 (Ohio Ct. App. 2022).
[25] *Id.* at 1075.
[26] Dennehy v. E. Windsor Reg'l Bd. of Educ., 284 A.3d 102, 409 Educ. L. Rep. 888 (N.J. 2022).
[27] 136 N.J. 494, 643 A.2d 600 (1994).

did not reach "the degree of recklessness described in *Crawn*,"[28] but the appellate court disagreed, finding that the time and context of when the injury occurred was more suitable for the simple standard of duty of care to which nonathletic school personnel are held.[29]

An appellate court in Indiana reversed and remanded a trial court's denial of summary judgment after a high school swimmer in Indiana filed suit against the diocese (i.e., the entity in charge of school operations) for allegedly allowing her to continue competing despite sustaining a concussion during her swim meet.[30] The appellate court argued that the trial court had erred in not granting summary judgment to the defendants, particularly after the diocese provided expert medical evidence from a neurologist that the plaintiff's head injuries were not worsened by participating in the remainder of the swim meet. The plaintiff did not provide any evidentiary support to counter the expert's argument, further supporting the defendant's summary judgment claim.

A former student-athlete sued individually and on behalf of a putative class who played for the University of Florida and incurred concussive head injuries. The plaintiff sued both the NCAA and the athletic conference to which the university belongs in a federal district court in Indiana, where the NCAA is headquartered, claiming negligence, fraudulent concealment, breach of express and implied contract, breach of express contract as a third-party beneficiary, and unjust enrichment for failing to implement adequate safety protocols despite having research data at its disposal that would indicate players with head injuries needed heightened care. The court granted the athletic conference's motion to dismiss for lack of jurisdiction, but allowed claims against the NCAA, minus unjust enrichment, to move forward.[31]

---

[28] Dennehy v. E. Windsor Reg'l Bd. of Educ., 284 A.3d 102, 409 Educ. L. Rep. 888 (N.J. 2022), at 203.

[29] *Id.* at 105–106 ("Indeed, the essence of plaintiff's theory of liability—that Fillmyer chose the wrong place and an unpropitious time to commence practice—is no different than the decisions that might be made by a biology teacher taking a class out to study marine life at the beach").

[30] Diocese of Ft. Wayne S. Bend, Inc. v. Gallegos, 203 N.E.3d 1080, 412 Educ. L. Rep. 868 (Ind. Ct. App. 2023)

[31] Richardson v. Southeastern Conf., 612 F. Supp. 3d 753, 412 Educ. L. Rep. 616 (N.D. Ill. 2020).

A state appellate court upheld summary judgment in favor of a university when a student-athlete and his mother filed suit after the student incurred an eye injury during a mandatory training exercise. The court premised its decision on a waiver of liability and assumption of risk form that was signed by the student and his mother.[32]

The family of a football player sued a private university after he died from a cardiac incident at football practice. The player had removed himself from the practice and complained to coaches of a tight chest and dizziness. This was not the first time he had similar episodes. The trainers put him in the shade to rest with water and took his vitals, but 45 minutes later he collapsed. A trial court granted summary judgment in favor of the university, but on appeal a court reversed, finding that though the player had signed two identical waivers acknowledging the risks of playing football, the language of the waiver was unenforceable, as it did not clearly express that he would be signing away his right to sue.[33]

First Amendment Issues

A district court granted in part and denied in part two cross-motions for summary judgment presented by both the plaintiffs and the defendants after a First Amendment suit arose from circumstances surrounding a high school cheerleading camp in Louisiana.[34] The plaintiffs comprised a trio of parents representing their children, who were allegedly subjected to having white athletic tape put over their mouths as a punitive measure for speaking excessively during one of their cheerleading practices. The crux of the court's First Amendment considerations were (a) whether the defendant high school could argue for summary judgment; (b) whether schools can regulate off-campus speech, as in the case of this summer camp; and (c) the extent to which the student-athletes' speech was disruptive during practice using the standard set in *Tinker v. Des Moines*.[35] The court denied the defendant's motion for summary judgment, holding that the

---

[32] Sinu v. Concordia Univ., 983 N.W.2d 511, 411 Educ. L. Rep. 342 (Neb. 2023).
[33] Estate of Blakely *ex rel.* Wilson v. Stetson Univ., Inc., 355 So.3d 476, 412 Educ. L. Rep. 885 (Fla. Dist. Ct. App. 2022).
[34] Haley v. DeSoto Parish Sch. Bd., 600 F. Supp. 3d 690, 410 Educ. L. Rep. 911 (W.D. La. 2022).
[35] 393 U.S. 503 (1969).

student-athletes were in a school-sponsored and regulated setting at the time of the incident; moreover, the sworn affidavits from the plaintiffs caused "genuine dispute as to whether the circumstances surrounding the taping incident present a situation where the children's speech was protected."[36] Although the court denied the plaintiffs' other First Amendment claim of retaliation by school officials, granting summary judgment for the defendants, they left open the free speech violations for later review.

A coach in Massachusetts claimed First Amendment retaliation for protected speech after receiving a nonrenewal notice for his position. The plaintiff argued his position was rescinded after he made a series of public statements in opposition to the school's handling of topics in its social studies curriculum, such as the Black Lives Matter movement.[37] It was clear, based on the facts of the case, that the coach's public comments did serve as the main motivation for his nonrenewal, and the court also argued that his speech was protected when communicating his concerns as a parent in the community. However, the court argued the school's decision was made appropriately by "countervailing government interests,"[38] referencing in particular the plaintiff's direct written attacks toward school administrators that would have likely resulted in a disruptive working relationship. Accordingly, they granted summary judgment to the school defendants.

Another coach filed suit after he was retaliated against for replacing a university-printed Black Lives Matter poster on his door with a handwritten sign that "[a]ll lives matter to Our Lord and Savior Jesus Christ." The plaintiff complied when the head coach requested that he remove the sign, but the plaintiff was dismissed several weeks later, allegedly for performance-related issues, and reassigned to research COVID-19 protocols in athletics. The plaintiff sued, claiming infringement of his First Amendment rights, and sought back pay, damages, attorney fees, and an injunction against the university. In its analysis, a federal district court in Illinois rejected an application of *Garcetti v. Ceballos*,[39] instead leaning on a 2022 U.S. Supreme Court ruling that favored

---

[36] *Id.* at 696.
[37] Flynn v. Forrest, 605 F. Supp. 3d 319, 411 Educ. L. Rep. 555 (D. Mass. 2022).
[38] *Id.* at 330 ("Flynn's personal attack of Welch is not entitled to First Amendment protection").
[39] 547 U.S. 410 (2006) (landmark holding that a public employee does not have First Amendment protection when speaking pursuant to their official duties).

a public high school football coach who prayed on the field after games, finding that because the prayers occurred during a time when coaches were allowed to attend to personal matters it did not fall within the ordinary scope of his duties.[40] The court in this case found that the plaintiff was not required to decorate his door in a certain way as condition of his employment, and was thus not acting in his official capacity when he placed the handwritten sign on his door. The court ruled that the coach's speech was protected by the First Amendment.[41]

A women's soccer player at a public university was dismissed from her team and lost her athletic scholarship after she raised her middle finger to a television camera during her team's post-game celebration. She sued the university and individual employees for violating her First Amendment and procedural due process rights, as well as Title IX—claiming that male student-athletes who acted similarly were not punished. A district court granted the university and its officials summary judgment on all claims. On appeal, the court remanded for further proceedings the plaintiff's Title IX claims, finding triable facts of disparate treatment based on sex. To the plaintiff's First Amendment and due process claims, the appellate court upheld the ruling that the university officials enjoyed qualified immunity.[42]

Bankruptcy

A former football operations employee was terminated from two universities for NCAA violations. Subsequently, the NCAA implemented sanctions against him that prohibited him from working at an NCAA-member institution through January 2032. The plaintiff filed for Chapter 7 bankruptcy and later added the NCAA as a defendant in a separate suit. A trial court dismissed his suit against the NCAA based on judicial estoppel because claims against the NCAA were not listed in his original bankruptcy filing. The Mississippi Supreme Court overturned that ruling, finding that his claim for declaratory relief was related solely to his ability to earn future income, which was separate from his bankruptcy

---

[40] Kennedy v. Bremerton Sch. Dist., 597 U.S. 507 (2022).
[41] Beathard v. Lyons, 620 F. Supp. 3d 775, 414 Educ. L. Rep. 847 (C.D. Ill. 2022).
[42] Radwan v. Manuel, 55 F.4th 101, 410 Educ. L. Rep. 39 (2d Cir. 2022).

filing, and he was not required to disclose a declaratory relief claim to the bankruptcy trustee.[43]

Employment

A trial court in New York unanimously denied the petition of a former per-session football coach to have his performance record—namely, his unsatisfactory rating for the Fall 2018 football season—to be expunged, allowing him to resume his coaching role. Given the considerable pattern of misbehavior leading to the unsatisfactory rating (e.g., multiple instances of drinking alcohol on school grounds and while operating a vehicle) and the subsequent lack of suitable performance by the football team, the court ruled that the dismissal was appropriate and procedurally fair for per-session employees.[44]

Conclusion

The legal issues in this chapter spanned student-athletes, coaches, and administrators in K–12 and higher education. From this review of 2023 cases, notable adjudication patterns emerged; among them were (a) equity concerns regarding transgender student-athlete participation, (b) liability parameters for school officials and coaches regarding student-athletes' physical safety, and (c) ongoing First Amendment disputes over ideological differences that test the public concern versus private citizen balance of coaches as school employees.

---

[43] Saunders v. Nat'l Collegiate Athletic Ass'n, 352 So. 3d 618, 411 Educ. L. Rep. 873 (Miss. 2022).

[44] Saunds v. Dept. of Educ. of City of N.Y., 177 N.Y.S.3d 231, 409 Educ. L. Rep. 908 (N.Y. App. Div. 2022).

Alphabetical List of Cases

A.M. by E.M. v. Indianapolis Public Schools

Balow v. Mich. State Univ.

Beathard v. Lyons

Billman v. Easton Area Sch. Dist.

Conley v. Wapakoneta City Sch. Dist. Bd. of Educ.

Dennehy v. E. Windsor Reg'l Bd. of Educ.

Diocese of Ft. Wayne S. Bend, Inc. v. Gallegos

Doe v. BMG Sports

E.H. ex rel. Herrera v. Valley Christian Acad.

Estate of Blakely ex rel. Wilson v. Stetson Univ.

Flynn v. Forrest

Garrett v. Ohio State Univ.

Haley v. DeSoto Parish Sch. Bd.

J.H. ex rel. Meudt-Antele v. Jefferson City Pub. Sch. Dist.

Kennedy v. Bremerton Sch. Dist.

MacIntyre v. Carroll Coll.

Ng v. Bd. of Regents of Univ. of Minn.

Radwan v. Manuel

Richardson v. Southeastern Conf.

Sacks v. Univ. of Minn.

Saunds v. Dept. of Educ. of City of N.Y.

Saunders v. Nat'l Collegiate Athletic Ass'n

Sinu v. Concordia Univ.

Slack ex rel. C.S. v. Copeland

Snyder-Hill v. Ohio State Univ.

Soule ex rel. Stanescu v. Conn. Ass'n of Schs.

Watkins v. Town of Webster

Federal Cases

United States Supreme Court

Kennedy v. Bremerton Sch. Dist.

Second Circuit

Radwan v. Manuel
Soule *ex rel.* Stanescu v. Conn. Ass'n of Schs.

Sixth Circuit

Garrett v. Ohio State Univ.
Snyder-Hill v. Ohio State Univ.

Seventh Circuit

Groves v. S. Bend Cmty. Sch. Corp.

Eighth Circuit

Ng v. Bd. of Regents of Univ. of Minn.

Ninth Circuit

MacIntyre v. Carroll Coll.

California
E.H. *ex rel.* Herrera v. Valley Christian Acad.

State and D.C. Cases
Alphabetical by state

Florida

Estate of Blakely *ex rel.* Wilson v. Stetson Univ.

Indiana

A.M. by E.M. v. Indianapolis Public Schools

Diocese of Ft. Wayne S. Bend

Illinois

Beathard v. Lyons

Richardson v. Southeastern Conf.

Louisiana

Slack *ex rel.* C.S. v. Copeland

Haley v. DeSoto Parish Sch. Bd.

Massachucetts

Flynn v. Forrest

Michigan

Balow v. Mich. State Univ.

Minnesota

Sacks v. Univ. of Minn.

Mississippi

Saunders v. Nat'l Collegiate Athletic Ass'n

Missouri

J.H. ex rel. Meudt-Antele v. Jefferson City Pub. Sch. Dist.

Nebraska

Sinu v. Concordia Univ.

New Jersey

Dennehy v. E. Windsor Reg'l Bd. of Educ.

New York

Saunds v. Dept. of Educ. of City of NY

Watkins v. Town of Webster

Ohio

Conley v. Wapakoneta City Sch. Dist. Bd. of Educ.

Doe v. BMG Sports

Pennsylvania

Billman v. Easton Area School District

CHAPTER 8

HIGHER EDUCATION FACULTY AND ADMINISTRATION

Marigold Hudock, Radomir Mitic,
and Jeffrey C. Sun

Continued on the next page...

Introduction

This chapter includes summaries of cases reported in 2023 that involved issues affecting higher education institutions (HEIs) and their administrators, staff, faculty, students, and families. The issues within this period included discrimination and harassment, First Amendment, due process, contracts, tenure, wrongful discharge, Family Medical Leave Act (FMLA) violations, workers' compensation, procedural issues in the law, environmental protections, intellectual property, property-related issues, crime-related matters, wage-related concerns, questions surrounding institutional governance, consumer protection concerns, student loan issues, and a case involving retirement.

When discussing discriminatory matters and constitutional violations, this chapter presented several short-form references. For instance, when raising issues around Title VI, these cases are referring to Title VI of the Civil Rights Act of 1964, those cases pertain to alleged discriminatory matters based on race, color, or national origin either due to the university denying participation or benefits associated with a university program. Similarly, Title VII refers to that part of the Civil Rights Act of 1964 prohibiting discrimination based on race, color, or national origin in the employment context. Also, when referencing Section 1981 or Section 1983, these short forms of the law refer to allegations of nongovernmental discrimination or governmental-sourced discrimination, respectively.

Collectively, the cases covered in this chapter summarize the key cases in 2023 addressing higher education matters involving faculty or administration. Accordingly, these cases will be instructive to administrators, scholars, and policymakers involved in various issues affecting HEIs.

Discrimination and Harassment

Race

The Seventh Circuit heard a case on appeal from Wisconsin involving a former employee who was allegedly discriminated and retaliated against based on race and national origin in violation of

Title VII.[1] The plaintiff was fired the day after reporting to the vice chancellor that his boss and the human resources department were violating Title VII through discriminatory hiring and promotion practices. The court found that the plaintiff's statements to the vice chancellor were a protected activity under Title VII, and the decision to terminate the plaintiff one day after he reported discriminatory and retaliatory behavior was sufficient to establish an inference of causation. Thus, the federal trial court's entry of summary judgment in favor of the university was reversed and remanded.

A university terminated an African American campus police officer based on his handling of a situation involving an intoxicated man found passed out in one of the university dormitories.[2] The former officer sued the Board of Trustees at the university for racial discrimination, retaliation, hostile work environment, and age discrimination. Initially, a federal trial court in Arkansas dismissed most of the claims except for race discrimination, hostile work environment, and retaliation, and the court granted the defendant's motion for summary judgment. The trial court ultimately decided that the university fired the officer for legitimate reasons, and the Eighth Circuit federal appellate court affirmed.

An African American, female professor sued a state university and its current and former law school deans alleging a culture of racism and sexism, along with retaliation by the deans.[3] The professor presented several examples in support of her claims, including secret recordings, negative evaluations by the deans, and negative comments regarding her concerns of bias. To succeed in her claims against the prior dean for a hostile work environment under §§ 1983 and 1981, the professor was required to show that the dean was acting under legal authority and his conduct deprived the professor of her equal protection rights under the Fourteenth Amendment. It was undisputed that the dean was acting under legal authority at the relevant times, so the only issue was whether the dean was personally involved in creating a hostile work

[1] Xiong v. Bd. of Regents of Univ. of Wis. Sys., 62 F.4th 350, 412 Educ. L. Rep. 472 (7th Cir. 2023).

[2] Thompson v. Univ. of Ark. Bd. of Trs., 52 F.4th 1039, 408 Educ. L. Rep. 721 (8th Cir. 2022).

[3] Sanders v. Univ. of Idaho by Bd. of Regents of Univ. of Idaho, 617 F. Supp. 3d 1200, 414 Educ. L. Rep. 140 (D. Idaho 2022).

environment. The federal trial court in Idaho allowed the professor's hostile environment claim to proceed, finding that a genuine issue of material fact existed as to whether the former dean was personally involved in the hostile work environment.

In Kansas, a university professor sued the university and individual employees for retaliation, harassment, and discrimination based on sex, race, and religion under Title VII, Title IX, and state law.[4] The professor, who describes herself as a woman, Native American, and Christian, served as both a professor of social work and as the director of a new Center for Combating Human Trafficking (CHHT). A male colleague was unhappy with the plaintiff's appointment to both roles and spread rumors in the department that the plaintiff exchanged sexual favors with university administrators for her job. These rumors persisted for years and were ignored by the university. Ultimately, the plaintiff was removed as the CHHT director and, eventually, CHHT was closed. The professor's race- and religion-based claims failed because she failed to allege facts connecting a race- or religion-based comment to her termination as CHHT director. However, the federal trial court in Kansas allowed the professor's claims under Title IX to proceed based on the university administrators' active avoidance of her sexual harassment, hostile work environment, and retaliatory harassment complaints stemming from the rumors spread by her colleague.

In Massachusetts, a Black, female former employee challenged the EEOC's dismissal of her discrimination claims in violation of Title VII and state law.[5] The employee alleged that, due to her race and gender, she was denied the opportunity for job reclassification within an appropriate time frame and for a salary properly aligned with her position. Under the relevant policy, reclassification is appropriate where the employee's duties and responsibilities have substantially changed. Here, the university argued that the employee's reclassification was decided by her professional development, as evidenced by her performance review, and not based on race or sex. The court found this rationale met the university's burden of providing a legitimate, nondiscriminatory

---

[4] Countryman-Roswurm v. Wichita State Univ., 618 F. Supp. 3d 1140, 414 Educ. L. Rep. 209 (D. Kan. 2022), No. 22-3160, 2023 WL 3451978 (10th Cir. May 15, 2023).

[5] Rucker v. President & Fellows of Harvard Coll., 621 F. Supp. 3d 212, 415 Educ. L. Rep. 25 (D. Mass. 2022).

reason for its employment action. Because the employee failed to show that the university's rationale was pretext for unlawful discrimination, her discrimination claims were properly dismissed.

In New York, a Black professor brought a racial discrimination claim against the administrators at a community college alleging racial discrimination, breach of contract, and harassment under Title VII and the New York State Human Rights Law.[6] The suit arose from a denial of course assignments and scheduling requests after having complained of racial discrimination. The defendants included the college, the faculty association and its president, and several senior leaders. The court dismissed claims against all defendants except for the racial discrimination claim against the department chair who was responsible for course scheduling. The court determined that none of the other defendants who were notified of the plaintiff's claims of discrimination influenced the personnel decisions of the department chair.

A Black professor was terminated from employment at a public university in Rhode Island after he and students used a class project to raise concerns of the university's commitment to diversity, equity, and inclusion.[7] The professor transmitted a document containing these concerns to university officials. These officials responded with a student complaint and ultimately placed the professor on administrative leave, alleging hostility and demeaning colleagues. After an investigation, the professor was terminated and then filed suit based on retaliation and discrimination. The university filed a motion to dismiss. The federal trial court held in favor of the professor, allowing the suit to proceed based on employment discrimination, defamation, and whistleblowing. However, the court sided with the university regarding the due process and breach of contract claims.

A Black male applicant for a campus police chief position filed suit after the university hired a younger, white female applicant for the job.[8] The defendant had modified job qualifications to enable the white female applicant to obtain the position and avoid hiring the Black male applicant, despite clear warnings from compliance officers and the fact that the plaintiff held higher credentials. The

---

[6] Felton v. Monroe Cmty. Coll., 579 F. Supp. 3d 400, 406 Educ. L. Rep. 215 (W.D.N.Y. 2022).
[7] Fosu v. Univ. of R.I., 590 F. Supp. 3d 451, 408 Educ. L. Rep. 345 (D.R.I. 2022).
[8] Blakely v. Austin Peay State Univ., 591 F. Supp. 3d 278, 408 Educ. L. Rep. 808 (M.D. Tenn. 2022).

plaintiff alleged race and age discrimination under Title VII of the Civil Rights Act and the Age Discrimination in Employment Act, and additionally asserted claims of emotional distress and fraud. The plaintiff conceded that the Eleventh Amendment barred his claims regarding age discrimination, fraud, and emotional distress, and so the court granted the motion to dismiss those specific claims. A federal trial court in Tennessee denied the motion to dismiss the claim regarding race discrimination, stating that only discovery could show whether the decision to hire the other applicant was discriminatory.

Sex/Sexual Orientation

On appeal from Arkansas, the Eighth Circuit affirmed a grant of summary judgment in favor of the college on a former female employee's claims under Title VII and state civil rights law.[9] The employee was terminated after using a disability-related slur toward a student during class. Additionally, the employee's nephew, who lived with the employee, and his friends physically attacked the student against whom the slur was used after class. Thus, the college presented a legitimate, nondiscriminatory reason for the plaintiff's termination, and the court found the college was not liable for sex discrimination, retaliation, or a hostile work environment under Title VII.

The Eighth Circuit upheld a Minnesota federal trial court decision in favor of a university accused of firing the plaintiff, a former female director of operations of the university's women's hockey team, for being gay.[10] The plaintiff also held the position of head softball coach. Despite having strong performance reviews, the plaintiff was fired from her duties as director of operations after the women's hockey head coach was fired. The university successfully argued that the dismissal was a common practice in intercollegiate athletics where a new coach typically hires their own staff. In addition, the university was able to point to other gay staff members who were retained on the coaching staff to show that the plaintiff's firing was not based on her sexual orientation.

---

[9] Walker-Swinton v. Philander Smith Coll., 62 F.4th 435, 412 Educ. L. Rep. 481 (8th Cir. 2023).

[10] Banford v. Bd. of Regents of Univ. of Minn., 43 F.4th 896, 406 Educ. L. Rep. 92 (8th Cir. 2022).

An employee for a university filed an internal complaint for gender discrimination when she noticed that her workplace gave preferential treatment to a male employee.[11] The university hired a law firm to handle the internal investigation and then notified the employee that her claim "could not be substantiated." The employee then filed a charge with the plaintiff, and the plaintiff asserted that the university had violated Title VII and the Equal Pay Act. The plaintiff and the university (the defendant) engaged in a number of disputes during the discovery phase and the plaintiff moved to compel discovery. The federal trial court in Washington D.C. denied the motion for reasons including that the documents from the university's internal investigation were protected by attorney-client privilege as well as work-product privilege.

The federal trial court in Connecticut granted a university's motion to dismiss a former associate professor's claims for sex-based discrimination and retaliation under Title IX.[12] The female professor was denied tenure based on negative teaching evaluations and later terminated. During her employment, the employee filed a complaint for sex discrimination based on an over-reliance on sex-biased teaching evaluations in faculty assessments, but the university found no wrongdoing after an investigation. Ultimately, the court held that Title IX did not provide a private remedy for employment discrimination claims, so the plaintiff's claim was dismissed.

A male former associate professor sued his employer, a private music college, for gender discrimination and retaliation under Title VII and state law.[13] The professor was terminated following complaints of sexual harassment from a student. The federal trial court in Massachusetts denied summary judgment on the professor's Title VII retaliation claim, finding insufficient evidence to prove the professor was terminated for a reason other than his in-class complaints about alleged bias in Title IX proceedings against him. However, summary judgment was granted on the

---

[11] U.S. E.E.O.C. v. George Wash. Univ., 342 F.R.D. 161, 409 Educ. L. Rep. 183 (D.D.C. 2022).

[12] Othon v. Wesleyan Univ., 612 F. Supp. 3d 35, 412 Educ. L. Rep. 587 (D. Conn. 2020).

[13] Farzinpour v. Berklee Coll. of Music, 616 F. Supp. 3d 98, 413 Educ. L. Rep. 693 (D. Mass. 2022).

Title VII claim because the college's actions were not sufficiently severe or pervasive to create a hostile work environment.

In Mississippi, a former faculty instructor brought suit in a federal trial court against the state university, its president, and her former supervisor under Title VII and § 1983 for sex-based harassment, discrimination, retaliation, and hostile work environment.[14] Specifically, the instructor argued that she was denied tenure and promotion because of her sex. The court first addressed the instructor's Title VII sex discrimination claim, finding the university's decision to deny tenure and promotion was not a discriminatory compensation decision. Additionally, the plaintiff's hostile work environment claim under Title VII failed because her alleged constructive discharge did not qualify as an unlawful employment practice. Thus, the instructor's Title VII claims were dismissed.

A professor in Texas alleged discrimination based on sex and pregnancy[15] when her tenure was denied after having her tenure probationary period extended to accommodate her pregnancy. The professor alleged that she was denied tenure stemming from gender stereotypes held by the dean and others. During trial, the plaintiff called a renowned social psychologist to provide expert testimony on gender stereotypes and bias in society. The university sought to exclude the expert testimony on the grounds that it was unreliable because it did not include evidence from a scientific study and did not show that gender stereotypes and bias existed at the university. A federal trial court ruled in favor of the university and excluded the testimony. Later, a jury awarded damages in favor of the professor on the basis of sex and pregnancy discrimination.

Age

In New York, an appellate court rejected a private university's motion to dismiss an employment discrimination suit seeking damages for breach of contract.[16] A professor alleged employment discrimination based on age. In response, the university filed a

---

[14] Bradley v. Bynum, 618 F. Supp. 3d 353, 414 Educ. L. Rep. 161 (S.D. Miss. 2022).
[15] Nikolova v. Univ. of Tex. at Austin, 585 F. Supp. 3d 936, 407 Educ. L. Rep. 762 (W.D. Tex. 2022).
[16] Rogoff v. Long Island Univ., 173 N.Y.S.3d 634, 407 Educ. L. Rep. 882 (N.Y. App. Div. 2022).

motion to dismiss based on its status as an educational institution. A lower court held that because the university did not provide evidence refuting the claims of the plaintiff, the motion to dismiss would be denied. The appellate court affirmed the decision.

A former university employee in Texas held a director-level position until a new president came in and informed the employee that her job title and duties would change, and her salary would be reduced.[17] The university then hired another employee who was 20 years younger than the plaintiff into a position that was equivalent to the plaintiff's director-level job. The plaintiff sued the university for age discrimination and retaliation. The trial court denied the university's plea to the jurisdiction, and the university appealed. The appellate court affirmed the trial court's decision regarding the age discrimination claim; however, it reversed and rendered the retaliation claim, stating that the plaintiff did not show a causation analysis between her engaging in a protected activity and experiencing an adverse employment action.

Disability

A former employee filed suit against a university and her former supervisors, alleging that her former workplace subjected her to disability discrimination, hostile work environment, and retaliation in violation of the Americans with Disabilities Act (ADA), the Family Medical Leave ACT (FMLA), and a state civil rights act.[18] A federal trial court in Iowa granted summary judgment in favor of the defendants, and the plaintiff appealed. The Eighth Circuit affirmed the trial court's decision on the grounds that there was insufficient evidence of pretext related to the complaints.

During her time working at a university medical school, a radiologist developed a medical condition.[19] Her employers decided to dismiss her on alleged performance-related issues, although a review of the plaintiff's work showed positive performance. The radiologist's employers also listed "retirement" as the official reason for her leaving the university. The radiologist sued the

---

[17] Tex. Tech Univ. Health Scis. Ctr.-El Paso v. Flores, 657 S.W.3d 502, 411 Educ. L. Rep. 841 (Tex. App. 2022).

[18] Corkrean v. Drake Univ., 55 F.4th 623, 410 Educ. L. Rep. 119 (8th Cir. 2022).

[19] Desai v. Univ. of Mass. Mem'l Med. Ctr., 605 F. Supp. 3d 255, 411 Educ. L. Rep. 536 (D. Mass. 2022).

university's medical center, medical group, medical school, hospital, and her former employers and supervising physicians, alleging discrimination based on her age, gender, and disability. The Massachusetts federal trial court partially granted summary judgment in favor of the defendants regarding the claims of gender and disability-based discrimination and held that the university's denial of one employee's requests was not an "adverse employment action." The court also granted summary judgment on some of the claims against the medical center, hospital, school, president of the medical group, and supervisors, holding that these entities were not liable.

In New York, a man who lived in an apartment leased by a private university was denied a lease renewal and mental health accommodation after the death of the previous leaseholder whom the man considered a surrogate mother.[20] After an investigation, a state agency found no discrimination by the university. The agency finding was overturned in state court after the agency did not appear at two pre-trial conferences. This decision was later overturned, and the claimant appealed to the state appellate court. The claimant then appealed this decision, alleging collusion between the state agency and the university. The state filed a motion to dismiss based on an untimely filing and a lack of subject matter jurisdiction, which was granted by the claims court.

Religion

A Jewish faculty member at a public community college sued their employer for religious discrimination after a series of anti-Semitic comments and being passed over for committee assignments.[21] After a federal court dismissed all federal claims with prejudice, a New York county court held that the professor did not file their claim within 90 days under the education law, and that the untimely notice of claim warranted dismissal. Further, the court held that even if the claim were sufficient, the plaintiff could not bring a second claim against the defendants due to the doctrine of collateral estoppel.

---

[20] Wiltz v. State, 175 N.Y.S.3d 172, 408 Educ. L. Rep. 509 (N.Y. Ct. Cl. 2022).
[21] Lax v. City Univ. of N.Y., 175 N.Y.S.3d 691, 408 Educ. L. Rep. 982 (N.Y. Sup. Ct. 2022).

Hostile Work Environment

A university dismissed a student from a medical residency program due to alleged unprofessionalism, failure to improve during a probationary period, communication issues, and failure to be present for an assignment.[22] The plaintiff brought action against the university, health services corporation, and doctors for retaliation, hostile work environment, due process violation, and breach of contract. In his statements, the plaintiff alleged that he experienced harassment and a hostile work environment due to his identity as a veteran. Both parties asked to exclude evidence. A federal trial court in Illinois declined to exclude statements made by the chief resident, evidence regarding surgical errors made by other residents, evidence that one of the doctors misinterpreted the plaintiff's military rank, emails made by other residents, and a defendant's deferment of military service. However, the court granted the defendants permission to exclude evidence regarding a racial slur made by a doctor. The court denied the plaintiff the opportunity to provide evidence regarding his military orders but granted the ability to dismiss any evidence regarding whether his spouse accessed or used patient medical records.

Retaliation

The Sixth Circuit heard a case on appeal from Ohio involving a female employee's unlawful retaliation claim under Title IX.[23] The employee was asked to resign as the Title IX coordinator after writing a letter to the student newspaper, against her supervisor's order, addressing the controversy surrounding an award given to a graduating student who was a sex offender. On appeal, the employee argued that she was not insubordinate. Specifically, she claimed the letter was a protected activity under Title IX, so it could not constitute insubordination. The federal trial court in Colorado disagreed, finding that the letter did not include accusations of intentional sex-based discrimination by the university, so it was not protected under Title IX. Further, the court found that the evidence supporting the employee's

---

[22] McDaniel v. Loyola Univ. Med. Ctr., 606 F. Supp. 3d 776, 411 Educ. L. Rep. 612 (N.D. Ill. 2022).
[23] Goldblum v. Univ. of Cincinnati, 62 F.4th 244, 412 Educ. L. Rep. 457 (6th Cir. 2023).

termination for insubordination and poor work performance was sufficient. Thus, the federal trial court's grant of summary judgment in favor of the university was affirmed.

A Hispanic, female doctor worked as an anesthesiologist and tenure-track assistant professor for a university and the Department of Veteran Affairs (VA).[24] She filed a report for dangerous conduct in a clinical setting and experienced retaliation, harassment, discrimination, and other hostile acts. She was eventually terminated and received several false complaints that were detrimental to her career. The plaintiff filed suit against the regents of the university for pregnancy discrimination, national origin discrimination, hostile work environment, retaliation under Title VII, and discrimination and retaliation under ADA and ADAAA. She additionally moved to proceed through the suit under a pseudonym. The court denied her motion for a pseudonym, stating that lawsuits were public events and pseudonyms were only used in unusual or highly sensitive cases.

First Amendment

The Ninth Circuit federal appellate court reversed and remanded the lower court's grant of a preliminary injunction that prevented the disclosure of letters appointing the appellees to serve on the university's animal care and use committee.[25] The appellees argued that the release of their appointment letters would violate their First Amendment rights of expressive association. On appeal from a federal trial court in Washington, the court found that the appellees' performance of their official duties was not protected by the First Amendment, so the disclosure of their appointment letters, which were considered public records, did not infringe upon their First Amendment rights.

The plaintiff worked as a urologist for a university, and the defendant worked as a professor of law at the same university.[26] The defendant criticized the plaintiff for testifying in a separate court case, and the plaintiff responded by filing suit saying that the defendant retaliated against him for engaging in protected speech. A federal trial court in Iowa dismissed the plaintiff's claims and

---

[24] Doe v. Regents of Univ. of Colo., 603 F. Supp. 3d 1014, 411 Educ. L. Rep. 486 (D. Colo. 2022).
[25] Sullivan v. Univ. of Wash., 60 F.4th 574, 412 Educ. L. Rep. 34 (9th Cir. 2023).
[26] Brown v. Linder (a), 56 F.4th 1140, 411 Educ. L. Rep. 35 (8th Cir. 2023).

the plaintiff appealed. The Eighth Circuit affirmed the trial court's decision, saying that the plaintiff failed to allege that the defendant was acting under color of state law. In a second case arising from the same facts, the plaintiff filed suit against the professor for violating his First Amendment rights and for defamation.[27] The defendant removed the action to federal court and moved to dismiss. The trial court held that the plaintiff failed to allege that the doctor acted under color of state law, that the professor's conduct did not violate the plaintiff's rights to freedom of speech, and the court declined to provide jurisdiction for defamation.

Several political science and law professors at a public university in Florida sued their employer on First Amendment grounds after being prohibited from providing expert testimony.[28] The university had instituted a conflicts of interest policy requiring faculty to report any potential conflict of interest. After reporting their intention to provide expert testimony in an election law case against the state, the university found their testimony in violation of the policy as the university is a state entity. The federal trial court held that such a prohibition was an unconstitutional suppression of the professors' free speech rights under the First Amendment.

A tenured professor at a university filed suit after the university restricted access to the use of Native American remains housed at the university.[29] The university claimed that it abided by a recently amended state law where it needed to prepare the remains to go back to a Native American tribe. However, the plaintiff claimed that the university enacted the policy in retaliation to her speaking out against the repatriation of Native American remains. A federal trial court in California held that the tribe was entitled to sovereign immunity and could not be joined in the case. The court also held that neither the comments made by the department chair against the plaintiff nor the plaintiff's loss of curational responsibilities qualified as an adverse employment action. Furthermore, the plaintiff failed to connect how her speech was a factor for the alleged adverse employment action. Thus, the court denied the plaintiff's motion for preliminary injunction and

---

[27] Brown v. Linder (b), 606 F. Supp. 3d 890, 411 Educ. L. Rep. 633 (S.D. Iowa 2022).

[28] Austin v. Univ. of Fla. Bd. of Trs., 580 F. Supp. 3d 1137, 406 Educ. L. Rep. 716 (N.D. Fla. 2022).

[29] Weiss v. Perez, 602 F. Supp. 3d 1279, 411 Educ. L. Rep. 291 (N.D. Cal. 2022).

partially granted the defendant's motion to dismiss. The court also granted the plaintiff leave to amend her complaint regarding retaliation.

Female former assistant professors at a public university in Colorado sued the university board of governors and officials alleging gender discrimination and retaliation under Title VII and Title IX, as well as violations of their First Amendment rights under § 1983.[30] Their claims arose from internal complaints of gender discrimination and public statements via social media posts and news outlets before the university decided not to reappoint them. The court noted that employees speaking out about work-related issues do not automatically speak as employees rather than private citizens. The court held that the plaintiffs were speaking as citizens, even though comments were made on the department's social media page and were largely addressed to students. Additionally, the statements focused on the broader situation at the university and not on the plaintiffs' personal grievances, so the statements were on a matter of public concern. Because the university failed to show that its interests outweighed the professors' free speech interests, and the professors sufficiently alleged that their statements were a motivating factor in their termination, the federal trial court dismissed the university's motion to dismiss.

Due Process

A federal trial court in Illinois dismissed a former tenured professor's § 1983 claim against the university's board of trustees claiming violations of his due process rights after his tenure was revoked and his employment terminated.[31] The professor was terminated for research misconduct, but he argued that the proceedings surrounding his termination were not procedurally sufficient or fair. Specifically, the professor argued that he was deprived of a property interest when his tenure was revoked and a liberty interest from his termination. The court found that the professor received sufficient notice of the charges against him, he was given an opportunity to respond to each of the charges, and the

---

[30] Cowden v. Bd. of Governors of Colo. State Univ. Sys. by and through Colo. State Univ.-Pueblo, 622 F. Supp. 3d 1019, 415 Educ. L. Rep. 146 (D. Colo. 2022).
[31] Wang v. Bd. of Trs. of Univ. of Ill., 612 F. Supp. 3d 739, 412 Educ. L. Rep. 602 (N.D. Ill. 2020).

final report fully explained the evidence against him. Thus, the professor failed to show a procedural due process violation that deprived him of his property or liberty interests.

Contracts

The Fourth Circuit affirmed the federal trial court in South Carolina's grant of summary judgment in favor of the college on a former professor's claims for wrongful termination, disability discrimination, retaliation, unlawful health inquiry, and gender discrimination.[32] While employed by the university, the professor complained of Title IX violations on behalf of students and mold or mildew in the building where her office was located that exacerbated her asthma. In response to her complaints of mold or mildew, a dean offered to move her office to a nearby building, but the professor declined. The college ultimately declined to renew the professor's contract due to performance concerns, professionalism, and conflicts with other faculty members and with students. In response, the professor allegedly made a number of threats against the college and specific faculty members, and the president decided to terminate her immediately. The court found that the professor's retaliation claim must fail because she was "not a good fit" for the college and due to the reports of threatening behavior. Further, the college did not violate the Americans with Disabilities Act (ADA) where the professor failed to properly request accommodations.

In Arizona, a former executive director for a human rights organization brought suit against the organization for retaliatory discharge and breach of contract claims.[33] In response, the organization countersued for indemnification to recover costs involved in resolving claims brought as a result of the former director's actions. The director's retaliatory discharge claim failed because the organization offered six legitimate, nonretaliatory reasons for termination, including failure to secure funding and other finance-related issues, a breakdown in the employment relationship, and failure to adhere to organizational processes. The federal trial court denied the director's motion for summary judgment on her breach of contract claim based on conflicting

---

[32] Lashley v. Spartanburg Methodist Church, 66 F.4th 168, 414 Educ. L. Rep. 523 (4th Cir. 2023).

[33] Gonzalez v. US Hum. Rts. Network, 617 F. Supp. 3d 1072, 414 Educ. L. Rep. 104 (D. Ariz. 2022).

evidence regarding the substance of the alleged oral employment contract. Finally, the court held that neither party was entitled to summary judgment on the organization's counterclaim for indemnification because genuine issues of material fact existed. Thus, the organization's motion for summary judgment was granted as to the retaliatory discharge claim, the director's motion for summary judgment was denied as to the breach of contract claim, and both parties were denied summary judgment on the organization's indemnification claim. An appeal to the Ninth Circuit has been filed and is currently pending in this case.

Two private universities in Missouri purchased property insurance policies from the defendant.[34] Due to the COVID-19 pandemic in 2020, the universities closed most of their campuses and sought to confirm insurance coverage under several provisions of the insurance contract. The insurance company responded that the policies did not cover losses due to COVID-19 as they did not constitute physical damage, and, even if considered physical damage, the losses would not be covered due to exclusions for "loss of use" and "contamination." The court held, however, that the universities may be entitled to coverage under a different provision for communicable diseases.

A university endowment foundation promised donors certain benefits, such as the best available seating and parking for football games.[35] In 2005, the foundation started to backtrack on the benefits previously promised to donors, and donors eventually filed suit. An insurer entered a contract with the university foundation in 2009, and the foundation asked the insurer to cover the defense regarding the conflict with the donors. The insurer refused, and the university foundation filed suit. Both parties filed cross-motions. A federal trial court in Texas concluded that the insurer's liability policy did not apply to the case occurring with the foundation. The court denied the defendant's motion for summary judgment and granted the insurer's motion for summary judgment.

When a university employee signed his employment letter, the university included a statement in the letter saying that all disagreements between the employee and the university would be

---

[34] Rockhurst Univ. v. Factory Mut. Ins. Co., 582 F. Supp. 3d 633, 406 Educ. L. Rep. 22 (W.D. Mo. 2022).

[35] Tex. A&M Univ. 12th Man Found. v. Hartford Lloyds Ins. Co., 596 F. Supp. 3d 788, 409 Educ. L. Rep. 871 (S.D. Tex. 2022).

solved through arbitration, not through a court or a trial.[36] The employee later filed suit against the university and a few unnamed defendants, claiming employment discrimination. A federal trial court in Washington held that the arbitration agreement was valid since the employee signed the letter that detailed the agreement and had the opportunity to read the terms. The trial court granted the university's motion to compel arbitration and dismissed the plaintiff's claims.

A private university in Wisconsin submitted a federal grant extension proposal to a granting agency with an error in the final budget figure.[37] The university alleged that a software bug was to blame for the error where some figures were double counted. Due to the last-minute nature of the submission, the university did not identify the error in the printout before submitting the proposal, leading to the proposal's rejection where it was otherwise strongly rated. The university sued for breach of contract in federal court for damages associated with the loss of the federal grant. The software company argued that its contract was for goods (the software) rather than a service, and therefore the university was not eligible for damages under the Uniform Commercial Code. The company further argued that there was no guarantee the grant would have been funded. The federal district court found favor of the software company and granted summary judgment on the basis that damages for goods were not governed by the Uniform Commercial Code.

A construction company contractor filed suit against a college board of trustees, asserting that the company never received full payment for its work on several campus projects.[38] The plaintiff's counsel initially stated that the construction company never received a reconciliation report with final payment. Later in court, the plaintiff admitted to receiving the report and depositing checks. Consequently, the judge awarded summary judgment in favor of the college. The plaintiff appealed and the appellate court in Florida dismissed the charges, stating that depositing the checks

---

[36] Okelo v. Antioch Univ., 601 F. Supp. 3d 894, 410 Educ. L. Rep. 1017 (W.D. Wash. 2022).

[37] Marquette Univ. v. Kuali, Inc., 584 F. Supp. 3d 720, 407 Educ. L. Rep. 575 (E.D. Wis. 2022).

[38] Const. Consulting, Inc. v. Dist. Bd. of Trs. of Broward Coll., 347 So.3d 14, 408 Educ. L. Rep. 1109 (Fla. Dist. Ct. App. 2022).

meant that the construction company accepted the college's payment as satisfactory.

A public university in Minnesota was sued by a wireless company alleging a breach of the contract to install an antenna system.[39] The university instead entered into agreements with cellphone carriers, depriving the plaintiff of exclusive income from a licensing agreement. After a settlement offer was rejected, a jury awarded the plaintiff financial compensation. An appellate court affirmed the jury's decision and award. While awaiting the appellate decision, both parties requested reimbursement for expert witness costs. The appellate court affirmed the award of all costs to the university, while awarding only a portion to the plaintiff.

A private college terminated two tenured music professors due to a financial decision to eliminate several academic programs and faculty.[40] Petitioners commenced a hybrid proceeding under article 78 and for breach of contract. The court dismissed the breach of contract claim and granted the article 78 petition, which the college appealed. An appellate court in New York held that the university did not terminate the professors for arbitrary or capricious reasons and that the breach of contract claim was subject to dismissal with prejudice. The court affirmed the previous decision with modifications.

Tenure

A Middle Eastern man began work as an untenured professor for a teaching-focused position at a private institution in Washington D.C.[41] The institution said it would reach a tenure decision in 3.5 years. While working at the university, the untenured professor consistently received below-average ratings on his course evaluations. He applied for tenure two years into the position, and the university president denied him tenure due to those evaluations. The professor then brought action against the university president on the grounds of racial discrimination and breach of contract. Both parties motioned for summary judgment.

---

[39] Capacity Wireless, LLC v. Bd. of Regents of Univ. of Minn., 978 N.W.2d 275, 406 Educ. L. Rep. 451 (Minn. Ct. App. 2022).

[40] Hansbrough v. Coll. of St. Rose, 177 N.Y.S.3d 735, 410 Educ. L. Rep. 479 (N.Y. App. Div. 2022).

[41] Moini v. Wrighton, 602 F. Supp. 3d 162, 411 Educ. L. Rep. 233 (D.D.C. 2022).

Although the federal trial court noted that perhaps the university unfairly weighted teaching evaluations in the tenure process, the university still had agency in determining how it evaluated its employees. Because the plaintiff failed to undermine the university's evidence, the court granted the president's motion and denied the professor's motion.

A federal trial court in Illinois granted the board of trustees' motion to dismiss a former tenured professor's § 1983 claims for due process violations, defamation, and false light after his tenure was revoked and his employment terminated.[42] The revocation of tenure and termination were the result of research misconduct relating to a grant application, but the professor argued that the proceedings that led up to his termination were unfair and deficient. To satisfy procedural due process requirements, the professor was entitled to oral or written notice of the allegations against him, an explanation of the evidence, and an opportunity to share his version of events before being terminated. Because the court found that all of these conditions were met, the procedural due process claims were dismissed.

In New York, an appellate court dismissed a claim from an assistant professor who was denied tenure based on the statute of limitations.[43] The lower court held that the university complied with established procedures and hence dismissed the plaintiff's case on the merits, but the case was timely filed. On appeal, the appellate court found that executive orders responding to the COVID-19 pandemic did not add 228 days to the statute of limitations but merely suspended the statute of limitations while they were in effect. The plaintiff's suit came a week after the statute of limitations had expired. The court also affirmed the case's dismissal on the merits.

Wrongful Discharge

A former flight instructor brought suit against the operator of a helicopter flight training school for wrongful discharge in violation of public policy prohibiting an employer from demanding

---

[42] Fei Wang v. Bd. of Trs. of Univ. of Ill., 612 F. Supp. 3d 739, 412 Educ. L. Rep. 602 (N.D. Ill. 2020).

[43] Roach v. Cornell Univ., 172 N.Y.S.3d 215, 406 Educ. L. Rep. 345 (N.Y. App. Div. 2022).

any sum of money as a condition of continued employment.[44] Specifically, the former employee alleged that his employer demanded 50% of any future fees he collected as a Federal Aviation Administration (FAA) certified pilot examiner as a condition of his continued employment. The Supreme Court of Connecticut first held that the type of fee-sharing the employer demanded constituted a "sum of money" under the statute. Further, there was a genuine issue of material fact as to whether there was an understanding that accepting the employer's demand for 50% of future fees was a requirement to continued employment. Thus, the appellate court's grant of summary judgment in favor of the employer was reversed and remanded.

A university terminated a police officer after the officer mishandled an incident where he pursued a juvenile on a bicycle.[45] The former officer challenged the termination under the state employment commission and requested disciplinary arbitration. The university objected to the officer's request, stating that disciplinary arbitration only applied to municipal officers. The state employment commission dismissed the objection and appointed an arbitrator anyway, and the university appealed. The appellate court sided with the university, agreeing that disciplinary arbitration did not apply. The state Supreme Court of New Jersey reversed the appellate court decision in favor of the plaintiff, stating that nonmunicipal police officers could still receive special disciplinary arbitration.

A university recruiter brought an action against the university and two coworkers for wrongful discharge, negligent retention or supervision of an employee, several claims related to sexual harassment, intentional infliction of mental and emotional distress, and violation of equal protection under the state constitution.[46] First, the Supreme Court of North Carolina granted the defendant's motion to dismiss, and the plaintiff appealed. The appellate court then affirmed and granted the plaintiff discretionary review. The university attempted to assert that it was protected by sovereign immunity. The court concluded that based on earlier precedent established by two Supreme Court decisions, the university's actions in registering as a nonprofit in

---

[44] Dunn v. Ne. Helicopters Flight Servs., 290 A.3d 780, 413 Educ. L. Rep. 901 (Conn. 2023).
[45] In re DiGuglielmo, 285 A.3d 305, 410 Educ. L. Rep. 438 (N.J. 2022).
[46] Farmer v. Troy Univ., 879 S.E.2d 124, 409 Educ. L. Rep. 402 (N.C. 2022).

the state where the plaintiff worked meant that the university waived its protections from sovereign immunity. The appellate court reversed and remanded the lower court's decision.

An appellate court in Louisiana affirmed the trial court's grant of summary judgment in favor of the university after a former professor alleged violations of state and federal law.[47] The professor received a jury duty summons requiring his service during the first week of the fall 2017 semester. While his supervisor approved the leave for jury duty, the professor failed to respond to numerous requests for his syllabus spanning multiple weeks. After the professor had been on leave for more than three weeks, only serving as a juror on four of those days, he discovered the trial was postponed due to weather-related damage and returned to work five days later. Less than a month after his return to work, the university held a termination hearing for the professor. This resulted in a recommendation for his termination and, ultimately, his dismissal. The professor brought this suit, alleging that his termination was based on his jury service. However, the court disagreed, holding that the professor's termination was due to his failure to perform his job duties both before and after his jury service. Thus, the professor's termination was proper.

In Mississippi, a former public university employee was terminated after a history of conflicts with a colleague resulted in a toxic environment within the department.[48] The termination followed a series of progressive disciplinary actions that included verbal notice, formal warning, and dismissal as a last resort. After the plaintiff received a verbal notice and formal warning, they were given the choice to resign or face dismissal. After not receiving the plaintiff's answer, the university terminated the employee. That employee then filed an appeal with a review board, to which the board affirmed the termination, and the decision was upheld by the university chancellor. The plaintiff sued, and the trial court held in favor of the university based on sufficient evidence for dismissal being provided at the review board. The appellate court affirmed the trial court's decision.

---

[47] Fugar v. Dillard Univ., 358 So.3d 168, 414 Educ. L. Rep. 774 (La. Ct. App. 2023).
[48] Avery v. Univ. of Miss., 346 So.3d 904, 408 Educ. L. Rep. 613 (Miss. Ct. App. 2022).

In Missouri, a former private university employee whose wrongful termination suit was dismissed and who was ordered to pay taxed costs to the university appealed a trial court's decision on the issue of paying costs.[49] The plaintiff argued the court erred in dismissing her claim and in assessing costs. The university countered by requesting sanctions imposed for a frivolous appeal. The appellate court affirmed the dismissal of plaintiff's claim and costs but declined to impose additional sanctions.

A public university fired an employee over a wage dispute.[50] The former employee filed suit against the university and the state for breach of contract, promissory estoppel, wrongful termination, negligent misrepresentation, intentional misrepresentation, intentional interference with a business expectancy, retaliation, and age discrimination. The plaintiff and the state reached a settlement agreement where the state paid the plaintiff $295,000 if the plaintiff agreed to drop all claims and to never work at the university again. A few months later, the plaintiff sued the state again and asserted that the no-hire provision violated a state public policy. The Washington appellate court concluded that the former employee waived the right to be rehired, affirming the trial court's decision.

Family Medical Leave Act (FMLA)

The Seventh Circuit affirmed an Illinois federal trial court's denial of an employee's motion for reconsideration.[51] The former employee took twelve weeks of FMLA leave, after which she failed to return to work or provide further documentation to extend her leave, so she was terminated. Additionally, while on FMLA leave, her supervisor withdrew the recommendation letter he had submitted in support of the employee's medical school applications. The employee then brought suit against the university and her former supervisor alleging a hostile work environment under Title VII, retaliation under the FMLA and Americans with Disabilities Act (ADA), and state law claims. The court held that the employee's retaliation claim under the FMLA was precluded, as her FMLA

---

[49] Owen v. Wash. Univ., 652 S.W.3d 349, 408 Educ. L. Rep. 580 (Mo. Ct. App. 2022).

[50] Elgiadi v. Wash. State Univ. Spokane, 519 P.3d 939, 409 Educ. L. Rep. 384 (Wash. Ct. App. 2022).

[51] Trahanas v. Nw. Univ., 64 F.4th 842, 413 Educ. L. Rep. 559 (7th Cir. 2023).

leave was not a motivating factor in her termination. Further, the employee did not show that she was injured by her supervisor withdrawing his recommendation letter and, regardless, the letter withdrawing support contained statements of opinion that were constitutionally protected. Therefore, she did not state a claim for retaliation under the FMLA.

A federal trial court in Indiana granted the college's motion for summary judgment on a former employee's claims for interference with her rights under FMLA.[52] The plaintiff, who worked as an administrative assistant for the information technology (IT) department, was reassigned to the position of administrative assistant in the graduate studies program when she returned from FMLA leave. To establish an interference claim under FMLA, an employee must show that "(1) she was eligible for the FMLA's protections; (2) her employer was covered by the FMLA; (3) she was entitled to FMLA leave; (4) she provided sufficient notice of her intent to take leave; and (5) her employer denied FMLA benefits to which she was entitled." Here, the court found that requiring the employee to attend a 30- to 60-minute meeting about her return to work did not interfere with her FMLA rights. Further, due to work restrictions, the employee was not entitled to be immediately reinstated to her former position, and a five-day delay in reinstatement did not interfere with her FMLA rights. Thus, the college was entitled to summary judgment.

A development associate for a university filed suit for violations of her rights under the Family Medical Leave Act (FMLA) against the university, her supervisor, several members of human resources, several members of the university compliance office, and the investigators for her complaints.[53] The investigators moved to dismiss. The federal trial court in Massachusetts granted the motion, stating that the investigators were not subject to liability under FMLA, and the plaintiff provided insufficient allegations to substantiate that the defendants acted with retaliation. The development associate also filed suit for violations of her FMLA rights against several members of human resources, again alleging retaliation. The defendants moved to dismiss. The same court granted the motion, stating that the defendants were not subject to liability under FMLA. The court also stated that the

---

[52] McManus v. St. Mary's Coll., 611 F. Supp. 3d 586, 412 Educ. L. Rep. 553 (N.D. Ind. 2020).

[53] Gregg v. Ne. Univ. (a), 599 F. Supp. 3d 9, 410 Educ. L. Rep. 611 (D. Mass. 2022).

plaintiff did not allege a claim of intentional malice, which was needed to prove there had been interference with her employment.[54]

Procedural Issues

Jurisdiction

The board for a university became concerned about the financial sustainability of the university's retirement system and issued the university a new fiscal plan.[55] The university opposed the new plan, and an association of faculty members filed suit to block the changes. The federal trial court in Puerto Rico dismissed the complaint for lack of jurisdiction, and the association appealed. The First Circuit affirmed the trial court's decision, holding that judicial review was not required for the board's actions in connection to the fiscal plan and that the trial court lacked jurisdiction.

The federal trial court in Puerto Rico granted the board of governors' motion to dismiss a former university president's claims under the First, Fifth, and Fourteenth Amendments.[56] The former president's contract with the university contained a forum selection clause which specified that any disputes would be addressed in the state trial court. In evaluating a forum selection clause, the court must determine whether the clause is permissive or mandatory, the scope of the clause, and whether the presumption of enforceability should apply. Here, the forum selection clause was mandatory, based on its use of the word "shall." Additionally, the forum selection clause was broad in scope, including any claim "'relating to' the 'execution' of the [c]ontract." Lastly, the court did not find any reason that the presumption of enforceability should not apply. Thus, the forum selection clause in the contract was valid and the case filed in federal court was dismissed.

---

[54] Gregg v. Ne. Univ. (b), 599 F. Supp. 3d 17, 410 Educ. L. Rep. 619 (D. Mass. 2022).
[55] In re Fin. Oversight & Mgmt. Bd. for P.R., 60 F.4th 9, 411 Educ. L. Rep. 980 (1st Cir. 2023).
[56] Haddock-Acevedo v. Bd. of Governors of Univ. of P.R., 615 F. Supp. 3d 78, 413 Educ. L. Rep. 161 (D.P.R. 2022).

A federal trial court in Tennessee granted the university's motion to transfer venue in a former employee's suit alleging retaliation in violation of Title VII and another civil rights statute.[57] Under Title VII, an action may be brought in the district in which the discriminatory/retaliatory act was committed, the relevant employment records are maintained, or the complainant would have worked had the discriminatory conduct not occurred. The university moved to transfer the case to the district in which the university, the former employee, all relevant employment records, and nearly all potential witnesses were located. The former employee did not challenge any of the university's assertions, instead arguing that the university failed to show any unreasonable hardship to the university or its witnesses by allowing the suit to proceed in the district where she filed. The court agreed with the university, finding that the location of documents and convenience of witnesses favored a transfer of venue.

The highest state court in New York reversed the trial court's decision to grant the defendant manufacturer's motion to dismiss based on a lack of personal jurisdiction.[58] The state of New York brought this breach of contract action on behalf of a public university against the manufacturer of unmanned aerial vehicles (UAVs), alleging that two UAVs purchased by the university did not function properly. The manufacturer, a Delaware corporation with headquarters in Michigan, argued that New York lacked personal jurisdiction to decide this case. The court disagreed, finding that the manufacturer was purposefully engaged in business activities in the state of New York; there was a substantial relationship between the manufacturer's business activities in New York and the contract, alleged breach, and potential damages at issue here; and allowing New York to exercise jurisdiction over the manufacturer did not violate due process.

An appellate court in Pennsylvania affirmed the trial court's decision denying the public university's motion for summary judgment on the plaintiff's claims related to workplace exposure to

---

[57] Van Cleave v. Univ. of S., 607 F. Supp. 3d 783, 411 Educ. L. Rep. 1040 (M.D. Tenn. 2022).

[58] State v. Vayu, Inc., 206 N.E.3d 1236, 414 Educ. L. Rep. 988 (N.Y. 2023).

asbestos and subsequent development of mesothelioma.[59] The plaintiff, a retired stationary engineer, brought common law claims, but the university argued that his claims must be filed with the Workers' Compensation Board as they fell under the Pennsylvania Occupational Disease Act (ODA). However, the court held that occupational diseases manifesting more than four years after an employee's last exposure to the hazardous material causing the disease is not limited to recovery under the ODA. Further, the university attempted to invoke the doctrine of primary jurisdiction, alleging the plaintiff was required to seek relief from the board before seeking judicial relief. Primary jurisdiction seeks to create "a workable relationship" between the judiciary and administrative agencies. Here, the court found no reason to allow the university to invoke primary jurisdiction; thus, the trial court properly denied summary judgment in favor of the university. The Supreme Court of Pennsylvania has since granted an appeal in this case.

Service of Process

In Louisiana, a former university librarian brought a wrongful termination suit against the university, directing that citation and service of process be made on the university.[60] The trial court granted the attorney general's declinatory exception of insufficient citation and service and dismissed the librarian's claims. The appellate court reversed and remanded, finding that the former librarian's failure to serve the attorney general within 90 days of filing the suit did not warrant dismissal for improper service and citation. Instead, the librarian should have been given an opportunity to request citation and service on the attorney general and the university's Office of Risk Management.

The New York Court of Claims, which addresses claims against the State of New York and some state agencies, denied a university's motion to dismiss for lack of jurisdiction on the retired employee's breach of contract claim.[61] Specifically, the retired

---

[59] Herold v. Univ. of Pittsburgh – of Commw. Sys. of Higher Educ., 291 A.3d 489, 414 Educ. L. Rep. 633 (Commw. Ct. Pa. 2023), appeal granted, 305 A.3d 957 (Pa. 2023).
[60] Thibodeaux v. McNeese State Univ., 354 So.3d 903, 412 Educ. L. Rep. 392 (La. Ct. App. 2023).
[61] Vazquez v. City Univ. of N.Y., 185 N.Y.S.3d 887, 414 Educ. L. Rep. 673 (Ct. Cl. N.Y. 2022).

employee alleged that the university failed to pay him for his accrued sick time and annual leave upon retirement. Under the relevant law, the employee had six months from the date of breach to file and serve the Office of the Attorney General (OAG) a copy of the claim either personally or by certified mail. Within that timeframe, the employee sent a copy of the claim to the OAG by regular mail. The defendant argued that the court lacked jurisdiction because the employee failed to properly serve the OAG. In response, and before the six months expired, the employee re-delivered his claim via personal service on the OAG. The university argued that this re-service did not satisfy jurisdictional requirements, but the court disagreed, holding that the employee's re-serving of his claim within the required timeframe cured the originally defective service.

Privilege

In Texas, the state university system filed suit against the attorney general challenging portions of an informal letter ruling that ordered the disclosure to records requesters of certain documents in an independent investigation report regarding the university's admissions policies.[62] The requesters intervened, seeking a declaratory judgment that all documents were public information and were not excepted from disclosure under the state Public Information Act, along with a writ of mandamus compelling the university to release the information. While the litigation was pending, the university system created a privilege log to track the documents it submitted to the attorney general and alleged they were all protected by attorney-client privilege. Specifically, it argued that documents it provided to the advisory firm contracted to review the admissions process were protected because the firm was acting as a "lawyer's representative." However, the firm did not fall within the statutory definition of a "lawyer's representative" as it was not "employed by the lawyer to assist in the rendition of professional legal services," so the materials disclosed during the investigation were not protected by attorney-client privilege.

---

[62] Franklin Ctr. for Gov't v. Univ. of Tex. Sys., 664 S.W.3d 371, 415 Educ. L. Rep. 399 (Tex. App. 2020).

Immunity

A former public university staff member brought a retaliation suit against their former department chair after allegedly being fired for complaining that they were going to be paid late.[63] The suit was brought against the department chair as an individual rather than against the institution under the Fair Labor Standards Act. The department chair argued entitlement to sovereign immunity under the Eleventh Amendment as well as qualified immunity. After a federal trial court in Texas held that the department chair was not entitled to either immunity, the Fifth Circuit reviewed both immunity claims. The court affirmed that sovereign immunity did not apply. However, the case was remanded to consider the question of qualified immunity and to determine whether qualified immunity applied under the Fair Labor Standards Act.

A police officer working at a private institution in Texas made a traffic stop for a student suspected of driving while intoxicated and subsequently killed the student by shooting him five times.[64] The student's parents sued both the university and the police officer. The university filed for summary judgment asserting that the police officer was protected by qualified immunity, which the trial court denied, and the university appealed. The appellate court affirmed the trial court's decision, stating there existed genuine evidence that precluded summary judgment regarding whether the officer acted in good faith.

Another appellate court in Texas affirmed a trial court's ruling that a public university was subject to the suit brought by a construction company.[65] The dispute stemmed from a subcontractor suing the construction company after not receiving payment due to a fraudulent bond that the university obtained. The university argued on grounds that it was not subject to the suit based on sovereign immunity, and that it did obtain a bond as required by law, albeit a fraudulent one. The trial court held that without a legitimate bond, the university could not invoke sovereign immunity. The appellate court affirmed this decision.

---

[63] Stramaski v. Lawley, 44 F.4th 318, 406 Educ. L. Rep. 168 (5th Cir. 2022).

[64] Univ. of the Incarnate Word v. Redus, 654 S.W.3d 169, 409 Educ. L. Rep. 553 (Tex. App. 2022).

[65] Univ. of Houston Sys. v. Ground Tex. Constr., Inc., 650 S.W.3d 832, 407 Educ. L. Rep. 964 (Tex. App. 2022).

Environmental Protections

In California, a petitioner sought review of an environmental impact report (EIR) for a university's long-range development plan and its plan to construct a student housing project that was issued under the California Environmental Quality Act (CEQA).[66] After the trial court denied the writ petition, the petitioner brought the current appeal arguing that the EIR failed to analyze an alternative to the development plan that would limit student enrollment, improperly restricted the scope of the plan to campus and properties close by, and failed to mitigate the environmental impacts of population growth and displacement that the plan would cause. The appellate court was unpersuaded by these arguments. In addition, the petitioner argued that the EIR did not justify the failure to consider alternative locations for the student housing project, which was set to be constructed on a historic landmark and an area known for political activity and protest, nor did it evaluate possible noise impacts on the residential neighborhoods surrounding campus. The court found merit in these arguments, reversing and remanding the case to fix the errors in the EIR.

Intellectual Property

In Louisiana, a dispute arose between the owners of the trademark of a phrase associated with a public historically black college and university (HBCU).[67] The patent owners sued the university's licensing agent and several licensees who produced and sold university merchandise bearing the trademarked phrase. The university never possessed a trademark on the phrase, despite it being the alma mater song for over 80 years. A federal trial court held that because the university could not join the suit as a matter of sovereign immunity, the case was dismissed. The Fifth Circuit affirmed the lower court decision.

A federal appeals court affirmed a Patent Trial and Appeal Board's decision on a patent infringement case brought by a public

---

[66] Make UC A Good Neighbor v. Regents of Univ. of Cal., 304 Cal. Rptr.3d 834, 412 Educ. L. Rep. 815 (Cal. Ct. App. 2023).

[67] Lee v. Anthony Lawrence Collection, 47 F.4th 262, 407 Educ. L. Rep. 459 (5th Cir. 2022).

university against two technology companies.[68] The case centered on three claims surrounding the method and apparatus for implementing a particular type of code. The board found that two of the claims were patentable. The federal appeals court affirmed.

A federal trial court in Pennsylvania denied the university's motion to dismiss an online retailer's counterclaim that the university's trademarks should be canceled because they were purely ornamental.[69] The question at issue here was whether, under the Lanham Act, a symbol identifies "the source of the goods if it merely creates an association between it and the trademark holder." The three marks at issue were a shortened version of the university's name, an old school logo that was phased out in 1987 and registered as a trademark 30 years later, and an image of the university seal. The online retailer argued that the marks were simply used as decoration and not to distinguish items from the university from others. The court held that a per se approach did not govern the determination of whether trademarks held by the university were purely ornamental. Instead, it found that a fact-intensive inquiry into whether consumers believed that the marks at issue signified university-authorized merchandise was appropriate.

The plaintiff worked in a university lab where another researcher stole and then published from the plaintiff's research materials.[70] The plaintiff made a report through the university. A university officer said the plaintiff should accept the defendant's apology, but the defendant did not return the stolen research materials or correct the published paper. Later, the defendant began to spread rumors that the plaintiff was under investigation for his research. During this time, the university began investigating the plaintiff, interviewing the plaintiff's lab staff and seizing several laboratory documents. The plaintiff continued to receive more investigations and accusations from the university regarding his research integrity, while the university failed to respond to the plaintiff's complaints about the other researcher. The plaintiff filed suit against the university and the other researcher for trade secret misappropriation, breach of contract,

---

[68] LSI Corp. v. Regents of Univ. of Minn., 43 F.4th 1349, 406 Educ. L. Rep. 122 (Fed. Cir. 2022).
[69] Pa. State Univ. v. Vintage Brand, LLC, 614 F. Supp. 3d 101, 412 Educ. L. Rep. 649 (M.D. Pa. 2022).
[70] Houser v. Feldman, 600 F. Supp. 3d 550, 410 Educ. L. Rep. 888 (E.D. Pa. 2022).

defamation, civil conspiracy, unjust enrichment, conversion, specific injunctive relief, and collective trust. The defendants moved to dismiss. A federal trial court in Pennsylvania granted the defendants' motions to dismiss regarding the breach of contract, misappropriation of trade secrets, and defamation claims. The court held that the plaintiff's claims regarding specific injunction and a constructive trust would be construed as *ad damnum* clauses.

Property-Related Issues

A federal trial court in Illinois granted the university's motion to dismiss the assignee's claims stemming from their purchase of a contractor's accounts receivable pursuant to a factoring agreement.[71] After the assignee purchased the accounts receivable and issued an invoice to the university for work completed, the university paid the subcontractors directly. It is unclear whether the university paid the assignee his share of the invoice. The court held that, under Illinois law, the letter from the assignee informing the university of the assignment did not amount to consideration for a separate contract between the two. Further, the assignee could not maintain an action for an open account under Illinois or Florida law because of the existence of a written contract, nor could the assignee maintain an account stated claim under Illinois law as there was a dispute over the amount owed, if any. Thus, the assignee's claims were dismissed.

Corporations that owned, managed, and operated a teaching hospital and clinics requested a refund of ad valorem taxes paid on the state university teaching hospital and clinics.[72] After their refund request was denied, the corporations filed suit for relief against the county's property appraiser, tax collector, and the executive director of the Florida Department of Revenue. Specifically, the corporations sought a declaration that their properties were immune from taxation. The trial court granted summary judgment in favor of the corporations, finding the state was the equitable owner of the properties at issue. The Florida appellate court affirmed, holding that the state, through the state

---

[71] AmeriFactors Fin. Grp., LLC v. Univ. of Chi., 619 F. Supp. 3d 842, 414 Educ. L. Rep. 378 (N.D. Ill. 2022).

[72] Solomon v. Shands Teaching Hosp. and Clinics, Inc., 353 So.3d 677, 411 Educ. L. Rep. 1275 (Fla. Dist. Ct. App. 2022).

university, was the equitable owner of the properties; thus, the properties were immune from ad valorem taxation.

In Indiana, a private university entered into agreement with a public utility company to install a private transmission line in an underground duct bank that the utility company sought as part of an eminent domain claim against a private company.[73] After discovering the agreement, the plaintiff sued on the basis that the private transmission line was not allowable under eminent domain. The trial court held that the public utility company could still obtain the property for a public purpose and that the private university's use was incidental. The appeals court reversed the decision, allowing the utility company to proceed with installing their line while preventing the private university's line to be installed.

The Supreme Court of Massachusetts found that the defendant, a private university in possession of photographs of enslaved persons, was required to return the photographs to one of the descendants.[74] After the plaintiff established identity as a descendant of the enslaved persons in the photographs, the university refused to turn over the photographs. The state supreme court upheld the trial court's finding that the property rights to the photographs rested with the photographer employed by the university rather than those depicted in the photographs. In addition, the state supreme court vacated the trial court's decision to dismiss the plaintiff's claim of emotional distress, given the university's behavior, and allowed the plaintiff to amend the complaint.

An appellate court in New Jersey dismissed a bidder's appeal after the bidder was not awarded a contract under a university hospital's request for proposals to design, construct, and operate a pharmacy at a hospital.[75] The primary issue on appeal was whether the university hospital was a state administrative agency, as the bidder argued. To determine whether an entity is a state administrative agency, the court considered the legislature's intent. Ultimately, the court held that the legislature did not

---

[73] 701 Niles, LLC v. AEP Ind. Mich. Transmission Co., Inc., 191 N.E.3d 931, 406 Educ. L. Rep. 372 (Ind. Ct. App. 2022).
[74] Lanier v. President & Fellows of Harvard Coll., 191 N.E.3d 1063, 406 Educ. L. Rep. 384 (Mass. 2022).
[75] In re Protest of Contract for Retail Pharmacy Design, Construction, Start-up, and Operation, Request for Proposal No. UH-P20-006, 290 A.3d 221, 413 Educ. L. Rep. 886 (N.J. Super. Ct. App. Div. 2023).

intend for the university hospital to be a state administrative agency; thus, its decisions were not directly appealable in court.

A borough within Pennsylvania filed suit for declaratory judgment against the state university system and one of its universities to establish that the charge related to stormwater management was not a tax from which the university system and university were immune.[76] The borough adopted a stormwater charge to cover operation, maintenance, and repair costs for a small storm sewer system it owned and operated. The university system argued that the charge was a tax because its revenue went toward providing a "'general benefit' [to] promote 'the welfare of all,'" while the borough argued that the charge was a fee because the amount owed was appealable, the revenue went into a specific fund for stormwater management, and only owners of developed land were required to pay the fee. The court ultimately agreed with the university system, holding that the stormwater charge was a general tax because the stormwater management system yielded a common benefit on all residents of the borough, as opposed to benefiting specific properties.

Crime-Related Issues

The defendant in this case opened a trade school for veterans.[77] While running the trade school, he lied on his application for VA approval. He additionally lied to enrolling students regarding the status of VA approval for the trade school and how much of the students' GI-Bill funds would be depleted. The defendant, in a federal trial court in Texas, was convicted of multiple wire fraud and money-laundering charges for running a scheme to defraud. After being sentenced and ordered to forfeit $72 million from the wire fraud, the defendant appealed. The Fifth Circuit affirmed the sentence but remanded and vacated the trial court's forfeiture order because the trial court incorrectly applied the definition of "proceeds."

A university brought action against a campus police officer for unlawful seizure, malicious prosecution, fabrication of evidence,

---

[76] Borough of W. Chester v. Pa. State Sys. of Higher Educ., 291 A.3d 455, 414 Educ. L. Rep. 620 (Commw. Ct. Pa. 2023).

[77] U.S. v. Davis, 53 F.4th 833, 409 Educ. L. Rep. 35 (5th Cir. 2022).

and indemnity under state law.[78] The officer previously stopped a Hispanic man, whom he then tackled to the ground and arrested. The defendant then intentionally failed to provide the video and audio recordings of the encounter to the prosecuting attorney who held the arrestee for trial. The defendant asked for dismissal of the claims and requested attorney fees, which the federal trial court in Oregon denied.

In Michigan, a defendant was charged with making false or misleading statements to a peace officer during a criminal investigation.[79] The defendant moved to quash the binding over. The trial court granted the motion and dismissed the case, and this appeal followed. To bind a defendant over for trial, the court "'must find probable cause that the defendant committed a felony' based on there being 'evidence of each element of the crime charged or evidence from which the elements may be inferred.'" The appellate court held that there was insufficient evidence to find that the statements made by the defendant were affirmatively false or misled law enforcement. Thus, the dismissal of the case against the defendant was affirmed.

In New York, a former student was sexually abused by a resident advisor.[80] The court denied the private university's motion to dismiss, finding that the plaintiff was able to show lack of consent under the Child Victims Act. The plaintiff argued that the university failed to adequately respond to reports of sexual assault and create a safe campus environment. The court held that universities have a duty to protect students from known risks of harm, and that the university could be held liable for negligence if it failed to take reasonable measures to address the risk of sexual assault on campus.

Wage-Related Issues

Former university hospital employees filed suit against the university board of regents stating that the university violated a state law by intentionally paying employees later than required.[81]

---

78 Univ. of Or. v. Phillips, 593 F. Supp. 3d 1062, 409 Educ. L. Rep. 169 (D. Or. 2022).

79 People v. Simon, 984 N.W.2d 800, 412 Educ. L. Rep. 318 (Mich. Ct. App. 2021).

80 Druger v. Syracuse Univ., 172 N.Y.S.3d 304, 406 Educ. L. Rep. 349 (N.Y. App. Div. 2022).

81 Myers v. Iowa Bd. of Regents, 594 F. Supp. 3d 1093, 409 Educ. L. Rep. 736 (S.D. Iowa 2022).

A federal trial court in Iowa held that the employment offer letters did not (a) constitute a written agreement to follow the timing provisions of the state law, (b) the language of the letters did not clearly reflect the state law, and (c) the university's failure to pay the former employees' vacation and sick days after their termination also was not covered by the state law. The court held the university liable for liquated damages, given that it had intentionally paid its employees late. Thus, the court partially granted the plaintiff's motion for summary judgment regarding the university's lateness but also dismissed the motion concerning the vacation and sick leave claim.

An appellate court in California affirmed the trial court's entry of judgment in favor of an adjunct professor on her wage statements claim and awarded her penalties and attorney fees, but affirmed the dismissal of her claims for unpaid wages.[82] Specifically, the professor alleged that adjunct professors were only paid for the dates listed in the employment contract (beginning on the first day of the semester and ending on the final day), but they were required to perform work outside of those dates without pay for tasks like preparing syllabi and other course materials before the semester began and grading exams and submitting final grades after the semester ended. After the trial court issued its decision, but before the current appeal, the legislature enacted a law that would benefit the university's case, and the university argued it should be applied retroactively. The court disagreed, holding that the legislative history and remedial purpose of the legislation did not overcome the presumption against retroactivity. Thus, the entry of judgment in favor of the professor on the wage statement claim was proper. However, her unpaid wages claim was preempted by federal law.

In Pennsylvania, a private college contracted with several union workers for a construction project paid for by public bonds issued by the county.[83] The unions argued that the project was "public work," and their members were entitled to prevailing wages for the work completed. The Department of Labor and Industry, Bureau of Labor Law Compliance found that the project was not a

---

[82] Gola v. Univ. of S.F., 90 Cal. App.5th 548, 414 Educ. L. Rep. 939 (Cal. Ct. App. 2023).

[83] Ursinus Coll. v. Prevailing Wage Appeals Bd., 280 A.3d 1113, 407 Educ. L. Rep. 846 (Pa. Commw. Ct. 2022).

"public work" and the union members were not entitled to prevailing wages; however, the state prevailing wage appeals board found in favor of the unions. The private college challenged this decision in state court, and the court held that the project was not a public work because the private college held the risk for repaying the bonds.

Governance-Related Issues

The Fifth Circuit affirmed a lower court's decision that a clinical teaching hospital affiliated with a public university did not engage in monopolistic behavior.[84] The issue stemmed from a dispute between the hospital's operator and a private nonprofit hospital. The private hospital donated funds to the university and made an agreement with the university to refer patients to the nonprofit hospital. The university hospital operator sued on antitrust grounds. A federal trial court in Louisiana dismissed based on failure to state a proper antitrust claim. The appeals court affirmed the decision.

A foreign country decided to provide some of its citizens full scholarships to a university in the United States.[85] The country would send the university money for the students' tuition directly, which became a problem whenever a student had funds left over because the university would use those extra funds toward expenses unrelated to the international students. The students initially filed suit, and the university had to pay back a sum of $202,000 to the country, but the litigation did not conclude. The country brought seven claims against the defendants, including declaratory judgment, accounting, unjust enrichment, conversion, negligent hiring, retention, monitoring, and supervision of its officials. The defendants motioned to dismiss on several grounds, claiming immunity. A federal trial court in Alabama held that the Eleventh Amendment protected the university officials within the scope of their official capacities. However, the trial court also held that the university officials were not entitled to immunity as individuals under the state constitution, nor were they entitled to state-agent immunity.

---

[84] BRFHH Shreveport, LLC v. Willis-Knighton Med. Ctr., 49 F.4th 520, 408 Educ. L. Rep. 84 (5th Cir. 2022).

[85] Fed. Republic of Nigeria v. Ala. State Univ., 604 F. Supp. 3d 1312, 411 Educ. L. Rep. 506 (M.D. Ala. 2022).

A federal trial court in Washington D.C. held that an alumnus of a public university may be entitled to records of a child sex abuse scandal under the Freedom of Information Act.[86] The case centered on two sets of email records: (1) emails that were "inadvertently overlooked" during a previous phase of the case, and (2) previously withheld records from a search of an email database and those reviewed by other government agencies as part of "remanded records." The court held that the Department of Justice did not provide sufficient justification to withhold the "inadvertently overlooked" emails from the FOIA request but did provide sufficient justification to withhold the "remanded records" from the plaintiff.

Several community college districts unsuccessfully petitioned the Supreme Court of California for reimbursement associated with state-mandated programs and services under the State of California Constitution.[87] Failure to meet the state mandate would jeopardize state aid. The community college districts filed a claim with the California Commission on State Mandates for reimbursement. The Commission argued that there was no legal obligation, and the loss of state aid was merely possible. A trial court affirmed the Commission's decision before being reversed by an appellate court. The Supreme Court agreed with the trial court that the districts were not compelled to comply with the mandate.

An assistant professor submitted several papers to academic journals, but the papers were retracted due to concerns about citations and plagiarism.[88] Shortly after that, the professor left her position and a third party issued an open records request for post-publication communication between the university, the professor, and the journals. When the university notified the professor, she did not want the materials released and filed suit. The court denied the professor's motion for preliminary injunction, and she appealed. The California appellate court affirmed the decision because it held that post-publication communications were public records, and the state public records act regarding exemptions from disclosure did not apply to post-publication communications.

---

[86] Bagwell v. U.S. Dept. of Just., 588 F. Supp. 3d 58, 408 Educ. L. Rep. 193 (D.D.C. 2022).
[87] Coast Cmty. Coll. Dist. v. Comm'n on State Mandates, 514 P.3d 854, 406 Educ. L. Rep. 958 (Cal. 2022).
[88] Iloh v. Regents of Univ. of Cal., 303 Cal.Rptr.3d 709, 411 Educ. L. Rep. 698 (Cal. Ct. App. 2023).

In California, an appellate court affirmed a trial court's decision that a private university's nursing program was required to obtain state board authorization prior to expanding its student enrollment from 500 to 850 per year over five years.[89] The state board provided examples of "substantive changes" which included a new campus, ownership, and agreements with institutions of higher education. Although the state board previously considered and declined to add enrollment changes to the list of examples, the trial court held that such a change required board approval.

An editor of a local newspaper filed suit against four university board members for holding a position with the state while residing outside of the state.[90] The defendants asserted that the state residency employment law only applied to public employees who received publicly funded salaries and that university board members held unpaid volunteer positions. Both the editor and the board members filed motions for summary judgment. The New Jersey trial court decided that the university and board members were not subject to the state act regarding residency requirements. The court denied the plaintiff's motion for summary judgment, granted the defendants' cross-motion for summary judgment, and dismissed the complaint with prejudice.

An appeals court in New Mexico affirmed a lower court's ruling that a private foundation that raises funds for a public university is not exempt from a public disclosure law.[91] The dispute arose when the plaintiff requested communications and financial records related to the naming rights for a sports facility at the public university. The court held that the private foundation acted as an extension of the public university and was subject to the public disclosure law.

A newspaper in New York filed a petition because the state education department denied the newspaper's open records request for records from public and private schools related to homeschooling.[92] The court dismissed the petition, and the newspaper appealed. The court held that the university's requests

---

[89] W. Coast Univ., Inc. v. Bd. of Reg. Nursing, 298 Cal.Rptr.3d 534, 407 Educ. L. Rep. 198 (Cal. Ct. App. 2022).

[90] Kratovil v. Angelson, 282 A.3d 651, 408 Educ. L. Rep. 903 (N.J. Super. Ct. 2020).

[91] Libit v. Univ. of N.M. Lobo Club, 516 P.3d 217, 407 Educ. L. Rep. 310 (N.M. Ct. App. 2022).

[92] Jewish Press, Inc. v. N.Y. State Educ. Dep't, 180 N.Y.S.3d 726, 411 Educ. L. Rep. 727 (N.Y. App. Div. 2023).

for records regarding school performance were not reasonably described. The court additionally stated that the newspaper failed to exhaust its administrative remedies regarding requests for protected records, affirming the trial court's decision.

A newspaper in Texas requested for a university to provide records related to students who went through the student conduct process and were found responsible of violence and sexual offenses.[93] The university denied the request, stating that FERPA did not require the disclosure. The newspaper filed a petition stating that FERPA allowed the release of information, motioned for summary judgment, and requested attorney fees. The university also motioned for summary judgment. The trial court sided with the plaintiff, but denied its request for attorney fees, and both parties appealed. The appellate court held that the university denied the Public Information Act (PIA) request without authority from the attorney general or court of law, and there was no compelling reason to withhold the information. The appellate court also revised and remanded the attorney fees decision.

Workers' Compensation

In 2020, a doctor diagnosed an associate university dean with bilateral wrists, carpal tunnel syndrome, and tendonitis.[94] The associate dean then filed a claim for workers' compensation benefits. However, during the hearing process she disclosed that she sought treatment previously in 2014 for issues with her hands. Due to the fact that the claimant failed to report this information, she failed to satisfy her duty to report and submit credible medical evidence connecting her injuries to her employment. The claimant appealed, and the New York appellate court affirmed that there was insufficient evidence that the plaintiff's employment had caused her injuries.

In New York, a nurse injured her left leg and both knees after slipping and falling on a wet floor.[95] Following a workers' compensation claim, the university filed for a reimbursement from

---

[93] Univ. of Tex. at Austin v. Gatehouse Media Tex. Holdings, II, Inc., 656 S.W.3d 791, 411 Educ. L. Rep. 398 (Tex. App. 2022).
[94] Yearwood v. Long Island Univ., 178 N.Y.S.3d 273, 410 Educ. L. Rep. 491 (N.Y. App. Div. 2022).
[95] O'Donnell v. Univ. of Rochester, 172 N.Y.S.3d 136, 406 Educ. L. Rep. 341 (N.Y. App. Div. 2022).

the Special Disability Fund due to the employee having preexisting conditions. After a workers' compensation law judge granted the university a reimbursement stemming from a conference sheet signed by the university and the Special Funds Group, a Workers' Compensation Board overturned the judge's decision. The court held that the conference sheet was not legally binding as it neither constituted a stipulation nor a settlement agreement and was not approved by the Board.

Consumer Protection

A previous founder and owner of a financial advisor company would solicit prospective students for money and demographic information while promising to enroll students in a financial aid program.[96] The company would then send the prospective student a booklet with generic financial aid information. After hundreds of complaints, the Consumer Financial Protection Bureau (CFCB) alleged that the defendant's conduct was deceptive and filed for summary judgment against the advisor and default judgment against the company. A federal trial court in California sided with CFPB, and the defendant appealed. The Ninth Circuit affirmed the previous decision, stating that the defendant fell under the CFPB's enforcement authority and created a deceptive impression through his solicitations.

Student Loans

A bankruptcy appellate panel affirmed a trial court's decision that a debtor who sought to discharge student loan debt under Chapter 7 bankruptcy was ineligible to do so.[97] The debtor was a former medical school student who did not complete medical residency after a conflict with the residency director. The plaintiff did not enter an income-based repayment program. The court applied the three-pronged *Brunner* test and found that the debtor did not demonstrate an undue hardship because they had not been motivated to seek a reasonable minimal standard of living.

A federal appeals court granted an appeal by several states seeking to stop a student loan debt discharge by the federal

---

[96] Consumer Fin. Prot. Bureau v. Aria, 54 F.4th 1168, 410 Educ. L. Rep. 32 (9th Cir. 2022).

[97] In re Parvizi, 641 B.R. 729, 406 Educ. L. Rep. 924 (1st Cir. 2022).

government under the Higher Education Relief Opportunities for Students (HEROES) Act.[98] The district court initially held that the states lacked standing to bring legal action, determining that it was a state-affiliated loan agency, not the states, that were harmed by the debt cancellation. The appellate court found that the relationship between the loan agency and the state of Missouri was sufficient for granting standing. This case later went before the U.S. Supreme Court and was decided in 2023, with the plaintiffs prevailing against the federal government that the student loan discharge was unlawful under the HEROES Act.

The Tenth Circuit affirmed a district court's decision that a debt collector's letter to the plaintiff's employer was not a violation of the Fair Debt Collection Practices Act (FDCPA).[99] The debt collector sent the letter to the employer to garnish the plaintiff's wages after the plaintiff defaulted on their student loan. The letter contained the logo of the federal student loan guaranty agency that employed the defendant to collect the debt. The plaintiff claimed that use of the logo was misleading and unfair. In dismissing the claim, the court held that the letter was not misleading nor unfair and thus did not constitute a violation of the FDCPA.

A student loan guaranty agency filed suit against the U.S. Department of Education in response to the Department's regulation limiting the agency's ability to assess recollection costs to borrowers who entered a loan repayment or rehabilitation agreement.[100] The federal trial court in Washington D.C. held that the agency lacked standing to sue regarding repayment but found that the Department was not able to restrict actions regarding rehabilitation agreements. In addition, the court held that the Department's regulation pertaining to the prohibition of assessing reasonable collection costs to borrowers who entered a loan prepayment agreement within 60 days was unlawful. This decision was later affirmed in part and reversed in part by the federal appeals court for Washington D.C., holding that the agency had standing to challenge the rule for both repayment and rehabilitation agreements, and that the Department had the

---

[98] Neb. v. Biden, 52 F.4th 1044, 408 Educ. L. Rep. 726 (8th Cir. 2022), *rev'd and remanded* 143 S. Ct. 2355 (2023).

[99] Tavernaro v. Pioneer Credit Recovery, Inc., 43 F.4th 1062, 406 Educ. L. Rep. 98 (10th Cir. 2022).

[100] Ascendium Educ. Sols., Inc. v. Cardona (a), 588 F. Supp. 3d 7, 408 Educ. L. Rep. 176 (D.D.C. 2022).

ability to prohibit the assessment of unreasonable collection costs.[101]

A federal trial court in New York found in favor of a borrower in a class action suit after a loan servicer failed to provide a loan verification certificate within the required 10-day period, resulting in extra payments.[102] The issue stemmed from the loan servicer hindering the borrowers from consolidating or prepaying their loans. In finding that the loan servicer engaged in misleading behavior, the court ordered both parties to engage in settlement talks.

Retirement

An appellate court in Mississippi reversed a lower court's decision denying non-duty-related disability retirement benefits.[103] The plaintiff, a registrar at a public university, retired after experiencing chronic pain. Later, plaintiff requested non-duty-related disability benefits as a result of a deteriorating form of arthritis. A series of medical examinations did not find consensus on the plaintiff's ability to return to work. The retirement system's appeals committee denied the disability benefits, and the plaintiff unsuccessfully filed a complaint in a trial court. The appellate court, however, held that the retirement system's appeals committee acted in an arbitrary and capricious manner by not considering the plaintiff's medical evidence and statements to the job requirements.

Conclusion

Among the cases presented, a handful latch onto ongoing political and cultural concerns and movements. The Supreme Court held that a student loan forgiveness program was unconstitutional, affecting millions of student loan borrowers across the United States. The First Circuit found that a student loan debtor who was unmotivated to seek a reasonable minimal

---

[101] Ascendium Educ. Sols., Inc. v. Cardona (b), 78 F.4th 470, 420 Educ. L. Rep. (D.C. Cir. 2023).

[102] Chery v. Conduent Educ. Servs., LLC, 581 F. Supp. 3d 436, 406 Educ. L. Rep. 804 (N.D.N.Y. 2022).

[103] Finley v. Pub. Emps.' Ret. Sys. of Miss., 346 So.3d 472, 408 Educ. L. Rep. 587 (Miss. Ct. App. 2022).

standard of living was not entitled to student loan forgiveness based on undue hardship. A federal trial court in Florida found that a public institution violates the First Amendment when it prohibits its employees from providing expert testimony in a legal case unrelated to the institution. Under the Child Victims Act in New York, an appellate court held that universities owe students a duty to protect them from known risks of harm, and, therefore, a university could be held liable for negligence where it fails to take reasonable measures to address the risk of sexual assault on campus. In Texas, an appellate court held that documents provided to an advisory firm employed by an attorney to review an institution's admissions process were not protected by attorney-client privilege. While the hot buttons do not all burn at the same temperature, the underlying issues remain inflamed.

Alphabetical List of Cases

701 Niles, LLC v. AEP Ind. Mich. Transmission Co., Inc.

AmeriFactors Fin. Group, LLC v. Univ. of Chi.

Ascendium Educ. Sols., Inc. v. Cardona (a)

Ascendium Educ. Sols., Inc. v. Cardona (b)

Austin v. Univ. of Fla. Bd. of Trs.

Avery v. Univ. of Miss.

Bagwell v. U.S. Dept. of Just.

Banford v. Bd. of Regents of Univ. of Minn.

Blakely v. Austin Peay State Univ.

Borough of West Chester v. Pa. State Sys. of Higher Educ.

Bradley v. Bynum

BRFHH Shreveport, LLC v. Willis-Knighton Med. Ctr.

Brown v. Linder (a)

Brown v. Linder (b)

Capacity Wireless, LLC v. Bd. of Regents of Univ. of Minn.

Chery v. Conduent Educ. Servs., LLC

Coast Cmty. Coll. Dist. v. Comm'n on State Mandates

Const. Consulting, Inc. v. Dist. Bd. of Trs. of Broward Coll.

Consumer Fin. Prot. Bureau v. Aria

Corkrean v. Drake Univ.

Countryman-Roswurm v. Wichita State Univ.

Cowden v. Bd. of Governors of Colo. State Univ. Sys. *ex rel.* Colo. State Univ.-Pueblo

Desai v. Univ. of Mass. Mem'l Med. Ctr.

Doe v. Regents of Univ. of Colo.

Druger v. Syracuse Univ.

Dunn v. Ne. Helicopters Flight Servs., LLC

Elgiadi v. Wash. State Univ. Spokane

Farmer v. Troy Univ.

Farzinpour v. Berklee Coll. of Music

Fed. Republic of Nigeria v. Ala. State Univ.

Fei Wang v. Bd. of Trs. of Univ. of Ill.

Felton v. Monroe Cmty. Coll.

Finley v. Pub. Emps.' Ret. Sys. of Miss.

Fosu v. Univ. of R.I.

Franklin Ctr. for Gov't v. Univ. of Tex. Sys.

Fugar v. Dillard Univ.

Gola v. Univ. of SF

Goldblum v. Univ. of Cincinnati

Gonzalez v. US Human Rights Network

Gregg v. Northeastern Univ. (a)

Gregg v. Northeastern Univ. (b)

Haddock-Acevedo v. Bd. of Governors of Univ. of P.R.

Hansbrough v. Coll. of St. Rose

Herold v. Univ. of Pittsburgh of Commw. Sys. of Higher Educ.

Houser v. Feldman

Iloh v. Regents of Univ. of Cal.

In re Contract for Retail Pharmacy Design, Constr., Start-up & Operation, Request for Proposal No. UH-P20-006

In re DiGuglielmo

In re Fin. Oversight & Mgmt. Bd. for P.R.

In re Parvizi

Jewish Press, Inc. v. N.Y. State Educ. Dep't

Kratovil v. Angelson

Lanier v. President & Fellows of Harvard Coll.

Lashley v. Spartanburg Methodist Coll.

Lax v. City Univ. of N.Y.

Federal Cases

First Circuit

In re Fin. Oversight & Mgmt. Bd. for P.R.
In re Parvizi

Massachusetts
Desai v. Univ. of Mass. Mem'l Med. Ctr.
Farzinpour v. Berklee Coll. of Music
Gregg v. Northeastern Univ. (a)
Gregg v. Northeastern Univ. (b)
Rucker v. President & Fellows of Harvard Coll.

Puerto Rico
Haddock-Acevedo v. Bd. of Governors of Univ. of P.R.

Rhode Island
Fosu v. Univ. of R.I.

Second Circuit

Connecticut
Othon v. Wesleyan Univ.

New York
Chery v. Conduent Educ. Servs., LLC
Felton v. Monroe Cmty. Coll.

Third Circuit

Pennsylvania
Houser v. Feldman
Pa. State Univ. v. Vintage Brand, LLC

Fourth Circuit

Lashley v. Spartanburg Methodist Coll.

Fifth Circuit

BRFHH Shreveport, LLC v. Willis-Knighton Med. Ctr.
Lee v. Anthony Lawrence Collection

Stramaski v. Lawley
U.S. v. Davis

Mississippi
Bradley v. Bynum

Texas
Nikolova v. Univ. of Tex. at Austin
Tex. A&M Univ. 12th Man Found. v. Hartford Lloyds Ins. Co.

Sixth Circuit

Goldblum v. Univ. of Cincinnati

Tennessee
Blakely v. Austin Peay State Univ.
Van Cleave v. Univ. of S.

Seventh Circuit

Trahanas v. Northwestern Univ.
Xiong v. Bd. of Regents of Univ. of Wis. Sys.

Illinois
AmeriFactors Fin. Group, LLC v. Univ. of Chi.
Fei Wang v. Bd. of Trs. of Univ. of Ill.
McDaniel v. Loyola Univ. Med. Ctr.
Wang v. Bd. of Trs. of Univ. of Ill.

Indiana
McManus v. St. Mary's Coll.

Wisconsin
Marquette Univ. v. Kuali, Inc.

Eighth Circuit

Banford v. Bd. of Regents of Univ. of Minn.
Brown v. Linder (a)
Corkrean v. Drake Univ.
Nebraska v. Biden
Thompson v. Univ. of Ark. Bd. of Trs.
Walker-Swinton v. Philander Smith Coll.

Iowa
Brown v. Linder (b)
Myers v. Iowa Bd. of Regents

Missouri
Rockhurst Univ. v. Factory Mut. Ins. Co.

Ninth Circuit

Consumer Fin. Prot. Bureau v. Aria
Sullivan v. Univ. of Wash.

Arizona
Gonzalez v. US Human Rights Network

California
Weiss v. Perez

Idaho
Sanders v. Univ. of Idaho *ex rel.* Bd. of Regents of Univ. of Idaho

Oregon
Univ. of Or. v. Phillips

Washington
Okelo v. Antioch Univ.

Tenth Circuit

Tavernaro v. Pioneer Credit Recovery, Inc.

Colorado
Cowden v. Bd. of Governors of Colo. State Univ. Sys. *ex rel.* Colo. State Univ.-Pueblo
Doe v. Regents of Univ. of Colo.

Kansas
Countryman-Roswurm v. Wichita State Univ.

Eleventh Circuit

Alabama
Fed. Republic of Nigeria v. Ala. State Univ.

Florida

Austin v. Univ. of Fla. Bd. of Trs.

D.C. Circuit

Ascendium Educ. Sols., Inc. v. Cardona (b)

D.C.

Ascendium Educ. Sols., Inc. v. Cardona (a)
Bagwell v. U.S. Dept. of Just.
Moini v. Wrighton
U.S. E.E.O.C. v. George Wash. Univ.

Federal Circuit

LSI Corp. v. Regents of Univ. of Minn.

State and D.C. Cases

California
Coast Cmty. Coll. Dist. v. Comm'n on State Mandates
Gola v. Univ. of SF
Iloh v. Regents of Univ. of Cal.
Make UC a Good Neighbor v. Regents of Univ. of Cal.
West Coast Univ., Inc. v. Bd. of Reg. Nursing

Connecticut
Dunn v. Ne. Helicopters Flight Servs., LLC

Florida
Const. Consulting, Inc. v. Dist. Bd. of Trs. of Broward Coll.
Solomon v. Shands Teaching Hosp. & Clinics, Inc.

Indiana
701 Niles, LLC v. AEP Ind. Mich. Transmission Co., Inc.

Louisiana
Fugar v. Dillard Univ.
Thibodeaux v. McNeese State Univ.

Massachusetts
Lanier v. President & Fellows of Harvard Coll.

Michigan
People v. Simon

Minnesota
Capacity Wireless, LLC v. Bd. of Regents of Univ. of Minn.

Mississippi
Avery v. Univ. of Miss.
Finley v. Pub. Emps.' Ret. Sys. of Miss.

Missouri
Owen v. Wash. Univ.

North Carolina
Farmer v. Troy Univ.

New Jersey
In re DiGuglielmo
In re Contract for Retail Pharmacy Design, Constr., Start-up & Operation, Request for Proposal No. UH-P20-006
Kratovil v. Angelson

New Mexico
Libit v. Univ. of N.M. Lobo Club

New York
State v. Vayu, Inc.
Druger v. Syracuse Univ.
Hansbrough v. Coll. of St. Rose
Jewish Press, Inc. v. N.Y. State Educ. Dep't
O'Donnell v. Univ. of Rochester
Roach v. Cornell Univ.
Rogoff v. Long Island Univ.
Yearwood v. Long Island Univ.
Vazquez v. City Univ. of N.Y.
Wiltz v. State
Lax v. City Univ. of N.Y.

Pennsylvania
Borough of West Chester v. Pa. State Sys. of Higher Educ.
Herold v. Univ. of Pittsburgh of Commw. Sys. of Higher Educ.
Ursinus College v. Prevailing Wage Appeals Bd.

Texas
Franklin Ctr. for Gov't v. Univ. of Tex. Sys.
Tex. Tech Univ. Health Scis. Ctr.-El Paso v. Flores
Univ. of Houston Sys. v. Ground Tex. Constr., Inc.
Univ. of Tex. at Austin v. Gatehouse Media Tex. Holdings, II, Inc.
Univ. of the Incarnate Word v. Redus

Washington
Elgiadi v. Wash. State Univ. Spokane

CHAPTER 9

STUDENTS IN HIGHER EDUCATION

Elizabeth T. Lugg, Joy Blanchard,
and Gillian P. Foss

Introduction

This chapter reviews cases reported in 2023 involving student-related matters in higher education. These cases dealt with academics; misconduct on academic grounds; torts including COVID-related actions; discrimination claims involving race, gender, and disability; and financial aid.

Academic and Curricular Matters

Challenges to Managerial Authority

An appellate court in Illinois upheld a trial court's dismissal of a breach of settlement suit brought against the University of Illinois Board of Trustees, which oversaw the purchase of John Marshall Law School (JMLS) into the University of Illinois state system in late 2018. The plaintiff was a former JMLS law student who was dismissed from the program in Summer 2018 following failure to meet the minimum GPA and an unsuccessful summer course that would have permitted readmittance in Fall 2018. The plaintiff, after being denied the opportunity to retake the summer development course in 2020 under the school's new designation, filed suit for breach of settlement, arguing that the shift from JMLS's status as a private institution to University of Illinois's position as a public entity meant that the university "assumed the contractual obligation in this case"[1] without the protection of sovereign immunity to shield from such liabilities. As the trial court had ruled, the appellate court affirmed that University of Illinois's position as a state entity maintained its sovereign immunity protections and, as such, would require the plaintiff's pursual of damages to be taken up in the court of claims rather than the circuit court setting.[2]

In Alabama a university graduate student sued three institutional employees on the premise of First and Fourteenth Amendment civil rights violations—specifically, that he was denied his constitutional rights to due process and free speech. The suit arose following accusations of plagiarism on a final course paper and subsequent failure of a comprehensive exam that was

---

[1] Abo-Saif v. Bd. of Trs. of Univ. of Ill., 207 N.E.3d 1131, 415 Educ. L. Rep. 326 (Ill. App. Ct. 2022), at 1135.

[2] *Id.* at 1138.

graded by one of the persons involved in the student's initial academic misconduct hearing process.[3] The plaintiff held that the accusations of plagiarism came from a content-based resentment of his conservative Christian views, on which he wrote the final paper that prompted the plagiarism investigation. The university defendants countered these claims on the basis of sovereign immunity as a public institution and Alabama's two-year statute of limitations, both of which were affirmed by the district court. Although the court acknowledged the possibility that the plaintiff's comprehensive exam grading process was impacted with one of his prior adjudicators as the sole grader, there was insufficient evidence to argue that the failing grade on the exams was provided in negative response to the student's viewpoints. Further, the court held that the institution provided the student with adequate remedies during the academic misconduct process that maintained his due process rights.[4]

On appeal, an appellate court in New York again denied a former student's motion to vacate a default judgment after the state's decade-plus effort to collect unpaid charges from the 2008–2009 academic year. The state plaintiff outlined the considerable due diligence taken to contact the former SUNY Fredonia student and collect the owed debts, including confirming the student's mailing address with the U.S. Postal Service for all mailed communication and finally serving the student with a court appearance in 2011, which she did not attend.[5] Additionally, court noted that the student did not file to dismiss the judgment of $10,010.27 against her until 2021 which it found was untimely and without merit.

Student Misconduct

Academic Misconduct

An appellate court in New York case, the court granted an article 78 petition from a student contesting a disciplinary board's decision to expel him from SUNY Maritime College. The court acknowledged that the institution had possible merit for the initial expulsion decision in November 2021, which came from two written accounts of supposed eyewitnesses that the student wielded a knife

---

[3] Melvin v. Troy Univ., 609 F. Supp. 3d 1262, 412 Educ. L. Rep. 179 (M.D. Ala. 2022).
[4] *Id.* at 1271.
[5] State v. Summers, 179 N.Y.S.3d 797, 411 Educ. L. Rep. 329 (N.Y. App. Div. 2022).

and used it to carve racial slurs into a residence hall elevator door.[6] Where the institution had erred was in the disciplinary investigation's appellate process once new information came to light, including university leaders' decision to withhold information from the university police department that provided contrasting accounts about the racial epithet having been carved into the elevator door prior to the general student body moving into the residence hall. As a result of this determination, which found the school's investigative process to be "arbitrary and capricious,"[7] the court directed the respondents to reinstate the student and expunge the accusations from the student's records.

Torts

After reversing and remanding the suit previously, the Eleventh Circuit ruled in favor, in part, of a former doctoral student who sued Grand Canyon University in Arizona on the grounds of breach of contract and intentional misrepresentation under the Arizona Consumer Fraud Act (ACFA).[8] At the crux of the plaintiff's complaint was that he enrolled in Grand Canyon University's Doctor of Education degree in 2015 under the assumption that he could complete the entirety of the program in 60 credit hours, dissertation included, only to have his process extended adversely by an alleged system that "requires students to take and pay for additional courses that would allow them to complete the dissertation"[9] without the support needed to do so. The court dismissed the plaintiff's ACFA argument pertaining to the 60 hours, finding that Grand Canyon University's contractual language made clear that 60 credit hours was the minimum threshold for completing the doctoral degree; however, the plaintiff was successful in arguing the good faith[10] doctrine of contract-related claims insofar as university officials failed to provide him

---

[6] Mozdziak v. State Univ. of N.Y. Maritime Coll., 179 N.Y.S.3d 210, 410 Educ. L. Rep. 764 (N.Y. App. Div. 2022).
[7] *Id.* at 592.
[8] Young v. Grand Canyon Univ., Inc., 57 F.4th 861, 411 Educ. L. Rep. 169 (11th Cir. 2023).
[9] *Id.* at 866.
[10] Id. at 874 ("Grand Canyon cannot accept tuition from Mr. Young, enroll him in the doctoral degree program, and then fail [as alleged] to give him the faculty support necessary to complete the program's requirements").

with the faculty resources he needed for that final degree requirement.

In Connecticut, two alumni from Sacred Heart University claimed they suffered from multiple torts inflicted by institutional personnel and another former student who had accused them of sexual assault, only to later rescind the accusations and admit guilt for false allegations.[11] Under deliberation for the Appellate Court of Connecticut was the trial court's prior granting of summary judgment in favor of Sacred Heart, and the court upheld this motion, finding one of the plaintiffs inaccurately interpreted the university handbook when arguing breach of contract. The plaintiff in question had been a student-athlete who was suspended from the institution during the sexual assault investigation and later withdrew from the university. Two years later, he was reinstated as a student without his football scholarship, and so the basis of his damages request was to recoup the financial loss that came with the scholarship revocation. Although the court agreed with the plaintiff that the private university's student handbook served as an enforceable contract in its tenets of due process and assumption of innocence over the course of an investigation, so too did the handbook have language allowing for "the dean of students to suspend *immediately* a student if the dean of students deems it necessary to preserve the benefit and welfare of the university's community."[12]

A group of undergraduate students in Illinois filed a class action lawsuit against Bradley University, holding that the online exam proctor software used by the institution (i.e., Respondus Monitor) violated Illinois Biometric Information Privacy Act (BIPA) provisions in its collection and maintenance of the students' information. The district court denied the plaintiffs' motion to leave to file a sur-reply, and granted the institution's motion to dismiss in part, holding that Bradley University's status as a private university under the Gramm-Leach-Bliley Act meant the use of the software for online proctoring purposes was part of the transactional institution–student relationship, thus providing an exemption to BIPA oversight.[13] However, the court did leave open the ability of the plaintiffs to cite additional authority on the basis

---

[11] Bradley v. Yovino, 291 A.3d 133, 414 Educ. L. Rep. 578 (Conn. App. Ct. 2023).
[12] *Id.* at 150.
[13] Duerr v. Bradley Univ., 590 F. Supp. 3d 1160, 408 Educ. L. Rep. 795 (C.D. Ill. 2022).

of the software's potentially invasive data collection and lack of institutional transparency regarding data retention.[14]

In another Illinois case, a district court denied a motion to dismiss pursued by 17 institutions after a collective of student plaintiffs claimed the universities violated the antitrust doctrine of Section 1 of the Sherman Act[15] in terms of need-based financial aid allocation. The 17 respondents represented consistently high-ranking private institutions (e.g., Brown University, Johns Hopkins University, University of Chicago) allegedly affiliated with the 568 Presidents Group, which—while presenting as a group operating a uniform approach to determine need-based financial aid—had become what the plaintiffs argued was a "price-fixing cartel"[16] whose antitrust violations actually resulted in higher overall net tuition prices for financial aid recipients. The court ruled that the plaintiffs successfully argued for the competitiveness of the relevant market (i.e., prestigious, private universities perennially in the top 25 of the *U.S. News & World Report* rankings), even for institutions that had since left the 568 Presidents Group. Furthermore, there was evidence of possible financial aid suppression in the form of institutions such as Harvard University, which had opted to not join the 568 Group due to concerns "that doing so would hinder their ability to provide larger aid awards."[17]

In a more successful case for a university respondent, the Supreme Court of Vermont upheld a trial court's granting of summary judgment after a former medical student at the University of Vermont Medical Center (UVMC) filed suit on the premise of breach of contract, employment discrimination, and failure to accommodate.[18] The medical center had opted not to renew the plaintiff's fellowship after the student missed substantial training time due to a series of physical and mental health tribulations requiring hospitalization. Such time spent out of the program led academic officials at the medical college to initially pursue improvement plans, but when nearing the

---

[14] *Id.* at 1167 ("Courts have found a defendant's failure to comply with a data-retention schedule sufficient to confer an Article III injury").

[15] Carbone v. Brown Univ., 621 F. Supp. 3d 878, 415 Educ. L. Rep. 68 (N.D. Ill. 2022).

[16] *Id.* at 883.

[17] *Id.* at 890.

[18] Kelly v. Univ. of Vt. Med. Ctr., 280 A.3d 366, 407 Educ. L. Rep. 186 (Vt. 2022).

completion date of the fellowship in June 2018, the plaintiff was informed that he would not be offered the opportunity to resume his training as a fellow at UVMC in the subsequent academic year. Upon review, the appellate court disputed all three of the plaintiff's claims, finding first that the fellowship decision was not an employment-related dismissal, but rather a denial to extend an academic fellowship on the grounds of insufficient academic progress that gave no indication of discrimination. Second, and relatedly, the decision to not extend the fellowship did not constitute an "adverse employment action"[19] as a disabled individual under the Fair Employment Practices Act. Lastly, the court ruled the breach of contract claim moot because the plaintiff did not quantify accurately nor prove damages from UVMC's decision.[20]

Another case involving a medical student emerged following New York Presbyterian Brooklyn Methodist Hospital's decision to deny admittance to an incoming pediatric resident from Saint George University School of Medicine, who had matched with the hospital as part of the National Resident Matching Program (NRMP).[21] The hospital unsuccessfully pursued a match waiver from NRMP after finding a series of antisemitic and homophobic postings from the student on social media that ran contrary to their values and typical patient demographic. Despite NRMP's denial of the waiver, the hospital continued to stand by their refusal to allow the plaintiff into the program, prompting him to sue for breach of contract. When reviewing the case, an appellate panel took issue with the trial court's order converting the preliminary injunction order to an article 78 proceeding for mandamus relief.[22] The court reversed that ruling on the grounds that the student had recourse under New York's Public Health and Planning Council complaint process that should have been exhausted first before taking the matter to court.

A second appellate court in New York found that former students from University provided factual and substantial evidence to revive Child Victims Act (CVA) grievances against the university, arguing negligent hiring by Syracuse University

---

[19] *Id.* at 457.
[20] *Id.* at 459.
[21] Khass v. N.Y. Presbyterian Brooklyn Methodist Hosp., 184 N.Y.S.3d 102, 412 Educ. L. Rep. 997 (N.Y. App. Div. 2023).
[22] *Id.* at 826.

officials insomuch that the plaintiffs were sexually abused by a former resident advisor who was also their camp counselor in Massachusetts from 1981–1982.[23] Although lower court rulings had denied the university's and Camp Greylock's motions to dismiss, they granted initial summary judgment, to which the plaintiffs appealed. Of the amended complaint, the appellate court found the plaintiff's arguments satisfied the prongs of negligence via the duty of care Syracuse University owed to the students as minors at camp and the positioning of the resident assistant into the camp counselor role, which caused "foreseeable harm";[24] moreover, the CVA parameters meant these claims were not time-barred.

In Texas an appellate court affirmed the denial of the University of the Incarnate Word (UIW)'s request for summary judgment in a wrongful death suit. The long-term negligence case first emerged in 2013 from the parents of a student whose off-campus traffic stop altercation with a campus police officer resulted in the student being fatally shot.[25] UIW unsuccessfully attempted to make the argument that, even as a private institution, their police department was eligible for governmental immunity as a state entity—moreover, the appeals court agreed with the trial court's earlier conviction that the escalated nature of the fatal encounter was enough to maintain dispute[26] over facts of the case, impeding UIW from being granted summary judgment.

COVID-19

Courts were kept busy by claims brought by students dissatisfied with the conversion of campus instruction to online learning precipitated by the regulations put in place during the onset of the COVID-19 pandemic.

The First Circuit ruled an appeal moot, considering that the complainants no longer attended the university. The plaintiffs had filed suit seeking declaratory and injunctive relief, arguing that the

---

[23] Shapiro v. Syracuse Univ., 173 N.Y.S.3d 769, 407 Educ. L. Rep. 885 (N.Y. App. Div. 2022).
[24] *Id.* at 772.
[25] Univ. of the Incarnate Word v. Redus, 654 S.W.3d 169, 409 Educ. L. Rep. 553 (Tex. App. 2022).
[26] *Id.* at 174.

university's COVID-19 vaccination policies were unconstitutional. The plaintiffs were seeking exemptions based on religious beliefs.[27]

In a case from New York, the parent of a student sought a partial refund of the tuition she paid prior to COVID-related shutdowns. The court Second Circuit upheld the district court's ruling that the parent lacked standing on her claims of breach of contract and unjust enrichment. However, the court did rule that the plaintiff had offered enough evidence of a possible implied contract claim to warrant further consideration and, thus, reversed in part and remanded the prior ruling for further proceedings. The court found that the university's marketing materials regarding the benefits of an in-person education and the descriptions of campus services and facilities potentially created an implied contractual promise of on-campus instruction.[28]

The Fifth Circuit heard two similar appeals. In the first, two former students of a private institution in Louisiana sued on behalf of a putative class of current and former students, seeking a partial refund of tuition and fees after the switch to online instruction denied them access to on-campus services. A district court dismissed the students' claims, but on appeal the court reversed and remanded, citing the university's marketing materials boasting the benefits of an on-campus education and the fact that the university charged substantially less for its programs designated as online degrees.[29] In the second case, the court remanded for further proceedings a plaintiff's alleged contract claims against a university in Texas, finding that the trial court erred in not considering whether the term "educational services" is an ambiguous term in the Financial Responsibility Agreement that all students signed prior to enrolling for the Spring 2020 semester. The plaintiff alleged that the FRA entitled her to the benefits promised of in-person instruction.[30]

The Seventh Circuit heard a pair of similar cases, as well. The first focused on procedural questions and whether a class action suit should be divided into two separate classes (one for tuition and one for fees). The appellate court vacated the district court's

---

[27] Harris v. Univ. of Mass. Lowell, 43 F.4th 187, 406 Educ. L. Rep. 22 (1st Cir. 2022).
[28] Rynasko v. N.Y. Univ., 63 F.4th 186, 413 Educ. L. Rep. 82 (2d Cir. 2023).
[29] Jones v. Adm'rs of Tulane Educ. Fund, 51 F.4th 101, 408 Educ. L. Rep. 680 (5th Cir. 2022).
[30] King v. Baylor Univ., 46 F.4th 344, 407 Educ. L. Rep. 69 (5th Cir. 2022).

certifications.[31] In the second case, the appellate court reversed and remanded a circuit court's decision to dismiss a student's claim seeking a partial refund of tuition and fees on behalf of the class of litigants he wanted to represent. The plaintiff claimed that an implied contract existed from the marketing materials the university utilized to tout the services offered in its on-campus programs. The court also noted that the registration bulletin made a distinction between courses offered on-campus and online and specifically designated some degree programs as online only. Undergraduate students were barred from registering for online classes unless given special permission and were required to live on campus during their first two years.[32]

A district court in California allowed to move forward a class action lawsuit challenging a university for reimbursement following the decision to move classes online. Though the university's catalog contained clauses permitting it to change policy and tuition rates without notice, the court found that nothing permitted it to change courses from an on-campus to online format. The court also noted that the registration bulletin identified an on-campus location for each course, thus providing students with an expectation that the course delivery would be in person. Though the state of California had orders in place that would have prevented on-campus delivery, the court still found that plaintiffs could pursue quasi-contractual claims.[33]

A federal trial court in Florida heard COVID-related cases related to a demand for reimbursement. In one, the court rejected the university's argument that it was immune under the newly enacted Florida Immunity Statute for Educational Institutions for Actions Related to the COVID-19 Pandemic. The court found that retroactive application of the Act unconstitutionally infringed on the plaintiffs' property rights. The plaintiffs alleged breach of contract for transitioning courses from on-campus to online and unjust enrichment for retaining the full amount of the plaintiffs' tuition.[34] In a second ruling regarding the same case, the court

---

[31] Eddlemon v. Bradley Univ., 65 F.4th 335, 414 Educ. L. Rep. 509 (7th Cir. 2023).
[32] Hernandez v. Ill. Inst. of Tech., 63 F.4th 661, 413 Educ. L. Rep. 108 (7th Cir. 2023).
[33] Arredondo v. Univ. of La Verne, 618 F. Supp. 3d 937, 414 Educ. L. Rep. 174 (C.D. Cal. 2022).
[34] Ferretti v. Nova Southeastern Univ., Inc. (a), 586 F. Supp. 3d 1260, 407 Educ. L. Rep. 811 (S.D. Fla. 2022).

dismissed with prejudice any claims for tuition, as well as fees related to on-campus instruction, and dismissed without prejudice claims related to itemized fees for on-campus services. The court cited a portion of the student-institution agreement that stated "[f]ace-to-face classes may also include some online instruction in addition to regular classroom instruction."[35]

In a third case, a federal trial court in Florida dismissed claims against a private campus housing provider, finding a valid enforceable contract existed regardless of the administrative decision of the adjacent university to move courses online. The plaintiffs argued that they should have been released from the terms of their lease and cited certain amenities (e.g., pool and fitness facilities) were unavailable due to COVID health precautions.[36]

In Illinois, a plaintiff filed a second amended complaint claiming unjust enrichment in a class action lawsuit seeking a refund for fees related to on-campus services not delivered following COVID-related campus shutdown. The district court ruled that because the financial responsibility agreement the plaintiff signed governed the relationship with the institution, the claim was dismissed with prejudice[37].

A Louisiana district court denied the plaintiff's motion for contempt and enforcement of a consent judgment when the university imposed reasonable masking requirements on unvaccinated students at the private medical college, citing the university did not act in a punitive or discriminatory manner when suspending the student. [38]

In Massachusetts, students filed two putative class actions, alleging breach of an implied contract and unjust enrichment, after the university transitioned from on-campus to online instruction. The court did not find that the student-institution contract obliging students to pay tuition and fees constituted a contract and only allowed for further proceedings to calculate damages between the

---

[35] Ferretti v. Nova Southeastern Univ., (b), 604 F. Supp. 3d 1330, 411 Educ. L. Rep. 517 (S.D. Fla. 2022).
[36] Longo v. Campus Advantage, Inc., 588 F. Supp. 3d 1286, 408 Educ. L. Rep. 260 (M.D. Fla. 2022).
[37] Buschauer v. Columbia Coll. Chicago, 579 F. Supp. 3d 1045, 406 Educ. L. Rep. 319 (N.D. Ill. 2022).
[38] Magliulo v. Edward Via Coll. of Osteopathic Med., 582 F. Supp. 3d 373, 406 Educ. L. Rep. 878 (W.D. La. 2022).

cost the university incurred running its online and in-person programs.[39]

A federal trial court in Ohio denied a university's motion to dismiss breach of contract claims related to tuition and professional liability insurance after a nursing student filed suit. The court noted language in the university's marketing materials guaranteeing a clinical environment and stating "that it is impossible to earn a BSN 100% online. As an ABSN student, you'll regularly attend hands-on skills labs at the ABSN Learning Center." The court did, however, grant the university's motion to dismiss breach of contract claims related to unused student activity fees.[40]

In Pennsylvania a federal trial court granted the university's motion to dismiss a class action lawsuit in which the plaintiff argued that the online experience was not equal to the on-campus experience, which also was more expensive. The court dismissed the breach of contract claims because the plaintiff could not point to a specific contractual guarantee for in-person classes.[41]

A federal trial court in Rhode Island granted summary judgment to a private university when three students filed breach of contract claims seeking refunds for student fees after the university shut down. The university provided all enrolled students with a 50% refund of housing fees, but utilized other fees (e.g., student activity and health services fee) to support students during the pandemic. The court noted that student organizations still received support during the transition to online learning and that health services were still available to students, including one of the plaintiffs who did not vacate the campus.[42]

Based on Texas's Pandemic Liability Protection Law, a district court ruled that a plaintiff's claims for breach of contract and unjust enrichment were barred. The court failed to find any specific provision in the student-institution contract where in-person instruction was promised. The suit was dismissed with prejudice.[43]

---

[39] In re Suffolk Univ. Covid Refund Litig., 616 F. Supp. 3d 115, 413 Educ. L. Rep. 710 (D. Mass. 2022).

[40] Miranda v. Xavier Univ., 594 F. Supp. 3d 961, 409 Educ. L. Rep. 673 (S.D. Ohio 2022).

[41] Brezinski v. Widener Univ., 582 F. Supp. 3d 257, 406 Educ. L. Rep. 22 (E.D. Pa. 2022).

[42] Choi v. Brown Univ., 594 F. Supp. 3d 452, 409 Educ. L. Rep. 662 (D.R.I. 2022).

[43] Hogan v. S. Methodist Univ., 595 F. Supp. 3d 559, 409 Educ. L. Rep. 795 (N.D. Tex. 2022).

In Virginia, a federal trial court declined to dismiss claims against a university for reimbursement of fees and residential fees. The plaintiffs argued that they did not receive the benefit of those services.[44]

The Supreme Court of Nebraska heard an appeal from an order denying injunctive relief to students who sought an exemption from the private university's vaccination requirements. The question before the court was whether the injunction was temporary (and, thus, not final nor appealable) or permanent. Utilizing the "four corners" doctrine, the court found ambiguity in the order. An examination of the record found that plaintiffs sought only a temporary injunction, which they were denied. The court found it lacked jurisdiction and dismissed the appeal.[45]

An appellate court in Florida court reversed a prior judgment that sovereign immunity did not bar a student's breach of contract claim against the public university. In its review, the court found that an express contract did not exist to overcome sovereign immunity.[46] The same court ruled differently when a public university appealed a trial court's denial of its motion to dismiss contract claims based on sovereign immunity. At issue was the collection of student fees for services not offered after the COVID shutdown. The court ruled without prejudice to allow the university to reassert its sovereign immunity if supported by facts.[47]

In a class action against a public university in Indiana for breach of contract and unjust enrichment, a state appellate court reversed a prior ruling that state law barred class actions against postsecondary educational institutions for claims of breach of contract and unjust enrichment arising from COVID-19. The court found that the newly enacted law conflicted with Indiana statute regulating class action procedures.[48]

---

[44] Student A v. Liberty Univ., Inc., 602 F. Supp. 3d 901, 411 Educ. L. Rep. 256 (W.D. Va. 2022).
[45] Ramaekers v. Creighton Univ., 978 N.W.2d 298, 406 Educ. L. Rep. 463 (Neb. 2022).
[46] Univ. of Fla. Bd. of Trs. v. Rojas, 351 So. 3d 1167, 411 Educ. L. Rep. 424 (Fla. Dist. Ct. App. 2022)
[47] Univ. of S. Fla. Bd. of Trs. v. Moore, 347 So.3d 545, 408 Educ. L. Rep. 1144 (Fla. Dist. Ct. App. 2022).
[48] Mellowitz v. Ball State Univ., 196 N.E.3d 1256, 408 Educ. L. Rep. 1008 (Ind. Ct. App. 2022).

Two separate class actions were brought against a public university by former students seeking partial fee and tuition refunds. The Kansas appellate court upheld the district court's dismissal of the unjust enrichment claims but reversed and remanded for further proceedings potential breach of contract claims.[49] In Michigan, an appellate court considered whether public institutions were liable to reimburse tuition and housing fees after shutting down. The court upheld the district court's finding that the plaintiffs failed to demonstrate any contractual obligations existed of a promise for in-person instruction.[50]

A North Carolina appellate court upheld a trial court's dismissal of unjust enrichment claims against a public university based on sovereign immunity but ruled that plaintiffs had sufficiently pled that an implied contract existed for claims to move forward. The court noted that the university charged different rates for on-campus and fully online programs and marketed the two types of instruction differently. Though the university offered prorated refunds for housing fees, it had not offered plaintiffs refunds for the tuition and fees it charged for on-campus programs.[51]

In New Jersey, an appellate court upheld dismissal of claims for breach of implied contract and unjust enrichment when a public university denied students a reimbursement for certain itemized on-campus services (e.g., campus parking permits) pursuant to the Emergency Health Powers Act previously passed by the state legislature.[52]

Ohio appellate courts heard numerous COVID-related claims. In one case, a group of plaintiffs sought certification of three classes: students seeking reimbursement for tuition, room and board, and mandatory student fees. The court reversed the grant of certification of classes, noting issue with the commonality and the predominance requirements. For example, in the tuition class, members would have little in common because they "enrolled in

---

[49] Minjarez-Almeida v. Kan. Bd. of Regents, 527 P.3d 931, 414 Educ. L. Rep. 1043 (Kan. Ct. App. 2023)

[50] Zwiker v. Lake Superior State Univ., 986 N.W.2d 427, 413 Educ. L. Rep. 445 (Mich. Ct. App. 2022).

[51] Dieckhaus v. Bd. of Governors of Univ. of N.C., 883 S.E.2d 106, 411 Educ. L. Rep. 1191 (N.C. Ct. App. 2023).

[52] Mueller v. Kean Univ., 287 A.3d 796, 411 Educ. L. Rep. 1147 (N.J. Super. Ct. App. Div. 2022).

different courses with different instructors who converted from in-person instruction to online instruction in different ways."[53]

In another case, the court reversed a trial court's certification of class for those who paid tuition and fees for on-campus instruction that was later converted to online instruction. The court cited a lack of information of who actually paid tuition and fees (e.g., student, parent or guardian, or other family member). Also, the court found that the plaintiff failed to show that all proposed class members were injured by the change in course delivery method.[54] An appeal in favor of class certification was ruled similarly. At issue was a dental student at a public university who paid various fees related to on-campus services. The court found that the trial court failed to conduct a rigorous analysis of commonality issues of dental students who paid the same fees.[55]

Discrimination

General

The first case alleged discrimination based on national origin.[56] Alberti, a former student from Switzerland, brought suit against defendant, University of Virginia, alleging that he was dismissed from the doctoral program and research assistantship because of his national origin, in violation of Title VI and Title VII of the Civil Rights Act of 1964. He also alleged retaliation. The student's supervising professor was a native of Italy. The student alleged that almost immediately the faculty member started to disparage everything Swiss, such as his education in Switzerland, the fact that he spoke a Swiss-German dialect, Swiss nationalism, and even Swiss grocery stores. After receiving two failing grades over two semesters, he was dismissed from the program. On appeal of a dismissal in favor of the faculty member, the Fourth Circuit Court affirmed that the student's exclusion was not based on national origin discrimination that alleged derogatory comments by his professor about his national origin were not causally connected to

---

53 Cross v. Univ. of Toledo, 10th Dist., 199 N.E.3d 699, 706; 410 Educ. L. Rep. 771 (Ohio Ct. App. 2022)

54 Duke v. Ohio Univ., 204 N.E.3d 752, 413 Educ. L. Rep. 409 (Ohio Ct. App. 2022)

55 McDermott v. Ohio State Univ., 205 N.E.3d 58, 413 Educ. L. Rep. 424 (Ohio Ct. App. 2022).

56 Alberti v. Rector & Visitors of Univ. of Va., 65 F.4th 151, 414 Educ. L. Rep. 493 (4th Cir. 2023)

his dismissal as they were not made proximate in time to the school's decision to terminate.

The plaintiffs in the next two cases were bringing suit under the Illinois Biometric Information Privacy Act (BIPA) In the case of *Patterson v. Respondus, Inc.,*[57] three putative class actions were filed by current and former students under the BIPA against a private university and the software company regarding software that was used to proctor online exams which used the students' webcam and microphone to monitor their examination environment. Plaintiffs alleged that this function was in violation of BIPA because it failed to obtain the students' informed consent to the collection of their biometric data, the handling and retention of that data, and the use of that data including disclosure to third parties. The defendants' motion to dismiss was granted in part and denied in part. As regarding the software company, the court held that the students lacked standing to assert a BIPA claim regarding retention of data, informed consent requirements, and profiting from the data, but they had stated a claim for violation of nondisclosure requirements. As regarding the university, the claims were not time-barred, but the students lacked standing for retention of the data or for profiting from the data and nondisclosure requirements. The students had stated a claim for violation of informed consent requirements.

The second case alleged similar claims.[58] During the pandemic, Northwestern University, like many other institutions, required students to use a proctoring software for taking exams outside of the classroom. This third-party software captured and stored various user data including biometric data. A plaintiff filed an action on behalf of herself and other similarly situated individuals alleging that the use of this software violated the Illinois Biometric Information Privacy Act (BIPA). Northwestern moved to dismiss. Granting the motion, the court held that the university was a "financial institution" under the Gramm-Leach-Bliley Act (GLBA) and therefore was not subject to the BIPA.

An African American student brought a Title XI and Title VI action, along with multiple claims under Massachusetts law, against Worcester Polytechnic Institute for conduct at an off-

---

[57] Patterson v. Respondus, Inc., 593 F. Supp. 3d 783, 409 Educ. L. Rep. 107 (N.D. Ill. 2022)

[58] Doe v. Northwestern Univ., 586 F. Supp. 3d 841, 407 Educ. L. Rep. 774 (N.D. Ill. 2022).

campus party.[59] Another student alleged that Bray had groped her breast at the party. A disciplinary hearing was held, and Bray was found in violation of the student code of conduct. The district court found that Bray's claims were insufficient under either the erroneous outcome theory or the selective enforcement theory to state a Title IX claim. The court also found that Bray's allegations were insufficient to state a Title VI claim.

The remaining seven cases in this category made claims of discrimination of their First Amendment rights to free speech, freedom of religion, or a combination of the two. In the first case, a doctoral student sued the university under Section 1983 action alleging violation of the First Amendment rights to free speech and violation of the Fourteenth Amendment right to equal protection and due process, as well as conspiracy to violate his civil rights. [60]This action arose from the refusal of a faculty member to teach him or administer general exams after Babinski voiced unpopular opinions in the professor's "Gender, Sexuality, and Performance" class, thereby resulting in his de facto expulsion from the program. When officials would not find that that the professor's behavior constituted a threat that required discipline, it was alleged that the faculty made the decision to neither teach or interact with him, nor serve on his dissertation committee. A federal trial court held that the defendant professor had qualified immunity from the First Amendment claim, but the failure of the professor to follow grade appeal procedures did not provide qualified immunity, so the case was allowed to proceed in part.

A student sued officials at a college in Rhode Island College alleging a violation of his First Amendment right to freedom of speech. A self-described "conservative libertarian,"[61] when officials planned to show the film "Fahrenheit 9/11", the student requested that they also show a conservative rebuttal film. He was told that the planned film upheld the ideology of the department and, if he was having difficulty with that ideology, perhaps he should consider a different career. Ultimately the student contacted the national free speech advocacy group Foundation for Individual

---

[59] Bray v. Worcester Polytechnic Inst., 596 F. Supp. 3d 142, 409 Educ. L. Rep. 837 (D. Mass. 2022).

[60] Babinski v. Queen, 621 F. Supp. 3d 632, 415 Educ. L. Rep. 47 (M.D. La. 2022). [reversed by Babinski v. Sosnowsky, 79 F.4th 515 (5th Cir. 2023)].

[61] Felkner v. Rhode Island Coll., 291 A.3d 1001, 414 Educ. L. Rep. 651 (R.I. 2023). [petition for certiorari filed].

Rights in Education (FIRE) as well as becoming more confrontative and vocal about his views, at times engaging in inappropriate behaviors. Once again, he was advised of the liberal ideology of social work and that he might be happier following a different career path. After first stating that his was not the first time that the student had appeared before the court, the defendants were granted summary judgment based on qualified immunity.

In 2013, the North Carolina General Assembly enacted the Opportunity Scholarship Program (OSP), which was intended to provide funds to assist students in paying tuition at any nonpublic school.[62] Students filed suit alleging that the funding of educational opportunities at religious schools violated the North Carolina Constitution, thereby violating their rights to religious liberty, free speech, education, and equal protection by subjecting them to religious discrimination. Moreover, it was alleged that the OSP was contrary to the purpose of education or any other public purpose. In a ruling by the trial court, a motion filed by the defendants to transfer the case to a three-judge panel was denied. On appeal, that decision was reversed on the grounds that the students' challenge to OSP was facial and thus required to be heard by a three-judge panel.

The issue in the fourth case was the use of student fees for speech, assembly, and public advocacy. A student in Minnesota filed suit alleging a violation of the First Amendment.[63] The suit arose from the decision to reject a proposed student-fee increase to help increase the plaintiff organization budget. One of the uses of the proposed increase would be for speech, assembly, and public advocacy. Before 2021, such a proposed fee increase had never been rejected. Plaintiffs alleged that the rejection was in direct relation to the defendant's dislike of the plaintiffs' speech and advocacy. The defendants moved to dismiss, and plaintiffs moved for a preliminary injunction. The defendants' motion was denied as regarding the plaintiffs' First Amendment retaliation claim and granted on all other respects. The plaintiffs' motion was denied.

In Idaho[64] plaintiffs, a group of law students, moved for a temporary restraining order, preliminary injunction, and expedited hearing in a suit they had filed against their university

---

[62] Kelly v. State, 878 S.E.2d 841, 408 Educ. L. Rep. 1085 (N.C. Ct. App. 2022).
[63] Minn. State Coll. Student Ass'n, Inc. v. Cowles, 620 F. Supp. 3d 835, 414 Educ. L. Rep. 874 (D. Minn. 2022).
[64] Perlot v. Green, 609 F. Supp. 3d 1106, 412 Educ. L. Rep. 157 (D. Idaho 2022).

and its officials for violation of their First Amendment rights of free speech and freedom of religion, as well as their Fourteenth Amendment right to due process. This lawsuit arose out of a discussion at a community event where plaintiffs voiced their opposition to same sex marriage. The university issued a no-contact order. The district court found that the no-contact order was a content-based restriction and was not the least restrictive means for accomplishing the goal of preventing a queer student from hearing speech with which she disagreed or creating a harmonious environment, that the comments did not constitute sexual harassment under Title IX, and that the law students showed likely harm from the university's issuance of the no-contact order. Moreover, the court held that the no-contact order was issued with virtually no due process. The plaintiffs' motion was granted.

Sabra and the American Muslims brought a §1983 action against the community college and a professor alleging that the inclusion in the professor's world politics course of a module on "Islamic Terrorism" violated the religion clause of the First Amendment.[65] The district court dismissed the case for lack of subject matter jurisdiction and failure to state a claim. On appeal, the judgment of the district court was affirmed, holding that a violation of the religion clause was not obvious. Issues of qualified immunity were appropriately resolved in a pre-discovery motion to dismiss.

In the final case, Speech First, Inc, brought an action challenging the defendant university's "anti-discrimination policy," alleging that it violated the students' First Amendment right to free speech.[66] The policy stated that students would be disciplined if they "subject an individual on the basis of their membership in a protected class to unlawful severe, pervasive, or persistent treatment." The university prohibited behavior that:

> (1) is humiliating, abusive, or threatening and denigrates or shows hostility or aversion towards an individual or group;

---

[65] Sabra v. Maricopa Cnty. Cmty. Coll. Dist., 44 F.4th 867, 406 Educ. L. Rep. 584 (9th Cir. 2022).

[66] Speech First, Inc. v. Khator, 603 F. Supp. 3d 480, 411 Educ. L. Rep. 483 (S.D. Tex. 2022).

> (2) creates an intimidating, hostile, or abusive learning, living, or working environment, or an environment that alters the conditions of learning, living, or working; or
> (3) causes an unreasonable interference with an individual's academic or work performance.

On May 13, 2022, the University changed its policy. The amendments to the policy eliminated the definition of behavior that constitutes harassment.[67] The plaintiff moved for a preliminary injunction against the enforcement of the policy. The court found that students had standing because the alleged injury, a violation of a constitutional right, was sufficient to confer standing. The fact that the university ceased enforcement of the policy was not sufficient to render the action moot. The plaintiff was likely to succeed on the merits; therefore, the injunction was granted.

Disability

Five cases dealt with claims of disability discrimination. A medical student filed suit alleging that he had a medical disability falling under the ADA.[68] When he was dismissed for academic reasons allegedly affected by his diagnosed medical disorder, he filed suit for violation of the ADA. The defendant moved to dismiss for failure to state a claim due to being time-barred. The district court granted the motion, holding that Evans had reason to know of his claims under the ADA from the date that he was dismissed, and he was not delayed in filing suit by internal grievance procedures entitling Evan to an equitable tolling of the statute. Moreover, the "continuing violations doctrine" was not applicable given the facts of the case.

In the next case, the plaintiff requested test-taking accommodations for her disabilities akin to the accommodations that had been granted by the university.[69] The defendant denied, and the plaintiff filed a complaint with the state. Her complaint was dismissed by the Montana Human Rights Bureau. On review

---

[67] 603 F. Supp. 3d 480 at 481

[68] Evans v. Vanderbilt Univ. Sch. of Med., 589 F. Supp. 3d 870, 408 Educ. L. Rep. 295 (M.D. Tenn. 2022).

[69] Zolnikov v. Nat. Bd. of Med. Exam'rs, 526 P.3d 1088, 414 Educ. L. Rep. 717 (Mont. 2023).

by the district court, the suit was dismissed as untimely. On appeal to the Supreme Court of Montana, the dismissal was upheld, holding that the discrimination accrued when the student was notified of the denial of her request for accommodations; therefore, her discrimination claim was time-barred.

The student in the third case was suffered from a documented medical disorder and sought accommodations from the University.[70] When accommodations were not provided and he was dismissed from the program, he filed suit for violation of the ADA. The University moved to dismiss, which was granted in part by the court. In finding for the defendants on the matter of accommodations, the court held that the 180-day statute of limitations began running when the university informed the plaintiff that it had decided to deny accommodations and dismiss him from the program. His request to remain in the program and receive practicum extension was a fundamental alternation and therefore was an unreasonable accommodation. It was therefore appropriately resolved with a motion to dismiss. The court found that the plaintiff did sufficiently state a claim for disparate treatment under the ADA, so that claim was not dismissed.

In the next case, the plaintiff was diagnosed with bipolar disorder.[71] When she was dismissed from her academic program, she filed suit alleging violation of the ADA. The defendant was granted summary judgment. On appeal, the court held that the plaintiff's pattern of unprofessional behavior, including repeated absences, supported the determination by the defendant that plaintiff was not qualified to participate in the program, so the decision was not arbitrary or capricious. Evidence presented supported the defendant's position that the plaintiff was not dismissed because of her disability but because of her unprofessional behavior. The summary judgment was affirmed.

The final case was brought by an individual who had been labeled a threat and suspended from campus.[72] The plaintiff brought suit under the ADA and the District of Columbia Human Rights Act against American University after she was suspended from the university. She alleged that the university assumed she was a threat and suspended her because of her mental health

---

[70] Frazier v. Pa. State Univ., 603 F. Supp. 3d 158, 411 Educ. L. Rep. 462 (M.D. Pa. 2022).
[71] Neal v. E. Carolina Univ., 53 F.4th 130, 408 Educ. L. Rep. 745 (4th Cir. 2022).
[72] Wheeler v. Am. Univ., 619 F.Supp.3d 1, 414 Educ. L. Rep. 263 (D.C. Cir. 2022).

disability. She also alleged a violation of the Fourth Amendment after officers unilaterally entered her apartment and seized items. A student had complained to the university that she had been accosted by a female student in a campus lab, and a professor had also complained of the plaintiff's behavior. Campus police entered her off-campus apartment and, although the plaintiff was calm, she was transported to the hospital where she was deemed a danger to herself and others. The defendant moved for pre-discovery summary judgment. The court found that the officers were entitled to qualified immunity for their actions, but that pre-discovery summary judgment was improper on the claims for disability discrimination and claims for unreasonable seizure and false arrest under the Fourth Amendment because genuine issues of material fact existed. Discovery was allowed to continue.

Gender and Sexual Harassment

Once again, sex discrimination/harassment was by far the most numerous category of litigation under discrimination.

The Circuit Court for the District of Columbia the rejected a plaintiff's cause of action as untimely. [73] The plaintiff, a third-year law student, was raped by Eastmond, a professor of physics at Howard. The two lived in the same building, which the defendant had recommended. The student reported the assault to both the defendant university and the police. She found the response from the university to be unsatisfactory on many levels, so she filed suit asserting discrimination and retaliation in violation of Title IX, negligence, and breach of fiduciary duty. Because the assault had occurred in 2017 and the lawsuit was not filed until 2020, the statute of limitations on all claims had tolled. The case was dismissed as untimely.

At issue in a second case before the District of Columbia Circuit was the expulsion of a student who was expelled on being accused of academic dishonesty for changing an answer on an examination.[74] She sued claiming breach of contract, alleging that the defendant failed to follow its policies, and a violation of Title IX alleging gender-based bias. The defendant moved to dismiss. In

[73] Doe v. Howard Univ., 594 F. Supp. 3d 52, 409 Educ. L. Rep. 649 (D.C. Cir. 2022).

[74] Smith v. Howard Univ., 605 F. Supp. 3d 103, 411 Educ. L. Rep. 527 (D.C. Cir. 2022).

denying the motion to dismiss, the court held that the District of Columbia's three-year limitations for personal injury claims governed the plaintiff's Title IX claim; therefore, it was timely. When looking at the pleadings, the plaintiff had plausibly alleged that the defendant discriminated against her under Title IX, as well as presenting a claim for breach of contract. The motion to dismiss was denied.

In a case from Rhode Island the First Circuit the claim of a violation of Title IX was combined with a claim of race discrimination.[75] The plaintiff sued the defendant university alleging that it had discriminated against him because of his race, gender, and disability, created a hostile environment, violated contractual agreements and procedural protections, and intentionally inflicted emotional distress when finding him in violation of the student code of conduct. The action arose out of an encounter between the plaintiff, an African American male, and a white woman outside of a bar. The details presented by each party differed as to who was the aggressor, agreeing only that there was a sexual encounter. Months after the encounter, the woman involved filed a complaint against the plaintiff, which started a multi-year process culminating in the plaintiff's suspension and a suicide attempt by him. The appellate court granted the defendant's motion for summary judgment on the claims of gender and race discrimination, finding insufficient evidence in the record. Regarding the claim for intentional infliction of emotional distress, the court denied summary judgment, finding that triable issues existed on the questions of whether the defendant's actions were extreme, outrageous, and intentionally reckless.

A male student was expelled for violating his college's sexual misconduct policy and sued, alleging violation of Title IX and various Massachusetts state tort laws.[76] The district court granted the defendant's motion to dismiss for failure to state a claim. On appeal, the court held that the Title IX claims alleging discrimination based on gender were not plausibly alleged and were dismissed. The state claims of breach of contract regarding review of the investigative report, lack of notice, and a fair and thorough investigation plausibly alleged that his reasonable expectations were not met because the defendant college did not follow the promises made in its sexual misconduct policy, and such

---

[75] Doe v. Brown Univ., 43 F.4th 195, 406 Educ. L. Rep. 30 (1st Cir. 2022).
[76] Doe v. Stonehill Coll., 55 F.4th 302, 410 Educ. L. Rep. 80 (1st Cir. 2022).

actions harmed the plaintiff's ability to defend himself and the ultimate outcome of the process. Therefore, those claims survived.

The First Circuit, in a case from Massachusetts, addressed a question of first impression regarding when it is appropriate for a party in a civil lawsuit in federal court to appear under a pseudonym. The male plaintiff and a female student engaged in an on-again-off-again sexual relationship from 2013 through 2015. In 2016, referring to a late-2015 encounter that had happened almost a year earlier, the female student filed a complaint against the plaintiff, who was expelled just prior to graduation. He filed suit alleging breach of contract, promissory estoppel, and denial of basic fairness, arguing that "MIT's investigation was infected by radical feminist anti-male bias to the point of presuming that the female complainant's story was . . . true." [77] At the same time, the plaintiff filed an ex parte motion to proceed by pseudonym. The motion was denied. On appeal, the court vacated the decision of the district court and remanded for further proceedings consistent with the elaborate thought process and tests enumerated by the court when balancing the need for privacy with the need for transparency in the judicial system. The court listed four paradigms to be considered in this balancing test: (1) fear of harm to a party to the action; (2) fear of harm to innocent non-parties to the action; (3) necessary to forestall a chilling effect on future litigants; and (4) confidentiality required by law.

A case in Texas focused on procedural.[78] The plaintiff was a male student who was disciplined for violation of university policies prohibiting sexual abuse and dating violence. He sued alleging claims of selective enforcement and erroneous outcome in violation of Title IX, as well as deprivation of due process. On appeal, the Fifth Circuit held that in deciding Title IX claims, the court must determine whether the alleged facts raise a plausible inference that the student was discriminated against on the basis of his sex. Gender bias by the university in connection with the disciplinary hearing in the instant case could not be inferred as required. In addition, the court held that due process did not require that students accused of sexual assault be permitted attorney-led, direct cross-examination of the alleged victim during the disciplinary hearings.

---

[77] Doe v. Mass. Inst. of Tech., 46 F.4th 61, 407 Educ. L. Rep. 32, 65-66(1st Cir. 2022).

[78] Overdam v Texas A&M Univ., 43 F.4th 522 (5th Cir. 2022).

Teacher-on-student sexual harassment was the basis of the next Title IX lawsuit. The plaintiff sued under Title IX alleging teacher-on-student hostile environment sexual harassment, teacher-on-student quid pro quo sexual harassment, as well as filing claims under the ADA and the Idaho Human Rights Act.[79] The claim arose out of a relationship between the plaintiff and a former faculty member at the defendant university. In the complaint, the plaintiff alleges that the faculty member had initiated an unwanted and emotionally abusive relationship when she was a student. The plaintiff alleged that when she reported his actions, the university failed to act. The defendant moved for summary judgment. The court held that factual issues existed as to the question of whether an appropriate person had actual knowledge of the behavior necessitating action under Title IX; as to the question of deliberate indifference on behalf of the defendant; and whether the defendant university, as a religious institution, had policies intended to discriminate against women. The claims were neither time-barred nor barred by Title IX religious exemption, or by the Free Exercise Clause of the First Amendment. Summary judgment on those issues would be inappropriate. As for the plaintiff's § 504 hostile educational environment claim, the Ninth Circuit does not recognize such a claim; thus, that claim was dismissed, but the state IHRA could be enforced.

In a case from Ohio, a student sued her college and various officials alleging a lack of due process in its investigative process of a Title IX complaint against him.[80] Other allegations included violations of Title IX and several state tort laws. After being removed to federal court, the plaintiff's complaint was dismissed by the district court. On appeal, the Sixth Circuit held that the district court had erred by not providing sufficient notice of its intention to dismiss nor providing the plaintiff sufficient opportunity to either respond to a notice of dismissal or to amend his complaint. However, the college was not a state actor and thus was not subject to federal due process requirements. Consequently, dismissal on the merits was appropriate. The plaintiff's Title IX selective enforcement claim was not ripe at the time of the filing of the complaint, and so dismissal on those grounds was appropriate.

---

[79] Stevens v. Brigham Young Univ.-Idaho, 588 F. Supp. 3d 1117, 408 Educ. L. Rep. 239 (D. Idaho 2022).

[80] Doe v. Oberlin Coll., 60 F.4th 345, 411 Educ. L. Rep. 988 (6th Cir. 2023).

After the college closed its investigation the plaintiff's selective enforcement claims and his state law claims ripened the claims so that a portion of the lawsuit could proceed.

In a case of professor-on-student harassment[81] the plaintiff sued alleging quid pro quo harassment and retaliation under Title IX, negligence, and breach of contract. The Title IX complaint arose from the sexually harassing behavior of a female chemistry professor against the plaintiff. When the male student ultimately rebuffed her advances and suggestions for a sexual relationship, she requested security stating that she felt threatened by the plaintiff, with those allegations becoming known around campus. After making a formal complaint, the plaintiff was evicted from his dormitory room, and later from campus entirely. Because of what the plaintiff claimed was harassment and retaliation from the defendant, he was constructively forced to withdraw prior to graduation, whence the Title IX claims. The breach of contract allegations came from a claim that the defendant moved to dismiss. The federal trial court in Maryland dismissed quid pro quo harassment and negligence claims but allowed the retaliation under Title IX and breach of contract charges to proceed. On the claim for quid pro quo harassment, the plaintiff failed to show deliberate indifference on behalf of the professor, and as for negligence, he did not prove an assumed duty by the defendant. The plaintiff did, however, plead sufficient facts to sustain an action for retaliation and breach of contract.

A second case from Maryland alleged professor-on-student sexual harassment.[82] This lawsuit arose out of alleged sexually harassing behavior of a professor, then 61 years old, toward a 17-year-old student. The defendant handed the student an envelope with her home address on the front and containing an assortment of poems, love notes, and a confession that he was sexually obsessed with her. The professor in question had been hired despite a criminal background including harassment and stalking. According to the plaintiff, no background check had been done, violating institutional procedures. During the harassment, he informed his supervisor of his behavior and, although he was threatened with termination, it was never done. The plaintiff

[81] Anderson v. Univ. of New England, 610 F.Supp.3d 306, 412 Educ. L. Rep. 210 (D. Me. 2022).

[82] Doe v. Cmty. Coll. of Balt. Cnty., 595 F. Supp. 3d 392, 409 Educ. L. Rep. 763 (D. Md. 2022).

suffered several mental health issues and was unable to finish her education. She sued alleging claims under state negligence, antidiscrimination, contract, and tort laws. The defendant's motion to dismiss was granted in part and denied in part. In making that determination, the court held that the state statute prohibiting discrimination in public places did not create a private right of action, and that the plaintiff could not bring a negligence claim against the county directly. Finally, the court stated that the doctrine of *in loco parentis* did not apply at the college level. As for the negligence claim, the plaintiff had stated a claim against the defendant regarding negligence in the hiring, training, supervising, and retaining of the professor.

A dispute from Wisconsin centered on the plaintiff's Title IX claim where university officials overturn a prior decision where a football player was expelled after being found responsible for third-degree sexual assault, and readmitted after he was acquitted of criminal sexual assault in state court.[83] Parties brought cross-motions for summary judgment. In granting the defendant's motion, the court held that the plaintiff's general anxiety about being on campus after the football player was readmitted was not severe enough to rise to indirect discrimination through deliberate indifference, as required under Title IX, nor was the decision to readmit direct discrimination under Title IX. The plaintiff had argued that the defendant's refusal to allow her to participate in the readmission decision amounted to deliberate indifference. The court disagreed, stating that there was no duty that arose to a violation of Title IX, and she offered no concrete examples of the hostile environment that she had to endure such as to deprive her of her educational opportunities.

In an article 78 decision an appellate court in New York affirmed in favor of university officials in determining that a student was responsible for violations of its student code of conduct and suspending him for two years.[84] The court held that there was substantial evidence supporting the defendant's determination, and that the sanction, a two-year suspension, was not so disproportionate as to be shocking to one's sense of fairness. The court concluded that the defendant institution had substantially

---

[83] Doe v. Bd. of Regents, 615 F. Supp. 3d 877, 413 Educ. L. Rep. 294 (W.D. Wis. 2022). [appeal filed].

[84] Doe v. Brockport, 186 N.Y.S.3d 458, 414 Educ. L. Rep. 970 (N.Y. App. Div. 2023).

adhered to its own procedural rules during the disciplinary proceeding and did not fail to act as a fair and detached fact finder.

In the next case, the plaintiff alleged that the defendant university violated Title IX during its handling of a complaint.[85] Specifically, he asserted claims based on gender bias and retaliation, as well as due process under state law, breach of contract, negligence, and vicarious liability. This suit arose out of a Title IX investigation where the plaintiff was found in violation of three policies regarding sexual assault and misuse of alcoholic beverages and was dismissed from the university. The defendants moved for summary judgment. As for the claims of gender-biased policies and procedures, issues of facts remained so that summary judgment would be inappropriate. In addition, summary judgment was not warranted on the common law due process, as well as breach of contract. The plaintiff had not chosen a proper comparator when naming his accuser and a female who had previously violated policies, nor had he established that he had engaged in a protected activity; therefore, summary judgment was granted on the claim of retaliation.

The plaintiff in a Georgia case was a female student attending a private women's college,[86] part of a consortium of four educational institutions. While a student at Spelman College, the plaintiff was raped by a student at Morehouse College. She became pregnant and terminated the pregnancy, after which she endured three years of stalking and harassment by the individual who had allegedly raped her. The plaintiff sued Morehouse and Clark, two colleges that were part of the consortium, alleging violation of Title IX based on the deliberate indifference to her report of sexual assault and alleged official policies permitting practices of sexual hostility and violence. Defendants moved to dismiss. Clark's motion to dismiss was granted, as the plaintiff failed to state a valid Title IX claim for deliberate indifference to student-on-student harassment against a university she did not attend. Morehouse's motion to dismiss was granted as to the plaintiff's claim regarding the institution's official policies. As for the claims that the male student engaged in conduct substantially within the control of the defendant Morehouse, the court found that

[85] Doe v. Dordt Univ., 616 F. Supp. 3d 872, 413 Educ. L. Rep. 803 (N.D. Iowa 2022).

[86] Doe v. Morehouse Coll., Inc., 622 F. Supp. 3d 1279, 415 Educ. L. Rep. 182 (N.D. Ga. 2022).

Morehouse College acted with deliberate indifference to harassment, that the plaintiff was denied her educational opportunities, and that she had standing to filed a Title IX complaint against the defendant college although she was not an enrolled student. The court denied the motion to dismiss.

Appropriate jury instructions were at the heart of a case from Pennsylvania.[87] The plaintiff filed a Title IX discrimination and retaliation suit alleging that the defendant had retaliated against her for exercising her rights under Title IX by her filing a report against two other students for sexual assault and then attempting to appeal the defendant's decision. There was disagreement as to the instructions given to the jury. The defendant proposed a causation instruction stating that the plaintiff had to demonstrate that the protected activity was the cause of the adverse action. The plaintiff disagreed and wanted the instruction to state that what needed to be shown was that retaliation was the motivating factor behind the adverse actions taken against her. The court denied the defendant's proposed instruction, holding that a college retaliates in violation of Title IX when the protected activity is the motivating factor for the adverse action.

In Oregon, the plaintiff was investigated for sexual misconduct and brought action in state court alleging violation of Title IX and the Due Process Clause, as well as asserting a state law claim for breach of contract.[88] Defendants moved to dismiss. Underlying the plaintiff's allegations was the belief that the defendants had been compelled to adopt unfair procedures to be in compliance with recent OCR guidance on the requirements in a 2011 "Dear Colleague" letter. The court granted the motion to dismiss, holding that the plaintiff adequately alleged neither discrimination based on sex under Title IX nor a clearly established property right in his continued enrollment to trigger due process protections. The court also found that the university did not violate the plaintiff's procedural due process, and its conduct did not constitute breach of contract. Finally, using the stigma-plus test, the court found the defendants not liable on the plaintiff's § 1983 due process claim. In conclusion, the court stated that the plaintiff's due process and contracts claims contained fatal flaws that could not be cured by amending the pleadings. His Title IX claim, however, could perhaps be amended to appropriately allege that defendants

---

[87] Doe v. Manor Coll., 587 F. Supp. 3d 249, 408 Educ. L. Rep. 168 (E.D. Pa. 2022).
[88] Doe v. Or. State Univ., 614 F. Supp. 3d 847, 412 Educ. L. Rep. 722 (D. Or. 2022).

intentionally discriminated against him because of his gender; therefore, the plaintiff was given 30 days to filed an amended Title IX claim.

Tolling of the statutes of limitations doomed many of the claims in a case from New York.[89] A male sued under Title IX alleging that the defendant college conducted a biased investigation of a complaint of sexual assault made by a female classmate. He claimed the defendant did not follow its procedures and did not provide him with appropriate notice of charges, nor was his roommate, who was present at the time of the alleged assault, interviewed as part of the investigation. The plaintiff brought eight causes of action including deliberate indifference, retaliation, hostile environment, violation of due process, and breach of express and implied contract that the investigation would be held in good faith and basic fairness. The defendant moved to dismiss. The court held that the governor's executive order tolling the state three-year limitation applied to the plaintiff's claim in state court. This order, however, did not apply to claims based on acts prior to the student returning to campus, and such claims were time-barred. While the plaintiff may have continued to feel the effects of what he claimed were discriminatory actions by the defendant during the adjudication of his case, such was not sufficient to allege a continuing violation to toll the statute. In addition, defendant college did not waive its Eleventh Amendment immunity to suit in federal court. Only the plaintiff's Title IX claims concerning his treatment upon returning to campus survived the motion to dismiss.

In a case from Colorado, the plaintiff was expelled from the defendant university for nonconsensual sexual contact.[90] He sued the university and named officials asserting claims for breach of contract, breach of the covenant of good faith and fair dealing, promissory estoppel, and negligence. The district court granted summary judgment for the defendants. On appeal, the court decided two questions of first impression: (1) whether the defendant's student sexual misconduct investigation procedures were sufficiently definite to be enforceable in contract, and (2) whether a private educational institution owes its students a tort duty when investigating and adjudicating claims of sexual

---

[89] Doe v. State Univ. of N.Y. Purchase Coll., 617 F. Supp. 3d 195, 414 Educ. L. Rep. 23 (S.D.N.Y. 2022).

[90] Doe v. Univ. of Denver, 516 P.3d 946, 407 Educ. L. Rep. 940 (Colo. App. 2022).

misconduct. The court held that the sexual misconduct policies were sufficiently definite to be enforceable, stating "Our holding is limited to concluding that the contractual term providing for a "thorough, impartial, and fair" investigation, coupled with the prescribed investigation requirements, is sufficiently definite and certain to be enforced under Colorado contract law." Regarding the second question, the court found that there was a duty of care to the students, independent of its contractual obligations, to adopt and implement fair procedures in investigating and adjudicating allegations against students. This duty did not extend to individuals of the defendant university. Because genuine issues of material fact existed as to the plaintiff's claims for breach of contract and breach of covenant of good faith and fair dealing, the granting of summary judgment was improper as to whether the university breached its duty of care.

Two medical students filed competing Title IX claims, each claiming the other sexually assaulted him.[91] After investigation, Doe was found in violation while the other student was not, because of evidence. Doe was expelled and sued the defendant university, moving for a preliminary injunction enjoining the enforcement of his expulsion during the pendency of the litigation. The irreparable harm alleged by plaintiff was a potential gap in his resume that would follow him for the remainder of his professional life. After reviewing the facts, including the fact that plaintiff already had a gap in his resume from an earlier leave of absence and the lack of urgency being shown by the plaintiff, the court denied the claim because a gap in his resume resulting from the plaintiff's expulsion did not constitute irreparable harm.

In a subsequent suit arising from the same set of facts, but after his expulsion, the plaintiff sued trustees of the college, seeking damages and injunctive relief for sex discrimination under Title IX and for breach of contract under New Hampshire law.[92] The defendants moved to dismiss for failure to state a claim. In the district court, in front of the same judge, the motion was granted in part and denied in part. The court held that plaintiff had stated a claim for erroneous-outcome sex discrimination under Title IX. The argument from the defendant that such could not occur

---

[91] Doe v. Trs. of Dartmouth Coll. (a), 597 F. Supp. 3d 511, 410 Educ. L. Rep. 179 (D.N.H. 2022).

[92] Doe v. Trs. of Dartmouth Coll. (b), 615 F. Supp. 3d 47, 413 Educ. L. Rep. 141 (D.N.H. 2022).

because both individuals were male, was irrelevant. Additionally, the plaintiff did not state a claim that the college selectively enforced its policies and processes regarding sexual misconduct on the basis of gender, as he did not allege that the severity of the penalty was based on gender—in fact, the plaintiff did not appear to take issue with the penalty imposed. The court also found that plaintiff did sufficiently state a claim for breach of contract for the college's failure to follow notice requirements of process policy, an action which arguably could have changed the outcome of the proceedings

The defendant did not, however, breach contractual obligation under its process policy to provide fair, thorough, and impartial investigation of the Title IX complaint by failing to properly apply the preponderance-of-evidence standard. Finally, the court found the plaintiff did state a claim for breach of contract for the defendant's failure to provide a fair and impartial investigation of the Title IX complaint due to gender-based discrimination and also did state a claim for breach of contract for the defendant's violation of its records policy. The defendant's motion was granted in part and denied in part.

The plaintiff in a Virginia case was a male graduate student from Iran who claimed that his advisor discriminated against him because of his sex, favoring female graduate students. The stress caused by the behavior and the hostile environment caused the plaintiff to voluntarily resign from the program. At about the same time, he was accused of sexual assault by a female student. After an investigation, he was found responsible and dismissed from the university. The plaintiff brought a §1983 due process claim action against the defendant university and officers and a claim under Title IX.[93] Defendants filed a motion to dismiss for failure to state a claim. The motion was granted on the basis that the plaintiff had failed to allege whether the individuals named had acted contrary to policy or had engaged in retaliatory behavior. In addition, the plaintiff failed to allege which policies conferred a property interest, which would create a right of due process under the Fourteenth Amendment. These claims, along with claims of a hostile environment based on sex and retaliation, were dismissed without prejudice, allowing the claims to be amended and refiled.

---

[93] Doe v. VA Polytechnic Inst. & State Univ., 617 F. Supp. 3d 412, 414 Educ. L. Rep. 58 (W.D. Va. 2022).

Wayne State University's School of Medicine puts a very high value on professionalism, so much that it is considered a competency that must be mastered to graduate from the school. Honesty is one of these core values. In this case, the plaintiff was dismissed from the university after being found responsible for harassing a fellow student online by sending fraudulent messages to gain control of her online accounts and pursue a relationship; such behavior was deemed unprofessional. The plaintiff, after being dismissed from the university, filed a lawsuit alleging violation of his Fourteenth Amendment right to due process and equal protection; violation of his rights to due process and fair and just treatment under the Michigan constitution; intentional infliction of emotional distress; violation of Title IX; and a claim for estoppel and reliance under state law.[94] Defendants moved for a summary judgment. The court held that the plaintiff's dismissal for unprofessional conduct was academic rather than disciplinary. As such, the court deferred to the judgment of the institution and found no violation of the student's substantive due process rights. The court stated that plaintiff had received sufficient process for an academic dismissal. As for the plaintiff's claims under the Michigan constitution, the court held that sovereign immunity barred the claims and, also looking at Michigan law, denied the plaintiff's promissory estoppel claim. The court held that the plaintiff's own texts and statements established articulable doubt on the school committee hearings as required to sustain a Title XI claim based on erroneous outcome theory. Finally, on the claim of intentional infliction of emotional distress, the behavior of the defendants did not constitute extreme and outrageous conduct which would make them liable. Summary judgment was granted.

A student in the physician assistant program at a university had academic difficulties from the start of the program. In the end, she was dismissed from the program for academic reasons. She sued the university, alleging breach of contract and violation of Title IX, and the university moved for summary judgment.[95] The court denied the motion, holding that there were genuine issues of material fact as to whether the contents of the student handbook created a contract between the plaintiff and the defendant.

---

[94] Eid v. Wayne State Univ., 599 F. Supp. 3d 513, 410 Educ. L. Rep. 631 (E.D. Mich. 2022).

[95] Kunche v. Univ. of Dubuque, 579 F. Supp. 3d 1071, 406 Educ. L. Rep. 326 (N.D. Iowa 2022).

Regarding the Title IX claim, the court held it was undisputed that the plaintiff participated in a protected activity under Title IX when she complained of sexual harassment and evidence of adverse reaction to that complaint. Therefore, genuine issues of material fact also precluded the granting of summary judgment on the Title IX claim. The motion was denied.

After a hearing, at which officials in New York expelled a student for violating the applicable code of conduct and was expelled, he unsuccessfully filed suit challenging the outcome.[96] In dismissing the plaintiff's petition, the court held that there was substantial evidence supporting the decision of the college. It also held that the plaintiff was provided with sufficient notice, satisfying his right of due process, and that the sanction was not so disproportionate to the offense that it would shock the conscience.

Something that is not often seen, in this case a plaintiff filed suit against a university, her alleged assailant, the assailant's sister, and university employees under Title IX, the Illinois Gender Violence Act (IGVA), and the Illinois Preventing Sexual Violence in Higher Education Act.[97] During the time in question, the plaintiff and the assailant's sisters were students at Augustana College. The alleged assailant was on campus as a guest and prospective student. The plaintiff was sexually assaulted by the alleged assailant at an off-campus bar when the plaintiff was highly intoxicated. His sister, when coming upon the scene, blamed the plaintiff and slapped her. According to the facts recited by the court, throughout the investigation of the assault the tone was more toward blaming the plaintiff, who was the victim, rather than ascertaining the facts. Before the plaintiff had filed her complaint, the alleged assailant had been admitted as a student to play on the lacrosse team. The defendants moved to dismiss. The court held that, because the assault took place at an off-campus bar that was outside the control of the university, student's claims for Title IX violation showing deliberate indifference could not be sustained. The court did find that the plaintiff had sufficiently pled a Title IX retaliation claim based on her reporting the sexual assault. As for the claims under state law against the employees of the university

---

[96] McGuinness v. Waters, 175 N.Y.S.3d 512, 408 Educ. L. Rep. 979 (N.Y. App. Div. 2022).

[97] O'Shea v. Augustana Coll., 593 F. Supp. 3d 838, 409 Educ. L. Rep. 151 (C.D. Ill. 2022).

who had conducted the investigation, the federal court declined to exercise supplemental jurisdiction.

In Texas the plaintiff was a university student who was suspended after a Title IX panel investigated two allegations of sexual assault by his former girlfriend.[98] The panel concluded that he was guilty of one of the allegations but found in his favor on the other. The plaintiff sued, alleging gender bias under Title IX and breach of contract. He also sought a temporary restraining order and preliminary injunction lifting his suspension. The plaintiff relied on an erroneous-outcome theory, and that gender bias was a motivating factor behind the erroneous outcome. He also claimed selective enforcement, alleging that the sanction chosen was affected by the student's gender.

To show erroneous outcome, the plaintiff was required to provide evidence that cast articulable doubt on the panel's decision. The court found that the panel's decision of finding violation on one allegation but not the other was illogical, applying evidence arbitrarily to one allegation but not the other. The irrationality of the panel's decision was indicative of gender bias and supported the plaintiff's gender bias claim. "Concluding that a thing is both true and not true is, by definition, erroneous."[99] The panel's exclusion of exculpatory evidence was further evidence of protentional bias, as was the defendant's erroneous consolidation of the two allegations into a single proceeding. The court found the evidence demonstrated that the defendant discriminated against the plaintiff because of his sex and that the plaintiff would face irreparable harm absent the injunction. The injunction was granted.

In *Tucker v. University of New Mexico Board of Regents*, the plaintiff was a law student[100] whose former husband was a law student at the same school. After being suspended, the plaintiff sued the law school, the board of regents, and the school's dean, alleging violations of Title IX, § 1983, the New Mexico Tort Claims Act, and the New Mexico Civil Rights Act. She alleged that defendants took no action when she reported that her ex-husband had violated an order of protection that she had against him and, when her academics suffered because of his harassment, the law

---

[98] Doe v. Tex. Christian Univ., 601 F. Supp. 3d 78, 410 Educ. L. Rep. 972 (N.D. Tex. 2022).
[99] 601 F.Supp.3d 78 at 88.
[100] Tucker v. Univ. of NM Bd. of Regents, 618 F. Supp. 3d 1201, 414 Educ. L. Rep. 238 (D.N.M. 2022).

school suspended her. The defendants moved to dismiss. The court held, regarding the Title IX claims, that the plaintiff had sufficiently alleged that defendants had actual knowledge of the harassment and, therefore, actual knowledge of the substantial risk she faced; that the sexual harassment was sufficiently severe and pervasive; and that defendants had shown deliberate indifference. As to her due process claims, the court held that the plaintiff did not state a due process claim under the Fourteenth Amendment, but did make sufficient allegations to support a claim against the school's dean for violations of the First Amendment and the Equal Protection Clause of the Fourteenth Amendment.

The final case in this category involved LGBTQ+ rights. A university's LGBTQ+ student group sued the university under the New York City's human rights law alleging discrimination based on sex for failure to recognize the group as an official student organization.[101] The defendant moved for summary judgment and was denied. Instead, the court granted the plaintiff partial summary judgment and issued a permanent injunction requiring the defendant to recognize the plaintiff as an official student organization. On appeal, the court found that the defendant was not a "religious corporation" under the law and, therefore, did not qualify for a religious exemption under the city's human rights laws. The court also found that denying recognition to the plaintiff was not essential to the central mission of the defendant university and would not violate First Amendments rights to freedom of expression and association.

Financial Aid

In *Akinlemibola v. National Collegiate Student Loan*, the plaintiff had taken out a private student loan which was then sold twice.[102] After being unsuccessful in an action against the lender, the defendant filed a breach of contract against the plaintiff. In response, the plaintiff filed a counterclaim claiming violations of the Fair Debt Collection Practices Act and Fair Credit Reporting Act, fraudulent misrepresentation, and defamation. The court granted summary judgment to the defendant on its claim and the

---

[101] YU Pride All. v. Yeshiva Univ., 180 N.Y.S.3d 141, 411 Educ. L. Rep. 714 (N.Y. App. Div. 2022).

[102] Akinlemibola v. Nat'l Collegiate Student Loan Tr. 2007-1, 205 N.E.3d 1014, 413 Educ. L. Rep. 959 (Ind. Ct. App. 2023).

counterclaim. The plaintiff appealed on the issues of whether the trial court abused its discretion in the admission of evidence, and whether it erred in granting summary judgment. The court of appeals held that the trial court acted within its discretion and summary judgment was appropriate.

Next was a consolidation of three cases against TransUnion for violation of the Fair Credit Reporting Act (FCRA) for reporting at the same time both a zero balance due to the creditor and a debt owed to the creditor that was 120 days past due.[103] The appellants had borrowed money from different lenders and made payments on those loans. When they stopped making payments for financial reasons, their lenders closed their accounts and transferred their loans. At the same time, the lenders made reports to TransUnion that the accounts were 120 days past due. Simultaneously, the institutions that had closed the accounts and transferred the debt, showed a zero balance on those closed accounts because they had transferred the past due accounts to another lender. Appellants claim this reporting was inaccurate, as no money was owed to the original lenders. In the current action, appellants challenged the standard applied by the district court to review the accuracy of the credit reports. The court, in answer to those questions, held that the standard used is the "reasonable reader" standard. To determine the accuracy of an entry in a report under that standard, the report must be read in its entirety. Only if the entry is inaccurate or ambiguous when read in isolation and in context of the report is it considered inaccurate under the FCRA. Using this standard, the court found the credit reports to be accurate. Accordingly, the district court did not err in dismissing the appellants' complaints.

The plaintiff in a student loan case sued the U.S. Secretary of Education and loan collection agency for its refusal to discharge loans that were taken out in his name by his son,[104] claiming he was a victim of fraud and identity theft. His ex-wife had forged his signature on the loan documents without his knowledge or consent. The department refused to discharge the loan because the plaintiff had not submitted a court order finding him to be a victim of identity theft, the plaintiff's son had benefited from the loan, the information on the promissory note was valid, the plaintiff was

---

[103] Bibbs v. TransUnion LLC, 43 F.4th 331, 406 Educ. L. Rep. 50 (3d Cir. 2022).
[104] Cianfrani v. Cardona, 620 F. Supp. 3d 200, 414 Educ. L. Rep. 811 (E.D. Pa. 2022).

aware of and had made payment on the loan, and the signature was deemed to be the plaintiff's signature. The court held that it could not substitute its reasoning for that of the department; since the decision was not arbitrary, capricious, an abuse of discretion, or otherwise not in accordance with the law, the department's motion for summary judgment was granted.

In an action for violation of the Fair Credit Report Act, the plaintiff alleged that the Pennsylvania Higher Education Assistance Agency was reporting an inaccurate notation of "account in dispute" to the credit agency.[105] The plaintiff claimed that the account was no longer in dispute and contacted the agencies to inform them that was no longer the case, requesting that they remove the notation. When this did not occur, the plaintiff alleged that the entities refused to remove the notation and that PHEAA failed to direct them to do so. As a result, the plaintiff alleged that he suffered damage to his credit rating and emotional damages. Defendants moved for judgment on the pleadings. In granting the defendants' motion, the court held that the plaintiff's letter to the credit agency was insufficient to allow the agency to remove the notation until the same was communicated by the lender. Consequently, there was no negligent violation of the FCRA.

The federal government created the Public Loan Forgiveness program (FLFP) in 2007. In this case, plaintiffs, a group of public servants, contacted the defendant company for information on repaying their loans. The result of that interaction was the filing of a putative class action alleging that the defendant had deceived them by telling them they were not eligible for the loan forgiveness program and then told them they were on track for loan forgiveness after they had chosen a different plan.[106] The plaintiffs alleged that these deceptive practices continued in violation of New York law. The district court certified the class for settlement purposes and a settlement was approved. Some who objected to the settlement appealed, arguing that the district court erred in entering a settlement where each named plaintiff received a service award of $15,000. On appeal, the court held that the class had standing and was appropriately certified; the settlement was fair, reasonable, and adequate; and that the service awards were appropriate.

---

[105] Hussey v. Equifax Info. Servs., LLC, 592 F. Supp. 3d 688, 408 Educ. L. Rep. 865 (W.D. Tenn. 2022).

[106] Hyland v. Navient Corp., 48 F.4th 110, 407 Educ. L. Rep. 519 (2d Cir. 2022).

A debtor objected to the Department of Education's claim in the amount of $13,832.77 asking that it be denied or, in the alternative, be held in abeyance until the issue of debt forgiveness programs was resolved by the court.[107] Although the court held that debtor had standing to object because of the nondischargeable nature of his loan, the potential of post-petition student loan forgiveness did not overcome the validity of the claim or that it was currently owing.

In the next case, the debtor, on behalf of himself and members of a putative nationwide class of borrowers who had received bankruptcy discharges, sued lenders that originated and/or serviced certain private loans.[108] The debtor sought determination that the loans had been discharged in the Chapter 7 bankruptcy, permanent injunctive relief, and award of actual damages for the lenders' alleged willful violations of discharge orders. The court granted the preliminary injunction motion in part, enjoining lenders from taking any acts to collect on loans that "exceed[ed] the cost of attendance," as defined by the Internal Revenue Code, and that had outstanding balances subject to collection. Lenders moved for stay pending appeal. The Bankruptcy Court held that the lenders did not show a strong likelihood of success on the merits, or that absent a stay they would suffer irreparable injury. The lenders' motion was denied.

In a subsequent case, debtors sought relief and a preliminary injunction against Navient Solutions, L.L.C. and Navient Credit Finance Corp. to prevent them from continuing their collection efforts on private student loans that plaintiffs claimed were within their Chapter 7 bankruptcy discharge.[109] Plaintiffs claimed that Navient had ignored this fact and continued collection efforts for at least the last 10 years. In ruling on the motion before it, the court made several holdings. It found that debtors did have standing and, because the relief sought was prohibitory and not mandatory, a showing of likely success on the merits was not required to prevail on the motion for a preliminary injunction. In addition, the court held that debtors showed a likelihood of success on the merits of the claims of discharge violations against Navient, and a

---

[107] In re Eriksen, 647 B.R. 192, 410 Educ. L. Rep. 692 (Bankr. N.D. Ohio 2022).
[108] In re Homaidan (a), 646 B.R. 550, 410 Educ. L. Rep. 383 (Bankr. E.D.N.Y. 2022).
[109] In re Homaidan (b), 650 B.R. 372, 415 Educ. L. Rep. 200 (Bankr. E.D.N.Y. 2022).

likelihood of irreparable injury in the absence of relief. The motion for preliminary injunction was granted in part, and Navient was restrained and enjoined from taking efforts to collect the debt.

A California debtor sought discharge of student loan debt due to undue hardship.[110] Reviewing the facts of the case, the bankruptcy court held that the debtor could not maintain a minimal standard of living and that the current circumstances were likely to persist for a significant portion of the repayment period. In addition, the low value of the education which the debtor had received could be considered evidence that those circumstances would persist. The debtor also had made a good faith effort to repay the loans. Therefore, the debtor established all three elements of the test for discharge, and it was granted.

Obtaining a private student loan to attend medical school abroad, a debtor sought a determination by the bankruptcy court that her debt fell outside the exception for student loan debt.[111] The court held that the rule to decide whether a loan was a qualified educational loan was to look at the specific purpose of the loan rather than how the funds from the loan were used. It was determined that debtor's loan was a qualified student loan and was nondischargeable.

A debtor filed for Chapter 7 bankruptcy, received a discharge, and the case was closed. No one challenged the dischargeability of any of his debts. Ten years later, the debtor brought a class action complaint against a creditor alleging violations of the discharge orders, seeking determination of dischargeability of debts that were outside scope of so-called "student loan" exception, and seeking relief under the California Consumer Credit Reporting Agencies Act (CCCRAA).[112] The debtor moved to certify the class. The bankruptcy court held that the debtor could move to sanction the creditor and to determine dischargeability both through the form of a class action. Proposing a class could be done without amending the original complaint. The creditor could not compel arbitration. Finally, the typicality requirement of proposed classes was satisfied, and the motion was granted.

An order was entered in a Chapter 13 bankruptcy which denied the award of fees charged by attorneys as administrative expenses to be paid through the Chapter 13 bankruptcy plan. In the order,

---

[110] In re Love, 649 B.R. 556, 413 Educ. L. Rep. 870 (Bkrtcy. E.D. Cal. 2023).
[111] In re Mazloom, 648 B.R. 1, 411 Educ. L. Rep. 1100 (Bankr. N.D.N.Y. 2023).
[112] In re Teran, 649 B.R. 794, 414 Educ. L. Rep. 920 (Bkrtcy. N.D. Cal. 2023).

the court determined that the fees for student loan assistance services were not in connection with the bankruptcy case, and could paid outside of the chapter 13 plan, but would not be awarded as administrative priority through the expedited fee approval process. The attorneys filed a motion to reconsider, in order to have them found to be beneficial and necessary expenses of the bankruptcy case and categorized as an administrative expense.[113] The court held that such a motion was an extraordinary remedy and should be used sparingly, and that the attorneys had not met their burden that such a remedy was necessary. "The Motion to Reconsider does not demonstrate an intervening change in the controlling law, put forth new evidence that was not available at trial, or show that there has been a clear error of law or a manifest injustice."[114]

In the state of Alaska, it is constitutionally mandated that unappropriated funds be placed in the Constitutional Budget Reserve, a type of savings account for the state. The Higher Education Investment fund (HEIF) was identified as being eligible for a sweep of unappropriated funds. When the Alaska legislature failed to pass a bill to prevent this action, the plaintiffs sued the state alleging that the funds could not be "swept" into the CBR fund.[115] On appeal, relying on precedent that had interpreted the constitutional provision and found those funds eligible, the court affirmed the lower court's decision that HEIF funds were "sweepable" and that the action of doing so did not violate the separation of powers doctrine.

A student group sued for declaratory and injunctive relief alleging that a Texas statute requiring that out-of-state U.S. citizens pay higher tuition rates than noncitizens not lawfully in the country, but who were residents of Texas, was preempted by federal law forbidding noncitizens not lawfully present in the country from receiving any postsecondary benefits not also available to U.S. citizens.[116] After holding that the plaintiff had standing to sue, that the university president and vice president for enrollment were "state officers" as required for an injunction to

---

[113] In re Welch, 647 B.R. 673, 411 Educ. L. Rep. 657 (Bankr. D.S.C. 2023).

[114] 647 B.R.673 at 677

[115] Short v. Office of Mgmt. & Budget, 520 P.3d 142, 409 Educ. L. Rep. 941 (Alaska 2022).

[116] Young Conservatives of Tex. Found. v. Univ. of N. Tex. (a), 597 F. Supp. 3d 1062, 410 Educ. L. Rep. 234 (E.D. Tex. 2022). [reversed and vacated by 73 F.4th 304 (5th Cir. 2023)].

issued, the court found that the Texas statute was void under conflict preemption and a permanent injunction was granted.

Under the same facts of the previous case, the university officials against whom the injunction was granted moved to stay the injunction pending appeal.[117] The motion was denied on the grounds that the injunction was not overly broad, any injury to the university was outweighed by the student group's probability of success on the merits, and that a stay of the injunction would substantially injure some of the group's members.

Conclusion

Cases involving students in higher education continued to occupy both state and federal courts. This chapter illustrated the balance courts strike in weighing students' rights and those of the institution and other governing bodies.

---

[117] Young Conservatives of Texas Found. v. Univ. of North Texas (b), 609 F.Supp.3d 504, 412 Educ. L. Rep. 125 (E.D. Tex. 2022).

Alphabetical List of Cases

Abo-Saif v. Bd. of Trs. of Univ. of Ill.

Akinlemibola v. Nat'l Collegiate Student Loan Tr. 2007-1

Alberti v. Rector & Visitors of Univ. of Va.

Anderson v. Univ. of New England

Arredondo v. Univ. of La Verne

Babinski v. Queen

Babinski v. Sosnowsky

Bibbs v. TransUnion LLC

Bradley v. Yovino

Bray v. Worcester Polytechnic Inst.

Brezinski v. Widener Univ.

Buschauer v. Columbia Coll. Chicago

Carbone v. Brown Univ.

Choi v. Brown Univ.

Cianfrani v. Cardona

Cross v. Univ. of Toledo, 10th Dist.

Dieckhaus v. Bd. of Governors of Univ. of N.C.

Doe v. Bd. of Regents

Doe v. Brockport

Doe v. Brown Univ.

Doe v. Cmty. Coll. of Balt. Cnty.

Doe v. Dordt Univ.

Doe v. Howard Univ.

Doe v. Manor Coll.

Doe v. Mass. Inst. of Tech.

Doe v. Morehouse Coll., Inc.

Doe v. Northwestern Univ.

Doe v. Oberlin Coll.

Doe v. Or. State Univ.

Doe v. State Univ. of N.Y. Purchase Coll.

Doe v. Stonehill Coll.

Doe v. Tex. Christian Univ.

Doe v. Trs. of Dartmouth Coll. (a)

Doe v. Trs. of Dartmouth Coll. (b)

Doe v. Univ. of Denver

Doe v. Univ. of Southern Indiana

Doe v. VA Polytechnic Inst. & State Univ.

Duerr v. Bradley Univ.

Duke v. Ohio Univ.

Eddlemon v. Bradley Univ. (b)

Eddlemon v. Bradley Univ. (a)

Eid v. Wayne State Univ.

Evans v. Vanderbilt Univ. Sch. of Med.

Felkner v. Rhode Island Coll.

Ferretti v. Nova Southeastern Univ., Inc. (a)

Ferretti v. Nova Southeastern Univ., Inc. (b)

Frazier v. Pa. State Univ.

Harris v. Univ. of Mass. Lowell

Hernandez v. Ill. Inst. of Tech.

Hogan v. S. Methodist Univ.

Hussey v. Equifax Info. Servs., LLC

Hyland v. Navient Corp

In re Eriksen

In re Homaidan

In re Homaidan

In re Love

In re Mazloom

Federal Cases

First Circuit

Maine
Anderson v. Univ. of New England

Massachusetts
Bray v. Worcester Polytechnic Inst.
Doe v. Mass. Inst. of Tech.
Doe v. Stonehill Coll.
Harris v. Univ. of Mass. Lowell

New Hampshire
Doe v. Trs. of Dartmouth Coll. (a)
Doe v. Trs. of Dartmouth Coll. (b)

Rhode Island
Choi v. Brown Univ.
Doe v. Brown Univ.
Felkner v. Rhode Island Coll.

Second Circuit

New York
Doe v. State Univ. of N.Y. Purchase Coll.
Hyland v. Navient Corp.
Morales v. N.Y. Univ.
Rynasko v. N.Y. Univ.

Third Circuit

Pennsylvania
Bibbs v. TransUnion, LLC
Brezinski v. Widener Univ.
Cianfrani v. Cardona
Doe v. Manor Coll.
Frazier v. Pa. State Univ.

Fourth Circuit

Maryland
Doe v. Cmty. Coll. of Balt. Cnty.

South Carolina
Neal v. E. Carolina Univ.

Virginia
Alberti v. Rector & Visitors of Univ. of Va.
Student A v. Liberty Univ., Inc.

West Virginia
Doe v. Va. Polytechnic Inst. & State Univ.

Fifth Circuit

Louisiana
Babinski v. Queen
Babinski v. Sosnowsky
Jones v. Adm'rs of Tulane Educ. Fund
Magliulo v. Edward Via Coll. of Osteopathic Med.

Texas
Doe v. Tex. Christian Univ.
Hogan v. S. Methodist Univ.
King v. Baylor Univ.
Overdam v. Texas A&M Univ.
Speech First, Inc. v. Khator
Young Conservatives of Tex. Found. v. Univ. of N. Tex. (a)
Young Conservatives of Tex. Found. v. Univ. of N. Tex. (b)

Sixth Circuit

Michigan
Eid v. Wayne State Univ.

Ohio
Doe v. Oberlin Coll.
Miranda v. Xavier Univ.

Tennessee
Evans v. Vanderbilt Univ. Sch. of Med.
Hussey v. Equifax Info. Servs., LLC

Seventh Circuit

Illinois
Buschauer v. Columbia Coll. Chicago
Carbone v. Brown Univ.
Doe v. Northwestern Univ.
Duerr v. Bradley Univ.
Eddlemon v. Bradley Univ. (a)
Eddlemon v. Bradley Univ. (b)
Hernandez v. Ill. Inst. of Tech.
O'Shea v. Augustana Coll.
Patterson v. Respondus, Inc.

Indiana
Doe v. Univ. of So. Indiana

Wisconsin
Doe v. Bd. of Regents

Eighth Circuit

Iowa
Doe v. Dordt Univ.
Kunche v. Univ. of Dubuque

Minnesota
Minn. State Coll. Student Ass'n, Inc. v. Cowles

Ninth Circuit

Arizona
Sabra v. Maricopa Cnty. Cmty. Coll. Dist.

California
Arredondo v. Univ. of La Verne

Idaho
Perlot v. Green
Stevens v. Brigham Young Univ.-Idaho

Oregon
Doe v. Or. State Univ.

Tenth Circuit

New Mexico
Tucker v. Univ. of N.M. Bd. of Regents

Eleventh Circuit

Alabama
Melvin v. Troy Univ.

Florida
Ferretti v. Nova Southeastern Univ., Inc. (a)
Ferretti v. Nova Southeastern Univ., Inc. (b)
Longo v. Campus Advantage, Inc.

Georgia
Doe v. Morehouse Coll., Inc.
Young v. Grand Canyon Univ., Inc.

D.C. Circuit

Doe v. Howard Univ.
Smith v. Howard Univ.
Wheeler v. Am. Univ.

United States Court of Federal Claims

Bankruptcy
In re Eriksen
In re Homaidan (a)
In re Homaidan (b)
In re Love
In re Mazloom
In re Suffolk Univ. Covid Refund Litig.
In re Teran
In re Welch

State and D.C. Cases

Alaska
Short v. Office of Mgmt. & Budget

Colorado
Doe v. Univ. of Denver

Connecticut
Bradley v. Yovino

Florida
Univ. of Fla. Bd. of Trs. v. Rojas
Univ. of S. Fla. Bd. of Trs. v. Moore

Illinois
Abo-Saif v. Bd. of Trs. of Univ. of Ill.

Indiana
Akinlemibola v. Nat'l Collegiate Student Loan Tr. 2007-1
Mellowitz v. Ball State Univ.

Kansas
Minjarez-Almeida v. Kan. Bd. of Regents
Wiedemann v. Fraternity

Michigan
Zwiker v. Lake Superior State Univ.

Montana
Zolnikov v. Nat. Bd. of Med. Exam'rs

Nebraska
Ramaekers v. Creighton Univ.

New Jersey
Mueller v. Kean Univ.

New York
Doe v. Brockport
Khass v. N.Y. Presbyterian Brooklyn Methodist Hosp.
McGuinness v. Waters
Mozdziak v. State Univ. of N.Y. Maritime Coll.

Shapiro v. Syracuse Univ.
State v. Summers
YU Pride All. v. Yeshiva Univ.

North Carolina
Dieckhaus v. Bd. of Governors of Univ. of N.C.
Kelly v. State
Lannan v. Bd. of Governors of Univ. of N.C.

Ohio
Cross v. Univ. of Toledo, 10th Dist.
Duke v. Ohio Univ.
McDermott v. Ohio State Univ.
Smith v. Ohio State Univ.

Texas
Univ. of the Incarnate Word v. Redus

Vermont
Kelly v. Univ. of Vermont Med. Ctr.

CHAPTER 10

FEDERAL AND STATE LEGISLATION

Amy L. Dagley and David L. Dagley

Continued on the next page...

Introduction

This chapter lists, categorizes, and details education-related legislative acts adopted by the United States Congress and each of the fifty state legislatures or general assemblies for the 2023 calendar year. The acts recorded herein include those directing or impacting educational institutions at the prekindergarten, K-12, community college, university, and graduate and professional school levels. The institutions affected by these acts include those in the public and private sectors.

The authors have provided the research for this chapter since the 1998 legislative year, in which the Congress and the individual state legislative bodies produced a total of only 253 education-related pieces of legislation. Since 1998, the amount of legislation grew by a factor of five, with a peak of 1,225 acts in 2011, and peaks of 1,480 acts in 2021 and 1,433 acts in 2023.

The research methodology for locating these acts changed greatly through the years. Through 2006 law libraries located near the authors contained a full complement of statutory codes for most jurisdictions as well as legislative service bulletins for a majority of the states. Consequently, a complete search for all fifty states could usually be accomplished by visually scanning annotations in the school codes or employing the content tables in legislative service bulletins.

As a result of the economic downturn in 2007 many law libraries cut expenditures by canceling subscriptions for printed state legislative service bulletins or annual updates of state statutory collections. While electronic versions of bills and bill summaries existed at that time, they were not readily available or in a similar format across the states. Some states placed electronic records on legislative websites, others placed them with their legislative service offices, the offices of the secretaries of state, or state archivists. Websites for state associations of school boards and school administrators occasionally posted legislative summaries for sessions where the public could access them. Eventually, more consolidated websites listing statutory acts emerged, especially HeinOnline, TheLAW.net, and Legiscan.com.

From these resources the authors visually scanned state-by-state lists of acts as being education-related and policy-impacting. The authors then gleaned the policy directions in the acts, attempting to summarize the legislative bodies' intent in one sentence. One-sentence summaries are beneficial in limiting print space for publication but carry the danger of misconstruing actual legislative intent. If readers are concerned about the accuracy of descriptions, they are encouraged to follow the citations and use them to locate the full texts of the bill.

The summary description of acts was loaded on a file listed by state, then sorted into the topical headings in the table of contents such as accountability and school reform, athletics, employment, or higher education. Within the topical headings, the authors qualitatively scanned the listings for similar subjects and organized them together, where possible.

The acts described in this chapter typically provide some policy direction. Consequently, appropriations acts are not reported except when the appropriation specifically funds a particular building or academic program. General appropriations acts,[1] appropriations for K-12 funding,[2] appropriations for higher education,[3] appropriations for state schools,[4] appropriations for state education entities[5] are not reported. Changes in state teacher retirement systems such as modifications of classification systems for new hires or adoption of alternative health insurance programs are not included. However, actions such as allowing retirees to temporarily return to service without loss of retirement benefits drive the policy of addressing staff shortages and would thus be included.

Resolutions in most instances make commendations, recognitions, and memorials. At times, resolutions express the general will or sentiment of legislatures, but without advancing them through the procedural rigors of legislative acts. On rare occasions, resolutions are reminders of earlier directions[6] or repudiate acts or resolutions from an executive branch entity such as a state school board.[7] Because resolutions represent the sentiment of legislative bodies, but do not direct a particular actions or policy outcomes, they are not usually reported in these materials. However, the authors note that resolutions seem to have

---

[1] *See, e.g.*, 2023 Del. Laws HB 195; 2023 Tex. Gen. Laws H.B. No. 1.
[2] *See, e.g.*, 2023 Alaska SB 140.
[3] *See, e.g.*, 2023 Ariz. Sess. Laws Ch. 140, H.B. 1727.
[4] *See, e.g.*, 2023 Ark Acts 869, S.B. 73.
[5] *See, e.g.*, 2023 N.D. Laws S.B. No. 2013.
[6] *See, e.g.*, 2023 Utah Laws HCR 10, in which Utah directed the state Board of Education to remind all LEAs of their obligation under statute to ensure the Pledge of Allegiance is recited in every classroom at the beginning of every school day.
[7] *See, e.g.*, 2023 Idaho Sess. Laws S.C.R. No. 107, in which Idaho rejected by concurrent resolution a rule of the state Board of Education regarding registration of postsecondary institutions as a proprietary school, as being inconsistent with legislative intent.

been used to direct state education entities infrequently last year, a development which contradicts the general rule that resolutions reflect mere legislative sentiments. For example, Maine used a resolution to direct its state Department of Education (DOE) and municipal bond bank to amend rules on its school facilities finance program and school revolving renovation fund.[8] Maine further adopted a resolution that its state Board of Education (BOE) study educator credential requirements.[9]

The authors also traced the history of bills with education-policy implications to learn whether they had been vetoed or survived vetoes. The 2023 legislative sessions had remarkably few education-related bills vetoed compared to previous years. Two notable vetoes included one in Iowa, relating to penalties for violation of its open meetings act,[10] and one in Kansas, purporting to standardize firearms safety programs in school systems.[11]

Federal Legislation

The first session of the 118th Congress, beginning January 3, 2023, was historically unproductive with only 33 laws recorded. Three of the laws passed in 2023 gave names to one post office and two Veterans Affairs Clinics. In the second session in 2024, Congress adopted 42 more laws. Only two laws related to education were enacted in 2023 as follows.

Congress amended the Elementary and Secondary Education Act of 1965[12] to clarify that the prohibition on the use of federal education funds for specified weapons does not apply to their use for training in archery, hunting, other shooting sports, or for culinary arts.[13]

Congress modified the age requirement for the Student Incentive Payment Program of the state maritime academies in the Changing Age-Determined Eligibility to Student Incentive Payments Act (CADETS Act). The change permits the Secretary to make an agreement under the relevant section[14] only with

---

[8] 2023 Me. Laws Ch. 44, S.P. 591, L.D. 1472.
[9] 2023 Me. Laws Ch. 54, H.P. 302, L.D. 485.
[10] 2023 Iowa HB 2539. Vetoed 5-17-2024.
[11] 2023 Kansas SB 2304. Vetoed 4-24-2023. House motion to override veto failed; veto sustained, 4-26-2023.
[12] 20 U.S.C. 7906(7).
[13] Pub. L. 118-17, H.R. 5110 (October 6, 2023).
[14] 46 U.S.C. § 51509.

qualified students who meet the age requirements for enlistments or commissions in the Navy Reserve when they graduate from the academy.[15]

State Legislation

Accountability and School Reform

Accountability and school reform efforts in 2023 saw limited changes in precipitating conditions for state takeovers, coupled with more direction in planning for improvement in lieu of takeovers. There were minor changes in assessments, including assurance of authority for virtual assessment and more concentration on performance reporting without a "letter grade" system. The dominant legislative measure for accountability and school reform was an increased focus on dropout prevention and credit recovery. This section describes these measures.

Three states enacted five bills regarding the process of state leadership taking control over individual school districts and three other states adopted four acts directing the creation of improvement plans. Arkansas changed the conditions under which a public school district must be administratively consolidated by its state BOE, within two years of its assumption of authority over a public school district.[16] In the same time frame of two years, Arkansas required its state BOE to establish the conditions under which a school board will be returned to local control.[17] However, Arkansas repealed special requirements placed on school districts with a ten percent or more minority population.[18]

Mississippi extended the date of repeal for the provision authorizing its state BOE to appoint a new five-member panel for the administration of a failing school district.[19] North Dakota gave the Superintendent of Public Instruction authority to intervene directly when a public school or school district is chronically low performing.[20]

---

[15] Pub. L. 118-7, S. 467 (June 30, 2023).
[16] 2023 Ark. Acts 543, H.B. 1504.
[17] 2023 Ark. Acts 633, S.B. 364.
[18] 2023 Ark. Acts 424, H.B. 1534.
[19] 2023 Miss. Laws SB 2812.
[20] 2023 N.D. Laws S.B. No. 2254.

California shifted the burden to post school accountability plans from the Superintendent of Public Instruction to the local and county school district or charter school.[21] In a measure addressing educational reform and planning for improvement, Connecticut added permission for local and regional school boards to request technical assistance.[22] Connecticut also required school boards to post their improvement plan on a website annually.[23] In a third act Connecticut extended a priority school grant of funding in its last year for one more year through June 2024.[24] Louisiana amended provisions for academic supports for low-performing students to require the program to include the third grade, rather than just grades 4-8; specified that the supports were aimed at the subjects of reading and mathematics; applied future requirements coming from its state BOE; called for one-on-one or small group instruction, at least three times a week, in thirty-minute minimum sessions, either embedded in or outside of school days o; and, provide high-quality tutoring services.[25]

Five states changed their assessment standards. Alabama amended its Alabama Literacy Act to authorize the literacy task force to approve assessments for three years, beginning with the 2023-24 school year, to direct the task force to evaluate the age appropriateness of program materials, and require the task force to make all rubrics and measurements used to analyze assessments publicly available.[26] Arkansas established the conditions under which public schools may offer statewide student assessments in virtual settings.[27] Kansas permitted students enrolled in online schools to participate in online state assessments.[28]

North Dakota required public school boards to administer assessments in grades K-10 at least twice annually in mathematics and reading using a state-provided interim assessment, or an interim assessment from a state-approved list of assessments.[29] Virginia permitted students enrolled in virtual school programs to

---

[21] 2023 Cal. Stat. Ch. 494, S.B. No. 609.
[22] 2023 Conn. Acts 167, Subst. S.B. No. 1, § 38.
[23] 2023 Conn. Acts 167, Subst. S.B. No. 1, § 4.
[24] 2023 Conn. Acts 2008, Subst. H.B. No. 5003, § 7.
[25] 2023 La. Acts No. 458, S.B. No. 177.
[26] 2023 Ala. Acts 417, H.B. 430.
[27] 2023 Ark. Acts 643, S.B. 432.
[28] 2023 Kan. Sess. Laws HB 2080.
[29] 2023 N.D. Laws S.B. No. 2028.

take beginning-of-year or mid-year growth assessments in a virtual setting, with measures taken to assure test security.[30]

Five states adopted seven acts directing more performance reporting from schools with two repealing "letter grade" school reporting systems. Arkansas mandated that each regular monthly meeting of a school district board of directors would feature a report or presentation regarding student achievement data or performance.[31] Additionally, Arkansas required that students who graduate with GEDs or transferred to home or private (including faith-based) school not be included in a school performance report on dropout rate.[32] California ordered its state DOE to report statewide summative accountability results from the California assessment of student performance and progress by October 15 each year.[33] Connecticut obligated the commissioner of education to conduct an audit of state and local testing requirements and administration.[34]

Maine expanded its commissioner's authority to review schools that are private schools enrolling 60% or more publicly funded students.[35] Virginia directed the commonwealth's BOE to create and maintain a parent data portal to display individual student assessment data on all state-supported assessments.[36] Virginia also ordered local boards to provide teachers, parents, principals, and other school leaders with their students' results on any standards of learning assessment or alternative assessment as soon as practicable after the assessment is administered.[37] Michigan repealed its A-F letter grade school rating system.[38] Utah ordered its state BOE to quit using letter grades to assign schools overall ratings and amended provisions on school turnaround leadership development.[39]

Six states pressed for more to be done in dropout prevention and credit recovery. Arizona amended provisions about it dropout recovery program to require reporting to its DOE about the

---

[30] 2023 Va. Acts Ch. 524, H.B. 1820.
[31] 2023 Ark. Acts 425, H.B. 1535.
[32] 2023 Ark. Acts 423, H.B. 1533.
[33] 2023 Cal. Stat. Ch. 177, S.B. No. 293.
[34] 2023 Conn. Acts 167, Subst. S.B. No. 1, § 25.
[35] 2023 Me. Laws Ch. 397, H.P. 916, L.D. 1420.
[36] 2023 Va. Acts Ch. 652, H.B. 1629; 2023 Va. Acts Ch. 653, S.B. 1329.
[37] 2023 Va. Acts Ch. 158, H.B. 2225; 2023 Va. Acts Ch. 159, S.B. 1253.
[38] 2023 Mich. Pub. Acts No. 34, H.B. 4166.
[39] 2023 Utah Laws H.B. 308.

academic progress of its students and that their individual plans specify whether children receive "wraparound services" defined as support services, including social work coaching sessions, trauma coaching sessions, or food and housing security coaching sessions.[40] Louisiana required the concurrence of a public school board prior to changing the exit code information assigned to a student in the data collection system.[41]

Oregon delineated requirements for the approval of recovery schools, which are schools identified for holistic efforts to provide credit recovery for students in danger of not graduating on time and which receive special funding for that purpose.[42] Pennsylvania renewed its credit recovery program for high school students at risk of not graduating in time.[43] Tennessee directed its state DOE to conduct a study of best practices for the use of ninth grade "on-track" indicators in state accountability systems, to prevent students from dropping out of high school.[44] Texas opened a dropout credit recovery program, expanding it to include charter schools and to allow offerings on campus, remotely or through hybrid delivery.[45]

Two states ordered reports on the graduation rate for special education students. California required its state DOE to report on its website the four- and five-year graduation rate for students with disabilities.[46] Indiana directed each school corporation to publish on its website the graduation rate for each high school, with an amended definition for "graduation," to include fuller descriptions of students who succeed or fail to graduate.[47]

Three states sought accountability through accreditation. Georgia permitted and encouraged, but did not require, accreditation of public schools, with guidance given as to the qualification of accrediting agencies.[48] Indiana adopted a process for national or regional accreditation agencies to be recognized by its state BOE, for accreditation for its nonpublic schools.[49] Montana

---

[40] 2023 Ariz. Sess. Laws Ch. 127, S.B. 1208.
[41] 2023 La. Acts No. 97, S.B. No. 45.
[42] 2023 Or. Laws Ch. 513, H.B. 2767.
[43] 2023 Pa. Laws Act No. 33, H.B. 301, Sec. 5.1.
[44] 2023 Tenn. Pub. Acts Ch. No. 322, H.B. No. 1295, Subs. S.B. No. 884.
[45] 2023 Tex. Gen. Laws S.B. No. 1647.
[46] 2023 Cal. Stat. Ch. 576, A.B. No. 1340.
[47] 2023 Ind. Acts P.L. 188, SB 380; 2023 Ind. Acts P.L. 160, HB 1635.
[48] 2023 Ga. Laws Act 252, S.B. 204.
[49] 2023 Ind. Acts P.L. 171, SB 100.

amended a provision on accreditation standards to specify that the economic impact statement must include an analysis of the ability of school boards to implement the standard within existing resources, including time.[50]

Four states asked for reports on instructional materials. Connecticut supplied a definition for "open educational resources" and required its state DOE to develop a model policy about data collection and report biennially (rather than annually) about open educational resources.[51] Louisiana required its state DOE to recognize a determination by school boards that textbooks or other instructional materials are of high quality, and that the review committee must include at least two teachers who hold a designation as a teacher leader advisor.[52] Utah created a process for local school boards or charter school governing boards to follow if the board chooses to adopt or approve instructional materials.[53] West Virginia directed school officials to publish adopted, up-to-date classroom curricula online at the beginning of each school year or within thirty days of when they were updated or adopted.[54]

Two states called for reports about enrollment. California obligated officials in its state DOE to report public school enrollment information in a manner that allows the public to determine class size for each school site easily.[55] Connecticut mandated an annual count in April of the number of students enrolled in public schools.[56]

Two states demanded more study about their accountability systems. Colorado created a task force to study the statewide K-12 education accountability system to address the contribution of resource inequities to differences in student performance.[57] Nevada created a subcommittee on educational accountability, from the interim finance legislative committee, and designated its membership, powers, and duties.[58]

Other acts related to accountability and school reform are described as follows. Connecticut required officials in its state DOE

---

[50] 2023 Mont. Laws H.B. 21.
[51] 2023 Conn. Acts 151, H.B. No. 6771.
[52] 2023 La. Acts No. 238, S.B. No. 46.
[53] 2023 Utah Laws S.B. 55.
[54] 2023 W. Va. Acts Ch. 128, S.B. 422.
[55] 2023 Cal. Stat. Ch. 614, S.B. No. 872.
[56] 2023 Conn. Acts 167, Subst. S.B. No. 1, § 37.
[57] 2023 Colo. Sess. Laws H.B. 1241.
[58] 2023 Nev. Stat. Ch. 494, AB 399.

and public schools to study, plan, implement, and report on school climate and culture.[59] Indiana obligated officials in its state DOE to report to the legislative council findings and recommendations about reducing the amount of redundant data required for schools to report to state agencies.[60] Nevada eliminated end-of-course final examinations.[61] New Hampshire required its DOE to provide the standing committees for education with copies of the laws and rules relative to education.[62]

Athletics

This section details legislative measures related to athletics. Ten states approved eleven acts on participation rules for student athletes. Arkansas addressed situations where students participate in school athletic activities on the same day they take part in non-school athletic activities with permissive language, except when sports are football, basketball, baseball, softball, or volleyball.[63] Arkansas also set aside a restriction for homeschooled students to participate in interscholastic athletics in public school attendance zones, allowing them to take part at nonresident public schools.[64]

Florida permitted full-time students in charter schools and virtual schools to participate in extracurricular activities at nonpublic schools.[65] Illinois required that a student alternative education plan must include information to parents or guardians about extracurricular activities which may be offered to pupils.[66] Kansas permitted homeschool and nonpublic school students to participate in interscholastic sports in public schools where they are residents.[67] Kentucky limited the authority of its interscholastic association to make participation rules for students before they enroll in ninth grade.[68]

---

[59] 2023 Conn. Acts 167, Subst. S.B. No. 1, §§ 48-54.
[60] 2023 Ind. Acts P.L. 250, HB 1638.
[61] 2023 Nev. Stat. Ch. 518, SB 9.
[62] 2023 N.H. Laws Ch. 197, HB 492.
[63] 2023 Ark. Acts 748, H.B. 1733.
[64] 2023 Ark. Acts 630, S.B. 361.
[65] 2023 Fla. Laws Ch. 113, S. 190. *See also*, 2023 Fla. Laws Ch. 97, H. 225.
[66] 2023 Ill. Laws P.A. 103-473, SB 183.
[67] 2023 Kan. Sess. Laws SB 113.
[68] 2023 Ky. Acts Ch. 93, SB 145.

Nebraska required school boards to adopt consistent policies for participation in extracurricular activities. This measure appeared to return authority for control of participation rules, from the athletic or activities association to each school board.[69] Nevada codified a prohibition against obligating pupils to participate in certain out-of-school activities as a condition of taking part in sports or cheer activities. For example, a coach cannot require participation in another activity as a condition of participation in the coach's sport.[70]

Tennessee specified that if homeschool students participate in LEA-sponsored interscholastic or extracurricular activities, then LEAs may request proof that the individuals received a health service or examination that is required for the LEA's students to participate in the activity or event.[71] Utah allowed nonpublic, home, charter, or online students to participate in extracurricular activities outside the student's public school of residence.[72] Virginia allowed school-age children of foreign service employees or civilian members of the armed forces to participate in extracurricular activities.[73]

Six states responded to the issue of gender identity by inserting participation rules in athletics. Alabama added to the prohibition for transgender athletes from competing in all non-coeducational school athletics. The act provided immunity for public K-12 schools, colleges, and universities for maintaining separate athletic teams, or sorting for biological male students, and prohibited retaliation taken against a student who reports an alleged violation of this act to an employee or representative of the public educational institutions.[74] Kansas directed that female student athletic teams can only include members who are biologically female.[75]

North Carolina required all teams participating in interscholastic or intramural athletic activities to be designated as male, female, or coeducational teams, and prohibited athletic teams designated as female teams from allowing a male, based on the male's reproductive biology and genetics at birth.[76] North

---

[69] 2023 Neb. Laws LB 705.
[70] 2023 Nev. Stat. Ch. 521, SB 196.
[71] 2023 Tenn. Pub. Acts Ch. No. 296, H.B. No. 252, Subs. S.B. No. 644.
[72] 2023 Utah Laws H.B. 209.
[73] 2023 Va. Acts Ch. 783, H.B. 1929.
[74] 2023 Ala. Acts 293, H.B. 261.
[75] 2023 Kan. Sess. Laws HB 2238.
[76] 2023 N.C. Sess. Laws Ch. 109, H.B. 574.

Dakota obligated public and nonpublic schools whose athletic teams compete against public schools to designate athletic teams as male, female, or coeducational, and prohibited teams or sports designated for females to be open to those the male sex, based individuals' non-ambiguous sex organs, chromosomes, and endogenous hormone profile at birth.[77]

Tennessee specified that, in connection with interscholastic athletic activities, students enrolled in nonpublic schools in the state are eligible to do so only in accordance with their sexes. This admonition does not prohibit students whose sex is female from participating on a male team's sport if the school does not offer a separate team for females.[78] Wyoming forbade males from competing on teams designated for female, described as the biological, physical condition of being male or female, determined by individuals' genetics and anatomies at birth.[79]

Gender identity was also a factor in a seventh act about athletics. Oklahoma directed that, if a suitable meeting room or area is not available, a coach may enter a locker room before, during, or after a school-sponsored athletic activity, if all students are fully clothed and the coach is accompanied by at least one other adult. If the coach is of the opposite sex of the students, the coach must be accompanied by a coach of the same sex as the students. A coach cannot be a student.[80]

Other athletics-related acts from 2023 are as follows. Alabama enacted an incentive program to provide athletic trainers in rural (1A, 2A, and 3A) schools and Title I schools, for grades 6-12.[81] South Carolina transferred authority over athletic trainers to the board of medical examiners.[82] New York changed the definition of "student athlete" to include 10th, 11th, and 12th graders, removing barriers for implementing compensation for student athletes for use of their name, image, or likeness (NIL).[83] North Dakota called for a legislative management study to assess the impact of the state high school activities association on students.[84]

---

[77] 2023 N.D. Laws H.B. No. 1249.
[78] 2023 Tenn. Pub. Acts Ch. No. 285, S.B. No. 1237, Subs. H.B. No. 306.
[79] 2023 Wyo. Sess. Laws Act No. 92, Ch. No. 191, S.F. 133.
[80] 2023 Okla. Sess. Laws S.B. No. 26.
[81] 2023 Ala. Acts 341, S.B. 267.
[82] 2023 S.C. Acts No. 77, S.B. 397.
[83] 2023 N.Y. Laws Ch. 154, A. 7107.
[84] 2023 N.D. Laws H.B. No. 1149.

Attendance, Promotion, and Graduation

This section discusses legislation passed in 2023 related to attendance, promotion, and graduation. Seven states enacted eight bills about compulsory attendance and truancy. Connecticut provided an exception allowing children who had not reached the age of five on or before the first day of September to be admitted by written request of their parents subject to assessments by school principals and appropriate certificated staff, to assure their enrollment is developmentally appropriate.[85]

Kentucky required that a report be made to the court of truancy cases when there is no action implemented by the response team within 90 days, and required a court-designated worker to make a finding if a diversion is failed due to lack of parental cooperation.[86] Maine directed officials in school administrative units with chronic absenteeism rates of 10% or higher to establish attendance review teams or committees to review chronic absences.[87] Maine then altered the notification law standards for superintendents bringing charges against parents for truancy.[88]

Nevada clarified in its compulsory attendance law that students must be in attendance for full school days in public schools for it to apply.[89] Rhode Island required compulsory attendance in kindergarten for all children who attained age 6 on or before September 1 of each school year.[90] Virginia made it mandatory rather than permissive for principals or their designees to notify parents of children who violate board policies or compulsory attendance rules which might result in suspensions or filing of court petitions.[91] Utah added duties to its state BOE and the director of juvenile justice and youth services to address chronic absenteeism.[92]

Four states passed bills about out-of-district attendance or open enrollment designations. Montana altered standards and procedures for granting permission for students to attend out-of-district schools, specifying that those who were expelled or are

---

[85] 2023 Conn. Acts 2008, Subst. H.B. No. 5003, § 1.
[86] 2023 Ky. Acts Ch. 105, HB 3.
[87] 2023 Me. Laws Ch. 480, H.P. 1191, L.D. 1861.
[88] 2023 Me. Laws Ch. 99, H.P. 408, L.D. 631.
[89] 2023 Nev. Stat. Ch. 206, AB 54, sec. 13.
[90] 2023 R.I. Pub. Laws S.B. 1090.
[91] 2023 Va. Acts Ch. 523, H.B. 1982.
[92] 2023 Utah Laws H.B. 400.

truant are ineligible for such attendance.[93] North Dakota specified that resident school boards may not deny open enrollment to approved virtual schools.[94] Tennessee allowed local education agencies (LEAs), its wording o school boards, which established virtual schools to enter into agreement with other LEAs that have not done so to provide it to their students.[95] West Virginia reenacted a provision regarding public schools' open enrollment policies,[96] to clarify when applications for transfers are denied due to prior suspensions or expulsions and the procedure for dealing with appeal of these actions.[97]

Twelve states adopted 15 acts on reciprocity to ease the transition for students when their parents transfer from one state to another or within states. Arizona corrected references adopting the interstate compact for educational opportunities for military children, from statutory "sections" to "chapters."[98] Arkansas amended its military child school transitions act to make it conform to the interstate compact adopted by other states.[99] Arkansas also required that a petitions by students to transfer districts be placed on the agendas of their boards for review and approval.[100] In a third act, Arkansas made minor changes in its school code such as modifying the reference to an "English language learner" to simply refer to an "English learner" and substituting "enhance and improve" with "accelerate" as to the transition of students from military families to transfer to other schools.[101]

California expressly provided access to the U.S. Space Force to participate in the interstate compact on educational opportunity for military children.[102] Idaho directed school boards to adopt policies governing the process for enrollment options, including in-district transfers; policies must be nondiscriminatory and include procedures for appeals.[103] Kentucky permitted students to have the option to remain in the same schools when changing residence

---

[93] 2023 Mont. Laws H.B. 203.
[94] 2023 N.D. Laws H.B. No. 1376.
[95] 2023 Tenn. Pub. Acts Ch. No. 111, S.B. No. 225, Subs. H.B. No. 588.
[96] W. VA. CODE § 18-5-16 (1931).
[97] 2023 W. Va. Acts Ch. 134, H.B. 2596.
[98] 2023 Ariz. Sess. Laws Ch. 151, H.B. 2599.
[99] 2023 Ark. Acts 636, S.B. 387.
[100] 2023 Ark. Acts 731, H.B. 1604.
[101] 2023 Ark. Acts 793, S.B. 573.
[102] 2023 Cal. Stat. Ch. 142, A.B. No. 1605.
[103] 2023 Idaho Sess. Laws Ch. 156, S.B. No. 1125.

within their districts.[104] Nevada ordered school boards, charter schools, and its university school for the profoundly gifted to take measures to accommodate students planning to move in or leave schools due to pending military transfers.[105]

Pennsylvania directed local boards to adopt policies on enrolling students so that when children whose parents or legal guardians are active-duty members of the military and received transfer orders, they may enroll prior to obtaining residency.[106] Similarly South Carolina allowed students whose military parents are being transferred to enroll in schools prior to becoming district residents.[107] Tennessee adopted the interstate compact on educational opportunity for children in military families by allowing them to enroll based on the transfers of their parent's transfer rather than waiting until they become district residents.[108]

Texas obligated school boards to transfer the children of service members to another campuses or districts subject to an agreement on their requests.[109] Texas then directed boards of trustees of school districts to transfer students whose parents are peace officers and request that they young ne moved to other campuses or districts.[110] Virginia removed barriers to educational success for school-age children of foreign service employees or civilian members of the armed forces by facilitating timely enrollment and student placement services by providing eligibility for educational programs including extracurricular activities.[111] Wyoming permitted parents on active military duty to have their children transferred from one school to another in a district unless the students are suspended or expelled.[112]

Four states added six acts on attendance and residency for specific situations. Arkansas amended the rule on districts of residence for children who reside on tracts of land located in two district, by taking into consideration the location of their places of

---

104 2023 Ky. Acts Ch. 158, SB 247.
105 2023 Nev. Stat. Ch. 90, AB 185.
106 2023 Pa. Laws Act No. 24, H.B. 1094.
107 2023 S.C. Acts No. 40, H.B. 3797.
108 2023 Tenn. Pub. Acts Ch. No. 257, S.B. No. 317, Subs. H.B. No. 1416.
109 2023 Tex. Gen. Laws H.B. No. 2892.
110 2023 Tex. Gen. Laws H.B. No. 1959.
111 2023 Va. Acts Ch. 783, H.B. 1929.
112 2023 Wyo. Sess. Laws Act No. 66, Ch. No. 130, S.F. 123.

residence.[113] Arkansas then amended its law to allow international exchange students to attend school while living with host families in districts.[114] In a third act Arkansas permitted students whose parents or guardians relocate them to different districts to complete their school years in the systems in which they were enrolled at the time of relocation.[115]

Louisiana specified residency requirements for parents or guardians of students participating in the Taylor Opportunity Program so the caregivers meet these criteria: live outside the U.S. or its territories; are not on active duty with the U.S. armed forces; were residents of and actually lived in Louisiana for at least 24 months preceding the dates they started living outside the U.S. or territories; and remained state residents through the date of the students' graduations from high school or completion of home study programs approved by its state BOE.[116]

North Dakota amended measures on the Center for Distance Education, now requiring school boards to pay for kindergarten costs there if requested by parents or guardians. The same act permitted the Center , through an agreement with a regionally accredited postsecondary institution, to provide high school and postsecondary credit for completing academic courses.[117] Oregon obligated boards to give notice of decisions not allowing students to enroll in virtual public charter schools within 10 days of receiving notice of their intention to do so.[118]

Nine states adopted 13 acts about excused absences. Arkansas provided an excused absence for children to accompany their parents to vote.[119] Arkansas next ensured excused absences for participation in 4-H, FFA, and other agriculture related organizations.[120] And, Arkansas adopted a Support for Pregnant and Parenting Student Act, which included such provisions as excused absences in connection with pregnancy and parenthood.[121] California limited a provision granting excused absences for

---

[113] 2023 Ark. Acts 43, H.B. 1112.
[114] 2023 Ark. Acts 426, H.B. 1030.
[115] 2023 Ark. Acts 189, S.B. 232.
[116] 2023 La. Acts No. 405, H.B. No. 327.
[117] 2023 N.D. Laws H.B. No. 1156.
[118] 2023 Or. Laws Ch. 434, H.B. 3204.
[119] 2023 Ark. Acts 621, S.B. 285.
[120] 2023 Ark. Acts 448, H.B. 1527.
[121] 2023 Ark. Acts 128, H.B. 1161.

attendance at religious retreats to one school day per year.[122] California excused absences for five days for the funerals of immediate family members and another three days for assessing the need for grief counseling.[123] Delaware provided an excused absence for mental health or behavioral health reasons.[124]

Louisiana provided an excused absence for up to three days in any school year related to students' mental or behavioral health in accord with board policy.[125] Nevada prohibited students in public schools from being deprived of any awards based on perfect attendance due to approved absences for religious observation.[126] New Jersey provided excused absences for students attending civic events.[127] Rhode Island decreed that policies for excused absences for participation in sports or extracurricular activities must include attending agricultural fairs.[128]

Texas removed a compulsory attendance requirement that excuses require documentation from clergy members or other religious leaders to observe "holy days." Rather, officials must accept notes from parents or those standing in for them.[129] Texas permitted excused absences for students to visit professional workplaces for career investigation days.[130] Wyoming approved excused absences for participating in programming or competitions sponsored by nationally recognized organizations and clubs promoting youth agricultural education or events associated with taking part in the annual state fair; the measure previously allowed excused absences only for students serving as exhibitors at the state fair.[131]

Four states addressed retention rules or situations where students may not be promoted to the next grade levels. Florida required schools to provide for students with disabilities to be retained in kindergarten at the discretion of their parents.[132] Louisiana prohibited the promotion of students who do not meet reading literacy standards by the end of third grade with

---

[122] 2023 Cal. Stat. Ch. 846, A.B. No. 1503.
[123] 2023 Cal. Stat. Ch. 601, S.B. No. 350.
[124] 2023 Del. Laws HB 3.
[125] 2023 La. Acts No. 318, H.B. No. 353.
[126] 2023 Nev. Stat. Ch. 95, AB 264.
[127] 2023 N.J. Pub. Laws c. 274, S. 2304.
[128] 2023 R.I. Pub. Laws H.B. 6507, S.B. 483.
[129] 2023 Tex. Gen. Laws H.B. No. 1212.
[130] 2023 Tex. Gen. Laws S.B. No. 68.
[131] 2023 Wyo. Sess. Laws Act No. 26, Ch. No. 47, H.B. 175.
[132] 2023 Fla. Laws Ch. 91, S. 290.

exceptions provided for limited English proficient students, those with disabilities or with Section 504 plans, who were retained twice in earlier years without meeting exceptional education criteria, or who identified as dyslexic.[133] Michigan repealed its third-grade retention provision without removing other provisions supporting the teaching of reading.[134] Likewise, Tennessee amended provisions on retaining third-graders not reading at grade level to allow specified students to advance to fourth grade with tutoring support while calling for reports from its state DOE on student retentions.[135]

Twelve states changed requirements for high school graduation through 14 acts; some of these modifications might interact with changes identified in the section for Curricular Requirements below). Alabama adopted the Alabama Credential Quality and Transparency Act obligating high school graduates to earn one or more college or career readiness indicators before graduating. Moreover, the act created an online registry, searchable by the public, which identifies industry-recognized degrees and certificates leading to employment and preparing students for the workplace.[136]

Arkansas directed its state BOE to establish a means by which public schools can award students high school diplomas before their presumptive graduation dates.[137] Arkansas ordered its division of elementary and secondary education to include in academic standards a means by which public school students may substitute comparable elective coursework in career and technical education for required core academic courses.[138] California added a specification for awarding a state seal of biliteracy by using a language proficiency assessment.[139]

Connecticut changed graduation standards beginning with the class of 2027 to include one credit in financial literacy.[140] Indiana added financial literacy as a requirement for graduation by 2028.[141] Nevada directed public high school students to be enrolled in

---

[133] 2023 La. Acts No. 422, H.B. No. 12.
[134] 2023 Mich. Pub. Acts No. 7, S.B. No. 12.
[135] 2023 Tenn. Pub. Acts Ch. No. 338, S.B. No. 300, Subs. H.B. No. 437.
[136] 2023 Ala. Acts 365, H.B. 109.
[137] 2023 Ark. Acts 662, S.B. 505.
[138] 2023 Ark. Acts 242, H.B. 1329.
[139] 2023 Cal. Stat. Ch. 326, A.B. No. 379.
[140] 2023 Conn. Acts 21, S.B. No. 1165.
[141] 2023 Ind. Acts P.L. 168, SB 35.

courses and credits to obtain college- or career-ready high school diplomas or their equivalent or more rigorous diplomas.[142] Oklahoma authorized school boards to issue high school diplomas to students in alternative assessment programs.[143] Oregon enables students to complete one half-credit of higher education and career path skills and one half-credit of personal financial literacy as needed for high school diplomas.[144] Oregon removed the provision for alternative graduation certificates issued by school boards or public charter schools as a means of proving graduation from high school.[145]

Pennsylvania mandated the completion of at least a one-half credit course in financial literacy during high school.[146] Washington permitted the withholding of graduation diplomas, but not transcripts or grades, of students who damaged to school board property valued more than $1,000 for the earlier of five years or until the amount owed is less than $1,000.[147] West Virginia enabled high school students to complete a one-credit course in personal finance as a prerequisite for graduation.[148] Wisconsin required students to complete a one-half credit course on personal financial literacy in order to graduate from high school.[149]

Four states dictated that career technology classes can be applied to high school graduation. Maine provided career and technical education students with credit toward high school graduation for work completed in career and technical education centers and regions.[150] Maryland directed county boards to issue high school diplomas where a P TECH (Pathways in Technology Early College High School) school is located immediately following completion of high school graduation requirements, regardless of whether students completed a pathway sequence.[151]

Virginia ordered its state BOE to develop guidelines and policies permitting students in grades 11 and 12 to earn one-half standard unit of credit per semester for employment in fields or

---

142 2023 Nev. Stat. Ch. 201, AB 241.
143 2023 Okla. Sess. Laws H.B. No. 1041.
144 2023 Or. Laws Ch. 564, S.B. 3.
145 2023 Or. Laws Ch. 202, S.B. 992.
146 2023 Pa. Laws Act No. 33, H.B. 301, Sec. 8.
147 2023 Wash Laws. Ch. 384, H.B. 1536.
148 2023 W. Va. Acts Ch.141, H.B. 3113.
149 2023 Wis. Laws Act 60, A.B. 109.
150 2023 Me. Laws Ch. 247, H.P. 269, L.D. 436.
151 2023 Md. Laws Ch. 741, H.B. 689; 2023 Md. Laws Ch. 742, S.B. 822.

industries or participation in fine arts programs for specified numbers of hours each week.[152] Washington revisited an earlier directive[153] to create multiple pathways for high school graduation, adding that students must complete a performance-based learning experience through which they demonstrates knowledge and skills in the real-world context.[154] Washington permitted public high school students to earn elective academic credit for paid work experience.[155]

Three states mandated completion of the Free Application for Federal Student Aid (FAFSA) before graduation. Indiana required senior-year students to complete and submit their FAFSA application by April 15 of the school year.[156] New Jersey ordered high school students to complete FAFSA financial aid forms.[157] Oklahoma obligated students to complete their FAFSA applications in order to qualify for their high school diplomas.[158]

Other course credit issues arising in 2023 are described as follows. Louisiana revised a measure on student community service, specifying that it cannot count toward academic course work or grades in public schools, nor may it be related to political activities.[159] Maine extended the time by three years, to 2026, which allowed applicants for high school diplomas who experienced delays during the pandemic.[160] Oregon directed officials in its state DOE to study means of improving the transfer of high school credits earned by pupils outside of the U.S.[161]

Tennessee permitted LEAs to award high school credit for courses they offer based on students' passing their final examinations without requiring them to enroll in the classes.[162] Tennessee increased, from one-half unit to one unit, the amount of elective credits students may receive for completing release-time religion classes if boards adopted policies permitting this

---

[152] 2023 Va. Acts Ch.145, S.B. 1277.
[153] Wash. Rev. Code § 28A.655.250 and .260.
[154] 2023 Wash Laws. Ch. 349, H.B. 1308.
[155] 2023 Wash Laws. Ch. 154, Subst. H.B. 1658.
[156] 2023 Ind. Acts P.L. 29, SB 167.
[157] 2023 N.J. Pub. Laws c. 295, A. 1181.
[158] 2023 Okla. Sess. Laws S.B. No. 93.
[159] 2023 La. Acts No. 346, H.B. No. 315.
[160] 2023 Me. Laws Ch. 171, S.P. 370, L.D. 873.
[161] 2023 Or. Laws Ch. 168, S.B. 940.
[162] 2023 Tenn. Pub. Acts Ch. No. 269, S.B. No. 838, Subs. H.B. No. 962.

practice.[163] Virginia permitted boards of education to award a posthumous high school diploma.[164]

Five states addressed school calendars. Arkansas changed the beginning date of the school year to on or after the Monday of the week in which August 19 falls, not earlier than August 14, and not later than August 26.[165] Rather than having private and faith-based schools to operate on terms not less than in public schools in their areas, Kentucky directed those schools to operate on terms as defined in its compulsory attendance law.[166] The code referenced for school calendars in Kentucky included over six pages of procedures, requirements, and alternative rules.[167]

New Mexico increased the number of instruction days beyond 185 for a five-day school weeks and more than 155 for four-day weeks.[168] Beginning the 2023-2024 school year, Pennsylvania provided a minimum of 180 days of instruction within school years or 900 hours of instruction at the elementary level or secondary levels.[169] Vermont mandated that homeschool study be at least 175 instructional days, obligating parents to notify the secretary of education within 10 business days when their children are withdrawn from home study.[170]

Four states adopted rules for alternative calendars. Arkansas allowed boards operating under alternative calendar to use varied methods of instruction to make up missed school days.[171] Florida created a year-round school pilot program to run for four years.[172] Iowa limited the number of school days in which instruction can be delivered primarily over the internet to five days or 30 hours, except in emergency situations or under rules adopted by its state BOE.[173] Maryland permitted county school boards to authorize superintendents to provide virtual education days in lieu of closing during severe weather.[174]

---

[163] 2023 Tenn. Pub. Acts Ch. No. 130, S.B. No. 987, Subs. H.B. No. 680.
[164] 2023 Va. Acts Ch. 7, H.B. 1514.
[165] 2023 Ark. Acts 26, H.B. 1122.
[166] KY. REV. STAT. § 158.070.
[167] 2023 Ky. Acts Ch. 154, SB 81.
[168] 2023 N.M. Laws Ch. 19, HB 130.
[169] 2023 Pa. Laws Act No. 56, H.B. No. 1507.
[170] 2023 Vt. Laws Ch. No. 66, H. 461.
[171] 2023 Ark. Acts 729, H.B. 1590.
[172] 2023 Fla. Laws Ch. 66, H. 891. *See also*, 2023 Fla. Laws Ch. 39, H. 1537.
[173] 2023 Iowa Acts SF 391.
[174] 2023 Md. Laws Ch. 804, S.B. 610.

Two states added material about class hours. Florida initiated a start time for middle school at 8:00 A.M. and 8.30 A.M. for high schools.[175] Illinois directed that the time students spend participating in supervised career development or work-based learning experiences must be counted toward the calculation of clock hours of schoolwork per day.[176]

Five states passed six bills about holidays. Colorado adopted Lunar New Year as a state holiday to celebrate Asian-American culture.[177] Illinois identified Constitution Day on September 17 as a commemorative holiday.[178] New York established Diwali as a holiday in public schools in the New York City.[179] In addition, New York declared Asian Lunar New Year a school holiday.[180] Rhode Island designated June 19 as a state holiday.[181] Texas required boards of trustees of school districts or governing bodies for charter schools to consider the dates of religious holy days or observances likely to be observed by students during periods set for administration of assessments.[182]

Four states addressed the General Education Development credential, or General Education Diploma (GED), or its equivalent. Arkansas mandated that passage of GED tests is considered equal to the receipt of high school diplomas.[183] Florida prohibited school boards from requiring students to complete courses before taking the high school equivalency examination unless they failed to pass practice tests.[184] Oregon ordered its state DOE to study the possibility of creating a high school equivalency diploma, aimed at unemancipated 16 and 17-year-old students.[185] Tennessee replaced references in its code to the general educational development credential with references to the high school equivalency credential.[186]

Six states recognized the right of graduating students to wear regalia signaling tribal or religious identity. Colorado permitted

---

[175] 2023 Fla. Laws Ch. 78, H. 733.
[176] 2023 Ill. Laws P.A. 103-560, HB 3814.
[177] 2023 Colo. Sess. Laws H.B. 1271.
[178] 2023 Ill. Laws P.A. 103-15, HB 1273.
[179] 2023 N.Y. Laws Ch. 629, A. 7769.
[180] 2023 N.Y. Laws Ch. 359, A. 7768.
[181] 2023 R.I. Pub. Laws H.B. 5380.
[182] 2023 Tex. Gen. Laws H.B. No. 1883.
[183] 2023 Ark. Acts 100, H.B. 1091.
[184] 2023 Fla. Laws Ch. 98, H. 265.
[185] 2023 Or. Laws Ch. 527, H.B. 3068.
[186] 2023 Tenn. Pub. Acts Ch. No. 114, S.B. No. 255, Subs. H.B. No. 74.

qualifying students to wear traditional tribal regalia to high school graduations.[187] Illinois directed its state BOE to make available to schools resource materials about students wearing or accessorizing their graduation attire with items used they use to associate with, identify, or declare their cultural, ethnic, or religious identities.[188]

Nevada established the right of public school students to wear traditional tribal regalia or recognized objects of religious or cultural significance at graduation ceremonies.[189] North Carolina allowed students enrolled in recognized Indian Tribes to wear objects of cultural significance as part of their regalia at graduation[190] Oklahoma permitted student members of Indian Tribes to wear tribal regalia during high school graduation.[191] Utah enabled students to wear recognized items of cultural or religious significance as adornments at a their graduations.[192]

Buildings and Grounds

This section describes 2023 acts about school buildings and grounds as follows. Five states approved six acts about school building projects. Arkansas called for the construction and addition of storm shelters for public schools.[193] California added locally funded school construction bonds to a pilot project allowing awards of multiple annual task order procurement contracts.[194] California also limited the cost of providing shaded paths to another part of school buildings to 20% of adjusted construction costs.[195] Maine raised the maximum school construction debt limit from $126 million to $150 million beginning fiscal year 2024 to expand access to school construction funding.[196] Maryland repealed the termination date on the eligibility of its school for the blind to receive funds from the public school construction program.[197] New

---

[187] 2023 Colo. Sess. Laws S.B. 202.
[188] 2023 Ill. Laws P.A. 103-463, SB 1446.
[189] 2023 Nev. Stat. Ch. 388, AB 73.
[190] 2023 N.C. Sess. Laws Ch. 43, H.B. 166.
[191] 2023 Okla. Sess. Laws S.B. No. 429.
[192] 2023 Utah Laws S.B. 103.
[193] 2023 Ark. Acts 764, S.B. 355.
[194] 2023 Cal. Stat. Ch. 523, A.B. No. 439.
[195] 2023 Cal. Stat. Ch. 489, S.B. No. 515.
[196] 2023 Me. Laws Ch. 462, H.P. 911, L.D. 1415.
[197] 2023 Md. Laws Ch. 639, S.B. 175; 2023 Md. Laws Ch. 640, H.B. 366.

York increased from $3 million to $4 million the cost of 10 school building improvement projects in different locations in the state.[198]

Six states permitted nine uses, sales, or leases for school property. Kentucky removed restrictions on the use and sale of property now held by the Lewis County Board of Education; the restrictions were adopted by an act passed in the 1880s.[199] Louisiana allowed the Cameron Parish School Board to sell or exchange sixteenth-section state lands.[200] Louisiana permitted the Natchitoches Parish School Board and its state BOE to sell school property.[201] Massachusetts authorized the city of Lynn to use park land for school purposes.[202] Massachusetts enabled the town of Tewksbury to lease the Louise Davy Trahan Elementary School for 99 years.[203] Mississippi allowed school boards to convey, sell, lease, or otherwise dispose of real property for residential, mixed-use, or other purposes.[204] Mississippi provided that no law, ordinance, or regulation shall prohibit, restrict, or interfere with a board's use of sixteenth-section lands to construct and operate school facilities.[205] Mississippi enabled governing authorities in the city of Gautier to enter public-private partnerships to construct inclusion playgrounds.[206] Boards in Anderson County, South Carolina, reassigned property in school district 1 to district 5.[207]

Six states enrolled seven acts about school environment, including air, temperature, water, and energy uses. Connecticut required local boards to conduct air quality inspections and report that data to its state DOE.[208] Connecticut also directed public schools to maintain thermal comfort ranges of 65– 80 degrees F..[209] Maine ordered that newly constructed or remodeled public schools be equipped with water bottle filling stations.[210]

---

[198] 2023 N.Y. Laws Ch. 569, A. 6431.
[199] 2023 Ky. Acts Ch. 155, SB 93. The relevant old act was cited as 1881-1882 Ky. Acts Ch. 701.
[200] 2023 La. Acts No. 58, H.B. No. 124.
[201] 2023 La. Acts No. 39, S.B. No. 59.
[202] 2023 Mass. Acts Ch. 94, H. 4448.
[203] 2023 Mass. Acts Ch. 59, S. 2582.
[204] 2023 Miss. Laws SB 2164.
[205] 2023 Miss. Laws SB 2751.
[206] 2023 Miss. Laws SB 3140.
[207] 2023 S.C. Acts No. 91, H.B. 3987.
[208] 2023 Conn. Acts 167, Subst. S.B. No. 1, §§ 43, 44.
[209] 2023 Conn. Acts 167, Subst. S.B. No. 1, § 45.
[210] 2023 Me. Laws Ch. 492, H.P. 604, L.D. 957.

Michigan mandated the adoption of clean drinking water quality standards for schools and childcare centers.[211] New Hampshire repealed its state BOE's authority to make rules about the installation of water bottle filling stations.[212] Oregon required school boards to perform functions designed to improve air quality in school buildings when updating or installing a heating, ventilation, and air conditioning or HVAC systems.[213] Utah authorized its state BOE to issue grants for energy and water consumption to meet the goal of reductions in usage.[214]

Six states addressed the need for buildings for charter schools. Florida revised charter school criteria for receiving capital outlay funds.[215] Idaho exempted some charter schools from having to demonstrate strong academic results to qualify for the public charter school facilities program.[216] Indiana channeled more funds to support charter school facilities and required public reporting by auditors about the use of the funds.[217] New Jersey added charter schools to the list of beneficiaries for funding school building projects.[218] Texas directed that political subdivisions such as counties and municipalities must consider open-enrollment charter schools the same as school districts for purposes of zoning, project permits, plats, business licenses, franchises, utility services, signage, land development, and other business interactions with political subdivisions.[219] West Virginia created a special revenue fund designated as its charter school stimulus fund to provide financial support for applicants for start-up costs of establishing charter schools.[220]

Other buildings and grounds-related legislation are described as follows. California added standards about the construction of all-gender restrooms in its main school-construction funding statute[221] for the state.[222] Delaware directed it secretary of education to publish and provide the general assembly with a

---

[211] 2023 Mich. Pub. Acts No. 154, H.B. No. 4341.
[212] 2023 N.H. Laws Ch. 6, HB 466.
[213] 2023 Or. Laws Ch. 525, H.B. 3031.
[214] 2023 Utah Laws H.B. 217.
[215] 2023 Fla. Laws Ch. 69, H. 1259.
[216] 2023 Idaho Sess. Laws Ch. 118, S.B. No. 1042.
[217] 2023 Ind. Acts P.L. 189, SB 391.
[218] 2023 N.J. Pub. Laws c. 311, A. 4496.
[219] 2023 Tex. Gen. Laws H.B. No. 1707.
[220] 2023 W. Va. Acts Ch.124, S.B. 47.
[221] The school building act is the Lewis F. Greene School Facilities Act of 1998.
[222] 2023 Cal. Stat. Ch. 227, S.B. No. 760.

report detailing requests for certificates of necessity not included in the proposed capital budget as well as reasons for the rejection.[223] Louisiana provided $10 per student to go into a fund for school facilities preservation.[224] Virginia ordered the commonwealth's BOE to make recommendations to the General Assembly regarding standards for maintenance, operations, renovation, and new construction of public elementary and secondary school buildings.[225] Other buildings and grounds-related acts are detailed in the section for School Safety such as efforts to "harden" schools from intruders

Curricular Requirements

This section details curricular requirements placed on schools. Nine states added financial literacy as a course offering with three of them including them as a graduation requirement. Alabama obligated students, beginning with those entering ninth grade in the 2024-25 school year, to complete a course in personal financial literacy and money management as a condition of graduation.[226] Connecticut changed graduation requirements beginning with the class of 2027 to include one credit in financial literacy.[227] Louisiana added financial literacy as a mandated high school course.[228] To legislative goals for public elementary and secondary schools, Montana added instruction in financial literacy defined as where students obtain the knowledge and skills required to succeed financially.[229]

Nevada specified that high school students must enroll in a financial literacy course.[230] Ohio added "capitalism" to its high school financial literacy standards.[231] Tennessee ordered public elementary and middle schools to provide information to its state DOE about financial literacy education provided in the schools.[232] West Virginia mandated that high school students complete a one-

---

[223] 2023 Del. Laws HB 169.
[224] 2023 La. Acts No. 55, H.B. No. 78.
[225] 2023 Va. Acts Ch. 752, S.B. 1124.
[226] 2023 Ala. Acts 179, H.B. 164.
[227] 2023 Conn. Acts 21, S.B. No. 1165.
[228] 2023 La. Acts No. 267, H.B. No. 103.
[229] 2023 Mont. Laws H.B. 535.
[230] 2023 Nev. Stat. Ch. 29, AB 274.
[231] 2023 Ohio Laws SB 17 (eff. 6-12-24).
[232] 2023 Tenn. Pub. Acts Ch. No. 310, H.B. No. 782, Subs. S.B. No. 971.

credit course in personal finance prior to graduation.[233] Wisconsin imposed a one-half credit of personal financial literacy course for graduation from high school.[234]

Six states passed seven acts about reading literacy. Connecticut implemented a comprehensive reading curriculum model for grades K-3.[235] Florida directed that reading instruction is phonics-based, not the three-cueing system or visual memory. The 106-page act also added mathematics proficiency as a marker at grade 4 and developed an online repository of digital science-of-reading materials, accessible by teachers, school leaders and parents.[236] Montana funded three early literacy-targeted interventions, school-based, home-based, and jump-start programming, for students not reading at grade level during four weeks between school years.[237]

North Dakota directed its state superintendent of public instruction to appoint a task force to review statutes about literacy, dyslexia, and related teacher training and report findings to the assembly.[238] Oregon created an early literacy success initiative aimed at children aged birth through five years.[239] Virginia extended the coverage of its literacy standards of learning, from grades K-3 to grades K-8.[240] Virginia next ordered each division to submit to its state DOE their literacy plans which identifies core literacy curricula, supplemental instructional practices and programs, and intervention programs.[241]

Four states weighed in on preferences for the teaching of sex education. Idaho provided a definition of abstinence to guide the delivery of sex education in public schools.[242] Indiana directed that schools, staff members, or vendors may not provide instruction on human sexuality to students in grades pre-K to 3.[243] Mississippi deleted the repealing date on requiring school boards to adopt policies on implementing abstinence-only or abstinence-plus

---

233 2023 W. Va. Acts Ch.141, H.B. 3113.
234 2023 Wis. Laws Act 60, A.B. 109.
235 2023 Conn. Acts 167, Subst. S.B. No. 1, § 20.
236 2023 Fla. Laws Ch. 108, H. 7039.
237 2023 Mont. Laws H.B. 352.
238 2023 N.D. Laws H.B. No. 1231.
239 2023 Or. Laws Ch. 534, H.B. 3198.
240 2023 Va. Acts Ch. 645, H.B. 1526; 2023 Va. Acts Ch. 646, S.B. 1175.
241 2023 Va. Acts Ch. 124, H.B. 2137.
242 2023 Idaho Sess. Laws Ch. 190, H.B. No. 228.
243 2023 Ind. Acts P.L. 248, HB 1608.

education into their health curricula.[244] North Dakota required school board curricula on growth and development and human sexuality to include high-definition ultrasound videos showing the development of the brain, heart, sex organs, and other vital organs in early fetal development as well as computer-generated, high-quality renderings or animations showing the process of fertilization and every stage of human development for every week of pregnancy until birth.[245]

Five states passed six acts on medically related subjects. Illinois obligated health courses to address the dangers of allergies through instruction, study, and discussion,.[246] Louisiana directed public high schools to instruct students about organ donation, integrating it into existing curricula in required courses.[247] New Jersey obligated school boards to provide instruction on the prevention of Lyme disease for K-12 students in their health education curricula.[248] Washington encouraged instruction in public schools on the importance of bone marrow donation.[249] Illinois ordered that mandatory health course in grades 9-12 school boards must provide instruction, study, and discussion on the dangers of fentanyl.[250] Texas called for the inclusion of fentanyl abuse prevention and drug poisoning awareness education in public schools.[251]

Three states added provisions regarding mental health with a focus on grief prevention in one of them. Arkansas created a mental health awareness week as an addition to public school curricula.[252] New Jersey directed school boards to instruct on grief as part of health education learning standards.[253] North Dakota renewed a provision to continue an evidence-based online virtual mental health and suicide prevention simulation-based training program for schools.[254]

Two states called for the construction of library learning standards to improve information literacy. California required its

---

[244] 2023 Miss. Laws HB 1390.
[245] 2023 N.D. Laws H.B. No. 1265.
[246] 2023 Ill. Laws P.A. 103-212, HB 3932.
[247] 2023 La. Acts No. 180, H.B. No. 289.
[248] 2023 N.J. Pub. Laws c. 60, S. 2463.
[249] 2023 Wash Laws. Ch. 219, S.B. 5065.
[250] 2023 Ill. Laws P.A. 103-365, HB 3924.
[251] 2023 Tex. Gen. Laws H.B. No. 3908.
[252] 2023 Ark. Acts 290, H.B. 1393.
[253] 2023 N.J. Pub. Laws c. 201, S. 3330.
[254] 2023 N.D. Laws H.B. No. 1312.

Instructional Quality Commission to consider the model library standards into the next revision of the English language arts/English language development curriculum framework after January 1, 2024, and consider including media literacy content at each grade level.[255] New Jersey directed its state DOE to develop student learning standards in information literacy.[256]

Three states dealt with their driver training courses. Rhode Island added instruction of the dangers of marijuana-impaired driving to its driver's education curriculum on approval by its state BOE.[257] Washington required driver training curricula to include instruction on sharing the road with large vehicles such as commercial vehicles and buses.[258] Wisconsin provided a grant program in its state DOE for a public school, technical college, or nonpublic, private, or tribal school to provide courses in driver's education.[259]

Three states took up water safety instruction. Arkansas directed public and charter schools to provide information to students regarding water safety courses and swimming lessons.[260] Georgia required public schools to provide students age 18 or older with water safety information annually.[261] In prior legislation requiring water-safety instruction in public schools, Illinois added the obligation that, water safety instruction must incorporate evidence-based water safety instructional materials and resources for students in grades K-6,.[262]

Three states compelled instruction in cursive writing. California called for handwriting instruction in cursive or joined italics as appropriate in grades 1 to 6.[263] Indiana required public elementary, charter, and state-accredited nonpublic schools to report to its state DOE whether they teach cursive writing.[264] New Hampshire ordered school boards to teach cursive writing and multiplication tables.[265]

---

[255] 2023 Cal. Stat. Ch. 815, A.B. No. 873.
[256] 2022 N.J. Pub. Laws c. 138, S. 588.
[257] 2023 R.I. Pub. Laws S.B. 667, H.B. 5768.
[258] 2023 Wash Laws. Ch. 30, H.B. 1540.
[259] 2023 Wis. Laws Act 86, A.B. 394.
[260] 2023 Ark. Acts 101, H.B. 1157.
[261] 2023 Ga. Laws Act 343, H.B. 402.
[262] 2023 Ill. Laws P.A. 103-567, HB 2104.
[263] 2023 Cal. Stat. Ch. 804, A.B. No. 446.
[264] 2023 Ind. Acts P.L. 169, SB 72.
[265] 2023 N.H. Laws Ch. 17, HB 170.

Two states demanded instruction in computer science. Hawaii directed its state BOE to work with its state DOE to analyze the necessary timeline and appropriate process for making computer science a graduation requirement by the 2030-31 school year.[266] North Carolina required its state BOE to include instruction in computer science in the standard course of study for middle and high school students.[267]

Two states approved additional state symbols. Louisiana adopted the pecan as the state nut.[268] North Dakota designated curling as the official state sport.[269]

Other curriculum-related acts enrolled in 2023 are described as follows.

Arkansas identified programs and activities that are approved for academic credit for community service.[270] Arkansas implemented health and safety courses in public high schools and charter schools to include information about breastfeeding.[271] Arkansas mandated that public schools teach about adoption awareness.[272] California obligated that science courses include emphasis on the causes and effects of climate change.[273] Colorado adopted a curriculum in grades 9 through 12 for instruction in cardiopulmonary resuscitation.[274] Colorado put a process in place to select students to participate in the review of state academic standards.[275]

Hawaii recognized American Sign Language (ASL) as a fully developed, autonomous, national language, with its own grammar, syntax, vocabulary, and cultural heritage.[276] Idaho called for the delivery of career education courses in grades 7-8.[277] Missouri allowed school boards and charter schools to offer elective social studies courses on the Hebrew scriptures and the New Testament.[278] New Hampshire altered curricular standards for

---

[266] 2023 Haw. Sess. Laws Act 174, HB 503.
[267] 2023 N.C. Sess. Laws Ch. 132, H.B. 8.
[268] 2023 La. Acts No. 123, H.B. No. 368.
[269] 2023 N.D. Laws S.B. No. 2229.
[270] 2023 Ark. Acts 720, H.B. 1489.
[271] 2023 Ark. Acts 732, H.B. 1526.
[272] 2023 Ark. Acts 637, S.B. 384.
[273] 2023 Cal. Stat. Ch. 426, A.B. No. 285.
[274] 2023 Colo. Sess. Laws S.B. 23.
[275] 2023 Colo. Sess. Laws S.B. 8.
[276] 2023 Haw. Sess. Laws Act 246, HB 834.
[277] 2023 Idaho Sess. Laws Ch. 243, H.B. No. 269.
[278] 2023 Mo. Laws S.B. 34.

civics education to begin in grades 6, 7, or 8, rather than in grade 8 only; this change specifies a half-year of study while adding civics education as a condition of high school graduation.[279] Oklahoma authorized school boards to offer law enforcement elective courses for high school juniors and seniors.[280] Pennsylvania directed school entities to conduct moments of silence during instructional hours for students and faculty to observe the anniversary of September 11, 2001.[281]

Washington required instruction on sex trafficking prevention and identification for students in grades 7-12.[282] West Virginia mandated the adoption and teaching in public schools of a technical transition mathematics class geared toward students interested in careers in the trades.[283] With respect to approval of an alternative curriculum outside the classroom in public and nonpublic schools, North Dakota simplified the procedural steps in obtaining approval, stating that the proposal must be submitted to the Superintendent of Public Instruction.[284] Washington directed that interdistrict cooperative agreements between school boards in skills centers must stipulate that approved state and local equivalency courses must be honored by all boards participating in the skills centers.[285]

Employment

This section reports employment-related legislation enacted in 2023 including salary and working conditions, leaves of absence, certification, professional development, and strategies for addressing employee shortages.

Eleven states enacted fourteen bills providing salary incentives to sign or retain employees. Alabama struck a requirement to set the salary for elected county superintendents before the start of their terms with a retroactive effective date of July 1, 2021.[286] Arkansas set a new minimum teacher compensation schedule.[287]

---

[279] 2023 N.H. Laws Ch. 226, SB 216.
[280] 2023 Okla. Sess. Laws H.B. No. 2265.
[281] 2023 Pa. Laws Act No. 25, H.B. No. 1097.
[282] 2023 Wash Laws. Ch. 328, S.B. 5355.
[283] 2023 W. Va. Acts Ch. 139, H.B. 3055.
[284] 2023 N.D. Laws H.B. No. 1521.
[285] 2023 Wash Laws. Ch. 407, Subst. S.B. 5617.
[286] 2023 Ala. Acts 410, S.B. 279.
[287] 2023 Ark. Acts 850, H.B. 1795.

Delaware allowed teachers who previously worked as paraprofessional in schools to receive partial credit toward placement on the teacher salary schedule to assure their teacher pay is not less than their prior pay.[288] Delaware clarified the types of certificates and their certifying agencies for placements on salary schedules for professionals providing auxiliary services such as speech pathologists, audiologists, counselors, school psychologists, nurses, occupational therapists, and physical therapists.[289]

Hawaii authorized consideration of wages of other employees in comparable positions when computing average weekly wages of injured public board members, police officers or chaplains, sheriff's deputies, volunteer firemen, and other listed employment categories.[290] Illinois raised the incentive from $1,500 to $2,250, for 45 hours of mentoring for its teaching excellence program.[291] Illinois also provided a bonus of $4,000 per year for two consecutive years as an incentive for retaining National Policy Board-certificated teachers.[292] Montana revised an act to increase teacher pay, specifying that teaching in the first three years without full certification does not qualify for the increase.[293] North Dakota modified a provision giving authority to school boards to give employees signing bonuses, specifying that they may not be paid until individuals are licensed and qualified for their roles by its Education Standards and Practices Board.[294]

Oklahoma set new statewide teacher salary schedules with minimum pay for beginning teachers at $39,601.[295] Tennessee increased base salaries for teachers.[296] Tennessee then directed that teachers receive their full salary and benefits during absences due to physical assaults or other violent criminal acts committed against them in the course of their employment.[297] West Virginia increased the state minimum salary schedule for beginning teachers starting at $36,597.[298] Utah extended the life of an

---

[288] 2023 Del. Laws SB 156.
[289] 2023 Del. Laws HB 231.
[290] 2023 Haw. Sess. Laws Act 195, SB 696.
[291] 2023 Ill. Laws P.A. 103-122, HB 1291.
[292] 2023 Ill. Laws P.A. 103-207, HB 3801.
[293] 2023 Mont. Laws H.B. 588.
[294] 2023 N.D. Laws H.B. No. 1187.
[295] 2023 Okla. Sess. Laws S.B. No. 1119.
[296] 2023 Tenn. Pub. Acts Ch. No. 437, H.B. No. 329, S.B. No. 281, Subs. H.B. No. 329.
[297] 2023 Tenn. Pub. Acts Ch. No. 343, S.B. No. 906, Subs. H.B. No. 1357.
[298] 2023 W. Va. Acts Ch. 242, S.B. 423.

incentive program for college students willing to teach in high-poverty schools.[299] Virginia ordered the commonwealth's DOE to convene a stakeholder group to study and make recommendations about competitive teacher pay.[300]

Ten states adopted 11 bills on leaves of absence. Alabama expanded sick leave by permitting public school employees eight weeks to attend to ill children or when they file adoption petitions, and allowing the use of sick leave to attend to adopted children who are three years of age or younger.[301] For leave as adverse employment actions California obligated that classified employee who are placed on involuntary leaves of absence while facing criminal charges, investigation, or pending administrative matter to receive full compensation if the matter is resolved in their favor.[302] Delaware amended school sick leave provisions clarify how it differs from personal leave.[303] Delaware further provided teachers the same protection to be absent without loss of pay as given to state merit employees.[304]

Georgia repealed a sunset provision with respect to the use of sick leave by public employees to care for immediate family members.[305] Louisiana approved up to 30 additional days of extended sick leave in a six-year period of employment for bus operators for personal illness related to pregnancy or the illness of infants or doctor visits.[306] Maryland required educational professionals employed by county boards of education, the Baltimore City School Board, or county public library systems, who transfer to the Juvenile Services Education Program, to receive credit as state employees for the purpose of calculating accrued leave.[307] New Jersey expanded the definition of being ill to include public emergencies such as a pandemic, for qualification for sick leave.[308]

Oregon increased the military leave of absence given to public employees who are members of the National Guard or reserves to

---

[299] 2023 Utah Laws S.B. 222.
[300] 2023 Va. Acts Ch. 725, S.B. 1215.
[301] 2023 Ala. Acts 352, H.B. 103.
[302] 2023 Cal. Stat. Ch. 331, A.B. No. 472.
[303] 2023 Del. Laws SB 61.
[304] 2023 Del. Laws SB 60.
[305] 2023 Ga. Laws Act 90, S.B. 61.
[306] 2023 La. Acts No. 133, H.B. No. 21.
[307] 2023 Md. Laws Ch. 672, H.B. 1047.
[308] 2023 N.J. Pub. Laws c. 95, A. 5060.

21 days.[309] South Carolina provided paid parental leave for school board employees on the birth of children or initial legal placements of a foster children.[310] Tennessee directed that employees for LEAs must be granted absences from work with pay for up to six work weeks after the birth or stillbirth of children or the adoption of newly placed minor children.[311] West Virginia increased the number of personal leave days granted to county board of education employees from four to five without regard to the causes for their absences.[312]

Fourteen states adopted 17 acts about mandatory subjects for professional development. Alabama adopted the School Principal Leadership and Mentoring Act with an accompanying development system. Under this act administrators must develop comprehensive professional learning plans including the identification of mentors beginning with the 2024-2025 school year with annual supplements of $10,000 for principals and $5,000 for assistant principals who complete the program contingent on future funding.[313]

Arkansas forbade its state BOE from including implicit bias as a requirement for certification or for professional development and prohibited schools from mandating training on this topic.[314] Arkansas adjusted the duty that professional development for licensed school staff must be delivered at least once during the 2023-2024 school year in the subject areas of family and community development and history; neither is required if they were taken before that school year.[315] Connecticut directed school nurses to receive at least 15 hours of professional development activities annually.[316] Connecticut also called for school nurses to undergo training about endometriosis, ordering its state DOE to establish an endometriosis data and biorepository program.[317]

Georgia directed its state DOE to require teachers in all programs licensed or commissioned by it to receive training on developmentally appropriate evidence-based literacy instruction

---

[309] 2023 Or. Laws Ch. 325, H.B. 2865.
[310] 2023 S.C. Acts No. 17, H.B. 3908.
[311] 2023 Tenn. Pub. Acts Ch. No. 399, H.B. No. 983, Subs. S.B. No. 1458.
[312] 2023 W. Va. Acts Ch. 302, H.B. 3547.
[313] 2023 Ala. Acts 340, S.B. 300.
[314] 2023 Ark. Acts 511, H.B. 1559.
[315] 2023 Ark. Acts 548, H.B. 1538.
[316] 2023 Conn. Acts 167, Subst. S.B. No. 1, § 35.
[317] 2023 Conn. Acts 67, H.B. No. 6672.

aligned with content standards.[318] Illinois mandated that in-service training at teacher institutes must include additional topics such as health conditions of students; social-emotional learning; developing cultural competency; identifying warning signs of mental illness and suicide behavior in youth; domestic and sexual violence; needs of expectant and parental youth; protection and accommodations for students; ethics; responding to child sex abuse and grooming; and violence prevention and conflict resolution.[319]

Kentucky implemented a performance-based professional development pilot project, directing the commonwealth's DOE to report on the project in 2027.[320] Louisiana obligated that foundational numeracy skills must be provided for teachers through professional development.[321] Michigan directed schools to provide information about sexual assault and harassment to students while encouraging professional development for staff on these topics.[322] New Jersey added a broader list of school employees who must participate in professional development for suicide prevention.[323] North Dakota gave discretionary authority for local school board administrators to recommend, and their boards to approve, professional development for their employees.[324]

Oklahoma altered the frequency of professional development for teachers on child abuse, sexual child abuse, and reporting of suspected abuse. These sessions must occur in the first year of newly employed, certificated teachers followed by another every fifth year.[325] Texas allowed school boards to provide school safety training courses to employees of nonpublic schools and other entities offering out-of-school-time care.[326] Virginia advanced the option for online training for school bus drivers in the operation of their vehicles and for instruction in Spanish.[327] Virginia directed that no public elementary or secondary school teacher can be made to participate more frequently than once every five years in training on test security violations.[328] West Virginia added a

---

[318] 2023 Ga. Laws Act 9, S.B. 538 § 2.
[319] 2023 Ill. Laws P.A. 103-542, HB 3690.
[320] 2023 Ky. Acts Ch. 40, SB 70.
[321] 2023 La. Acts No. 260, S.B. No. 163.
[322] 2023 Mich. Pub. Acts No. 57, S.B. No. 66.
[323] 2023 N.J. Pub. Laws c. 111, S. 528.
[324] 2023 N.D. Laws H.B. No. 1386.
[325] 2023 Okla. Sess. Laws H.B. No. 1441.
[326] 2023 Tex. Gen. Laws H.B. No. 1905.
[327] 2023 Va. Acts Ch. 156, H.B. 1928.
[328] 2023 Va. Acts Ch. 641, H.B. 2457.

provision, the Third Grade Success Act, focused on achievement in reading and mathematics by the end of third grade, through teacher training in instructional delivery and tracking measures of improvement.[329]

Tennessee decreed that professional development cannot include what it called "implicit bias training," prohibiting public education entities such as local boards, charter schools, its state department, or state board from requiring educators or other employees to complete or participate in implicit bias training or to take adverse employment action against those why refuse to do so.[330]

Two states adopted provisions describing administrator contracts. Nevada designated the first three years of contracts for principals as probationary periods with requisite procedures for continuing employment.[331] Washington permitted contracts between boards and principals to be for terms of up to three years if principals were employed as such for three or more consecutive years; were recommended by their superintendents as candidate for two- or three-year contracts because they demonstrated the ability to stabilize instructional practices and received comprehensive performance ratings of level 3 or above in their most recent comprehensive performance evaluations; and met the school board's requirements for satisfying updated records checks.[332]

Nine states adopted 14 union-related acts. Arkansas prohibited public employers from deducting dues, fees, or contributions from payments to their employees on behalf of professional or labor organizations or political funds while requiring applications for labor organization membership to contain notices of public school employees' rights to join or refrain from joining them.[333] Hawaii specified that exclusive representatives of public employees need not provide grievance representation to collective bargaining unit members who do not pay dues.[334] Illinois obligated renewals of school charters to include union neutrality clauses.[335] Illinois next permitted teacher

[329] 2023 W. Va. Acts Ch. 138, H.B. 3035.
[330] 2023 Tenn. Pub. Acts Ch. No. 438, S.B. No. 102, Subs. H.B. No. 158.
[331] 2023 Nev. Stat. Ch. 171, SB 292.
[332] 2023 Wash Laws. Ch. 362, S.B. 5175.
[333] 2023 Ark. Acts 776, S.B. 473.
[334] 2023 Haw. Sess. Laws Act 150, HB 1205.
[335] 2023 Ill. Laws P.A. 103-416, HB 1120.

members of statewide association representing them, and who are elected by membership to represent them in federal advocacy work to spend up to 10 days during school terms in those jobs.[336]

Maine provided additional protections for public school employees who were subjected to dangerous behavior and who are covered by collective bargaining agreements by requiring that disputes arising out of incidents of dangerous behavior are subject to the dispute resolution process of their bargaining contracts.[337] Maine added a provision in its public sector bargaining law in public schools on the duty to bargain within 10 days of requests for meetings with the following exceptions: "as long as the parties have not otherwise agreed in a prior written contract, except that explicit waivers of collective bargaining over wages, hours, working conditions and contract grievance arbitration in a prior written contract may not be enforced for purposes of this paragraph." [338]

Michigan removed a prohibition against deductions from public employees' wages for political purposes.[339] Michigan removed a ban on the collection of dues from public school employees for membership in labor organizations.[340] Michigan removed a public school employer's decision to contract with third parties for non-instructional support services as subject to its collective bargaining law.[341] Nevada clarified that the hiring of staff by principals of local school precincts must conform to applicable collective bargaining agreements.[342]

New York obligated employers to provide the home addresses of employees of bargaining units to their organizations.[343] New York ratified the collective bargaining agreement between a city school board with population of one million or more persons to reduce class sizes beginning September 2023 and to be achieved by September of 2028, with annual reporting requirements.[344] Rhode Island called for its council on elementary and secondary education to ratify the collective bargaining agreement for the public school

---

[336] 2023 Ill. Laws P.A. 103-308, HB 2392.
[337] 2023 Me. Laws Ch. 493, S.P. 770, L.D. 1898.
[338] 2023 Me. Laws Ch. 95, H.P. 690, L.D. 1095.
[339] 2023 Mich. Pub. Acts No. 243, H.B. No. 4230.
[340] 2023 Mich. Pub. Acts No. 114, H.B. No. 4233.
[341] 2023 Mich. Pub. Acts No. 143, H.B. No. 4356.
[342] 2023 Nev. Stat. Ch. 276, SB 282.
[343] 2023 N.Y. Laws Ch. 677, A. 7157.
[344] 2023 N.Y. Laws Ch. 86, S. 843.

district for Providence.[345] Texas prohibited local education agencies from deducting dues from wages for professional employees' organizations.[346]

Seven states enrolled acts on benefits and other working conditions. Georgia provided planning periods for teachers in grades K-12.[347] Illinois stated that educational support personnel shall not be required to work on legal school holidays.[348] Kentucky provided excess liability coverage for certificated employees of public schools.[349] New York allowed benefit costs for transportation employees for the Goshen Central School District.[350] Oregon directed its state DOE to study the appropriate methodology for determining the workload for school health care workers.[351] Virginia defined the terms "direct counseling" and "program planning" to clarify the duty that school counselors spend 80% of their workday in direct counseling.[352] Texas permitted school boards to hire teachers with supplemental contracts for initial lesson plan design or instructional material selection.[353]

Two states addressed grievance policies. Arkansas allowed school boards to consolidate grievances into groups when individual grievances are the same.[354] Montana required local boards to adopt grievance policies addressing formal and informal resolution of complaints, informs grievants about them, provides printed versions of them on request, and accepts for filing formal complaints submitted within 30 days of the completion of informal resolutions.[355]

Twelve states passed 18 bills about certification for teachers, counselors, administrators, and other professional personnel. Arkansas permitted public school administrators and secondary teachers to receive enhanced licensure after beginning with alternative certificates.[356] In the first of three actions, California funded an award of $495 for teachers to enroll in the National

---

[345] 2023 R.I. Pub. Laws H.B. 5773, S.B. 190.
[346] 2023 Tenn. Pub. Acts Ch. No. 437, H.B. No. 329, S.B. No. 281, Subs. H.B. No. 329.
[347] 2023 Ga. Laws Act 256, H.B. 340.
[348] 2023 Ill. Laws P.A. 103-395, SB 2017.
[349] 2023 Ky. Acts Ch. 99, SB 3.
[350] 2023 N.Y. Laws Ch. 595, S. 6441.
[351] 2023 Or. Laws Ch. 503, H.B. 2618.
[352] 2023 Va. Acts Ch. 347, H.B. 2187.
[353] 2023 Tex. Gen. Laws H.B. No. 1605.
[354] 2023 Ark. Acts 745, H.B. 1691.
[355] 2023 Mont. Laws H.B. 504.
[356] 2023 Ark. Acts 416, H.B. 1463.

Board for Professional Teacher Standards certification program when working in high-priority schools; the existing provision awards $25,000 for those who finish the program.[357] California then directed its Commission on Teacher Credentialing to convene a workgroup on credentialing for instruction in computer science.[358] Finally, California reinstated the requirement that school superintendents must have credentials for theirs jobs as set forth by the Commission on Teacher Credentialing.[359]

Georgia directed its Professional Standards Commission, with other agencies

in consultation, to create a school safety and anti-gang endorsement for eligible certificated professional personnel.[360] Hawaii reinstated the exemption from the behavior analyst licensing requirement for teachers working in collaboration with licensed behavior analysts or licensed psychologists.[361] Illinois authorized the creation and award of teacher licenses for special content area and grade levels subsequent to the original teaching certificate.[362] When hiring or assigning physical education, music, or visual arts teachers, Illinois directed school boards to place a priority on hiring or assigning of certificated teachers.[363]

Iowa permitted school practitioners with master's or doctoral degrees and 10 years of licensed service to have their licenses renewed.[364] Iowa added to the requirements for persons serving as school counselors, based on programs developed to show that they support the curricular goals of their schools by offering responsive services addressing the growth and developmental needs of students.[365] Michigan called for coursework in reading instruction for advancement to a professional certificate.[366] Mississippi specified that computer science instruction must be provided by appropriately endorsed teachers for computer science courses which award Carnegie units, or by licensed teachers and

[357] 2023 Cal. Stat. Ch. 819, A.B. No. 908.
[358] 2023 Cal. Stat. Ch. 834, A.B. No. 1251.
[359] 2023 Cal. Stat. Ch. 273, A.B. No. 872.
[360] 2023 Ga. Laws Act 7, H.B. 147.
[361] 2023 Haw. Sess. Laws Act 167, SB 1340.
[362] 2023 Ill. Laws P.A. 103-157, HB 2442.
[363] 2023 Ill. Laws P.A. 103-46, HB 3402.
[364] 2023 Iowa Acts HF 672.
[365] 2023 Iowa Acts SF 391.
[366] 2023 Mich. Pub. Acts No. 110, S.B. No. 161.

paraprofessionals under the supervision of appropriately endorsed teachers for computer science.[367]

New Mexico created a vocational education licensure track for teachers.[368] New Mexico next provided funding as an incentive for teachers certificated by the national board for professional teaching standards.[369] North Carolina created a provisional one-year assistant principal license, renewable once, which allows teachers in administrator preparation programs to serve as assistant principals while completing internships.[370] North Dakota added to certification standards for elementary teachers, specifying the instruction of scientifically based, evidence-based, and research-based curricula plus the use of systematic direct instruction to ensure that all students obtain necessary early reading skills.[371]

Texas specified that the qualifications for certification as school counselors do not include experience as classroom teacher.[372] Rhode Island changed the subject matter requirements for the Fast-Track Principal Certification Program, adding supervision of school personnel and deleting program evaluation/data analysis to the list of subjects.[373]

Thirteen states adopted 18 acts on interstate reciprocity for certificates. Alabama amended its Military Family Jobs Opportunity Act to permit spouses of civil servants employed by the U.S. Department of Defense to receive reciprocity for professional licensure.[374] Alabama adopted the interstate teacher mobility compact to allow certification reciprocity for teachers in 10 states; the act does not become operational until the tenth state adopts the act.[375] Colorado adopted the Interstate Teacher Mobility Compact to allow teachers to move more easily across state lines.[376] Florida adopted the Interstate Teacher Mobility Compact which authorizes teacher licenses in one member state to become licensed in other member states.[377]

---

[367] 2023 Miss. Laws SB 2586.
[368] 2023 N.M. Laws Ch. 128, SB 417.
[369] 2023 N.M. Laws Ch. 145, HB 181.
[370] 2023 N.C. Sess. Laws Ch. 125, H.B. 432.
[371] 2023 N.D. Laws H.B. No. 1231.
[372] 2023 Tex. Gen. Laws S.B. No. 798.
[373] 2023 R.I. Pub. Laws S.B. 496.
[374] 2023 Ala. Acts 200, S.B.37.
[375] 2023 Ala. Acts 234, S.B. 46.
[376] 2023 Colo. Sess. Laws H.B. 1064.
[377] 2023 Fla. Laws Ch.165, H. 1125.

Iowa permitted license applicants from out-of-state with full licensure from another state or country with verification from an institution and transcripts.[378]

Kansas enacted the Interstate Teacher Mobility Compact to recognize equivalent teacher licenses across member states.[379] Nebraska adopted the Interstate Teacher Mobility Compact,[380] as did Nevada[381] and Oklahoma.[382] Oregon enacted the Interstate Teacher Mobility Compact to facility mobility of teachers across member states with the goal of supporting teachers through a new pathway to licensure.[383] Pennsylvania adopted the Interstate Teacher Mobility Compact.[384]

Louisiana first ordered its state board of elementary and secondary education to grant five-year teaching certificates to applicants with out-of-state teaching certificates.[385] Louisiana then amended teacher certification standards by allowing teaching experience out-of-state or in nonpublic schools to be credited for certification.[386] Michigan directed its state superintendent of education to provide reciprocity for out-of-state school counselors.[387] Michigan next made it easier for teachers in other states to have their certificates recognized there.[388]

In the first of two acts Montana provided educator certification reciprocity for military members or their spouses with teaching licenses from other states.[389] Montana adopted the interstate compact providing reciprocity for licensure of audiologists and speech-language pathologists.[390] Vermont adopted the audiology and speech-language pathology interstate compact, to facilitate interstate practice of professionals in those fields.[391]

Seven states amended their retirement programs through nine acts to address teacher and other employee shortages by allowing

---

[378] 2023 Iowa Acts HF 614.
[379] 2023 Kan. Sess. Laws SB 66.
[380] 2023 Neb. Laws LB 298.
[381] 2023 Nev. Stat. Ch. 139, SB 442.
[382] 2023 Okla. Sess. Laws S.B. No. 467.
[383] 2023 Or. Laws Ch. 218, S.B. 279.
[384] 2023 Pa. Laws Act No. 33, H.B. 301, Sec. 5.
[385] 2023 La. Acts No. 371, H.B. No. 472.
[386] 2023 La. Acts No. 63, H.B. No. 191.
[387] 2023 Mich. Pub. Acts No. 111, S.B. No. 162.
[388] 2023 Mich. Pub. Acts No. 110, S.B. No. 161.
[389] 2023 Mont. Laws H.B. 583.
[390] 2023 Mont. Laws S.B. 214.
[391] 2023 Vt. Laws Ch. No. 36, H. 86.

retirees to come out of retirement and work for time periods without losing their retirement benefits. Alabama permitted those classified as law enforcement officers prior to their retirement in the Employees' Retirement System to return to work as a school resource officers at a maximum pay of $52,000 per year without interfering with their pension until December 31, 2026.[392]

Maine permitted retired teachers and educational technicians to be recertificated and return to service if they have not been retired for more than five years.[393] In a second act Maine directed universities to submit report to a legislative committee about the state teacher residency program while calling for its Education Policy Research Institute to study the development of career ladders for educators. Both directives were aimed at addressing teacher shortages through financial assistance and career advancement opportunities.[394] Michigan permitted retired public school employees to return to work without forfeiting retirement benefits if their annual pay as teachers is no more than $15,100.[395]

New Jersey permitted retired teachers and professional staff personnel to return to work for two years without having to reenroll in the retirement system.[396] Virginia reduced from 12 to six months the time period teachers, bus drivers, school administrators, or school security officers may return to work and continue to collect retirement benefits.[397] Washington changed its teacher retirement system by allowing members who retired on or after September 1, 2008, and chose the 3% per year reduction provided at that time to have their retirement allowances recalculated. The preliminary language in this act asserted that the change repealed restrictions on benefits, including the right to return to service without losing retirement benefits.[398]

West Virginia allowed county school boards to contract with retired teachers to provide tutoring in reading and mathematics to support one-on-one intervention for students.[399] In addition, West

---

[392] 2023 Ala. Acts 334, H.B. 41.
[393] 2023 Me. Laws Ch. 442, S.P. 311, L.D. 753.
[394] 2023 Me. Laws Ch. 469, S.P. 640, L.D. 1608.
[395] 2023 Mich. Pub. Acts No. 147, H.B. No. 4752.
[396] 2023 N.J. Pub. Laws c. 121, S. 3798.
[397] 2023 Va. Acts Ch. 690, S.B. 1289; 2023 Va. Acts Ch. 692, S.B. 1170; 2023 Va. Acts Ch. 707, H.B. 1630.
[398] 2023 Wash Laws. Ch. 410, Subst. H.B. 1056.
[399] 2023 W. Va. Acts Ch. 132, S.B. 688.

Virginia permitted retired bus operators to work as substitutes without affecting their monthly retirement benefits.[400]

Four states adopted measures to set aside limits on the use of substitute teachers. Illinois permitted school boards to hire substitute teachers to continue to work in the same vacant positions for 90 calendar days or until the end of a semester.[401] Nevada allowed student teachers to be employed as substitutes.[402] Pennsylvania permitted those in student teacher programs to serve as substitutes for no more than 10 days in their classrooms.[403] Rhode Island permitted substitute teachers and post-retirement employees to exceed the 90-day cap on post-retirement employment with conditions on the permission.[404]

Two states enable professional employees to work without certificates for a time to fill positions temporarily. For permitting instruction given by uncertificated teachers Arkansas raised the time limit from 30 to 60 consecutive school days.[405] California obligated local boards to report to a legislative committee when they used their authority to hire vocational nurses supervised by certificated school nurse to fill vacant positions.[406]

Seven states, through nine acts, authorized professional employees to work without certificates, high school diplomas, associate's degrees, or under manufactured job titles to place them in classrooms. California exempted participants currently enrolled in or having completed programs to support bilingual teacher education in languages identified in the act from specified requirements applicable to teachers.[407] Delaware directed its state DOE to coordinate with its department of labor to create a program to places aspiring teachers in paid positions in schools while they complete the training and schooling necessary to receive certification.[408] Louisiana permitted its state Board of Elementary and Secondary Education to create an associate educator program

---

[400] 2023 W. Va. Acts Ch. 298, H.B. 2346.
[401] 2023 Ill. Laws P.A. 103-193, HB 3442.
[402] 2023 Nev. Stat. Ch. 403, SB 291.
[403] 2023 Pa. Laws Act No. 33, H.B. 301, Sec. 5.
[404] 2023 R.I. Pub. Laws S.B. 20, H.B. 5040.
[405] 2023 Ark. Acts 732, H.B. 1609.
[406] 2023 Cal. Stat. Ch. 853, A.B. No. 1722.
[407] 2023 Cal. Stat. Ch. 830, A.B. No. 1127.
[408] 2023 Del. Laws HB 138.

which would allow persons with associate's degrees to serve as teachers.[409]

North Dakota amended a provision permitting individuals to teach with high schools diploma with relevant work experience and specialized training in the subject areas, except in elementary education, mathematics, science, language arts, and social studies. The amendment permitted persons to teach special education for no more than two years but allowed the award of special education certificates while still enrolled in a bachelor's programs in special education.[410] North Dakota amended a provision allowing its education standards and practices board to issue a three-year permit for individuals to teach if local school administrators submit written requests indicating their inability to locate qualified personnel. The amendment allowed the permit to be extended for four more years to seven if the individuals are enrolled in teacher education programs.[411]

Pennsylvania recreated a staff position of classroom monitor for those who served as paraprofessional but had not yet gained teacher certification.[412] Tennessee permitted person with active industry licenses or credential relevant to career and technical education courses to provide instruction under constant supervision of licensed teachers.[413] In addition, Tennessee enables its commissioner of education to issue an endorsement exemption to individuals as teachers of elementary physical education if the directors of schools or charter school apply for such an exemption because they are unable to secure a qualified teachers.[414]

Texas added an associate or baccalaureate degree in early childhood education as a qualifying requirement for receiving a certificate as a prekindergarten teacher.[415] Texas also permitted the award of temporary certificates to teach career and technical education for military service members and first responders with relevant training.[416]

Other methods to address staff shortages through creative certification practices involved the use of paid externships,

---

[409] 2023 La. Acts No. 99, S.B. No. 81.
[410] 2023 N.D. Laws H.B. No. 1304.
[411] 2023 N.D. Laws S.B. No. 2070.
[412] 2023 Pa. Laws Act No. 33, H.B. 301, Sec. 8.
[413] 2023 Tenn. Pub. Acts Ch. No. 344, S.B. No. 967, Subs. H.B. No. 662.
[414] 2023 Tenn. Pub. Acts Ch. No. 280, S.B. No. 1070, Subs. H.B. No. 897.
[415] 2023 Tex. Gen. Laws H.B. No. 2729.
[416] 2023 Tex. Gen. Laws H.B. No. 621.

apprenticeships, residencies, and practice teaching experiences are described as follows. Colorado added a track for obtaining K-12 teacher certification in one of the STEM, science, technology, engineering, and mathematics, areas, through externship program. The act includes its own repeal effective September 1, 2025.[417] Colorado created another path for teacher certification by way of affiliated bachelor's degree programs led by "apprentice mentor teachers."[418] Connecticut created adjunct faculty permits to allow university faculty to teach in public schools.[419]

Delaware allowed its state DOE to issue initial or continuing licenses to JROC instructor who has been certificated by the U.S. Department of Defense.[420] Connecticut established an educator apprenticeship initiative to allow participants to gain teaching experience while working in a school.[421] Idaho provided teacher apprenticeships as a means of allowing individuals in training to work for pay while performing practice teaching.[422]

Montana created a teacher residency program, matching teacher-leaders from districts and resident teachers in teacher education programs; those serving as resident teachers may receive pay in their final years of training.[423] Nebraska created an alternative track to full certification through one-year teacher apprenticeships.[424] Tennessee allowed its Commissioner of Education to grant individuals pursuing clinical experience in educator preparation programs temporary permit to teach when licensed teachers cannot be secured.[425]

Nine states enacted 10 bills fashioning alternative certificate programs to secure more professional staff. Kentucky changed its alternative, provisional certification period from two to four years for Option 6 certificates and five years for Option 7 certificates.[426] Maine established an alternative certification pathway for educational technicians in public schools to address staff shortages.[427] Maryland altered the qualifications for early

---

[417] 2023 Colo. Sess. Laws H.B. 1198.
[418] 2023 Colo. Sess. Laws S.B. 87.
[419] 2023 Conn. Acts 167, Subst. S.B. No. 1, § 15.
[420] 2023 Del. Laws HB 163.
[421] 2023 Conn. Acts 167, Subst. S.B. No. 1, § 8.
[422] 2023 Idaho Sess. Laws Ch. 175, S.B. No. 1069.
[423] 2023 Mont. Laws H.B. 833.
[424] 2023 Neb. Laws LB 705.
[425] 2023 Tenn. Pub. Acts Ch. No. 284, S.B. No. 1221, Subs. H.B. No. 424.
[426] 2023 Ky. Acts Ch 54, SB 49.
[427] 2023 Me. Laws Ch. 200, H.P. 880, L.D. 1366.

childhood education teachers through an alternative teacher preparation program with provision for financial assistance from its Higher Education Commission.[428]

Montana created an alternative teacher certificate credential for persons with bachelor's degrees, a short course from the Indian Education for All program, successful criminal background checks, and completion of alternative teacher education programs.[429] Nebraska adopted alternative teaching certificates which provide fast tracks to classroom with two years of college and passing subject matter tests.[430] New Hampshire permitted local boards to extend a one-year certificates of teaching eligibility for second consecutive school years.[431] New Jersey permitted its state BOE to authorize alternative teaching certificates.[432]

In an earlier measure that created an alternative teacher pathway, Oklahoma changed the definition of a "provider" for alternative certificates to include entities that established partnerships with accredited institutions of higher education.[433] Virginia directed its commonwealth's BOE to extend provisional teacher licenses for at least one, but no more than two, additional years.[434] Virginia also permitted local school boards to employ clinical psychologists to serve as a school psychologist with a provisional license for three years with an allowance for two-year extensions subject to approval of the division superintendent and the psychologist's making progress for full licensure.[435]

Another method designed to attract more professional education staff was to provide financial assistance as an incentive to seek certification with three states adopting five such acts. Maryland altered the qualifications for early childhood education teacher certification through alternative teacher preparation programs with provision for financial assistance from its Higher Education Commission.[436] Minnesota provided $1.925 million in grant funds for underrepresented student teachers.[437] Further,

---

[428] 2023 Md. Laws Ch. 627, H.B. 1219.
[429] 2023 Mont. Laws S.B. 373.
[430] 2023 Neb. Laws LB 705.
[431] 2023 N.H. Laws Ch. 64, HB 654.
[432] 2023 N.J. Pub. Laws c. 180, S. 1553.
[433] 2023 Okla. Sess. Laws H.B. No. 2679.
[434] 2023 Va. Acts Ch. 800, H.B. 2375.
[435] 2023 Va. Acts Ch. 348, H.B. 2124, 2023 Va. Acts Ch. 349, S.B. 1043.
[436] 2023 Md. Laws Ch. 627, H.B. 1219.
[437] 2023 Minn. Laws Ch. 41, sec. 1, subd. 26, HF 2073.

Minnesota provided $1.0 million in grant funds for student loan repayments for teachers in shortage areas.[438] In a third act Minnesota provided $1.3 million in grants to student teachers to address educator shortages.[439] Pennsylvania initiated a grant program to pay student teachers a stipend of $10,000, with an additional 5,000 for pursuing certification in high-need areas.[440]

Scholarships designated for teachers may be appealing means of attracting and retaining more teachers. Five states added such scholarships last year. New Mexico amended a scholarship program to produce more teachers by allowing licensed teachers to participate in it to pursue graduate study and by enabling them to attend classes part-time.[441] New Jersey created a pilot program for its state DOE to assist veterans in obtaining teacher certification.[442] North Dakota appropriated funds to its Department of Public Instruction to support the paraprofessional-to-teacher program.[443] Oklahoma changed the name of a scholarship program designed to attract persons to enter the teaching profession to the "Inspired to Teach" program.[444] Utah broadened the scope of its "grow your own educator" pipeline program to include individuals seeking to become school psychologists and school social workers.[445] Many more scholarships are reported in the Higher Education section of this chapter.

Four states enacted bills to increase the pool of paraeducators and classified employees to address a shortage of noncertificated employees,. Connecticut directed its Commissioner of Education to establish a model program for training paraeducators for students in grades 9-12.[446] Iowa clarified that para-educator certificates may be issued to applicant who are at least 18 years of age.[447] Kentucky allowed school boards to hire classified employees without high school diplomas or the equivalent if they provides them with opportunities to obtain high school GEDs at no cost.[448] Washington added to the qualifications necessary to serve as paraeducator

---

[438] 2023 Minn. Laws Ch. 41, sec. 1, subd. 27, HF 2073.
[439] 2023 Minn. Laws Ch. 41, sec. 1, subd. 25, HF 2073.
[440] 2023 Pa. Laws Act No. 33, H.B. 301, Sec. 9.
[441] 2023 N.M. Laws Ch. 201, SB 307.
[442] 2023 N.J. Pub. Laws c. 215, S. 2764.
[443] 2023 N.D. Laws S.B. No. 2032.
[444] 2023 Okla. Sess. Laws H.B. No. 2559.
[445] 2023 Utah Laws H.B. 190.
[446] 2023 Conn. Acts 167, Subst. S.B. No. 1, § 29.
[447] 2023 Iowa Acts HF 256.
[448] 2023 Ky. Acts Ch. 68 HB 32.

assessments to demonstrate knowledge of, and the ability to assist in, instruction in reading, writing, and mathematics.[449]

Other miscellaneous actions designed to attract and retain teachers, other professionals, and noncertificated employees are detailed as follows. California directed its Teacher Credentialing Commission to contract with a public relations organization to develop a public awareness campaign highlighting the value and benefits of a career in education.[450] Hawaii authorized its School Facilities Authority to partner with public and private agencies to develop housing on or off campus for teacher educators and staff and to develop classrooms.[451] Illinois permitted its Student Assistance Commission to reduce the amount owed on certain high-need scholarship programs such as for special education or minority teachers, for service in schools.[452]

Kentucky ordered the commonwealth's DOE to administer exit surveys from school personnel when leaving their jobs.[453] Pennsylvania obligated the commonwealth's DOE to establish and maintain a public job posting internet database, enabling school entities to post employee vacancies.[454] Virginia adopted a teacher reengagement program to address instructional personnel shortages and COVID-19 pandemic-related student learning loss.[455]

Four states called for more study of the causes and means of mitigating school employee shortages. Connecticut created a working group to study funding, accountability measure, financial reporting, and financial impact. A central topic to be studied was compensation, benefits, retention, as well as recruitment of teachers, paraprofessionals, and social workers.[456] Nevada revised the name and mission of its task force for recruitment and retention of teachers to include education support personnel as members while adding the words "education support" in its name and mission.[457] New York obligated its Commissioner of Education to issue guidance for developing programs to attract

[449] 2023 Wash Laws. Ch. 17, Subst. H.B. 1015.
[450] 2023 Cal. Stat. Ch. 671, A.B. No. 934.
[451] 2023 Haw. Sess. Laws Act 172, SB 941.
[452] 2023 Ill. Laws P.A. 103-448, HB 3498.
[453] 2023 Ky. Acts Ch. 164, HB 319.
[454] 2023 Pa. Laws Act No. 35, S.B. 843, Sec. 4.
[455] 2023 Va. Acts Ch. 429, H.B. 1762.
[456] 2023 Conn. Acts 167, Subst. S.B. No. 1, § 36.
[457] 2023 Nev. Stat. Ch. 273, SB 71.

underrepresented candidates into teaching and to identify funding available for this purpose.[458] Oregon directed its state DOE to develop and implement a plan to establish and maintain a statewide data system on the education workforce in the state.[459]

Four states sought more evaluation data. Illinois redirected its state BOE to report, rather than analyze and assess, teacher evaluation data from all schools.[460] Illinois then paused the use of performance tests for teacher certification candidates while creating a task force to evaluate potential teacher assessment systems.[461] Michigan changed its teacher and administrative evaluation systems by eliminating student test scores as a factor in ratings.[462] West Virginia asked for more data and an explanation for personnel evaluations for classroom teachers, principals, and assistant principals in public schools.[463]

Another four states added six acts with First Amendment speech or religion applications in employment. Kentucky prohibited school boards from punishing employees for engaging in private religious expression otherwise protected by the First Amendment absent showings of engaging in actual coercion.[464] Pennsylvania repealed a long-standing banning against public school teachers wearing religious garb or insignia.[465] Tennessee stated that teachers or other employee of public schools or LEA need not refer to students using their preferred pronouns if they are inconsistent with their biological sex. The act provides immunity for teachers and other school employee.[466]

In the first of three laws Texas permitted public schools to employ chaplains or permit them to serve as volunteers.[467] Texas then protected teachers from disciplinary proceedings for allegations that they violated the Establishment Clause.[468] In addition, Texas directed that teachers in public elementary or

---

[458] 2023 N.Y. Laws Ch. 350, A. 68.
[459] 2023 Or. Laws Ch. 592, S.B. 283.
[460] 2023 Ill. Laws P.A. 103-452, HB 3570.
[461] 2023 Ill. Laws P.A. 103-488, SB 1488.
[462] 2023 Mich. Pub. Acts No. 224, S.B. No. 395; 2023 Mich. Pub. Acts No. 225, S.B. No. 396.
[463] 2023 W. Va. Acts Ch.299, H.B. 2597.
[464] 2023 Ky. Acts Ch. 89, HB 547.
[465] 2023 Pa. Laws Act No. 26, S.B. 84.
[466] 2023 Tenn. Pub. Acts Ch. No. 448, S.B. No. 466, Subs. H.B. No. 1269.
[467] 2023 Tex. Gen. Laws S.B. No. 763.
[468] 2023 Tex. Gen. Laws H.B. No. 1605.

secondary schools may not be prohibited from displaying posters or framed copies of the National Mott in their classrooms.[469]

Four states provided immunity for school personnel and their employers in specified situations. Alabama provided immunity for public K-12 schools, colleges, and universities for maintaining separate athletic teams or sorting for biological male students, and prohibited retaliation against students who report alleged violations of this act to institutional employees or officials.[470] Louisiana granted immunity from civil liability and criminal prosecution for teachers, principals, or administrators in public schools approved nonpublic schools who intervene and act in justifiable defense to protect student or employees unless their intervention was maliciously, willfully, and deliberately intended to cause bodily harm.[471] Rhode Island provided immunity from liability for school employees who work with students and compensation for injuries they receive.[472] Tennessee allowed immunity for teachers or other school employee who refuse to use another's preferred pronoun.[473]

Three states addressed circumstances related to certificate revocation. New Hampshire prohibited the employment or volunteering of educators whose certifications are revoked or suspended.[474] Tennessee added substitute language to assure that linkages are recognized between criminal behaviors and the revocation of educator licenses.[475] Virginia declared that if courts reverses founded complaints of child abuse or neglect against teachers who licenses are revoked, the commonwealth's BOE must consider reinstating them on request of the teachers.[476]

Four states adopted provisions about adverse employment actions such as reductions-in-force (RIF) or dismissal. Arkansas amended criteria for the layoffs and recalls of employees in school districts under RIF policies, diminishing seniority as a criterion.[477] California prohibited boards from terminating the employment of superintendents or assistant superintendents without cause at

---

[469] 2023 Tex. Gen. Laws H.B. No. 2012.
[470] 2023 Ala. Acts 293, H.B. 261.
[471] 2023 La. Acts No. 56, H.B. No. 86.
[472] 2023 R.I. Pub. Laws S.B. 381, H.B. 5564.
[473] 2023 Tenn. Pub. Acts Ch. No. 448, S.B. No. 466, Subs. H.B. No. 1269.
[474] 2023 N.H. Laws Ch. 164, SB 136.
[475] 2023 Tenn. Pub. Acts Ch. No. 267, S.B. No. 744, Subs. H.B. No. 529.
[476] 2023 Va. Acts Ch. 771, H.B. 1550.
[477] 2023 Ark Acts 780, S.B. 510.

special or emergency meetings or within 30 days of reorganizations after board membership changes.[478]

Michigan forbade seniority as being used as the sole factor in filling school vacancies, allowing it to serve as a tiebreaker for candidates with otherwise equal ratings.[479] North Dakota clarified that when school employees whose position are substantially funded by grant funds or temporary funding sources received advance notice of these contract term before accepting the jobs, school board need not report these action to the state's Educational Standards and Practices Board.[480]

Other employment-related acts passed in the last legislative year are described as follows. Arizona required school boards or charter schools to classify each candidate enrolled in classroom-based preparation programs they provide as paid employee.[481] Arizona next permitted boards in small school districts to hire substitute teachers who may be related to their members but the former must recuse on matters relating to the latter.[482] Arkansas added to the provision mandating the existence of school board personnel policy committees, describing membership, including classified employees,[483] and elections of their members.[484] Also, Arkansas prohibited superintendents from making positive employment recommendation if they have knowledge of probable cause that employees engaged in sexual misconduct with minors.[485]

California set the maximum retirement income at 70% of median final income of all members retiring in the same fiscal year.[486] North Dakota defined a probationary teachers as those teaching for less than two years in school districts.[487] Oregon directed school boards and charter schools to designate civil rights coordinators.[488] Texas provided employment preference for

---

[478] 2023 Cal. Stat. Ch. 875, S.B. No. 494.
[479] 2023 Mich. Pub. Acts No. 116, H.B. 4820.
[480] 2023 N.D. Laws H.B. No. 1259.
[481] 2023 Ariz. Sess. Laws Ch. 88, H.B. 2057.
[482] 2023 Ariz. Sess. Laws Ch. 115, S.B. 1584.
[483] 2023 Ark. Acts 782, S.B. 514.
[484] 2023 Ark. Acts 781, S.B. 512.
[485] 2023 Ark. Acts 792, S.B. 572.
[486] 2023 Cal. Stat. Ch. 885, S.B. No. 765.
[487] 2023 N.D. Laws S.B. No. 2284, sec. 2.
[488] 2023 Or. Laws Ch. 243, H.B. 2281.

military members and their spouses for positions with state offices and agencies.[489]

Finance and School Business

This section describes finance and school business-related bills states adopted in 2023. Fifteen acts from 21 states fashioned new funding formulae for K-12 schools. Colorado amended the school funding formula statewide base of $7,478.16 for general inflation,[490] plus $598.25 additional funds for special education funding.[491] Florida removed a factor in a calculation that would have reduced school funding for boards failing to meet class size requirements.[492] Maine directed its department of education to analyze data on the essential programs and services funding formula and its allocation methodology.[493] Minnesota adopted an education finance bill with formulae and seven directives in sections 1-7.[494] Mississippi increased the minimum funding levels for early learning students, to $2,500 for full-day and $1,250 for half-day students.[495]

Montana created a school equalization and property tax reduction account as part of an effort to provide school funding equalization mechanisms.[496] Montana included students in offsite instructional settings and in remote instruction for calculating the number of pupils for school funding purposes.[497] New Hampshire approved a formula for the payment of transporting students to career and technical education.[498] New Mexico changed its school funding formula to boost at-risk and art programs, and to increase administrator pay.[499] Oklahoma determined that students attending virtual charter school alternative education programs for abbreviated days will count in full attendance for purposes of computing average daily attendance and membership.[500]

---

[489] 2023 Tex. Gen. Laws S.B. No. 1376.
[490] 2023 Colo. Sess. Laws S.B. 287.
[491] 2023 Colo. Sess. Laws S.B. 99.
[492] 2023 Fla. Laws Ch. 104, H. 633.
[493] 2023 Me. Laws Ch. 118, H.P. 732, L.D. 1160.
[494] 2023 Minn. Laws Ch. 55, HF 2497.
[495] 2023 Miss. Laws HB 817.
[496] 2023 Mont. Laws H.B. 587.
[497] 2023 Mont. Laws H.B. 214.
[498] 2023 N.H. Laws Ch. 130, HB 364.
[499] 2023 N.M. Laws Ch. 148, HB 199.
[500] 2023 Okla. Sess. Laws H.B. No. 2180.

Oregon required a separate calculation of virtual public charter schools' average daily membership when the boards supporting them lose funds because of decrease in average daily membership from the prior year.[501] Oregon preserved additional funding for small districts which merge with one or more other systems.[502] Oregon ordered boards to designate students' schools or programs of enrollment such that only pupils with school identification numbers are included in average daily membership.[503] Pennsylvania permitted high school students enrolled in dual credit courses to be included in school entities' average daily membership.[504] South Dakota revised property tax levies for boards and state aid funding formulae.[505]

Texas initiated an allotment in the school foundation program, supporting nonpublic students to participate in university interscholastic league activities.[506] Texas then amended its school funding formula so that non-enrolled students may participate in university interscholastic league activities the same as those who are enrolled.[507] Utah increased from 4% to 5% the distributed amount of average market amount of the state school fund as the basic factor for the funding formula to be paid to its school and instructional trust fund office.[508] Utah next expanded statewide online education programs to include grade 6, funding additional middle school credits in the formula to support the extra expenses.[509] Utah provided contingent additional funds in the minimum school funding program to help boards with decreased enrollment to be "held harmless" for the following fiscal year.[510] Washington ordered a performance audit of special education programming and the funding formula supporting them.[511]

Georgia provided 19 homestead exemptions for ad valorum taxes for school districts as follows: Heard County;[512] Gwinnett

---

[501] 2023 Or. Laws Ch. 571, S.B. 278.
[502] 2023 Or. Laws Ch. 332, H.B. 3135.
[503] 2023 Or. Laws Ch. 197, S.B. 923.
[504] 2023 Pa. Laws Act No. 52, H.B. No. 1258.
[505] 2023 S.D. Laws S.B. 24.
[506] 2023 Tex. Gen. Laws H.B. No. 3708.
[507] 2023 Tex. Gen. Laws H.B. No. 699.
[508] 2023 Utah Laws H.B. 421.
[509] 2023 Utah Laws S.B. 45.
[510] 2023 Utah Laws H.B. 394.
[511] 2023 Wash Laws. Ch. 417, Subst. H.B. 1436.
[512] 2023 Ga. Laws Act 277 H.B. 395.

County in the amount of $4,000;[513] an additional exemption for Gwinnet County in the amount of $2,000 of the assessed value of the homestead for residents 65 years and older;[514] Early County in the amount of $150,000 of assessed valuation;[515] Whitfield County in the amount of $150,000 of assessed valuation;[516] an additional exemption for Whitfield County taxes in the amount of $30,000 of assessed valuation for residents age 65 or older;[517] the City of Dalton in the amount of $150,000;[518] an additional exemption for the City of Dalton in the amount of $75,000 for residents age 65 or older;[519] another exemption for the City of Dalton in the amount of $150,000 for residents age 65 or older;[520] for Twiggs County in the amount of $15,000;[521] for Catoosa County in the amount of $75,000, with a continued benefit to unmarried surviving spouses;[522] for Bartow County for $15,000, subject to voter approval;[523] for Forsyth County above the adjusted base per year, subject to voter approval;[524] for Dekalb County in the amount of $14,000;[525] for Newton County at $30,000, with an income cap at $100,552, subject to approval of the voters;[526] for the City of Decatur at $200,000, subject to approval of the voters;[527] for Oconee County based on a comparison to the base year;[528] for Oconee County in an additional amount of $3,000, subject to voter approval;[529] and for Oconee County for those over age 75, subject to voter approval.[530]

Rhode Island authorized bond issues in nine jurisdictions while Tennessee permitted bond issues in one district. Rhode Island allowed the town of Lincoln to issue bonds in an amount up to $25 million for improvement of elementary schools[531] and enabled the

---

[513] 2023 Ga. Laws Act 296, H.B. 711.
[514] 2023 Ga. Laws Act 309, H.B. 748.
[515] 2023 Ga. Laws Act 330, S.B. 302.
[516] 2023 Ga. Laws Act 311, H.B. 753.
[517] 2023 Ga. Laws Act 323, H.B. 787.
[518] 2023 Ga. Laws Act 316, H.B. 762.
[519] 2023 Ga. Laws Act 314, H.B. 758.
[520] 2023 Ga. Laws Act 209, H.B. 756.
[521] 2023 Ga. Laws Act 220, H.B. 805.
[522] 2023 Ga. Laws Act 123, H.B. 511.
[523] 2023 Ga. Laws Act 106, H.B. 118.
[524] 2023 Ga. Laws Act 194, H.B. 717.
[525] 2023 Ga. Laws Act 154, H.B. 594.
[526] 2023 Ga. Laws Act 139, S.B. 311.
[527] 2023 Ga. Laws Act 128, S.B. 288.
[528] 2023 Ga. Laws Act 43, H.B. 767.
[529] 2023 Ga. Laws Act 42, H.B. 766.
[530] 2023 Ga. Laws Act 46, H.B. 770.
[531] 2023 R.I. Pub. Laws H.B. 6454, S.B. 1069.

town of Cumberland to issue bonds in an amount up to $52 million for improvement of school facilities.[532] Rhode Island empowered the Bristol Warren regional school board to issue bonds in an amount up to $200 million for a new high school and other school facilities,[533] and enabled the town of North Kingston to issue bonds in an amount up to $167.46 million for school facilities, including a new middle school.[534]

Rhode Island permitted the town of Barrington to issue bonds in an amount up to $250 million for school facility improvements[535] and the town of South Kingston to issue bonds for up to $125 million to finance purchase, construction, and improvements for a new high school and athletic facilities.[536] Rhode Island empowered the town of East Greenwich to issue not more than $180 million in bonds to finance the acquisition, construction, improvement, renovation, and furnishing of public schools and facilities.[537] Rhode Island authorized the town of Middletown to issue up to $190 million in bonds to finance school construction and renovation,[538] and approved the issuance of $1 million in bonds by the town of Scituate to finance a water project for its high school and middle school.[539] Tennessee permitted the Franklin special school district in Williamson County to issue bonds or notes in an amount not to exceed $20 million.[540]

Three states addressed restrictions on bond issues. Maine amended laws governing bonding restrictions for school administrative units by increasing the time for maturity, from 25 to 30 years.[541] New York repealed a requirement of a one-year waiting period for a capital improvement when school boards or municipal corporations or district corporations issue indebtedness to finance costs of preparation of plans and specifications.[542] Oklahoma directed school boards to post information on their websites about issuing bonds prior to bond elections.[543]

---

[532] 2023 R.I. Pub. Laws H.B. 6479, S.B. 1091.
[533] 2023 R.I. Pub. Laws H.B. 6455, S.B. 1073.
[534] 2023 R.I. Pub. Laws H.B. 6429, S.B. 1076.
[535] 2023 R.I. Pub. Laws H.B. 6404, S.B. 980.
[536] 2023 R.I. Pub. Laws S.B. 994, H.B. 6276.
[537] 2023 R.I. Pub. Laws H.B. 6376, S.B. 981.
[538] 2023 R.I. Pub. Laws H.B. 5526, S.B. 206.
[539] 2023 R.I. Pub. Laws S.B. 995, H.B. 6355.
[540] 2023 Tenn. Priv. Acts Ch. No. 9, H.B. No. 1536, Subs. S.B. No. 1513.
[541] 2023 Me. Laws Ch. 210, H.P. 153, L.D. 232.
[542] 2023 N.Y. Laws Ch. 592, S. 5655.
[543] 2023 Okla. Sess. Laws H.B. No. 1445.

Six states changed their standards for bidding contracts. Alabama increased the threshold for competitively bid contracts from $15,000 to $40,000; beginning in 2027 the competitive bid minimum will be tied to the Consumer Price Index (CPI).[544] Georgia set the threshold at $50,000 for bids for school construction and equipment in Richmond County.[545] Illinois amended its public sector bid law to provide a preference for bids from companies employing former coal miners.[546] Kentucky increased the threshold amount at which local government contracts must be bid, from $30,000 to $40,000.[547] Minnesota changed the requisite publicity timeline from 20-60 days to 48-60 days before referenda for bonds or solicitations of bids to invite public comment.[548] New Jersey permitted some public school contracts to be awarded by state purchasing agents rather than by bid.[549]

Four states altered procedures for approving school board budgets. California amended a posting requirement for budgets and hearings, to permit these to be placed websites instead of being printed in newspapers.[550] Maine lengthened the time, from 30 to 45 calendar days allowed between regional school unit budget meetings and budget validation referenda.[551] New Jersey eliminated votes on budgets for Type II districts in April elections except when proposing to spend above legislative caps.[552] New Hampshire increased, from $5,000 to $20,000, the amount of anticipated funds for which boards must conduct prior public hearings.[553]

Five states approved six acts about insurance programs. Indiana directed its state DOE to create a list of personal liability insurers that offer personal liability insurance policies for teachers and to post the list on its website.[554] Mississippi created a task force to advise the legislature on school employees' life and health insurance plans.[555] Montana created a school district health

---

[544] 2023 Ala. Acts 203, H.B. 65.
[545] 2023 Ga. Laws Act 304, H.B. 733.
[546] 2023 Ill. Laws P.A. 103-570, HB 2878.
[547] 2023 Ky. Acts Ch. 152, HB 522.
[548] 2023 Minn. Laws Ch. 55, sec. 3, HF 2497.
[549] 2023 N.J. Pub. Laws c. 252, A. 5501.
[550] 2023 Cal. Stat. Ch. 811, AB. No. 721.
[551] 2023 Me. Laws Ch. 256, H.P. 658, L.D. 1022.
[552] 2023 N.J. Pub. Laws c. 289, S. 4209.
[553] 2023 N.H. Laws Ch. 38, HB 207.
[554] 2023 Ind. Acts P.L. 196, SB 443.
[555] 2023 Miss. Laws SB 2623.

insurance trust to stabilize health insurance costs for school employees.[556] Nevada permitted boards of trustees of school districts to purchase liability insurance for pupils participating in work-based learning programs.[557] New York allowed the Auburn Enlarged City School District to establish an insurance reserve fund.[558] New York also enabled the Cleveland Hill Union Free School District to establish an insurance reserve fund.[559]

Four states enacted five provisions on sinking funds or sub funds. Colorado provided specialized funding for what it called facility schools needing specialized services beyond what is available from school districts of residence.[560] Michigan allowed public boards to use a school sinking fund for financing school transportation.[561] Washington obligated all school districts of the second class to create depreciation sub-funds to reserve funds for future facility and equipment needs.[562] West Virginia created a special revenue fund designated as the Charter School Stimulus Fund to provide financial support for applicants seeing to open and charter schools.[563] West Virginia then created a special revenue fund to provide resources for CPR instruction to high school students.[564]

Ten states mandated adherence to generally accepted accounting practices in school districts. With respect to program-based accounting, Connecticut directed its state DOE to publish program-based accounting of school expenditures, financial comparisons between school districts, and student enrollment and demographic statistics on their websites annually.[565] Maine required called for annual financial audits of nonpublic schools approved for tuition purposes.[566]

As to purchasing and receivables, Alabama directed public K-12 schools and their boards to accept cash as a form of payment along with other form of payment to school-sponsored sporting

---

[556] 2023 Mont. Laws H.B. 332.
[557] 2023 Nev. Stat. Ch. 256, AB 207.
[558] 2023 N.Y. Laws Ch. 598, S. 6667.
[559] 2023 N.Y. Laws Ch. 589, S. 3611.
[560] 2023 Colo. Sess. Laws S.B. 219.
[561] 2023 Mich. Pub. Acts No. 26, S.B. No. 63.
[562] 2023 Wash Laws. Ch. 402, S.B. 5403.
[563] 2023 W. Va. Acts Ch.124, S.B. 47.
[564] 2023 W. Va. Acts Ch. 130, S.B. 469.
[565] 2023 Conn. Acts 167, Subst. S.B. No. 1, § 1.
[566] 2023 Me. Laws Ch. 112, H.P. 68, L.D. 100.

events open to the public.[567] Mississippi authorized its state DOE to provide EEF classroom supply procurement cards or credentials for a digital purchasing solution to eligible teachers employed by charter schools.[568] New Mexico excluded the purchase of instructional materials from procurement through its state purchasing agent.[569]

Three states addressed rules about reimbursements. Illinois required its state BOE to reimburse not less than 15 cents or the actual cost, whichever is less, to nonprofit welfare centers for each free breakfast or lunch they serve.[570] Oregon directed its state DOE to make biennial transfers to the state military department to pay costs of educational services provided through the programs the latter operates for at-risk youth.[571] Rhode Island dictated that services provided by certificated school psychologists and school social workers be included as health care-related services for Medicaid reimbursement.[572]

Two states altered rules on reporting revenue and expenditures. Rhode Island called for every board and council on elementary and secondary education to report each fiscal year on revenue and expenditures from the All American Rescue plan, elementary and secondary school emergency relief, and state and local recovery funds.[573] New Hampshire repealed a requirement that its state Commissioner of Education must report each payment made in a fiscal year by the state to a chartered public school.[574]

With respect to cash reserves, South Carolina permitted school districts 2 and 4 in Dorchester County to exceed the limit on cash reserves for fiscal years 2023-2024 and 2024-2025.[575]

Other finance and school business-related acts passed in 2023 are described as follows. Louisiana permitted the Monroe City School Board to levy an ad valorem tax for funding early childhood care and education.[576] Montana altered the method for determining

---

[567] 2023 Ala. Acts 355, H.B. 364.
[568] 2023 Miss. Laws HB 1173.
[569] 2023 N.M. Laws Ch. 149, HB 226.
[570] 2023 Ill. Laws P.A. 103-532, HB 2471.
[571] 2023 Or. Laws Ch. 587, S.B. 1034.
[572] 2023 R.I. Pub. Laws H.B. 5010, S.B. 869.
[573] 2023 R.I. Pub. Laws H.B. 6128, S.B. 767.
[574] 2023 N.H. Laws Ch. 27, HB 71.
[575] 2023 S.C. Acts No. 95, H.B. 3254.
[576] 2023 La. Acts No. 361, H.B. No. 56.

fees for teaching and specialist certificates by repealing set fee amounts and directing its state superintendent of public instruction to set a fee amount to allow a special state account to never be more than twice the previous amount appropriated.[577] Montana mandated follow-up reporting from education entities, including its state superintendent of public instruction and state library, about the impacts of education-related appropriations in the general appropriations act.[578] New Hampshire allowed parents to pay the difference between receiving school tuitions cost and the tuition cap assessed by their sending boards.[579]

North Dakota specified that its state Superintendent of Public Instruction, rather than state Board For Career and Technical Education, sets the fees for services provided by the center for distance education.[580] North Dakota added a provision that allowed its state treasurer to withhold funds due or payable to school boards after the public finance authority or paying agents indicate financial issues impact their ability to pay its bills.[581] North Dakota obligated local boards to report to the Superintendent of Public Instruction and to legislative management on the categories and amount spent on school safety and security measures during previous school years.[582] Oregon permitted its state DOE to adjust the amounts charged for distribution of agricultural products received from the U.S. Department of Agriculture for school food programs.[583] Utah repealed the obligation that LEAs notify others before disposing of undamaged textbooks, ordering its state DOE to make rules about textbook disposal.[584]

Governance and School Leadership

This section lists governance and school leadership-related acts adopted in 2023, beginning with state-level entities, state school boards, state schools, and state commissions. Eleven states enacted 13 bills regarding state level entities. Florida added the School for Competitive Academics to the education-related entities

[577] 2023 Mont. Laws H.B. 403.
[578] 2023 Mont. Laws H.B. 946.
[579] 2023 N.H. Laws Ch. 185, SB 275.
[580] 2023 N.D. Laws S.B. No. 2269.
[581] 2023 N.D. Laws H.B. No. 1125.
[582] 2023 N.D. Laws H.B. No. 1337.
[583] 2023 Or. Laws Ch. 570, S.B. 215.
[584] 2023 Utah Laws H.B. 494.

described in the school code.[585] Georgia established the State Council on Literacy to conduct comprehensive reviews of birth to postsecondary programs, for the alignment of student support for such programs, and other issues related to improving literacy outcomes for students in the state.[586] Hawaii moved the authority to appoint the executive director of the School Facilities Authority, from the governor to the facilities authority board.[587] Maine increased funding for the School of Science and Mathematics to pay for free room and board, in addition to free tuition, for students.[588]

Montana created a board to manage and protect data from workforce authorities and education entities, to ensure the data is used to benefit the people of the state in a secure manner and for improving decisions regarding career training and workforce pathways.[589] North Carolina provided that two schools for the deaf and a school for the blind are governed by boards of trustees; however, the act clarified that its state BOE maintains general supervision over the schools.[590] Oklahoma created a statewide Charter School Board, which was given control over approval, review, supervision, and closure of charter schools.[591] Oregon moved up the date at which the Teacher Standards and Practices Commission would lose its authority to collect fees from educator preparation providers, based on number of license applications.[592]

Oregon increased membership on its state BOE to include an additional representative of a congressional district and to add a member working as a classified staff member for a public school or education service district.[593] Pennsylvania renamed schools for the physically and mentally handicapped as "schools for children with physical or intellectual disabilities" and renamed truant schools "alternative schools."[594] Pennsylvania initiated a quarterly reporting system of items sought by the legislature from the commonwealth's DOE.[595] Rhode Island added the Teacher of the

---

[585] 2023 Fla. Laws Ch. 245, H. 5101.
[586] 2023 Ga. Laws Act 8, S.B. 211.
[587] 2023 Haw. Sess. Laws Act 61, SB 531.
[588] 2023 Me. Laws Ch. 464, S.P. 576, L.D. 1458.
[589] 2023 Mont. Laws H.B. 949.
[590] 2023 N.C. Sess. Laws Ch. 10, H.B. 11.
[591] 2023 Okla. Sess. Laws S.B. No. 516.
[592] 2023 Or. Laws Ch. 501, H.B. 2609.
[593] 2023 Or. Laws Ch. 440, H.B. 3383.
[594] 2023 Pa. Laws Act No. 33, H.B. 301, Sec. 1.
[595] 2023 Pa. Laws Act No. 33, H.B. 301, Sec. 9.

Yean *ex officio* member of its state BOE and as an *ex officio* member of the council on elementary and secondary education.[596] Tennessee extended the state Textbook and Instructional Materials Quality Commission to June 30, 2027.[597] And Tennessee extended the existence of the Energy Efficient Schools Council to June 30, 2027.[598] Utah directed that when its state BOE makes a request of LEAs, it must include a justification and statement that the information is not available elsewhere with a deadline for receipt of information and the penalties for noncompliance.[599]

Seven states passed eight acts on the terms of office of local school board members. Arkansas specified the term of board members so that if no one has filed to serve unexpired terms of vacating members, they shall be deemed vacant and filled by procedures set forth in its general election law.[600] Georgia repealed a provision which had removed board member term limits for the seven-member Board of Education of McDuffie County.[601] Idaho amended provisions regarding the terms of office of school board trustees, specifying that those elected to trustee zones can complete the trustee's term if the trustee zone changes.[602] New York changed the dates of commencing or concluding the governance terms for board members of the schools in New York City.[603]

South Dakota allowed school boards to modify the length of terms of service for members to allow boards to conduct joint elections.[604] North Carolina reduced the terms, from six years to four years, for board members in Granville County.[605] Texas permitted independent school boards to change by resolution the terms of their trustees, to create staggered terms.[606] Texas also allowed persons who retire from active duty or civilian service while serving terms as members of the boards of trustees of

---

[596] 2023 R.I. Pub. Laws S.B. 182, H.B. 6052.
[597] 2023 Tenn. Pub. Acts Ch. No. 136, H.B. No. 221, Subs. S.B. No. 55.
[598] 2023 Tenn. Pub. Acts Ch. No. 7, S.B. No. 47, Subs. H.B. No. 213.
[599] 2023 Utah Laws S.B. 257, Sec. 1.
[600] 2023 Ark. Acts 750, H.B. 1739.
[601] 2023 Ga. Laws Act 126, S.B. 108.
[602] 2023 Idaho Sess. Laws Ch. 241, H.B. No. 240.
[603] 2023 N.Y. Laws Ch. 71, S. 813.
[604] 2023 S.D. Laws H.B. 1123.
[605] 2023 N.C. Sess. Laws Ch. 2, H.B. 30.
[606] 2023 Tex. Gen. Laws H.B. No. 2285.

military reserve school districts to continue to do so for the remainder of their terms.[607]

Two states changed provisions about student members of local school boards, through six acts. California authorized school boards to add student members under the age of 18 if candidates who are at least age 18 are unavailable.[608] California permitted students serving as pupil members of boards to receive course credit or financial compensation for doing so.[609] In the first of four acts about student board members Maryland altered the authority of those in Prince George's County school, enabling them to vote on certain matters.[610] Second, Maryland added a student member to the Kent County board.[611] Third, Maryland altered the voting rights of and process for selecting a student member of the Baltimore City Board of School Commissioners, clarifying that their pupil may not vote on matters relating to personnel and collective bargaining.[612] Fourth, Maryland allowed the student member of the Baltimore County Board of Education to vote on capital and operating budget matters.[613]

Two states addressed non-voting school board members who are not student members. Mississippi revised the board membership for agricultural high schools, permitting county superintendents of education to serve as *ex officio* nonvoting members.[614] Nevada added four non-voting members to the boards of trustees of school districts with 75,000 or more students. At present, Clark County is the only district meeting this requirement.[615] Two states mandated annual training of board members. Connecticut directed that newly elected local board members and regional board members must complete the training program offered by its state BOE.[616] Tennessee directed that annual training for governing board members for charter schools must be approved by its state BOE.[617]

---

[607] 2023 Tex. Gen. Laws H.B. No. 4210.
[608] 2023 Cal. Stat. Ch. 437, A.B. No. 417.
[609] 2023 Cal. Stat. Ch. 321, A.B. No. 275.
[610] 2023 Md. Laws Ch. 793, H.B. 1079.
[611] 2023 Md. Laws 674, S.B. 402; 2023 Md. Laws 675, H.B. 402.
[612] 2023 Md. Laws Ch. 764, S.B. 31; 2023 Md. Laws Ch. 765, H.B. 153.
[613] 2023 Md. Laws Ch. 785, H.B. 175.
[614] 2023 Miss. Laws SB 2360.
[615] 2023 Nev. Stat. Ch. 187, AB 175.
[616] 2023 Conn. Acts 167, Subst. S.B. No. 1, §§ 2 and 3.
[617] 2023 Tenn. Pub. Acts Ch. No. 92, S.B. No. 577, Subs. H.B. No. 359.

Three states changed the physical boundaries or procedure for setting them for specified school districts. Georgia set the procedure for modifying the boundaries of the school system in the city of Buford, adding that the boundaries for the Hall County school system, which Buford annexed would remain the same.[618] North Carolina altered the boundaries of the school administrative unit for Whiteville City.[619] Oregon obligated county governing boards to provide its state DOE with records about changes to school district boundaries.[620]

As noted in previous years, various states in the South changed the membership numbers and election districts. In this vein, the following school board member changes are listed by district as follows. Georgia divided Dooly,[621] Hart,[622] Taylor,[623] Bartow,[624] and Seminole Counties into five election districts.[625] Further, Georgia divided Rabun County into five election districts, with five members;[626] the City of Decatur into four election districts, with one member for each and a fifth elected at large;[627] and Dodge County into seven election districts with seven board members.[628]

North Carolina changed membership on the school board for Johnston County now based on the district of residency;[629] it additionally decreased the size of the board of education for Nash County to seven members.[630] South Carolina reapportioned the seven election districts from which members of the school board for Spartanburg County School District 7 will be elected.[631] South Carolina reapportioned the election districts from which members of the school board Spartanburg County must be elected.[632] South Carolina reapportioned the single-member election districts from which members of the board for Rock Hill School District 3 in York

---

[618] 2023 Ga. Laws Act 276, H.B. 156.
[619] 2023 N.C. Sess. Laws Ch. 143, S.B. 68.
[620] 2023 Or. Laws Ch. 8, S.B. 271.
[621] 2023 Ga. Laws Act 293, H.B. 700.
[622] 2023 Ga. Laws Act 308, H.B. 743.
[623] 2023 Ga. Laws Act 283, H.B. 610.
[624] 2023 Ga. Laws Act 275, H.B. 117.
[625] 2023 Ga. Laws Act 97, H.B. 49.
[626] 2023 Ga. Laws Act 151, H.B. 587.
[627] 2023 Ga. Laws 127, S.B. 287.
[628] 2023 Ga. Laws Act 134, S.B. 301.
[629] 2023 N.C. Sess. Laws Ch. 143, S.B. 68.
[630] 2023 N.C. Sess. Laws Ch. 37, S.B. 248.
[631] 2023 S.C. Acts No. 98, H.B. 4216.
[632] 2023 S.C. Acts No. 97, H.B. 4215.

County will be elected.[633] Tennessee permitted the school board in Monroe County to have 10, rather than nine, members, subject to local approval.[634]

Seven states passed bills about reorganizing or consolidating local school districts. Arkansas amended the authority of its state BOE to require an administrative reorganization for with less than 350 students.[635] Georgia continued the charter for the Academy of Social Circle but created a body politic, the Board of Education of Social Circle with a chairperson elected at large and four members elected to serve in four education districts.[636] Illinois authorized school districts previously under authority of the trustees of schools of Northfield and Maine Townships to withdraw from it.[637]

Maine repealed and replaced the charter of the Boothbay-Boothbay Harbor Community School District.[638] New Hampshire amended the procedures required for boards to withdraw from cooperative school districts including having a supermajority of three-fifths of voters present.[639] South Carolina consolidated three school districts into one for Barnwell County.[640] West Virginia required county boards of education, before making final decisions to close or consolidate schools, to prepare and reduce to writing its reasons and supporting data for closing or consolidation and an impact statement on its choice.[641]

Ten states adopted 15 acts on whether school board members are elected or appointed and the procedures under either system. Arkansas clarified the candidate filing period for local school boards so that for November elections in odd-number years it will coincide with the one-week period ending 90 days before a November election in even-number years.[642] California required school boards to post information on vacancies on their websites in addition to printing it in newspapers.[643] Georgia set qualifications for election as board members in the Atlanta Independent School

---

[633] 2023 S.C. Acts No. 101, S.B. 764.
[634] 2023 Tenn. Priv. Acts Ch. No.11, H.B. No. 1551, Subs. S.B. No. 1543.
[635] 2023 Ark. Acts 461, S.B. 262.
[636] 2023 Ga. Laws Act 214, H.B. 775.
[637] 2023 Ill. Laws P.A. 103-144, HB 2160.
[638] 2023 Me. Laws Ch. 12, H.P. 1149, L.D. 1786.
[639] 2023 N.H. Laws Ch. 136, HB 530.
[640] 2023 S.C. Acts No. 92, S.B. 654.
[641] 2023 W. Va. Acts Ch. 125, S.B. 51.
[642] 2023 Ark. Acts 276, S.B. 276.
[643] 2023 Cal. Stat. Ch. 68, A.B. No. 1326.

System, including being 18 years old, district residents city elector, and not being one of its employees.[644]

Indiana changed the timing by which candidates for school boards must file petitions for nomination.[645] Maryland moved the timing of the annual election of the officers for the Talbot County Board of Education to be at its last meeting at the end of each calendar year or at the annual December meeting.[646] Maryland ordered the school board nominating commission for Baltimore County to conduct a public hearing on the selection of a nominee for a single vacancy on the board.[647] Maryland next directed the seven elected members of the Baltimore County Board of Education to be chosen in gubernatorial election years while required the four appointed members to be named in presidential election years.[648]

In the first of four acts North Carolina provided for partisan elections for school board members for Catawba County, Hickory City, the cities of Newton and Conover City, Polk County,[649] and for Pamlico County.[650] North Carolina changed the dates and methods of election for the board of education for Franklin County to a nonpartisan primary election.[651] North Carolina changed the school board for Thomasville City from appointed to elected members.[652] North Dakota directed candidates seeking elected school district offices to file campaign contribution statements as required by state law.[653]

Oklahoma prohibited the appointment of persons who serves on school boards under supervision by its state BOE.[654] South Carolina changed election procedures for members of the Williamsburg County board, requiring individuals to file statements of candidacy with the county elections board rather than file petitions.[655] South Carolina changed the method of electing the seven members of the board for Summerville School

---

644 2023 Ga. Laws Act 327, H.B. 792. 2023 Ga. Laws Act 331, S.B. 317.

645 2023 Ind. Acts P.L. 34, SB 177.

646 2023 Md. Laws Ch. 782, H.B. 656; 2023 Md. Laws Ch. 783, S.B. 302.

647 2023 Md. Laws Ch. 787, H.B. 348.

648 2023 Md. Laws Ch. 786, H.B. 210.

649 2023 N.C. Sess. Laws Ch. 32, H.B. 66.

650 2023 N.C. Sess. Laws Ch. 22, S.B. 286.

651 2023 N.C. Sess. Laws Ch. 17, H.B. 452.

652 2023 N.C. Sess. Laws Ch. 1, H.B. 27.

653 2023 N.D. Laws H.B. No. 1257.

654 2023 Okla. Sess. Laws H.B. No. 2678.

655 2023 S.C. Acts No. 100, S.B. 360.

District 2, from at-large to single-member election districts.[656] Texas permitted the boards in independent districts to conduct general elections for officers on a date other than the November uniform election date to change the date to the November date.[657]

Eight states changed their open meetings laws, especially regarding teleconferencing. California required local legislative bodies to make findings of a continuing emergency within 45 days to permit continued use of teleconferencing for meetings.[658] Illinois amended its open meetings act to permit a quorum of public board members who are physically present to allow a member to attend by remote means due to circumstances such as childcare needs.[659] Louisiana permitted specified governing bodies to meet by electronic means; school boards appear to meet these criteria.[660]

New Hampshire amended its open meeting law by directing public bodies to review meeting minutes withheld from public disclosure at least every 10 years to determine whether they should continue to be kept private; minutes not reviewed after 10 years must be made public.[661] Tennessee ordered local boards to enact policies on the use of electronic media, incorporating required provisions, including a quorum of members physically present at meetings; the electronic attendance is due to statutorily identified reasons; those participating electronically can be visibly identified by the chair; and, the number of times attendance is by electronic means is limited to two times for work reasons and three times for illness, inclement weather, or family emergency; there is no constraint on members who are absent due to military service.[662]

Utah amended its Open Meetings Act obligating school boards to enact policies allowing public comment at their meetings while permitted public bodies and local boards of special service district to convene and conduct electronic meetings when provided for as exceptions.[663] To the list of items not disclosable under its public meetings law Utah added consideration of loan applications if public discussion would disclose personal financial information, nonpublic trade secrets, or nonpublic business information which

---

[656] 2023 S.C. Acts No. 96, H.B. 3961.
[657] 2023 Tex. Gen. Laws S.B. No. 1131.
[658] 2023 Cal. Stat. Ch. 534, A.B. No. 557.
[659] 2023 Ill. Laws P.A. 103-311, HB 2447.
[660] 2023 La. Acts No. 393, S.B. No. 201.
[661] 2023 N.H. Laws Ch. 189, HB 321.
[662] 2023 Tenn. Pub. Acts Ch. No. 350, S.B. No. 1268, Subs. H.B. No. 1324.
[663] 2023 Utah Laws H.B. 21.

would reasonably be expected to result in unfair competitive injuries.[664] Until July 4, 2024 Vermont permitted a quorum or more of public bodies to attend regular, special, or emergency meetings by electronic means without being present at designated locations.[665] West Virginia amended its open meetings law to permit the use of virtual meetings in emergency situations.[666]

Six states adopted seven acts on school board meeting management. Arizona required school boards and other public bodies to plan for convening public meetings in locations providing sufficient seating for expected attendance at the sessions; this does not require moving to a larger location.[667] Arizona also changed the calendar for conducting school board organizational meeting from "January 1-15" to "in January."[668] Delaware directed local boards and charter schools to allow public comments on each item before they vote on measures.[669] Hawaii encouraged its state school board to maintain recordings of its meetings on a website and provide them to state archives.[670]

Illinois obligated school boards to have public voted with community comment before doing so when approving contracts for district administrative assessments.[671] Nevada restricted the ability of boards of trustees to act in regular or special meetings on items added to agendas posted after 11:59 p.m. on the day of the sessions.[672] North Dakota added a provision directing before regularly scheduled board meetings members must be given opportunities to participate in voluntary recitation of the Pledge of Allegiance.[673]

Montana adopted an unusual act impacting public boards for both K-12 schools and higher education as the legislature required its Board of Public Education and the Board of Regents to meet at least once yearly as the combined state BOE, for the purpose of long-range planning, coordinating, and evaluating policies and programs for the state's public educational system.[674]

---

[664] 2023 Utah Laws S.B. 245.
[665] 2023 Vt. Laws Ch. No. 1, H. 42.
[666] 2023 W. Va. Acts Ch. 169, H.B. 3146.
[667] 2023 Ariz. Sess. Laws Ch. 23, S.B. 127.
[668] 2023 Ariz. Sess. Laws Ch. 180, H.B. 2663.
[669] 2023 Del. Laws HB 34.
[670] 2023 Haw. Sess. Laws Act 125, HB 712.
[671] 2023 Ill. Laws P.A. 103-393, SB 1993.
[672] 2023 Nev. Stat. Ch., 182, AB 65.
[673] 2023 N.D. Laws H.B. No. 1120.
[674] 2023 Mont. Laws H.B. 531.

Nine states enacted 12 acts about open records. Arizona permitted public and charter schools to satisfy regulatory posting requirements by making the link to schools' webpages.[675] Arkansas required records custodians to respond in writing to requests for records under the Freedom of Information Act in the new timeline it set.[676] Illinois amended its Public Record Act to protect electronic medical records and information on demographic data from disclosure.[677] Indiana directed state archives and record administrators to adopt procedures to retain original papers for a time, convert them to electronic format, and provide for their destruction.[678]

Montana amended its public record law by ordering its state BOE and local boards to record their public meetings in audio and video formats.[679] Montana ordered its Office of Public Instruction to create a repository, accessible by website, to provides information, including about how to contact current members of local school board.[680] North Dakota called for archiving of recordings of school board meetings and to make them available to the public on request.[681] Oklahoma added more types of information not subject to disclosure under its public records law, including school risk and vulnerability assessments as well as recommendations to increase security in schools.[682]

Virginia amended its Freedom of Information Act to permit local public bodies to provide persons requesting records to receive electronic copies of them.[683] Virginia made medical and educational records declared confidential by law to remain so after being archived by The Library of Virginia.[684] Washington amended its public records law to exempt disclosure of personal information about students enrolled or previously enrolled in local education agencies and in records pertaining to them, including correspondences.[685] Washington modified its public records law to specify that requests for recordings required to be maintained by

---

[675] 2023 Ariz. Sess. Laws Ch. 170, H.B. 2060.
[676] 2023 Ark. Acts 879, S.B. 830.
[677] 2023 Ill. Laws P.A. 103-554, SB 1670.
[678] 2023 Ind. Acts P.L. 246, HB 1591.
[679] 2023 Mont. Laws H.B. 890.
[680] 2023 Mont. Laws H.B. 811.
[681] 2023 N.D. Laws H.B. No. 1270.
[682] 2023 Okla. Sess. Laws S.B. No. 100.
[683] 2023 Va. Acts Ch. 534, H.B. 2006.
[684] 2023 Va. Acts Ch. 126, H.B. 1844; 2023 Va. Acts Ch. 127, S.B. 1024.
[685] 2023 Wash Laws. Ch. 182, Subst. S.B. 5127.

school district boards of directors shall only be considered valid when the dates of the recording, or a range of dates, is specified in requests. When searching for and providing identifiable recordings, boards must not consider search criteria except dates.[686]

Georgia changed school board member compensation for 11 boards while two other jurisdictions did so with some discretion given to the local boards. Georgia set the compensation for board members for Cook County to $1,000 per month;[687] in Coweta County to $950 per month;[688] in Floyd County to $1,000 per month;[689] in McIntosh County to $300 per day for members and $375 per day for the chair;[690] and in Ben Hill County to $300 per month for members and $350 per month for the chair;[691] for members in Savannah and Chatham County to $25,000 per annum and $35,000 for the chair;[692] in Carroll County to $1,000 per month for members, $1,200 per month for the chair, and $1,100 per month for the vice chairman;[693] in Mitchell County to $400 per month for members and $450 for the chair;[694] in Brantley County to $800 per month, plus $75 for each additional meeting, limited to 12 extra meetings in a year;[695] and in Franklin County at 8% of the monthly salary of a beginning teacher with zero years' service on salary step E and a T-4 certificate, and 10% of the monthly salary at the same salary step for the board chair.[696] Mississippi raised the annual salary for board members to range, based on district size, from $4,000 to $6,000.[697] Oregon allowed boards to choose to give directors monthly stipends, allowing individuals to refuse these payments.[698]

Three states added provisions guiding ethical conduct by school board members. Arkansas amended provisions on cause for removal of a local board members to include violation of ethical

---

[686] 2023 Wash Laws. Ch. 67, H.B. 1210.
[687] 2023 Ga. Laws Act 284, H.B. 619.
[688] 2023 Ga. Laws Act 295, H.B. 707.
[689] 2023 Ga. Laws Act 287, H.B. 649.
[690] 2023 Ga. Laws Act 300, H.B. 723.
[691] 2023 Ga. Laws Act 289, H.B. 676.
[692] 2023 Ga. Laws Act 294, H.B. 702.
[693] 2023 Ga. Laws Act 149, H.B. 580.
[694] 2023 Ga. Laws Act 93, H.B. 11.
[695] 2023 Ga. Laws Act 115, H.B. 255.
[696] 2023 Ga. Laws Act 192, H.B. 715.
[697] 2023 Miss. Laws SB 2749.
[698] 2023 Or. Laws Ch. 321, H.B. 2753.

guidelines and prohibitions articulated in state law, and not just felonies.[699] Montana mandated disclosure of the use of taxpayer funds for lobbying by local governments and school boards.[700] Utah clarified the process for ethics complaints about local board members by requiring that they be reviewed by the political subdivision's ethics review commission and prohibited schools board from create local review commissions.[701]

Other governance-related acts are detailed as follows. Kentucky placed the appointment or reappointment of its state Commissioner of Education to be subject to consent of the Senate while set term limits for the appointment at four years.[702] Kentucky next included school boards in the definition of local government for the purpose of entering public-private partnerships.[703] Maine amended its definition of "educational Institution" under the state Human Rights Act to include those that are for a single-sex.[704] Maryland changed the title of the administrative leader of the Prince George's County school system from Chief Executive Officer to County Superintendent.[705]

Montana removed language referencing teaching certificates as a qualification to serve as state Superintendent of Public Instruction.[706] North Dakota directed that in long-term planning school boards must include plans for academic achievement and progress toward state goals.[707] Rhode Island repealed a requirement that school committee policy manual musts be kept in libraries and administrative building, instead directing that they be made available on board website.[708] Utah permitted school boards to enter into collective agreements with one another for resource sharing for services such as student transportation.[709] West Virginia allowed county boards to meet with other bodies to explore and discuss the feasibility of consolidating districts or sharing services.[710] Wyoming enabled its Board of Cooperative

---

[699] 2023 Ark. Acts 883, S.B. 543.
[700] 2023 Mont. Laws S.B. 358.
[701] 2023 Utah Laws S.B. 227.
[702] 2023 Ky. Acts Ch. 134, SB 107.
[703] 2023 Ky. Acts Ch. 41, SB 69.
[704] 2023 Me. Laws Ch. 188, H.P. 1165, L.D. 1833.
[705] 2023 Md. Laws Ch. 792, H.B.437.
[706] 2023 Mont. Laws H.B. 181.
[707] 2023 N.D. Laws S.B. No. 2284, sec. 1.
[708] 2023 R.I. Pub. Laws S.B. 494, H.B. 5671.
[709] 2023 Utah Laws S.B. 143.
[710] 2023 W. Va. Acts Ch. 126, S.B. 99.

Educational Services to act as a LEAs for the purpose of applying for and receiving state and federal grants.[711]

Parental and Student Rights

This section describes 2023 legislative acts about parental and student rights, beginning with extensive expressions of parental rights carrying that label. Six states enacted seven bills described as "parental rights acts." Alabama placed language in its school code about court decisions recognizing that parents have a fundamental right to direct the upbringing of their children and that the government may not burden it absent a compelling governmental interest accompanied by the least restrictive means possible to further that interest.[712]

Kentucky required school boards, at the beginning of academic years or on enrollment, to notify parents of health and mental health services provided about to human sexuality, contraception, or family planning. In addition, the law directs boards their employees to respect parental rights to make decisions regarding the upbringing and control of their children through procedures encouraging students to discuss mental or physical health or life issues with their parents.[713]

Montana adopted an extensive statement of parental rights over the upbringing of their children, including to choose public, private, faith-based, or home schooling; over student records; to consent before school employee make audio-visual recordings of their children; to provide consent for biometric scanning or DNA recording; to opt out of personal evaluation, analysis, survey, or data collection, except data for student's educational records; and excused absences for religious reasons.[714] In a second parental rights act, Montana addressed permission needed for participation in extracurricular and other activities; the use of pronouns not matching birth genders; and directing requiring boards to adopt policies promoting parental involvement in the schools their children attend.[715]

---

[711] 2023 Wyo. Sess. Laws Act No. 38, Ch. No. 82, H.B. 31.
[712] 2023 Ala. Acts 555, H.B. 6.
[713] 2023 Ky. Acts Ch. 132, SB 150.
[714] 2023 Mont. Laws H.B. 676.
[715] 2023 Mont. Laws S.B. 518.

North Carolina adopted a Parents' Bill of Rights starting with the right to direct the education and care of their children. Other rights include a prohibition on biometric scans or collection of blood of their young and limitations on taking videos of their children.[716] North Dakota adopted an act stating that parents retain the right and duty to exercise primary control over the care, supervision, upbringing, and education of their children; that pupils have the right to protection from abuse and neglect; and the state has a compelling interest in preventing, assessing, investigating, addressing, and prosecuting abuse and neglect.[717]

Tennessee called for the adoption of policies allowing parents or legal guardians access to review all surveys, analyses, or evaluations, prior to being administered to the children in their care; this requires LEAs to obtain prior written, informed, and voluntarily signed consent of a parents or legal guardian before children participates in these matters if they have not reached the 18.[718]

Five states adopted nine acts regarding First Amendment religious rights for parents and students. Arkansas adopted a Religious Viewpoint Anti-Discrimination Act, which required boards to treat public school students' voluntary expressions of religious viewpoints on otherwise permissible subjects in the same manner they treats voluntary expression on secular or other viewpoint on otherwise permissible topics.[719] Arkansas also prohibited discussion by state government entities based on an individual's religious beliefs and adopted a state-level Religious Freedom Restoration Act, which articulated using the rule in *Wisconsin v. Yoder*[720] to deploy higher scrutiny by the court in analyzing claims under the act.[721]

Idaho asserted that no public colleges, public school boards, or charter schools may take adverse action against persons for praying in school at any time they are otherwise free to engage in personal conversation or other personal conduct. Likewise, those colleges and schools may not act against individuals who refuse to participate in prayers.[722] Idaho required public schools and

---

716 2023 N.C. Sess. Laws Ch. 106, S.B. 49.
717 2023 N.D. Laws H.B. No. 1362.
718 2023 Tenn. Pub. Acts Ch. No. 353, S.B. No. 1443, Subs. H.B. No. 727.
719 2023 Ark. Acts 778, S.B. 556.
720 406 U.S. 205 (1972).
721 2023 Ark. Acts 773, H.B. 1615.
722 2023 Idaho Sess. Laws Ch. 239, H.B. No. 182.

institutions of higher education to display the National Motto, "In God We Trust," with the U.S. or state flag.[723] Louisiana mandated the display of the National Motto in public elementary, secondary, and postsecondary education classrooms.[724] Louisiana authorized public high schools to offer an introductory course on the history and literature of the Bible.[725]

Montana permitted students to read from the Bible or other religious material during free reading time; further, if schools, classes, or courses have requirements for self-selected reading, pupils must be allowed to read from the Bible or other religious materials. The act directed that prayer is permitted in a school, on school grounds and at school-sponsored events, but persons may not be compelled to pray and that school days may begin with prayer.[726] Montana specified that students cannot be prohibited from initiating or participating in conversations about religion, religious beliefs, or religious practices with peers or teachers.[727] Utah directed that athletic associations and educational organizations may not prohibit student athletes from wearing religious clothing or other clothing displaying their athlete's beliefs while participating. The act obligates athletic associations and educational entities to provide the clothing if the association or entity requires clothing to be a certain material, style, or color.[728]

Twelve states enacted 14 provisions arising from the culture issues surrounding gender identity. Arkansas adopted a "given name" act, which prohibited requiring public school employees to use persons' preferred pronoun, name, or title without parental consent.[729] California provided for the sealing of records for gender changes, sex identifiers, or name changes.[730]

Florida mandated exclusive use of restrooms and changing facilities by gender and prohibited persons from willfully entering those designated for the opposite sex.[731] Florida next added a definition of "sex" as meaning the clarification of a person as either female or male, based on the organization of such person for a

---

[723] 2023 Idaho Sess. Laws Ch. 148, H.B. No. 202.
[724] 2023 La. Acts No. 264, H.B. No. 8.
[725] 2023 La. Acts No. 215, H.B. No. 68.
[726] 2023 Mont. Laws H.B. 745.
[727] 2023 Mont. Laws H.B. 744.
[728] 2023 Utah Laws H.B. 163.
[729] 2023 Ark. Acts 542, H.B. 1468.
[730] 2023 Cal. Stat. Ch. 221, A.B. No. 223.
[731] 2023 Fla. Laws Ch. 106, H. 1521.

specific reproductive role, as revealed by the individual's sex chromosomes, naturally occurring sex hormones, and internal and external genitalia present at birth. The definition was followed by direction that personal titles and pronouns will correspond to the definition above.[732]

Idaho required all public school restrooms or changing facilities accessible by multiple persons at the same time to be designated for use by males or females only may only be used by members of those sexes. Sex was defined in the final clause as "generally recognizable at birth that defines an individual as male or female." The act provided a private cause of action for students who encounter persons of the opposite sex in those facilities.[733] Illinois provided that any multiple occupancy restroom may be identified as an all-gender multiple-occupancy restroom and designated for use by persons of any gender.[734]

Iowa prohibited persons from entering single and multiple occupancy restrooms or changing areas and other facilities in elementary and secondary schools not corresponding with their biological sexes.[735] Kansas required boards to provide separate accommodations for students of each biological sex on overnight school -sponsored trips.[736] Montana defined "sex" in terms of chromosomes, XX and XY, and production of either male gametes or sperm or female gametes as eggs, relating this definition to a separate provision prohibiting males from participating in female sports.[737] Montana also specified that it is not an unlawful discriminatory practice for students to call peers by the student's legal name or refer to them by their sexes.[738]

New York added gender identity or expression as a protected class for purposes of its human rights law.[739] North Dakota adopted provisions relating to accommodations for transgender students, specifying that school boards, public schools, and/or their teachers may not adopt policies requiring or prohibiting individuals from using students' preferred gender pronouns, but forbidding pupils

---

[732] 2023 Fla. Laws Ch. 105, H. 1069.
[733] 2023 Idaho Sess. Laws Ch. 50, H.B. No. 92.
[734] 2023 Ill. Laws P.A. 103-518, HB 1286.
[735] 2023 Iowa Acts SF 482.
[736] 2023 Kan. Sess. Laws HB 2138.
[737] 2023 Mont. Laws S.B. 458.
[738] 2023 Mont. Laws H.B. 361.
[739] 2023 N.Y. Laws Ch. 305, A. 7355.

from using restrooms not coinciding with their biological sexes.[740] Tennessee defined "sex" as a person's immutable biological sex as determined by anatomy and genetics existing at the time of birth and evidence of a person's biological sex.[741] Utah ordered schools and governing board to ensure parental rights to access the educational record of their children, including on gender identity, prohibiting changes of gender identity in records without their consent.[742]

Five states passed acts about data privacy. Arkansas adopted a Student Data Vendor Security Act to increase security and transparency in the sharing and use of student data with and by third-party vendors. The act specified that contracts with vendors must include provisions safeguarding the privacy and security of personally identifiable student information.[743] Florida forbade operators who manage student data from knowingly providing personal information about students.[744] Montana removed the opt-in requirement for releasing student assessment data, such as ACT scores, to institutions of higher education and scholarship organizations.[745]

North Dakota specified that information that reasonably may identify minor children, including their names, dates of birth, addresses, parental names, and images obtained by its Education Standards and Practices Board during disciplinary actions is exempt from disclosure under the public records law.[746] Utah prohibited education entities from sharing student data with federal agencies except as required by federal law.[747]

Twelve states enrolled 17 bills on student food and meals. Arkansas created the means for students qualified to receive reduced-price meals to receive free meals at school.[748] California loosened restrictions on students receiving additional entrées from second meals during school days.[749] Colorado provided funding to supplement school meals budgets under its "health school meals"

---

[740] 2023 N.D. Laws H.B. No. 1522.
[741] 2023 Tenn. Pub. Acts Ch. No. 486, S.B. No. 1440, Subs. H.B. No. 239.
[742] 2023 Utah Laws S.B. 100.
[743] 2023 Ark. Acts 754, H.B. 1757.
[744] 2023 Fla. Laws Ch. 170, S. 662.
[745] 2023 Mont. Laws S.B. 480.
[746] 2023 N.D. Laws S.B. No. 2099.
[747] 2023 Utah Laws S.B. 265.
[748] 2023 Ark. Acts 656, S.B. 477.
[749] 2023 Cal. Stat. Ch. 318, A.B. No. 95.

program.[750] Connecticut directed its Department of Agriculture to consult with its state DOE to administer the local food for the school incentive program.[751] Connecticut obligated school boards to post information online about the nutritional value of school meals and to permit lunch providers to serve whole milk.[752]

Louisiana ordered school lunch programs to provide free breakfast and lunch for all eligible students while appropriating funds to make up the excess costs.[753] Maine established a grant program for school lunches for meal equipment and program improvements.[754] Maine encouraged flexibility in mealtimes and packaging of meals to send home with students to maximize the distribution of free summer lunches for children.[755] Maine next allowed the Local Foods Fund for Public Schools to be used for processed and value-added Maine food products.[756]

New Jersey obligated eligible nonpublic schools to provide meals for all students under a state anti-hunger act.[757] New Jersey required schools to remind parents continuously that school lunch applications may be submitted at any time during school years, specifying that the application must be submitted in hard copy.[758] New Jersey permitted school boards to transfer food waste to other schools to compost food waste.[759] New Mexico obligated schools to offer one breakfast and lunch at no cost to students who request meals without consideration of the their eligibility for free or reduced-price meal.[760]

North Dakota prohibited a USDA-subsidized school lunch programs from denying or substituting full meals to students requesting one, forbidding them from identifying or stigmatizing pupils who receives free or reduced-price meals or incur debt in their school lunch accounts.[761] Vermont directed school board to offer the same breakfast and lunch program to each qualified student under the National School Lunch Act and Child Nutrition

[750] 2023 Colo. Sess. Laws S.B. 221.
[751] 2023 Conn. Acts 167, Subst. S.B. No. 1, § 26.
[752] 2023 Conn. Acts 159, H.B. No. 6880.
[753] 2023 La. Acts No. 305, H.B. No. 282.
[754] 2023 Me. Laws Ch. 457, H.P. 755, L.D. 1183.
[755] 2023 Me. Laws Ch. 181, H.P. 594, L.D. 947.
[756] 2023 Me. Laws Ch. 101, S.P. 392, L.D. 921.
[757] 2023 N.J. Pub. Laws c. 336, A. 5684.
[758] 2023 N.J. Pub. Laws c. 530, S. 530.
[759] 2023 N.J. Pub. Laws c. 193, S. 3153.
[760] 2023 N.M. Laws Ch. 30, SB 4.
[761] 2023 N.D. Laws H.B. No. 1494.

Act.[762] Virginia dictated that at any back-to-school night parents of enrolled students receive information about free and reduced-price school meals.[763] Washington obligated boards to provide breakfast and lunch each school day to students who requests either or both, at no charge and without consideration of their eligibility for free or reduced-price meals.[764]

Six states assured the availability of menstrual products in schools. California expanded the provision of free menstrual products for grades 6-12 to include grades 3-12.[765] Florida authorized school boards to make menstrual hygiene products available at no charge in their schools.[766] Minnesota directed school boards and charter schools to provide students in grades 4-12 with access to menstrual products at no charge.[767] New Jersey directed its state DOE to reimburse schools for the costs of providing free menstrual products.[768]

New York dictated that menstrual products to be offered free in nonpublic schools.[769] Moreover, New York replaced all instances of the words or variations of the words feminine hygiene products and sanitary napkins with the words menstrual products and pads.[770] Mississippi enabled local boards to make feminine hygiene products available, at no cost to students, in bathrooms or nurses offices in schools housing grades 6 through 12.[771]

Four states acted to ensure that harmful materials do not reach students. Arkansas enables schools to prevent materials harmful to minors from being accessed by the internet.[772] Kentucky defined what is "harmful to minors," directing local school boards to adopt complaint resolution policies to address parental complaints about materials harmful to minors.[773] Louisiana ordered libraries to adopt and implement policy language to limit the access of minors to sexually explicit materials.[774] Mississippi

---

762 2023 Vt. Laws Ch. No. 64, H. 165.
763 2023 Va. Acts Ch. 125, H.B. 2021.
764 2023 Wash Laws. Ch. 379, 2nd Subst. H.B. 1238.
765 2023 Cal. Stat. Ch. 421, A.B. No. 230.
766 2023 Fla. Laws Ch. 100, H. 389.
767 2023 Minn. Laws Ch. 55, sec. 1, HF 2497.
768 2023 N.J. Pub. Laws c. 147, S. 1221.
769 2023 N.Y. Laws Approval Memo. 31, S. 5913.
770 2023 N.Y. Laws Ch. 650, S. 1522.
771 2023 Miss. Laws HB 1264.
772 2023 Ark. Acts 612, S.B. 66.
773 2023 Ky. Acts Ch. 120, SB 5.
774 2023 La. Acts No. 436, S.B. No. 7.

regulates pornographic media exposure to children in K-12 schools as well as digital and online resources provided by K-12 vendors.[775]

Two states acted to help students when they are transitioning into new schools. California added provisions to assure that students classified as pupils participating in newcomer programs receive assistance to be integrated into their curricula.[776] Hawaii required the parents or legal guardians of minors, rather than the students, to produce the necessary student records when transferring schools, but clarified that emancipated minors may produce their own records.[777]

Three states passed legislation on the availability of materials in libraries and delineated procedures for their removal. Indiana required the governing bodies of school corporations or charter schools to have created catalogues of materials available in their school libraries along with procedure for parents or guardians to request that materials be removed from them.[778] Iowa mandated that K-12 library programs have only age-appropriate materials and set up a series of sanctions for violations of this standard culminate with loss of their licenses.[779] Maryland added to a provision delineating three conditions when public, previously free association, libraries, or school, college, or university libraries may disclose individuals' circulation records: if necessary for their reasonable operations, with the persons' written consent, or by subpoena or court order.[780]

Three states adopted acts supporting student voting rights. Louisiana designated the first Tuesday after the first Monday in May annually as high school seniors voter registration day.[781] New York directed local boards of education, BOCES, charter schools, and nonpublic schools to adopt policies to promote student voter registration.[782] Tennessee obligated high schools to inform each senior that on reaching the age of 18 they may be eligible to vote while providing them with information from the secretary of state about voter eligibility and registration.[783]

---

[775] 2023 Miss. Laws HB 1315.
[776] 2023 Cal. Stat. Ch. 342, A.B. No. 714.
[777] 2023 Haw. Sess. Laws Act 168, HB 1045.
[778] 2023 Ind. Acts P.L. 234, HB 1447.
[779] 2023 Iowa Acts SF 496.
[780] 2023 Md. Laws Ch. 737, S.B. 846.
[781] 2023 La. Acts No. 79, H.B. No. 316.
[782] 2023 N.Y. Laws Ch. 478, S. 1733.
[783] 2023 Tenn. Pub. Acts Ch. No. 444, S.B. No. 346, Subs. H.B. No. 933.

Two states addressed school recesses. Louisiana called for public schools to provide at least one recess period per day in K-5 schools.[784] Washington directed that for each school day exceeding five hours in duration public schools must provide a minimum of 30 minutes of recess for students in K-5 and grade 6 who attend an elementary school.[785]

Two states acted to improve case management for foster students. Colorado created the Fostering Success voucher program in its state DOE, to provide vouchers to foster students and provide developmentally appropriate case management for eligible recipients.[786] Colorado called for the continuation of school placement for foster children as their housing situations change.[787]

Other measures adopted by legislative bodies in 2023 on parental and student rights are detailed as follows. Arkansas prohibited public and charter schools from entering transactions to offer or provide abortion referrals as a fourth abortion-related prohibition.[788] Arkansas next prohibited discrimination based on natural or cultural hairstyles in public schools.[789] California specified the rights of parents to audio record meetings for Section 504 planning.[790]

In the first of three acts Florida required local boards to inform students and parents of accelerated, academic, and career planning options.[791] Florida ordered boards to act annually to certify and provide evidence that instruction related to African American history does not indoctrinate a particular viewpoint; this law appeared to create a rebuttable presumption with school boards having the burden of production and proof that instruction does not indoctrinate.[792] Florida obligated schools to provide for students with disabilities to be retained in kindergarten at the discretion of parents.[793] Florida mandated that schools create comprehensive plans for student progression.[794] Georgia required public schools

---

[784] 2023 La. Acts No. 219, H.B. No. 121.
[785] 2023 Wash Laws. Ch. 272, Subst. S.B. 5257.
[786] 2023 Colo. Sess. Laws S.B. 82.
[787] 2023 Colo. Sess. Laws H.B. 1089.
[788] 2023 Ark. Acts 653, S.B. 466.
[789] 2023 Ark. Acts 514, H.B. 1576.
[790] 2023 Cal. Stat. Ch. 81, A.B. No. 87.
[791] 2023 Fla. Laws Ch. 89, S. 196.
[792] 2023 Fla. Laws Ch. 103, H. 551.
[793] 2023 Fla. Laws Ch. 91, S. 290.
[794] 2023 Fla. Laws Ch. 91, S. 290.

to provide parents and guardians of students under 18 with water safety information annually.[795]

Hawaii declared that when police officers have custody of children under age 8, they shall have contact with legal counsel and a parent or legal guardian.[796] Illinois dictated that school boards provide parents of students with disabilities with information about their career and technical education opportunities.[797] Minnesota funded student-parent support initiative grants to assist expectant parents and parents or legal guardians of young children.[798] Nebraska allowed parents and guardians to challenge the appointment of hearing officers for suspension and expulsion hearings due to perceived bias.[799]

New York directed schools to expand access to advanced courses to improve educational equity by providing early notification to parents and students of the benefits and opportunities offered in these classes as well as automatic enrollment opportunities.[800] New York also required boards of education or trustees serving high school students with no districtwide or school building peer-selected student governments to establish at least one student government organization in each district or school.[801]

In the first of a trilogy of laws North Dakota added failure to demonstrate proficiency in a standards-based grading system to a list of failures triggering inquiries into whether, after two years of high school, students should be provided an alternative curricula.[802] North Dakota allowed students with military connections, medical conditions rendering them unable to attend school physically, or moving in or out-of-state to have their educational needs accommodated through virtual instruction.[803] North Dakota permitted boards to adopt policies enabling private tutors to provide services on school premises.[804] Oklahoma

---

[795] 2023 Ga. Laws Act 343, H.B. 402.
[796] 2023 Haw. Sess. Laws 180, HB 781.
[797] 2023 Ill. Laws P.A. 103-181, HB 3224.
[798] 2023 Minn. Laws Ch. 41, sec.16, HF 2073.
[799] 2023 Neb. Laws LB 705.
[800] 2023 N.Y. Laws Ch. 355, A. 514.
[801] 2023 N.Y. Laws Ch. 357, S. 1732.
[802] 2023 N.D. Laws H.B. No. 1131.
[803] 2023 N.D. Laws H.B. No. 1132.
[804] 2023 N.D. Laws S.B. No. 2284, sec. 5.

required its state DOE to adopt a form to report on student homelessness.[805]

Oregon directed its state DOE to develop and implement statewide education plans for students who are Native Hawaiian or Pacific Islanders.[806] Oregon adopted provisions on surveys administered in schools to give parents and guardians the right to review the materials and to decline participating, also affording students the right to refuse to take part, and to describe procedures for communicating the outcome of surveys.[807] Tennessee obligated LEAs and public charter school to provide high school seniors, rather than all students generally, opportunities to take nationally recognized assessments.[808]

A new act in Utah obligated LEAs to provide an annual assurance to its state BOE that their professional learning, administrative functions as well as instructional and curricular materials are consistent with principles of individual freedom listed in its provisions.[809] Utah forbade the use of "vaccine passports" for access to public accommodations, with exceptions for school vaccines and those provided by governance authority of public institutions of higher education.[810] Utah addressed parental engagement by acknowledging their right to access to school records, directing its state BOE to create the ability to track records through information management systems while providing a parent portal for data mandated by statute, including school comparison data. The act further called for the appointment of parental engagement specialists.[811] West Virginia passed an act to support and define the free speech rights of student journalists in public high schools.[812]

Program Development

This section lists and describes legislation related to program development in the 2023 legislative year beginning with career technology, career readiness, and apprenticeship programs, as

---

[805] 2023 Okla. Sess. Laws H.B. No. 1029.
[806] 2023 Or. Laws Ch. 530, H.B. 3144.
[807] 2023 Or. Laws Ch. 505, H.B. 2656.
[808] 2023 Tenn. Pub. Acts Ch. No. 439, S.B. No. 198, Subs. H.B. No. 250.
[809] 2023 Utah Laws H.B. 427.
[810] 2023 Utah Laws H.B. 131.
[811] 2023 Utah Laws H.B. 249.
[812] 2023 W. Va. Acts Ch. 175, S.B. 121.

described below. Nine states approved 10 acts on career technology programs. Arkansas initiated the use of a weighted course credit system for career and technical education to assure equal academic recognition with college-bound students.[813] Connecticut created a working group to determine feasibility, cost, and planning for development of an aerospace advanced manufacturing high school.[814] Idaho established the Career Ready Students Program to create greater opportunities for career and technical education in grades 7-12.[815]

Minnesota enabled the creation of a Career and Technical Education Consortium to develop new career pathways and programs as well as to develop highly trained and knowledgeable students equipped with technical and workplace skills needed by regional employers; the consortium creates a conduit for grant funds.[816] Montana directed its state Superintendent of Public Instruction to allocate performance grants to career and technical student organizations including Future Farmers of America, Family Career and Community Leaders of America, and Distributive Education Clubs of American.[817] New Jersey required state agencies to promote the creation of career pathways for students in manufacturing.[818]

New Jersey then created an award program to recognize outstanding students in career and technical education.[819] North Dakota appropriated funds to its Department of Career and Technical Education for career exploration software.[820] South Dakota provided grants to its state DOE for supporting career and technical education.[821] Wyoming established competitive grants for public schools to purchase career and technical education supplies, materials, and equipment.[822]

Three states added acts about career and college readiness. Montana increased funding for advanced opportunity aid to accelerate career and college readiness of students, based on

---

[813] 2023 Ark. Acts 654, S.B. 470.

[814] 2023 Conn. Acts 167, Subst. S.B. No. 1, § 34.

[815] 2023 Idaho Sess. Laws Ch. 231, H.B. No. 267.

[816] 2023 Minn. Laws Ch. 55, sec. 6, HF 2497.

[817] 2023 Mont. Laws H.B. 382.

[818] 2023 N.J. Pub. Laws c. 268, S. 659.

[819] 2023 N.J. Pub. Laws c. 47, A. 1791.

[820] 2023 N.D. Laws H.B. No. 1232.

[821] 2023 S.D. Laws S.B. 59.

[822] 2023 Wyo. Sess. Laws Act No. 94, Ch. No. 164, H.B. 33.

learning plans adopted by school boards.[823] Oregon directed its state DOE to study how to increase access to advanced instruction, for the purpose of preparing students for college and careers.[824] Washington amended its "high school and beyond" planning function to prepare students for college or work by beginning the planning in seventh grade and attempting to standardize online functions to improve accessibility for students throughout the state.[825]

Eight states enrolled bills about apprenticeship programs. Colorado adopted an Apprenticeship Navigator Program to be piloted in one rural and one non-rural district. The navigators are full-time employees of its state DOE who develop information materials, construct a job board for apprenticeship programs, and find ways to incorporate registered apprenticeship programs into the state's career planning.[826] Connecticut permitted local boards to partner with employers in aerospace or aviation industries to provide apprenticeships.[827] Florida provided a tax credit for businesses that employ apprentices.[828] Montana granted a tax credit for employers providing education and training in trades in the amount of $2,000 per employee, capped at $25,000 annually.[829]

Iowa passed legislation to support the adoption of apprenticeships including an act to create an Office of Apprenticeship in the Department of Workforce Development.[830] Kansas expanded apprenticeships with businesses, healthcare organizations, and nonprofit organizations through tax credits and grants, and the development of teaching apprenticeships through a grant program.[831] Washington required its office of the Superintendent of Public Instruction and Educational Service District to establish a regional apprenticeship preparation pilot program.[832] Wyoming directed its Department of Workforce

---

[823] 2023 Mont. Laws H.B. 257.
[824] 2023 Or. Laws Ch. 186, S.B. 736.
[825] 2023 Wash Laws. Ch. 271, 2nd Subst. S.B. 5243.
[826] 2023 Colo. Sess. Laws H.B. 1212.
[827] 2023 Conn. Acts 167, Subst. S.B. No. 1, § 28.
[828] 2023 Fla. Laws Ch. 81, S. 240. *See also*, companion bills 2023 Fla. Laws Ch. 245, S. 196 and 2023 Fla. Laws Ch. 89 S. 2502.
[829] 2023 Mont. Laws H.B. 245.
[830] 2023 Iowa Acts SF 318.
[831] 2023 Kan. Sess. Laws HB 2292.
[832] 2023 Wash Laws. Ch. 128, 2nd Subst. H.B. 1013.

Services to provide information to secondary students on apprenticeship and on-the-job training programs.[833]

Seven states adopted programs on reading literacy while one repealed a program to move to another system of addressing the teaching of reading. Georgia adopted the Early Literacy Act, built on the science of reading, defined as the body of research identifying evidence-based approaches of explicitly and systematically teaching students to read, including foundational literacy skills to enable children to develop reading skills needed to meet state standards. The act ordered its state BOE to establish policies, rules and regulations necessary to implement metrics for measuring literacy and approve high-quality instructional materials for teaching reading in grades K-3.[834] Illinois directed its state BOE to adopt and make available a rubric by which boards may evaluate, select, and implement evidence-based, culturally inclusive core reading instruction programs.[835]

Indiana enabled its state BOE to prepare and submit a report on the adoption of the science of reading including its five essential components in reading instruction: phonemic awareness, phonics, fluency, vocabulary, and comprehension.[836] Kentucky established a commonwealth-wide reading research center.[837] New Hampshire allowed its state DOE to employ a staff member who is a reading specialist.[838] New Mexico mandated that the reading materials fund in the state treasury be used to purchase elementary literacy materials that are aligned to the science of reading.[839] Oklahoma authorized the creation of a pilot program to employ a literacy instruction team in its state DOE.[840] Utah repealed its Interventions for Reading Difficulties program.[841]

Four states passed five measures on behavioral and mental health. Delaware adopted a provision to provide more behavioral health supports to school boards and charter schools after a school-connected traumatic event, such as the death of a student or

[833] 2023 Wyo. Sess. Laws Act No. 23, Ch. No. 42, S.F. 78.
[834] 2023 Ga. Laws Act 9, S.B. 538 § 3.
[835] 2023 Ill. Laws P.A. 103-402, SB 2243.
[836] 2023 Ind. Acts P. L. 243, HB 1558. *See also*, 2023 Ind. Acts P.L. 245, HB 1590.
[837] 2023 Ky. Acts Ch. 55, SB 156.
[838] 2023 N.H. Laws Ch. 47, HB 604.
[839] 2023 N.M. Laws Ch. 165, HB 481.
[840] 2023 Okla. Sess. Laws S.B. No. 1118.
[841] 2023 Utah Laws H.B. 182.

educator.[842] Missouri changed the name of the one-half credit in health education required by its state BOE to health and family education, directing it to convene a work group to develop and recommend performance standards and curricula in health and family education with an emphasis on behavioral health.[843] Nebraska ordered each administrator, teacher, paraprofessional school nurse, and counselor to receive behavior awareness training, updated annually.[844] Nebraska established a mental health training program.[845] Utah allowed behavioral support personnel to work with school mental health professionals and required its state BOE to provide guidance to LEAs for staffing structure and support.[846]

Three states addressed early childhood programming, while five passed measures about prekindergarten and kindergarten programming. Maine directed its DOE to study the Educare model for publicly funded statewide early childhood education programs and report its findings to a legislative committee.[847] Nevada funded a grant program through the Early Childhood Literacy and Readiness account to support early childhood learning.[848] Tennessee obligated its state DOE to conduct a statewide needs analysis for preschool education, directing it to create a task force to assist in developing a strategic plan for preschool education.[849]

Illinois moved back to 2027-2028 a directive to establish all-day kindergarten.[850] Oregon renamed its prekindergarten program a "prenatal to kindergarten program" to reflect the expansion of its purposes and goals.[851] Rhode Island ordered school boards to provide full-day kindergarten.[852] Utah made all-day kindergarten available in all LEAs with the option remaining for half-day kindergarten.[853] Washington established a transition to

---

[842] 2023 Del. Laws HB 4.
[843] 2023 Mo. Laws H.B. No. 447.
[844] 2023 Neb. Laws LB 705.
[845] 2023 Neb. Laws LB 705.
[846] 2023 Utah Laws H.B. 411.
[847] 2023 Me. Laws Ch. 116, H.P. 453, L.D. 684.
[848] 2023 Nev. Stat. Ch. 387, AB 400.
[849] 2023 Tenn. Pub. Acts Ch. No. 340, S.B. No. 355, Subs. H.B. No. 1150.
[850] 2023 Ill. Laws P.A. 103-410, HB 2396.
[851] 2023 Or. Laws Ch. 547, H.B. 3435.
[852] 2023 R.I. Pub. Laws S.B. 1090.
[853] 2023 Utah Laws H.B. 477.

kindergarten program to assist students of kindergarten age but who are not ready for it.[854]

Two states added provisions supporting dual language programs. Illinois asked its advisory council on bilingual education to report to its general assembly on how to provide incentives for dual language instruction in schools.[855] Utah added funding for its dual language program and prohibited LEAs from providing foreign language instruction by seeking or accepting funding from restricted foreign entities.[856]

Two states sought more support for English language learner (ELL) programs. Utah directed its state BOE to allocate funding for instructional materials and licenses used for ELL instruction and support.[857] Virginia directed its DOE to convene a stakeholder work group to make recommendations to assist ELL students to obtain access to paid, work-based learning programs.[858]

Other legislation occurring in 2023 related to program development is described as follows. Arkansas directed its Division of Elementary and Secondary Education to create an agricultural education pilot program in public elementary schools.[859] Colorado created an adult high school program in its state BOE for students aged 21 and older, permitting it to develop online and face-to-face courses, in consultation with a nonprofit organization.[860] Colorado revised a program for a Student Leadership Institute, setting specific criteria for student selection.[861] Colorado adopted a "train-the-trainer" training framework to develop educators into subject matter experts who can teach peers to improve the teaching of mathematics.[862]

Connecticut called for the establishment of a family resource center in each elementary school.[863] Florida renamed an early childhood music education program to recognize its graduation from "pilot" status.[864] Kentucky established the Kentucky Guard Youth Challenge Program in its Department of Military Affairs as

[854] 2023 Wash Laws. Ch. 420, H.B. 1550.
[855] 2023 Ill. Laws P.A. 103-362, HB 3822.
[856] 2023 Utah Laws H.B. 161.
[857] 2023 Utah Laws H.B. 154.
[858] 2023 Va. Acts Ch. 480, S.B. 1430.
[859] 2023 Ark. Acts 243, H.B. 1336.
[860] 2023 Colo. Sess. Laws S.B. 3.
[861] 2023 Colo. Sess. Laws S.B. 86.
[862] 2023 Colo. Sess. Laws H.B. 1231.
[863] 2023 Conn. Acts 167, Subst. S.B. No. 1, § 4.
[864] 2023 Fla. Laws Ch. 168, S. 478.

an alternative educational program in which student attendees are marked present at school while attending the program.[865] Missouri directed its Department of Elementary and Secondary Education to select language development milestones to develop resources for parents in addition to monitoring and tracking expressive and receptive language acquisition and developmental stages for children who are deaf or hard of hearing.[866]

Montana created a program with grant funds to assist children aging out of foster care to meet their educational, vocational, and professional goals without accruing personal debt.[867] Nebraska directed its state DOE, Department of Health and Human Services, Office of Probation Administration, and state court administration to enter into a memorandum of agreement for data sharing on students under jurisdiction of the juvenile courts for system-wide coordination of programming.[868] Nevada appropriated funds to support the state Center for Civic Engagement in connection with its role in civic education programs at the elementary, middle school, and high school levels.[869]

New Jersey created a pilot program in its state DOE to assist high school seniors transitioning to higher education.[870] Oklahoma amended requirements for a state-private sector initiative for at-risk students to change the private sector match ratio from a 2–1, to a 1.5–1 basis.[871] Oregon required its State University Extension Service to collaborate with its state DOE to identify to collect student data about the maintenance of outdoor school programs.[872] Pennsylvania initiated an Opportunity Scholarship Program, a tax-credit based savings program beginning in kindergarten and continuing through high school until students are ready to enter college.[873]

Tennessee enabled LEAs to conduct summer learning camps and after-school learning mini-camps annually instead of only in the summers in 2021 and 2022.[874] Utah provided block grant

---

865 2023 Ky. Acts Ch. 151, HB 244.
866 2023 Mo. Laws H.B. No. 447.
867 2023 Mont. Laws H.B. 482.
868 2023 Neb. Laws LB 705, sec. 122.
869 2023 Nev. Stat. Ch. 238, SB 285.
870 2023 N.J. Pub. Laws c. 272, S. 2076.
871 2023 Okla. Sess. Laws (1st Spec. Sess.) S.B. No. 29.
872 2023 Or. Laws Ch. 526, H.B. 3037.
873 2023 Pa. Laws Act No. 33, H.B. 301, Sec. 10.1.
874 2023 Tenn. Pub. Acts Ch. No. 144, S.B. No. 249, Subs. H.B. No. 68.

funding for substance abuse prevention, gang prevention, and intervention programs.[875] Washington amended a grant program for assisting students who are homeless to provide examples of support which can be paid for from its funds.[876] Washington directed local boards to select a grade level to implement universal screening procedures for each student for the purpose of increasing equity in the identification of children who traditionally are not referred for highly capable programs and services; the legislation visualized a fast track for highly capable students.[877]

School Choice

This section details and describes school choice provisions adopted by state legislative bodies in 2023. Much of the school choice-related activity from year to year has addressed charter schools. This was the case again last year with 11 states enacting 12 bills about charter school approval and reauthorization. Alabama amended its charter school law to require local authorizers to reapply every five years to continue authorizing charter schools.[878] Georgia provided for transition of charter schools, from an alternative charter school to a state chartered special school, and designated a funding formula for the changed school.[879] Idaho amended charter school-enabling legislation to allow schools to contract with an educational services providers to offer comprehensive educational administration and management services.[880]

Illinois required any renewals of school charters to include union neutrality clauses.[881] Montana authorized the establishment of charter schools with its state BOE as the authorizing authority.[882] North Carolina gave authority for all the rules for the operation and approval of charter schools to its state BOE.[883] North Carolina also forbade its state BOE from considering any alleged impact on local school administrative units in the areas served by

---

[875] 2023 Utah Laws H.B. 16.
[876] 2023 Wash Laws. Ch. 386, H.B. 1622.
[877] 2023 Wash Laws. Ch. 265, Subst. S.B. 5072.
[878] 2023 Ala. Acts 420, H.B. 363.
[879] 2023 Ga. Laws Act 342, H.B. 87.
[880] 2023 Idaho Sess. Laws Ch. 268, H.B. No. 113.
[881] 2023 Ill. Laws P.A. 103-416, HB 1120.
[882] 2023 Mont. Laws H.B. 549.
[883] 2023 N.C. Sess. Laws Ch. 110, H.B. 618.

charter schools when deciding whether to grant, renew, amend, or terminate charters.[884] Oklahoma created a statewide charter board which to approve, review, supervision, and closure of such schools.[885]

Oregon added special procedures for approval in situations where a charter school applies for location in a non-sponsoring so that its board must give its written permission.[886] Tennessee extended the public charter school commission to June 30, 2026.[887] Utah added the board of trustees of a private, nonprofit accredited college or university in the state to the named entities empowered to authorize charter schools.[888] Wyoming changed the process for approval and renewal of charter schools by creating a state Charter School Authorizing Board.[889]

Readers' attention is drawn to the fact that five of the acts about charter school approval had the effect of it from the local to the state level; another two states added oversight for charter schools. Maine directed its Charter School Commission or its representative to provide an annual report to a legislative committee on the status of charter schools.[890] Washington created greater oversight for charter schools by adding more reporting requirements such as in achievement and the number of noncertificated staff as well as more training for administrators and governance boards.[891]

Four states wrestled with the revocation or dissolution of charter schools. New Hampshire established a committee to study the dissolution process for chartered public schools.[892] Tennessee provided an exemption for automatic revocation of public charter school agreements by removing the priority lists issued in 2022 and 2023 as a cause for revocation.[893] Utah adopted new procedures for closing charter schools.[894] West Virginia ensured the repayment of retirement contributions and delinquent retirement contributions

---

[884] 2023 N.C. Sess. Laws Ch. 107, H.B. 219.
[885] 2023 Okla. Sess. Laws S.B. No. 516.
[886] 2023 Or. Laws Ch. 163, S.B. 767.
[887] 2023 Tenn. Pub. Acts Ch. No. 106, S.B. No. 64, Subs. H.B. No. 230.
[888] 2023 Utah Laws S.B. 65
[889] 2023 Wyo. Sess. Laws Act No. 80, Ch. No. 179, S.B. 174.
[890] 2023 Me. Laws Ch. 183, H.P. 684, L.D. 1089.
[891] 2023 Wash Laws. Ch. 356, Subst. H.B. 1744
[892] 2023 N.H. Laws Ch. 90, HB 550.
[893] 2023 Tenn. Pub. Acts Ch. No. 290, H.B. No. 36, Subs. S.B. No. 881.
[894] 2023 Utah Laws H. B. 134.

for employees when charter school close or are succeeded by other entities.[895]

Five states added six acts about charter school buildings. Idaho exempted some charter schools from having to demonstrate strong academic results to qualify for the Public Charter School Facilities Program.[896] Indiana channeled more funds to support charter school facilities, calling for reporting by auditors about the use of the funds.[897] Florida revised its charter school criteria for receiving capital outlay funds.[898] New Jersey added charter schools to the list of beneficiaries for funding school building projects.[899]

West Virginia created a special revenue fund, the Charter School Stimulus Fund, to provide financial support for applicants and charter schools for start-up costs.[900] West Virginia clarified the access of charter schools to public school monies, particularly with respect to a school safety fund.[901] Wyoming required lease agreements for charter schools to identify the amount to be spent on major building maintenance separately from the total list of expenditures.[902]

Two states created new timelines for charter school approvals. Colorado set its new timeline for reviewing applications roughly at 18 months before projected opening of a charter schools.[903] Texas increased from 18 to 36 months the timeline needed for written notice to its commission before establishing new or expanded open-enrollment charter schools.[904]

Two states experimented with new types of schools of choice called community schools and community choice schools. Illinois allowed community schools to be private schools.[905] Montana enabled the creation of community choice schools and virtual community choice schools through local community choice commissions by local school boards. The legislation affords these

---

[895] 2023 W. Va. Acts Ch. 129, S.B. 453.
[896] 2023 Idaho Sess. Laws Ch. 118, S.B. No. 1042.
[897] 2023 Ind. Acts P.L. 189, SB 391.
[898] 2023 Fla. Laws Ch. 69, H. 1259.
[899] 2023 N.J. Pub. Laws c. 311, A. 4496.
[900] 2023 W. Va. Acts Ch.124, S.B. 47.
[901] 2023 W. Va. Acts Ch. 140, H.B. 3084.
[902] 2023 Wyo. Sess. Laws Act No. 77, Ch. No. 166, S.F. 83.
[903] 2023 Colo. Sess. Laws H.B. 1025.
[904] 2023 Tex. Gen. Laws H.B. No. 2109.
[905] 2023 Ill. Laws P.A. 103-265, SB 2391.

certain amounts of self-government in pursuit of the educational goals articulated in their charters.[906]

Four states altered tax credits for paying for nonpublic school expenses. Alabama amended the Alabama Accountability Act, a school choice bill to increase the number of qualifying schools participating in the program to increase the family income threshold to participate to 250% of the poverty level of $62,000 and allow students to continue in the program until the family's annual income exceeds 350% of $87,000 of the poverty level. The bill increased the maximum scholarship amount to $10,000 for all students instead of $5,000 to $10,000, depending on grade level.[907]

Louisiana raised the permissible individual income tax deduction for elementary and secondary school tuition for home school expenses, for fees, and other expenses for quality public educations from a maximum of $5,000 per child to $6,000 per child.[908] Oklahoma provided tax credits for taxpayers participating in parental school choice by paying tuition for nonpublic schooling.[909] Tennessee expanded the eligibility criteria for education savings accounts to include students zoned to attend LEAs identified as priority schools in 2015, 2017, 2018, and 2021.[910]

Arkansas passed three acts permitting students to transfer to a better school and another state permitted students to transfer to nonpublic schools. First, Arkansas amended its Opportunity Public School Choice Act to allow students older than 18 to transfer to a better-performing public school if the present public school is rated as in need of intensive support.[911] Arkansas then protected the rights of students to transfer under the Public Choice Act, except for transfers due to recruiting of athletes.[912] Third, Arkansas created an exception for kindergarten students who had attended a nonresident preschool for the prior year, so that their transfer does not count toward the 3% cap on participation in the Public School Choice Act.[913] New Hampshire enabled the designation by

---

[906] 2023 Mont. Laws H.B. 562.
[907] 2023 Ala. Acts 418, S.B. 263.
[908] 2023 La. Acts No. 423, H.B. No. 32.
[909] 2023 Okla. Sess. Laws H.B. No. 1934.
[910] 2023 Tenn. Pub. Acts Ch. No. 328, S.B. No. 12, Subs. H.B. No. 433.
[911] 2023 Ark. Acts 790, S.B. 570.
[912] 2023 Ark. Acts 768, S.B. 400.
[913] 2023 Ark. Acts129, H.B. 1185.

its state BOE that students may be served at nonpublic, not just public schools, due to manifest educational hardships.[914]

Three states enacted bills regarding homeschools or home-centered schools. Montana directed local school boards to enroll students into a public school setting on a part-time basis, while they are enrolled in a nonpublic school or homeschool.[915] Wyoming removed a restriction that a home-based educational program is restricted to only one family unit.[916] Utah allowed LEAs to provide a home-centered, school-supported enrollment option allowing students to complete a portion of coursework from home. However, the act prohibited home school students from participating in home-centered, school-sponsored programs.[917]

In the first of two other acts on school choice, Nebraska provided textbooks for K-12 students in nonpublic school.[918] Illinois amended its state Global Scholar Certification Program to allow it to be awarded to students in public or nonpublic high schools.[919]

School Safety

This section itemizes student discipline-related acts from legislatures and assemblies during the 2023 calendar year. It describes student discipline, substance abuse prevention, medication management, harassment, and school safety measures designed to provide security and safety for students.

Thirteen states enrolled 19 acts on student discipline policy. Arizona amended student discipline policy requirements by permitting two school days of suspensions with an aggregate of no more than 10 per year for students in grades K-4.[920] Arkansas adopted a Student Due Process and Protection Act revising procedural protections for discipline hearings referencing *Goss v. Lopez*[921] while incorporating subsequent Eighth Circuit decisions and a university-level disciplinary case from the Seventh

[914] 2023 N.H. Laws Ch. 59, SB 77.
[915] 2023 Mont. Laws H.B. 396.
[916] 2023 Wyo. Sess. Laws Act No. 13, Ch. No. 16, H.B. 70.
[917] 2023 Utah Laws H.B. 185.
[918] 2023 Neb. Laws LB 705.
[919] 2023 Ill. Laws P.A. 103-352, HB 3522.
[920] 2023 Ariz. Sess. Laws Ch. 176, H.B. 2460.
[921] 419 US. 565, 574 (1975).

Circuit.[922] Arkansas also repealed a requirement in the Digital Learning Act of 2013 that public school boards and charter schools must offer courses to expelled students.[923] California limited suspensions and expulsions of students in the lower grade levels for willful defiance of school authorities.[924]

Colorado created a task force to study the disproportionate application of disciplinary consequences, identify alternative approaches to discipline, and recommend legislative changes to address discipline.[925] Colorado rewrote a provision permitting the use of hearing officials for expulsion hearings and guiding procedural aspects of the hearings.[926] Illinois required that student alternative education plans must include information to parents or guardians about extracurricular activities which may be offered to pupils.[927]

Kentucky directed local boards to expel students for at least 12 months if the student makes threats that pose a danger to other students or staff. Superintendents are empowered to provide alternative consequences including different placements.[928] Michigan prohibited public school boards from expelling or suspending pupils for more than 10 school days for actions they took immediately preceding, immediately following, or that could be reasonably tied to incidents in which they reported being sexual assaulted or when staff members reported the same.[929] Montana provided that students may use reasonable and necessary physical force for self-protection or to help others if physically attacked.[930]

Nebraska directed school boards to establish dress code and grooming policies consistent with the model policy adopted by its state department, which incorporates the philosophy of limiting the loss of learning time due to suspensions. An interesting provision prohibited school staff from cutting students' hair.[931] Nebraska allowed parents and guardians to challenge the appointment of hearing officers for suspension and expulsion

---

922 2023 Ark. Acts 470, S.B. 365. The other case referenced in the act was *Doe v. Purdue Univ.*, 927 F.3d 652 (7th Cir. 2019).

923 2023 Ark. Acts 724, H.B. 1539.

924 2023 Cal. Stat. Ch. 597, S.B. No. 274.

925 2023 Colo. Sess. Laws S.B. 29.

926 2023 Colo. Sess. Laws H.B. 1291.

927 2023 Ill. Laws P.A. 103-473, SB 183.

928 2023 Ky. Acts Ch. 76, HB 538.

929 2023 Mich. Pub. Acts No. 51, H.B. No. 4125.

930 2023 Mont. Laws H.B. 450.

931 2023 Neb. Laws LB 298.

hearings due to perceived bias.[932] Nevada repealed a requirement for the use of restorative disciplinary practices in public schools, charter schools, and the University School for Profoundly Gifted Students, instead calling for progressive discipline plans based on restorative justice.[933]

In addition to coats Oklahoma added shoes, hand and head coverings, except religious head coverings, as other items which may be removed while conducting warrantless searches.[934] Pennsylvania permitted school entities to seek juvenile court jurisdiction when dealing with students whose behaviors impede the learning of themselves or others.[935] In a separate section, this act specified that the existence of behaviors impeding learning is not a sufficient rationale for interrupting special education services.[936] Pennsylvania substituted its Safe Schools Program, rather than adopting interventions designed to redirect youth who commit minor offenses in school from exclusionary disciplinary practices or formal processing in the juvenile justice system, while still holding them accountable for their actions.[937]

Tennessee released school director, or superintendents, from having to assign students in grades 7-12 who were suspended for more than 10 days or expelled for violent or threatened violent acts to alternative schools if such changes might endanger the safety of students or staff there.[938] Tennessee next added to the list of zero tolerance offenses for students bringing firearm to school, committing aggravated assaults or assaults causing injury to school employee or peers, unlawful possession of drugs or controlled substances, or threatening mass violence on school property or at school-related activities. The revised provision continued the authority of the directors to provide consequence on case-by-case bases.[939]

Five states banned corporal punishment while one gave parents waiver power, and another adopted procedural steps for its use. Colorado forbade school employees or volunteers from using

---

[932] 2023 Neb. Laws LB 705.
[933] 2023 Nev. Stat. Ch. 149, AB 285.
[934] 2023 Okla. Sess. Laws H.B. No. 1634.
[935] 2023 Pa. Laws Act No. 33, H.B. 301, Sec. 10.2.
[936] 2023 Pa. Laws Act No. 33, H.B. 301, Sec. 15.
[937] 2023 Pa. Laws Act No. 33, H.B. 301, Sec. 11.
[938] 2023 Tenn. Pub. Acts Ch. No. 279, S.B. No. 1069, Subs. H.B. No. 826.
[939] 2023 Tenn. Pub. Acts Ch. No. 299, H.B. No. 340, Subs. S.B. No. 190.

corporal punishment.[940] Idaho prohibited corporal punishment and disallowed restraint or seclusion as forms of discipline or classroom management.[941] Louisiana proscribed the use of corporal punishment in public school unless students' parents or legal guardians provides written consent for its use.[942] Maryland directed its state BOE not to issue approval certificates to schools lacking policies prohibiting corporal punishment.[943] New York banned the use of corporal punishment in schools as defined by its Commissioner of Education.[944]

Tennessee added procedural steps prior for administering corporal punishment including documenting actions educators take to address students' behavior, providing (presumably other) consequences to them to address their actions, consulting with their parents or guardians, and considering the need to conduct initial evaluations to determine whether children are eligible for special education services.[945] West Virginia rewrote provisions on classroom discipline to clarify that teachers may exclude unruly students from their classes while disciplinary control then rests with the principal. Educators may move students to other locations, including alternative classrooms or schools, but prohibiting corporal punishment. Officials must load records of disciplinary actions into a statewide data system with no repercussions permitted against teachers.[946]

Instead of disciplinary consequences Delaware mandated that students be referred to a school-based mental health or behavioral health specialists after the second unduplicated infraction resulting in out-of-school suspensions in a semester.[947] Nevada ordered the suspensions or expulsions of students in charter schools or its university school for the profoundly gifted to be consistent with the punishments in other public schools.[948]

Eight states enacted bills implementing training and locations of equipment to provide cardiopulmonary resuscitation (CPR) and the use of automated external defibrillators (AEDs). Alabama

---

[940] 2023 Colo. Sess. Laws H.B. 1191.
[941] 2023 Idaho Sess. Laws Ch. 246, H.B. No. 281.
[942] 2023 La. Acts No. 268, H.B. No. 242.
[943] 2023 Md. Laws Ch. 671, H.B. 185.
[944] 2023 N.Y. Laws Ch. 551, A. 5010.
[945] 2023 Tenn. Pub. Acts Ch. No. 275, S.B. No. 972, Subs. H.B. No. 995.
[946] 2023 W. Va. Acts Ch. 301, H.B. 2890.
[947] 2023 Del. Laws HB 174.
[948] 2023 Nev. Stat. Ch. 150, AB 330.

enacted the Tyrell Spencer Act obligating coaches to receive training and obey health and safety guidelines about sudden cardiac arrest. This act added to existing CPR and AED standards, charging its state BOE with approving training requirements, guidelines, information materials, directing its activities associations with providing training. Under the act's terms at the beginning of the 2024-2025 school year parents or guardian and student-athletes must sign cardiac prevention acknowledgements form prior to participating.[949]

Indiana called on coaches, extracurricular activity leaders, drama and music leaders, and band leaders to ensure that operating AEDs are in proximity to where they work.[950] Kentucky directed boards to obligate schools maintain portable AEDs in their middle and high school, at school-sponsored events, and to create policies and procedures guiding their use.[951] Louisiana mandated that AEDs must be on the premises of all educational institutions and at sponsored athletic events.[952] Mississippi created a grant program, administered by its Department of Health, to place AEDs in public and charter schools.[953]

New Mexico required coaches employed by school boards to be certificated in CPR and trained in the use of AEDs.[954] Texas ordered instruction in cardiopulmonary resuscitation and use of AEDs in public schools.[955] Virginia directed local boards to develop plans for the placement, care, and use of AEDs in every public elementary and secondary school.[956]

Ten states adopted 12 acts designed to protect students from opioid overdoses. Arkansas called for opioid overdose rescue kits to be located on the premises of its public high schools and state-supported institution of higher education.[957] California first encouraged schools to adopt opioid safety programs.[958] California then obligated educators to inform parents or guardians annually about the dangers of synthetic drugs.[959] Illinois ordered public and

---

[949] 2023 Ala. Acts 235, H.B. 45.
[950] 2023 Ind. Acts P.L. 187, SB 246.
[951] 2023 Ky. Acts Ch. 165, HB 331.
[952] 2023 La. Acts No. 234, S.B. No. 12.
[953] 2023 Miss. Laws SB 2750.
[954] 2023 N.M. Laws Ch. 178, SB 450.
[955] 2023 Tex. Gen. Laws H.B. No. 4375.
[956] 2023 Va. Acts Ch. 767, S.B. 1453.
[957] 2023 Ark. Acts 811, H.B. 1514.
[958] 2023 Cal. Stat. Ch. 856, S.B. No. 10.
[959] 2023 Cal. Stat. Ch. 123, A.B. No. 8889.

nonpublic schools to make reasonable efforts to stock opioid antagonists in anticipation of potential shortages of supply.[960] Illinois next directed its state BOE, in conjunction with its Department of Health Services and the Opioid Advisory Council, to develop and update substance abuse prevention and recovery resource materials for public elementary and secondary schools.[961] Mississippi authorized school authorities to store and administer opioid antagonists.[962]

Maine required public schools to offer training for secondary school students on the administration of naloxone hydrochloride.[963] Minnesota mandated that school boards and charter schools to maintain a supply of opiate antagonists or nasal naloxone at their school sites.[964] Oklahoma allowed schools to store and administer emergency opioid antagonists.[965] Oregon permitted prescribing, obtaining, storing, and administering short-acting opioid antagonists; although the measure speaks to uses in the larger society, educational entities qualify for the provisions.[966] South Dakota enabled employers to acquire and make available on their premises opioid antagonists dispensed or distributed by licensed health care professionals; as broadly stated, the act appears to include school board and postsecondary employers.[967] Texas directed school boards to adopt policies on maintenance, administration, and disposal of opioid antagonists.[968]

Three states passed legislation on protecting students from substance abuse. Colorado formed a Secondary School Substance Abuse Committee in its state DOE to provide means of identifying student substance abuse and refer students to treatment resources.[969] Washington required school boards to link their websites to information from the Department of Health to address substance use trends; overdose symptoms and responses; and the secure storage of prescription drugs, over-the-counter medications, and firearms and ammunition.[970] Wisconsin adopted operational

---

[960] 2023 Ill. Laws P.A. 103-348, HB 3428.
[961] 2023 Ill. Laws P.A. 103-399, SB 2223.
[962] 2023 Miss. Laws SB 2336.
[963] 2023 Me. Laws Ch. 460, S.P. 533, L.D. 1315.
[964] 2023 Minn. Laws Ch. 55, sec. 2, HF 2497.
[965] 2023 Okla. Sess. Laws S.B. No. 710.
[966] 2023 Or. Laws Ch. 593, H.B. 2395.
[967] 2023 S.D. Laws H.B. 1162.
[968] 2023 Tex. Gen. Laws S.B. No. 629.
[969] 2023 Colo. Sess. Laws H.B. 1008.
[970] 2023 Wash Laws. Ch. 173, H.B. 1230.

and planning grants for recovery high schools to support those designed for pupils in recovery from a substance use or mental health disorders coexisting with substance use disorders.[971]

Eight states added 12 acts on medications, other substances, and their management and administration. California called for schools to store epinephrine auto-injectors in accessible locations, permitting their use by volunteers and trained personnel.[972] California further allowed school officials to stock emergency albuterol inhalers and provided immunity for their administration.[973] Georgia mandated that school boards stock undesignated, ready-to-use glucagon to administer treatment for severe hypoglycemia.[974] Illinois obligated after-school programs to permit children with severe or potentially life-threatening allergies to possess, self-administer, and use epinephrine auto-injector or inhalers.[975] Illinois permitted public and nonpublic schools to maintain supplies of undesignated oxygen tanks in secure location to provide access for persons with developmental disabilities.[976]

New York directed schools to provide teachers with written information on the use of epinephrine auto-injectors.[977] Oklahoma allowed school boards to stock glucagon for diabetes management, subject to written permission from parents.[978] South Carolina rewrote its law authorizing the use of epinephrine auto-injectors in schools, now referring to it as the authorization to use "lifesaving medication," thus broadening the range of medications that may be used in emergency situations.[979] South Carolina permitted students to use sunscreen at school or at school events, with permission of parents.[980]

Virginia empowered licensed athletic trainers under contract with local school boards to administer albuterol, and exempted them from liability in administering albuterol.[981] Virginia amended another provision authorizing the possession and administration of epinephrine to assure an appropriate, weight-

---

[971] 2023 Wis. Laws Act 72, S.B. 267.
[972] 2023 Cal. Stat. Ch.588, A.B. No. 1651.
[973] 2023 Cal. Stat. Ch. 574, A.B. No. 1283.
[974] 2023 Ga. Laws Act 10, H.B. 440.
[975] 2023 Ill. Laws P.A. 103-438, HB 2949.
[976] 2023 Ill. Laws P.A. 103-196, HB 3613.
[977] 2023 N.Y. Laws Ch. 422, S. 209.
[978] 2023 Okla. Sess. Laws S.B. No. 147.
[979] 2023 S.C. Acts No. 47, H.B. 4122.
[980] 2023 S.C. Acts No. 21, S.B. 256.
[981] 2023 Va. Acts Ch. 569, H.B. 2429.

based dosage of the drug is available in residences in which family day homes operate.[982] Wisconsin replaced the term "epinephrine auto-injector" with "epinephrine delivery system" in a section allowing schools to administer it.[983]

Two states approved measures to protect students from allergens. Maryland required each county board, before the start of the 2024-2025 school year, to adopt and implement guidelines to reduce the risk of exposure to anaphylactic major food allergens in classrooms and commons areas.[984] Texas directed school food service personnel to receive training on protecting against allergies.[985]

Two states enacted legislation promoting the provision of health services in schools. Hawaii replaced the title of "school health aides" with "school health assistants," authorizing the latter to administer medications with the approval of a health care professional.[986] New Mexico initiated the creation and operation of school-based health centers in public schools.[987]

Two states advocated for the creation of individual health plans for students with specified medical conditions. Alabama directed its state BOE to create guidelines for students with adrenal insufficiency to assure they receive individual health plans including the presence of on-site nurses or trained unlicensed medical assistants before, during, and after school activities; a guarantee of inclusion on school activities; and access to injectable medication through school nurses or trained school employees.[988] Arkansas required the adoption of an individualized health plan to acknowledge and prepare for health care needs of a student diagnosed with a seizure disorder.[989]

Eight states adopted nine measures based on criminal law to dissuade perpetrators who might injure or commit crimes against students.[990] Alabama made it a Class B felony to discharge firearms on school property with exceptions provided, such as land leased from school system or situations where board approved

---

[982] 2023 Va. Acts Ch. 123, S.B. 1146; 2023 Va. Acts Ch. 122, H.B. 2140.
[983] 2023 Wis. Laws Act 27, S.B. 7.
[984] 2023 Md. Laws Ch. 770, H.B. 78.
[985] 2023 Tex. Gen. Laws S.B. No. 812.
[986] 2023 Haw. Sess. Laws Act 173, SB 1344.
[987] 2023 N.M. Laws Ch. 48, SB 397.
[988] 2023 Ala. Acts 75, S.B. 52.
[989] 2023 Ark. Acts 286, H.B. 1315.
[990] 2023 Ark. Acts 811, H.B. 1514.

events involve use of firearms.[991] Arkansas created the criminal offense of sexual indecency with a child.[992] Arkansas added to the criminal code the offense of furnishing obscene materials by a library.[993] Delaware made possession of a firearm in a school safety zone a class E felony.[994]

Kentucky defined "hazing" and established a Class D felony of hazing in the first degree and a Class A misdemeanor of hazing in the second degree.[995] . Mississippi adopted a new criminal law to regulate pornographic media exposure to children.[996] Tennessee made it a Class E felony for book publishers, distributors, or sellers to sell or distribute obscene matter knowingly to public K-12 school.[997] Washington added the crime of felony hazing to its criminal law.[998] West Virginia created a new criminal offense about sexual contact with, sexual intrusion, or sexual abuse of students by school employees.[999]

Three states instituted the duty to report offenses. Iowa permitted ombudsmen to investigate reports of violence in classrooms or on school property for licensed school employees and file reports to the state DOE and the Board of Educational Examiners. The act included a new section describing the procedures for reporting incidents of school violence.[1000] Tennessee added the Director of Schools as a person to whom a principal must report direct knowledge of assaults and batteries or vandalism by students on school property endangering the lives, health, or safety of others.[1001] Virginia transferred the duty to provide information about instances of felony or class 1 misdemeanors in schools, from the division superintendent to the person designated as its safety director.[1002]

Ten states adopted 13 acts on harassment and bullying. California ordered its state interscholastic federation to report and be available for hearings with legislative committees on racial

---

[991] 2023 Ala. Acts 370, H.B. 34.
[992] 2023 Ark. Acts 619, S.B. 270.
[993] 2023 Ark. Acts 372, S.B. 81.
[994] 2023 Del. Laws HB 201.
[995] 2023 Ky. Acts Ch. 110, SB 9.
[996] 2023 Miss. Laws SB 2346.
[997] 2023 Tenn. Pub. Acts Ch. No. 278, S.B. No. 1059, Subs. H.B. No. 841.
[998] 2023 Wash Laws. Ch. 196, H.B. 1002.
[999] 2023 W. Va. Acts Ch. 100, S.B. 187.
[1000] 2023 Iowa Acts HF 604.
[1001] 2023 Tenn. Pub. Acts Ch. No. 153, S.B. No. 1155, Subs. H.B. No. 892.
[1002] 2023 Va. Acts Ch. 283, S.B. 821; 2023 Va. Acts Ch. 282, H.B. 1704.

discrimination, harassment, or hazing occurring at high school sporting games.[1003] California also recommended that school boards address both the perpetrators and victims of racist bullying, harassment, or intimidation, by incorporating restorative justice practices in their discipline plans.[1004] In a third act, California directed its state DOE to develop and post on its website a model policy and related resources on body shaming.[1005] Colorado required local boards and charter schools to have detailed policies on harassment and discrimination.[1006]

Indiana amended its school bullying provision to require that disciplinary rules must include timetables, usually within five days, for reporting incidents to parents of both the targeted student and the alleged perpetrator; the changes provided for sharing of disciplinary policies with parents.[1007] Indiana called for a more robust bullying prevention program, tied to school safety planning.[1008] Maryland mandated that public schools provide information to students, faculty, staff, and parents regarding who serves as their Title IX coordinators and the process for filing sexual misconduct complaints.[1009]

Nevada obligated that students in work-based learning programs receive instruction about harassment and its reporting in the workplace, developing and maintaining healthy relationships, and identifying signs of predatory behavior.[1010] North Carolina updated a provision on inappropriate relationships between students and school personnel by strengthening reporting standards, inserting a provision resulting in the forfeiture of retirement benefits due to misconduct, and calling for the use of videos to inform students about misconduct.[1011]

Nevada specified that schools have the responsibility to determine whether workplaces are suitable settings for student in work-placed learning programs.[1012] Oregon modified a provision requiring its state BOE to adopt standards for school boards on

---

[1003] 2023 Cal. Stat. Ch. 366, A.B. No. 1327.
[1004] 2023 Cal. Stat. Ch. 22, A.B. No. 115.
[1005] 2023 Cal. Stat. Ch. 791, A.B. No. 10.
[1006] 2023 Colo. Sess. Laws S.B. 296.
[1007] 2023 Ind. Acts P.L. 238, HB 1483.
[1008] 2023 Ind. Acts P.L. 150, HB 1492.
[1009] 2023 Md. Laws Ch. 678, H.B. 16.
[1010] 2023 Nev. Stat. Ch. 222, AB 256.
[1011] 2023 N.C. Sess. Laws Ch. 128, H.B. 142.
[1012] 2023 Nev. Stat. Ch. 222, AB 256.

sexual harassment policies, to include a statutory definition of "consent" in the directive.[1013] Virginia amended a provision mandating policies against bullying that principals or their designee must notify the parents of students involved in alleged incident within 24 hours, rather than five school days.[1014] Washington ordered its Office of the Superintendent of Public Instruction to develop and periodically update model student handbook language on policies and complaint procedures related to discrimination, including sexual harassment and addressing transgender students, and information about policies and complaint procedures related to harassment, intimidation, and bullying.[1015]

Thirteen states passed 18 acts on school safety plans. California called for the development of comprehensive school safety plans including for charter schools to include procedures to assess and respond to reports of dangerous, violent, or unlawful activity at their schools, school activities, or on school buses.[1016] California then stated that school safety plans must include adaptations for students with disabilities.[1017] Finally, California required comprehensive school safety plans for grades 7 to 12 to include the development of a protocol for students at risk.[1018] Florida created a school mapping data grant program within its state DOE to provide information in digital formats to assist first responders for use in emergencies and for conducting safety drills.[1019]

Illinois obligated school building emergency and crisis response plan protocols to include measures on how local law enforcement officers can rapidly enter buildings in emergencies.[1020] Indiana added critical incidence digital mapping to its school safety plan directives with the development of a multidisciplinary threat assessment teams to review and improve them.[1021] Louisiana mandated that school boards create policies based on standards supplied by legislation on surveillance and security systems,

---

[1013] 2023 Or. Laws Ch. 242, H.B. 2280.
[1014] 2023 Va. Acts Ch. 296, H.B. 1592; 2023 Va. Acts Ch. 297, S.B. 1072.
[1015] 2023 Wash Laws. Ch. 242, Subst. H.B. 1207.
[1016] 2023 Cal. Stat. Ch. 626, S.B. No. 671.
[1017] 2023 Cal. Stat. Ch. 599, S.B. No. 323.
[1018] 2023 Cal. Stat. Ch. 856, S.B. No. 10.
[1019] 2023 Fla. Laws Ch. 99, H. 301.
[1020] 2023 Ill. Laws P.A. 103-194, HB 3559.
[1021] 2023 Ind. Acts P.L. 150, HB 1492.

adding that data on such systems are not subject to its Open Records Act.[1022] Louisiana then declared that local boards must revise their school safety plans by creating district threat assessment teams.[1023] In a third act, Louisiana obligated school administrators, on being informed of risks of threats, must first notify those at risk before informing others.[1024]

Montana specified that school safety plans must be updated annually and contain threat assessment protocols along with the identification of threat assessment teams that meet at least monthly.[1025] New Jersey called for documentation and incorporation of the needs of students with disabilities in making emergency plans.[1026] North Carolina decreed that public school units must establish teams to assess threats when such behavior is communicated.[1027] Oregon required school boards to provide electronic communication to parents and guardians of students as well as employees working when safety threat actions occurred.[1028] Texas mandated the recognition of confidentiality for public school employees who report potential threats to schools' threat assessment and safety support school teams.[1029] Texas also dictated that parents or guardians must be notified before threat assessment team may speak with their children and afford them the right to be present.[1030]

Utah codified and enlarged emergency plans its state BOE devised on, informing LEAs or schools to develop emergency preparedness and response plans for active threats, emergency preparedness, standard response protocols coordinated with community stakeholders, and identifying necessary components of the above materials.[1031] Virginia amended a provision about threat assessment team members, specify that new members must complete an initial training and a refresher every three years.[1032] West Virginia added state fire marshals, along with law enforcement and first responders, to persons who must receive

---

[1022] 2023 La. Acts No. 301, H.B. No. 213.
[1023] 2023 La. Acts No. 334, S.B. No. 207.
[1024] 2023 La. Acts No. 164, H.B. No. 348.
[1025] 2023 Mont. Laws S.B. 213.
[1026] 2023 N.J. Pub. Laws c. 212, S. 2057.
[1027] 2023 N.C. Sess. Laws Ch. 78, H.B. 605.
[1028] 2023 Or. Laws Ch. 560, H.B. 3584.
[1029] 2023 Tex. Gen. Laws S.B. No. 1720.
[1030] 2023 Tex. Gen. Laws H.B. No. 473.
[1031] 2023 Utah Laws H.B. 140.
[1032] 2023 Va. Acts Ch. 295, S.B. 1359.

information on school safety standards from their crisis response plans.[1033]

Six states enacted seven bills about school safety drills. Arkansas amended a section on fire drills[1034] by removing the directive that exterior school doors and exits must be unlocked during school hours.[1035] Connecticut ordered its Department of Emergency Services and Public Protection to consult with its state DOE to determine effectiveness and efficiency of current school safety drills as well as their effect on the mental health of students.[1036] Georgia obligated elementary and secondary schools to create trained seizure action plans to respond to students' needs for support services to address their needs safely.[1037]

Hawaii established a one-year critical emergency response pilot program in its state DOE to create a critical emergency response team for a school in central Oahu.[1038] Additionally, Hawaii called on its state DOE to work with other entities to develop and implement active shooter training programs in all public and charter schools. The act permits public and charter school students to decline to participate in the program.[1039] To a provision about school safety training and drills, Oregon encouraged the instruction of students on preparing for and recovering from natural disaster events, including fires, earthquakes, and safety threats.[1040] Vermont decreed that local boards adopt policies mandating each school site to conduct options-based response drills in the fall and spring of each academic year.[1041]

Nine states adopted 12 provisions on criminal background checks. California imposed limits on criminal background checks for those providing work experience opportunities.[1042] Colorado permitted local boards to employ school-based therapists, including psychologists, social workers, marriage and family therapists, and licensed professional counselors, after they undergo successful

---

[1033] 2023 W. Va. Acts Ch. 127, S.B. 275.
[1034] ARK. CODE ANN. § 20-22-1011(a).
[1035] 2023 Ark. Acts 9, S.B. 4, H.B. 1005.
[1036] 2023 Conn. Spec. Acts 31, Subst. H.B. No. 6846.
[1037] 2023 Ga. Laws Act 11, S.B. 45.
[1038] 2023 Haw. Sess. Laws Act 143, SB 830.
[1039] 2023 Haw. Sess. Laws Act 53, HB 1329.
[1040] 2023 Or. Laws Ch. 517, H.B. 2902.
[1041] 2023 Vt. Laws Ch. No. 29, S. 138.
[1042] 2023 Cal. Stat. Ch. 616, S.B. No. 531.

criminal background checks.[1043] Delaware directed its state-level bureau of investigation to provide subsequent arrest notifications to its state DOE for criminal background checks for those possessing teacher certificates.[1044] Indiana directed officials in school corporations, charter schools, and nonpublic schools to use expanded criminal background checks when available.[1045]

Nevada added the need for criminal background checks for volunteers in charter schools, employees of a unified school for profoundly gifted students, and all school board employees with unsupervised access to students.[1046] New Hampshire obligated school transportation monitors to undergo criminal background checks before employment.[1047] New Mexico changed the procedures for criminal background checks for school employees to align with federal law.[1048] Texas allowed accredited nonpublic schools and the Texas Education Agency (TEA), its state DOE to have access to criminal background check information.[1049]

Virginia called on its School for the Deaf and the Blind to perform criminal background checks on teachers with unsupervised access to students.[1050] Virginia enabled governing boards or administrators of nonpublic elementary or secondary schools to disclose information in records about criminal background checks with its Council for Private Education.[1051] Virginia added solicitation of sex crimes, or child abuse and neglect, as offenses preventing individuals from working in schools.[1052]

Three states added five acts about the use of seclusion and restraint. California added the duty to post reports about the uses of seclusion and restraint to its state DOE.[1053] California next mandated reports on the use of restraints or seclusion on a website in addition to paper copies provided to its state DOE.[1054] New Hampshire prohibited the use of prone restraints for children,

---

1043 2023 Colo. Sess. Laws S.B. 4.
1044 2023 Del. Laws HB 181.
1045 2023 Ind. Acts P.L. 110, SB 342.
1046 2023 Nev. Stat. Ch. 498, AB 503.
1047 2023 N.H. Laws Ch. 55, SB 39.
1048 2023 N.M. Laws Ch. 177, SB 383.
1049 2023 Tex. Gen. Laws S.B. No. 1471.
1050 2023 Va. Acts Ch. 670, S.B. 825.
1051 2023 Va. Acts Ch. 253, H.B. 1701.
1052 2023 Va. Acts Ch. 703, H.B. 1822.
1053 2023 Cal. Stat. Ch. 582, A.B. No. 1466.
1054 2023 Cal. Stat. Ch. 582, A.B. No. 1466.

described in the measure as being restrained face-down, without the ability to move, as inherently dangerous.[1055] In addition, New Hampshire declared that seclusion never be used explicitly or implicitly in schools or treatment facilities as punishments or discipline of children.[1056] Oregon modified its rules for records about the use of seclusion or restraint of children in care programs or public education to include photographs, audio or video recordings among others, specifying that records may not be destroyed, edited, concealed, or altered in any way.[1057]

Six states enacted bills aimed at preventing child abuse. California directed its agency receiving child abuse reports to seek additional information from nonmandatory reporters prior to initiating investigations.[1058] Colorado obligated its state DOE to convene a training meeting for school resource officers to discuss best practices in responding to "Safe2Tell" reports.[1059] Iowa amended provisions for complaints of child abuse against school employees, indicating that employees must be 18 or older, striking an applicable age limit of under 12 for abused students.[1060]

Tennessee instituted prohibitions against employing individuals its Department of Children's Services found to have committed child abuse to public charter schools and its state BOE, in the same manner this applies to other educational entities. The act likewise applied to loss of teacher licenses.[1061] Oregon directed its Department of Human Services to investigate and determine the public education program that was responsible for founded reports of child abuse.[1062] Oregon required its state DOE and law enforcement agencies to make available information they receive during investigations of suspected sexual conduct or child abuse to its Teacher Standards and Practices Commission.[1063] Utah banned those who committed child abuse from exempting their children from mandatory school attendance.[1064]

[1055] 2023 N.H. Laws Ch. 153, HB 491.
[1056] 2023 N.H. Laws Ch. 75, SB 179.
[1057] 2023 Or. Laws Ch. 204, S.B. 1024.
[1058] 2023 Cal. Stat. Ch. 434, A.B. No. 391.
[1059] 2023 Colo. Sess. Laws S.B. 70. "Safe2Tell reports" are codified at COLO. REV. STAT. § 22-32-146.
[1060] 2023 Iowa Acts HF 430.
[1061] 2023 Tenn. Pub. Acts Ch. No. 222, S.B. No. 743, Subs. H.B. No. 459.
[1062] 2023 Or. Laws Ch. 581, S.B. 790.
[1063] 2023 Or. Laws Ch. 131, S.B. 218.
[1064] 2023 Utah Laws H.B. 305.

Five states passed six acts on the use of law enforcement and school resource officers (SROs). Connecticut called for memoranda of understandings between schools and SROs, posted on school websites about the duties, procedures regarding restraint of students, use of firearms, school-based arrests, reporting any investigations, and behavioral interventions of these officers.[1065] Kentucky permitted private and faith-based schools to enter memoranda of understandings with local law enforcement agencies of the state police department to provide SROs who are employees of those agencies.[1066]

Tennessee permitted nonpublic schools and local governments to contract for SROs to serve the former.[1067] Texas prohibited peace officers or SROs from using physical restraints, chemical irritants, or tasers on public school students.[1068] Texas next permitted memoranda of understanding between public and nonpublic schools to authorize the marshal of one school to act in the other school during an event at which both schools participate.[1069] Virginia amended its SRO grants programs for equipment necessary for uniformed SROs, school security officers, and other school safety personnel, which cannot be used to purchase firearms, handcuffs or other wrist constraints, or stun weapons.[1070]

Four states enacted provisions with respect to firearms and other weapons. Indiana authorized the use of public funds for providing specialized firearm training for teachers.[1071] Mississippi empowered trained individuals within its Office of Homeland Security to carry concealed firearms as part of their duties to protect schools and students.[1072] Tennessee provided an exemption from the offense of possessing or carrying a weapon on school property when an adult carries or possesses a pocketknife that remains concealed while on school property.[1073] Texas directed providers of active shooter training in public schools and

---

1065 2023 Conn. Acts 167, Subst. S.B. No. 1, § 72.
1066 2023 Ky. Acts Ch. 104, SB 540.
1067 2023 Tenn. Pub. Acts Ch. No. 87, S.B. No. 315, Subs. H.B. No. 1456.
1068 2023 Tex. Gen. Laws S.B. No. 133.
1069 2023 Tex. Gen. Laws H.B. No. 3623.
1070 2023 Va. Acts Ch. 609, H.B. 1691; 2023 Va. Acts Ch. 610, S.B. 1099.
1071 2023 Ind. Acts P.L. 218, HB 1177.
1072 2023 Miss. Laws SB 2079.
1073 2023 Tenn. Pub. Acts Ch. No. 142, S.B. No. 172, Subs. H.B. No. 159.

institutions of higher education to obtain certification issued by its state Commission on Law Enforcement.[1074]

Seven states adopted measures to provide greater safety through lockdowns and construction techniques to "harden" schools. Arkansas required exterior doors to be closed and locked during school hours except during transition times.[1075] To increase school safety, Maine directed school administrative units to ensure that new or renovated elementary and secondary schools are equipped with interlocking door controller technology which refers to areas in between two doors separating the interior of schools from their exterior where both cannot be opened at the same time.[1076] New York mandated the use of design principles and strategies, under guidance of its commissioner of education as part of a comprehensive approach to provide safe, secure, and healthy school environments.[1077]

Pennsylvania provided targeted school safety grants for nonpublic schools.[1078] Tennessee amended its school safety law by replacing the provision on safety plans and security systems; adding representatives from police associations to the state School Safety Center; adding standards about armed intruders, incident command, and emergency safety bus drills; ordering school building exterior doors to be locked; and incorporating more secure "hardened" construction in new buildings after July 1, 2023.[1079] Texas added provisions for construction improvements as part of a program to improve student safety in schools.[1080] West Virginia provided charter schools with access to its safe schools fund for audiovisual sources for school safety training and "hardening" school facilities against violent incidents.[1081]

Two states adopted means of providing surveillance of school facilities. Alabama directed local boards of education to install, maintain, and operate video cameras in self-contained special-education classrooms, contingent on available funding.[1082] West

---

[1074] 2023 Tex. Gen. Laws S.B. No. 999.
[1075] 2023 Ark. Acts 787, S.B. 554.
[1076] 2023 Me. Laws Ch. 452, S.P. 104, L.D. 204.
[1077] 2023 N.Y. Laws Ch. 529, A. 286.
[1078] 2023 Pa. Laws Act No. 33, H.B. 301, Sec. 19.
[1079] 2023 Tenn. Pub. Acts Ch. No. 367, H.B. No. 322, Subs. S.B. No. 274.
[1080] 2023 Tex. Gen. Laws H.B. No. 3.
[1081] 2023 W. Va. Acts Ch. 137, H.B. 2827.
[1082] 2023 Ala. Acts 527, S.B. 56.

Virginia called for the placement of audio recording devices in restrooms of self-contained classrooms.[1083]

Three states adopted acts about concussions. Delaware improved its 2016 Concussion Protection Act[1084] by giving the Division of Public Health regulatory control in recommending concussion prevention protocols.[1085] Nevada obligated its Superintendent of Public Instruction to adopt policy regarding treatment of head injuries, thereby modifying rules of its Interscholastic Activities Association.[1086] Texas permitted school boards or charter schools to use any persons licensed under its State Occupations Code as a member of the concussion oversight team in consideration of removing public school students from interschool athletic activities due to suspected concussions.[1087]

Five states enacted bills about suicide prevention. Delaware adopted a correction on contact information on suicide prevention services to be printed on public school students' identification cards in grades 7 to 12.[1088] Iowa required public schools to include the crisis hotline telephone and text numbers as well as the internet address for the "Your Life Iowa" suicide prevention program on student identification cards.[1089] Virginia directed public schools to provide suicide and crisis lifeline telephone numbers on student identification cards.[1090] West Virginia obligated public schools covering grades 6-12 to print information on suicide prevention resources on student identification cards.[1091] New Jersey created an advisory council to report on suicide prevention instruction in public schools.[1092]

Five states approved the recognition of school zones where dangerous or criminal activities can yield greater consequences. Florida allowed counties and municipalities to enforce speed limits in school zones through speed detection systems.[1093] Kentucky prohibited registered sex offenders from loitering within 1,000 feet

---

[1083] 2023 W. Va. Acts Ch. 143, H.B. 3271.
[1084] 2016 Del. Laws HB 404.
[1085] 2023 Del. Laws HB 193.
[1086] 2023 Nev. Stat. Ch. 219, SB 80.
[1087] 2023 Tex. Gen. Laws H.B. No. 1002.
[1088] 2023 Del. Laws HB 137.
[1089] 2023 Iowa Acts HF 602.
[1090] 2023 Va. Acts Ch. 223, S.B. 1044.
[1091] 2023 W. Va. Acts Ch. 142, H.B. 3218.
[1092] 2023 N.J. Pub. Laws c. 270, S. 1662.
[1093] 2023 Fla. Laws Ch. 174, H. 657.

of school grounds, playgrounds, and daycares.[1094] New York started a school speed zone camera demonstration program in Albany with its authorization set to repeal in 2028.[1095] Tennessee amended a prohibition on needle and hypodermic syringe exchange programs operating within 1,000 feet of schools, making it applicable statewide rather than only in larger cities.[1096] Virginia increased the maximum boundaries of school crossing zones from 600 to 750 feet from school limits.[1097]

Rhode Island provided school zone exemptions against alcohol sales in five locations while Texas exempted a proscription of alcohol use in school zones. Rhode Island additionally allowed its Board of Licenses for Providence to exempt retailers located at 566 Plainfield Street and 777 Elmwood Avenue for alcoholic beverage licenses;[1098] empowered its Board of Licenses for Providence to exempt a business located at 225 Waterman Street from a prohibition about proximity to schools and churches for a Class B or Class BV (liquor) license;[1099] allowed East Providence to grant a retailer's Class B license to property located at 136 Taunton Avenue;[1100] exempted a retailer at 499 Hope Street in Bristol from a 200-foot distance requirement from schools or churches for a Class BV license;[1101] and permitted the South Kingston to exempt retailers located at 357 Main Street from a prohibition about proximity to schools and churches for a Class BV license.[1102] Texas permitted consumption, possession, and sale of alcoholic beverages at performing arts facilities in districts meeting the size and location requirements specified in the act.[1103]

Two states enacted bills on safety for students moving to and from school. Hawaii created an advisory committee to develop a comprehensive plan for helping students to get safely to and from school.[1104] Louisiana ordered elementary schools to develop and

---

[1094] 2023 Ky. Acts Ch. 109, SB 80.
[1095] 2023 N.Y. Laws Ch. 500, A. 7043.
[1096] 2023 Tenn. Pub. Acts Ch. No. 256, S.B. No. 292, Subs. H.B. 275.
[1097] 2023 Va. Acts Ch. 84, H.B. 2104.
[1098] 2023 R.I. Pub. Laws H.B. 6450, S.B. 669.
[1099] 2023 R.I. Pub. Laws H.B. 5289.
[1100] 2023 R.I. Pub. Laws H.B. 6492, S.B. 38.
[1101] 2023 R.I. Pub. Laws S.B. 1018.
[1102] 2023 R.I. Pub. Laws S.B. 1019, H.B. 6345.
[1103] 2023 Tex. Gen. Laws H.B. No. 1825.
[1104] 2023 Haw. Sess. Laws Act 244, HB 600.

deploy safety protocols for elementary students who are dropped off or picked up from school.[1105]

Three states added provisions for dental and vision screening. Delaware required public and charter schools to provide kindergarten students with oral health screenings by the end of the school year and to notify their parents or guardians.[1106] For dental screenings in public schools, Pennsylvania permitted screenings by public health dental hygiene practitioners.[1107] Texas allowed the use of electronic eye charts for vision screening in public or nonpublic schools.[1108]

Two states approved the placement of trauma kits in schools for bleeding control. Colorado directed its state DOE to distribute kits described as "stop the bleed" control kits to each school that chooses to administer "stop the bleed" training.[1109] Illinois enabled local boards to provide and maintain on-site trauma kits at their schools for bleeding emergencies.[1110]

Two states created state entities to coordinate school safety. Colorado began its Office of School Safety, obligating its director to hire a grants manager while calling for the formation of a crisis response unit.[1111] South Carolina established the Center for School Safety and Targeted Violence in its state law enforcement division.[1112]

Three states adopted four measures mandating studies for school safety. Nevada established a committee to study responses to power-based violence in schools.[1113] Nevada also created an advisory committee to study and make recommendations about the safety and well-being of public school staff.[1114] New Jersey formed a task force to study school security and safety issues in addition to making recommendations for improvement.[1115] Utah created a school safety task force charged with developing justifications, duties, and scope of authority of its security chief in the

---

1105 2023 La. Acts No. 362, H.B. No. 169.
1106 2023 Del. Laws HB 83.
1107 2023 Pa. Laws Act No. 55, H.B. No. 1478.
1108 2023 Tex. Gen. Laws H.B. No. 1297.
1109 2023 Colo. Sess. Laws H.B. 1213.
1110 2023 Ill. Laws P.A. 103-128, HB 1561.
1111 2023 Colo. Sess. Laws S.B. 241.
1112 2023 S.C. Acts No. 79, H.B. 3360.
1113 2023 Nev. Stat. Ch. 504, AB 245.
1114 2023 Nev. Stat. Ch. 263, AB 72.
1115 2023 N.J. Pub. Laws c. 218, S. 3079.

Department of Police Services, obligating all schools to conduct threat assessments.[1116]

Other school safety-related acts enacted in 2023 are described as follows. Arkansas placed controls on sleeping arrangements for public school or charter school students on overnight school trips; law requires K-12 multiple occupancy restrooms and changing rooms designated as male or female, specifying that their use must conform to students' sexes designated by their birth certificate.[1117] Illinois prohibited schools serving students in grades K–8 from scheduling pesticide applications on school grounds during class day.[1118] Illinois then directed its state BOE to develop a school district-level Children's Adversity Index to measure community childhood trauma exposure for students.[1119]

South Dakota permitted school boards to adopt policies about students who are registered sex offenders so they may receive instruction by remote, distance learning, or alternative education programs.[1120] Texas allowed spectators at extracurricular athletic activities to be removed for conduct intentionally, knowingly, or recklessly causing bodily injuries to referees, judges, or other officials of the activities.[1121] Texas removed the requirement that nonpublic schools must post signs about penalties for human trafficking but keeping it in public schools.[1122]

Students with Disabilities

This section describes 2023 legislative acts about students with disabilities. Four states updated terminology describing disabilities. Kansas modified definitions for children with disabilities in special education by replacing the terms "emotional disturbance" with the terms "emotional disability."[1123] New York replaced the terms "mentally retarded," "mental retardation," and variants thereof with "developmentally disabled" and "developmental disability" in its school code.[1124] Pennsylvania

[1116] 2023 Utah Laws H.B. 61.
[1117] 2023 Ark. Acts 317, H.B. 1156.
[1118] 2023 Ill. Laws P.A. 103-496, SB 1772.
[1119] 2023 Ill. Laws P.A. 103-413, HB 342.
[1120] 2023 S.D. Laws S.B. 168.
[1121] 2023 Tex. Gen. Laws H.B. No. 2484.
[1122] 2023 Tex. Gen. Laws S.B. No. 2069.
[1123] 2023 Kan. Sess. Laws HB 2322.
[1124] 2023 N.Y. Laws Ch. 371, S. 4041.

updated references to students with disabilities in its state special education code to refer to "disabilities," "hearing impaired," "visually impaired," "intellectually disabled," "brain injured," and "emotionally disabled."[1125] Rhode Island substituted the terms "mentally retarded" and "retarded" with "intellectual or developmental disability" in its statutes.[1126]

Four states adopted acts about dyslexia. Louisiana directed its state Board of Elementary and Secondary Education to adopt a screening instrument for dyslexia, requiring local boards to screen students for dyslexia.[1127] Nebraska required boards and its state DOE to collect and report information with respect to dyslexia and other learning disabilities.[1128] New Hampshire mandated additional screening for dyslexia and related disorders in grades K-2, and provided greater funding for meeting the needs of these students.[1129] Texas set standards for evaluating and identifying students with dyslexia, defined dyslexia as a disability, and set standards for leading an IEP team for a student with dyslexia.[1130]

Through three acts two states mandated that school safety planning include the needs of students with disabilities. Illinois required IEP teams to address in accommodations necessitated by natural disasters or active shooter incidents.[1131] Illinois permitted public and nonpublic schools to maintain a supply of undesignated oxygen tanks in secure locations to provide access for persons with developmental disabilities.[1132] New Jersey called for documentation and incorporation of the needs of students with dishabilles in making emergency plans.[1133]

Other acts related to students with disabilities are described as follows. Colorado directed its state DOE to enter into a service agreement with a nonprofit organization to create and maintain a list of attorneys to represent a parent in a due process hearing for a child's special education program.[1134] Colorado mandated the availability of translation services for parents with communication

---

[1125] 2023 Pa. Laws Act No. 33, H.B. 301, Sec. 11.
[1126] 2023 R.I. Pub. Laws S.B. 722, H.B. 5755.
[1127] 2023 La. Acts No. 266, H.B. No. 69.
[1128] 2023 Neb. Laws LB 298.
[1129] 2023 N.H. Laws Ch. 151, HB 377.
[1130] 2023 Tex. Gen. Laws H.B. No. 3928.
[1131] 2023 Ill. Laws P.A. 103-197, HB 3680.
[1132] 2023 Ill. Laws P.A. 103-196, HB 3613.
[1133] 2023 N.J. Pub. Laws c. 212, S. 2057.
[1134] 2023 Colo. Sess. Laws H.B. 1168.

barriers for IEP meetings.[1135] Delaware clarified that if school boards deny requests to transport special education students, the state will pay 70% of costs.[1136] Florida required IEPs to contain information on the legal rights and responsibilities that transfer to students at age 18.[1137] Florida obligated schools to provide for students with disabilities to be retained in kindergarten at the discretion of their parents.[1138]

Hawaii adopted the national instructional materials accessibility standard[1139] to require state schools to provide timely availability of accessible instructional materials and technology for students eligible for services under the IDEA.[1140] Louisiana directed the state Board of Elementary and Secondary Education to report to legislative committees regarding school board compliance with special education requirements.[1141] Maine defined a "state agency client" to identify students with disabilities who are in the care or custody, or both, of the Department of Health and Human Services or of the Department of Corrections.[1142] Maine amended state special education law to specify that a person who is continuing an educational placement until the person attains 22 years of age has the right to participate in career and technical education courses. The bill also changed the descriptions of three of the 12 identified types of disability.[1143]

Maryland directed that a child with a disability who needs special education and related services that cannot be provided in a public county, regional, or state program shall be placed in an appropriate nonpublic educational program that offers these services.[1144] Maryland required the recording of student disability data by specific disability category in its longitudinal data system.[1145] Minnesota added pupils who are provided an individualized educational program in special education to be included in the definition of "English learners."[1146] Montana

---

[1135] 2023 Colo. Sess. Laws H.B. 1263.
[1136] 2023 Del. Laws HB 81.
[1137] 2023 Fla. Laws Ch. 96, H. 19.
[1138] 2023 Fla. Laws Ch. 91, S. 290.
[1139] 20 U.S.C. § 1474(e).
[1140] 2023 Haw. Sess. Laws Act 254, HB 388.
[1141] 2023 La. Acts No. 346, H.B. No. 315.
[1142] 2023 Me. Laws Ch. 449, H.P. 49, L.D. 79.
[1143] 2023 Me. Laws Ch. 450, H.P. 66, L.D. 98.
[1144] 2023 Md. Laws Ch. 648, H.B. 448.
[1145] 2023 Md. Laws Ch. 778, H.B. 320.
[1146] 2023 Minn. Laws Ch. 55, sec. 7, HF 2497.

created a Special Needs Equal Opportunity Education Savings Account, from which the state superintendent of public instruction may draw to reimburse parents of special needs students for tuition, fees, textbooks, software, instructional materials, online courses, therapies, assessment tests, and other related services.[1147]

New Hampshire amended the rules for alternative dispute resolution in special education, to allow the parties to mutually agree to continue conferring after the original 30-day period.[1148] New Hampshire specified that special education services must continue through age 21, inclusive.[1149] Oregon added provisions to address or protect instructional time for students with disabilities who are permitted to be served by abbreviated school days.[1150] Oregon required that school board employees working with students with specialized needs such as IEPs, a Section 504 plan, or behavior intervention plans have access to student records and be consulted when plans are formulated or changed.[1151] Rhode Island required every public school district to post and maintain a link on its website concerning the its special education local advisory committee, or provide contact information for the committee.[1152]

Tennessee established a Deaf Mentor and Parent Advisor Program to assist families in implementing bilingual and bicultural home-based programming for children who are deaf, hard of hearing, or attendees of the state schools for the deaf and blind.[1153] Texas required school boards and charter schools to provide information about the state's Driving with Disability Program for the driver's education curriculum, for the purpose of helping students with disabilities in their communications with peace officers in traffic stops.[1154]

Virginia directed its Standards of Learning Task Force to assess the effectiveness of assessments for students with disabilities.[1155] Virginia directed the commonwealth's BOE to shorten the deadline of 65 business days from the date or receipt of

---

1147 2023 Mont. Laws H.B. 393.
1148 2023 N.H. Laws Ch. 72, SB. 135.
1149 2023 N.H. Laws Ch. 7, HB 501.
1150 2023 Or. Laws Ch. 290, S.B. 819.
1151 2023 Or. Laws Ch. 161, S.B. 756.
1152 2023 R.I. Pub. Laws S.B. 489, H.B. 5668.
1153 2023 Tenn. Pub. Acts Ch. No. 327, S.B. No. 4, Subs. H.B. No. 435.
1154 2023 Tex. Gen. Laws S.B. No. 2304.
1155 2023 Va. Acts Ch. 157, H.B. 1884.

referral for an initial evaluation or a reevaluation of a child to determine eligibility for special services and related services.[1156] Virginia required each public high school to publicly identify on its website the faculty member responsible for school transition planning and coordination for special education students.[1157]

Washington authorized its state BOE to establish standards for authorizing, monitoring, and investigating nonpublic schools approved by its state BOE, other private in-state entities, and out-of-state programs that contract with school boards to provide special education and related services to children with disabilities.[1158] Wyoming directed its state BOE to establish requirements for students with disabilities under federal special education law to obtain a high school certificate of completion to be issued by local boards, consistent with the student's IEP.[1159]

Technology

This section details technology-related legislation adopted last year. Arkansas allowed school boards to hire a computer science teacher at each of their high schools.[1160] Hawaii directed state schools to provide timely availability of accessible instructional materials and technology for students eligible for services under the IDEA.[1161] Illinois authorized its state BOE to create a competitive grant program to support the development and enhancement of computer science programs in K-12 schools.[1162]

Nevada funded replacement of computer hardware and software for its state DOE. Updating hardware and software seemed to occur by stand-alone bills across many state agencies in the state.[1163] New Hampshire allowed the use of technology platforms in career exploration or career technical education, excluding those uses from the definition of a "social media account."[1164] New Mexico amended a provision on the use of technology in education to highlight digital citizenship and

---

[1156] 2023 Va. Acts Ch. 4, H.B. 1492.
[1157] 2023 Va. Acts Ch. 280, H.B. 1554; 2023 Va. Acts Ch. 281, S.B. 943.
[1158] 2023 Wash Laws. Ch. 436, 2nd Subst. S.B. 5315.
[1159] 2023 Wyo. Sess. Laws Act No. 62, Ch. No. 114, S.F. 98.
[1160] 2023 Ark. Acts 635, S.B. 378.
[1161] 2023 Haw. Sess. Laws Act 254, HB 388.
[1162] 2023 Ill. Laws P.A. 103-264, SB 2374.
[1163] 2023 Nev. Stat. Ch. 367, SB 500.
[1164] 2023 N.H. Laws Ch. 225, SB 213.

strengthen digital equity where all learners have the information, support, and skills to equitably access digital information.[1165]

Utah amended provisions of the statewide online education program to require its state BOE to provide a longer notice timeline for changes to the approval of an online course, establish a deadline for making a payment to a course provider, obligating its state BOE to create an approval process for new course offerings.[1166] Vermont convened a technology advisory group to assist the work of the Ethnic and Social Equity Standards Advising Work Group.[1167]

Transportation

This section describes school transportation-related legislative acts from 2023. Six states adopted seven acts concerning measures to protect stopped school buses and their passengers. Florida permitted school boards to install and operate school bus infraction detection systems.[1168] Illinois raised the fine for passing a stopped school bus from $300 to $500.[1169] Pennsylvania approved a pilot program providing for automated enforcement of failure to stop for a school bus with flashing red lights and automated speed enforcement.[1170] Pennsylvania also permitted automated enforcement of failure to stop for a school bus with flashing red lights.[1171] Tennessee amended the code on the offense of passing stopped school busses to authorize the use of video cameras and to address evidentiary rules and who is empowered to review the videos.[1172] Virginia extended from 10 to 30 business days the deadline for issuing summonses for alleged violations of passing stopped school buses to prove that motor vehicles passed stopped buses.[1173]

Two states increased the planned service life of school buses. Maryland extended the service life of school vehicles in Anne Arundel County, from 12 years to 15 years.[1174] New Jersey

---

[1165] 2023 N.M. Laws Ch. 161, HB 401.
[1166] 2023 Utah Laws S.B. 167.
[1167] 2023 Vt. Laws Ch. No. 66, H. 461.
[1168] 2023 Fla. Laws Ch. 171, S. 766.
[1169] 2023 Ill. Laws P.A. 103-404, SB 2340.
[1170] 2023 Pa. Laws Act No. 38, H.B. No. 1284.
[1171] 2023 Pa. Laws Act No. 19, S.B. 851.
[1172] 2023 Tenn. Pub. Acts Ch. No. 179, S.B. No. 1281, Subs. H.B. No. 818.
[1173] 2023 Va. Acts Ch. 401, H.B. 1995; 2023 Va. Acts Ch. 402, S.B. 868.
[1174] 2023 Md. Laws Ch. 64, H.B. 492.

extended the useful life of school buses to 20 years. The legislative history for this provision indicates that the previous useful life for school buses has been 10, 12, and 15 years.[1175]

Two states added laws about public school transportation for students in nonpublic schools. New Jersey established a consortiums to provide to provide transportation for students attending nonpublic schools.[1176] This appears to continue a tradition of support for transportation for students attending faith-based school under the "Child Benefit" theory enunciated in *Everson v. Board of Education.*[1177] Minnesota allowed the payment of state aid for excess costs of transportation for pupils to and from area learning centers.[1178]

Other transportation-related acts are listed as follows. Colorado created a task force to study improvements in school transportation.[1179] Delaware set targets for the purchase of electric school buses in the coming years.[1180] Delaware clarified that if school boards deny requests to transport special education students, the state will pay 70% of costs.[1181] Illinois permitted school boards to contract for pupil transportation for any time periods they deem appropriate rather than terms of up to three years.[1182] Kentucky expanded the time frame for school bus drivers to have physical examinations from 12 to 24 months.[1183] Louisiana provided free rites of passage over all bridges and roads, except the Greater New Orleans Expressway, for all students on school buses.[1184]

Maine required that school bus doors must be equipped with technology to prevent doors from closing on persons' limbs or other body parts, if the vehicles were manufactured in 2025 or later.[1185] Minnesota permitted school boards and nonpublic schools to agree mutually to written plans for them to provide transportation for nonpublic pupils to their schools.[1186]

[1175] 2023 N.J. Pub. Laws c. 144, A. 5329.
[1176] 2023 N.J. Pub. Laws c. 326, A. 5412.
[1177] 330 U.S. 1 (1947), *reh'g denied*, 330 U.S. 855, (1947).
[1178] 2023 Minn. Laws Ch. 55, sec. 5, HF 2497.
[1179] 2023 Colo. Sess. Laws S.B. 94.
[1180] 2023 Del. Laws HB 10.
[1181] 2023 Del. Laws HB 81.
[1182] 2023 Ill. Laws P.A. 103-430, HB 2235.
[1183] 2023 Ky. Acts Ch. 121, HB 13.
[1184] 2023 La. Acts No. 114, H.B. No. 83.
[1185] 2023 Me. Laws Ch. 423, H.P. 37, L.D. 62.
[1186] 2023 Minn. Laws Ch. 55, sec. 4, HF 2497.

New Hampshire approved the transportation of students to career and technical education programs.[1187] Oklahoma authorized the transportation of students living outside district boundaries and off regular bus routes.[1188] Oregon directed its state BOE to approve rules for reimbursing school boards expenses for alternative transportation costs[1189]. Oregon increased the eligibility for Safe Routes to School grants, by doubling the distance of the routes to two miles from the school and by making the grants available to high schools.[1190]

Tennessee required that the registration fee for one school bus owned by a person under contract with LEAs to provide transportation services is equal to the fee charged for buses owned by LEAs.[1191] Tennessee allowed school bus drivers to use portable electronic devices for navigation of their vehicles and keeping accurate accounting of student pick-up and drop-off locations.[1192] Tennessee transferred authority from its state BOE to local boards over the annual physical and mental examinations, reports, and certification revocation of school bus drivers.[1193]

Texas specified that nepotism rules in public employment do not apply to hiring of school bus drivers if boards of trustees approve the appointments.[1194] Virginia provided the option for online training for school bus drivers in Spanish.[1195] West Virginia clarified that vehicles with capacities larger than 10 passengers may be used to transport students but no more than 10 at one time.[1196] Wisconsin permitted school board members to serve as volunteer school bus drivers.[1197]

Higher Education

In eight of the last ten years higher education-related legislation has been the category with the most acts, a situation

[1187] 2023 N.H. Laws Ch. 130, HB 364.
[1188] 2023 Okla. Sess. Laws H.B. No. 2314.
[1189] 2023 Or. Laws Ch. 524, H.B. 3014.
[1190] 2023 Or. Laws Ch. 400, H.B. 2099.
[1191] 2023 Tenn. Pub. Acts Ch. No. 462, S.B. No. 815, Subs. H.B. No. 1144.
[1192] 2023 Tenn. Pub. Acts Ch. No. 210, S.B. No. 1434, Subs. H.B. No. 1321.
[1193] 2023 Tenn. Pub. Acts Ch. No. 122, S.B. No. 579, Subs. H.B. No. 258.
[1194] 2023 Tex. Gen. Laws H.B. No. 1789.
[1195] 2023 Va. Acts Ch. 156, H.B. 1928.
[1196] 2023 W. Va. Acts Ch.135, H.B. 2607.
[1197] 2023 Wis. Laws Act 26, A.B. 233.

that remained true last year. This section categorizes and describes legislation concerning higher education in 2023.

Governance in Higher Education

Two states amended statutes on the powers and responsibilities of the state's higher education system and it operates. Utah amended membership and duties of its state Board of Higher Education and the appointment process. The act required the University of Utah to provide administrative support for the board and specified that its authority is exercised through the commissioner and its executive committee. The act mandates the adoption through a public process a statewide succession plan to develop potential institutional presidents from within the system.[1198] West Virginia amended state law to change rulemaking authority in higher education to provide more transparency in the creation of rules and reviews by the Legislative Oversight Commission on Educational Accountability.[1199]

Two states supplemented the powers statements of their governing boards with reference to high-level administrators. Maryland indicated that its Secretary of Higher Education is appointed by and serves at the pleasure of the governor with consent of the senate.[1200] Virginia made it permissive, rather than mandatory, that the chief executive officer of the Virginia Commonwealth University health system must hold the title of vice president for health sciences at that university.[1201]

Three states created new institutions of higher education. Louisiana established a state maritime academy within the University of Louisiana System.[1202] Nevada appropriated funds to add weighted student credit hours to support the acquisition of Sierra Nevada College into the state system of higher education.[1203] New Jersey approved the merger between Bloomfield College and Montclair State University.[1204]

Four states changed the membership and numbers of governing boards. Kansas reapportioned the districts of members of the Board

---

[1198] 2023 Utah Laws S.B. 146.
[1199] 2023 W. Va. Acts Ch.177, S.B. 543.
[1200] 2023 Md. Laws Ch. 634, H.B. 923.
[1201] 2023 Va. Acts Ch. 734, S.B. 1499.
[1202] 2023 La. Acts No. 231, H.B. No. 258.
[1203] 2023 Nev. Stat. Ch. 312, AB 494.
[1204] 2023 N.J. Pub. Laws c. 65, S. 3848.

of Regents for Washburn University who are appointed by the city of Topeka.[1205] Nevada reduced the elected members of the board of trustees for the university system from 13 to nine members, lowering their terms of office from six to four years.[1206] Illinois directed that the chair and vice chair of community college boards must be one of its member but the secretary need not be a member.[1207] Oregon changed the composition of governing boards for public universities by creating a process to include undergraduate and graduate students as well as faculty and non-faculty staff among nonvoting members.[1208] Oregon added one faculty member and one non-faculty staff member as voting members of the board of directors for its health and science university.[1209]

Two states added student members to governing boards with one an advisory vote. Maryland authorized the Board of Regents of the university system to provide a grant to the student member serving in the first year of the individual's term.[1210] California gave student members of governing boards of a community college an advisory vote on matters they are considering.[1211]

Three states addressed the timing of governing board meetings and the term for board members. Louisiana simplified the timing for the January meeting of university governing boards to require that they occur in January.[1212] Montana directed its Board of Public Education and Board of Regents to meet at least once annually as the combined state BOE, for the purpose of long-range planning, coordinating and evaluating policies and programs for its public educational system.[1213] South Dakota limited members of the Board of Technical Education to three consecutive three-year terms.[1214]

Two states changed their Open Meetings Act with respect to governing boards. New Hampshire modified open meeting requirements for state boards meeting remotely, mandating that at least one-third of their members be present at the actual meeting site.[1215] North Dakota obligated its state Board of Higher

---

[1205] 2023 Kan. Sess. Laws HB 2092.
[1206] 2023 Nev. Stat. Ch. 72, AB 118.
[1207] 2023 Ill. Laws P.A. 103-278, HB 1133.
[1208] 2023 Or. Laws Ch. 280, S.B. 273.
[1209] 2023 Or. Laws Ch. 178, S.B. 423.
[1210] 2023 Md. Laws Ch. 750, H.B. 428; 2023 Md. Laws Ch. 751, S.B. 142.
[1211] 2023 Cal. Stat. Ch. 103, A.B. No. 1541.
[1212] 2023 La. Acts No. 6, H.B. No. 6.
[1213] 2023 Mont. Laws H.B. 531.
[1214] 2023 S.D. Laws H.B. 1056.
[1215] 2023 N.H. Laws Ch. 188, HB 308.

Education to establish a policy ensuring transparent communication between its members on all topics relating to the specific powers and duties under section 6 of article VIII of the State Constitution and state Century Code.[1216]

Two states modified their open records law. Montana amended its public record law by directing its Board of Regents of higher education to record their public meetings in audio and video formats.[1217] North Dakota indicated that the working papers of the compliance officer of the North Dakota university system are not disclosable under state records laws.[1218]

Five states initiated the creation of state-level entities or provided authority or direction to them. Connecticut permitted the establishment of a foundation for Connecticut State Community College.[1219] Florida established a timeline for the appointment of a member of the Higher Educational Facilities Financing Authority.[1220] Mississippi enabled state institutions of higher education to appoint staff to perform the duties of the Commission on Accreditation.[1221] South Carolina transferred authority for statewide education and workforce development to its Department of Employment and Workforce.[1222] Virginia directed its Advisory Board on Teacher Education and Licensure to make recommendations on teacher recruitment and retention.[1223]

Four states passed five acts on operational oversight of private proprietary schools. Illinois amended provisions on the oversight of private colleges about unfair, misleading, or deceptive practices, so that when courts order institutions to reimburse students for loans, any monetary rewards must be refunded to the state Student Assistance Commission.[1224] Illinois then permitted its board of higher education to issue a cease and desist order to private businesses or vocational schools operating without mandated permits under the threat of civil penalties.[1225]

[1216] 2023 N.D. Laws S.B. No. 2343.
[1217] 2023 Mont. Laws H.B. 890.
[1218] 2023 N.D. Laws H.B. No. 1226.
[1219] 2023 Conn. Acts 3, S.B. No. 1106.
[1220] 2023 Fla. Laws Ch. 92, S. 598.
[1221] 2023 Miss. Laws SB 2581.
[1222] 2023 S.C. Acts No. 67, H.B. 3726.
[1223] 2023 Va. Acts Ch. 748, S.B. 1052.
[1224] 2023 Ill. Laws P.A. 103-536, HB 2898.
[1225] 2023 Ill. Laws P.A. 103-288, HB 2041.

Oklahoma directed its Board of Regents for Higher Education to make and enforce policies about private, out-of-state degree institutions operating there so they must meet the same standards of academic quality and fiscal responsibility as public higher education institutions (HEIs).[1226] Utah adopted a revised act for oversight of postsecondary proprietary schools with certification under the authority of its Division of Consumer Protection.[1227] Under the theory that because proprietary schools need oversight, loan companies funding them should mandate oversight, Nevada ordered licensure and regulatory control over companies providing student loans by its Commissioner of Financial Institutions.[1228]

Five states adopted six acts on building contracts, leases, and taxes. Florida directed the board of governors of its university system to develop regulations for boards of trustees about contracting for building construction for new or existing facilities.[1229] Mississippi increased the length of time that Mississippi State University may lease land for public-private partnership student housing, by permitting two additional options for renewals not to exceed 10 years, and one additional option for a renewal period not to exceed five years.[1230] New York enlarged the share of proceeds from land leases permitted at the State University at Purchase to support current full-time faculty positions.[1231] New York authorized the State University of New York at Buffalo to lease lands for the relocation and operation of the Leonardo da Vinci High School.[1232]

Washington raised the threshold for public bids for construction, renovation, or demolition contracts at Evergreen State College, or any regional or state university, to $110,000, or $90,000 if the work involves one trade or craft area.[1233] Rhode Island amended property tax exemptions for property owned by a private HEIs when occupied by tenants.[1234]

Seven states adopted laws guiding finance and accounting for HEIs. Maryland empowered the Board of Regents for its university

---

[1226] 2023 Okla. Sess. Laws S.B. No. 550.
[1227] 2023 Utah Laws S.B. 180.
[1228] 2023 Nev. Stat. Ch. 466, AB 332.
[1229] 2023 Fla. Laws Ch. 95, S. 7062.
[1230] 2023 Miss. Laws SB 2590.
[1231] 2023 N.Y. Laws Ch. 562, A. 5806.
[1232] 2023 N.Y. Laws Ch. 603, S. 7443.
[1233] 2023 Wash Laws. Ch. 97, S.B. 5385.
[1234] 2023 R.I. Pub. Laws S.B. 924.

system to make transfers of not more than $150 million, to establish quasi-endowment funds.[1235] Minnesota passed a higher education finance and policy bill which is mostly funding formulae for various programs.[1236] New Jersey ordered public HEIs to provide financial reports and enabled its Secretary of Higher Education to appoint a state monitor for institutions exhibiting financial instability.[1237] Oklahoma added to the Board of Regents' power to issue obligations for the university system, under the name of the Regional University System of Education.[1238]

Pennsylvania renewed a public information transparency law, requiring public HEIs to provide data on budgets, salaries, and other financial matters.[1239] Utah allowed its state Board of Higher Education to supplement funding with private contributions, permitting it to name a Promise Partner Grant after a business that funded it, and removed the requirement for institutions to evaluate partner award recipients.[1240] Virginia increased the maximum reimbursement for public institutions of higher education from $3,000 to $4,000 for each completed noncredit workforce training program per eligible student.[1241]

Two states modified accreditation standards for HEIs. North Dakota amended its requirements for postsecondary career schools, to specify that those operating in the state offer full-stack software engineering courses need not be accredited.[1242] West Virginia permitted HEIs to use nationally recognized accrediting agencies for their accreditation.[1243]

Two states addressed agricultural research. Hawaii appropriated funds to the University of Hawaii for statewide research into ornamental ginger pathogens, prevention of their spreading, and development of pathogen-free ornamental ginger plants.[1244] Maine directed the University of Maine to provide cooperative extension education regarding meat and poultry processing.[1245]

[1235] 2023 Md. Laws Ch. 735, S.B. 426.
[1236] 2023 Minn. Laws Ch. 41, HF 2073.
[1237] 2023 N.J. Pub. Laws c. 115, S. 3406.
[1238] 2023 Okla. Sess. Laws S.B. No. 86.
[1239] 2023 Pa. Laws Act No. 29, H.B. 1556.
[1240] 2023 Utah Laws H.B. 197.
[1241] 2023 Va. Acts Ch. 5, H.B. 2194; 2023 Va. Acts Ch. 6, S.B. 1422.
[1242] 2023 N.D. Laws S.B. No. 2145.
[1243] 2023 W. Va. Acts Ch. 176, S.B. 488.
[1244] 2023 Haw. Sess. Laws Act 258, HB 306.
[1245] 2023 Me. Laws Ch. 473, H.P. 1131, L.D. 1767.

Other acts passed in 2023 related to governance in higher education are described as follows. California urged the University of California[1246] both to report progress toward completing repatriation under the California Native American Graves Protection Act of 2001[1247] and to forbid the use of Native American human remains or cultural items for purposes of teaching or research.[1248] Louisiana prohibited public HEIs from contracting with gaming entities on marketing and promotions.[1249] Similarly, Maryland ordered HEIs not to contract with gaming entities if they receives compensation for student participation.[1250] Oklahoma allowed members of postsecondary governing boards to audit courses of HEIs but cannot earn academic credit for doing so.[1251]

Tennessee allowed adjunct faculty to enroll in one course consisting of no more than four credit hours or 120 clock hours per term at a community college or college of applied technology.[1252] Tennessee prohibited public postsecondary institutions that provide internet access to students, faculty, staff, or the public to allow individuals to access a social media platforms using their network if the platforms are operated or hosted by a company based in the People's Republic of China.[1253] Texas forbade academic boycotts of foreign countries by public HEIs.[1254] Texas next extended compliance programming directed at public HEIs, their officers, and employees to their agents, contractors, subcontractors, or other persons acting on their behalf.[1255]

Employees in Higher Education

Legislatures adopted very few acts on employment in higher education last year. Three states enacted bills related to salaries of employees or employees of vendors serving HEIs. California required vendors to pay employees at the rate reported or indicated

---

[1246] Note: California's legislature has the power to direct the California State University (CSU) system but can only request action by the University of California (UC) system.
[1247] 2001 Cal. Stat. AB 978.
[1248] 2023 Cal. Stat. Ch. 639, A.B. No. 226.
[1249] 2023 La. Acts No. 105, S.B. No. 191.
[1250] 2023 Md. Laws Ch. 700, H.B. 802; 2023 Md. Laws Ch. 701, S.B. 620.
[1251] 2023 Okla. Sess. Laws H.B. No. 2094.
[1252] 2023 Tenn. Pub. Acts Ch. No. 339, S.B. No. 301, Subs. H.B. No. 961.
[1253] 2023 Tenn. Pub. Acts Ch. No. 152, S.B. No. 834, Subs. H.B. No. 1445.
[1254] 2023 Tex. Gen. Laws S.B. No. 1517.
[1255] 2023 Tex. Gen. Laws S.B. No. 336.

in contracts for services with its UC system.[1256] Oklahoma appropriated funds to state HEIs for increased faculty salaries.[1257] New York implemented an agreement between the state and an employee organization, providing for the adjustment of salaries of persons in the professional service in state universities.[1258]

Other acts passed last year related to employees in higher education are listed as follows. Arkansas adopted a law to direct the practices of personnel management in public HEIs.[1259] Florida prohibited public HEIs from mandating loyalty political tests as a condition of employment.[1260] New York authorized CREF to merge with TIAA,[1261] with the former ceasing to be a corporate entity and the latter remaining as the surviving entity. TIAA manages retirement accounts for university faculty and staff.[1262] Texas the permitted issuance of temporary teaching certificates for experienced persons as instructors for the Community College of the Air Force.[1263] Washington designated graduate students serving in roles such as teaching, staff, laboratory, faculty, and research assistants, as employees eligible to engage in collective bargaining with their HEIs.[1264]

Academics in Higher Education

Much of what HEIs accomplish is done through programs, especially academic programs. Last year, nine states approved 10 acts directing the activity of teacher education and administrator preparation programs. Alabama set prerequisites for approval by its state BOE of programs providing alternative teacher education preparation. Programs must operate in at least five states successfully, for at least 10 years, and provide evidence that they certificated at least 10,000 teachers in the U.S.[1265] Indiana added subjects to be included in teacher certification programs including youth suicide awareness and prevention, bullying prevention, child

---

[1256] 2023 Cal. Stat. Ch. 480, S.B. No. 27.
[1257] 2023 Okla. Sess. Laws HB 1004.
[1258] 2023 N.Y. Laws Ch. 189, S. 7575.
[1259] 2023 Ark. Acts 778, S.B. 491.
[1260] 2023 Fla. Laws Ch. 83, H. 931.
[1261] CREF is the College Retirement Equities Fund; TIAA is the Teachers Insurance and Annuity Association.
[1262] 2023 N.Y. Laws Ch. S. 2679.
[1263] 2023 Tex. Gen. Laws S.B. No. 544.
[1264] 2023 Wash Laws. Ch. 115, Subst. S.B. 5238.
[1265] 2023 Ala. Acts 451, H.B. 342.

abuse and neglect, lockout provisions, and assessment training; the state repealed other subjects, including criminal gang awareness and information regarding homeless students.[1266]

Louisiana provided a work-around for applicants who have not attained the requisite 2.20 average on a 4.00 scale for entrance into teacher education programs. Students can receive conditional admission if they achieves 3.00 grade point averages after the first 12 hours or course work or by demonstrating competence through programs such as those offered by school boards that do not grade them.[1267] Louisiana next dictated that foundational numeracy skills must be taught in teacher education programs.[1268] Maryland directed teacher education programs to include teaching through virtual education as a program component.[1269] Nebraska obligated HEIs to provide assurances that instructors in teacher education programs are competent to teach program courses.[1270]

New Jersey prohibited HEIs from limiting the number of community college credits that may be applied toward teacher education and certification programs.[1271] Tennessee permitted local boards of education to contract with accredited private colleges or universities, domiciled in the state to provide training for the delivery of practice teaching experience for students in teacher education.[1272] Wisconsin called on teacher preparatory programs to demonstrate that they provide instruction to prepares candidates to teach reading and language arts using science-based early reading instruction rather than incorporating 3-cueing.[1273] North Carolina directed its state BOE to adopt rules for granting approval to administrator preparation programs under guidance specified by its legislature.[1274]

Seven states enacted nine bills about dual credit or dual enrollment programs. Connecticut ordered its state DOE, local and regional school boards and HEIs to expand opportunities for dual credit enrollment for high school students.[1275] Georgia determined

---

[1266] 2023 Ind. Acts P.L. 200, SB 486.
[1267] 2023 La. Acts No. 392, S.B. No. 197.
[1268] 2023 La. Acts No. 347, H.B. No. 326.
[1269] 2023 Md. Laws Ch. 804, S.B. 610.
[1270] 2023 Neb. Laws LB 705.
[1271] 2023 N.J. Pub. Laws c. 251, A. 5417.
[1272] 2023 Tenn. Pub. Acts Ch. No. 435, S.B. 1231, Subs. H.B. 1232.
[1273] 2023 Wis. Laws Act 20, A.B. 321.
[1274] 2023 N.C. Sess. Laws Ch. 125, H.B. 432.
[1275] 2023 Conn. Acts 167, Subst. S.B. No. 1, § 32.

that students participating in a dual enrollment program shall be eligible to access HOPE grant funds for career, technical, and agricultural education courses irrespective of whether they reached the maximum credit hour cap.[1276] South Dakota ordered its Board of Education Standards to establish a uniform method for school boards to calculate the amount of high school credit students receive for completing postsecondary courses.[1277]

Tennessee allowed public postsecondary schools to charge dual enrollment tuition or fees in an amount exceeds that of students' dual enrollment grants for charges such as textbooks, special examination fees, and industry certification fees.[1278] Virginia obligated the commonwealth's BOE to develop guidelines and policies for prioritizing to the maximum extent practicable dual enrollment programs, such as the Passport Dual Credit Program, the Certificate of General Studies Program, and the New Economy Workforce Credential Grant Program, which allow high school students to receive college credit.[1279] Virginia then directed its DOE to authorize nonprofit organizations with demonstrated evidence of positive student outcomes to provide, through public-private partnerships, schools for adults to earn industry-recognized credentials or dual college credit.[1280]

Washington decreed that its HEIs provide enrollment and registration in college for high school courses in which students are eligible to receive college credits available at no cost for them in ninth through twelfth grades at public high schools.[1281] West Virginia included Potomac State College as an eligible participant in its "learn and earn" program in which students may earn college credit and paychecks while seeking industry certifications.[1282] West Virginia established a dual enrollment pilot program to be administered by its Higher Education Policy Commission and the Council for Community and Technical College with assistance from its state DOE. [1283]

Three states addressed work training programs. Kentucky provided funding for attendance in a high-demand work sector

---

[1276] 2023 Ga. Laws Act 54, S.B. 86.
[1277] 2023 S.D. Laws S.B. 182.
[1278] 2023 Tenn. Pub. Acts Ch. No. 227, S.B. No. 1408, Subs. H.B. No. 957.
[1279] 2023 Va. Acts Ch. 479, S.B. 1281.
[1280] 2023 Va. Acts Ch. 454, S.B. 1019; 2023 Va. Acts Ch. 453, H.B. 1726.
[1281] 2023 Wash Laws. Ch. 314, Sec. Subst. S.B. 5048.
[1282] 2023 W. Va. Acts Ch. 33, 1st Extraordinary Sess., H.B. 144.
[1283] 2023 W. Va. Acts Ch. 178, H.B. 2005.

training programs at proprietary schools including agriculture and the top five high-demand work sectors as determined by its Workforce Innovation Board.[1284] Maine appropriated funds for and directed its community college system to invest in an educational technician training program to address shortages in public schools.[1285] Michigan extended a sunset provision for jobs training programs in community colleges, to 2033.[1286]

Three states addressed college pathways programs. Nebraska established a college pathways program and granted funds to assist students receiving associate and baccalaureate degrees.[1287] Nevada funded a grant to expand undergraduate and graduate nursing programs.[1288] Washington ordered HEIs to enter into data-sharing agreements with the office of the Superintendent of Public Instruction to facilitate the transfer of high school student directory information for the purpose of informing them of in-state postsecondary educational opportunities.[1289]

Two states called for the award of high school diplomas to participants in workforce education programs. Texas enacted a high school diploma program to permit adult students enrolled in workforce education programs at public junior colleges to earn high school diplomas simultaneously.[1290] Utah required LEAs to issue high school diplomas to students who receive associate's degrees with 60 credit hours or industry certificates with 500 hours of instruction.[1291]

Five states added six acts about care on campuses. Connecticut obligated public HEIs with residential campuses to establish plans for access to reproductive health care services for students.[1292] Maryland directed public HEIs to develop and implement provision for reproductive health services for students.[1293] Maryland also required a study of policies and procedures adopted by HEIs on access to mental health care.[1294]

[1284] 2023 Ky. Acts Ch. 67, SB 54.
[1285] 2023 Me. Laws Ch. 453, H.P. 217, L.D. 343.
[1286] 2023 Mich. Pub. Acts No. 186, H.B. No. 4573.
[1287] 2023 Neb. Laws LB 705.
[1288] 2023 Nev. Stat. Ch. 421, SB 375.
[1289] 2023 Wash Laws. Ch. 406, 2nd Subst. S.B. 5593.
[1290] 2023 Tex. Gen. Laws S.B. No. 2139.
[1291] 2023 Utah Laws S.B. 257, Sec. 2.
[1292] 2023 Conn. Acts 41, Subst. H.B. No. 1108.
[1293] 2023 Md. Laws Ch. 250, S.B. 341; 2023 Md. Laws Ch. 251, H.B. 477.
[1294] 2023 Md. Laws Ch. 401, S.B. 263; 2023 Md. Laws Ch. 402, H.B.573.

Michigan forbade pregnant and parenting student services offices in HEIs from offering referrals for abortion services.[1295] New York provided access to medication abortion prescription drugs at state and city university campuses by employing or contracting with individuals who can prescribe such drugs or by make referrals.[1296] Virginia directed the commonwealth's board for community colleges to standardize health care-related programs across institutions.[1297]

Three states passed four acts about providing academic services for students with disabilities. California authorized its state university system to establish and maintain inclusive college programs for students with disabilities.[1298] Minnesota called for the offering of inclusive higher education technical assistance centers to provide equal access for students with intellectual disabilities through a credentialed program[1299] and made available inclusive higher education grants for those with intellectual disabilities.[1300] Texas obligated its Higher Education Coordinating Board to study best practices for assisting students with autism spectrum disorder.[1301]

Two states provided support for distance education in community colleges. California allowed career development and college preparation courses at community colleges to be offered via face-to-face and by distance education.[1302] Wyoming changed the definition of "distance education class" to include a designation of a level one, two, or three courses; for purposes of funding community colleges, the levels are to be determined by course content.[1303]

Other acts passed in 2023 related to programs in HEIs are detailed as follows. California encouraged community colleges to create mathematics, engineering, science, and achievement (MESA) programs while identifying and assisting students who can participate in the program.[1304] California allowed the CSU

[1295] 2023 Mich. Pub. Acts No. 207, S.B. No. 477.
[1296] 2023 N.Y. Laws Ch. 129, A., 1395.
[1297] 2023 Va. Acts Ch. 542, S.B. 1286; 2023 Va. Acts Ch. 212, S.B. 1172.
[1298] 2023 Cal. Stat. Ch. 654, A.B. No. 447.
[1299] 2023 Minn. Laws Ch. 41, sec. 5, HF 2073.
[1300] 2023 Minn. Laws Ch. 41, sec. 6, HF 2073.
[1301] 2023 Tex. Gen. Laws S.B. No. 55.
[1302] 2023 Cal. Stat. Ch. 450, A.B. No. 634.
[1303] 2023 Wyo. Sess. Laws Act No. 7, Ch. No. 2, H.B. 29.
[1304] 2023 Cal. Stat. Ch. 872, S.B. No. 444.

system to award professional or applied doctoral degrees statewide that do not duplicate doctoral degrees from the UC system.[1305] California allowed community colleges to offer courses in a language other than English without obligating students to be enrolled concurrently in English versions of the same classes.[1306] California permitted community colleges to substitute Lincoln or Washington holidays for the Lunar New Year.[1307]

Indiana permitted its Commission For Higher Education to create an education and career support services pilot program to provide career and support services to adult students of HEIs.[1308] Oregon directed its Higher Education Coordinating Commission and Department of Corrections to enter into a memorandum of understanding on educational programs delivered in corrections facilities.[1309] Oregon then permitted community colleges to offer Bachelor of Science in nursing degrees.[1310]

New York directed boards of trustees for the state and city universities as well as community colleges to adopt policies to award degrees posthumously.[1311] Rhode Island decided that individuals may earn bachelors' degree in its public HEIs by earning credits through apprenticeships.[1312] Utah removed a provision limiting its state BOE from allocating funds for an International Baccalaureate (IB) program, aligning such funding with other early college program funding.[1313]

Students in Higher Education

Scholarships for teachers address two policy goals: making college affordable and addressing staffing shortages in the public schools. Last year, nine states funded 11 teacher scholarships, as follows. Connecticut created an Aspiring Educator Diversity Scholarship program.[1314] Indiana initiated a Next Generation Hoosier Educators Scholarship program, which provides one-time

---

[1305] 2023 Cal. Stat. Ch. 663, A.B. No. 656.
[1306] 2023 Cal. Stat. Ch. 559, A.B. No. 1096.
[1307] 2023 Cal. Stat. Ch. 517, A.B. No. 264.
[1308] 2023 Ind. Acts P.L. 216, HB 1160.
[1309] 2023 Or. Laws Ch. 279, S.B. 269.
[1310] 2023 Or. Laws Ch. 287, S.B. 523.
[1311] 2023 N.Y. Laws Ch. 549, A. 4942.
[1312] 2023 R.I. Pub. Laws S.B. 178, H.B. 6477.
[1313] 2023 Utah Laws H.B. 189.
[1314] 2023 Conn. Acts 167, Subst. S.B. No. 1, § 11.

scholarships for individuals transitioning from another field into teaching.[1315] Indiana next increased the amount awarded for the Next Generation Hoosier teacher scholarships from $7,500 to $10,000.[1316] Nebraska adopted the Door to College Scholarship Act which provides monetary incentives for teacher recruitment and retention in high-need areas.[1317]

New Mexico amended a scholarship program to produce more teachers by allowing licensed teachers to participate in the program to pursue graduate study, and by permitting recipients to attend school part time.[1318] Oklahoma changed the name of a scholarship program designed to attract persons to become teachers to the "Inspired to Teach" program.[1319] Oregon created a scholarship for early childhood and education professionals particularly working in areas regarding mental health and behavioral services.[1320] Oregon increased the number of scholarships awarded by the Higher Education Coordinating Commission to diverse teacher candidates.[1321]
South Dakota expanded eligibility for teachers to receive tuition and fee benefits for taking university courses for teachers in public school, accredited schools, or Head Start programs.[1322] Tennessee created a scholarship for future teachers.[1323] Texas established a future teachers scholarship for students attending public HEIs.[1324]

Six states adopted scholarships for persons connected to the military. Idaho modified language for eligibility for scholarships for children of members of the armed forces and public safety officers by removing the requirement that their parents must be "totally and permanently disabled," replacing it with "determined to be unemployable."[1325] Louisiana created a National Guard scholarship program to cover the cost of mandatory fees for members attending state public HEIs[1326] Oklahoma channeled funds to more specific purposes to state institutions of higher

---

[1315] 2023 Ind. Acts P.L. 242, HB 1528.
[1316] 2023 Ind. Acts P.L. 161, HB 1637.
[1317] 2023 Neb. Laws LB 705.
[1318] 2023 N.M. Laws Ch. 201, SB 307.
[1319] 2023 Okla. Sess. Laws H.B. No. 2559.
[1320] 2023 Or. Laws Ch. 609, H.B. 3561.
[1321] 2023 Or. Laws Ch. 431, H.B. 3178.
[1322] 2023 S.D. Laws S.B. 118.
[1323] 2023 Tenn. Pub. Acts Ch. No. 381, H.B. No. 432, Subs. S.B. No. 1220.
[1324] 2023 Tex. Gen. Laws H.B. No. 4363.
[1325] 2023 Idaho Sess. Laws Ch. 260, H.B. No. 219.
[1326] 2023 La. Acts No. 279, H.B. No. 485.

education, such as for general scholarships and scholarships to members of the National Guard.[1327]

South Dakota provided free tuition at institutions governed by its Board of Technical Education for children and spouses of disabled or deceased members of the National Guard.[1328] South Dakota then amended its statute providing tuition payments for members of the National Guard, specifying that federal tuition benefits do not include payments by the U.S. Department of Veterans Affairs.[1329] Vermont provided the same tuition rate as in-state tuition for members of the National Guard or a non-Vermont approved postsecondary institutions.[1330] Virginia permitted public HEIs to enter into special arrangement contracts with the Department of Military Affairs to provide reduced-rate tuition charges for members of the National Guard.[1331]

Three states funded tribal scholarships. Minnesota appropriated $8.5 million for its American Indian Scholars Program, with roughly half going equally to the University of Minnesota and half to state colleges.[1332] Montana amended its Tribal Computer Programming Scholarship Program to include elementary and secondary teachers, not just high school teachers.[1333] Oregon established a Tribal Student Grant Program to increase college participation for members of Indian Tribes.[1334]

Fourteen states funded 17 other types of scholarships. Arkansas added vocational technical schools and technical institutes as approved institutions for students to participate in its Academic Challenge Scholarship Program.[1335] Colorado created a program to provide higher education financial assistance to students who perform youth mentorships.[1336] Colorado created a universal high school scholarship program for students pursuing in-demand or high-priority postsecondary pathways identified by its state Office of Economic Development.[1337] Florida increased the number of students receiving its Family Empowerment

---

[1327] 2023 Okla. Sess. Laws (1st Spec. Sess.) S.B. No. 28.
[1328] 2023 S.D. Laws H.B. 1046.
[1329] 2023 S.D. Laws H.B. 1039.
[1330] 2023 Vt. Laws Ch. No. 66, H. 461.
[1331] 2023 Va. Acts Ch. 638 S.B. 955.
[1332] 2023 Minn. Laws Ch. 41, sec. 1, subd. 41, HF 2073.
[1333] 2023 Mont. Laws H.B. 346.
[1334] 2023 Or. Laws Ch. 558, H.B. 3565.
[1335] 2023 Ark. Acts 539, H.B. 1417.
[1336] 2023 Colo. Sess. Laws S.B. 149.
[1337] 2023 Colo. Sess. Laws S.B. 205.

Scholarship.[1338] For access to a HOPE Scholarship, Georgia replaced the ACT score of 26 with one calculated annually by its state Student Finance Commission.[1339]

Illinois recast its iGROW Scholarship to the iGROW Technology Scholarship.[1340] Illinois repealed a pilot program for its Aim High grant program.[1341] Minnesota created its North Star Promise Scholarship Program, to benefit state students.[1342] At the same time, Minnesota funded early learning scholarships, Head Start, early childhood education programs, and modifications to early education programs.[1343] Mississippi created a dual enrollment/dual credit scholarship program.[1344] Then Nevada also prohibited its Board of Regents from denying tuition-free status at state universities based on immigration status.[1345] Rhode Island created its Hope Scholarship pilot program to provide two-year scholarships to juniors and seniors at Rhode Island College.[1346]

South Dakota increased the scholarship award amount for its Opportunity Scholarships.[1347] Tennessee allowed students who earns their first baccalaureate degrees in less time than projected to continue to receive a HOPE Scholarship to pursue an advanced degree.[1348] Utah increased funding for the Special Needs Opportunity Scholarship Program.[1349] Virginia extended the *Brown v. Board of Education* scholarship program for lineal and collateral descendants domiciled or residing in Virginia between 1954 and 1964 for whom schools were closed to avoid desegregation.[1350] West Virginia included West Virginia Junior College as an institution eligible to accept PROMISE scholarship recipients.[1351]

Two other states enacted scholarship bills expressly for adult students. Indiana created a career scholarship account fund to

---

[1338] 2023 Fla. Laws Ch. 328, H. 773 (3rd Spec. Session).
[1339] 2023 Ga. Laws Act 52, H.B. 607.
[1340] 2023 Ill. Laws P.A. 103-519, HB 1378.
[1341] 2023 Ill. Laws P.A. 103-516, HB 301.
[1342] 2023 Minn. Laws Ch. 41, Sec. 19, HF 2073.
[1343] 2023 Minn. Laws Ch. 54, HF 2292.
[1344] 2023 Miss. Laws SB 2487.
[1345] 2023 Nev. Stat. Ch. 281, AB 226.
[1346] 2023 R.I. Pub. Laws S.B. 77, H.B. 5099.
[1347] 2023 S.D. Laws H.B. 1055.
[1348] 2023 Tenn. Pub. Acts Ch. No. 368, H.B. No. 27, Subs. S.B. No. 74.
[1349] 2023 Utah Laws H.B. 398.
[1350] 2023 Va. Acts Ch. 605, H.B. 1419; 2023 Va. Acts Ch. 606, S.B. 1498.
[1351] 2023 W. Va. Acts Ch. 181, H.B. 3224.

assist adult students with education and workforce development.[1352] Kansas adopted an Adult Learner Grant Act to permit adult learners to pursue fields of study including career technical education credentials.[1353]

Seven states approved eight acts offering free tuition for military-connected students. California amended a provision for free tuition for children of veterans, specifying that the application was limited to children who whose family incomes are below the federal and state poverty level.[1354] Florida clarified qualifications for the award of tuition its pays to limit awards to spouses or children of deceased or disabled service members.[1355] Iowa modified provisions in its tuition grants program including removing a limit of eight semesters for full-time students.[1356]

Louisiana granted an exemption for disabled veterans who do not qualify for a 100% exemption to pay the uncovered tuition and fees.[1357] Nevada waived tuition charges at state HEIs for students with parents who received Purple Hearts.[1358] North Dakota offered free tuition to public HEIs for dependents of disabled veterans or those killed in action.[1359] Oklahoma provided in-state tuition payments for family members and members of the armed forces.[1360]

Two states adopted other tuition grants or waivers. Oregon permitted the waiver of tuition and fees for former foster children to pursue initial undergraduate degrees.[1361] New Jersey authorized awards of annual summer tuition grants for students in HEIs.[1362]

Two states granted resident status for tuition purposes for undocumented aliens. California exempted the nonresident tuition fee at community colleges when students' residences are near the California-Mexico border.[1363] Utah provided residency for higher education tuition purposes for aliens with special immigration

---

[1352] 2023 Ind. Acts P.L. 202, HB 1002.
[1353] 2023 Kan. Sess. Laws SB 123.
[1354] 2023 Cal. Stat. Ch. 695, A.B. No. 1745.
[1355] 2023 Fla. Laws Ch. 279, H. 339.
[1356] 2023 Iowa Acts HF 421.
[1357] 2023 La. Acts No. 224, H.B. No. 167.
[1358] 2023 Nev. Stat. Ch. 471, AB 279.
[1359] 2023 N.D. Laws H.B. No. 1196.
[1360] 2023 Okla. Sess. Laws H.B. No. 2663.
[1361] 2023 Or. Laws Ch. 179, S.B. 449.
[1362] 2023 N.J. Pub. Laws c. 283, S. 3987.
[1363] 2023 Cal. Stat. Ch. 796, A.B. No. 91.

visas or who were granted refugee status or other temporary protected status.[1364]

Three states adopted measures aimed to address affordability and staff shortages. Iowa created an educational savings account program to assist with payment for higher education instructional costs.[1365] Virginia initiated a reduced tuition rate at Norfolk State University and Virginia State University for out-of-state students who have completed at least 30 credit hours of coursework and are enrolled in programs leading to employment in high-demand teaching fields.[1366] Washington amended provisions for student loan programs in higher education, offering examples of graduate programs considered in high demand such as health care, behavioral and mental health, early education, K-12 education, higher education, law enforcement, and public safety.[1367]

Two states directed their HEIs to provide more information and transparency regarding the costs of education. California required each campus of its community college and state university systems to display the estimated costs for each course prominently along with costs for course materials and fees for no less than an annually increasing percentage up to 75%, by January of each year.[1368] Iowa directed its state Board of Regents to provide information related to the average income and student debt of institution graduates to undergraduates.[1369]

Four states passed measures to use FAFSA as a means of making college more affordable. Iowa created its educational savings account program to assist with payment for higher education instructional costs.[1370] Hawaii exempted community college students enrolled in certification programs from completing FAFSA each year to be eligible for community college scholarships.[1371] New Jersey removed the expected family contribution from the calculation of financial need, resulting in public HEIs reducing student financial aid.[1372] Maine expanded access to postsecondary education for low-income parents by

---

[1364] 2023 Utah Laws H.B. 102.
[1365] 2023 Iowa Acts HF 68.
[1366] 2023 Va. Acts Ch. 696, H.B. 2272; 2023 Va. Acts Ch. 697, S.B. 1448.
[1367] 2023 Wash Laws. Ch. 389, H.B. 1823.
[1368] 2023 Cal. Stat. Ch. 660, A.B. No. 607.
[1369] 2023 Iowa Acts HF 135.
[1370] 2023 Iowa Acts HF 68.
[1371] 2023 Haw. Sess. Laws Act 57, SB 1151.
[1372] 2023 N.J. Pub. Laws c. 317, A. 4814.

raising the permissible income level from 185% to 225% of the nonfarm income official poverty line, thereby impacting FAFSA calculations.[1373]

Three states adopted measures to make textbooks and instructional materials more affordable. Louisiana initiated a pilot program for affordable digital textbook and learning materials.[1374] Texas provided pilot program financial assistance to public junior colleges, public technical institutes, and public state colleges to transition to digital instructional materials.[1375] West Virginia permitted governing boards for state HEIs to work with vendors to establish courseware and book fees at lump sum or credit hour bases provided that opt-out option are available to students in advance of the start of each academic term.[1376]

Three states severed the connection between debt to HEIs and access to transcripts. Maryland prohibited HEIs from refusing to provide transcripts or taking other punitive measures regarding student's transcript requests because they owes a debt to the institutions.[1377] Nevada forbade the board of trustees for its university system from charging students higher fees to obtain transcripts due to outstanding debts.[1378] Oregon prohibited postsecondary institutions of education based in the state from refusing to provide transcripts to current or former students because the individuals owed them debts.[1379]

Six states enacted bills on First Amendment speech and religion rights. Arizona amended a provision on speech for university and community college students, specifying that officials may regulate economic activity on their campuses.[1380] Arkansas adopted an act on free speech at state-supported HEIs.[1381] Maryland required its public HEIs to adopt written policies providing reasonable academic accommodations for students to practice sincerely held faith-based or religious beliefs.[1382] North Dakota codified a ban on discrimination and a

---

[1373] 2023 Me. Laws Ch. 21, H.P. 9, L.D. 5.
[1374] 2023 La. Acts No. 128, H.B. No. 644.
[1375] 2023 Tex. Gen. Laws H.B. No. 2177.
[1376] 2023 W. Va. Acts Ch. 184, H.B. 3555.
[1377] 2023 Md. Laws Ch. 748, S.B. 248; 2023 Md. Laws Ch. 749, H.B. 384.
[1378] 2023 Nev. Stat. Ch. 28, AB 212.
[1379] 2023 Or. Laws Ch. 284, S.B. 424.
[1380] 2023 Ariz. Sess. Laws Ch. 184, S.B. 1013.
[1381] 2023 Ark. Acts 614, S.B. 125.
[1382] 2023 Md. Laws Ch. 634, H.B. 923.

ban on specified concept training in its HEIs, listing listed offending beliefs but closing by paying homage to the First Amendment.[1383] Texas directed that instructional personnel in public HEIs may not be prohibited from displaying posters or framed copies of the National Motto in their classrooms.[1384] West Virginia passed an act to support and define the free speech rights of student journalists in HEIs.[1385]

Two states passed acts challenging the First Amendment protections for diversity, equity, and inclusion (DEI) on college campuses. Tennessee enacted the Higher Education Freedom of Expression and Transparency Act. Besides seeking equality in access to universities as places for speech, the act focused on the role of divisive concepts on campuses, placing a spotlight on the role of a person whose job title includes DEI.[1386] Texas required the governing board of HEIs to ensure that, except as mandated by federal law, they do not establish or maintain DEI officers or contracts for services of DEI offices, and mandatory monitoring of DEI activities; the act forbade preferences for the employment of persons based on race, sex, color, ethnicity, or national origin.[1387]

Three states enacted bills relating to the issue of gender identity. Arkansas adopted a "given name" act, which prohibited requiring employees of state-supported HEIs to use persons' preferred pronoun, names, or titles without parental consent.[1388] California directed California State University and the University of California to permit students, staff, and faculty to update records on name changes or gender identification.[1389] North Dakota directed that public and private HEIs designate their athletic teams as male, female, or coeducational, prohibiting athletic teams or sport designated for females from being open to males based on individuals' non-ambiguous sex organs, chromosomes, and endogenous hormone profiles at birth.[1390]

Three states adopted bills on college admissions. California prohibited students from being denied admission to community college apprenticeships and internship training programs because

---

[1383] 2023 N.D. Laws S.B. No. 2247.
[1384] 2023 Tex. Gen. Laws H.B. No. 2012.
[1385] 2023 W. Va. Acts Ch. 175, S.B. 121.
[1386] 2023 Tenn. Pub. Acts Ch. No. 268, S.B. No. 817, Subs. H.B. No. 1376.
[1387] 2023 Tex. Gen. Laws S.B. No. 17.
[1388] 2023 Ark. Acts 542, H.B. 1468.
[1389] 2023 Cal. Stat. Ch. 222, A.B. No. 760.
[1390] 2023 N.D. Laws H.B. No. 1489.

they used individual tax ID numbers for purposes of a background check.[1391] Illinois required community colleges to create four-year uniform admission system pilot programs to admit transfer students for each semester of the program.[1392] Texas discontinued the use class rankings in determining eligibility of applicants with nontraditional secondary education experiences such as homeschool or virtual instruction for admission to HEIs.[1393]

Another three states enacted four acts on college enrollment and registration. California required its CSU system and requested its UC system to adopt priority enrollment plans for first responders.[1394] Colorado directed all HEIs that are not regionally accredited to provide incoming students with enrollment agreements or contracts before enrolling.[1395] Colorado also removed a previous obligation for students to register for the U.S. Selective Service System in order to be eligible to enroll in state-supported HEIs.[1396] Texas provided early registration preference for parenting students at HEIs.[1397]

Four states joined the Purple Star program which provides liaison services to assist students connected to the military. Florida defined a "military student" as a one enrolled in a public HEIs and on active duty for the purposes of providing liaison services, assistance, and participation in the Higher Education Purple Star campus program.[1398] Indiana adopted the Purple Star Program to recognize veterans pursuing higher education.[1399] Wyoming provided for the designation of Purple Star schools that take specific actions to assist military-connected students.[1400] Louisiana allowed the designation of postsecondary educational institution as veteran-friendly campuses to last for two instead of one year.[1401]

Two states borrowed from the ideas of the Purple Star program, expanding it to require the appointment of an ombudsperson to assist all students in their transition into college. Texas required HEIs to designate employees as liaison officers for

---

[1391] 2023 Cal. Stat. Ch. 73, S.B. No. 467.
[1392] 2023 Ill. Laws P.A. 103-205, HB 3760.
[1393] 2023 Tex. Gen. Laws H.B. No. 3993.
[1394] 2023 Cal. Stat. Ch. 643, A.B. No. 255.
[1395] 2023 Colo. Sess. Laws S.B. 281.
[1396] 2023 Colo. Sess. Laws H.B. 1261.
[1397] 2023 Tex. Gen. Laws S.B. No. 459.
[1398] 2023 Fla. Laws Ch. 160, S. 732.
[1399] 2023 Ind. Acts P.L. 49, SB 384.
[1400] 2023 Wyo. Sess. Laws Act No. 50, Ch. No. 75, H.B. 56.
[1401] 2023 La. Acts No. 53, H.B. No. 72.

current or incoming students with children younger than 18 years old to assist them with connections to resources.[1402] Washington ordered all public HEIs and the tribal college to have benefits navigators assigned at least 75% of full-time, not to be divided between two or more staff, to assist students in accessing public benefits such as housing, food, and childcare.[1403]

Two states called for better articulation and seamless transfers of college credit. Colorado changed a provision on students receiving associate degrees through the CORE (COlorado RE-engaged) curriculum, thereby permitting 15 or more credit hours from prior institutions.[1404] Illinois amended its Articulation Initiative Act for transfer of courses between community colleges and universities, by requiring public HEIs to have up to four core courses in each major.[1405]

Two states addressed student hunger on their campuses. Illinois directed its state Board of Higher Education to establish a hunger-free campus grant program for its public HEIs.[1406] Minnesota appropriated $1.0 million in funds for hunger-free campus grants.[1407]

Two states seemed to place the duty of remediating students on community colleges. Illinois obligated community college districts, on request from local school boards, to provide individual disaggregated data on student enrollment in community college remediation courses.[1408] Tennessee permitted its state university and its system to work with two-year institutions governed by its Board of Regents to provide remedial or developmental courses or coursework, regardless of whether they provide those courses.[1409]

Other acts related to students in higher education are detailed as follows. Arkansas prohibited discrimination based on natural or cultural hairstyles in two- and four-year HEIs Illinois directed that student profile information collected by high schools be made to public HEIs in a timely manner.[1410] Indiana ordered its Commission for Higher Education to cooperate with its

---

[1402] 2023 Tex. Gen. Laws H.B. No. 1361.
[1403] 2023 Wash Laws. Ch. 421, H.B. 1559.
[1404] 2023 Colo. Sess. Laws H.B. 1262.
[1405] 2023 Ill. Laws P.A. 103-469, SB 2288.
[1406] 2023 Ill. Laws P.A. 103-435, HB 2528.
[1407] 2023 Minn. Laws Ch. 41, sec. 1, subd. 35, HF 2073.
[1408] 2023 Ill. Laws P.A. 103-401, SB 2240.
[1409] 2023 Tenn. Pub. Acts Ch. No. 289, H.B. No. 29, Subs. S.B. 89.
[1410] 2023 Ill. Laws P.A. 103-204, HB 3759.

Department of Education to identify students who meet the requirements to participate in its Twenty-First Century Scholars Program.[1411] Minnesota required HEIs to provide access to menstrual products free of charge.[1412] Texas called for ed recognition of the right to confidentiality for information about people who were aided in accessing postsecondary education; the act mandated the distribution of information about postsecondary education and career opportunities.[1413]

Texas obligated officials in colleges or universities receiving state aid or support which do not offer at least a three-semester hour undergraduate course on state history to contract with an institution that has such a course for delivery.[1414] Texas forbade officials in HEIs from obligating parenting students under the age of 16 to take leaves of absence, withdraw, limit their studies, participate in alternative programs, change majors, degrees, or certification programs, refrain from participating in any courses, activities or programs, solely because of their status as pregnant or parenting.[1415]

Virginia directed the governing boards of each baccalaureate public HEIs to adopt policies requiring that participation in internships or work-based learning experiences be integrated into students' degree programs so as not to extend the time to complete their studies.[1416] Virginia ordered public HEIs maintaining and operating university housing during scheduled intersessions to provide access to the it at no cost for homeless students eligible for a grant for this purpose.[1417] Wisconsin added an exemption regarding motor vehicles bearing special registration plates issued to disabled veteran, so that university parking rules or regulations are consistent with governmental ordinances.[1418]

Athletics in Higher Education

Two issues dominated legislative interests in athletics in higher education: the management of name, image, and likeness (NIL); and participation rules arising from gender identity. Seven

---

[1411] 2023 Ind. Acts P.L. 235, HB 1449.
[1412] 2023 Minn. Laws Ch. 41, sec. 1, HF 2073.
[1413] 2023 Tex. Gen. Laws H.B. No. 2920.
[1414] 2023 Tex. Gen. Laws S.B. No. 427.
[1415] 2023 Tex. Gen. Laws S.B. No. 412.
[1416] 2023 Va. Acts Ch. 758, S.B. 1280.
[1417] 2023 Va. Acts Ch.33, H.B. 1403.
[1418] 2023 Wis. Laws Act 59, H.B. 49.

states passed acts weighing in on how NIL will work in their HEIs. Arkansas amended a Student-Athlete Publicity Rights Act to permit HEIs, their supporting foundations, or its authorized entities to identify, create, facilitate, and otherwise enable opportunities for student-athletes to earn compensation for the commercial use of their publicity rights.[1419] California removed a requirement for HEIs to rely exclusively on revenue derived from media rights for intercollegiate athletics to defray the costs of affording benefits to student-athletes.[1420]

Colorado permitted HEIs to identify, create, solicit, facilitate, and otherwise empower opportunities for student-athletes to earn compensation for the use of their NILs following their consent to do so.[1421] Missouri amended provisions about student-athletes' rights related to the use of their NILs to address the relationship between and among themselves, college athletics associations, and a postsecondary educational institutions, as well as "unique identifiers" such as seals, logos, emblems, mottos, and the like.[1422] New Mexico removed a prohibition against postsecondary educational institutions arranging compensation for the use of a student-athlete's NILs.[1423] Oklahoma amended its law regarding student-athletes' NILs by prohibiting postsecondary institutions from identifying, enabling, or supporting opportunities for individuals to earn compensation for NIL activities.[1424] Texas altered rules governing athletic associations and HEIs to permit NIL accommodation and compensation for student-athletes.[1425]

Two states prohibited athletic participation based on their definitions of gender rather than athletes' own gender identities. Alabama added to the prohibition for transgender athletes from competing in all non-coeducational school athletics. The act provided immunity for public K-12 schools, colleges, and universities for maintaining separate athletic teams or sorting for biological male students while prohibiting retaliation against students who reports alleged violation of the act to an employee or representative of the public educational institutions.[1426] Texas

---

[1419] 2023 Ark. Acts 589, H.B. 1649.
[1420] 2023 Cal. Stat. Ch. 625, S.B. No. 661.
[1421] 2023 Colo. Sess. Laws S.B. 293.
[1422] 2023 Mo. Laws H.B. No. 447.
[1423] 2023 N.M. Laws Ch. 105, SB 219.
[1424] 2023 Okla. Sess. Laws S.B. No. 840.
[1425] 2023 Tex. Gen. Laws H.B. No. 2804.
[1426] 2023 Ala. Acts 293, H.B. 261.

obligated students in HEIs participating in intercollegiate athletic competitions to compete based on biological sex.[1427]

Safety in Higher Education

The dominant legislative response on safety in HEIs last year addressed sexual assault and harassment, with four states enacting seven bills. California directed governing boards of HEIs to provide a sexual assault forensic medical evaluation and transportation of victims.[1428] Also, California required or requested its governing boards over higher education that when hiring new employees to seek information on any claims of sexual harassment in the prior seven years.[1429] In a third act, California obligated the CSU system to report investigations and outcomes of sexual harassment complaints posted on its website annually.[1430] Hawaii obligated the University of Hawaii to ensure that individual who participate in university disciplinary processes to have training or experience in handling sexual misconduct complaints and in campus disciplinary processes.[1431]

Virginia included the Virginia Military Institute (VMI) as a public HEI with the duty to report acts of sexual violence; however, the provision stipulated that the VMI Superintendent may require cadets who discloses instances of substance abuse to attend drug or substance use disorder counseling.[1432] Virginia directed the governing board of its public HEIs to develop and implement policies on human trafficking awareness and prevention training programs to be delivered at first-year orientation.[1433] Washington added to a provision on sexual misconduct in colleges and universities, requiring professional associations to adopt codes of conduct forbidding sexual misconduct at academic activities or events while establishing investigative procedures for allegations of code violations.[1434]

Three states enacted bills with respect to police services. Georgia established a unified campus police force through a

---

[1427] 2023 Tex. Gen. Laws S.B. No. 15.
[1428] 2023 Cal. Stat. Ch. 564, A.B. No 1138.
[1429] 2023 Cal. Stat. Ch. 415, S.B. No. 791.
[1430] 2023 Cal. Stat. Ch. 417, S.B. No. 808.
[1431] 2023 Haw. Sess. Laws Act 76, HB 554.
[1432] 2023 Va. Acts Ch. 160, H.B. 1870.
[1433] 2023 Va. Acts Ch. 30, H.B. 1555; 2023 Va. Acts Ch. 31, S.B. 1373.
[1434] 2023 Wash Laws. Ch. 79, 2nd Subst. H.B. 1522.

memorandum of understanding entered by colleges or universities with local police jurisdictions.[1435] Louisiana required the heads of law enforcement or criminal justice agencies located within the parishes of the campuses of a postsecondary institution to execute memoranda of understanding within 30 days of making proposal about campus security.[1436] Virginia enabled its School for the Deaf and Blind to establish and maintain a campus security department.[1437]

Four states fostered efforts to prevent suicide in HEIs. New Jersey ordered HEIs to implement suicide prevention programming and raise awareness about available mental health services.[1438] Tennessee directed public HEIs, when issuing new identifications cards to students, to include contact information for crisis and suicide prevention on them.[1439] Virginia obligated public HEIs to provide suicide and crisis lifeline telephone numbers on student identification cards.[1440] West Virginia mandated that both public and private HEIs print information on suicide prevention resources on student identification cards.[1441]

Three states passed bills on the dangers of fentanyl and other opioids. California required its CSU system and recommended that its UC system use fentanyl test strips to assist in student safety.[1442] South Dakota permitted employers to acquire and make available opioid antagonists dispensed or distributed by licensed health care professionals. As broadly stated, the act appeared to include school boards and postsecondary employers.[1443] Texas added public HEIs along with first responders, Emergency Medical Technicians, and public schools, to receive opioid antagonists in a program authorizing distributions.[1444]

Two states adopted acts about firearms on campuses. Tennessee added to the list of persons permitted to carry handguns on property of a public HEIs by including law enforcement officers who retired in good standing and with 20 years of service.[1445] West

---

[1435] 2023 Ga. Laws Act 266, H.B. 142.
[1436] 2023 La. Acts No. 211, S.B. No. 202.
[1437] 2023 Va. Acts Ch. 428, S.B. 826.
[1438] 2023 N.J. Pub. Laws c. 168, A. 1176.
[1439] 2023 Tenn. Pub. Acts Ch. No. 190, S.B. No. 350, Subs. H.B. No. 294.
[1440] 2023 Va. Acts Ch. 223, S.B. 1044.
[1441] 2023 W. Va. Acts Ch. 142, H.B. 3218.
[1442] 2023 Cal. Stat. Ch. 525, A.B. No. 461.
[1443] 2023 S.D. Laws H.B. 1162.
[1444] 2023 Tex. Gen. Laws S.B. No. 867.
[1445] 2023 Tenn. Pub. Acts Ch. No. 149, S.B. No. 515, Subs. H.B. 723.

Virginia blocked higher education authorities from restricting or regulating the carrying of concealed pistols or revolvers on campuses of HEIs and legislated permission for individuals with concealed carry permits to carry such weapons on campus property.[1446]

Other acts related to student safety and well-being in HEIs are described as follows. Colorado mandated the placement of epinephrine auto-injectors in HEIs.[1447] Connecticut prohibited HEIs from receiving money or profiting from directly soliciting students to gamble online.[1448] California required its CSU system and recommended that its UC system use an affidavit of application for legal immunization to accompany financial aid requests.[1449] New York directed colleges to implement plans to investigate of hate crimes on their campuses, to inform incoming students about hate crime prevention measures, and to post campus crime statistics on their websites.[1450]

Texas amended a provision about reporting of hazing in HEIs to discharge the duty by reporting to peace or law enforcement officers, not just to deans or other campus officials.[1451] Virginia called for the creation of threat assessment teams for public HEIs on preliminary determinations that individuals pose articulable and significant threats of violence to others, to obtain criminal history records and notify the campus police department, local law enforcement, and the threatening individual, and the commonwealth attorney within 24 hours of doing so.[1452]

Conclusion

This chapter describes and sorts legislative acts adopted by the United States Congress and each of the fifty state legislatures-general assemblies during the 2023 calendar year. The second author began researching and reporting for this chapter with the 1998 legislative year when only five education-related acts were reported at the federal level and 253 education-related acts were enacted by state legislative bodies. This chapter reported 1,480

[1446] 2023 W. Va. Acts Ch. 174, S.B. 10.
[1447] 2023 Colo. Sess. Laws S.B. 299.
[1448] 2023 Conn. Acts 68, H.B. No. 5232.
[1449] 2023 Cal. Stat. Ch. 584, A.B. No. 1540.
[1450] 2023 N.Y. Laws Ch. 191, A. 3694.
[1451] 2023 Tex. Gen. Laws S.B. No. 37.
[1452] 2023 Va. Acts Ch. 226, H.B. 1916; 2023 Va. Acts Ch. 227, S.B. 910.

education-related legislative acts for the 2021 legislative year, 1,319 acts in 2022, and 1,433 acts in 2023. Table 1 at the end of this chapter represents the continuing trend of accelerating numbers of education-related acts since 1998 with peaks in 2011, 2019, 2021, and 2023.

The data in Table 1 demonstrate that legislative bodies produced more education-related legislation in 2021 than any time since 1998, with 1,480 acts in the later year. In 2020, the year marking the height of the COVID-19 pandemic, the total dropped to 799 acts. In *The Yearbook of Education Law 2021* the authors speculated not only that the decreased number of acts in 2020 was due to the COVID-19 pandemic but also observed that the data showed there is a trough in the numbers in presidential election years.

Readers are invited to recognize that the categories dividing this chapter have generally remained unchanged since 1998 with one exception. Because there were no acts regarding professional development in 2010, the major heading for "Professional Development" was folded into the "Employment" section in 2011. Sorting each year's acts into consistent categories from year to year can help readers in spotting new policy initiatives as they emerge. Sorting the acts again within the category of subject headings can be used to acknowledge emerging trends as well as differences in approaches adopted in different jurisdictions. Table 2 at the end of this chapter provides the number of acts reported in each category of education-related legislation passed in 2023.

In 2023 higher education-related legislation represented the largest number of legislative acts among the subject headings for this chapter, with 253 acts. In 1998 13 states enacted 18 acts about higher education. In 1999 16 states added 35 more acts regarding higher education. From 2000 to 2005, on average, 29 states annually adopted 54 acts related to higher education. Then the amount of higher education-related legislation accelerated dramatically each year until 2011, with 94 acts in 2006; 170 acts in 2007; 151 acts in 2008; 141 acts in 2009; 218 acts in 2010; 257 acts in 2011.

The first decade of the new century marked a change as legislatures started treated higher education more like K-12 schools with more direct involvement about their internal operations. In subsequent years the number of higher education-related acts remained relatively high as follows: 150 in 2012; 147 in 2013; 151 in 2014; 173 in 2015; 102 in 2016; 147 in 2017; 167 in 2018; 263 in 2019; 152 in 2020; 314 in 2021; 249 in 2022; and 253 in 2023. In the current decade higher education-related legislation was the most numerous legislative category except in 2022 when the category of governance and school leadership acts had the most new laws.

A leading concern of legislative bodies regarding higher education in 2023 was affordability. Scholarships and tuition waivers were offered largely to four groups of students who might go into teaching, are connected to the military, are members of Native American tribes, and are adults desiring to go to college later in life. A similar number of scholarships were inaugurated or amended to encourage participation in various programs such as for dual credits and career technology.

Legislatures directed Officials in HEIs to provide more transparency and information about the costs of education, to plan for ease of credit transfers between institutions and programs, to spare the expense of wasted courses, and to plan pathways for students progressing through their institutions. Additionally, legislatures ordered these officials to do more to ease the transition of students into college through enrollment assistance, priority in registration, and the availability of personnel to serve as liaisons between enrollees and their institutions.

The term "pathways" has matured and changed since it first appeared in legislation in 2019. The term first seemed to refer to legislative decisions to put more resources into career technology programs beginning in middle school before projecting into community colleges and career technology institutions. By 2021 the term connoted the need for students to be made more aware of careers not needing college educations. The term incorporated the use of internships, paid apprenticeships, and industry certification. By 2022 and 2023, the term expanded to refer not only to the earlier meanings but also the need to plan various paths, to know where the paths cross, and to provide options for students to change paths more than once.

A recurring policy direction has been greater requirements for governing authorities to provide better oversight of private proprietary schools. Such oversight has included the need to ferret out unfair, misleading, or deceptive practices in recruitment and program delivery. Other measures included the right to issue cease and desist orders against schools with the possibility of civil penalties. One state directed its Board of Regents to fashion policy to judge whether private schools meet the same standards of academic quality and fiscal responsibility as public ones while another extended oversight of postsecondary proprietary schools to the companies providing student loan.

The authors previously reported that legislators first interceded directly in academic programs in public HEIs in 2000 and over the years when they did their interventions usually involved teacher education programs. Twelve such acts were recorded in 2021 with 14 more in 2022. In 2023, 10 acts provided divergent direction to teacher education and administrator preparation programs with some of them increasing requirements and others providing ways to assist students in becoming certificated to teach more quickly.

States continued to address concerns about the safety and well-being of students in higher education settings as expressed by more legislation on hazing, harassment, sexual harassment, and sexual assault. More attention was given in 2023 to health care services on campus with greater focus on mental health issues. A new feature last year in on-campus health care services was directions on reproductive health care with opposing views in a few states on what services may be provided with respect to advice or assistance related to abortion.

Legislation on sports in higher education addressed two topics. The first involved direction for athletic programs in accommodating student-athletes' right to negotiate agreements for the use of their name, image, or likeness. The second topic concerned gender identity including who may participate in which sports and which names and pronouns can be used to address persons.

In 2023 legislation about First Amendment speech and religion rights of students and faculty recurred. Legislatures in 2022 deployed the public forum doctrine to describe what was permitted that is likely to invite litigation. Under the banner of prohibiting discrimination some states banned the teaching of specific concepts. Likewise, some states proscribed diversity, equity, and inclusion programs in public HEIs. Legislation prescribing or proscribing beliefs or specified concepts in higher education or legislation about gender identity are evidence of the culture wars in our society. They are further evidence that understanding of the role of higher education as a "marketplace of ideas"[1453] is fading.

[1453] Abrams v. U.S., 250 U.S. 616 (1919) (Holmes, J. dissenting).

Legislation related to school employment was the second-most-common category of legislation in 2023, with 204 acts recorded. The number of employment-related acts averaged 65 annually from 2000-2005; 85 in 2006; 157 in 2007; 107 in 2008; 113 in 2009; 151 in 2010; 183 in 2011; 127 in 2012; 95 in 2013; 94 in 2014; 102 in 2015; 57 in 2016; 124 in 2017; 155 in 2018; 148 in 2019; 98 in 2020; 156 in 2021; 167 in 2022, and 204 in 2023. More recently school employment-related legislation has competed with school safety for second place among the most numerous.

In the 2023 calendar year legislative bodies accelerated their agendas to address shortages in the availability of teachers and other educational staff, adopting a multitude of strategies to meet this policy goal. Various states provided salary incentives such as signing bonuses to sign or retain employees. Another incentive method appearing in five acts was designed to attract more professional education staff by providing financial assistance as an incentive to seek certification. Scholarships designated for existing teachers to return to school to seek higher certifications, and therefore higher pay, might be an appealing means of retaining teachers. Other states added scholarships last year to attract beginning students into teacher education programs the most dominant financial incentive method even though it takes by far the longest time to bear fruit.

In some states uncertificated persons were simply permitted to teach. A few states permitted professional employees to work without certificates for a time as a means of temporarily filling positions. In one instance, the time was extended from 30 to 60 days. In another, a local board was only required to report the situation to a legislative committee with no mention of repercussion. In other states, professional employees, usually teachers, were permitted to work without certificates, with only high school diplomas, associate's degrees, or under manufactured job titles to place them in classrooms. A few states allowed uncertificated persons to teach on enrolling in teacher education program. Another method for allowing uncertificated persons to teach was to allow practice teachers to serve as teachers and be paid, sometimes with the experience renamed as another activity such as an externship residency, or apprenticeship.

Other states addressed their labor shortages by extending the time substitute teachers may teach during school years or setting aside limits on the use of substitute. Some states enacted bills to increase the pool of paraeducators and classified employees, while a few renaming their positions with a teacher's aide becoming a classroom monitor, implying thereby the endowment of new abilities.

Certificate reciprocity was a popular method of possibly increasing the pool of potential teachers and other professionals, many through an interstate reciprocity agreements. Multiple states enacted bills to fashion more alternative certificate programs to secure more professional staff. Moreover, other states amended their retirement programs to allow retirees to come out of retirement and work for a time, without losing their retirement benefits. Other strategies to increase the supply of teachers included the initiation of public relations campaigns, directions to place job postings on state websites, providing student loan assistance, and reviving the use of teacherages or housing for teachers.

Legislation regarding First Amendment issues from the Establishment, Free Exercise Clauses, and Speech appeared in the Employment section of this chapter. More First Amendment legislation was recorded in the section for Parental and Student Rights because these acts impact students, not employees. One state prohibited a school board from punishing employees for engaging in private religious expression otherwise protected by the First Amendment, absent a showing of actual coercion. Another state protected teachers from disciplinary proceedings for allegations that they violated the Establishment Clause. A third state provided immunity for teachers who refuse to refer to students by their preferred names or pronouns. Another state permitted boards to hire school chaplains.

A troubling piece of legislation required school boards to certify annually and provide evidence that instruction related to African American history does not indoctrinate a particular viewpoint. The act appeared to create a rebuttable presumption, with boards having the burden of production and proof, that the instruction does not indoctrinate. How does one prove a negative? At common law, absence of evidence proves the negative.[1454] How does the superintendent annually certify and provide evidence that evidence does not exist?

State legislative bodies adopted 202 school safety-related acts in 2023, making it the third most numerous category. By

---

[1454] Positive proof is that which directly establishes the fact in question, as opposed to negative proof, which establishes the fact by showing that its opposite is not or cannot be true. *See* BLACK'S LAW DICTIONARY 1215 (6th ed. 1990).

comparison, legislatures adopted 107 school safety-related acts in 1999, the year of violence at Columbine High School and 100 more each of the next two years. For 2002 to 2004, about 50 school safety acts were passed annually. The following number of acts were signed into law subsequently: 81 in 2005; 70 in 2006; 122 in 2007; 81 in 2008; 97 in 2009, 54 in 2010; 87 in 2011; 55 in 2012; 88 in 2013; 88 in 2014; 110 in 2015; 115 in 2016; 120 in 2017; 155 in 2018; 190 in 2019; 100 in 2020; 135 in 2021; 118 in 2022, and 202 in 2023. School safety was the most numerous category of legislation only once during the 2010s, in 2016. In the other years, it alternated second and third place with employment.

The most numerous type of school safety-related legislation in 2023 was student discipline policy with 29 acts adopted when included with laws on corporal punishment. Most of the new disciplinary policy requirements appear to be equitable, reasonable, and fair. One state limited suspensions and expulsions of students in the lower grades for willful defiance of school authorities. Another state prohibited public boards from expelling or suspending students for more than 10 school days for actions they took immediately preceding or following or that could be reasonably tied to incidents in which they reported being sexually assaulted or when staff members reported the assault. Even in situations where students' behaviors can warrant 12 months of expulsion, superintendents were empowered to recommend alternative consequence including alternative placement.

A few of the policy requirements were procedural in nature such as permitting student to challenge the appointment of hearing officers for perceived biases or requiring referrals to school-based mental health or behavioral health specialists for students after their second unduplicated infractions resulting in out-of-school suspensions in given semester. An interesting provision in one act prohibited school staff from cutting students' hair.

Colorado, Idaho, Maryland, New York, and West Virginia banned the use of corporal punishment. Additionally, Louisiana prohibited its use unless students' parents or legal guardians provided written consent for its use. Tennessee permitted corporal punishment while adding procedures, including documenting previous consequences given, conferring with parents, and considering evaluation for eligibility for special education.

The second most numerous types of school safety-related legislation in 2023 addressed school safety plans and drills with 25 acts recorded. Some of these acts mandated the creation of threat assessment teams to inform plan revisions. One feature added to safety plans was the need to map the facilities to speed law enforcement to the scene. Another feature was the obligation to address the needs of students with disabilities in implementing plans.

Safety drills were enhanced to address a variety of threats including fire, tornados, earthquakes, floods, extreme cold, extreme heat, active shooter situations, and medical emergencies. Through practice with the drills, threat assessment teams had to include more personnel from other agencies besides law enforcement such as fire departments, fire marshals, emergency management specialists, and search and rescue specialists. One state codified the duty to assess the impact of safety drills on students' mental health.

Taken together, medically related legislation in 2023 totaled 40 acts, including CPR and AEDs. opioid antagonists, substance abuse recovery, stocking and administration of medications, protection from allergens, and individual health plans.

Dealing with harassment and bullying continued to be an important policy prescription. The acts against harassment connoted a separation into two types, the bullying type of harassment and sexual harassment but may represent a false dichotomy. This may be an inapt separation because body shaming is undoubtedly both bullying and sexual harassment while teacher in inappropriate relationships with students are undoubtedly both. Perhaps harassment represents a spectrum of bad behavior.

In the category of Student Choice multiple states moved the authority to approve and renew charter schools from local boards to state entities such as state school boards or new commissions or boards designed for this purpose.

An emerging trend was the adoption of new legislation to stake claims for positions in our nation's current culture wars. The category of Parental and Student Rights ballooned from 74 acts in 2022, to 99 in 2023. Six states enrolled seven acts with broad statements about parental rights with nearly all of them reciting their fundamental rights to direct the upbringing of their children. One state adopted two parental rights acts with one focused on privacy issues such as records, DNA scanning, and participation in surveys. The other channeled issues related to gender identity through parents.

In a separate grouping of gender identity issues, 14 acts asserted the rights of school officials rather than parents to choose which names or pronouns are used for students, which restrooms they can use, and/or which sports they may pursue. In another grouping of nine acts states articulated the rights of students with respect to the Free Exercise Clause of the First Amendment including religious speech, prayer, Bible reading, and the wearing or posting of religious symbols. One state adopted a state-level Religious Freedom Restoration Act requiring courts to apply greater scrutiny when analyzing claims under its provisions.

Table 1. *Education-Related Legislative Acts by Year*

Years	Acts Reported
1998	253
1999–2001	430*
2002–2006	630*
2007–2009	890*
2010	1,050
2011	1,050
2012	830
2013	922
2014	819
2015	864
2016	671
2017	960
2018	919
2019	1,233
2020	799
2021	1,480
2022	1,319
2023	1,433

Note. * = On average, annually

Table 2. *Education-Related Legislative Acts by Category*

Category	Acts Reported
Federal Legislation	2
State Legislation	
Accountability and School Reform	48
Athletics	22
Attendance, Promotion, and Graduation	103
Buildings and Grounds	32
Curricular Requirements	68
Employment	204
Finance and School Business	95
Governance and School Leadership	127
Parental and Student Rights	99
Program Development	65
School Choice	40
School Safety	202
Students with Disabilities	36
Technology	8
Transportation	29
Higher Education	253

Made in the USA
Las Vegas, NV
07 July 2026

50435819R00295